Wissenschaftliche Untersuchungen
zum Neuen Testament · 2. Reihe

Herausgeber / Editor
Jörg Frey (Zürich)

Mitherausgeber / Associate Editors
Markus Bockmuehl (Oxford)
James A. Kelhoffer (Uppsala)
Hans-Josef Klauck (Chicago, IL)
Tobias Nicklas (Regensburg)

355

Isaac W. Oliver

Torah Praxis after 70 CE

Reading Matthew and Luke-Acts as Jewish Texts

WIPF & STOCK · Eugene, Oregon

Wipf and Stock Publishers
199 W 8th Ave, Suite 3
Eugene, OR 97401

Torah Praxis after 70 CE
Reading Matthew and Luke-Acts as Jewish Texts
By Oliver, Isaac Wilk
Copyright © 2013 Mohr Siebeck All rights reserved.
Softcover ISBN-13: 978-1-6667-7310-1
Publication date 3/13/2023
Previously published by Mohr Siebeck, 2013

To my Father, Benoni Batista de Oliveira ז"ל

Sou caipira, Pirapora
Nossa Senhora de Aparecida
Ilumina a mina escura
E funda o trem da minha vida
("Romaria" by Renato Teixeira de Oliveira)

Preface to the Second Printing

Ten years have passed since *Torah Praxis* was first published. To my delight, the main arguments of the book have withstood the test of time. They have, furthermore, contributed to a much wider and ongoing appreciation of the New Testament documents within their Second Temple Jewish matrix.[1] The *communis opinio* that long supposed that Luke was a "Gentile Christian" who grew disinterested in all things Jewish is gradually fading away as his writings are resituated within their original Jewish habitat next to other early Christian works.[2]

in *Torah Praxis,* I experimented reading Luke-Acts alongside the Gospel of Matthew simply *as* Jewish works.[3] Many interpreters end up relegating the Jewish context of the New Testament documents to the background, failing to appreciate fully its import. I attempted to present Matthew and Luke-Acts in a manner that would prevent their Jewish texture from going unnoticed. Matthew and Luke-Acts were deliberately chosen for comparison because of their perceived relationships to first-century Judaism. Matthew, on the one hand, has been called the "most Jewish" Gospel of the New Testament. This assessment stems mainly from its perspective on the Torah.[4] It has been customary, on the other hand, to view Luke as someone who knew or cared little about anything

---

1. Like many specialists, I refer to the Second Temple period as extending beyond 70 CE to the Bar Kokhba Revolt. See Daniel M. Gurtner and Loren T. Stuckenbruck, eds., *T&T Clark Encyclopedia of Second Temple Judaism*, 2 vols. (New York: T&T Clark, 2020), 1:1–4.

2. The Fourteenth Nangeroni Meeting on "Luke and Acts with(in) Second Temple Judaism," which took place in Rome from June 26–29, 2022, testifies to a significant shift in Lukan studies. Experts in early Judaism and New Testament studies demonstrated in various ways the heuristic promise of investigating Luke and Acts in Jewish contexts, especially in relation to Second Temple works hitherto neglected in Lukan studies (e.g., the Jewish Pseudepigrapha and the Dead Sea Scrolls). A volume based on the conference is set to come out in the near future.

3. The hyphen in Luke-Acts expresses my belief that Luke and Acts can be interpreted coherently as compositions redacted by an author who nevertheless drew from and edited multiple sources.

4. W. D. Davies and D. C. Allison, *The Gospel According to Saint Matthew*, ICC, 3 vols., repr. 2010 (London: T&T Clark, 1988), 1:25: "Perhaps the most impressive of these [themes that imply Jewish authorship] is the gospel's understanding of the Torah, especially as this is set forth in the programmatic 5.17–20."

related to Torah observance because of his alleged Gentile background.[5] Since I found this dichotomy unconvincing, I analyzed Matthew and Luke's views on three practices that were commonly associated with Judaism in antiquity: the Sabbath, the Jewish dietary (or "kosher") laws, and circumcision. Assessing how Matthew and Luke related to these three central markers of Jewish identity seemed like a promising way to evaluate their Jewish character.

I concluded that both Matthew and Luke affirmed in their respective ways the observance of these Jewish practices. Based on the criterion of Torah observance, Luke was just as Jewish as Matthew. Ethnic and ecclesiological considerations are key for reaching this conclusion. Like many Jews in antiquity, Luke did not expect *Gentiles* to observe all of the commandments of the Mosaic Torah. This is apparent from Luke's depiction of the "Apostolic Decree." According to Acts, the "Jerusalem Council" established that Gentile followers of Jesus did not need to keep the *entire* Torah but only four commandments. This verdict was reached, however, under the assumption that *Jewish* followers of Jesus would continue to uphold the Torah in all of its facets. Nowhere in Acts are Jews granted license to abandon their ancestral practices. When we consider that many Jews from the Second Temple period and Late Antiquity made similar distinctions, Luke's perspective is not striking at all. For example, the rabbinic Noahide Laws, which are already anticipated in works such as Jubilees, only require Gentiles to observe seven commandments without implying that Jews are exempt from keeping the Torah.

When I began working on my dissertation, scholars were intensely debating David Sim's work on Matthew. Sim argued that Matthew expected Gentiles to become full proselytes of Judaism as part of their confession of Jesus.[6] Unfortunately, Matthew did not compose a work akin to the Acts of the Apostles, which could further assist in determining whether he expected Gentile followers of Jesus to observe the Torah in its totality. If the Didache stems from the same social-historical milieu, it would suggest that Matthew did *not* demand Gentiles to fulfill such things as the Sabbath or (male) circumcision, which Jewish followers of Jesus, on the other hand, were to continue doing. The Didache encourages Gentile Jesus-followers to bear the "yoke of the Lord" as much as they can. Yet it only commands them to refrain from food offered to idols (6:2–3).[7] Recognizing that Matthew is a Torah-

---

5. I refer to Matthew and Luke in the masculine form because I continue to believe that they were men. Joan E. Taylor, "Paul's Significant Other in the 'We' Passages," in *Who Created Christianity? Fresh Approaches to the Relationship between Paul and Jesus* (Grand Rapids, MI: Hendrickson, 2020), 125–56, suggests that the author of the "we-passages" in Acts was a woman, possibly Thecla, because of the author's self-effacing tendency to remain unnamed. Anonymity does draw further attention to Paul, the main hero of the "we-passages," but does not help determine the author's gender.

6. David Sim, *The Gospel of Matthew and Christian Judaism: The History and Social Setting of the Matthean Community* (Edinburgh: T&T Clark, 1998), 246–54.

7. John Kampen, *Matthew within Sectarian Judaism* (New Haven: Yale University Press,

affirming Gospel, I nevertheless posited that its author only expected *Jews* to keep the entire Torah. The Great Commission, though it exhorts Jesus' disciples to teach the nations to obey everything that Jesus has commanded them, does not clarify whether certain Mosaic commandments are incumbent upon Jews only. The evidence in my opinion remains insufficient to conclude that Matthew expected Gentiles to become Jewish proselytes in the fullest sense of the term.

Some reviewers of my book were drawn by my suggestions on the *author* of Luke-Acts. My efforts, however, focused on the Jewish *perspective* in Luke's *text*, without assuming anything about the author's ethnic background. When I stated that "Luke is Jewish till proven Gentile,"[8] I intended to break away from common (mis)conceptions about Luke and Judaism that remain entrenched in assumptions about his supposed non-Jewish background. I went as far as to declare that "Luke the Gentile is dead."[9] One reviewer deemed this provocative obituary to be premature.[10] However, in a recent dissertation, Joshua Smith argues for the Jewish *authorship* of Luke-Acts in an unprecedent manner.[11] The time may be right after all to provide Luke the Gentile with a proper burial.

Chapter Fifteen, which covers the Apostolic Decree, is the only section in *Torah Praxis* that I would significantly rewrite if I had the time and occasion.[12]

2019) is helpful for understanding Matthew in light of pre-70 Judean texts and contexts. Matthew, however, must simultaneously be compared with other first-century "Christian" writings to understand how a text that shares affinities with sectarian documents discovered in the Judean desert could also contribute to the development of gospel texts and traditions that ultimately found their way into the Christian canon. Documents such as the Gospels of Mark and Luke, the Acts of the Apostles, the Letters of Paul, or the Didache, are just as relevant as texts from Qumran for evaluating Matthew "within sectarian Judaism," especially if the First Gospel was composed after 70. For a further discussion, see Isaac W. Oliver, "The Jewishness of Matthew within the Diversity of the Jesus Movement: Insights from Early Christian, Jewish, and Islamic Receptions of Matthew 5:17" (paper presented at the Fourth Enoch Colloquium, 12 November, 2020).

8. *Torah Praxis,* 447.

9. *Torah Praxis,* 450.

10. Boris Repschinski, review of *Torah Praxis after 70 CE*, by Isaac W. Oliver, *Bibelwissenschaften und historische Theologie*, 233–234 (234): "Wenn am Ende des Buches Vf. den Tod des ‚heidnischen Lukas' feiert (450), scheint mir dies doch ein voreiliges Begräbnis zu sein."

11. Joshua Paul Smith, "Luke Was Not a Christian: Interdisciplinary Perspectives on the Jewish Authorship of Luke and Acts" (PhD diss., University of Denver, 2021).

12. For my halakhic-historical analysis (pp. 148–60) of Jesus' burial on a Passover (according to the Synoptics), I overlooked Tobit 2:1–9, which apparently claims that Tobit removed the dead body of an Israelite on a festival day (Shavuot) but waited until sunset to bury it. For a discussion of the (im)purity of hides in 4QMMT, English readers can now consult Vered Noam, "Pharisaic Halakah as Emerging from 4QMMT," in *The Pharisees,* ed. Joseph Sievers and Amy-Jill Levine (Grand Rapids: Eerdmans, 2021), 55–79. I did not analyze the passages on hides in 4QMMT in any detail because of their fragmentary nature (see my brief comment on p. 331 n. 30). These texts do not alter my main argument about Luke's views on Jewish purity laws in reference to Simon the tanner, who is mentioned in passing in Acts chs. 9–10 (see Chapter

I confess that I struggled in this chapter to compare adequately the Apostolic Decree with its rabbinic counterpart, the Noahide Laws. Since the Apostolic Decree prohibits Gentile believers from eating blood as well as strangled meat, it seemed to me to be more demanding in its requirements than the rabbinic Noahide Laws, which only forbid Gentiles from eating blood (or a limb) from a *living animal*. To highlight this difference, I claimed that the Apostolic Decree dealt with "moral" *and* "ritual" matters.[13] The truth, however, as Holger Zellentin has recently pointed out, is that the apostolic interdiction against eating blood or strangled meat is just as moral in its concern as its rabbinic parallel.[14] Long ago, Jacob Milgrom identified this ethical concern in his magisterial commentary on Leviticus. He underlined that the laws in Lev 17 on blood and carcasses apply to the Israelite and the *ger* alike and pointed back to the bipartite commandment in Gen 9:4–6 that forbids humanity from committing bloodshed and eating blood. According to Milgrom, Gen 9:4–6 expresses the "fundamental premise that human beings can curb their violent nature through ritual means, specificall , a dietary discipline that will necessarily drive home the point that all life (*nepeš*), shared also by animals, is inviolable, except—in the case of meat—when conceded by God."[15] Milgrom went on to state that the "principle of the inviolability of life was sharpened by the provision in the Levitical Holiness Code that required all meat for the table to be first slaughtered at the altar. Failure to dash the blood of the animal on the altar was tantamount to murder."[16]

Both the Apostolic Decree and the rabbinic Noahide Laws differ in how non-Israelites should put this ethical principle into practice. The difference is partly exegetical. The Levitical Holiness Code concedes that Israelites and *gerim* can under certain circumstances eat carrion if they subsequently purify themselves (Lev 17:15–16). By contrast, Deuteronomy categorically forbids Israelites—but not *gerim*—from eating carrion (Deut 14:21). Thus, the Levitical Holiness code originally posited that the consumption of carrion only caused *ritual* impurity. Jews from the Second Temple period onwards tried to resolve this discrepancy in various ways.[17] Some Second Temple works, Acts included, taught that Israelites and non-Israelites must refrain from eating blood and

Ten of *Torah Praxis*).

13. I was also influenced by Markus Bockmuehl, *Jewish Law in Gentile Churches: Halakhah and the Beginning of Christian Public Ethics* (Edinburgh: T&T Clark, 2000) 166; "The Noachide Commandments and New Testament Ethics: With Special Reference to Acts 15 and Pauline Halakhah," *Revue Biblique* 102 (1995): 72–101 (95): "the decree addresses both 'moral' and 'ritual' offences."

14. Holger Zellentin, *Law Beyond Israel: From the Bible to the Qur'an* (Oxford: Oxford University Press, 2022), 62 n. 56.

15. Jacob Milgrom, *Leviticus*, 3 vols., AB 3–3B (New York: Doubleday, 1991–2001), 1:48.

16. Milgrom, *Leviticus*, 1:49.

17. For more details, see *Torah Praxis*, 392.

carrion. Rabbinic *halakhah*, however, ruled that Gentiles could eat the carcass of an animal, in conformity with Deut 14:21.

In this regard, I find Zellentin's nomenclature of "prohibited" and "regulated" impurity especially helpful. Regulated impurity represents a type of *permitted* impurity that is inevitable as its results from certain natural functions such as sexual intercourse or menstruation. It is temporary and departs after a predetermined period accompanied by certain purification rites. Prohibited impurity, on the other hand, is "contracted through acts such as idolatry, the shedding of human blood, or the consumption of animal blood, and by committing sexual transgressions."[18] The distinction between these two types of impurity, as Zellentin observes, is not absolute. Thus, neglecting the rules on regulated impurity can gave way to prohibited impurity, which is a serious matter, as no method of purification enables its removal, save for punishment or atonement. Best not to commit prohibited acts in the first place to avoid this precarious situation.

Some will immediately notice that Zellentin's classification of "regulated" and "prohibited" impurity is virtually identical to how Jonathan Klawans' defines "ritual" and "moral" impurity. Indeed, I adopted Klawans' terminology in my book when I analyzed some of the purity laws in Matthew and Luke-Acts. Nevertheless, the pair "ritual" and "moral" can occasionally obscure matters. First, it recalls how some arbitrarily distinguish between the "ceremonial" and "moral" commandments of the Mosaic Torah, based on the belief that Jesus only upheld the Ten Commandments, God's universal "moral" law, but abrogated the "ceremonial" laws of the Torah. In reality, the Decalogue also encompasses the ritual or "ceremonial" domain (e.g., the Sabbath commandment) while moral concerns are interspersed throughout pentateuchal Law. The confusion generated by this terminology is evident in the way that New Testament scholarship has treated the Apostolic Decree. Consider, for example, how the late textual critic of the New Testament, Bruce Metzger, discussed the variant readings of the Apostolic Decree in Acts. Most witnesses list four items, including the prohibition against eating strangled meat. Some texts omit any reference to *porneia* (illicit sexual practices), while the so-called Western text substitutes strangled meat with the Golden Rule in its negative form. Metzger phrased the issue as follows:

> (1) Are Gentiles commanded to abstain from four things (food offered to idols, blood, strangled meat, and unchastity) or from three (omitting either strangled meat or unchastity); and (2) are the three or four prohibitions entirely ceremonial, or entirely ethical, or a combination of both kinds?[19]

---

18. Zellentin, *Law Beyond Israel*, 12–13.

19. Bruce M. Metzger, *A Textual Commentary on the Greek New Testament*, 2nd ed. (Stuttgart: United Bible Societies, 1994), 379.

Representing the majority view, Metzger supported the priority of the fourfold decree that includes the interdiction against eating strangled meat. Some, however, continue to favor the Western text. Whatever the case, discussions of this textual critical problem should not mistakenly oppose the decree's moral dimension against its supposed ritual components. All readings of Acts attest rather to what Zellentin calls *prohibitive* (or moral) impurity. In fact, the "Western" text of Acts approximates the rabbinic Noahide Laws by allowing Gentiles to eat blood and strangled meat, while the majority (and probably original) reading of Acts aligns with the position attested in Second Temple Jewish works such as Jubilees and the Temple Scroll that ban eating any blood or carrion.

It is evident from what is stated above that I see Leviticus chs. 17–18 as relevant background for illuminating the Apostolic Decree. Indeed, I endorsed this position in *Torah Praxis*, claiming that the Apostolic Decree should be read in light of Lev 17–18 along with the commandments given to Noah and his children in Gen 9. However, I soon started to doubt my position after encountering an article that proposed an alternative view.[20] I am happy to say though that I can now sleep at night in peace, knowing that Zellentin has established the connection between Lev 17–18 and the Apostolic Decree once and for all.[21] Zellentin solves a riddle that has challenged the majority view: Why does the Apostolic Decree not include other biblical laws that concern the *ger* if it depends on Lev 17–18? The answer lies in the decree's focus on *purity*. Thus, the Apostolic Decree does not, for example, require Gentile followers of Jesus to keep the Sabbath, since its observance does not deal directly with purity matters. In Acts, James endorses the Apostolic Decree by alluding to the reading of Moses on the Sabbath in the Jewish synagogues but without mentioning the Decalogue, which provides no rules about blood or strangled meat. The apostolic prohibition against eating strangled meat can only make sense in light of Leviticus 17. Zellentin's research undergirds this point by showing how Christians throughout Late Antiquity understood the Apostolic Decree in connection to Lev 17–18.

The Apostolic Decree therefore was designed to preserve the moral purity of Gentiles who had joined the Jesus movement.[22] These, according to Peter

---

20. Todd Hanneken, "Moses Has His Interpreters: Understanding the Legal Exegesis in Acts 15 from the Precedent in *Jubilees*," *CBQ* 77 (2015): 686–706.

21. In addition to his groundbreaking book *Law Beyond Israel*, see Holger Zellentin, *The Qur'ān's Legal Culture: The Didascalia as a Point of Departure* (Tübingen: Mohr Siebeck, 2013); "Judaeo-Christian Legal Culture and the Qur'ān: The Case of Ritual Slaughter and the Consumption of Animal Blood," in *Jewish Christianity and the Origins of Islam: Papers Presented at the Colloquium Held in Washington DC, October 29–31, 2015 (8th ASMEA Conference)*, ed. Francisco del Río Sánchez (Turnhout: Brepols, 2018), 117–59. W. Gil Shin, "Holy Land Sanctity for Every Greco-Roman City: Rethinking the Lukan Apostolic Decree (Acts 15:19–21)," *JBL* 141.3 (2022): 553–74, further strengthens the connection between the Apostolic Decree and Lev 17–18 but doesn't interact with Holger Zellentin or my book.

22. Shin, "Holy Land," 557 n. 16, dismisses the connection between the Apostolic Decree

in Acts, had undergone an internal purification, having received the gift of the sacred spirit (15:7–9).²³ To mark and safeguard their new holy status, they were to refrain from the *pollutions* of idolatry, *porneia,* blood, and strangled meat (15:20). The observance of these laws, however, had a *secondary*, practical outcome: it could facilitate table fellowship between Jewish and Gentile followers of Jesus. In Luke's estimation, once it had been clearly established that Gentile Christ-followers committed themselves to abide by the purity laws of the Apostolic Decree, Jewish disciples of Jesus had no reason to refuse their fellowship. The story of Cornelius relates this important lesson. Previously, Peter had hesitated even to enter the Roman centurion's house (Acts 10:28). Eventually, he came to the understanding that God-fearing Gentiles like Cornelius who confessed Jesus' lordship should not be treated as regular (or "pagan") Gentiles. The sacred spirit had descended upon Cornelius and his household, who in turn were baptized in the name of Jesus. These events signaled that Gentile Christ-followers had been purified and sanctifie . Only then did Peter accept Cornelius' invitation to lodge at his residence. We can certainly assume that Luke did not believe that such fellowship led Peter to transgress the Torah. When he reported back to the Jewish *ekklesia* in Jerusalem, Peter provided no indication of breaking the Law of Moses during his stayover at Cornelius' house (11:1–18). No confession of eating pork or other forbidden meats, let alone food offered to idols, blood, or carrion.

The Clementine *Homilies* and *Recognitions* offer a similar understanding of the functions I have proposed for the Apostolic Decree.²⁴ As in Acts, the laws in the Clementine literature that Gentiles are expected to observe revolve around purity. For example, the *Homilies* instruct Gentile followers of Jesus to "have no share with the table of demons, that is, food offered to idols, dead animals, strangled meats, animals torn by wild beasts, blood," since they must "not live

---

in Acts 15 and moral impurity because Cornelius is described in Acts 10:2 as a "pious" man. However, Gentile God-fearers did not necessarily abandon their pagan customs even if they sympathized with Judaism and the Jewish community. It was Jewish followers of Jesus who demanded that Gentile abandon entirely their idolatrous and (from a Jewish standpoint) immoral ways in order to become Christians. See Paula Fredriksen, "What 'Parting of the Ways'? Jews, Gentiles, and the Ancient Mediterranean City," in *The Ways That Never Parted*, ed. Adam H. Becker and Annette Yoshiko Reed (Tübingen: Mohr Siebeck; repr. Minneapolis: Fortress, 2007), 35–63. "Genealogical impurity" (as defined by Christine Hayes and suggested by Matthew Thiessen) may help us understand the Cornelius episode. See Chapter Ten for my discussion of this view. In any case, even if Luke thought that Gentiles were genealogically impure, he expected them to uphold the purity required by laws of the Apostolic Decree once they joined the Jesus movement.

23. For my usage of "sacred spirit" instead of the traditional "Holy Spirit," see *Torah Praxis*, 360–61.

24. Karin Heder Zetterholm, "Jewish Teachings for Gentiles in the Pseudo-Clementine *Homilies*: A Jewish Reception of Ideas in Paul and Acts Shaped by a Jewish Milieu?" *Journal of the Jewish Movement in Its Jewish Setting* 6 (2019): 68–87.

impurely" (μὴ ἀκαθάρτως βιοῦν).²⁵ The *Recognitions* share similar concerns about impurity: Gentile Jesus-followers should not "participate in the tables of demons, that is, eat animals sacrificed [to idols], blood, or carrion that has been strangled," since it defiles the soul and the body (4.36.4). Hence the rite of baptism, which assists in purifying Gentiles from the pollution of idolatry and all immorality.²⁶

However, in the Clementines, observance of such laws does not only concern purity. It also involves table fellowship between Jews and non-Jews. Peter raises this issue in both the *Homilies* and the *Recognitions*:

> We do not enjoy the table of Gentiles (τραπέζης ἐθνῶν), in as much as we cannot feast with them (συνεστιᾶσθαι αὐτοῖς) because they live impurely (διὰ τὸ ἀκαθάρτως αὐτοὺς βιοῦν).²⁷

> But we pay attention also to something else, not to share our table with Gentiles (*mensam cum gentilibus non habere communem*).²⁸

According to these passages, Torah-observant Jews such as Peter do not share the same table with Gentiles because of their impurity.²⁹ Peter clarifies though that after Gentiles undergo baptism and commit themselves to refrain from impure activity, "we then eat with them" (τότε αὐτοῖς συναλιζόμεθα).³⁰ Giovanni Bazzana, who has written extensively on the Clementine literature, concludes that its regulations for Gentiles are meant to "enable the coexistence of Christ-followers who are Jews with those who are not."³¹

I retain therefore my position that the Apostolic Decree was built on the laws of Lev 17–18 as well as commandments from Genesis that were associated with

---

25. *Hom.* 7.8.1. Similarly, *Hom.* 7.4.2 tells Gentile Christians to keep away from the table of demons, dead flesh, and blood and to "wash themselves from all defilement" (ἐκ παντὸς ἀπολούεσθαι λύματος). My translations of the Clementine corpus are based on Bernard Rehm's edition, which is referenced in the bibliography of this book.

26. See *Hom.* 7.8.1; 9.23.2; 13.4.3. On the importance of baptism in Ps.-Clem as a purificatory rite, see Zetterholm, "Jewish Teachings for Gentiles," 74–75.

27. *Hom.* 13.4.3.

28. *Rec.* 7.29.3.

29. Cf. *Hom.* 13.11.4; *Rec.* 7.36.4. Shin, "Holy Land," 3, is correct when he states that the Apostolic Decree in Acts does not represent a practical compromise to accommodate the demands of different factions within the Jesus movement. Observance of the decree's stipulation is *necessary* (I would say mandatory) for Gentile Jesus-followers. Shin, however, overlooks the Clementine traditions when he refers to the "wide acknowledgment of the use of the prohibitions in the early church without mention of table fellowship" (559 n. 23).

30. *Hom.* 13.4.3–4; cf. *Rec.* 7.29.3.

31. Giovanni Bazzana, "Paul among His Enemies? Exploring Potential Pauline Theological Traits in Pseudo-Clementines," in *The Early Reception of Paul the Second Temple Jew*, ed. Isaac W. Oliver and Gabriele Boccaccini, Library of Second Temple Studies 92 (London: T&T Clark, 2018), 120–30 (127).

Noah. Already before the Apostolic Decree, the book of Jubilees interpreted some of the biblical laws given to Noah's descendants, including the regulations on blood(shed) in Gen 9:4–6, in light of Lev 17–18.[32] Following Cana Werman, I believe that the legislation of the Apostolic Decree stems from a combined reading of Gen 9 with Lev 17–18.[33] Interestingly, early rabbinic expositions of the Noahide Laws refer to the same biblical passages.[34] Thus, the Apostolic Decree and the rabbinic Noahide Laws represent two parallel interpretations of biblical information deemed legally relevant for Gentiles.

I wish to end this new preface with an expression of gratitude. The reprint of my book would not be possible without the support of Robin Parry, from Wipf and Stock, who showed personal interest in my work. As always, I remember my father, Benoni Batista de Oliveira, hoping that my work fulfills in some indirect way the endeavors that he wished to pursue in his lifetime.

January 6, 2023

Isaac W. Oliver/de Oliveira
Bradley University

---

32. Hanneken, "Moses Has His Interpreters," overlooks this connection.

33. Cana Werman "The Concept of Holiness and the Requirements of Purity in Second Temple and Tannaic Literature," in *Purity and Holiness: The Heritage of Leviticus*, eds. Marcel J. H. M. Poorthuis and Joshua Schwartz, Jewish and Christian Perspectives Series 2 (Brill: Leiden, 2000), 163–79 (168).

34. See Zellentin, *Law Beyond Israel,* 63–77.

Preface

This monograph is a revised version of my PhD thesis, which was submitted to the Department of Near Eastern Studies of the University of Michigan in June 2012. I revised a considerable portion of this dissertation, incorporating and interacting with additional primary and secondary sources when I worked as a post-doctoral fellow at the Frankel Institute for Advanced Judaic Studies (University of Michigan) during the fall of 2012.

First and foremost, I would like to thank my advisor, Gabriele Boccaccini, for his support in so many endeavors as well as for his original and sophisticated input that led to the creation and fruition of this project. I have learned much about Middle Judaism (we both include the Jesus movement under this rubric) by sitting at the feet of this Italian maestro. His charisma and ability to create bridges between different academic communities at the international level through his tireless efforts in founding and facilitating the various activities related to the Enoch Seminar continually inspire and remind us all not only to explore texts but also to foster positive human relationships.

I thank Daniel Boyarin for serving as a member of my dissertation committee. As I embarked on this project, I was unaware that Boyarin was writing a book about the canonical gospels – read as Jewish texts. This turned out to be the most serendipitous of events. His feedback has been invaluable. Professors Ray Van Dam, Ellen Muehlberger, and Rachel Neis from the University of Michigan provided me with great suggestions and important corrections about my presentation, style, and argumentation. I thank them for their professional and academic support that reaches far beyond this project.

I am also greatly indebted to Mark Kinzer for encouraging me to select and pursue this topic. Kinzer, who also earned his PhD at Michigan under the tutorship of Jarl Fossum and Gabriele Boccaccini, introduced me to the writings of Jacob Jervell. Indeed, a special story about Luke runs deep in the history of the Department of Near Eastern Studies at Michigan. Kinzer tells me that Fossum, a student of Jervell, taught the Gospel of Luke and the Acts of the Apostles at Michigan from his professor's perspective, which in turn was handed down and accepted by Kinzer and now me. May this chain of tradition continue to be transmitted!

Many others need to be thanked. I am indebted to professor Jörg Frey for accepting this monograph for publication. William Loader shared encouraging words during and after my visit to the Department of Theology of Murdoch University (Perth, Australia) and found time in his busy schedule to look through my dissertation. Aharon Shemesh kindly agreed to read my chapter dealing with the Apostolic Decree in the Acts of the Apostles and provided useful comments and references. Richard Kalmin looked at a draft of my paper, "Breaking Passover to Keep the Sabbath: The Burial of Jesus and the Halakic Dilemma as Embedded within the Synoptic Narratives," presented at the Midwest Society of Biblical Literature in 2011 and now part of chapter 5 of this book. He greatly assisted me with comments on halakic discussions and my usage of rabbinic literature related to this matter. Of course, I bear full responsibility for the interpretation of this material and any other shortcomings.

The Faculty of Theology of the University of Copenhagen honored me with an invitation to share my research in Denmark on April 9 and 10, 2013. I especially thank Kasper Dalgaard for initiating and organizing this event as well as professors Heike Omerzu, Mogens Müller, Troels Engberg-Pedersen, Ingrid Hjelm, and many others, for their kind and honest feedback. I should not fail to thank the participants of the Fourth Graduate Enoch Seminar at the University of Notre Dame for reading and discussing my chapter on food laws in Acts chs. 10–11 as well as the participants of the Unit of Sabbath in Text and Tradition of the Society of Biblical Literature for their input on my research on the Sabbath in Luke-Acts. Many stimulating conversations with various members of the Enoch Seminar, especially Lutz Doering, Daniel Stökl, Andreas Bedenbender, and Anders Klostergaard Petersen, have helped me in more than one way.

The Rackham Graduate School (University of Michigan) provided me with two fantastic fellowships, the Rackham Merit Fellowship and the Rackham Predoctoral Fellowship, which allowed me to devote my time and energy to research and completing my dissertation within a reasonable time frame. The Jean & Samuel Frankel Center for Judaic Studies granted generous funding during the summers for study and sharing my research in Europe and Israel. I also thank the Department of Near Eastern Studies of the University of Michigan for supplying additional funding during the summers. I cherish the advice and reactions to my work shared by the members of the Frankel Institute for Advanced Judaic Studies of 2012. Finally, Bradley University provided me with a Research Excellence and Development (REC) Summer Stipend to finish revising and editing this book during the summer of 2013.

Colleagues, friends, and family have provided immense wisdom and support. I thank Luca Marulli (University of Strasbourg) as well as Jason

Zurawski, Deborah Forger, Jason von Ehrenkrook, Rodney Caruthers, and James Waddell from the Department of Near Eastern Studies at Michigan for the friendly, critical, and extended conversations. My colleagues, Daniel Getz, Robert Fuller, Jason Zaborowski, Andrew Kelley, Vlad Niculescu, and Michael Greene at the Department of Philosophy and Religious Studies of Bradley University have been incredibly supportive. Marc Gottlieb has been a guardian angel and a personal mentor. I also extend a special thanks to my mother, Susan. Matteo Silvestri and Hervé Gonzalez from the University of Lausanne greatly assisted me with accessing and using the excellent library for biblical studies of their institution during my annual summer stays in France and Switzerland. Last but not least, Ségolène, thank you for your patience and support throughout our six-year stay in Michigan during which three kids were born and raised!

October 16, 2013

Isaac W. (de) Olive(i)r(a)
Bradley University

Table of Contents

Preface to the Second Printing..VII
Preface..XVII

Chapter 1: Introduction 1
Introduction 1
Who Was Jewish Anyways? Two Jews, Three Opinions 5
Torah Practice and the Problem with "Jewish Christianity" 10
The Judaization and Gentilization of Matthew and Luke-Acts 18
Present State of Research 22
Matthew and Luke, Why not Mark? 32
Methodological Considerations 33
Thesis and Summary of Chapters 39

Part I
Sabbath Keeping in Matthew and Luke-Acts

Chapter 2: Non-Controversial Sabbath Episodes 45
The Sabbath in Antiquity 45
   A Marker of Jewish Identity 45
   Did Jews Treat Minor Diseases on the Sabbath? 47
Introduction to the Non-Controversial Sabbath Episodes 53
An Unclean Spirit in the Synagogue of Capernaum 54
   Literary Context 54
   Analysis 56
Going out of the Law for an In-Law? Healing Peter's Mother-in-Law 61
   Literary Context 61
   Analysis 61

Healing the Masses after Sunset 65
   Literary Context 65
   Analysis 66

Rejection in Nazareth 69
   Literary Context 69
   Analysis of Luke 4:16–30 70
   A Lukan Sabbath Theology and Praxis in the Sermon
   Delivered in Nazareth? 74

Conclusion 78

Chapter 3: Plucking Grain on the Sabbath 80

Matthew 12:1–8 80
   Introduction 80
   Literary Context 81
   Determining the Controversy 87
   The Nob Incident 92
   Additional Matthean Arguments 95

Luke 6:1–5 99
   Literary Context 99
   Analysis 102

Excursus: Why Is Mark 2:27 Missing in Matthew and Luke? 105

Conclusion 112

Chapter 4: Healing on the Sabbath 114

Introduction 114

Healing the Withered Hand: Matt 12:9–14 114
   Literary Context 114
   Analysis 115

Healing the Withered Hand: Luke 6:6–11 124
   Analysis 124

Excursus: Luke 6:11 in Modern Translation 127

Healing the Crippled Woman: Luke 13:10–17 130
   Literary Context 130
   Analysis 132

Healing on the Sabbath in Pharisaic Space: Luke 14:1–6 138

Literary Context 138
   Analysis 139
Conclusion 145

Chapter 5: Burying on the Sabbath 147

Introduction 147

Breaking Passover to Keep the Sabbath? 148

Do Joseph and the Women Perform Work on the Sabbath? ... 161

When Do the Women Visit Jesus' Tomb? 163

Matthew's Polemics against the Pharisees and their Sabbath keeping .. 165

Conclusion 166

Chapter 6: Traveling on the Sabbath 170

Introduction 170

Literary Context and Analysis 170

Matt 24:20 and Modern Scholarship 177

Conclusion 182

Conclusion on Sabbath Keeping in Matthew and Luke 182
   Matthew's Sabbath Repertoire 182
   Luke's Sabbath Repertoire 184
   Matthean and Lukan Sabbath Theologies Compared 186
   Matthean and Lukan Sabbath Praxis 188

Chapter 7: The Sabbath in the Acts of the Apostles 194

Introduction 194

Respecting the Sabbath Limits: Acts 1:12 194
   Literary Context 194
   Redactional Analysis 197
   Interpretation 199

Visiting the Synagogue at Antioch of Pisidia 204
   Key Verses 204
   Literary Context 204
   Interpretation 209

Reading Moses on the Sabbath: Acts 15:21 211
    Literary Context 211
    Redactional Analysis 212
    Interpretation 213

Worshiping Outdoors on the Sabbath: Acts 16:12–15 216
    Literary Context 216
    Analysis 216

More Sabbath Services in the Synagogue: Acts 17:2 and 18:4 220
    Literary Context 220
    Redactional Analysis 221

When Do the Followers of Jesus "Break Bread"? Acts 20:7–12 222
    Literary Context 222
    Analysis 222

Conclusion 233

Part II
Food Laws in Matthew and Luke-Acts

Chapter 8: Food Laws in Matthew 241

Food Laws and Jewish Identity in Antiquity 241

Food Laws in Matthew and Luke-Acts: Preliminary Observations 251

Hand Washing before Eating: Matt 15:1–20 255
    Literary Context 255
    Literary Structure 257
    Halakic Analysis: Hand Washing before Meals 257
    Redactional Analysis 264

Pigs, Dogs, Gnats, and Camels: Matt 7:6 and 23:24 276
    Key Verses 276
    Literary Context 276
    Analysis 278

Non-Kosher Food in Impure Vessels: Matt 23:25–26 288
    Literary Context 288
    Interpretation 288

Conclusion 292

Chapter 9: Food Laws in Luke 294

Introduction 294

Perfecting Pharisaic Purity: Luke 11:37–41 294
    Literary Context 294
    Redactional Analysis 296
    Interpretation 298

The Commission of the Seventy-Two: Luke 10:1–11 304
    Literary Context 304
    Redactional Features 306
    Interpretation 309

Conclusion 319

Chapter 10: The Cornelius Episode 320

Introduction 320

Literary Context 321

Literary Structure 323

Redactional Analysis 325

The Insignificance of Simon the Tanner 327

Cornelius: Righteous Gentile among the Nations 337

Peter's Vision: A Story about Gentiles, Not Food 340

Distinguishing between Gentile Impurity and Profaneness ... 345

Entering and Lodging in a Gentile House 357

The Baptism of the Sacred Spirit 360

The Jerusalem Report 362

Conclusion 363

Chapter 11: The Apostolic Decree 365

Introduction 365

Literary Context 366

The Moral and Ritual Scope of the Decree 368

Lev 17–18 and the Apostolic Decree 370

Idolatry 371
Porneia 375
Strangled Meat 380
Blood 390
Conclusion 394

Part III
Circumcision in Matthew and Luke-Acts

Chapter 12: Circumcision in Matthew and Luke-Acts 401
Introduction 401
Matthew and the Circumcision Debate in Recent Scholarship 403
The Circumcision of John the Baptist and Jesus 410
    Introduction 410
    Passage 412
    Redactional Analysis 412
    Naming and Circumcising Jewish Boys 414
    The Importance of Eighth-Day Circumcision 416
    The Purification of the Parturient and Her Child 417
    The Presentation and Redemption of the Firstborn 421
Circumcision in Acts 7:8 427
Paul's Circumcision of Timothy: Acts 16:1–3 430
Conclusion 435

Chapter 13: Conclusion 439

Bibliography 453

Index of Ancient Sources 487
Index of Modern Authors 513
Index of Subjects 521

Chapter 1

Introduction to Matthew and Luke-Acts

Introduction

These are exciting times for exploring any topic relating early Christianity to its original Jewish matrix. How fortunate we are to lie far away from those days when many Christian theologians and historians felt anxious about the Jewish heritage embedded in their Christian tradition. From the historical Jesus to the apostle Paul, many are the scholars of Christian provenance who have affirmed in positive terms the Jewishness of these two foundational figures. This tendency has also been reciprocated among several Jewish scholars, first with the historical Jesus, and eventually even with Paul who had previously been viewed, and still is by some, as a Jewish apostate and the first "Christian."[1] Ever since the publication of E. P. Sanders' *Paul and Palestinian Judaism*,[2] many Christian scholars have finally heeded to George Foot Moore's prophetic cry against Christian misrepresentations and stigmatizations of rabbinic Judaism.[3] The fascinating discoveries of the Dead Sea Scrolls and the new intellectual and ecumenical atmosphere reigning after World War II have only encouraged and accelerated the process of recovering the diversity of Second Temple Judaism, which in turn has brought the early Jesus movement, at least some of it, back to its original Jewish pastures.

All of these commendable acts and formative events highlight the scholarly achievements made during the second half of the twentieth century in the fields of biblical studies, ancient Judaism, and early Christianity. But new frontiers of exploration and methodological considerations are

---

[1] Jewish scholars who have affirmed the Jewishness of Jesus or Paul include Claude G. Montefiore, Joseph Klausner, David Flusser, Samuel Sandmel, Alan F. Segal, Geza Vermes, Daniel Boyarin, Paula Fredriksen, and Mark Nanos, to name a few. Further references can be found in the ever-expanding www.4enoch.org, created by Gabriele Boccaccini (2009). For the "older," less favorable view of Paul as the inventor of Christianity, seen as a religion in radical discontinuity from Judaism, see Hyam Maccoby, *The Mythmaker, Paul and the Invention of Christianity* (London: Weidenfeld & Nicolson, 1986).

[2] E. P. Sanders, *Paul and Palestinian Judaism: A Comparison of Patterns of Religion* (Philadelphia, Pa.: Fortress, 1977).

[3] George Foot Moore, "Christian Writers on Judaism," *HTR* 14 (1921): 197–254.

constantly emerging in the world of academia. The beginning of the third millennium has already generated its share of new proposals concerning Jewish-Christian relations in Late Antiquity that open fresh opportunities to revisit the documents now incorporated in the New Testament. Thus, the many articles compiled in the volume, *The Ways That Never Parted*, propose moving away from pinpointing an early date when Judaism and Christianity became distinct, autonomous entities everywhere throughout the Greco-Roman and Near Eastern worlds of Late Antiquity.[4] While popular opinion continues to imagine that Jesus almost immediately founded a new religion upon his arrival on the earthly scene, specialists of early Judaism and Christianity have traditionally issued the bill of divorce between Jews and Christians at a slightly later time. As mentioned earlier, some blame Paul as the primary culprit for initiating this process of separation. Others, however, turn their gaze toward 70 CE and consider this date as the watershed moment when Jews made their way to Yavneh and developed what eventually became "rabbinic Judaism," while one of the last remnants of Christians firmly attached to Judaism settled in Pella never again to reincorporate themselves into Jewish society.[5] Until recently, the

---

[4] Adam H. Becker and Annette Yoshiko Reed, eds., *The Ways That Never Parted* (Minneapolis: Fortress, 2007); cf. Daniel Boyarin, *Borderlines: The Partition of Judaeo-Christianity* (Philadelphia, Pa.: University of Pennsylvania Press, 2004). Cf. Cf. Seth Schwartz, *Imperialism and Jewish Society, 200 B.C.E. to 640 C.E.* (Princeton: Princeton University Press, 2011); Judith Lieu, *Neither Jew nor Greek? Constructing Early Christianity* (Studies of the New Testament and Its World; London: T&T Clark, 2002), 11–29. "Late Antiquity" normally refers to a period after the composition of the documents included in the New Testament. The point is that if no definitive separation between the entities we are accustomed to calling Judaism and Christianity occurred everywhere during the third, fourth, or even fifth centuries of the Common Era, then a reassessment of the emergence and development of the nascent Jesus movement during the first century of its existence is certainly warranted.

[5] By no means does this constitute an antiquated view about the relations between Jews and Christians after 70 CE. On the contrary, it is very much alive at the beginning of the third millennium. See, for example, Donald A. Hagner, "Paul as a Jewish Believer – According to His Letters," in *Jewish Believers in Jesus: The Early Centuries* (eds. Oskar Skarsaune and Reidar Hvalvik; Peabody, Mass.; Hendrickson, 2007), 118–20: "Two questions are debated by scholars today. First, when can we speak of Christianity? And, second, when did the church break with the synagogue? As for the first, the answer depends on what we mean by the word…. As for the second question, it would seem wise not to think in terms of a specific date for the break of the church from the synagogue. We undoubtedly have to reckon with a process taking place in different locations at different rates of speed. Dating the supposed break circa 85–90 C.E., during the work of the Yavneh rabbis and the adding of the 'benediction' of the *minim* to the Eighteen Benedictions, to my mind is much too late. Tensions were great virtually from the start, and only increased with the passing of time. Paul knew the reality of Jewish opposition to the message he preached (cf. 2 Cor 11:23–25). There were clear points of vital im-

Second Jewish Revolt (c.132–35 CE) was considered the *terminus ad quem* for any ongoing and meaningful overlap between Jews and Christians.[6]

More recently, the proposals offered in *The Ways That Never Parted* herald a fresh approach for understanding Jewish-Christian relations, denying any real and complete separation between Jews and Christians everywhere during the first three or four centuries of the Common Era.[7]

---

portance, especially, the destruction of Jerusalem in 70, but it is likely, in my opinion, that the church and the synagogue were obviously separate entities before the end of the first century." Even in the prestigious Hermeneia series, similar perspectives on the breach between Judaism and Christianity continue to thrive. Thus, Richard I. Pervo, *Acts: A Commentary* (Hermeneia; Minneapolis: Fortress, 2009), 685: "Judaism and Christianity began to emerge as clearly distinct entities c. 90 CE. A generation later, Luke was engaged in retrojecting this separation to the 'primitive' period. This is a normal tactic of an established body that wishes to maintain and protect its boundaries by dating its foundation as early as possible. The separation of 'Christians' from 'Jews' is an accomplished fact." Menahem Mor, *The Bar-Kochba Revolt: Its Extent and Effect* [in Hebrew] (Israel Exploration Society; Jerusalem: Yad Izhak Ben-Zvi, 1991), 187–90, treats "Jewish Christians" as part of the *non-Jewish* population during the Second Revolt. See also his later article, "The Geographical Scope of the Bar Kokhba Revolt," in *The Bar Kokhba War Reconsidered: New Perspectives on the Second Jewish Revolt against Rome* (ed. Peter Schäfer; TSAJ 100; Tübingen: Mohr Siebeck, 2002), 108.

[6] James D.G. Dunn in his *The Partings of the Ways between Christianity and Judaism and Their Significance for the Character of Christianity* (2d ed.; London: SCM, 2006), advocates this position, but the preface to the second edition of his book (xxii–xxiv) provides a corrective in response to the views proposed in the book, *The Ways That Never Parted*. On Jewish followers of Jesus during the Bar Kokhba Revolt and the question of the "parting of the ways," see Isaac W. Oliver, "Jewish Followers of Jesus and the Bar Kokhba Revolt: Re-examining the Christian Sources," in *The Psychological Dynamics of Revolution: Religious Revolts* (vol. 1 of *Winning Revolutions: The Psychology of Successful Revolts for Freedom, Fairness, and Rights*; ed. J. Harold Ellens; Santa Barbara, Calif.: Praeger, 2014).

[7] From an intellectual point of view, one could argue that Christianity *never* parted from Judaism, since it represents until this day one of the many possible outcomes and developments of the Jewish genius in the aftermath of 70 CE. Gabriele Boccaccini, *Middle Judaism: Jewish Thought, 300 BCE. to 200 CE* (Minneapolis: Fortress, 1991), 17–18, notes: "Among the many possible Judaisms, Christianity is one of those which has been realized in history. It did happen at the beginning of the Common Era that a particular multinational Judaism called Christianity – which through its faith in Jesus as the Messiah gave a different meaning to obeying the law – became highly successful among Gentiles, that the gentile members very soon composed the overwhelming majority of this community, and that the strong (and reciprocal) debate against other Jewish groups gradually turned, first into bitter hostility against all other Jews (that is, against all non-Christian Jews), and then against the Jews *tout court* (including the Christian Jews) in a sort of *damnatio memoria* of their own roots. However, neither a different way of understanding the law nor a claimed otherness nor the emergence of anti-Jewish attitudes does away with the Jewishness of Christianity.... For a historian of religion, Rabbinism and Christianity are simply different Judaisms."

This new framework, despite its critics,[8] invites scholars to revisit the relationship of the Jesus movement of the first century with its Jewish environment. If there was no complete and final separation between Judaism and Christianity before the fourth century CE, then certainly the boundaries between the two remained fluid even after the destruction of the temple in 70, the period when Matthew and Luke most likely composed their works.[9] It is therefore misleading and anachronistic to speak of the Jewish "background" or Jewish "roots" when relating early "Christian" (also an anachronism for the first century) texts of the New Testament to the Judaism of that time. From a historical point of view, there is no Jewish background of the New Testament because this literary corpus contains what were originally Jewish documents.

The experiment throughout this monograph involves reading three texts from the New Testament, the Gospel of Matthew along with the Gospel of Luke and the Acts of the Apostles "simply" *as Jewish* texts. This experiment, though rather novel in the case of Luke, is not unprecedented in the history of research.[10] Moving beyond the widespread, by now, almost superfluous recognition of the Jewishness of the historical Jesus, Paul, or even Matthew, the latter so often perceived as the most "Jewish" of all gospels, I am wondering how far the boundaries of Jewishness can be

---

[8] Marius Heemstra, *The Fiscus Judaicus and the Parting of the Ways* (WUNT 2.277; Tübingen: Mohr Siebeck, 2010), points to the important yet overlooked dimension in the discussion on the "parting of the ways," that is, the Roman perspective on Jews and Christians. Heemstra looks at how the *fiscus Judaicus* played an integral role in the process of the formation of Jewish and Christian identities. I full heartedly agree with Heemstra's call to pay closer attention to this third dimension. Nevertheless, perhaps he overstates some of his findings when he concludes that "the decisive separation between Judaism as we know it today and Christianity as we know it today, took place at the end of the first century, as the combined result of a decision by representatives of mainstream Judaism…and the Roman redefinition of the taxpayers to the *fiscus Judaicus*" (189). A closer treatment of the gospel of Matthew could prove worthwhile, given the likely indications that the "Matthean community" paid the *fiscus Judaicus*. See Anthony Saldarini, *Matthew's Christian-Jewish Community* (Chicago Studies in the History of Judaism; Chicago: University of Chicago Press, 1994), 144–45. Heemstra dismisses this possibility in a footnote with no argumentation (p. 63 n. 125). Leonard V. Rutgers, *Making Myths: Jews in Early Christian Identity Formation* (Leuven: Peeters, 2009) mounts a stirring critique against the *Ways That Never Parted*, but his comments address more the period of Late Antiquity and need not deter us.

[9] By employing the names "Matthew" and "Luke" I do not imply that these historical figures actually wrote the (anonymous) documents attributed to them in subsequent Christian tradition. I simply use these names out of convenience and convention to designate the final authors of these writings.

[10] As I revised this work, a stimulating session on Acts and the Parting of the Ways in light of Second Temple Judaism was held at the Society of Biblical Literature on November 18, 2012.

pushed in order to include texts that have normally and normatively been considered to be "Gentile Christian" documents. Do the bounds of pluriform Early Judaism even need to be stretched so far to accommodate writings ascribed to an author such as Luke, the Gentile Christian *par excellence* in Christian imagination and tradition, into a Jewish environment? Or have terminological epithets and conceptual presuppositions created an artificial embryo that enables Luke's works to subsist continually as the single non-Jewish documents in the Jewish hall of fame of New Testament writings, coloring and governing the interpretation of themes such as Torah observance in Luke-Acts? What would happen if we would temporarily suspend ascribing terms such as "Gentile Christian" to Luke-Acts and begin with the assumption that these two works are just as Jewish as the gospel of Matthew?

Who Was Jewish Anyways? Two Jews, Three Opinions

Ascribing the epithet "Jewish" to any ancient document or author requires clarifying what is meant by such terminology.[11] Just as in our day Jewishness remains a contested category, with various Jewish groups continually and vigorously debating the definition(s) of Jewish identity, so in antiquity Jewishness could be perceived in a variety of ways by both outsiders (i.e., those non-Jews who did not belong to or identify with a particular Jewish community) and insiders (those Jews who were affiliated with and re-

---

[11] Steve Mason, "Jews, Judaeans, Judaizing, Judaism: Problems of Categorization in Ancient History," *JSJ* 38 (2007): 457–512, pleads with historians to discard the usage of the term, "Jew(s)," in their treatments of ancient history. He writes: "According to both insiders and outsiders, the Ἰουδαῖοι (just like Egyptians, Syrians, Romans, etc.) were an *ethnos* with all of the accoutrements" (484). Using the term "Jews" or even "Judaism" for describing ancient Jewry can be misleading as these words may, among other things, convey the impression that Jewish identity in antiquity should be understood primarily from a religious perspective, that ancient "Judaism" constituted a "religion" much like Christianity. Being a Judean in antiquity, however, was not simply a matter of religion, education, or even geographical provenance, as Mason notes, but involved the representation of an entire local culture in a manner similar to being Egyptian, Libyan, or Greek (490). In fact, Mason, Boyarin, and others assert that the phenomenon of religion, as a discrete category of human experience, disembedded from a local culture, is foreign to the ancient civilizations of the Greco-Roman world and the product of the Christianization of the west. During the first two centuries of the Common Era, we should speak of a Judean culture or civilization rather than of a Judaism, especially if by the latter a religion is primarily in view. Cf. Boyarin, *Borderlines*, 224–25. Nevertheless, for the purposes of this inquiry, I still use the terms "Jew(s)," "Jewish," or even "Judaism," since their usage is so deeply entrenched in the history of research and in order to encourage new readings of Matthew and Luke-Acts.

mained attached to a local Jewish community). As Cohen in his work on Jewish identity claims, "uncertainty of Jewishness in antiquity curiously prefigures the uncertainty of Jewishness in modern times."[12] Jewishness, then, was and will always remain, for better or for worse, a variable, non-constant category, open to different definitions and vulnerable to appropriations by various groups of people who wish to declare themselves in some sense as being legitimately "Jewish."

We might begin with the "ethnic" criterion as a means of exploring Jewish identity in antiquity: "The Jews (Judaeans) of antiquity constituted an *ethnos*, an ethnic group. They were a named group, attached to a specific territory, whose members shared a sense of common origins, claimed a common and distinctive history and destiny, possessed one or more distinctive characteristics, and felt a sense of collective uniqueness and solidarity."[13] The ethnic criterion, however, posed several challenging questions for defining Jewish identity in antiquity. Special borderline cases (e.g., Gentile converts, children of only one Jewish parent, etc.) required further clarification and highlighted certain Jewish anxieties over the vulnerable permeability and inevitable trespassing of Jewish-Gentile borders. Hayes highlights the views shared by certain groups of the Second Temple period who held onto the notion of what she dubs "genealogical purity." The authors of Ezra-Nehemiah, the book of *Jubilees,* and 4QMMT only recognized the Jewishness of those individuals whose parents were *both* Jewish (father and mother). For such Jews, to qualify as a Jew (or a Judean), a person had to stem from a pure genealogical tree undefiled by Gentile ancestry: "Groups that defined their Jewishness mostly or exclusively in genealogical terms established an impermeable boundary between Jews and Gentiles. Not only was it impossible for Gentiles to become Jews, but also violations of the genealogical distinction between the two groups (i.e., interethnic sexual unions) were anathema."[14]

Thiessen has recently pointed to the importance of genealogical purity in conjunction with the timing of *eighth-day* circumcision for Jewish male infants as a means for certain Jewish groups throughout the late Second Temple period to demarcate more clearly their Jewish identity. Not only were Jews supposed to belong to a pure Jewish genealogical stock, but they also were to circumcise their sons on the eighth day. The belief in and

---

[12] Shaye J. D. Cohen, *The Beginnings of Jewishness: Boundaries, Varieties, Uncertainties* (Berkeley, Calif.: University of California Press, 1999), 346. Cf. Martin Goodman, *Rome and Jerusalem: The Clash of Ancient Civilizations* (London: Allen Lane, 2007), 168.

[13] Cohen, *The Beginnings of Jewishness*, 7.

[14] Christine E. Hayes, *Gentile Impurities and Jewish Identities: Intermarriage and Conversion from the Bible to the Talmud* (Oxford: Oxford University Press, 2002), 8–9.

practice of eighth-day circumcision allowed these Jews to distinguish themselves from other non-Jewish peoples from Syria and elsewhere who also practiced circumcision. The exclusive affirmation of eighth-day circumcision also denied the possibility for conversion to Judaism even if Gentile males would be willing to undergo circumcision.[15] Jewish circumcision had to occur on the eighth day, not earlier or later. In the eyes of such Jews, any other type of circumcision was deemed worthless for establishing Jewish identity.

Not all ancient Jews held on to this stringent notion of genealogical purity and narrow timeframe for performing circumcision. They tolerated a certain permeability that enabled Gentiles to cross over and become fully Jewish by converting to Judaism. They also accepted the Jewishness of individuals who did not have an impeccable genealogical record, but were children of only one Jewish parent, either the mother (the matrilineal principle) or the father (the patrilineal principle), depending on the Jewish circle.[16]

The ethnic criterion has recently been used as a means for discussing the Jewishness of members who belonged to the Jesus movement. This is essentially the path adopted by Skarsaune and Hvalvik in the volume, *Jewish Believers in Jesus*:

> In this book, by the term "Jewish believers in Jesus" we mean "Jews by birth or conversion who in one way or another believed Jesus was their savior." We have chosen to focus on the criterion of ethnicity rather than the criterion of ideology. Many, perhaps most, histories of "Jewish Christianity" or the like, have done the opposite. The basic definition of who is a Jewish Christian is derived from the definition of which theology and praxis the person in question embraces. One can then either disregard the question of ethnic origin completely, or restrict the term "Jewish Christian" to those Jews who believed in Jesus, and at the same time continued a wholly Jewish way of life.[17]

The application of the criterion of ethnicity allows Skarsaune and many of his colleagues to appreciate the Jewish provenance of a number of "Christian" authors and texts from antiquity. On the other hand, this approach completely diminishes the importance of Torah observance as a marker of

---

[15] Matthew Thiessen, *Contesting Conversion: Genealogy, Circumcision, and Identity in Ancient Judaism and Christianity* (Oxford: Oxford University Press, 2011).

[16] The rabbis eventually championed the view that Jewishness was transmitted through the mother, while other Jews believed it was transmitted through the father. More on this topic in chapter 12 of Part III dealing with circumcision, particularly the section on Timothy's circumcision in Acts 16:1–3.

[17] Oskar Skarsaune, "Jewish Believers in Jesus in Antiquity – Problems of Definition, Method, and Sources," in *Jewish Believers in Jesus*, 3–4. Martin S. Jaffee, *Early Judaism* (Upper Saddle River, N.J.: Prentice Hall, 1997), also highlights the Jewish ideal of belonging to a people stemming from the same physical ancestors (at least in the Jewish imagination) as a meaningful criterion for defining Judaism.

Jewishness for "Christian" and non-Christian Jews alike. Moreover, many of the collaborators of this volume work under certain commonly held assumptions concerning the ethnic origins of a number of authors of the New Testament: Matthew and to a certain extent John are the only canonical gospels discussed in the volume as possibly written by ethnic Jews. Missing are treatments of Mark and Luke. Is this because most of the authors of this volume assume that these gospel writers were ethnically Gentile?[18] In the same volume, the Acts of the Apostles is brought to the reader's attention only in so far as it can provide information about the Jewishness of the historical Paul rather than Luke himself. In the end, despite its splendid resourcefulness, the volume perpetuates the traditional understanding about "Jewish Christians." Authors and writings of the Jesus movement considered as probable Jewish candidates essentially and unsurprisingly amount to Paul, the Jerusalem Church, the gospel of Matthew, segments from the *Pseudo-Clementine* writings, Ebionites, Nazoreans, and other little, insignificant "heretical" sects.[19]

The importance of Jewish Law and its observance, therefore, cannot be underestimated in assessing the potential Jewishness of any author or text from antiquity. Of course, I wish not to reduce exploring or establishing Jewish identity according to the criterion of the observance of the Mosaic Torah. There were certain Jews, such as the so-called Hellenizers, who sought to break away from what was perceived by other Jews as the fundamentals of Jewish observance: keeping the Sabbath, food laws, and circumcision, among other things. Despite their break away from these practices, these Hellenizers, Maccabean propaganda notwithstanding, may have continued to view themselves as Jewish.[20] Schäfer and others would have us think that such Jews did not evaporate from the historical scene once the Maccabean revolt was over, but survived well up until Bar Kokh-

---

[18] It is indeed curious that a treatment of Mark is left out of this volume, since according to Christian tradition the author of the second canonical gospel was a Jew. I obviously do not claim that the Christian tradition is historically reliable on this point, only that a treatment of Mark's Jewishness deserves attention.

[19] One of the exceptions and more interesting chapters in the book would be Torleif Elgvin's consideration of many of the so-called Old Testament Pseudepigrapha as "Jewish Christian." See his "Jewish Christian Editing of the Old Testament Pseudepigrapha," in *Jewish Believers in Jesus*, 278–304.

[20] Gabriele Boccaccini, *The Roots of Rabbinic Judaism* (Grand Rapids, Mich.: Eerdmans, 2002), 162: "The Maccabean propaganda presents Antiochus's measures in Judah not as the result of intra-Jewish conflicts but as the last chapter and inevitable outcome of the opposition between Hellenism and Judaism (1 Macc 1:1–10)"; Jaffee, *Early Judaism*, 40: "From the perspective of hindsight…it is clear that the debate was not between Judaism and Hellenism as opposed forces, but really over the degree to which an already Hellenized Judaism would self-consciously conform even further to international cultural norms."

ba's day and might have even been partly responsible for triggering the Second Revolt against Hadrian.[21] Boccaccini also notes that the Mosaic Torah remains conspicuously absent from earlier strata of Enochic literature, although he acknowledges changes occurred in post-Maccabean times when, thanks to the book of *Jubilees*, Moses emerged as an important figure in the Enochic movement. In the end, then, "Enochians," like the Essenes, would have observed the Torah, though they certainly would have felt that the Mosaic tradition needed a supplement both to understand and repair this world.[22] In a similar vein, even *if* Paul did view the Torah as having in a real sense met its end after the crucifixion and resurrection of Jesus, this would not imply that he ceased to view himself as a Jew.[23] Other Jews, such as the so-called allegorizers, whom Philo condemns for abandoning the literal observance of Jewish customs, might have nonetheless viewed themselves as living out the true intent of the Torah and remaining in a real sense "Jewish." We could also speculate with Kraemer and others about the archaeological evidence and to what extent Jews in Palestine and elsewhere had assimilated into their "pagan" environment and no longer observed some of the central tenets of the Mosaic Torah,[24] though positing, as Schwartz does, that Judaism with its core unifying ideology centered on God-Torah-Temple essentially disappeared after 70 and especially 135 CE, only to remerge some two centuries later thanks to the successful rise of Christianity and the Christianization of the Roman Empire, probably exaggerates the decline of keeping Jewish customs persisting throughout antiquity.[25]

Despite these important caveats, the literary evidence available thus far shows that many Jews (and many non-Jews) considered the observance of central Mosaic commandments such as the Sabbath, kashrut, or circumcision as fundamental markers of Jewish identity and expression.[26] In fact,

---

[21] Peter Schäfer, *Der Bar Kokhba-Aufstand: Studien zum zweiten jüdischen Krieg gegen Rom* (TSAJ 1; Tübingen: Mohr Siebeck, 1981).

[22] Gabriele Boccaccini, *Beyond the Essene Hypothesis: The Parting of the Ways between Qumran and Enochic Judaism* (Grand Rapids, Mich.: Eerdmans, 1998), 167.

[23] Daniel Boyarin, *A Radical Jew: Paul and the Politics of Identity* (Berkeley, Calif.: University of California Press, 1994), 2.

[24] David Kraemer, "Food, Eating, and Meals," in *The Oxford Handbook of Jewish Daily Life in Roman Palestine* (ed. Catherine Hezser; Oxford: Oxford University Press, 2010), 403–19.

[25] Seth Schwartz, *Imperialism and Jewish Society, 200 B.C.E. to 640 C.E.* (Princeton, N.J.: Princeton University Press, 2001). For one review critiquing Schwartz's diachronic reconstruction of early Judaism, see Yaron Z. Eliav, review of Seth Schwartz, *Imperialism and Jewish Society, Prooftexts* 24 (2004): 116–28.

[26] Cohen, *The Beginnings of Jewishness,* 62: "The observance of Jewish laws was perhaps a somewhat more reliable indicator of Jewishness than presence in a Jewish neighborhood or association with known Jews, but it was hardly infallible."

even the *selective* or eclectic appropriation and observance of certain Jewish customs by Gentiles could in principle lead other Greeks and Romans to labeling or even libeling such non-Jews as "Jewish."[27] Any affirmation, then, on the part of Christians of the observance of Jewish custom could at least insinuate to non-Jews their affiliation or at least proximity to Judaism. Consequently, it is through the lens of Torah practice that I have chosen to explore the Jewishness of the works penned by both Matthew and Luke, even though there exist many other ways, not discussed here, of assessing the Jewish character of an ancient author or text, including ideology (eschatology, messianic expectations, "apocalypticism," attitude toward Gentiles, etc.), literary genre, or usage of Jewish scriptures (e.g., Luke's appropriation of the Septuagint). Indeed, Matthew's positive attitude toward the Torah (e.g., Matt 5:17–20) has often served as a cornerstone for establishing the Jewishness of his gospel. But if Luke's writings affirm the observance of the Torah and display an equally remarkable expertise on Jewish legal matters, do they not provide a perspective that in the end is just as Jewish as Matthew's?

Further Terminological Considerations: Torah Practice and the Problem with "Jewish Christianity"

Any study of the history of research on "Jewish Christianity" or "Jewish Christians" reveals a long and confusing debate about what is really meant by the usage of such terminology.[28] The label "Jewish Christian(ity)" has been ascribed to multiple texts and groups, becoming a "rubber bag term, applied to a host of phenomena yet saying nothing with any clarity about the phenomena that would warrant this specific label."[29] Like the terms

---

[27] Cohen, *The Beginnings of Jewishness*, 58–62.

[28] On the history of research and the terminological problems, see Daniel Boyarin, "Rethinking *Jewish Christianity*: An Argument for Dismantling a Dubious Category (To Which is Appended a Correction of My Borderlines)," *JQR* 99 (2009): 7–36; Matt Jackson-McCabe, "What's in a Name? The Problem of 'Jewish Christianity,'" in *Jewish Christianity Reconsidered: Rethinking Ancient Groups and Texts* (ed. Matt Jackson-McCabe; Minneapolis: Fortress, 2007), 7–38; James Carleton Paget, "The Definition of the Terms Jewish Christian and Jewish Christianity in the History of Research," in *Jewish Believers in Jesus*, 22–48; Simon Claude Mimouni, *Le judéo-christianisme ancien: essais historiques* (Paris: Cerf, 1998), 40–42; 68–71; 458–93; Carsten Colpe, *Das Siegel der Propheten: historische Beziehungen zwischen Judentum, Judenchristentum, Heidentum und frühem Islam* (Arbeiten zur neutestamentliche Theologie und Zeitgeschichte 3; Berlin: Institut Kirche und Judentum, 1990), 38–42.

[29] Bruce Malina, "Jewish Christianity or Christian Judaism: Toward a Hypothetical Definition," *JSJ* 7 (1976): 46.

"gnostic" or "Gnosticism," the label "Jewish-Christian" has often been equated unfavorably with heresy, syncretism, or sectarianism by ancient heresiological discourse and even modern scholarship.[30] Mimouni's description of German scholarship on "Jewish Christianity" during the nineteenth and much of the twentieth century is quite sobering:

> Starting from the 19th century, German theology did not stop extracting Christianity from its Jewish roots, even throwing back all of the period of the emergence of the Christian movement to the fringes of heresy – except for Paul and the Pauline trend. The closure of this process, loaded with consequences at the epistemological and methodological level, would be the approach of W. Bauer, for whom heterodoxy precedes orthodoxy, this latter giving birth to *Frühkatholizismus* only toward the end of the 2nd century. As for Jesus, following Hegel, the German theologians of this period extracted him more and more from his Jewish world, along with R. Bultmann going as far as to make him a being almost completely ahistorical – the "Jesus of faith" in opposition to the "Jesus of history." All of these historical constructions of Christianity in its beginnings rest essentially upon a negation of Judaism, on an extraction of the movement of the disciples of Jesus from its life setting, falling neither on Judaism nor paganism, but on a philosophy, the Christian philosophy, as if this latter had been a religion.[31]

Up until the second half of the twentieth century and even beyond, it was crucial for many to sanitize Paul from his Jewish element, to posit the Jewish-Christian ideology of Peter or James, the brother of Jesus, against the emerging (and superior) Greek-Christian and Hellenistic-universal branch of the church,[32] or, finally, to reduce the phenomenon of Torah

---

[30] See Karen L. King, *What is Gnosticism?* (Cambridge, Mass.: Harvard University Press, 2003), who discusses the ways in which early Christian polemicists' discourse of orthodoxy and heresy have been intertwined with twentieth-century scholarship on Gnosticism and has distorted our understanding of ancient texts. The story of "Jewish Christianity" seems painfully similar.

[31] My translation: "À partir du XIXe siècle, la théologie allemande n'a eu de cesse d'extraire le christianisme de ses origines juives, renvoyant même toute la période de l'émergence du mouvement chrétien aux franges de l'hérésie – à l'exception de Paul et du courant paulinien. L'aboutissement de ce procédé, lourd de conséquences sur le plan épistémologique et méthodologique, sera la démarche de W. Bauer, pour qui l'hétérodoxie est antérieure à l'orthodoxie, cette dernière ne donnant naissance au *Frühkatholizismus* que vers la fin du IIe siècle. Quant à Jésus, suivant Hegel, les théologiens allemands de cette époque l'ont de plus en plus extrait de son monde juif, allant jusqu'à en faire, avec R. Bultmann, un être presque totalement ahistorique – le "Jésus de la foi" en opposition au "Jésus de l'histoire." Toutes ces constructions historiques du christianisme en ses débuts reposent essentiellement sur une négation du judaïsme, sur une extraction du mouvement des disciples de Jésus de son milieu de vie, ne reposant plus alors ni sur le judaïsme ni sur le paganisme, mais sur une philosophie, la philosophie chrétienne, comme si cette dernière avait été alors une religion" (Mimouni, *Le judéo-christianisme ancien*, 463 n. 1).

[32] Ferdinand Christian Baur especially confronted Jewish Christianity with Pauline Christianity. For Baur, Pauline Christianity stood for the superior and universal Christian ideals in contrast to the particularism of Jewish Christianity, imprisoned in its national-

observant Jewish Christians in the aftermath of 70 CE to the marginal and insignificant heretical pockets of "Ebionites" and "Nazoreans."[33]

However, the period after World War II witnessed important shifts in the study of Jewish Christianity, as many Christian specialists now seemed ready to acknowledge the Jewish heritage of their Christian tradition. The cardinal Jean Daniélou went the furthest in this acclamation, placing all of Christianity until the middle of the second century CE under the rubric of Jewish Christianity.[34] In his loose usage of the concept and the term, Daniélou did not imply that all early Christians belonged to the Jewish community and observed the Torah. Rather, Christians at this time expressed themselves within a literary and ideological framework that borrowed from Jewish patterns of thought and expression. His rather vague definition of Jewish Christianity, therefore, was comprehensive enough to include virtually all authors of the first one hundred years or so of Christian history, since most Christian writers of this period used Jewish categories and concepts to express their thoughts and beliefs.

---

ism and legalism. True to his application of Hegelian philosophical principles to the study of church history, Baur believed that Christianity made its entrance into human history at a time when Judaism and "paganism" had long fallen into decay. His views on Judaism represent nothing more than a refined Protestant "Hegelian supersessionism" of the traditional Christian teaching on replacement theology. Nevertheless, his serious appreciation of the phenomenon of Torah observant "Jewish Christians" cannot be underestimated in any historical inquiry on the history of the Jesus movement. See Ferdinand Christian Baur, *The Church History of the First Three Centuries* (trans. Allan Menzies; 2 vols.; London: Williams and Norgate, 1878), especially volume 1. On the roots of the study of ancient Jewish Christianity in the Enlightenment in early eighteenth-century England and its impact on German scholars of the nineteenth century such as Baur and the so-called Tübingen School, see F. Stanley Jones, ed., *The Rediscovery of Jewish Christianity: From Toland to Baur* (History of Biblical Studies 5; Atlanta: Society of Biblical Literature, 2012).

[33] These heretical groups are often presented as *the* official representatives of "Jewish Christians" in standard introductions to the New Testament. Thus, for example, Bart D. Ehrman's *The New Testament: A Historical Introduction to the Early Christian Writings* (Oxford: Oxford University Press, 2008), 205–8, includes under the rubric of "Jewish Christian Gospels," only the extra-canonical writings known as "The Gospel of the Nazareans," "The Gospel of the Ebionites," and "the Gospel of the Hebrews." I argue that other gospels such as Matthew and Luke should also be labeled as such, if we mean by this term that they represent "Jews who had converted to belief in Jesus as the messiah but who nonetheless continued to maintain their Jewish identity, keeping kosher food laws, observing the sabbath, circumcising their baby boys, praying in the direction of Jerusalem, and engaging in a number of other Jewish practices" (Ehrman, *The New Testament,* 206). Since so many still employ the term "Jewish Christian" in a way that excludes canonical authors such Luke and even Matthew from this category, I prefer to discard the term altogether.

[34] Jean Daniélou, *Théologie du judéo-christianisme* (2d ed.; Histoire des doctrines chrétiennes avant Nicée 1; Tournai: Desclée, 1991).

In some ways, Daniélou anticipated the "The Ways That Never Parted" model by globally affirming the Jewish dimension of nascent Christianity, at least during the first century of its existence. Some, however, criticized the arbitrariness of his chronological schematization of church history, which he artificially divided into three periods: Jewish, Greek, and Latin.[35] Why did the Jewish Christian phase suddenly cease in the first half of the second century to make place for a Greek period of church history? What happened to the afterlife of Jewish Christianity in the subsequent centuries after Bar Kokhba until Constantine and beyond? Most strikingly, Daniélou omitted from his volume on Jewish Christianity the treatment of any New Testament text! These documents, after all, were all written during the timeframe he labeled as Jewish Christian. As Robert Murray astutely states, "the supreme monument of Jewish Christianity is the New Testament itself."[36]

Nonetheless, we retain from Daniélou's research a sincere desire to affirm in a comprehensive way the pervasive Jewish fabric encompassing all of early Christianity during its formative stages. More than Daniélou, however, I feel the need to signal the ongoing importance of the question of the observance of the Torah during the formative stages of the Jesus movement after 70 CE Torah praxis was not important only for James and the church of Jerusalem or, later on, the so-called Ebionites and Nazoreans, as Daniélou presumed, but for other members of the Jesus movement as well such as Matthew and Luke.[37] On the other hand, like Daniélou, I fully agree that Jewishness should not be reduced to the criterion of Torah practice. Once again, there were Jews, whether followers of Jesus or not, who might not have viewed the observance of the Torah as the primary index for measuring their Jewishness. Nevertheless, employing the criterion of Torah observance remains an efficient and practical way for concretely assessing the Jewishness of many ancient authors and texts. It is no historical accident that the decline of the observance of the Sabbath, kashrut, circumcision, and other Jewish customs among followers of Jesus coincides with the disappearance of a visible, corporate body of Jewish disciples of Jesus from the historical scene.[38]

---

[35] The criticisms against Daniélou's work are best summarized by Robert A. Kraft, "In Search of 'Jewish Christianity' and its 'Theology': Problems of Definition and Methodology," *RSR* 60 (1972): 81–92.

[36] Robert Murray, "Defining Judaeo-Christianity," *HeyJ* 15 (1974): 308.

[37] Daniélou, *Théologie du judéo-christianisme*, 35–37.

[38] On the observance of Jewish customs among *Gentile* Christians see Michele Murray, *Playing a Jewish Game: Gentile Christian Judaizing in the First and Second Centuries CE* (Studies in Christianity and Judaism/Études sur le christianisme et le judaïsme 13; Waterloo, Ontario: Wilfrid Laurier University Press, 2004).

The French historian Marcel Simon, who carried out his research around the same time as Daniélou but described the phenomenon of Jewish Christianity in fundamentally different ways, especially signaled the importance of employing the criterion of Torah praxis for any inquiry on ancient Jewish Christianity.[39] First of all, for Simon, it was possible to speak of several Jewish Christianities.[40] Simon categorized Jewish Christians (*judéo-chrétiens*) in at least two different ways: the ethnic and religious sense. The former sense designated ethnic Jews who converted to the Christian faith; the latter referred to Christians whose religion contained Jewish elements, particularly those related to Torah observance.[41] Simon did not agree in fusing the two criteria into one definition, finding it too restrictive and arguing that there were "converted" Jews, such as Paul, who had ceased practicing their ancestral customs but remained Jewish, just as there were non-Jews among the ranks of Judaizers who were not ethnically Jewish but observed numerous precepts of the Torah.[42] Simon even added a third category under the rubric of *judéo-christianisme*: "syncretizing" sects, described by ancient heresiologists as not only Judaizing in their practice but also embracing doctrines radically different from orthodoxy.[43] Today, many would view Simon's usage and understanding of much of his terminology ("syncretistic," "gnostic," etc.) as problematic, and the various groups he has listed as "Jewish Christian" has assisted in generating the ongoing confusion about the phenomena this terminology actually circumscribes. Ultimately, Simon spelled out his preference for the criteri-

---

[39] Marcel Simon, *Verus Israël. Études sur les relations entre chrétiens et juifs dans l'empire romain (135-425)* (2d ed.; Paris: É. de Boccard, 1964).

[40] Thus anticipating Raymond Brown, "Not Jewish Christianity and Gentile Christianity but Types of Jewish/Gentile Christianity," *CBQ* 45 (1983): 74–79.

[41] Simon, *Verus Israël*, 277: "Il peut désigner, d'une part, les Juifs convertis à la foi chrétienne, les chrétiens issus d'Israël; il s'applique, d'autre part, à ceux des chrétiens dont la religion reste mêlée d'éléments judaïques et qui, en particulier, continuent de se plier à tout ou partie des observances."

[42] Ibid., 277. L. Marchal fused both criteria together in his definition of Jewish Christians. See his "Judéo-chrétiens," in *Dictionnaire de théologie catholique* (eds. A. Vacant et al.; 15 vols.; Paris: Letouzey et Ané, 1899–1950), 8.2.1681–1709. Marchal defined Jewish Christians as "les chrétiens d'origine juive qui associent les observances de la religion mosaïque aux croyances et aux pratiques chrétiennes." More recently, Mimouni has readopted Marchal's definition (see below).

[43] "Un troisième type de judéo-christianisme est représenté par l'ensemble de ces sectes syncrétisantes décrites par les hérésiologues et qui, non contentes de judaïser dans la pratique, professent en outre des doctrines radicalement et cette fois positivement différentes de celles de la grande Eglise" (Simon, *Verus Israël*, 280).

on of Torah praxis for assessing Jewish Christianity, since he viewed ancient Judaism primarily as an "orthopraxy" rather than an "orthodoxy."[44]

One of the problems with employing the criterion of praxis involves *measuring* the degree of Torah observance to determine the Jewishness of a given text or group. Since practices will vary according to location, social conditions, and religious beliefs, where does the line of demarcation begin and end when employing this criterion to assess whether a text or group qualifies as Jewish Christian?[45] Simon pointed to Acts 15 as a means for distinguishing Jewish Christians from the rest of Christianity: Jewish Christians went beyond the minimal requirements of the so-called Apostolic Decree, while Gentile Christians only observed the basic commandments of the decree. Simon's proposal brings us close to Boyarin's call to focus (without employing the problematic nomenclature, "Jewish Christian") on collecting and analyzing the "evidence for followers of Jesus who continued to observe the Torah or newly came to observe the Torah and the different varieties of such Christians at different times as well as those Christians who abandoned the Law, even the minimal requirements imposed, as it were, by the Gentile Christian author of Acts on his fellow gentiles...."[46]

This is precisely the task set out in this monograph: to demonstrate that the authors of Matthew and Luke-Acts affirm the observance of the Mosaic Torah *in its totality*, a maximalist measurement and assessment of their Jewishness according to criterion of Torah praxis. The brief presentation about the tortuous history of the usage of the terms "Jewish Christian" and "Jewish Christianity" sufficiently warrants suspending the usage of such confusing and problematic terminology for the time being. Its usage has been too intertwined with heresiological discourse, theological prejudice,

---

[44] Marcel Simon, "Problèmes du judéo-christianisme," in *Aspects du judéo-christianisme: Colloque de Strasbourg 23–25 avril 1964* (Bibliothèque des centres d'études supérieures spécialisés: Travaux du centre d'études supérieures d'histoire des religions de Strasbourg; Paris: Presses Universitaires de France, 1965), 1–16. Also in his postscript to *Verus Israël*: "En fait le critère le plus sûr, sinon absolument le seul, dont nous disposions pour caractériser et délimiter le judéo-christianisme reste encore l'observance. Au même titre que le judaïsme, le judéo-christianisme est d'abord une orthopraxie. Il se distingue par une attitude fondamentalement légaliste et par son attachement à une observance non pas simplement apparentée dans son esprit, mais bien identique à celle du judaïsme et qu'il retient en totalité ou en partie" (p. 27).

[45] Giovanni Filoramo and Claudio Gianotto, "Introduzione," in *Verus Israel: Nuove prospettive sul giudeocristianesimo. Atti del Colloquio di Torino (4-5 novembre 1999)* (eds. Giovanni Filoramo and Claudio Gianotto; Brescia: Paideia Editrice, 2001), 13–14, underline this problem.

[46] Boyarin, "Rethinking Jewish Christianity," 33. I am delighted that after examining my research Boyarin no longer views Luke-Acts as Gentile Christian texts.

and conceptual and terminological confusion.⁴⁷ Even Daniélou, as we saw, who used the term Jewish-Christian in a very wide sense, left out from his *magnum opus* on Jewish Christianity the treatment of the entire New Testament. It comes as no surprise that not one of the recent conferences and edited volumes devoted to the subject of "Jewish Christianity" has included Luke's writings into the discussion. The terminology continues to conceal traditional presuppositions that govern the scope of scholarly investigation.⁴⁸ It seems that whenever the term "Jewish Christian" pops up, it leads, for the most part, to a confined interest in Elkesaites, Ebionites, Nazoreans, the *Pseudo-Clementine* literature, the Jerusalem Church headed by James, or finally the gospel of Matthew, at the cost of ignoring other potential Jewish candidates such as Luke's writings. For some, the term "Jewish *Christian*" also implies there is something intrinsically non-Jewish about said documents that officially licenses omitting any real and serious engagement with ancient Jewish sources for their elucidation.⁴⁹ Consequently, I have also chosen to leave out of my research the very usage of the term "Christian," even though it appears in Acts (11:26; 26:28). I have no problem employing the term "Christian"; modern presuppositions surrounding this epithet concern me. For too long, the word "Christian," like the term "church" (I used instead the Greek term *ekklesia* or speak simply

---

⁴⁷ These comments also apply to a lesser extent to the terms "Christian Jew" or "Christian Judaism." For the time being, it seems better to set this jargon aside and focus on assessing the phenomenon of Torah observance in the Jesus movement.

⁴⁸ A treatment of Luke and his writings as Jewish Christian is missing in Skarsaune and Hvalvik, eds., *Jewish Believers in Jesus*; McCabe, ed., *Jewish Christianity Reconsidered*; Simon Claude Mimouni, ed., *Le judéo-christianisme dans tous ses états: Actes du colloque de Jérusalem 6-10 1998* (Paris: Cerf, 2001). In Peter J. Tomson and Doris Lambers-Petry, eds., *The Image of the Judaeo-Christians in Ancient Jewish and Christian Literature* (WUNT 158; Tübingen: Mohr Siebeck, 2003), one will find the excellent article by Daniel Stökl Ben Ezra, "'Christians' Observing 'Jewish' Festivals of Autumn," 53–73, which, in my opinion, includes an interesting and compelling proposal that the author of Acts observed Yom Kippur. Nevertheless, the article does not focus on Luke as a Jewish Christian. Likewise, Filoramo and Gianotto, *Verus Israel: Nuove prospettive sul giudeo cristianesimo*, includes no treatment of Luke's writings as Jewish Christian although it contains one article (not dealing directly with Luke) by Jürgen Wehnert who has written an important monograph on the Apostolic Decree, emphasizing, among other things, Luke's affirmation of the observance of the Law. See his *Die Reinheit des "christlichen Gottesvolkes" aus Juden und Heiden* (FRLANT 173; Göttingen: Vandenhoeck & Ruprecht, 1997). A treatment of Luke-Acts and Jewish Christianity is also missing in the older volume dedicated to Jean Daniélou, *Judéo-Christianisme: Recherches historiques et théologiques offertes en hommage au Cardinal Jean Daniélou* (Recherches de science religieuse; Paris: Éditions Beauchesne, 1972).

⁴⁹ Cf. John W. Marshall, "John's Jewish (Christian?) Apocalypse?" in *Jewish Christianity Reconsidered*, 233–56, who, for similar reasons, prefers to qualify the Revelation of John simply as "Jewish" rather than "Jewish-Christian."

of the "Jesus movement"), demarcates an autonomous group or space lying outside the Jewish realm. This assumption may accurately describe the contemporary scene where church and synagogue exist as two independent and autonomous entities, but this reality hardly reflects the social and historical circumstances in Luke's time.[50]

For the time being, then, I use the pedantic formulation of "Jewish followers of Jesus" and "Gentile followers of Jesus." By "Jewish followers of Jesus," I mean simply that such persons are Jewish in an ethnic sense: they are of Jewish ancestry (through either one or both parents). Gentile followers of Jesus, on the other hand, are those members of the Jesus movement who do not have Jewish ancestry. Within both camps can be found a variety of persons who observe Jewish ritual commandments to various degrees, ranging from a maximalist tendency that strives to keep the Torah as much as possible, to a minimalist approach that is highly selective in or entirely dismissive of observing the rituals aspects of Jewish tradition.[51]

Qualifying Matthew and Luke-Acts simply as "Jewish" will challenge specialists in ancient Judaism and Christianity to reconsider their understanding and configuration of Jewish and Christian texts alike, which are still compartmentalized according to academic fields of discipline and specialization such as "early Christian studies" and "early Judaism." By proclaiming such literature as Jewish, it will anchor even more this "Christian" literature in its Jewish matrix, unveil more fully the pluriform nature

---

[50] Contra Pervo, *Acts,* 294: "The advent of the adjective "Christian" (v.26d) marks the followers of Jesus as a body recognized by outsiders as distinct from Judaism." But do the terms "Pharisees" or "Sadducees," which also appear in Acts, refer to bodies outside of Judaism? What about Acts 24:5, where the Jesus movement is described as part of Judaism, as the "sect (αἱρέσεως) of the Nazarenes," the very same kind of language his contemporary, Josephus, uses to describe the different Jewish "sects" (Sadducees, Pharisees, Essenes, and Zealots) of his time? Pervo, on p. 294 n. 46, claims that since Luke is familiar with the word "Christian," it is not anachronistic to use such terminology when commenting on Acts. I argue that it is anachronistic to use this term, if we understand it as referring to an entity entirely distinct from Judaism. Luke's usage of the term "Christian" need not refer to a group outside Judaism. Even outsiders who designated the followers of the Jesus movement as such may still have viewed them as belonging to a Jewish group of a certain (messianic) tendency. The term simply means "messianists." Cf. Hugh J. Schonfield, *Proclaiming the Messiah: The Life and Letters of Paul, Envoy to the Nations* (London: Open Gate, 1997), 37.

[51] I prefer the terms "follower" or "disciple" than "believer" (even if the latter appears frequently in the New Testament), which Skarsaune currently employs. See Skarsaune, "Jewish Believers in Jesus in Antiquity," 3–21. Personally, I find the term too loaded with contemporary self-referential overtones that risk reducing the essence of the identity of ancient followers of Jesus to confessional beliefs. The terms "follower" or "disciple" of Jesus signal not only adherence to theological beliefs, but also fidelity to a certain way of living, to ancestral customs so intimately tied to ethnicity.

of ancient Judaism, and radically challenge many cherished presuppositions about the Jesus movement and its relationship to ancient Jewry.

The Judaization and Gentilization of Matthew and Luke-Acts

Scholars agree that the period after 1945 marked an important transition in the study of both Matthew and Luke-Acts.[52] Ever since, many New Testament specialists have employed redaction criticism (*Redaktionsgeschichte*), which had evolved out of its parent, form criticism (*Formgeschichte*), in order to detect the intentions, ideology, and situation of the final authors of the canonical gospels. Scholars in the aftermath of World War Two began to focus on the *final* stages of the literary development of these traditions, on the reworking and shaping of the literary sources and material available to the evangelists who gave the final shape to the texts as we now have them, whereas previous investigators had focused on the traditions in the synoptic gospels in their oral and written forms in order to unearth insights about the earliest *ekklesia* as well as the historical Jesus by breaking down these materials into their smaller units and reconstructing their supposed original *Sitz im Leben*. By performing such an analysis, many hoped to produce a history of the later stages of the Jesus movement during the end of the first century, to unearth the *Tendenz* of the redactor of each gospel.

---

[52] The discussion here on the history of research can only cover certain aspects related to the Jewish nature of these writings and their relationship to the theme of the Jewish Law. For a general discussion on the history of research on Matthew until 1980, see Graham N. Stanton, "The Origin and Purpose of Matthew's Gospel: Matthean Scholarship from 1945-1980," *ANRW* 25.3: 1889–951. See also, Donald Senior, *What Are They Saying about Matthew?* (rev. and enl. ed.; New York: Paulist, 1996), especially pp. 62–73. Paul Foster, *Community, Law, and Mission in Matthew's Gospel* (WUNT 2.177; Tübingen: Mohr Siebeck, 2004), 22–77, is extremely helpful for providing a discussion on more recent works, especially social-scientific treatments. For Luke, see François Bovon, *Luke the Theologian: Fifty-five Years of Research (1950-2005)* (2d ed.; Waco, Tex.: Baylor University Press, 2006). For a discussion on the history of research on Luke in so far as his Gentile or Jewish identity and attitude toward the Law are concerned, see Matthias Klinghardt, *Gesetz und Volk Gottes* (WUNT 2.32; Tübingen: Mohr Siebeck, 1988), 1–9; Kalervo Salo, *Luke's Treatment of the Law: A Redaction-Critical Investigation* (AASF.DHL 57; Helsinki: Suomalainen Tiedeakatemia, 1991), 13–41; William R.G. Loader, *Jesus' Attitude towards the Law* (WUNT 2.97; Tübingen: Mohr Siebeck, 1997), 137–54 (on Matthew); 273–300 (on Luke); Rick Strelan, *Luke the Priest: The Authority of the Author of the Third Gospel* (Burlington, Vt.: Ashgate, 2008), 26–30. Joseph B. Tyson, *Luke, Judaism, and the Scholars: Critical Approaches to Luke-Acts* (Columbia, S.C.: University of South Carolina, 1999) is also very helpful.

Bornkamm was among the first to apply a thorough redaction-critical analysis to the Gospel of Matthew.[53] Initially, Bornkamm set the study of Matthew on a progressive track, emphasizing the redactor's allegiance to Judaism and engagement in an *intra muros* debate with other Jewish peers.[54] Unfortunately, Bornkamm subsequently backed away from his initial thesis, declaring that the Matthean community knew itself to have been cut off from the Jewish community and to have no longer gathered for the sake of the Torah but rather in the name of Jesus.[55] The tendency to view Matthew as separate (*extra muros*) from Judaism became the dominant view for the next two decades.[56] Not until the late eighties would the pendulum swing back and replace Matthew within the parameters of pluriform Judaism.

With the momentum building in favor of viewing Matthew as a representative of *the* decisive rupture between Christians and Jews, it would not take long for redactional critics to relegate the more "Jewish" features of Matthew into their supposed earlier strata of tradition, hoping thereby to restrict the historical relevance of this material to a primitive "Jewish Christian" stage when the Jesus movement had not yet parted its way from the "synagogue across the street."[57] While many of these redaction critics assumed that the first apostolic generation of followers of Jesus remained faithful to Torah observance, they claimed that the author of Matthew had detached himself from such duties. The "'Jewish' material, judged antithetic to the gospel's universalistic outlook," was "viewed as old lace: still

---

[53] Günther Bornkamm, Gerhard Barth, and Heinz Joachim Held, eds., *Tradition and Interpretation in Matthew* (trans. Percy Scott; Philadelphia, Pa.: Westminster Press, 1963).

[54] This is the position Bornkamm advocated in his article "End-Expectation and Church in Matthew," in *Tradition and Interpretation in Matthew*, 15–51. In this article Bornkamm argued that Matthew was still attached to the Law and Judaism (p. 22).

[55] Günther Bornkamm, "The Authority to 'Bind' and 'Loose' in the Church in Matthew's Gospel: The Problem of Sources in Matthew's Gospel," in *Jesus and Man's Hope* (ed. Donald G. Miller; 2 vols.; Pittsburgh, Pa.: Pittsburgh Theological Seminary, 1970), 1:41.

[56] According to Stanton, the position that views Matthew as having recently broken away from Judaism prevailed up until the 1980s. See Stanton, "The Origin and Purpose of Matthew's Gospel," 1914.

[57] According to Élian Cuvillier, "Torah Observance and Radicalization in the First Gospel. Matthew and First-Century Judaism: A Contribution to the Debate," *NTS* 55 (2009): 159, n. 46, the expression is usually attributed to Krister Stendahl, *The School of St. Matthew* (ASNU 20; Uppsala: C. W. K. Gleerup, Lund, 1954).

valued by the community that preserved them, but no longer of practical use."⁵⁸

This bifurcation of Matthew into traditional (=Jewish-Christian) and redactional layers (=Gentile Christian) led some to go as far as dismissing the very Jewish identity of the author of the first canonical gospel. Ever since the days of Papias (Eusebius, *Hist. eccl.* 3.39.16), it had become customary in Christian tradition to view the gospel of Matthew as written by a Jew who had penned his work for the "Hebrews." But in the ecumenical climate of the post-World War Two era, when many scholars were trying to deal with the anti-Semitic legacy of Christianity, Matthew's Jewishness came under serious attack.⁵⁹ Clark was one of the first during that era to argue against the Jewish identity of Matthew. He believed that the rejection of Israel was a central theme in the gospel of Matthew. Consequently, a Gentile wrote this work.⁶⁰ Nepper-Christensen also denied that Matthew was a Jewish-Christian, distinguishing between traditions the evangelist received on the one hand and his own emphases on the other.⁶¹ In a similar vein, Wolfgang Trilling claimed that the Matthean community had developed out of an earlier Jewish Christian base to form a predominantly Gentile Christian stock. Accordingly, the final redactor of Matthew could only address Gentile Christian, universal concerns: "Matthäus als der Endredaktor denkt entschieden heidenchristlich-universal."⁶²

During the first three decades after 1945, Luke's writings underwent a remarkably similar assessment as the gospel of his sibling Matthew. The

---

⁵⁸ Amy-Jill Levine, *The Social and Ethnic Dimensions of Matthean Salvation History: "Go nowhere among the Gentiles. . ." (Matt. 10:5b)* (Studies in Bible and Early Christianity 14; Lewiston, N.Y.: The Edwin Mellen Press, 1988), 276.

⁵⁹ The "anti-Semitic" elements in Matthew have also led some Jewish scholars to question the Jewish origins of Matthew. So, for example, the late David Flusser, "Anti-Jewish Sentiment in the Gospel of Matthew," in *Judaism of the Second Temple Period. Vol. 2: The Jewish Sages and Their Literature* (trans. Azzan Yadin; Grand Rapids, Mich.: Eerdmans, 2009), 351–53; Herbert W. Basser, *The Mind behind the Gospels: A Commentary to Matthew 1–14* (Boston, Mass.: Academic Studies Press, 2009), 7.

⁶⁰ Kenneth Willis Clark, "The Gentile Bias in Matthew," *JBL* 66 (1947): 165–72. Cf. John P. Meier, *The Vision of Matthew: Christ, Church, and Morality in the First Gospel* (New York: Paulist, 1979), 22, who asserts the Gentile identity of the author on different grounds: "...a learned Gentile scholar, not a learned Jewish scholar."

⁶¹ Poul Nepper-Christensen, *Das Matthäusevangelium, ein judenchristliches Evangelium?* (ATDan 1; Aarhus: Universitetsforlaget, 1958), especially pp. 202–7.

⁶² Wolfgang Trilling, *Das wahre Israel: Studien zur Theologie des Matthäus-Evangeliums* (SANT 10; Munich: Kösel-Verlag, 1964), 215. Georg Strecker drew sharp distinctions between a supposed "Jewish Christian" phase and a latter Gentile redactional stage in the Gospel of Matthew. See Georg Strecker, *Der Weg Gerechtigkeit: Untersuchung zur Theologie des Matthäus* (FRLANT 82; Göttingen: Vandenhoeck & Ruprecht, 1962), especially pp. 15–35.

rather singular and dissident voice of Jervell, too prophetic for that time, did not dissuade the majority of his New Testament redaction critics from restricting the more Jewish elements of Luke-Acts to the traditional strata Luke had inherited from his sources. Theological schemes of *Heilsgeschichte* ("salvation history") conveniently came to the forefront for those who needed to minimize the significance of the many favorable references in Luke-Acts toward Torah observance. These interpreters maintained that the positive descriptions concerning Torah observance in Luke-Acts could not inform the modern reader about Luke's own praxis, because Judaism and Jerusalem allegedly lay so far behind in the mind of the Gentile Christian author who could only concern himself about "universal" matters rather than "petty" halakic debates. For such interpreters and even many today, Luke has given up on Judaism, gazing with fixed admiration westward toward Rome with his back turned to Jerusalem.

Particularly the work of the late and influential Conzelmann, the progenitor of the redaction-critical approach to Luke-Acts, has led many away from appreciating Luke's special relationship to and affirmation of Judaism in all of its aspects. Conzelmann, who argued that Luke should be viewed more as a "theologian" than a "historian," artificially divided Luke-Acts into three discrete epochs of "salvation history": 1) the period of Israel 2) the period of Jesus 3) and the period of the church.[63] For Conzelmann, only the first period of salvation history belonged to the "time of the Law and prophecy."[64] By the third period of salvation history, the Law had lost its special footing and had been "given up on principle by the Church."[65] Conzelmann's *Heilsgeschichte* scheme, however, clashes with the consistent Lukan portrait of Jesus and his Jewish followers as faithful Torah observers *throughout* the narration in both Luke and Acts. Even after recounting the so-called Jerusalem Council, which Conzelmann curiously interpreted as marking the "actual separation of the Church from the Temple and the Law,"[66] Luke depicts Paul as continually observing the Torah, circumcising Timothy (!), visiting the temple, and affirming his allegiance to the Pharisaic party as well as the ancestral customs of the Jewish people. Conzelmann seemed dimly aware of this Achillean heel that could lead to the downfall of his entire *Heilsgeschichte* empire. He resorted to dismissing the significance of the presentation in Acts of Paul as Torah observant on the grounds that Luke was merely reminiscing about

---

[63] Hans Conzelmann, *The Theology of St. Luke* (trans. Geoffrey Buswell; New York: Harper & Row, 1961), 16.

[64] Hans Conzelmann, *Acts of the Apostles* (Hermeneia; trans. James Limburg et al.; Philadelphia, Pa.: Fortress, 1987), xlv.

[65] Conzelmann, *The Theology of St. Luke*, 147.

[66] Ibid.

an earlier period of church history that necessitated a literary adjustment and fine-tuning of Paul as a Law abiding Jew.[67] In Luke's time though, the *ekklesia* had totally detached itself from the Law. The circular reasoning worked surprisingly well. Regrettably, it won the hearts of many New Testament exegetes and still affects contemporary scholarship.[68]

In many ways, then, Matthew and Luke drew similar lots in the immediate post-war period: New Testament specialists generally applied redactional critical readings to the writings of both authors, often relegating the Jewish elements recorded therein to earlier strata of a fossilized period bearing no relevance for understanding the *Sitz im Leben* of the gospel authors. In Matthew's case, however, as we shall see, scholars from the last two decades of the twentieth century would refine their application of redaction criticism and raise social critical considerations that would lead to a complete "rejudaization" of the first canonical gospel. Unfortunately, these methodological processes and considerations have not yet fully revolutionized the classical perception of Luke, still viewed by many as an ignorant Gentile Christian, hostile to Judaism – this despite the protests of certain specialists who state otherwise.

Present State of Research

That the Gospel of Matthew currently enjoys the status of being the most "Jewish" of all gospels can be easily verified through a quick perusal of various popular and academic works on the New Testament.[69] Those responsible for the decisive shift away from the Gentile Matthew of the 1960s and 1970s to the Jewish Matthew of our time, include, among others, Overman,[70] Levine, and Saldarini, the latter strongly emphasizing

---

[67] Ibid.

[68] Pervo's otherwise excellent commentary on Acts treats Luke's attitude toward Judaism like his predecessor Conzelmann. See Pervo, *Acts*, 283 (the Jewish Law is for Luke merely a "superstition"); 544 (projection of Justin Martyr's attitude towards the Jewish Law onto Acts).

[69] Craig A. Evans, "The Jewish Christian Gospel Tradition," in *Jewish Believers in Jesus*, 242: "The Gospel of Matthew has been traditionally viewed as the most Jewish of the four New Testament Gospels. Whereas the Jewish authorship of Mark and John is disputed, almost everyone agrees that the Matthean Gospel was composed by a Jew." Evans' omission of considering Luke as a Jew is quite telling. Ehrman, *The New Testament*, 206: "…the Gospel of Matthew is in many respects the most Jewish of our Gospels"; L. Michael White, "The Gospel of Matthew: Jesus as the New Moses," [cited on 13 February, 2012]. Online: http://www.pbs.org/wgbh/pages/frontline/shows/religion/story/matthew.html: "Matthew is the most Jewish of all the gospels."

[70] J. Andrew Overman, Matthew's Gospel and Formative Judaism: The Social World of the Matthean Community (Minneapolis: Fortress, 1990).

reading the gospel of Matthew as part of "the post-70 Jewish debate over how Judaism was to be lived and how that way of life was to be articulated in order to insure the survival of the Jewish community without the Temple and its related political institutions."[71] For Saldarini and others it is imperative to read Matthew "with other Jewish post-destruction literature, such as the apocalyptic works 2 Baruch, 4 Ezra and Apocalypse of Abraham, early strata of the Mishnah, and Josephus," works that "envision Judaism in new circumstances, reorganize its central symbols, determine the precise will of God, and propose a course of action for the faithful community."[72] Scholars such as Saldarini tend to place Matthew and his audience within Judaism, as still belonging to Jewish society – *intra muros*, to use the currency employed by Matthean scholars to describe this complex relationship.

Others, however, have not followed this trend. Hagner, for example, sees Matthew as representing a Jewish form of Christianity rather than a Christian form of Judaism (two categories that for our purposes are misleading and have been discarded from this inquiry, although the term "Christian Judaism" is certainly preferable to "Jewish Christianity").[73] Hagner exaggerates the supposed "radical newness" contained in the Gospel of Matthew. He asserts that there were several "new things" in the Matthean air the Judaism of that time could not handle, including among others: the eschatological announcement and arrival of the messiah and the kingdom, the belief in the messiah as a unique manifestation of God, the claim that the messiah must die a death of a criminal for the forgiveness of sins, obedience to God centered upon Jesus, not the Law, the inclusion of Gentiles into the Jewish community, and Matthew's supposedly "high Christology." It is becoming more apparent, however, that many of these beliefs, once thought to be unique to early Christianity, find their antecedents within the Jewish world of thought and practice or at least can be

---

[71] Anthony J. Saldarini, "The Gospel of Matthew and Jewish-Christian Conflict in Galilee," in *The Galilee in Late Antiquity* (ed. L. Levine; New York: Jewish Theological Seminary of America, 1992), 24. See also Saldarini's *Matthew's Christian-Jewish Community* (Chicago Studies in the History of Judaism; Chicago: University of Chicago Press, 1994); Overman, *Matthew's Gospel and Formative Judaism,* 4, and much of the first two chapters of that work. We should add David C. Sim, *The Gospel of Matthew and Christian Judaism: The History and Social Setting of the Matthean Community* (Studies in the New Testament and Its World. Edinburgh: T&T Clark, 1998), within the same trajectory.

[72] Saldarini, "The Gospel of Matthew and Jewish-Christian Conflict in Galilee," 24.

[73] Donald A. Hagner, "Matthew: Apostate, Reformer, Revolutionary," *NTS* 49 (2003): 193–209; "Matthew: Christian Judaism or Jewish Christianity?" in *The Face of the New Testament Studies: A Survey of Recent Research* (Scot McKnight and Grant R. Osborne, eds.; Grand Rapids, Mich.: Baker Academic, 2004), 263–82.

understood as natural developments emerging from within a Jewish context.[74] Hagner's approach to the *intra/extra muros* debate, in the end, relies too heavily on doctrinal matters and neglects the social, political, and economic factors for explaining the "parting of the ways."[75]

Some scholars employing, like Saldarini, social-scientific approaches to the gospel of Matthew, nevertheless, view Matthew and his audience as having parted ways with Jewry and Torah observance. In his treatment of the so-called Matthean Antitheses (Matt 5:21–48), Foster concludes that Matthew's approach to the Torah is occasionally supersessionary. While much of his research proves insightful and useful, Foster underestimates some of the ancient Jewish parallels relevant for assessing Matthew's interpretation of certain halakic matters. Thus, Foster highlights the Matthean critique of the misusage of oaths, going as far as implying that the Mosaic legislation on oaths is viewed by Matthew as an evil.[76] While noting the Josephan reference to the Essene abstention from oaths, Foster dismisses this matter with a mere footnote, relying on the standard model that equates the "community of Qumran" with the Essenes: "However, the extant material from Qumran demonstrates that group members were required to use an oath as part of the entrance rite into the community (1QS 5.7–9). On this basis it appears best to speak of an aversion towards oaths at Qumran and not a total prohibition."[77]

But can the Matthean antithesis on oaths be understood along similar lines, as a hyperbolic statement, which resembled the praxis reflected in the *Rule of the Community*? Besides noting the problems involved in equating the Essenes in Josephus' writings with the group(s) responsible for the production of the diverse documents found near Qumran, the language Josephus uses to describe the Essene view on oaths should be appreciated: "they esteem it worse than perjury (ἐπιορκίας); for they say that he who cannot be believed without [swearing by] God is already condemned" (*J.W.* 2:135)."[78] The language in Josephus could also be taken as supersessionary and imply that the Essenes even viewed some of the Mosaic legislation as evil. Josephus, on the other hand, highlights the strict Essene adherence to the Torah, and so we should seek for better explanations accounting for their perspective on oaths. This applies to Matthew's case

---

[74] See especially Boyarin's *Borderlines*.

[75] See Warren Carter, "Matthew's Gospel: Jewish Christianity, Christian Judaism, or Neither?" in *Jewish Christianity Reconsidered*, 155–80, for an assessment of Hagner's thesis, favoring Saldarini's conclusions, but also calling upon Matthean scholars to move on and appreciate Matthew's outlook toward the Roman Empire.

[76] Foster, *Community, Law, and Mission*, 118.

[77] Ibid., 115 n. 76.

[78] All translations of Josephus cited in this work are by William Whiston, The *Works of Josephus: Complete and Unabridged* (Peabody, Mass.: Hendrickson Publishers, 1987).

as well. For Matthew as well as Josephus' Essenes, none of the aspects of the Mosaic Torah is evil per se; human nature is the real problem.[79] While agreeing with Foster that Jesus constitutes the primary source of authority for Matthew and his readers, I find it unlikely that Matthew would have deemed his perspective on the Law to be supersessionary. Even if tensions undeniably existed between Matthew's audience(s) and the local Jewish communities, it is still better to view the gospel of Matthew as a Jewish text that strongly affirms the observance of the Torah.[80] Runesson's approach is to be commended for inviting us to view Matthew as participating within an intra-Jewish debate between Pharisees and followers of Jesus who were (formerly) related to the Pharisaic party.[81]

As noted earlier, the author of Luke and the Acts of the Apostles has still not enjoyed an equal share with Matthew in the process of rejudaization. If Matthew is viewed as the most Jewish of all gospels, the two tomes penned by Luke are still regarded by conventional scholarship and certainly by most Christian clergy and lay members as the most "Greek" or "Hellenistic" documents within the New Testament corpus.[82] Because of the

---

[79] Cf. *1 En.* 98:4, which decries the institution of slavery, though legislated in the Mosaic Torah, and traces its origins back to the rise of human oppression.

[80] The more one delves into the ancient Jewish sources, the less radical many of the statements in the gospel of Matthew vis-à-vis Jewish Law and custom appear to be. A case in point would be the statement appearing in Matt 8:22, "let the dead bury their own dead," (cf. Luke 10:60). Matthew's Jesus is not encouraging Jews to neglect the duty to bury their loved ones, but probably referring to the practice of *secondary* burial that involved gathering and placing the bones of the deceased in ossuaries, which was observed during the Second Temple period. See Craig A. Evans, *Jesus and the Ossuaries* (Waco, Tex.: Baylor University Press, 2003), 13. Outside the corpus of Jewish writings produced by the Jesus movement, one thinks of the duty of מת מצוה, which according to rabbinic standards, obliges a priest or a nazirite to acquire impurity in order to care for a neglected corpse (e.g., *m. Naz.* 7:1). One could argue that this rabbinic command "contradicts" the written Torah (Lev 21:1–3, 11; Num 6:7), but probably we should not understand this rabbinic approach in a supersessionist way any more than the Matthean antitheses that seemingly clash with the Mosaic Law but are actually designed to exhort followers of Jesus to exceed the righteousness of the Pharisees. On the clash between the מת מצוה and the Mosaic Torah, see Thomas Kazen, *Jesus and Purity Halakhah: Was Jesus Indifferent to Impurity?* (ConBNT 38; Winona Lake, Ind.: Eisenbrauns, 2010), 195, citing Jacob Mann, "Jesus and the Sadducean Priests: Luke 10. 25–37," *JQR* 6 (1915–1916): 415–22.

[81] Anders Runesson, "Rethinking Early Jewish-Christian Relations: Matthean Community History as Pharisaic Intragroup Conflict," *JBL* 127 (2008): 95–132.

[82] G. B. Caird, *The Gospel of St. Luke* (PNTC; Baltimore, Md.: Penguin Books, 1963), 105; Walter Schmithals, *Das Evangelium nach Lukas* (ZBK.NT 3.1; Zurich: Theologischer, 1980), 9: "zweifellos ein Heidenchrist, und er schreibt für Heidenchristen"; Bart J. Koet, *Five Studies on Interpretation of Scripture in Luke-Acts* (SNTA 14; Leuven: University Press, 1989), 22: "The *communis opinio* is that the theology of Luke-Acts is clearly Gentile Christian and that Luke-Acts has been written for a predominantly Gen-

allegedly universal concepts and positive outlook toward the Gentile and Roman worlds appearing within his writings, many assert that Luke, in contradistinction to Matthew, and following in the footsteps of his predecessor and mentor Paul, so the narrative goes, rejects the validity of Torah observance. In spite of the newest perspectives on Paul and his attitude toward the Jewish Law as well as fresh proposals for understanding the "parting of the ways," Luke continues to be caricatured as ignorant of Jewish practice and opposed to its observance even by the most prominent of scholars who adopt the latest trends on Jewish-Christian relations. Thus, in a stimulating and interesting article in the edited volume, *The Ways That Never Parted,* Gager unfortunately perpetuates the stereotyped picture of Luke as the abrogator of the Law and harbinger of Christian anti-Judaism. Gager rightly and commendably argues against the trend of viewing the phenomenon of "Jewish Christianity" as quickly disappearing from the historical scene. He also perspicaciously critiques the common misperception of a rapid and inevitable "parting of the ways" between Judaism and Christianity in Late Antiquity (not the historical period explored in this inquiry but still pertinent for my argument). Gager even goes as far as postulating that "Jewish Christianity" could well have survived into the Islamic period.[83] On the other hand, the scholar, well known for his thought provoking work on Paul,[84] deviates from his progressive trajectory of thinking when he blames the author of Acts for generating misunderstandings concerning "Jewish Christianity" and the "parting of the ways." Gager commences his attack against Luke by stating: "Contrary to the ideologically determined picture of Acts, early Christianity did not move unidirectionally toward Rome but multi-directionally into every corner of the Mediterranean world and beyond...."[85] He then adds:

---

tile audience"; Raymond E. Brown, *The Birth of the Messiah: A Commentary on the Infancy Narratives in the Gospels of Matthew and Luke* (ABRL; New York: Doubleday, 1993), 235–39; Darrell L. Bock, *Luke* (2 vols.; BECNT 3; Grand Rapids, Mich.: Baker Books, 1994), 1:6; Anthony J. Saldarini, "Interpretation of Luke-Acts and Implications for Jewish-Christian Dialogue," *Word & World* 12 (1992): 37–42; Goodman, *Rome and Jerusalem,* 516.

[83] John G. Gager, "Did Jewish Christians See the Rise of Islam?" in *The Ways That Never Parted,* 361–72.

[84] John G. Gager, *Reinventing Paul* (New York: Oxford University Press, 2000). Others who follow in Gager's trajectory on Paul include Mark Nanos, *The Mystery of Romans: The Jewish Context of Paul's Letter* (Minneapolis: Fortress, 1996); *The Irony of Galatians: Paul's Letter in First-Century Context* (Minneapolis: Fortress, 2002); Pamela Michelle Eisenbaum, *Paul Was Not a Christian: The Real Message of a Misunderstood Apostle* (New York: HarperOne, 2009); previously and especially, Lloyd Gaston (to whom Gager is indebted), *Paul and the Torah* (Vancouver: University of British Columbia Press, 1987).

[85] Gager, "Did Jewish Christians See the Rise of Islam?" 367.

Contrary to the portrait in Acts, Paul did not repudiate Judaism – or those whom we call Jewish Christians; instead, he focused entirely on his mission to Gentiles, insisting simply that Gentile believers had no need to observe the customs and practices of the Torah. The author of Acts has deliberately drafted Paul to serve for his own anti-Jewish and anti-Jewish-Christian message. Here it is worth noting that just as Paul advocates a "two-door" road to salvation, with different paths for Jews and Gentiles, so at least some Jewish-Christian groups advanced a similar "two-doors" scenario.[86]

Gager also holds Luke responsible for depicting Peter as allegedly abandoning the Jewish Law (Acts 11), which would reflect Luke's own theological agenda rather than historical reality.[87] If for Gager the ways never really parted between Judaism and Christianity, and "Jewish Christianity" enjoyed such longevity so as to see the dawn of Islam, the author of Luke-Acts, on the other hand, had already parted company from the Judaism of his time. My point is not to single out Gager nor downplay the significant contributions he has made to further our understanding of ancient Judaism and Christianity, only to highlight an unfortunate misunderstanding of Luke-Acts that underscores and justifies the need to revisit these issues in a manner that does justice to Luke's writings. To every assertion made recently by Gager and others, counter arguments can be offered that seriously question such claims. First of all, it is far from certain whether the author of Luke-Acts is moving "uni-directionally toward Rome" rather than "multi-directionally into every corner of the Mediterranean world and beyond." The opening of Acts (1:8) already contains a trajectory that is *multi*-directional: "You will be my witnesses in Jerusalem, in all Judea and Samaria, and to the ends of the earth." While Luke undeniably ends his narrative in Rome, he brings the reader along with Paul time and time again back to *Jerusalem*.[88] Luke regrets that the holy city of Jerusalem "is

---

[86] Ibid., 367.

[87] Ibid., 368.

[88] Joseph Shulam, introduction to *A Commentary on the Jewish Roots of Acts,* by Hilary Le Cornu with Joseph Shulam (2 vols.; Jerusalem: Academon, 2003), 1:xxx: "While most Western scholars presume Luke wrote Acts for a predominantly gentile audience – the book being written in Greek and Paul, as Luke's mentor, being the Apostles [*sic*] to the Gentiles – it seems more likely to me that it was written for the Jewish community in Jerusalem. The general structure of the book places the story of the Jerusalem community, and Peter's annals, at the beginning of the account. The book opens with Peter's and the early Jerusalem community's faithfulness to Jesus and the community, and closes with Paul affirming his loyalty to the people of Israel and to the traditions of the fathers before the Jewish leadership in Rome. Paul's struggles with the Sanhedrin, Agrippa, and Festus over his faithfulness to the Law and the Prophets (cf. 22–26, 28) would not serve any understandable function for Gentiles in the diaspora. Since one third of the book of Acts is devoted to episodes in Jerusalem and Caesarea it seems likely that Luke was addressing an audience in Jerusalem rather than one in Rome." Cf. Strelan, *Luke the Priest*, 115, also suggesting a Palestinian locale for Luke. Although I am not convinced that Luke originally came from Palestine or wrote to a Palestinian audience, I do find

trampled on by the Gentiles, *until the times of the Gentiles are fulfilled*" (Luke 21:24; emphasis mine), and never denies the hope for the restoration of the kingdom of Israel (Acts 1:8), only postponing it until the unknown time of the Parousia.[89] In the meantime, Luke rejoices that the word of God and the good news about the Jewish messiah and king Jesus flow out of Zion to the rest of the world, conquering even Rome, which, vis-à-vis Jerusalem, lies at the extremities of the earth, not at the center.[90]

As to the claim that Luke's Paul repudiates Judaism, such an assertion is impossible to support when one looks more closely at the portrait of Paul in Acts. Luke repeatedly portrays Paul as faithfully attending the synagogue on the Sabbath,[91] keeping Jewish festivals such as Shavuot/Pentecost (20:16) and Yom Kippur (27:9),[92] attending the temple in Jerusalem and partaking in its rituals (21:24), affirming his fidelity to the Torah and Jewish customs (28:17), and even circumcising Timothy (16:3)![93] As for Peter's supposed abandonment of Torah observance, the book of Acts does not claim that Peter entered the house of just any uncircumcised Gentile but that of Cornelius said to be "a devout man who feared God" (10:2), well-spoken of by the whole Jewish nation (10:22). In Acts 11, Peter never acknowledges to have eaten anything forbidden for a Jew in Cornelius' house. As I argue in chapter 10 of this book, the vision Peter sees at Joppa with the instruction to eat forbidden meats does not endorse abandoning kosher rules. The point of the vision is that God-fearing Gentiles, who have now accepted the good news, are no longer considered morally impure since they have received the sacred spirit like the rest of the Jewish followers of Jesus (11:17). In fact, the so-called

---

Shulam's comments noteworthy for pointing out how Rome does *not* lie at the center of Luke's worldview. Jerusalem is the navel of Luke's universe, and Rome is only an object for Jewish evangelistic conquest via the proclamation of God's word flowing out of Zion.

[89] Loader, *Jesus' Attitude towards the Law,* 382: "For Luke Jerusalem remains the holy city and the place of hope. There is more going on here than can be explained by the valid observations about the role of Jerusalem in salvation historical terms as the goal of Jesus' ministry and the beginning point of the church. Already Paul keeps coming back to Jerusalem. For Luke, Jesus will come to Jerusalem as its Messiah. It will be liberated from the Gentiles who in Luke's time now desecrate it after the disaster of 70CE."

[90] I hope to develop these thoughts in a subsequent work dealing with Luke's attitude toward the Roman Empire. At this stage, I remain content in proving Luke's Jewishness by highlighting his affirmation of the Torah. For further secondary references to Acts 1:8, see the first section of chapter 7 of this monograph, which deals with traveling on the Sabbath in Acts 1:12.

[91] Acts 13:14–15; 14:1; 17:1, 10, 17; 18:4, 19, 26; 19:8.

[92] On the observance of Yom Kippur by the author of Acts see Stökl, *The Impact of Yom Kippur on Early Christianity*; "'Christians' Observing 'Jewish' Festivals of Autumn," in *The Image of the Judaeo-Christians,* 53–73.

[93] On Timothy's circumcision, see chapter 12 of this book.

Apostolic Decree in Acts 15 implies that Gentile followers of Jesus are obliged to keep a minimal set of Mosaic requirements, some of which overlap with Jewish food laws. As for Jewish followers of Jesus, Peter included, Luke assumes that they continue to bear the entire yoke of the Torah.

Several decades ago, before Sanders had even written his seminal *Paul and Palestinian Judaism* and before the so-called New Perspective on Paul had begun to fructify, Jervell had provided a remarkably new perspective on Luke-Acts, claiming them to be "Jewish Christian" documents written by a Torah observant Jew.[94] The results of this original thinker, who argued on behalf of the Jewishness of what seemed at that time to be the most Gentile of New Testament candidates, are worth quoting here at length:

> The Jewishness of Acts, compared to all other New Testament writings, is conspicuous: in the pre-Pauline christology, in the ecclesiology; where the church is Israel; in the soteriology, with the promises of salvation given only to Israel; in the law, the Torah, with its full validity for all Jews in the church; in Paul being the missionary to Israel and the Dispersion. For years scholars were nearly unanimous in viewing Acts as a Gentile-Christian document, written by a Gentile Christian for Gentile Christians. This is not tenable any longer, as it is based to a great extent upon the idea that after 70 AD Jewish Christianity had disappeared, was of no importance, existing only as a marginal feature outside the church. And so no Jewish Christian could have written a book like Acts after 70 AD. But Jewish Christianity was an important and widely spread part of the church throughout the first century. That Luke was able to write Greek in a good style does not show that he was a Gentile – many Jews did so. In spite of his ability to write decent Greek he does so only seldom and sporadically. Most of his work he presents in what may be called biblical Greek, clearly influenced by the Septuagint, a Jewish book, written for Jews and not for Gentiles. Luke's stylistic home was the synagogue. He was a Jewish Christian.[95]

In the 1970s, the time was not yet ripe for New Testament scholarship to swallow the revolutionary perspective on Luke-Acts Jervell had to offer, although a number of specialists have always sympathized with various points of his thesis.[96] The study of the diversity of Second Temple Judaism

---

[94] Jacob Jervell, *Luke and the People of God: A New Look at Luke-Acts* (Minneapolis: Augsburg, 1972); "The Mighty Minority," *ST* 34 (1980): 13–38; "The Church of the Jews and Godfearers," in *Luke-Acts and the Jewish People: Eight Critical Perspectives* (ed. Joseph B. Tyson; Minneapolis: Augsburg, 1988), 11–20; *The Theology of the Acts of the Apostles* (Cambridge: Cambridge University Press, 1996).

[95] Jervell, *The Theology of the Acts of the Apostles*, 4–5.

[96] Some of those who would sympathize or coincide with *certain* aspects of Jervell's work include, among others, Donald Juel, *Luke-Acts: The Promise of History* (Atlanta: John Knox, 1983), 101–12; Robert L. Brawley, *Luke-Acts and the Jews: Conflict, Apology, and Conciliation* (SBLMS 33; Atlanta: Scholars Press, 1987); Robert C. Tannehill, *The Narrative Unity of Luke-Acts: A Literary Interpretation. Vol. 1.: The Gospel according to Luke* (Foundations and Facets; Philadelphia, Pa.: Fortress, 1986); especially the overlooked Marilyn Salmon, "Insider or Outsider? Luke's Relationship with Judaism" in

was only burgeoning. Scholars were still uncovering the Jewishness of the historical Jesus and, to a lesser extent, that of Paul. Neusner was only beginning to talk about "formative Judaism" rather than "normative Judaism" to describe the Jewish history of post-70.[97] Many scholars still held on to what are by now considered outdated schemes and hyphenations concerning normative "Pharisaic-Rabbinic" Judaism and "orthodox-Christianity" as the sole legitimate survivors of Second Temple Judaism in the aftermath of 70 CE. In such an intellectual environment, there was little room to accommodate a set of writings such as Luke-Acts into its Jewish matrix. One prominent interpreter of Luke-Acts would criticize Jervell for having Judaized Luke "to the limit."[98]

Thankfully, our understanding of pluriform Judaism has dramatically changed since then. Now that contemporary scholarship appreciates more fully the diversity of post-70 Judaism, ancient Jews of all colors and strands, including those who believed in Jesus, can be reincorporated into the diverse spectrum of ancient Jewry. The recent publication of *The Jewish Annotated New Testament* is only the latest manifestation of an ongoing affirmation to see the entire New Testament as a literary corpus of Jewish heritage.[99] What is more, some are moving beyond appreciating the Jewish "heritage" of the New Testament to viewing all of its writings as Jewish documents. Jervell, all of the sudden, no longer seems so radical. Even German scholarship is beginning to appreciate his work.[100]

Luke-Acts and the Jewish People, 76–82; David L. Tiede, *Luke* (ACNT; Minneapolis: Augsburg Publishing House, 1988), 20, claiming Luke was not a Gentile who was indifferent to the Law and was more intent than Paul that Christians observe the Law. We cannot forget the works of Klinghardt, Wehnert, Loader, and more recently Thiessen, cited throughout this monograph.

[97] Jacob Neusner, *From Politics to Piety: The Emergence of Pharisaic Judaism* (Englewoods Cliff, N.J.: Prentice Hall, 1973); *Rabbinic Traditions about the Pharisees before 70* (3 vols.; Leiden: Brill, 1973); "The Formation of Rabbinic Judaism: Yavneh from A.D. 70–100," *ANRW* 19.2:3–42.

[98] Bovon, *Luke the Theologian,* 406.

[99] Amy-Jill Levine and Marc Zvi Brettler, eds., *The Jewish Annotated New Testament* (Oxford: Oxford University Press, 2011). This does not mean that the contributors of this volume believe that all of the New Testament documents were written by Jews, only that a firm knowledge of ancient Judaism is important for the elucidation of these Christian texts – common currency these days. The task now, in my opinion, is to move on and see what hermeneutical promise lies in reading these New Testament texts simply as Jewish documents. Unfortunately, even in this latest volume, Levine shares the *communis opinio* that the gospel of Luke is a Gentile writing (p. 97).

[100] Jervell has complained about the German neglect of his work. See Jacob Jervell, "Retrospect and Prospect in Luke-Acts Interpretation," in *SBL Seminar Papers, 1991* (SBLSP 30; ed. Eugene H. Lovering; Atlanta: Scholars Press, 1991), 384: "The books have made almost no impact whatever on the German-European scene, at least until two years ago when M. Klinghardt's monograph, *Gesetz und Volk Gottes* appeared. Dogmas

In certain circles, the pendulum is indeed swinging to the other extreme. Strelan goes as far as arguing that Luke was a Jewish priest![101] Although I am not convinced that we can make such a precise determination about Luke's professional background, I do find some of Strelan's comments regarding the relationship of authorship and authority quite instructive for affirming the Jewishness of Luke: "What authority would a Gentile have, in the years between 70 and 90 CE, to interpret the traditions of Israel in the way that Luke does? What authority would a god-fearer of that time have to interpret and to transmit the Jesus traditions? What authority would a Jew have to interpret Paul, the apostle to the Gentiles?"[102] These questions merit careful consideration. How credible would a Gentile author arguing on behalf of the continuity of the Jesus movement with its Jewish heritage appear to those Jews of the end of the first century CE who were suspicious of the apostasy of Jewish followers of Jesus from the foundational practices of Judaism? A Torah observant Jewish disciple of Jesus would certainly prove a more trustworthy and authoritative candidate than a law-free Gentile Christian ignorant about Judaism for composing a tractate arguing on behalf of Paul's Jewishness and fidelity to the Torah. My primary goal, however, throughout this monograph, is first to demonstrate that the *perspective* formulated in the writings of Luke-Acts is indeed Jewish in its affirmation of Torah observance before making claims about

---

in the history of exegesis are long-lived! It is a great mystery that I was asked to be the successor of E. Haenchen in writing the commentary on Acts for the Meyer Series." Jervell adds: "It is perhaps no coincidence that of the reviews of my work, 90% have been in English and French, 10% in other languages, and none in German" (384 n. 8). Since his publication of his commentary on Acts in German for the Meyer Series, *Die Apostelgeschichte* (KEK; Göttingen: Vandenhoeck & Ruprecht, 1998), German scholarship has begun to appreciate his work more fully. Positive treatments of Jervell's works now include Andrea J. Mayer-Haas, *"Geschenk aus Gottes Schatzkammer (bSchab 10b)": Jesus und der Sabbat im Spiegel der neutestamentlichen Schriften* (NTAbh 43; Münster: Aschendorff, 2003), 382: "Die andauernde Existenz von *gesetzesobservanten* Judenchristen – andere Judenchristen zeigt die Apostelgeschichte nicht – in der Kirche ist ein Zeichen für die Kontinuität von Kirche und Israel" (citing Jervell on p. 382 n. 522) and Jürgen Wehnert, *Die Reinheit*. Before the appearance of Jervell's commentary in German, appreciative responses to Jervell's work included Klinghardt's *Gesetz und Volk Gottes* and to a certain extent Gerhard Lohfink, *Die Sammlung Israels: Eine Untersuchung zur lukanischen Ekklesiologie* (München: Kösel, 1975). Even the attempt by Roland Deines, "Das Aposteldekret – Halacha für Heidenchristen oder christliche Rücksichtnahme auf jüdische Tabus?" in *Jewish Identity in the Greco-Roman World* (eds. Jörg Frey, Daniel R. Schwartz, and Stephanie Gripentrog; Ancient Judaism and Early Christianity 71; Leiden: Brill, 2007), 323–98, to refute Jervell and Wehnert shows that German scholarship is finally taking due notice of Jervell's work.

[101] Strelan, *Luke the Priest*. I would like to thank Anthony Kent, student of Strelan, for drawing my attention to this work.

[102] Strelan, *Luke the Priest*, 103.

the identity of the author, a point I return to at the conclusion of this work. In other words, I am trying to argue that the *writings* of Luke-Acts are just as Jewish as Matthew's gospel. In the end though, I think this thesis will have some ramifications for assessing the identity of the authors responsible for the composition of such documents and for situating them within the world of ancient Jewry.

Matthew and Luke, Why not Mark?

As I have shared and discussed my project with various people at conferences, seminars, and other venues, many have asked why I have not included the gospel of Mark into my inquiry. The initial answer I gave to this question was rather straightforward: the gospel of Mark, so I firmly believed, announces the abrogation of the ritual aspects of the Jewish Law, including kashrut. This can be clearly seen in the parenthetical phrase of Mark 7:19, "thus he declared all foods clean." At least according to the criterion of Torah praxis, Mark could not be as Jewish as Matthew and Luke. Then Boyarin shared with me the draft of his book dealing with the gospel of Mark, which has since then been published.[103] At the very least, his work has demonstrated that we cannot rush making easy conclusions concerning Mark and his attitude toward the Law. When the parenthetical statement is removed from Mark ch. 7, it becomes quite clear that Mark is only condemning the subordination of moral concerns to the practice of ritual purity. Mark 7 does not even mount a critique against kashrut, a different matter altogether, and even Mark 7:19b can be read in a way that does not declare the abrogation of kosher laws.[104] Nevertheless, too much work had already been done to turn back and include a thorough analysis of Mark in this monograph. An inquiry into the attitude of Matthew and Luke toward Jewish Law, is, I suppose, already an ambitious project for any scholar. Mark, however, does provide an important platform for my research as a means for exploring Matthew and Luke's perspectives on the Jewish Law, since I work under the assumption that both Matthew and Luke used a copy of Mark when composing their gospels, though I hope my thesis stands regardless of how one reconstructs the complicated literary relationship between the synoptic gospels.[105] Suffice to state that I no

---

[103] Daniel Boyarin, *The Jewish Gospels: The Story of the Jewish Christ* (New York: New Press, 2012).

[104] See especially Daniel Stökl Ben Ezra, "Markus-Evangelium," *RAC* 24 (2010): 173–207. I thank Stökl for sharing this reference with me.

[105] Eric Franklin, *Luke: Interpreter of Paul, Critic of Matthew* (JSNTSup 92; Sheffield: JSOT Press, 1994), seeks to disprove the existence of Q, and argues that Luke used

longer work under my previous assumption concerning Mark's dismantlement of the ritual aspects of the Torah when assessing how Matthew and Luke modified the Markan traditions they incorporated into their gospels.[106] However, I do detect a mutual concern on the part of Matthew and Luke to eliminate certain misunderstandings the wording of the Markan gospel could generate concerning the abrogation of Torah observance (even if it was not Mark's intent to insinuate such interpretations). In other words, in their appropriation of the gospel of Mark, Matthew and Luke rewrite and modify some of the Markan materials in order to clarify that the Torah has not been cancelled.

Methodological Considerations

Initially, I was set on applying a purely compositional critical approach to Matthew and Luke-Acts. Nevertheless, I inevitably found myself gravitating toward diachronic questions, wondering whether a tradition recorded in Matthew and Luke reflected their attitude toward a certain matter or whether such material merely represented a traditional view that the synoptic evangelists had chosen to preserve in their writings. My analysis, therefore, although primarily interested in analyzing Matthew and Luke-Acts synchronically, at times deviates from this trajectory when considering certain diachronic developments that might clarify Matthew and Luke's stance toward the Law. These occasional deviations force me to apply a

---

Matthew in a highly critical way as he composed his own gospel. I do not share Franklin's views concerning Luke's downplaying the significance of the Law as a marker of identity for the *ekklesia*. I find Franklin relies too heavily on his own solution to the synoptic problem when underscoring the supposed discrepancies between Matthew and Luke on the Law.

[106] The significance of the usage and appropriation of Mark by Matthew and Luke, therefore, for the exploration of their Jewishness must be revisited. Both Boris Repschinski, *The Controversy Stories in the Gospel of Matthew. Their Redaction, Form and Relevance for the Relationship between the Matthean Community and Formative Judaism* (FRLAT 189; Göttingen: Vandenhoeck & Ruprecht, 2000), 349 and Foster, *Community, Law and Mission,* 75–76, operate under the assumption that Mark is a Gentile text when assessing Matthew's Jewishness and reworking of Mark's gospel. See also David C. Sim, "Matthew's Use of Mark: Did Matthew Intend to Supplement or to Replace His Primary Source?" *NTS* 57 (2011): 176–92, who works under the assumption that Mark is a "law-free" gospel. Earlier, Samuel Sandmel, *Anti-Semitism in the New Testament?* (Philadelphia, Pa.: Fortress, 1978), 48: "In short, Mark is a tract on behalf of Gentile Christianity, contending that Christianity has only negative connections with Judaism into which it had been born. Matthew and Luke seemed to disagree with this connection. In writing their Gospels they used Mark. But they were not reluctant to alter what they found in Mark to be uncongenial."

redactional critical analysis to Matthew and Luke with the aim of better appreciating their attitude toward the Jewish Law. Overall, my interest lies primarily in the final layers of composition of Matthew and Luke, that is, in reading these texts in a holistic way, as literary products that inform us about the worldviews of their final authors. Therefore, I stray between composition criticism and redaction criticism even though I do not think that a purely redactional critical approach proves essential for defending my thesis. The redactional method only underscores and further clarifies what I see as a mutual concern on the part of Matthew and Luke to affirm the perpetuation of Torah practice. Consequently, my thesis does not hinge entirely on accepting the so-called Two Source Hypothesis to the synoptic problem, which is increasingly under attack, even though I assume Markan priority in my analysis of Matthew and Luke.[107]

I still find William Thompson's distinction between redaction and composition criticism quite helpful for clarifying what I am trying to carry out in this monograph:

> I call myself a composition-critic rather than a redaction-critic. My basic methodological presupposition is that Matthew's editorial activity – whether it be called redaction or composition – was so thorough-going and proceeded out of such a unique vision that it transformed all that he touched. Hence, I am not so much interested in separating tradition from redaction, nor in confronting Matthew with his sources (Mark, Q, and *Sondergut*) in an effort to discover his uniqueness vis-à-vis the material he inherited. Instead, I will attempt to discover one of the evangelist's historical perspectives by accepting his final composition as an intelligible whole and by working with the end-product of his editorial activity.[108]

I do confront Matthew and Luke more than Thompson with their sources (especially Mark) even if I do not systematically strive to reconstruct a history about the sources available and traditions handed down to the synoptic writers. Like Thomson and other composition critics, I view redactional activity primarily as an authorial and creative process. Modifying, deleting, and adding material to sources do not constitute a passive, editorial process, but stem from a dynamic creativity that can inform us about the perspectives of the final "redactors," in our case, Matthew and Luke.

---

[107] For a growing skepticism towards the Two-Source Hypothesis, see Mogens Müller, "Luke–the Fourth Gospel?" in *Voces Clamantium in Deserto: Essays in Honor of Kari Syreeni* (eds. Sven-Olav Back and Matti Kankaanniemi; Studier exegetik och judaistik utgivna av Teologiska fakulteten vid Åbo Akademi 11; Åbo: Teologiska fakulteten vid Åbo Akademi, 2012), 231–42; Matthias Klinghardt, "The Marcionite Gospel and the Synoptic Problem: A New Suggestion," *NovT* 50 (2008): 1–27. I thank professor Müller for sharing an offprint of his article.

[108] William Thompson, "An Historical Perspective on the Gospel of Matthew," *JBL* 93 (1974): 244 n. 2.

I assume, like many, that both Matthew and Luke-Acts were written *after* 70 CE. For example, it seems clear to me that both Matthew and Luke rewrote Mark 13 in light of the destruction of the temple of Jerusalem.[109] Matthew and Luke, therefore, can inform us about the ongoing importance of the Torah for segments of the Jesus movement living after 70 CE.[110]

I also accept the authorial unity of Luke-Acts in spite of the recent attempt to question this long held and cherished thesis.[111] My work does not prove that the same author who wrote the gospel of Luke also composed the book of Acts. Nevertheless, the coherence and consistent affirmation in both works concerning the place of the Torah within the Jesus movement is striking. If the author of Acts did not compose the gospel of Luke, he certainly read and appropriated it in such a way that both volumes now attributed to Luke can be read as the work of one writer.

My inquiry is historical because of my interest in exploring what Matthew and Luke-Acts could have meant in their original contexts in light of what we know about ancient Judaism and the Greco-Roman world of that period. I am, therefore, not limiting myself to reading Matthew and Luke-Acts through literary methods that ignore the importance of seriously engaging with the cultural-historical context in which said texts were written. Many secondary works, primarily of exegetical and theological nature, approach Matthew and Luke-Acts using a variety of literary-critical tools, including what is called in biblical studies as "narrative criticism." Because these literary-critical approaches can often prioritize an autonomous reading of ancient canonical texts without granting sufficient weight to historical-cultural considerations and their original Jewish contexts, they occasionally arrive, in my opinion, to erroneous interpretations about the

---

[109] See chapter 6 and its treatment of Matthew 24:20.

[110] Probably the *terminus ad quem* for Matthew and Luke-Acts should be 132 CE, as no reference to the Bar Kokhba Revolt appears in either of these writings. On the dating of Luke-Acts, see Joseph B. Tyson, *Marcion and Luke-Acts: A Defining Struggle* (Columbia, S.C.: University of South Carolina Press, 2006), 1–23.

[111] Patricia Walters, *The Assumed Authorial Unity of Luke and Acts: A Reassessment of the Evidence* (SNTSMS 145; Cambridge: Cambridge University Press, 2009). A number of reviewers express reservations about Walters' revisionist thesis. More time and research are needed before making any hasty conclusions concerning her work. See, for the time being, Paul Foster, review of Patricia Walters, *The Assumed Authorial Unity of Luke and Acts*, *ExpTim* 121 (2010): 264–65; Joel B. Green, review of Patricia Walters, *The Assumed Authorial Unity of Luke and Acts*, *RBL* [http://www.bookreviews.org] (2009); Richard I. Pervo, review of Patricia Walters, *The Assumed Authorial Unity of Luke and Acts: A Reassessment of the Evidence*, *RBL* [http://www.bookreviews.org] (2009).

worldviews contained in the New Testament writings.[112] This becomes quite apparent in various treatments by New Testament exegetes about the relationship and attitude of the Jesus movement to Judaism and the Torah. Often where some New Testament exegetes declare Matthew and Luke are making a "radical" statement about Jewish practice that would mark a supposed shift away from its observance, it becomes apparent, after a careful assessment of ancient halakah, that these interpreters have overstated their cases, if not misread the primary texts.

I try my best, then, to draw from the ancient Jewish sources as well as the best of secondary scholarship on the topic of ancient Jewish Law. In addition to employing redaction/composition criticism, I assess Matthew and Luke-Acts from a "halakic-critical" approach. Many studies on the relationship between the Torah and the Jesus movement often tend to approach this topic by autonomously exegeting a New Testament document independently from a thorough engagement with the alternative halakic positions voiced in the Second Temple and early rabbinic sources. For the section on Sabbath keeping, Doering's monumental work in German on Sabbath halakot has been very informative.[113] For matters related to purity laws and kashrut, two systems that must be properly distinguished from one another, I recognize my indebtedness to the works of Hayes, Kazen, Klawans, Maccoby, Milgrom, and Sanders, among others.[114] The works of Kraemer, Rosenblum, and Freidenreich have provided me with a lot of "food for thought," as far as Jewish food laws are concerned.[115]

---

[112] See Foster, *Community, Law, and Mission*, 15–17, for a concise and excellent discussion of the limitations of literary criticism and the dangers involved of neglecting the historical method.

[113] Lutz Doering, *Schabbat: Sabbathhalacha und –praxis im antiken Judentum und Urchristentum* (TSAJ 78; Tübingen: Mohr Siebeck, 1999). I also interact extensively with Andrea Mayer-Haas, *Geschenk aus Gottes Schatzkammer*.

[114] Hayes, *Gentile Impurities*; Kazen, *Jesus and the Purity Halakhah*; Jonathan Klawans, *Impurity and Sin in Ancient Judaism* (New York: Oxford University Press, 2000); Hyam Maccoby, *Ritual and Morality: The Ritual Purity System and Its Place in Judaism* (Cambridge: Cambridge University Press, 1999); Jacob Milgrom, *Leviticus* (3 vols.; AB 3–3B; New York: Doubleday, 1991–2001); E. P. Sanders, *Jewish Law from Jesus to the Mishnah* (Philadelphia, Pa.: Trinity Press International, 1990); "Jewish Association with Gentiles and Galatians 2:11–14," in *The Conversation Continues: Essays on Paul and John Presented to J. Louis Martyn* (eds. Robert Fortna and Beverly Gaventa; Nashville, Tenn.: Abingdon, 1990), 170–88; *Judaism: Practice and Belief 63 BCE–66 CE* (Philadelphia, Pa.: Trinity Press International, 1992).

[115] David Kraemer, *Jewish Eating and Identity through the Ages* (New York: Routledge, 2007); Jordan D. Rosenblum, *Food and Identity in Early Rabbinic Judaism* (Cambridge: Cambridge University Press, 2010); David M. Freidenreich, *Foreigners and Their Food: Constructing Otherness in Jewish, Christian, and Islamic Law* (Berkeley, Calif.: University of California Press, 2011).

Regarding circumcision, I have found the works of Cohen, Rubin, and Thiessen very instructive.[116] Many other important secondary works appear in references in the pertinent chapters and bibliography of this book.

One final note should be made concerning the usage of rabbinic sources in this work. I am quite aware of the historical and methodological problems involved in using rabbinic texts written "much after" the time of Matthew and Luke by a group of (elite?) Jews representing only *one* (insignificant?) stream of Judaism in Late Antiquity who frequently engaged in theoretical debates that do not necessarily reflect the halakic practices and social reality on the ground of other non-rabbinic Jews living in Palestine, let alone the Diaspora. Nevertheless, I do not belong to the school of persuasion that describes rabbinic literature as "too late, therefore, irrelevant for the study of the New Testament." First of all, the chronological gap that divides the earliest rabbinic document, that is, the Mishnah, from Matthew and Luke is not so great as some imagine, particularly since Matthew, Luke, and Acts may have been written as late as the first quarter of the second century CE, that is, about *less than a century* before the Mishnah reached its *final* form.[117] The Mishnah and other Tannaitic texts certainly contain earlier materials, which, of course, must be examined on an individual basis. In my opinion, the tremendous interest on the part of the rabbinic sages in halakic matters is too significant to be overlooked in an inquiry on Matthew and Luke-Acts that focuses on matters related to Torah observance.[118] At times, the rabbinic documents provide the only

---

[116] Shaye Cohen, *Why Aren't Jewish Women Circumcised?* (Berkeley, Calif.: University of California Press, 2005); Nissan Rubin, *Beginning of Life; Rites of Birth, Circumcision, and Redemption of the First-Born in the Talmud and Midrash* [in Hebrew] (Tel Aviv: Ha-Kibbuts Ha-Meuhad, 1995); Thiessen, *Contesting Conversion*.

[117] On the late dating of Matthew, see David C. Sim, "Reconstructing the Social and Religious Milieu of Matthew: Methods, Sources, and Possible Results," in *Matthew, James, and Didache: Three Related Documents in their Jewish and Christian Settings* (eds. Huub van de Sandt and Jürgen K. Zangenberg; SBLSymS 45; Atlanta: Society of Biblical Literature, 2008), 13–41; On the late dating of Luke and Acts see J.C. O'Neill, *The Theology of Acts in its Historical Setting* (2d ed.; London: S.P.C.K., 1970); Richard Pervo, *Dating Acts: Between the Evangelists and the Apologists* (Santa Rosa, Calif.: Polebridge, 2006).

[118] Why then not also consult patristic and classical ("pagan") sources of a later time? My answer to this question is equally positive, albeit by advising careful and critical scrutiny of these materials. Nevertheless, because my project experiments reading Matthew and Luke-Acts as *Jewish* texts and focuses on *halakic* issues and the question of the observance of the Mosaic Torah, the patristic and classical sources carry limited weight for the purposes of this inquiry. First, the patristic authors mainly arrived to the conclusion that the Torah no longer carried any relevance for the *ekklesia* in so far as the "ceremonial" (a term I dislike) aspects were concerned. Sabbath, kashrut, and circumcision lost their place in the early church, being replaced with other customs (e.g., Sunday worship), discarded altogether, or allegorized into spiritual metaphors and ethics. Occa-

literary evidence, admittedly from a later date and particular provenance, for discussing certain halakic issues in Matthew and Luke-Acts. For example, besides the gospels, only the rabbinic literature records reservations about performing healings of minor illnesses on the Sabbath (the entire Second Temple literary corpus is silent on this topic). I treat this problem in the introduction to Part I dealing with the Sabbath, and find it impossible to overlook the rabbinic evidence, which can only enhance our discussion on this matter. In my chapter on burial and Sabbath keeping in Matthew and Luke, I point to the halakic dilemma embedded in the synoptic portrayal of Jesus' burial: although Joseph of Arimathea rushes to bury Jesus before sunset in order to avoid desecrating the Sabbath, the synoptic narratives imply that Jesus was buried on another holy day, Passover. How would Jews deal with the issue of burying a corpse when a holy day fell before or after the Sabbath? To my knowledge, no Second Temple Jewish source deals with this halakic matter besides some later (Amoraic) rabbinic texts.

This should not, of course, entail treating the rabbinic corpus as a timeless, monolithic entity, as if chronology and historical-critical (as well as other) considerations do not apply to these texts. Obviously, it is always preferable to refer to Tannaitic traditions when they prove pertinent, but even then, methodological and historical issues abound (reliability of the attribution of sayings, reflection of actual praxis, pertinence of such passages for the analysis of non-rabbinic Jewish texts, diachronic issues, etc.). Nevertheless, I still maintain that the rabbinic literature should at least be consulted as a *heuristic* device to explore how other Jews dealt with halakic questions Matthew and Luke-Acts mention. Therefore, I often solicit the rabbinic documents as a means for *imagining* and *exploring* halakic scenarios embedded within the documents now contained in the New Testament. At times, I even cite Rashi and Maimonides in my research! However, I do not do so acritically *à la* Strack and Billerbeck. Rather, citing Rashi or Maimonides for me is just like citing Neusner or Sanders. They represent *secondary* sources that can enlighten certain halakic problems that arise in my treatments of Sabbath keeping, purity laws, kashrut, and circumcision. As the rabbinic saying goes, "Who is wise? He that

---

sionally, I point out this process in works such as *Pseudo-Barnabas* to illustrate precisely what Luke and Matthew are *not* stating. As for the classical sources, I show at the introduction of each major part of this monograph how Greeks and Romans perceived Jewish custom. Nevertheless, these sources only provide an outsider's (and at times polemical) look into the world of Jewish praxis, and often do not assist in shedding light on the halakic intricacies and debates recorded in Matthew and Luke-Acts.

learns from all men, as it is written, *From all my teachers have I got understanding*" (*Avot* 4:1).[119]

Thesis and Summary of Chapters

Luke's writings affirm the observance of the Torah to the same degree as the gospel of Matthew. Both authors, who lived during the tumultuous aftermath of 70 CE, expected other Jewish followers of Jesus to continue observing the Jewish Law *in toto* and Gentiles to keep moral or ethical commandments and even certain purity and dietary laws from the Mosaic Torah so as to enable Jewish-Gentile fellowship within the Jesus movement. According to the criterion of Torah praxis, Luke and Acts prove to be just as Jewish as Matthew. The evidence from both Matthew and Luke-Acts suggests that the issue of Torah practice continued to play an important role in the Jesus movement and that there was a body of Torah observant Jewish followers of Jesus even after 70 CE, significant enough for Matthew and Luke to concern themselves with the question of the observance of Jewish customs. In the conclusion to this monograph, I posit that Matthew and Luke representing two different strands or tendencies of Judaism, one more akin to but in bitter conflict with Palestinian, Pharisaic Judaism, the other reflecting a Diasporan and Hellenistic form of Judaism, albeit indebted to Jewish tradition and thought originating from Palestine. Both Matthew and Luke-Acts (and by extension many other early "Christian" writings) are like Jewish prisms refracting light that illuminates our understanding of the ongoing diversity of post-70 Judaism found in other Jewish writings from this period.

Part I explores the question of Sabbath keeping in Matthew and Luke-Acts. Neither Matthew nor Luke declares the abrogation of the Sabbath. Instead, they only argue about *how* the Sabbath should be observed, not about the legitimacy of the Sabbath institution itself. The Introduction to Part I, which can be found in Chapter 2, provides a brief overview of the Sabbath in antiquity and its treatment in Matthew and Luke-Acts. Chapter 2 also contains an analysis of the passages on the Sabbath in Matthew and Luke where no controversy about the Sabbath institution is recorded. Chapters 3 and 4 assess the controversies in Matthew and Luke about plucking grain and healing on the Sabbath. These controversy stories do not point to an abrogation of Sabbath keeping; they only seek to justify the Sabbath praxis of Jesus and his first followers when it deviates from "normative" conventions. Chapter 5 deals with Jesus' burial and the depiction

---

[119] All translations from the Mishnah, unless otherwise indicated, are taken from Herbert Danby, *The Mishnah* (London: Humphrey Milford, 1938).

of the Sabbath keeping of Joseph of Arimathea and the disciples of Jesus. Here, I explore the halakic dilemma mentioned earlier regarding the burial of Jesus on a holy day (Passover) that falls next to a Sabbath. Chapter 6 treats the topic of traveling on the Sabbath in the gospel of Matthew. In this chapter, I seek to strengthen the thesis made by others that Matthew refrains from traveling on the Sabbath. In fact, I argue that Matt 24:20, when read in its literary, eschatological, and halakic contexts, marks an important shift within the narration that directly addresses Matthew's readers and informs us about their attitude toward Sabbath keeping. The conclusion of Part I provides a detailed summary and synthesis of my analysis of Sabbath keeping in Matthew and Luke.

Finally, I dedicate chapter 7 to the question of Sabbath keeping in the book of Acts. Whereas the gospel of Luke contains several controversies about the Sabbath keeping of Jesus and his first disciples, in Acts, no debate whatsoever about Sabbath keeping arises. The contrast between the gospel of Luke, which reports the highest number of Sabbath controversies of all gospels, and Acts, which records none at all, is striking and must be accounted for. I suggest that the Sabbath controversies in the synoptics, particularly in Luke's case, tell us more about Jesus' authority than the Sabbath praxis of the gospel writers. We should avoid accepting simplistic, linear, and teleological constructions positing that the Jesus movement inevitably moved away from the Jewish Law as time passed by. On the contrary, I propose that the Sabbath praxis of certain followers of Jesus could have been more "conservative" than the historical Jesus himself.

Part II covers another important marker of Jewish identity: Jewish food laws or, kashrut, to use a rabbinic term. In this section, I find myself inevitably dealing with purity laws as well, but the focus involves assessing Matthew and Luke's attitude toward kosher laws. While many Jews of the Second Temple period argued about how they should observe the purity system (e.g., washing hands before eating), it seems that most, or at least many, of them agreed on the basic and fundamental necessity to observe kashrut (e.g., refraining from eating forbidden foods such as pork).[120] Matthew and Luke align themselves with this "mainstream" Jewish consensus on the question of kashrut. The Introduction to Part II presents the topic of kashrut, distinguishing it from the Jewish system of purity laws. I find it important to appreciate the distinctions between both systems, for many have made conclusions concerning kashrut in passages of the New Testament that deal primarily with the domain of ritual (im)purity. Chapter 8 surveys Jewish food laws in Matthew, while chapter 9 covers the same topic in the gospel of Luke. I find nothing in either of the two gospels that

---

[120] However, see Kraemer, "Food, Eating, and Meals," 403–19; *Jewish Eating and Identity*, 123–45, for a discussion about Jews disregarding various aspects of kashrut.

speaks against the observance of kashrut. Chapters 10 and 11 deal with the Cornelius episode and the Apostolic Decree in Acts, respectively. These two important chapters show that Luke is really arguing on behalf of the moral purification of Gentile followers of Jesus, not the abrogation of kashrut. In fact, through his affirmation of the Apostolic Decree, Luke presupposes that Jewish followers of Jesus will continue to observe the Jewish Law in its entirety and even expects Gentiles to observe some aspects of the Mosaic legislation that enable them to preserve their newly acquired purity and respect the ritual concerns of their Jewish comrades.

Part III, which looks at the question of circumcision, is the shortest of all three sections. Although Matthew does not explicitly refer to this topic, I suggest that his position on the matter would probably have been similar to Luke's: Jewish (male) followers of Jesus should continue to observe circumcision, while Gentile followers of Jesus need not undergo circumcision. Especially in this section of my research, I discover an intimate and thorough knowledge on the part of Luke about Jewish tradition and halakah.

With these three markers of Jewish identity, Sabbath, kashrut, and circumcision, I hope to have sufficiently highlighted Matthew and Luke's mutual appreciation for the perpetuation of Torah observance. Other aspects of Torah praxis could have been covered, but they go well beyond the limits possible for this inquiry. Nevertheless, many other important issues concerning Torah praxis are dealt with along the way (purity, redemption of the first born, etc.), particularly in Parts II and III, and the concluding chapter of this work provide a synthesis and sense of closure that tie some of the loose ends necessary for comprehending the complex topic of Torah praxis and the Jewish character of Matthew and Luke-Acts.

Part I

Sabbath Keeping in Matthew and Luke-Acts

Chapter 2

Non-Controversial Sabbath Episodes

*"An entire cessation of all the affairs of life
on each seventh day is a Jewish institution,
and is not prescribed by the laws of any other people."*
(Isaac DiIsraeli)[1]

"Two ministering angels accompany man on the eve of the Sabbath from the synagogue to his home, one a good [angel] and one an evil [one]. And when he arrives home and finds the lamp burning, the table laid and the couch [bed] covered with a spread, the good angel exclaims, 'May it be even thus on another Sabbath [too],' and the evil angel unwillingly responds 'amen.' But if not, the evil angel exclaims, 'May it be even thus on another Sabbath [too],' and the good angel unwillingly responds, 'amen.'"
(*B. Shabb.* 119b)[2]

The Sabbath in Antiquity

A Marker of Jewish Identity

For generations the Sabbath has accompanied the Jews throughout their exile, functioning as one of the distinctive markers of identity that sets the Jewish people apart from other cultures. Many Jews, both in ancient and modern times, have viewed the Sabbath as an exclusive and perpetual covenantal sign between God and the people of Israel (Exod 31:17).[3] One popular saying, penned by the famous Israeli writer Ahad Haam, captures the traditional Jewish esteem for the Sabbath as an institution that has served to guarantee the survival and flourishing of the Jewish common-

---

[1] Isaac Disraeli, *The Genius of Judaism* (London: Edward Moxon, 1833), 126.

[2] All translations of the Bavli, unless otherwise indicated, are taken from the Soncino edition.

[3] Some Jews in antiquity, however, such as Philo, understood the Sabbath in broader, cosmic terms as a "day of festival for all people, and the birthday of the world" (*Opif.* 89), and did not restrict the Sabbath in covenantal terms as other ancient Jews did (e.g., the author of the book of *Jubilees* 2:19–21). For Philo's view on the Sabbath, see Herold Weiss, *A Day of Gladness: The Sabbath among Jews and Christians in Antiquity* (Columbia, S.C.: University of South Carolina Press, 2003), 32–51. Translations of Philo, unless otherwise indicated, are taken from *The Works of Philo: New Updated Edition* (trans. C. D. Yonge; n.p.: Hendrickson, 1993).

wealth throughout its long and perilous history: "more than the Jews have kept the Sabbath, the Sabbath has kept them."[4]

For outsiders, more precisely, of Greco-Roman provenance, "the observance of the Sabbath was one of the best known Jewish customs."[5] Judging from the ancient classical sources, the Sabbath seems to have been popular among many non-Jews as well. Juvenal (c. 60–130 CE), in addition to singling out the Jewish abstention from eating pork and the practice of circumcision, mockingly notes the infiltration of Sabbath keeping into Roman society:

> Some who have had a father who reveres the Sabbath, worship nothing but the clouds, and the divinity of the heavens, and see no difference between eating swine's flesh, from which their father abstained, and that of man; and in time they take to circumcision (Saturae XIV, 96–99).[6]

Juvenal further belittles this fictional paternal character, representative of Gentiles attracted to Judaism, for giving up "every seventh day to idleness, keeping it apart from all the concerns of life" (*Saturae* XIV, 104–105). Seneca (end of first century BCE. to 65 CE), in his work *De superstitione,* also expresses similar disdain over the diffusion of Jewish customs throughout the Roman Empire, declaring that "by introducing one day of rest in every seven they lose in idleness almost a seventh of their life, and by failing to act in times of urgency they often suffer loss."[7] The stoic philosopher proceeds indulging in his lamentation and disparagement, complaining about the widespread approval of Jewish customs throughout the Greco-Roman world, famously and hyperbolically declaring, "the vanquished have given laws to their victors."[8]

---

[4] Translation mine. Ahad Haam, *Kol Kitve Ahad Haam* (Tel Aviv: Dvir, 1965), 286: יותר משישראל שמרו את השבת שמרה השבת אותם.

[5] Harry Joshua Leon, *The Jews of Ancient Rome* (Philadelphia: Jewish Publication Society of America, 1960), 3. For a list of Greco-Roman references to the Sabbath see the index of Menahem Stern, *Greek and Latin Authors on Jews and Judaism* (3 vols.; Jerusalem: The Israel Academy of Sciences and Humanities, 1984), 3:146. All translations of Greek and Latin authors on Jews are taken from Stern's edition. For further discussion on the Sabbath in ancient non-Jewish sources, see Klinghardt, *Gesetz und Volkes Gottes*, 244–52; Heather A. McKay, *Sabbath and Synagogue: The Question of Sabbath Worship in Ancient Judaism* (Leiden: Brill, 2001), 89–131.

[6] The full passage with further comments can be found in Stern, *Greek and Latin Authors,* 2:102–7.

[7] *De superstitione,* apud: Augustine, *De civitate Dei* VI, 11.

[8] Ibid.: "*victi victoribus leges dederunt.*" Such vilification, however, usually proceeds from a selective group of Roman elitist writings that do not represent the views of all ancient non-Jews, many of who were curious about and drawn to Jewish tradition. See Doering, *Schabbat,* 286–89, for a brief discussion of the evidence for Gentile attraction toward the Sabbath.

Did Jews Treat Minor Diseases on the Sabbath?

Given the prominent profile of the Sabbath, as evidenced in the Jewish and non-Jewish sources, it only seems natural to start this inquiry with an assessment of the Sabbath in the gospels of Matthew and Luke as well as the Acts of the Apostles. However, before engaging in this endeavor, a central aspect regarding Sabbath keeping, which appears prominently throughout Matthew and Luke, needs to be dealt with in this introduction.[9] In the fourth volume of his gigantic project on the historical Jesus, Meier has highlighted the absence of any passage in Second Temple Jewish sources forbidding healing on the Sabbath. Meier fully exploits this silence in order to paint a picture of the historical Jesus (not the object of this study) in total harmony with and conforming to the non-sectarian halakic practices of his day. After surveying the pertinent sources, from the Jewish scriptures all the way to the early rabbinic literature, Meier concludes:

> The overall impression one gets from these and other rabbinic texts, when viewed in the context of the total absence of any prohibition of healing on the sabbath in the pre-70 period (notably in Jubilees and the Damascus Document), is that the post-70 rabbis had developed a new type of sabbath prohibition concerning healing, enshrined literarily for the first time in the Mishna. From the start, the newly formulated prohibition was not without its inconsistencies and disputed points, and further wiggle room continued to be created in later stages of rabbinic writings.[10]

Meier thinks that the gospel texts reporting controversies over Jesus' Sabbath healings reveal a "disconnect" with Jewish views on this matter. Their alleged ignorance about Jewish halakah encourages Meier to reaffirm his premonition regarding such pericopes, dubbed "controversy stories" or "dispute stories" (*Streitgespräche*) by form critics: their meaning remains unclear.[11] Meier's thesis implies that the Jewish followers of Jesus living in Palestine prior to 70 CE would have been responsible for creating such

---

[9] There is no need here to provide a survey on Sabbath halakah during the Second Temple period, since other specialists have already performed this work. Instead, I will cite the pertinent primary and secondary sources at various points throughout Part I when necessary. The reference work for any aspect of Sabbath halakah in ancient Judaism is Doering's *Schabbat*. Other (less exhaustive) surveys can be found in the works of Mayer-Haas, *Geschenk*, 32–80; John P. Meier, *A Marginal Jew: Rethinking the Historical Jesus. Volume Four: Law and Love* (New Haven: Yale University Press, 2009), 234–52; Weiss, *A Day of Gladness*, 10–31; Yong-Eui Yang, *Jesus and the Sabbath in Matthew's Gospel* (JSNTSup 139; Sheffield: Sheffield Academic Press, 1997), 21–99.

[10] Meier, *Marginal Jew*, 4:251. Before Meier, others who already pointed to the absence of pre-Tannaitic (besides the gospels) objections to healing on the Sabbath include Doering, *Schabbat*, 566–78; Mayer-Haas, *Geschenk*, 214.

[11] Meier, *Marginal Jew*, 4:254.

"senseless" stories either for polemical, apologetic reasons or for internal consumption.[12]

Despite the noble and welcomed effort to place the historical Jesus within his original Jewish halakic framework, Meier's thesis regarding the issue of Sabbath healings during the first century proves unconvincing on several grounds. First, it seems very unlikely that all of the first *Jewish* followers of Jesus, who were responsible for the generation of such stories, should be as ignorant of Jewish custom as to conjure up such halakic phantoms. However idealized, polemical, or apologetic such stories may be – and they certainly are, as the traditional studies of form criticism have amply demonstrated – for them to make any sense, a real objection to Sabbath healings of *non-life-threatening conditions* needs to be heard in the voice of the opponents, usually Pharisees. Surely, somewhere during the development of such stories, a member of the Jesus movement could have pointed out and erased such halakic incongruities if Sabbath healings were indeed acceptable among all Jews in the pre-70 era. Unless one imagines a sudden widespread prohibition against healing, emerging only and immediately after 70 CE, the same charge of logical absurdity and ignorance regarding Jewish custom would also have to be held against the redactors of Mark, Matthew (certainly no ignoramus of Jewish affairs), Luke, and John, since none of these gospel writers corrects the supposedly blatant halakic errors regarding Sabbath healings in the traditions handed down to them.

The manifold repetitions and widespread agreement among all four canonical gospels make it more than likely that certain ancient Jews felt uncomfortable with the execution of such therapeutic acts on the Sabbath. In my opinion, the gospel literature should be taken more seriously as evidence for Jewish halakic practices otherwise unattested for in the first century even while undergoing the *same* rigorous historical-critical inquiry any other Second Temple Jewish text would receive at the hands of modern scholars. Obviously, we should not expect to find complete accuracy or unbiased portrayals in the canonical gospels regarding the halakic practices of other Jewish groups, but to deny such accounts any historical basis regarding halakic matters before taking them seriously encourages skepticism beyond reasonable proportion. Hence, one of the many reasons for my preference in qualifying such literature simply as *Jewish* rather than "Christian." The latter label can too easily lead to setting this literature completely aside from an inquiry on Second Temple Judaism and dismiss its descriptions about Jewish custom and thought. In our justified efforts to recover the Jewish Jesus, we should not forget the very Jewish nature and provenance of much of the primary evidence used to reconstruct the histor-

---

[12] Cf. Meier, *Marginal Jew,* 4:279.

ical portrait of this enigmatic and elusive figure. Especially by beholding the *synoptic* writings do we discover the *Jewish* Jesus. "The Synoptic Jesus lived as a law-abiding Jew."[13] Lutz Doering's comments are right on mark regarding the usage of early "Christian" literature for elucidating ancient Jewish halakah:

> The rabbis did not invent halakhah, it was in various forms already quite developed in the first century. But early Jewish halakhic texts tend to cover only selected aspects of legally structured life. At times, when we ask for halakah and practice in the New Testament we cannot simply take a Jewish source and "adduce" it for comparison. Sometimes the New Testament is the earliest evidence for a certain regulation.[14]

In addition to the gospel texts, the admittedly later rabbinic literature also reveals a certain reticence among some (rabbinic) Jews toward healing minor diseases on the Sabbath.[15] To illustrate this point further, Doering discusses the issue of *piquah nefesh* (פיקוח נפש) – a rabbinic term and concept that is rooted in the halakic developments of the Second Temple period. Briefly stated, the ancient rabbis granted license for suspending the Sabbath when human life is in danger. This concept seems to have developed in tandem with the question of engaging in warfare on the Sabbath, an issue that acutely arose during the Maccabean wars. For obvious strategic and pragmatic reasons, the Maccabeans eventually decreed that fighting was permissible on the Sabbath (1 Macc 2:39–41; *Ant.* 12:276).[16] Besides justifying warfare on the Sabbath, some Jews also devised ways for saving human life on the Sabbath in more "normal" circumstances.[17] For example, what should be done if a person would fall into a well or body of water on the Sabbath? According to the stringent opinions voiced in certain texts from the Dead Sea Scrolls, Jews could not *break* the Sabbath in such circumstances in order to save a human. This strict position on the matter maintained that a Jewish person should in this scenario try to pull the endangered human out of the water with bare hands or clothes, but

---

[13] Sanders, *Jewish Law from Jesus to the Mishnah*, 90. Sanders makes this pronouncement but does not perceive its implications for understanding the perspectives of the *synoptic authors*. Instead, like Meier, he only emphasizes the Jewishness and Torah observance of the historical Jesus, but overlooks the very Jewish provenance of the synoptic writings that have preserved the Torah abiding Jewish Jesus for us.

[14] Lutz Doering, "Much Ado about Nothing? Jesus' Sabbath Healings and their Halakhic Implications Revisited," in *Judaistik und neutestamentliche Wissenschaft* (ed. Lutz Doering et al.; FRLANT 226; Göttingen: Vandenhoeck & Ruprecht, 2008), 229 (emphasis mine).

[15] On this matter, see much of Doering's "Much Ado about Nothing?" 215–41.

[16] Doering, *Schabbat*, 547–54. A tradition recorded in *Jubilees* 50:12 still holds on to the older, more stringent practice of not engaging in battle on the Sabbath. See Doering, *Schabbat*, 107–8.

[17] See Doering, *Schabbat*, 201–4; 232–35.

not use instruments forbidden to Jews to carry on the Sabbath (CD 11:16–17; 4Q265 6:6–7). This stringent view attempted to uphold simultaneously two fundamental values should they clash with one another: preserving human life while also honoring the sanctity of the Sabbath.[18]

However, alternative halakic routes existed to deal with this problem. For example, the rabbinic sages allowed suspending the Sabbath in almost any way in order to save someone's life.[19] Doering points to one text in which certain rabbis even permitted Jews to save life without seeking permission from the *Beit Din* (*t. Shabb.* 15:11). These rabbinic sages may have made this qualification because some Jews were still reluctant in their own day to save human life out of concern for respecting the Sabbath. Hence, the rabbinic effort to devise ways of encouraging Jews to save life even without their "official consent."[20] Given the reluctance among certain Jews to even save life on the Sabbath, one wonders how first century Jews would have responded to less mitigating conditions (chronic diseases, minor illnesses, etc.) that were not life-threatening. At least the later rabbinic evidence expresses substantial reservation toward caring about less serious conditions on the Sabbath.[21] Passages such as *m. Shabb.* 14:3 (one may not consume hyssop on the Sabbath since it is not food for healthy people), *m. Shabb.* 14:4 (prohibition against sucking vinegar out of concern for one's teeth; prohibition against applying wine or vinegar on the body to relieve one's loins), and *m. Shabb.* 22:6 (e.g., one may not induce vomiting, straighten the limb of a child, pour cold water on a dislocated hand or foot, and so on) attest to the opposition among certain rabbinic sages against intentionally performing healings of minor conditions on the Sabbath.

Meier, however, following Sanders, contends that such rabbinic positions prohibit performing healings that involve physical labor. The Jesus we discover in the canonical gospels, on the other hand, often heals the sick merely through *oral* pronouncement:

Indeed, more than any other sabbath dispute story, Mark 3:1–6 is a glaring example of this difficulty [i.e., determining how a 1st century Jew would object to such a Sabbath

---

[18] Doering, *Schabbat,* 566–68.

[19] *T. Shabb.* 15[16]:17: one can break the Sabbath to save life in any circumstance, save for idolatry, sexual immorality, and bloodshed (כל דבר עומד בפני פקוח נפש חוץ מע"ז וגלוי עריות ושפיכות דמים). Cf. *m. Yoma* 8:6; *t. Shabb.* 9[10]:22; 15[16]:11, 15.

[20] Doering, *Schabbat,* 230. I do *not* take this injunction as evidence that "common" Jews would have felt a need to consult with rabbinic authorities on such matters. Nevertheless, I do think that such rabbinic passages, along with the evidence from the gospels, point toward a hesitation on the part of some ancient Jews to break the Sabbath in order to save human life.

[21] The evidence is discussed by Doering, "Much Ado about Nothing?" 232–35.

healing]. For, in the healing of the man with the withered hand, Jesus literally *does nothing*. He simply issues two brief, simple commands to the afflicted man....[22]

However, lest we suddenly forget the *ideal*, generalizing nature of such pericopes, which do not report history *wie es eigentlich gewesen*, it could well be that during his healing performances the historical Jesus "used some form of 'physical action' which is not recorded."[23] In any case, other passages in the gospels do record physical applications. One readily thinks of John 9:6: "he spat on the ground and made mud with the saliva and spread the mud on the man's eyes."[24] In the gospels of Mark and Luke, some passages describe physical gestures such as holding the hand, laying hands, or helping someone stand up (Mark 1:31; Luke 13:13; 14:4).[25] None of the gospels, however, really concerns itself with the *mode* of Jesus' healings. They provide the reader with generalizing, concise stories that conceal a halakic debate concerning intentional healings of minor diseases on the Sabbath. Read against this halakic backdrop, such stories become comprehensible despite their inaccuracies and biases: when Jesus performs minor cures on the Sabbath, controversy arises.

Doering also brings to the foreground the prohibition against *talking* about work in certain passages from the Dead Sea Scrolls and rabbinic literature (e.g., CD 10:19; 4Q264a 1:5–8; *b. Shabb.* 113b; 150a).[26] Appar-

---

[22] Meier, *Marginal Jew,* 4:254, following Sanders, *Jewish Law from Jesus to the Mishnah*, 21. See already Geza Vermes, *Jesus the Jew: A Historian's Reading of the Gospels* (Philadelphia: Fortress, 1981), 25.

[23] Graham Stanton, *The Gospels and Jesus* (2d ed.; Oxford: Oxford University Press, 2002), 228. Cf. Doering, "Much Ado about Nothing?" 229.

[24] For the purposes of this inquiry, I do not deal with the gospel of John and its (ir?)relevance for reconstructing the historical Jesus. My goal is to illustrate how intentional healings of minor diseases, whether through physical or oral means, were objectionable to certain Jews – the gospels serving as the primary evidence to prove this point.

[25] Luke, however, primarily focuses on testifying to the power and authority of Jesus' *word* as I argue in the subsequent chapters.

[26] Doering, "Much Ado about Nothing?" 234. Even the very thought of work is proscribed in certain texts (Philo, *Mos.* 2:21; *Lev. Rab.* 34:16 on Lev 25:35; *y. Shabb.* 15:3 15 a–b, etc.). See Doering, *Schabbat*, 348–352. Meier, *Marginal Jew*, 4:254, to bolster his thesis, brings up the incident in the prayer house of Tiberias during which a debate occurred on the Sabbath regarding political affairs and military action (Josephus, *Life* 276–279): "Apparently, forceful speech exhorting or ordering others to undertake forceful action was not considered by any Jew present in the 'prayer house' to be a violation of the sabbath rest. Why should Jesus' two short commands, which do not urge any action that would be illicit on the sabbath, constitute such a violation?" The reference to Josephus carries limited weight. The debate takes place during a time of war (First Jewish Revolt). Consequently, such an occurrence may have been exceptional, deviating from normal convention. Moreover, these Jewish members of Tiberias *debate* about what to do *after* the Sabbath, while Jesus *pronounces* words that *generate* a change in the human's condition on the Sabbath proper. Furthermore, this pericope may suggest that

ently, the House of Shammai might have even forbidden praying for the sick on the Sabbath (*t. Shabb.* 16:22). If any overlap can be imagined between Pharisees and the Tannaim – a supposition I find by no means absurd, if not, by any means, assured – then it certainly seems possible that some Pharisees and maybe even some other Jews (e.g., Essenes, Qumranites, etc.) would have objected to caring for minor diseases on the Sabbath.[27] Doering concludes that *"first century Pharisees are likely to have considered an immediate therapy of a non-life threatening disease unlawful, even if effected by mere word."*[28]

The position advocated by Meier and others in the end also results to an argumentum e silentio, since to the best of my knowledge no Second Temple Jewish document besides the canonical gospels ever records a healing episode occurring during the Sabbath. Could such a remarkable silence in the sources indicate that many first-century Jews did indeed avoid treating minor diseases on the Sabbath? When such scenarios finally do emerge, some Jews either contest (the gospel evidence) or strongly discourage, if not forbid (the rabbinic evidence), such actions. Moreover, Meier's thesis raises the question of why healings of minor conditions suddenly became an issue in the post-70 era. Why were rabbinic sages making such qualifications on this issue, if no real reluctance or debate existed prior to 70? To see the rabbinic evidence as collectively representing a sudden and more stringent position on the matter, even stricter than their Qumranic and Essene counterparts, seems unlikely.[29] Rather, one might tentatively sug-

---

Josephus tries to observe carefully the Sabbath limits despite the pressing circumstances. On this point, see Doering, *Schabbat,* 494–95.

[27] This observation should not encourage a return to the romantic, outdated narrative that sees the Pharisees and then the rabbis as the immediate leaders of a "normative" Judaism in post-70 Palestine, let alone the Diaspora.

[28] Doering, "Much Ado about Nothing?" 235. Perhaps, the Pharisaic objection to performing minor cures on the Sabbath stemmed from a desire to refrain from creating "change" or altering natural circumstances on this holy day. In other words, some Jews of the Second Temple period and beyond objected to healing on the Sabbath because they viewed such an act as a "creative" performance that would transform the condition of the human from one state (sick) to another (healed). Such a transformative, creative act may have been viewed as unnecessary "work" that could be postponed until after the Sabbath. *Imitatio Dei,* Jews were supposed to refrain from "creating," in this case, healing, on the Sabbath. Cf. Peter J. Tomson, *'If this be from Heaven. . .': Jesus and the New Testament Authors in Their Relationship to Judaism* (Sheffield: Sheffield Academic Press, 2001), 154: "Not one of the synoptic accounts reports that Jesus prepares a medicine: he does not execute a single 'work' that is forbidden on the Sabbath, as that was later summarized in a rabbinic formulation (*m. Šab.* 7.2). Healing, however, entails a change in circumstances and the issue is how this is viewed."

[29] In many instances, rabbinic halakah tends to be more lenient than sectarian positions from the pre-70 era (e.g., the sect of Qumran). For example, *Jub.* 50:12 prohibits one from being on a ship on the Sabbath, while rabbinic tradition allows for such a

gest that prior to 70 certain Jews (e.g., Qumranites, Essenes, some Pharisees, etc.) objected to treating minor diseases on the Sabbath and that later on the rabbinic sages allowed for some "wiggle room" in this domain even if they preferred to postpone performing Sabbath healings to normal weekdays. To be sure, many "common" Jews would probably have ignored the injunctions of rabbis, Essenes, Pharisees, and the like, and probably cared for their sick on the Sabbath at their own discretion. I argue that it is precisely this segment of the Jewish people, the so-called "people of the land," that Matthew could have been seeking to win over by appealing to their customs and "common sense."[30] Throughout Part I of this book, I work under the assumption that certain Jews of the first century CE objected to performing minor cures on the Sabbath. This approach, in my opinion, best accounts for the presence of reports on controversies over Sabbath healings in the synoptic gospels.

Introduction to the Non-Controversial Sabbath Episodes in Matthew and Luke

The episodes in Matthew and Luke discussed in this chapter occur in Sabbath settings that do not deal directly with the question of Sabbath keeping. In other words, these stories happen *on* the Sabbath but are not really *about* the Sabbath.[31] Nevertheless, even if these passages do not deal di-

---

possibility in certain conditions (e.g., *Sifre Deut* Pisqa 203; *Midr. Tann.* on Deut 20:20; *m. Shabb.* 16:8). See Doering, *Schabbat,* 99–100 and chapter 7 in this monograph dealing with Sabbath traveling in Acts. *Jub.* 50:12 prohibits fighting on the Sabbath; rabbinic tradition permits (*t. Eruv.* 3:7). While CD 11:16–17 and 4Q265 6:6–7 prohibit using instruments to draw a human from the water on the Sabbath, many rabbis would certainly not object to this act. The list could be easily multiplied (e.g., saving an animal from a well on the Sabbath: Qumran forbids; rabbis allow at least for one to provide the animal with food; see chapter 5 of this monograph). Is it not better to posit that the rabbis loosened a previous legislation against healings of minor diseases on the Sabbath that categorically prohibited such actions?

[30] I do not intend to revive an older scholarly dichotomy that ties the emergence of "Christianity" with the *Am Haarets* ("people of the land") and completely opposes these against the Pharisees/rabbinic sages. Many "normal" Jews may have been equally attracted to Pharisaic practice. Consequently, it seems better to see both the Matthean followers of Jesus and the Pharisees as competing with another to gain control over the masses of "common" Jews who lived throughout Galilee. See already Aharon Oppenheimer, *The ʿAm Ha-Aretz: A Study in the Social History of the Jewish People in the Hellenistic-Roman Period* (ALGHJ 8; Leiden: Brill, 1977), 1–22.

[31] Mayer-Haas, *Geschenk,* 136 n. 2: "Bei den Textanalysen wird unterschieden zwischen den beiden Texten, die *am* Sabbat handeln…und den Texten, die *vom* Sabbat

rectly with Sabbath keeping, it is important to analyze them carefully in order to obtain a global perspective on Matthew and Luke's attitude toward the Sabbath institution. First of all, these passages illustrate how Matthew and Luke (and even Mark) are not always set on reporting controversies about Sabbath keeping when they refer to this holy day in their writings. In fact, these episodes show that the synoptic authors can often depict the Sabbath in positive terms, free from polemics. This is especially true of Luke, as he highlights Jesus' attendance of the synagogue on the Sabbath more than any other gospel writer does. In Luke's case, we also discover a great deal about what happens on the Sabbath in a synagogue setting. Can this information tell us anything about Luke and his readers? To answer this question, I begin by analyzing those Markan passages that both Matthew and Luke have reworked, appropriated, and at times even eliminated. I then conclude with an assessment of a pericope unique to Luke's gospel (Luke 4:16–30) that also contains no disputes about Sabbath keeping.

An Unclean Spirit in the Synagogue of Capernaum: Mark 1:21–28; Matt 7:28–29; Luke 4:31–37[32]

Literary Context

The first reference in Mark to the Sabbath appears within a larger literary unit (1:21–39).[33] In its first subunit (vv. 21–28), Mark depicts Jesus teaching with authority on the Sabbath in the synagogue of one of his favorite Galilean towns, Capernaum. According to Mark, Jesus succeeds in winning the admiration of the local crowd through his authoritative manner of teaching. It is during this visit on the Sabbath to the synagogue that Jesus also expels an evil spirit from one of the congregants. After this exorcism, Mark's Jesus cures on the same day the mother-in-law of Simon Peter during a visit to the latter's house (vv. 29–31), meaning that this healing also takes place on the Sabbath.

---

handeln." Meier, *Marginal Jew,* 4:252, includes such stories under the rubric of "miracles on the Sabbath that do not provoke a dispute."

[32] All citations from the New Testament (and the Hebrew Bible) are taken from the New Revised Standard Version. I critique the NRSV and other versions of the Bible at different junctures where I believe my analysis can improve or correct the modern translations.

[33] Mayer-Haas, *Geschenk,* 139, views Mark 1:21–39 as one unit although within this segment of Mark the Sabbath day ends in v. 34, since according to v. 3 Jesus goes out to pray in a deserted place "in the morning, while it was still very dark." This chronological reference marks a transition into the following day of the new week.

Matthew does not follow Mark's narration of the events, leaving out the story about the man tormented by an unclean spirit in the synagogue of Capernaum, while placing the material found in Mark 1:22, which describes the amazement of the crowds at Jesus' authority, at the conclusion to the Sermon on the Mount (Matt 7:28–29). As a result, the crowds marvel at Jesus' teaching and authority, but, unlike Mark (1:21–22), there is no hint in Matthew that this event occurs on the Sabbath day.[34]

This leaves us with the assessment of Luke's version of the episode, which, unlike Matthew, does retain the Markan material within its Sabbath setting. Luke, however, has placed the Markan material in a different sequence. Unlike Mark, who places Jesus' visit to the synagogue of Capernaum after the calling of the first disciples (1:16–20), Luke reverses the order of events: the calling of the disciples appears only after Jesus' visit to the synagogue of Capernaum on the Sabbath (5:1–11).[35] In addition, before visiting Capernaum, the Lukan Jesus experiences rejection in Nazareth, his hometown (4:16–30). According to Luke, this event also occurs on a Sabbath. Luke's relocation of Jesus' visit to Capernaum immediately after his rejection in Nazareth is by no means accidental.[36] During this marking event, the Lukan Jesus delivers on the Sabbath in the synagogue a programmatic message closely linked to the reading from the Isaiah scroll (Isa 61:1, 2; 58:6), announcing release and freedom to those captive and suffering oppression (4:18–19). Immediately after his departure from Nazareth, the readers of Luke witness the very concretization of that pro-

---

[34] Matthew relocates the reference in Mark 1:21a to Jesus' departure from Nazareth to Capernaum to Matt 4:13. Traces of Mark 1:28 appear in Matt 4:24a: "So his fame spread throughout all Syria, and they brought to him all the sick, those who were afflicted with various diseases and pains, demoniacs, epileptics, and paralytics, and he cured them." Cf. also Mark 1:24 ("What have you to do with us, Jesus of Nazareth? Have you come to destroy us? I know who you are, the Holy One of God.") with Matt 8:29b ("What have you to do with us, Son of God? Have you come here to torment us before the time?"). The material introducing the Sermon on the Mount in Matt 5:1 is based in part on Mark 1:21. See Ulrich Luz, *Matthew* (3 vols.; Hermeneia; Minneapolis: Fortress, 2001–2007), 1:182.

[35] Hence the different singular and plural verbs in Mark and Luke: in Mark 1:21, *they* (i.e., Jesus and his first disciples) enter into the synagogue of Capernaum on the Sabbath (εἰσπορεύονται), while in Luke 4:31 only Jesus arrives in Capernaum (κατῆλθεν), since he officially calls his first disciples only in 5:1–11. The address to Jesus in Luke 5:5 ("master") already signifies a certain recognition of Jesus' authority on Peter's part even before Jesus calls him to become a "fisher of people." Peter addresses Jesus in this manner because of the healing of his mother-in-law in 4:39. However, he becomes a full-blown disciple of Jesus only after the official call in 5:10.

[36] Correctly, George E. Rice, "Luke 4:31–44: Release for the Captives," *AUSS* 20 (1982): 23–28. Cf. Ulrich Busse, *Die Wunder des Propheten Jesus: Die Rezeption, Komposition und Interpretation der Wundertradition im Evangelium des Lukas* (Forschung zur Bibel 24; Stuttgart: Katholisches Bibelwerk, 1977), 58.

phetic announcement when Jesus releases a man from an unclean spirit in the synagogue of Capernaum (4:31–37) – an event that also occurs on a Sabbath. In this way, Luke situates on the Sabbath day both the proclamation and the materialization of the theme of release from captivity promised and fulfilled by Jesus.

Analysis

As noted earlier, Luke follows Mark in situating Jesus teaching in the synagogue on the Sabbath day (Mark 1:21: "τοῖς σάββασιν εἰσελθὼν εἰς τὴν συναγωγὴν ἐδίδασκεν"; Luke 4:31: "καὶ ἦν διδάσκων αὐτοὺς ἐν τοῖς σάββασιν"). The Greek word for "Sabbath" appears in Mark 1:21 and Luke 4:31 in the plural. Mark employs the plural form to mean that Jesus entered into the synagogue of Capernaum and taught there (εἰσελθὼν εἰς τὴν συναγωγὴν ἐδίδασκεν) on a *single Sabbath day* (τοῖς σάββασιν). The usage of the plural in the singular sense is not uncommon in "Jewish Greek": it appears elsewhere in the synoptic tradition as well as in the Septuagint.[37] Luke, however, probably uses the plural dative τοῖς σάββασιν in this instance to mean that Jesus taught in Capernaum during *several Sabbaths*. This becomes more apparent when we observe how Luke has reworked Mark's text. According to Luke, Jesus "entered" (κατῆλθεν: in the aorist, probably signaling a simple aspect occurring in the past once) into the city of Capernaum and "was teaching" (ἦν διδάσκων) – the periphrastic construction suggesting in this instance the continuous, repeated force of an action – "on the *Sabbaths*" (ἐν τοῖς σάββασιν). With these verbal constructions, Luke insinuates that Jesus traveled once to Capernaum but spent several Sabbaths teaching in the local synagogue during his visit. This particular usage of the plural in Greek for the noun Sabbath corresponds to Luke's intention elsewhere to underline Jesus' *habitual* attendance of the synagogue on the Sabbath day.[38]

Besides retaining Mark's Sabbath setting, Luke also preserves much of the Markan wording, albeit with some modifications in style and language, eliminating, for example, the characteristic Markan usage of εὐθύς ("im-

---

[37] Matt 12:1; 28:1; τὰ σάββατα: Exod 16:29; 31:14, 16; τὴν ἡμέραν τῶν σαββάτων: Exod 20:8; Deut 5:12; Jer 17:21.

[38] Luke 13:10, Ἦν δὲ διδάσκων ἐν μιᾷ τῶν συναγωγῶν ἐν τοῖς σάββασιν, can also be translated as: "and he was teaching in one of the synagogues on the *Sabbaths* (or on each Sabbath)." When Luke wants to signal that an act occurred only on one Sabbath he does so by employing various other constructions such as τῇ ἡμέρᾳ τῶν σαββάτων (Luke 4:16; Acts 13:14; 16:13); ἐν σαββάτῳ (Luke 6:1); ἐν ἑτέρῳ σαββάτῳ (Luke 6:6); σαββάτῳ (Luke 14:1); τῷ ἐρχομένῳ σαββάτῳ (Acts 13:44).

mediately"; cf. Mark 1:21, 23 and Luke 4:31, 33).[39] Luke also makes some significant changes to Mark's pericope. For example, Luke prefers to highlight the verbal aspect of Jesus' teaching, referring to it as "this word" (Luke 4:36: τίς ὁ λόγος οὗτος; instead of Mark 1:27: τί ἐστιν τοῦτο;), and eliminates Mark's description of Jesus' instruction in terms of *novelty* (1:27: διδαχὴ καινή), emphasizing, as elsewhere, the continuity of Jesus' message with the Jewish tradition.[40] In addition, Luke eliminates Mark's polemical rhetoric: whereas Mark declares that Jesus "taught them as one having authority, and not as the scribes" (Mark 1:22), Luke claims that Jesus simply "spoke with authority" (4:32).[41] By contrast, Matthew's wording of the crowd's reaction to Jesus' teaching, which concludes the Sermon on the Mount, seems more alienated from and antagonistic toward the scribal establishment, since it directly contrasts Jesus' authority with the instruction of *"their* scribes" (7:29).[42]

---

[39] As is well known, the Greek word εὐθύς appears only once in Luke (6:49), five times in Matthew, but no less than forty times in Mark. See Mayer-Haas, *Geschenk,* 296–97, for a more detailed redactional discussion of this Markan passage by Luke.

[40] Cf. François Bovon, *Luke 1* (Hermeneia; Minneapolis: Fortress, 2002), 159, who views the omission as revealing Luke's concern over new, deceptive teachings. See also Mayer-Haas, *Geschenk,* 298; Helmut Merkel, "Israel im lukanischen Werk," *NTS* 40 (1994): 371–98.

[41] This accords with Luke's more nuanced portrayal of the conflicts between Jesus and his disciples and the scribes and Pharisees ("scribes" in Luke should not always be equated with Pharisees). Mayer-Haas, *Geschenk,* 298, claims Luke has deleted the polemical rhetoric in Mark 1:22 because it deters from his intent to emphasize the authority of Jesus' λόγος. While this deletion may serve that immediate function in the context of this pericope, overall, it underscores Luke's less hostile portrait of the scribes and particularly the Pharisees.

[42] Much has been made of the presence of the distancing pronoun in Matthew (cf. Matt 4:23; 9:35; 10:17; 13:54) in an ongoing scholarly debate about whether Matthew and his presumed community should be located *intra muros* or *extra muros* with respect to the wider Jewish society. Luz, *Matthew,* 1:390, commenting on Matt 7:29, sides with the *extra muros* camp: "With the possessive pronoun 'their' Matthew indicates that the separation between the Jesus community and Judaism has already taken place. The Jewish scribes are on the 'other' side. The people who are astonished stand in the middle between 'their' scribes and Jesus." Cf. Sim's retort to the *extra muros* view: "Once we understand Matthew's community as a sectarian group in conflict with a Jewish body, then it seems more appropriate to speak of a Jewish sect within Judaism than of a Christian sect outside Judaism. The important sociological evidence Stanton compiles from Qumran in fact points precisely in this direction. The Qumran community, which bears all the hallmarks of a sectarian group, completely renounced mainstream Jewish society by moving to the shores of the Dead Sea and living in isolation from it. But no-one would contend that its considerable differences with and rejection of the remainder of Jewish society entailed that it no longer considered itself to be Jewish. The evidence for the sectarian nature of the Matthean community should not be interpreted any differently" (Sim, *The Gospel of Matthew and Christian Judaism*, 5). See also Runesson, "Re-

Both Mark and Luke report the intrusion of an individual possessed by an unclean clean spirit (Mark 1:23: ἄνθρωπος ἐν πνεύματι ἀκαθάρτῳ; Luke 4:33: ἄνθρωπος ἔχων πνεῦμα δαιμονίου ἀκαθάρτου) into the synagogue where Jesus teaches. Jesus, however, is able to neutralize the spirit with little difficulty, which only excites further amazement among the members of the synagogue of Capernaum. Neither of the two gospel narrators seems concerned about the timing of Jesus' act, which occurs on a Sabbath. Because of his apparent nonchalance over the timing of Jesus' exorcism, some commentators have argued that Sabbath keeping was no longer an issue of interest for Mark.[43] However, this argument from silence can also be read in the opposite direction. Andrea Mayer-Haas emphasizes that the gospel of Mark never makes any depreciating remarks against the Sabbath institution. She goes as far as suggesting that Mark 1:21–28 (as well as 3:1–6; 6:1–6) even contain hints of a Christian Sabbath worship, which may have included scriptural readings accompanied by christo-centric teachings.[44] In Luke's case, it seems very unlikely that he intends to downgrade the importance of the Sabbath to the level of irrelevance, given his strong interest elsewhere in this topic and his desire to portray the *ekklesia* as the legitimate embodiment of Israel. In several other passages, Luke provides numerous justifications for Jesus' attitude toward the Sabbath, suggesting an ongoing concern for honoring and preserving the Sabbath institution.

Some have pointed out that no explicit prohibition against the performance of exorcisms on the Sabbath appears in Second Temple Jewish literature.[45] Could this silence account for the absence of any rationalization or justification in the pericopes of Mark and Luke on behalf of Jesus' performance of an exorcism on the Sabbath?[46] Not even the canonical gospels contain any Jewish objection to performing exorcisms on the Sabbath. It is difficult, however, to determine whether ancient Jews would have halakically distinguished between the performance of an exorcism and the healing of minor diseases on the Sabbath. To complicate the problem further, Luke, in particular, blurs the lines between demonic posses-

---

thinking Early Jewish-Christian Relations," 95–132, who proposes reading some of the pronominal references to "their synagogues" in Matthew in a more restrictive way, as referring to synagogues of Pharisaic association.

[43] Dieter Lührmann, *Das Markusevangelium* (HNT 3; Tübingen: Mohr Siebeck, 1987), 49, 65; Heikki Sariola, *Markus und das Gesetz: Eine redaktionskritische Untersuchung* (AASF.DHL 56; Helsinki: Suomalainen Tiedeakatemia, 1990), 113.

[44] Mayer-Haas, *Geschenk*, 148–49.

[45] Mayer-Haas, *Geschenk*, 418; Yang, *Jesus and the Sabbath*, 246.

[46] This silence would also suggest that Matthew did not delete this episode because of his uneasiness with its occurrence on the Sabbath. But see Bornkamm, "End-Expectation and Church in Matthew," 31 n. 2.

sion and physical diseases. Western readers should not neatly divide these two categories, since Luke (and probably many other ancient people) would have perceived the source of many of the physical ailments affecting human beings as ultimately stemming from demonic forces and causes.[47] Luke may have viewed Jesus' healings of physical ailments on the Sabbath as all the more justifiable, almost on par with life-threatening conditions, because of their demonic origination. Interestingly, a mishnaic passages allows one to extinguish a light on the Sabbath (this is considered "work" according to the rabbis) for fear of Gentiles, robbers, an *evil spirit* (רוח רעה), or in order to allow a sick person (whose life is endangered) to sleep.[48] It could be that some Jews viewed demonic possession as a life-

---

[47] For example, Luke makes little distinction between exorcism and healing when depicting Jesus as equally rebuking (ἐπετίμησεν) an unclean spirit (4:35) and a physical ailment (i.e., the fever of Simon Peter's mother-in-law, 4:39). The overlap between demonic possession and other sicknesses appears again in Luke 4:41 where the demonically possessed seem to be part of the "sick" in v. 40. Jesus first heals the "sick with various kinds of diseases" (v.40) and (as a result?) demons, whom Jesus rebukes (ἐπιτιμῶν), "also came out of many" (v.41). Cf. the similar overlap between sickness and demonic possession in Luke 9:2, 6.

[48] In Philip Blackman's translation of the Mishnah, רוח רעה is translated as "melancholia" and rationally understood as referring to hypochondria or depression (so Soncino's translation of *b. Shabb.* 29b). This understanding of the term seems to go back to Maimonides, a doctor with a rationalist tendency, who claimed that רוח רעה referred to different types of melancholia (see his commentary on *m. Shabb.* 2:5). This is possible, but historically it is somewhat misleading, as it deters from appreciating the ancient and widespread belief in demonic agents as responsible for causing sickness and trauma. Cf. Danby's translation of the Mishnah, which sticks to a literal translation of the term. See also Jastrow, "רוח," 1458. Gideon Bohak, "Jewish Exorcism before and after the Destruction of the Second Temple," in *Was 70 CE a Wathershed in Jewish History?* 285, also understands this mishnah as referring to demons. Perhaps *m. Shabb.* 2:5 is not referring specifically to depression, but any sort of demonic attack. The juxtaposition of the "evil spirit" to the two preceding items concerning fear for Gentiles and robbers conveys the impression of some kind of external agent potentially detecting and attacking a Jewish home because of the candle lit therein. On the other hand, the fourth item in *m. Shabb.* 2:5 refers to sickness, possibly suggesting that רוח רעה designates some kind of mental or psychological condition, which is nevertheless attributed from the rabbinic point of view to a demon (see Rashi, in his commentary on *b. Shabb.* 29b, who states that the evil spirit "comes upon" the person). Maimonides claims that the darkness helps assuage a specific type of hypochondria or depression. Indeed, it is interesting that this mishnah refers to the practice of *extinguishing* rather than lighting a fire in order to repel the evil spirit. The Soncino English edition of the Bavli cites J. Bergmann, "Zur Geschichte religiöser Bräuche," *MGWJ* 5/6 (1927): 161–71, which contains references to the reverse practice among ancient people, namely, to light a fire in order to scare away demons. One should also take note of *m. Eruv.* 4:1, which states that if non-Jews or an evil spirit carries a Jew off (beyond 2000 cubits) on the Sabbath, that person may not move further than four cubits. However, if the Gentiles or evil spirit brings back the Jew, it is as if that person had never been carried away. Once again Blackman rationalizes this mishnah by translat-

threatening condition and were willing in certain cases to intervene on the Sabbath on behalf of the tormented person. One thinks of the story of the man of Gerasenes who was tormented by an impure spirit to the point that he would walk around naked in the desert and tombs (Luke 8:26–29), or the case of a father's son who was possessed by a spirit that would make him mute and even suicidal by casting him into fire and water (Mark 9:14–29; Luke 9:37–43a). These conditions are indeed dangerous for the affected person who might even pose a threat to the members of his or her community. Since Luke seems to think that diseases generally originate from demonic sources, he views Jesus' intervention on the Sabbath on behalf of the sick as entirely justified. In other words, he might be underscoring the theme of demonic origination in order to legitimate Jesus' healing ministry and extend its application on the Sabbath to cases where a person's life is not imminently under threat. In the subsequent sections and chapters on the Sabbath, I explore and develop this Lukan theme more fully. In any case, the absence of any apologia in Luke on behalf of Jesus' Sabbath exorcism and healing may simply stem from Luke's eagerness to signal how the eschatological and prophetic message announced by Jesus in Nazareth (4:16–30) immediately and concretely plays out in his itinerant ministry. The time to defend Jesus' approach to the Sabbath will come shortly in the subsequent narration of events, but first Luke is determined to flesh out Jesus' eschatological portfolio and to highlight his messianic authority.[49]

In Matthew's case, other reasons for his deletion of this episode have been proposed, including his reservation toward the practice of exorcism in general.[50] While this proposal may suffice to explain Matthew's deletion of Mark's episode on exorcism, it does not account for his relocation of the other healing events from the same Markan pericope. As will be shown, by reconfiguring all of these Markan episodes into non-Sabbath settings, Matthew provides a narrative that always contains a defense of Jesus' Sabbath keeping whenever such an issue arises.[51] Too much should not be

---

ing רוח רעה as "lunacy," but it seems more likely that the Tannaim envisage an external, demonic agent as responsible for the attack, even if "lunacy" is indeed the correct scientific (and modern) diagnosis for such behavior.

[49] Some of these comments apply to Mark as well, since he also focuses at this point in exalting Jesus' authority. See Loader, *Jesus' Attitude towards the Law,* 16, 307.

[50] See discussion in Mayer-Haas, *Geschenk,* 417–18, with bibliographical references on the topic. According to Mayer-Haas, in Mark 1:23–28, the features describing this exorcism that bother Matthew the most include: the demonic, the demon's resistance to the exorcist by openly identifying Jesus by name, the command silencing the demon as well as the graphic description of the demon's withdrawal from the victim's body.

[51] The suggestion provided by Yang, *Jesus and the Sabbath,* 246, for Matthew's deletion of the Sabbath settings for said episodes is based on a problematic and misguided projection of Jewish "legalism" that did not bother most Jews in antiquity: "He [i.e.,

read into this, however, since the Matthean modifications of Mark's gospel in these instances may stem more from literary preferences than ideological factors.⁵²

Going out of the Law for an In-Law?
Healing Peter's Mother-in-Law:
Mark 1:29–31; Matt 8:14–15; Luke 4:38–39

Literary Context

After reporting the exorcism in the synagogue of Capernaum, Mark has Jesus immediately (εὐθύς) leave the synagogue and enter into the house of Simon and Andrew where he heals their mother-in-law. This implies that for Mark this healing occurs on the same day, that is, on a Sabbath (1:29–31), and he explicitly refers to sunset in the subsequent verse after the healing episode (1:32). Luke also assumes that the healing takes place on the same Sabbath: "After leaving the synagogue he entered Simon's house" (Luke 4:38). Together, the two Lukan episodes reporting the exorcism of the man in the synagogue and the healing of Peter's mother-in-law point back to Jesus' eschatological message announced in the synagogue of Nazareth (4:16–30). They demonstrate how the oppressed among Israel experience in concrete terms liberation from their suffering and sickness thanks to Jesus' ministry of healing.

Matthew preserves this episode but places it in a setting completely divorced from the Sabbath. In its Matthean context, the episode occurs in the midst of a series of healings, after the cleansing of a leper and the healing of the centurion's servant (Matt 8:1–13), and before the healing of the masses (8:16–17). Since Matthew locates this episode outside its Sabbath environment, I will only analyze Luke's account more closely.

Analysis

Luke describes the physical condition of Peter's mother-in-law in slightly more severe terms than Mark. While Mark states that the mother-in-law lay in bed with a fever (κατέκειτο πυρέσσουσα), Luke augments the gravity of her condition by claiming that she suffered from a *high* fever (ἦν

Matthew] may well have refrained intentionally from using the phrase in order to avoid an unnecessary misunderstanding by the members in his community who had a legalistic tendency – a misunderstanding that they were to worship on the sabbath after the example of Jesus."

⁵² Robert Banks, *Jesus and the Law in the Synoptic Tradition* (SNTSMS 28; Cambridge: Cambridge University Press, 1975), 127.

συνεχομένη πυρετῷ μεγάλῳ).⁵³ Luke also describes the administration of the healing with significantly different verbal features. In Mark, Jesus takes the woman by the hand and lifts her up (1:31), but Luke does not refer to physical contact, instead Jesus merely stands over her and rebukes (ἐπετίμησεν) the fever (4:39). With the verbal reference to "rebuking," Luke sends the reader's attention back to the preceding pericope where Jesus also "rebukes" (ἐπετίμησεν) the evil spirit tormenting the man at the synagogue of Capernaum (4:35). Physical sickness and demonic possession are always closely related in Luke's worldview.⁵⁴ This depiction in turn accentuates the authority of Jesus' verbal utterance: standing with authority over Peter's mother-in-law, Jesus only needs to summon the power of his word in order to repudiate her (demonic) fever (v. 39). Luke's stress on Jesus' verbal utterance also recalls the reaction of the crowd at the synagogue of Capernaum: "What kind of utterance is this (τίς ὁ λόγος οὗτος)? For with authority and power he commands the unclean spirits, and out they come" (4:36).⁵⁵

After the healing, according to both Mark and Luke, Peter's mother-in-law rises and serves (διηκόνει) Jesus as well as those present with him. Mark and Luke provide no indication that they view such activity as infringing on the sanctity of the Sabbath. Here the verb "διακονέω" means simply to "perform duties," to "render assistance" or to "serve someone" by waiting at the table and offering food and drink, services the mother-in-law previously was unable to perform because of her condition. Luke does not define what kind of "work" was involved in performing this hospitable service. Like Mark, his text remains extremely terse.⁵⁶ The mother-in-law's prompt attendance to the guests and household members testifies to the efficacy of Jesus' healing powers and confirms his authority.⁵⁷

As in the preceding episode on exorcism, Luke reveals no concern over possible reproaches Jesus' act could have raised among his Jewish peers as far as Sabbath observance is concerned. Some scholars even wonder whether such a report contains any act that goes against Jewish codes of Sabbath conduct. After all, certain halakic discussions within early rabbinic literature, admittedly written after the time of Luke, grant license for

---

⁵³ Bovon, *Luke 1*, 163.

⁵⁴ Loader, *Jesus' Attitude towards the Law,* 307: "In 4:38–39 Luke rewrites Mark's account of the healing of Peter's mother-in-law (1:29–31) turning it into an exorcism." Mayer-Haas, *Geschenk,* 300: "Die von Markus vorgegebene Heilungserzählung wird im Lukasevangelium zu einem Exorzismus, der die Vollmacht und Kraft Jesu, die in seinem Wort zum Ausdruck kommen, demonstriert."

⁵⁵ Cf. Mayer-Haas, *Geschenk,* 302.

⁵⁶ Mayer-Haas, *Geschenk,* 150:"die kürzeste neutestamentliche Wundergeschichte."

⁵⁷ Michael Wolter, *Das Lukasevangelium* (HNT 5; Tübingen: Mohr Siebeck, 2008), 204–5.

treating any illness deemed to be life-threatening. According to *m. Yoma* 8:6, R. Mattyah b. Heresh even allows one to administer herbs on the Sabbath to an individual with a sore throat if there is doubt concerning the person's ability to survive (ספק נפשות). R. Mattyah b. Heresh's lenient position stretches the application of the rule that calls for suspending the Sabbath in life-threatening circumstances to rather doubtful cases where human life *may* be under threat: "Whenever there is doubt whether life is in danger this overrides the Sabbath" (*m. Yoma* 8:6: וכל ספק נפשות דוחה את השבת). Epstein also points to a rabbinic halakah that permits healing through "whispering," that is, pronouncing through incantation, on the Sabbath of conditions not viewed as life-threatening.[58] Of course, the rabbinic evidence stems from a later period and a particular Jewish circle. Does it suggest that Luke could have heightened the gravity of Peter's mother-in-law's condition ("a *high* fever") and highlighted Jesus' *verbal rebuke* (in contrast to Mark's reference to the physical act of lifting her hands) in order to conform Jesus' actions to Jewish practice?[59] We recall furthermore the demonic dimension Luke ascribes to the mother-in-law's illness: Jesus has to "reprimand" her fever.[60] Does Luke underline the supernatural severity of her psychosomatic condition, interpreting Jesus' response more as an act of rescue (i.e., an exorcism) than as a healing in order to present this episode in terms that are more palatable to other Jews? Throughout his gospel, Luke consistently points to the demonic dimension of the physical ailments assailing Jesus' "patients." As we shall see, this

---

[58] Jacob Nahum Epstein, *Introduction to Tannaitic Literature: Mishna, Tosephta and Halakhic Midrashim* [in Hebrew] (Jerusalem: Magnes, 1957), 280–281, citing *t. Shabb.* 7[8]:23, *y. Shabb.* 14:3 [14c], *b. Sanh.* 101a as examples. Epstein's remarks on this matter have directly or indirectly influenced the positions of several prominent scholars regarding the stance of the historical Jesus vis-à-vis Sabbath healings, including David Flusser, *The Sage from Galilee: Rediscovering Jesus' Genius* (4th ed.; Grand Rapids, Mich.: Eerdmans, 2007), 39; E. P. Sanders, *Jesus and Judaism* (London: SCM Press, 1985), 266; *Jewish Law from Jesus to the Mishnah*, 21; Vermes, *Jesus the Jew*, 25, and most recently (and indirectly via Sanders) Meier, *Marginal Jew*, 4:254. I find the usage of these particular rabbinic passage for the interpretation of the synoptic pericopes on the Sabbath problematic on several grounds (see introduction to this chapter as well the ensuing discussion in chapters 2, 3 and 4).

[59] Even in Mark's case, some commentators like Robert Horton Gundry, *Mark: A Commentary on His Apology for the Cross* (Grand Rapids, Mich.: Eerdmans, 1993), 286 and Joachim Gnilka, *Das Evangelium nach Markus* (2 vols.; EKKNT 2; Zurich: Neukirchener Verlag, 1978), 1:84, claim that the gospel writer emphasizes the severity of the mother-in-law's condition.

[60] Some have also detected in Mark an overlap between "exorcism" and "healing," since the mother-in-law's fever is said to have "left her" (ἀφῆκεν αὐτὴν ὁ πυρετός), suggesting that fever, like an unclean spirit, can leave the body. See Adela Yarbro Collins, *Mark* (Hermeneia; Minneapolis: Fortress, 2007), 174. Luke, however, makes the link between the two categories more explicit.

standard reference to demonic origins, which are responsible for human suffering, plays an integral role in Luke's attempt to justify Jesus' need to intervene on the Sabbath on behalf of the oppressed children of Israel. Demonic cruelty demands immediate divine intervention, making it lawful for Jesus to do good and save life on the Sabbath (Luke 6:9).

Nevertheless, such observations should not invite over-interpreting a passage that contains no deliberate concern for Sabbath controversies or interest in sophisticated, halakic debates about Sabbath keeping. First, Epstein's remarks on rabbinic halakah for the understanding of the Sabbath healing and exorcism episodes in the gospel accounts prove inadequate. The key passage mentioned by Epstein (*t. Shabb.* 7:23) refers to "whispering," a particular type of utterance, which never appears in any passage reporting one of Jesus' healings or exorcisms. According to the synoptic gospels, Jesus never whispers over his subjects or pronounces incantations, as the Toseftan passage presumes, but openly proclaims his healings and exorcisms in the public domain. Second, as Doering points out, the usage of whispering in these rabbinic passages is restricted to particular cases: whispering over the (evil?) eye[61] and over snake or scorpion bites. Some of these conditions certainly can be life-threatening (e.g., poisonous snakebites) or may at least seriously jeopardize a person's health, if not remove life altogether (scorpion bites can be fatal for children and frail people).[62] By contrast, Luke has Jesus heal persons suffering from less acute conditions (a man with a withered hand, a "bent" woman, and a person with "dropsy"). But, once again, Luke deems these conditions serious enough to demand immediate attention and treatment partly because of the demonic dimension he attributes to the generation of such physical ailments.[63]

---

[61] For the textual problems regarding the reference to either the "eye" or the "evil eye," in *t. Shabb.* 7[8]:23, see Doering, "Much Ado about Nothing?" 220–22. The evil eye was viewed as a very dangerous threat, potentially leading to fatality. Cf. Rivka Ulmer, *The Evil Eye in the Bible and in Rabbinic Literature* (Hoboken, N.J.: Ktav, 1994), 26: "In the rabbinic mind, the evil eye was the cause of inexplicable deaths."

[62] Some commentators even assume that only life-threatening conditions are presupposed in this passage. So Berndt Schaller, "Jesus und der Sabbat. Franz-Delitzsch-Vorlesung 1992," in *Fundamenta Judaica: Studien zum antiken Judentum und zum Neuen Testament* (eds. Lutz Doering and Annette Steudel; SUNT 25; Göttingen: Vandenhoeck & Ruprecht:, 2001), 133; Michael Becker, *Wunder und Wundertäter im frührabbinischen Judentum: Studien zum Phänomen und seiner Überlieferung im Horizont von Magie und Dämonismus* (WUNT 2.144; Tübingen: Mohr Siebeck, 2002), 180. However, Doering, "Much Ado about Nothing?" 221–22, concedes that acute conditions are also envisioned in *t. Shabb.* 7[8]:23. A further problem, which Doering points out, involves the ambiguity over the *curative* or *preventive* nature of such acts.

[63] Luke purposefully exploits this ambiguity, I will continually argue, in order to highlight the serious conditions of Jesus' "patients," downplay his trespassing of the Sabbath, and underline his authority. I hesitate to embark with the point made by

Fitzmyer's comments on the Lukan reference to "high fever" are probably closer to the mark: Luke wants his readers to understand that it will take a very powerful deed to remove the fever.[64] Furthermore, at the narrative level, this healing occurs in the intimate realm of "insiders," in the home of Simon Peter, for Luke, a soon-to-be disciple of Jesus (Luke 5:1–11), and away from the immediate sight of potential opponents.[65] At this point of his narrative, Luke remains more interested in showcasing Jesus' messianic credentials and abilities, in affirming the fulfillment of Jesus' eschatological program announced in Nazareth, rather than in engaging in polemics about the Sabbath, which will receive their ample share of attention in subsequent sections of his gospel.

Healing the Masses after Sunset:
Mark 1:32–34; Matt 8:16–17; Luke 4:40–41

Literary Context

After healing Peter's mother-in-law, according to Mark and Luke, Jesus proceeds to care for people *en masse*, but this episode presumably takes place *after* the Sabbath.[66] For Matthew, once again, this event, like the preceding one, does not occur on the Sabbath. Matthew, however, does retain and place this episode immediately after the healing of Peter's mother-in-law, but both incidents occur within a different narrative setting, completely divorced from the Sabbath, in a so-called "miracle-cycle" (the

---

Doering, "Much Ado about Nothing?" 224, who fully contrasts the *magical* dimension in the rabbinic passages solicited by Epstein with the *therapeutic* practices (or simply "healings") of Jesus as they appear in the canonical gospels: "*There is no way from the conceded magical 'whispering' on certain severe wounds or threats to Jesus' acts of healing on the Sabbath.*" Being ignorant on how ancients would have conceptually distinguished both acts, and wishing to avoid ancient and modern polemics regarding Jesus' status as magician vs. healer, I happily leave the question open to discussion.

[64] Joseph A. Fitzmyer, *The Gospel according to Luke* (2 vols.; AB 28–28A; Garden City: Doubleday, 1981–1985), 1:550.

[65] Meier, *A Marginal Jew*, 4:253: "The reasons for the absence of a dispute here are patent: the healing occurs in a private house, the people in the house are disciples of Jesus along with (presumably) their relatives or friends, and it is precisely this group of people who speak to Jesus about the afflicted woman."

[66] Mark 1:32: "that evening, at sundown" (ὀψίας δὲ γενομένης ὅτε ἔδυ ὁ ἥλιος). Luke 4:40 is less cumbersome than Mark's "doublet," reading simply "as the sun was setting" (δύνοντος δὲ τοῦ ἡλίου). Luke's abbreviation hardly needs to be interpreted as "obscuring Mark's attention to the sabbath observance of these people" (John Nolland, *Luke* [2 vols.; WBC 35A–C; Dallas: Word Books, 1989–1993], 1:213), but simply as a stylistic improvement of Mark's superfluous language.

Wunderzyklus of Matt 8:1–9:35), which immediately follows the Sermon on the Mount.[67]

Analysis

Is the chronological reference in Luke (following Mark) insignificant or does it signal that mass healings should wait until after the Sabbath, even if in exceptional cases treatments of individuals are allowed for on the seventh day? Once again, such an inquiry may be demanding too much from the text and even be raising the wrong questions. Mayer-Haas offers an intriguing proposal concerning Mark's perspective on Sabbath keeping in this pericope: Mark does not object to performing healings on the Sabbath (1:21–31), he is worried about *bearing* (ἔφερον, v. 32) sick people on the Sabbath, perhaps even concerned about trespassing the travel limits imposed on the Sabbath (תחום שבת).[68] With respect to Luke, she even sees a more heightened concern to remove any suspicion about breaking the Sabbath. Thus, she claims that Luke employs the verb ἤγαγον ("led" or "brought") instead of Mark's ἔφερον ("bore" or "carried") in order to show that the people living in the more distant places around Capernaum began to lead out their sick right before the Sabbath ended, but waited until sunset before traveling beyond the Sabbath limits (2000 cubits = c. 1 km).

---

[67] Mayer-Haas, *Geschenk*, 418. Notice again the problematic speculations of Yang, *Jesus and the Sabbath*, 250: "…Matthew misses Mark's witness…that the ordinary Jews in the time of Jesus observed at least some of the sabbath regulations (e.g. carrying, travelling, healing) quite faithfully…he may…have thought of the possibility that such a witness could have encouraged some members of his community to be legalistically bound to the rabbinic sabbath regulations – a tendency which probably was a real threat to his community."

[68] Mayer-Haas, *Geschenk*, 156: "Nicht die Heilungen am Sabbat sind für den Evangelisten verboten, sondern das Tragen der Kranken!" Mark 1:32–34, in Mayer-Haas' opinion, is entirely redactional (p. 155). Cf. Alfred E. J. Rawlinson, *The Gospel according St Mark* (6th ed.; WC; London: Methuen, 1925), 18; Vincent Taylor, *The Gospel according to St Mark* (London: Macmillan, 1935), 180; Collins, *Mark*, 175–76: "The fact that the people of Capernaum waited until the sun had gone down to bring the sick and possessed to Jesus implies that either the activity of bringing them or healing them, or perhaps both, is unlawful on the Sabbath. If such is indeed implied, then it is noteworthy that Mark's Jesus nevertheless exorcises (vv. 21–28) and heals (vv. 29–31) on the Sabbath." See also Morna D. Hooker, *A Commentary on the Gospel according to St Mark* (BNTC; London: A & C Black, 1991), 71. Daniel A. Carson, "Jesus and the Sabbath in the Four Gospels," in *From Sabbath to Lord's Day: A Biblical, Historical and Theological Investigation* (ed. Daniel A. Carson; Grand Rapids, Mich.: Zondervan, 1982), 60, following Caird, *The Gospel of Luke*, 89, claims that Mark and Luke seek to portray the crowd as more scrupulous in their Sabbath keeping than Jesus. This is probably the wrong way of treating the issue. Gundry, *Mark*, 87, is closer to the mark when he states that the scene stresses "the alacrity with which the people bring their sick and demon-possessed once the Sabbath has ended."

Mayer-Haas also claims that Luke removes the verb φέρω because it refers to the idea of "carrying" from one domain to the other, an act that is forbidden on the Sabbath. Finally, Mayer-Haas points out that Luke's Jesus *lays hands* on the sick (v.40) only after the Sabbath is over, while during the Sabbath proper he simply emits verbal utterances when performing miracles (in contrast to the Markan Jesus who grabs the mother-in-law *by the hand* in Mark 1:31).[69]

Doering, however, dismisses Mayer-Haas' reading of Luke's substitution of ἤγαγον for ἔφερον as purely "imaginative and speculative."[70] He also questions whether φέρειν in Mark 1:32 should be understood in the technical sense Mayer-Haas restricts it to, arguing that it could simply mean, "to bring." At least in Mark 2:3, Mark does clarify when the verb φέρειν denotes "carrying" by providing additional qualifiers: "some people came, bringing (φέροντες) to him a paralyzed man, *carried* (αἰρόμενον) by four of them."[71] While in this pericope Luke's Jesus only employs speech to heal and exorcise on the Sabbath, elsewhere in the gospel of Luke Jesus does lay hands on the Sabbath (13:13).[72] Consequently, the Lukan switch from verbal pronouncement on the Sabbath to physical action after sunset should not be overstated.

In any case, the cumulative effect of Luke's portrayal of the three episodes assessed thus far (the exorcism in the synagogue of Capernaum, the healing of Peter's mother-in-law, and the healings of the masses after sunset) hardly proves to be dramatically offensive from a halakic point of view: on one Sabbath, Jesus merely utters some words to repel a demon and a fever of *demonic* origin, highlighting the gravity of the patients' condition, and cares for the sick people *en masse* only after sunset. As he reports these incidents, Luke feels no need to employ halakic or theological arguments in order to justify Jesus' actions. Probably some ancient Jews would have been displeased with the Lukan presentation of Jesus' actions on the Sabbath, claiming that the treatment of non-life-threatening

---

[69] Mayer-Haas, *Geschenk*, 301. Fitzmyer claims that the imposition of hands as a physical gesture for healing is unknown in the Hebrew Bible and rabbinic literature, although it does appear in 1Qap Gen^{ar} 20:28–29 where Abram prays for Pharaoh, laying his hands on his head to exorcise the evil spirit tormenting him. See Fitzmyer, *The Gospel according to Luke,* 1:553.

[70] Lutz Doering, "Sabbath Laws in the New Testament," in *The New Testament and Rabbinic Literature* (eds. Reimund Bieringer et al.; Supplements to the Journal for the Study of Judaism 136; Leiden: Brill, 2010), 251 n. 187.

[71] Doering, "Sabbath Laws," 187. Doering also refers to certain rabbinic texts such as *m. Shabb.* 10:5 and *t. Shabb.* 8[9]:18 that do not condemn carrying a living person on a bed on the Sabbath. See Doering, "Sabbath Laws," 187 n. 188. But cf. CD 11:11.

[72] Although even in Luke 13:13, as will be shown, it is not entirely clear whether the laying of hands is actually performed as part of the healing.

conditions could have waited until after the Sabbath was over so as to honor the sanctity of the seventh day (cf. Luke 13:14). Luke, as we will see, will answer to such objections by pointing to the demonic origins of the ailments afflicting the children of Israel: they are "semi-life-threatening" conditions due to demonic oppression that require Jesus to intervene and do good on the Sabbath day in order to deliver Jews from the tyrannical bonds of Satan (cf. 6:9; 13:16). Nevertheless, Luke does not fully develop this argument at this juncture of his narrative.

On the other hand, we note – and this is an important point – that Luke does not polemicize at all against the institution of the Sabbath in any of the three episodes assessed above. Instead, he uses Mark's material primarily to highlight Jesus' authority, to demonstrate how his therapeutic ministry fulfills the programmatic speech delivered one Sabbath in the synagogue of Nazareth. Moreover, it is remarkable that Luke feels no need to elucidate the terms related to the Sabbath institution that appear in these three episodes. These features include chronological terms such as "on the Sabbath" (Luke 4:31: τοῖς σάββασιν), the announcement of the arrival of sunset (Luke 4:40: δύνοντος δὲ τοῦ ἡλίου), the latter phrase possibly pointing toward a Jewish demarcation of time in which the new halakic day begins at sunset, as well as the reference to the Jewish custom of attending and teaching in the synagogue on the Sabbath (4:31). Luke's readers seem sufficiently acquainted with the Jewish institution of Sabbath to be able to understand these terms and appreciate the narrated episodes without further explanation.[73] Luke's description of the Sabbath in these episodes may not provide us with any extensive information about the Sabbath praxis of Luke and his readers, but they also do not furnish much material to fuel a Christian protest and polemic against Sabbath keeping. At this point, all that may be said with certainty is that Luke assumes his readers are familiar with the Sabbath and the environment of the synagogue, and that the portrayal in these three episodes of Jesus' Sabbath praxis is compatible

---

[73] Some may argue that even many non-Christian Gentiles would be familiar with basic terms such as the "Sabbath" and "synagogue" (hardly an exclusively Jewish term), although the reference to the ending of a halakic day at sunset probably would have escaped the knowledge of many Gentiles. Nevertheless, I find the multiple references to Jewish holy days and practices throughout Luke-Acts, which Luke almost never explains to his audience, most remarkable. The usage of Jewish measurement to describe the topography of Jerusalem in Acts 1:12, for example, is striking (see chapter 7). The cumulative effect of the usage of such Jewish features, without further explanation, challenges the *communis opinio* that views Luke's audience as primarily "Gentile Christian." Undoubtedly, Luke imagines that Gentiles will read his gospel, but he assumes a lot of knowledge on their part about Jewish tradition and likely envisages a Jewish readership that can also appreciate the halakic and theological intricacies of his Jewish gospel.

with the Lukan Torah observant Jesus one discovers elsewhere in Luke's gospel. As for Matthew, by relocating all three episodes in non-Sabbath settings, he never portrays Jesus engaging in questionable activities on the Sabbath without providing justification.[74]

Rejection in Nazareth:
Mark 6:1–6; Matt 13:53–58; Luke 4:16–30

Literary Context

Mark 6:1–6 reports no debate about Sabbath keeping but centers on the rejection of Jesus by the inhabitants of Nazareth during his hometown visit to the synagogue on the Sabbath. As usual, Matthew eliminates Mark's reference to the Sabbath (cf. Mark 6:2 with Matt 13:54).[75] Luke, on the other hand, follows Mark by explicitly situating this event on a Sabbath. However, he places this episode *before* Jesus' visit to Capernaum, which was assessed in the previous sections.[76] In addition, Luke significantly augments this section with material unattested in any of the other gospels.[77]

---

[74] Cf. Mayer-Haas, *Geschenk*, 421. I argued earlier that we should not read too much into this Matthean feature, which may stem more from literary preferences than theological factors. Contra Yang, *Jesus and the Sabbath,* 251: "Matthew's probable omissions of and modifications...may perhaps rather indicate that Matthew is more concerned about the legalistic tendency of his community – that is why he sometimes modifies the cotexts of and sometimes even omits certain passages/phrases which he thinks might unnecessarily encourage a legalistic observance of the sabbath."

[75] Nevertheless, Matthew might still assume a Sabbath setting for this episode, since Jesus teaches in the synagogue. Notice, once again, the problematic statement in Yang, *Jesus and the Sabbath,* 256, claiming that Matthew omits the reference to the Sabbath "in order not to cause any unnecessary misunderstanding that one must visit the synagogue and worship on the sabbath after the example of Jesus."

[76] Luke 4:31–37 (visit at Capernaum synagogue, exorcism); 4:38–39 (healing of Peter's mother-in-law); 4:40–41 (healing of the masses after sunset) all take place *after* Jesus' visit to Nazareth (4:16–30; Mark 6:1–6), while in Mark they take place beforehand (1:21–34).

[77] Scholars debate about the sources as well as the amount of redactional activity exerted in crafting this section of Luke. Some posit a great proportion of redaction for this section. In this avenue, Busse maintains that Luke has composed the episode in 4:16–30 basing himself on Q, Mark 1:14 f. and 6:1–6. See Ulrich Busse, *Das Nazareth-Manifest: Eine Einführung in das lukanische Jesusbild nach Lk 4, 16–30* (SBS 91; Stuttgart: Katholisches Bibelwerk, 1978), 5. See also Bovon's discussion in *Luke 1*, 150. Some, however, think that Luke has employed another *Vorlage* because his version of the story deviates so much from Mark 6:1–6 and 1:14 f. For an overview of the discussion, see Mayer-Haas, *Geschenk*, 285–89. Regardless of the sources lurking behind 4:16–30, there

Analysis of Luke 4:16–30

The opening of the Lukan scene, which is based on Mark 6:1–2, contains several Lukan features: "When he came to Nazareth, where he had been brought up, he went to the synagogue on the sabbath day (ἐν τῇ ἡμέρᾳ τῶν σαββάτων εἰς τὴν συναγωγήν), as was his custom (κατὰ τὸ εἰωθός)" (4:16). The phrases ἐν τῇ ἡμέρᾳ τῶν σαββάτων as well as κατὰ τὸ εἰωθός are Lukan literary constructions, appearing with similar wording elsewhere in Luke as well as the book of Acts.[78]

Upon his entry into the synagogue of Nazareth, Luke's Jesus reads and expounds the Jewish scriptures in ways that point toward his mission to fulfill God's plan of redemption for Israel and the nations. Teaching accompanied by readings and messianic interpretations of scripture is a Lukan leitmotif appearing throughout Luke and Acts and one of the main tasks Luke has Jesus and his Jewish followers perform in the synagogue and in other private and public domains.[79] The detailed description of the ritual of reading from the scrolls on the Sabbath in the synagogue reveals Luke's own acquaintance with such settings. Quite significantly, Luke feels no need to elaborate nor elucidate the following features to his readers: the act of rising to read the scriptures (ἀνέστη ἀναγνῶναι), the procedure of unrolling a scroll and locating the proper section for reading (ἐπεδόθη αὐτῷ βιβλίον τοῦ προφήτου Ἠσαΐου καὶ ἀναπτύξας τὸ βιβλίον εὗρεν τὸν τόπον οὗ ἦν γεγραμμένον), the removal of the scroll and its transferal to the synagogue attendant (ὑπηρέτης; 4:20), as well as the ensuing exposition of the Jewish scriptures (4:21 f.). All of these elements are taken for granted and require no clarification for the audience reading or listening to this episode.

These observations may shed some light on the *Sitz im Leben* of Luke and his audience. Some think the episode recalls a historical event that

---

can be no doubt regarding Luke's appropriation of this section, given the strong presence of Lukan style and literary creativity as well as central themes compatible with his worldview. Undoubtedly, much of 4:16–17 as well as v. 20 are redactional. The same applies to vv. 28–30, which mirror Paul's experience in Diasporan synagogues as reported in the book of Acts (see ch. 7 of this book). On the other hand, the materials in 4:17–19, given the remarkable parallels with certain Qumran writings (see discussion below), as well as vv. 25–27 may be traditional.

[78] Cf. Luke 14:5: "ἐν ἡμέρᾳ τοῦ σαββάτου"; Luke 2:42: "And when he was twelve years old, they went up as usual (κατὰ τὸ ἔθος) for the festival"; Acts 13:4: "εἰς τὴν συναγωγὴν τῇ ἡμέρᾳ τῶν σαββάτων"; Acts 16:13: "τῇ τε ἡμέρᾳ τῶν σαββάτων"; Acts 17:2: "And Paul went in, *as was his custom* (κατὰ δὲ τὸ εἰωθός), and on three sabbath days argued with them from the scriptures."

[79] Luke 24:27; Acts 8:28–30; 13:15, 16, 27; 15:21; 17:2–3, 11.

occurred in the synagogue of Nazareth.[80] Its current form though is marked by features that serve Luke's theological interests. For example, the citation and reworking of the passages from Isaiah 61:1–2 and 58:6, which Luke's Jesus reads, presuppose a text resembling the Greek Septuagint rather than a Hebrew *Vorlage*.[81] Luke also treasures tying Jesus' ministry with the fulfillment of prophecies from the Jewish scriptures. Consequently, he has Jesus or his followers read and expound from scriptures throughout Luke-Acts, often within synagogue settings on the Sabbath. These depictions, then, may mirror Luke's acquaintance and experience with Diasporan synagogues where it was customary to read and expound upon portions of the Septuagint every Sabbath.[82] Finally, the stories of

---

[80] For discussions on the supposed historicity of the events reported in Luke ch. 4, see Hugh Anderson, "Broadening Horizons: the Rejection at Nazareth Pericope of Luke 4.16–30 in Light of Recent Critical Trends," *Int* 18 (1964): 259–75; Bruce Chilton, "Announcement in Nazareth: An Analysis of Luke 4.16–21," in *Gospel Perspectives: Studies of History and Tradition in the Four Gospels, Vol. 2* (eds. R. T. France and David Wenham; Sheffield: JSOT, 1981), 147–72; David Hill, "The Rejection of Jesus at Nazareth (Luke iv 16–30)," *NovT* 13 (1971): 161–80.

[81] Fitzmyer, *Luke*, 532; Mayer-Haas, *Geschenk*, 270, 292 n. 200. On the other hand, the content of the Isaian reading in Luke 4:18–19 resembles in remarkable ways the messianic proclamation found in the Messianic Apocalypse (4Q521). See ensuing discussion below. It cannot be ruled out, therefore, that while Luke definitely colors this pericope with contours stemming from his own experience with the Hellenistic-Diasporan synagogue, he also solicits and draws from Palestinian traditions and messianic readings of Isaiah. Luke knows a great deal about Jewish life and thought in the Diaspora but is also heavily indebted to Jewish tradition from Palestine. He draws from both. See the conclusion to this monograph where I further develop this point.

[82] This is not to deny the importance the reading of scripture could have enjoyed even in synagogues in Palestine, especially in a post-70 setting, although we cannot underestimate the oral culture and pervasive illiteracy of that time. In addition, if Luke is a Diasporan Jew, as I suggest in the conclusion of this book, and since the many features in this scene are unattested in any other gospel, it becomes likely that Diasporan experience of Jewish life has shaped to a certain extent the narrative at this point. Fitzmyer, *Luke*, 1:526–27: "…vv. 17–21, suits a distinctive Lucan concern, and is probably better ascribed to Luke's own pen." Would a humble town like Nazareth have a scroll of Isaiah as Luke presumes? Josephus, *J.W.* 2:228–231; *Ant.* 20:113–117, refers to the destruction of a scroll in the village of Bet Horon by a Roman soldier. So it is possible. Luke also describes Jesus' hometown as a πόλις. Is he thereby projecting a Diasporan urban Jewish setting upon the rural environment of Nazareth? The synagogue atmosphere described in this Lukan pericope also recalls scenes described by Philo about the public reading of scriptures in Diasporan synagogues. See Philo, *Somn.* 2:127; *Prob.* 81–83; *Legat.* 156–157, 311–13. Cf. Josephus, *Ant.* 16:43 and *Ag. Ap.* 2:175 as well as Acts 13:14–15. Cf. McKay, *Sabbath and Synagogue*, 164: "It seems to me that Luke's stories involving 'synagogues' can tell us little or nothing about synagogues in Galilee at the time of Jesus, but rather describe later synagogues elsewhere." For an alternative view defending Luke 4:16–21 as reflective of synagogue practices in Palestine, see Anders Runesson, *The*

Elijah and Elisha, which anticipate the mission to the Gentiles, also serve Lukan interests even if this material may be traditional.[83]

What can such features and observations tell us about Luke's attitude toward the Sabbath? Many have rightly detected Luke's desire to portray Jesus as a pious Jew who regularly attends the synagogue on the Sabbath.[84] The prepositional phrase "according to his custom" only underscores this motif. Nevertheless, some have dismissed this explanation, preferring instead to portray Luke's Jesus as a "missionary opportunist." Rordorf summarizes this position well:

> This behaviour does not necessarily mean that Jesus was a zealous observer of the Jewish law or that he was very strict about the sabbath commandment. It stands to reason that Jesus used the opportunity to deliver his message in the synagogue where people were assembled on the sabbath.[85]

For Rordorf and others, Luke's main aim is to highlight the custom and authority of Jesus' *teaching* rather than his Sabbath keeping. The Lukan Jesus, like the Paul of Acts (e.g., Acts 17:1–2), only adapts to the local culture, "playing the Jew" in order to convince his compatriots about more important theological issues. This anachronistic missiological projection proves unconvincing on several grounds. First, the preposition κατά followed by a noun in the accusative frequently appears in Luke-Acts in contexts that have nothing to do with missionary activity but emphasize the fidelity of Jesus and his followers to Jewish custom.[86] Salo rightly

---

Origins of the Synagogue: A Social-Historical Study (ConBNT 37; Stockholm: Almqvist & Wiksell, 2001), 213–20.

[83] Klinghardt, *Gesetz und Volk Gottes,* 236–37, sees the theme of a Gentile mission as reflecting an ongoing controversy between Luke and the rest of Jewish society regarding the proclamation of the gospel to non-Jews. This problem reemerges in some key passages in Acts (see chapter 7).

[84] Fitzmyer, *Luke,* 1:530; Loader, *Jesus' Attitude towards the Law,* 305; I. Howard Marshall, *The Gospel of Luke: A Commentary on the Greek Text* (NIGTC; Exeter: Pater Noster, 1978), 181; Samuele Bacchiocchi, *Divine Rest for Human Restlessness* (Rome: Pontifical Gregorian University Press, 1980), 145–46, even maintains that the evangelist sets the Sabbath practice of Jesus as a model for his readers to follow. Cf. Mayer-Haas, *Geschenk,* 267–68, 294–95.

[85] Willy Rordorf, *Sunday: The History of the Day of Rest and Worship in the Earliest Centuries of the Christian Church* (trans. A. A. K. Graham; London: SCM Press, 1968), 67–68. Others who embrace this position include Max M. B. Turner, "The Sabbath, Sunday, and the Law in Luke/Acts," in *From Sabbath to Lord's Day,* 101–2; Yang, *Jesus and the Sabbath,* 244, who imposes the not very helpful distinction between "tradition" and Torah. Both items were quite important for Jews – the concept of tradition not enjoying the subordinate, at times, negative status it carries in certain Christian circles today.

[86] "He was chosen by lot, according to the custom of the priesthood (κατὰ τὸ ἔθος)" (1:9); "When the time came for their purification according to the law of Moses (κατὰ

dismisses the missiological interpretation by pointing out that κατὰ τὸ εἰωθὸς appears within the phrase εἰσῆλθεν...ἐν τῇ ἡμέρᾳ τῶν σαββάτων εἰς τὴν συναγωγὴν: "It is much easier to assume that the phrase κατὰ τὸ εἰωθὸς is linked to the clause where it is found and not the next one (καὶ ἀνέστη ἀναγνῶναι)."[87] Finally, the reductionist missiological reading of Luke 4:16 does not do justice to the wider theological concern of Luke to depict Jesus, Peter, Paul, and his other central Jewish protagonists as faithful Torah observant Jews. Luke's wider portrait makes it clear that his Jewish protagonists are not simply masquerading as Jews in order to gain converts, but observing Torah in its own right, "*Torah lishmah*," as the rabbis would put it.

Mayer-Haas suggests that the description of synagogue life in Luke 4 as well as in the book of Acts reflects the Sabbath worship practiced by Luke and his circle(s). On the Sabbath day, Luke and his circle apply christological readings to the Jewish scriptures.[88] Mayer-Haas' interpretation largely depends on how one reconstructs the historical framework and social dynamics governing the relations between Luke and his followers and the wider Jewish community. Are "Lukan followers of Jesus" still attending the synagogue, *partly* in an attempt to win over other Jews to their movement? Do some of them attend the synagogue and then christologically elucidate the scriptures in their private homes? Given the state of the evidence, it is difficult to answer these concrete questions with any exactitude and confidence. It is apparent though that Luke is thoroughly familiar with

---

τὸν νόμον Μωϋσέως), they brought him up to Jerusalem to present him to the Lord" (2:22); "and they offered a sacrifice according to what is stated in the law of the Lord (κατὰ τὸ εἰρημένον ἐν τῷ νόμῳ κυρίου)" (2:24); "and when the parents brought in the child Jesus, to do for him what was customary under the law (κατὰ τὸ εἰθισμένον τοῦ νόμου)" (2:27); "When they had finished everything required by the law of the Lord (πάντα τὰ κατὰ τὸν νόμον κυρίου)" (2:39); "And when he was twelve years old, they went up as usual (κατὰ τὸ ἔθος) for the festival" (2:42); "He came out and went, as was his custom (κατὰ τὸ ἔθος), to the Mount of Olives; and the disciples followed him" (22:39); Then they returned, and prepared spices and ointments. On the sabbath they rested according to the commandment (κατὰ τὴν ἐντολήν)" (23:56); "And Paul went in, as was his custom (κατὰ τὸ εἰωθὸς), and on three sabbath days argued with them from the scriptures" (Acts 17:2); "A certain Ananias, who was a devout man according to the law (κατὰ τὸν νόμον) and well spoken of by all the Jews living there" (Acts 22:12); "I have belonged to the strictest sect of our religion (κατὰ τὴν ἀκριβεστάτην αἵρεσιν τῆς ἡμετέρας θρησκείας) and lived as a Pharisee (Acts 26:5).

[87] Salo, *Luke's Treatment of the Law,* 68.
[88] Mayer-Haas, *Geschenk*, 295: "Daß der Sabbat als typischer Zeitpunkt des jüdischen Synagogengottesdienstes mit Schriftlesung in den lukanischen Erzählungen nicht verschwiegen, sondern eigens hervorgehoben wird, ist ein Hinweis auf den Zeitpunkt, an dem die gemeinschaftliche christliche Schriftauslegung im Umkreis des Evangelisten stattfand."

synagogue life – an indication of his own interaction with such settings on the Sabbath. Luke's knowledge about Judaism is not solely "bookish," derived from a private, individualistic reading of the Septuagint, but stems from his own organic connection with the Jewish community.[89] Through his depiction of Jesus' (and later Paul's) attendance of the synagogue on the Sabbath, we learn a good deal about Luke's own experience and acquaintance with this Jewish environment.

A Lukan Sabbath Theology and Praxis in the Sermon Delivered in Nazareth?

Another main element in this pericope, important for the assessment of Luke's understanding of the Sabbath, concerns the actual timing and content of the reading and sermon delivered in the synagogue of Nazareth, particularly the substance of 4:18–21. Many scholars agree that Luke 4:16–30 serves as a programmatic preface for Jesus' public mission in the gospel of Luke.[90] But should we ascribe any particular importance to the fact that Luke's Jesus delivers the sermon on the Sabbath itself? Moreover, could the choice of the scripture reading mentioned in 4:18–21, with its eschatological language related to the sabbatical-jubilee year, inform the reader about a particular Lukan theology of the Sabbath?

The scriptural passages that Jesus reads according to Luke are taken from Isaiah 61:1–2 and part of 58:6. They are fused together in Luke 4:18–19 in the following way:

The Spirit of the Lord is upon me, because he has anointed me to bring good news to the poor.
He has sent me to proclaim *release* (ἄφεσιν) to the captives and recovery of sight to the blind (Luke 4:18a=Isa 61:1a),
to let the oppressed go *free* (ἐν ἀφέσει) (Luke 4:18b=Isa 58:6),
to proclaim the year of the Lord's favor (Luke 4:19=Isa 61:2).

The phrase from Isa 58:6, "to let the oppressed go free," has been incorporated into Luke 4:18–19 with Isa 61:1–2 to form one reading. As an ensemble, the Isaian verses promise comfort to the oppressed who comprise, among others, the poor (πτωχοῖς) – a group dear to Luke's heart – as well as the sick and other suffering persons.[91] Luke views Jesus as the one anointed and appointed by the spirit of God to carry out this program. More importantly for our analysis, Luke believes that Jesus has been cho-

---

[89] Contra Brown, *The Birth of the Messiah*, 449 n. 14. In chapter 12, I further critique the notion that Luke has derived his knowledge of Judaism solely from an autonomous, private reading of the LXX.

[90] See Yang, *Jesus and the Sabbath*, 251 n. 34, for secondary references.

[91] The word πτωχός appears in Luke more than in any other gospel. See Luke 6:20; 7:22; 14:13, 21; 16:20, 22; 18:22; 19:8.

sen to "proclaim" (LXX: κηρύξαι; MT: לקרא) *release* (ἄφεσις) to the "captives" (αἰχμαλώτοις). The reference to "release" appears several times in Luke, mostly in connection to the announcement of forgiveness of sins.[92] By inserting the phrase from Isa 58:6, "to let the oppressed go *free*" (ἀποστεῖλαι τεθραυσμένους ἐν ἀφέσει), Luke repeats the theme of release twice within the short span of one verse. Interestingly enough, the Paul of Acts also uses this word in a sermon delivered in a synagogue on the Sabbath.[93] The Septuagint employs the word ἄφεσις in Isa 61:1 to translate the Hebrew דרור, which along with the verb לקרא recalls Lev 25:10: "And you shall hallow the fiftieth year and you shall proclaim (וקראתם) liberty (דרור/ἄφεσιν) throughout the land to all its inhabitants...." Ideally, the establishment of the sabbatical year of the jubilee was designed to guarantee the emancipation of slaves and those covered in debt. Some of its language and themes were readapted for newer purposes in Isaiah 61. Luke has in turn interpreted Isaiah 61:1–2 and its jubilary language in an eschatological way, centering its fulfillment on the ministry of Jesus. By Luke's time, some Jews had already applied an eschatological interpretation to Isa 61:1–2. Thus, 11Q13 (Melchizedek) eschatologically appropriates Isa 61, although the beneficiaries of the Isaian prophecies belong to a select group, who are promised, among other things, freedom from the oppression of the evil spirits of Belial (11Q13 2:12–25).[94] Luke's eschatological-social horizon, however, is broader. He does not restrict the benefits promised in

---

[92] Luke 1:77; 3:3; 24:27; Acts 2:38; 5:31; 10:43; 13:38; 26:18.

[93] Acts 13:38. There, however, the word is used in the sense of "release" (i.e., forgiveness) from sins, whereas Luke 4:18–19 refers to the theme of deliverance from oppression and captivity.

[94] Similarly, 4Q521 2ii + 4:1–13: "[For the hea]vens and the earth shall listen to His Messiah....For the Lord seeks the pious and calls the righteous by name. Over the humble His spirit hovers, and He renews the faithful in His strength. For He will honour the pious upon the th[ro]ne of His eternal kingdom, '*setting prisoners free, opening the eyes of the blind, raising up those who are bo*[*wed down*' (Ps 146:7-8). And for [ev]er (?) I (?) shall hold fast [to] the [ho]peful and pious []. A man's rewa[rd for]good [wor]k[s] shall not be delayed and the Lord shall do glorious things which have not been done, just as He s[aid.] For He shall heal the critically wounded, He shall revive the dead, '*He shall send good news to the afflicted,*' (Isa 61:1) He shall sati[sfy] the [poo]r, He shall lead the uprooted, and the hungry He shall enrich (?)." All translations of the Dead Sea Scrolls are taken from Donald W. Perry and Emmanuel Tov, eds., *The Dead Sea Scrolls Reader* (6 vols.; Leiden: Brill, 2004–2005). The manner in which Isa 58:6 and 61:1–2 are read, combined, and eschatologically understood in Luke resemble (yet differ) in remarkable ways how 4Q521 and 11Q13 messianically and eschatologically reread Isa 61. Therefore, despite the septuagintal language of Isa 58:6 and 61:1–2, as cited in Luke 4:18–19, I am inclined to view this material as traditional (Luke may have then modified its wording to conform it to his beloved LXX). Perhaps, Luke added Isa 58:6 into 61:1–2 to highlight the theme of "release," so important for his worldview (see discussion below).

Isa 61 to one elected group, but envisions its blessings as contagiously affecting the poor and afflicted in general.

Significant for our discussion is the reference to the theme of release, which appears here and elsewhere in Luke. For example, in Luke 13:16, Jesus "releases" on the Sabbath day a crippled woman who had been bound by Satan for eighteen years.[95] As noted earlier in this chapter, Luke frequently connects the contraction of physical ailments with evil, demonic forces. Interestingly, Luke often has Jesus release such persons from their sufferings on the Sabbath.[96] In fact, Luke contains more healings occurring on the Sabbath than any other gospel.[97] Are there enough clues and cues in Luke to warrant reading Luke 14:18–21 as containing a particular theology of the Sabbath, viewed as a day *especially meant for* healing and assisting the poor, hungry, and oppressed? Does Luke conceive of the Sabbath as a particularly opportune and appropriate moment for performing healings of non-life-threatening conditions or does he view it as a major halakic obstacle that has to be creatively bypassed in order to make such healings appear justifiable? In other words, does Luke develop a theology of the Sabbath as a day fitting for and symbolic of healing, a time when followers of Jesus are *especially* to perform healings? Or does he justify Jesus' Sabbath performances as occurring *in spite of* the institution of the Sabbath? I offer here a preliminary answer to this question, which is further addressed in other chapters and the conclusion of Part I.

The late Samuel Bacchiocchi is probably best known as the main proponent of the former possibility. He goes as far as proclaiming that the Sabbath functioned in the early stages of the Jesus movement as a sort of memorial for recalling Jesus' redemptive activity, since Jesus, at least according to Luke, essentially begins his ministry on a Sabbath, delivers his inaugural address in the language of the eschatological sabbatical jubilee, and performs healings on the Sabbath. In practical terms, Bacchiocchi thinks that early followers of Jesus viewed the Sabbath as a particularly appropriate day for performing healings, as a sabbatical commemoration of redemption and rest.[98] Unfortunately, Bacchiocchi never applied a histori-

---

[95] "And ought not this woman, a daughter of Abraham whom Satan bound for eighteen long years, be set free ($λυθῆναι$) from this bondage on the sabbath day?" The passage receives its full treatment in chapter 4 of this book.

[96] I have already discussed the examples in Luke 4:31–37 and vv. 38–39.

[97] Luke 13:10–17 and 14:1–6 contain two additional Sabbath episodes that appear only in Luke. The multiplication of Sabbath pericopes in which healings occur hardly translates into a Lukan contempt for Sabbath keeping. On the contrary, as will be shown, it underscores the ongoing pertinence of the issue for the author of Luke-Acts.

[98] Samuele Bacchiocchi, *From Sabbath to Sunday: A Historical Investigation of the Rise of Sunday Observance in Early Christianity* (Rome: Pontifical Gregorian University, 1977), 37–38; Cf. Paul K. Jewett, *Lord's Day: A Theological Guide to the Christian Day*

cal-critical reading to canonical literature, indiscriminately ascribing his wide sweeping claims to the New Testament as a whole. The fact that his reading coincided with his own confessional standing also generated further suspicion.[99] But more recently Mayer-Haas, who certainly does apply a rigorous historical-critical analysis to canonical literature, also maintains that the redactional placement of the motif of release and the healing of the crippled women on the Sabbath marks the beginning of the development of a Christian Sabbath theology that combines a Jewish understanding of the Sabbath with the concept of eschatological redemption.[100]

Several observations, however, call for further refinement of this thesis, lest we overstate Luke's claims about *Jesus'* healings on the Sabbath. As has been noted, Luke employs *jubilary* language in Jesus' inaugural address, expressive of a sabbatical *year*, which remains connected to the concept of the *weekly* Sabbath only in an indirect way. On the other hand, one may argue that Luke has left traces for the development of a Sabbath theology, since he intentionally includes the word "release" no fewer than three times in sermons delivered on the Sabbath by two of his major protagonists, Jesus and Paul (twice in Luke 4:18 and once in Acts 13:38), and explicitly describes the condition of the crippled woman in terms of bondage and release (Luke 13:1–7). Surely, Luke must have perceived such textual and thematic interconnections, since they stem from the compositional creativity of his own pen. Nevertheless, Luke seems to have only planted the seeds for a Sabbath theology that did not fully germinate in the longer course of early Christian history. In addition, it should be pointed out that Luke's Jesus does not carry out his programmatic message delivered in Luke 4:18–21 solely on the Sabbath but on other days as well. This becomes very clear in Luke 7:21–22 where Jesus, in his defense, reminds the disciples of John the Baptist that he is curing "many people of diseases, plagues, and evil spirits" as well as restoring the sight of the blind (v. 21). Jesus orders John's disciples to report to their master what they have witnessed: "the blind receive their sight, the lame walk, the lepers are cleansed, the deaf hear, the dead are raised, the poor have good news

---

of Worship (Grand Rapids, Mich.: Eerdmans, 1971), 42: "Hence we have in Jesus' healings on the Sabbath, not only acts of love, compassion and mercy, but true 'sabbatical acts,' acts which show that the Messianic Sabbath, the fulfillment of the Sabbath rest of the Old Testament, has broken into our world. Therefore the Sabbath, of all days, is the most appropriate for healing."

[99] Many of the articles compiled by Carson in *From Sabbath to Lord's Day* seek to refute Bacchiocchi's claims. Unfortunately, some of the authors of this compilation also apply a non-critical reading of canonical literature that in the end defends a certain confessional orientation. On this problem, see the preface in Weiss, *A Day of Gladness*, 4–6.

[100] Mayer-Haas, *Geschenk*, 295–96.

brought to them" (v. 22). No chronological parameters appear in this section of Luke that would limit bestowing such blessings only on the Sabbath day. The recipients who benefit from Jesus' marvelous ministry receive such blessings on any given day. For Luke, the programmatic mission as foretold in Isa 61:1–2 and 58:6 and announced in Luke 4:18 takes place not only on the Sabbath but also on a daily and uninterrupted basis.

These observations show that Luke does not restrict Jesus' healing ministry to the weekly Sabbath to claim this day as *the* particular, commemorative moment most suitable for performing such actions. On the other hand, Luke seems to have set a basis that invites interpreting the Sabbath as a day symbolizing eschatological rest and liberation from demonic oppression and physical suffering. The other extreme that posits viewing the Lukan Jesus as either healing on the Sabbath *despite* its sanctity, or, worse, claims that Sabbath keeping is no longer a relevant issue for Luke proves even less convincing.[101] The Sabbath may not be *the most* or *only* appropriate day for Luke's Jesus to carry out his liberating ministry, but it certainly is an *appropriate* time for him to accomplish his eschatological mission. Jewish tradition attributes various motifs and theological themes to the Sabbath, and Luke seems to connect the commemoration of eschatological redemption and liberation from demonic oppression, human suffering, and captivity with the Sabbath institution. By positing such a link, Luke can justify Jesus' healings on the Sabbath without implying that the institution of the Sabbath has met its end.

Conclusion

The episodes assessed above relate nothing about a supposed abrogation of the Sabbath. Neither do they present the Sabbath in a negative light. While some ancient Jews would have objected to the synoptic presentation of Jesus healing non-life-threatening conditions on the Sabbath, none of the synoptic authors overly concerns themselves with this matter at this juncture of their narration. Matthew, as we saw, removes all of Mark's explicit references to the Sabbath in these episodes. By doing so, he has Jesus perform questionable acts (from a halakic point of view) on the Sabbath only in episodes where controversies arise and Jesus defends himself against his opponents' criticism. Luke, by contrast, retains the Sabbath settings that Mark uses to frame his stories. He even highlights in positive terms Jesus' regular attendance of the synagogue on the Sabbath. In 4:16–30, Luke displays his acquaintance with the world of the ancient syna-

---

[101] Contra Turner, "The Sabbath, Sunday, and the Law in Luke/Acts," 101–2, 107; Yang, *Jesus and the Sabbath,* 253–55.

gogue, which, remarkably, he feels no need to explicate to his readers who seem equally informed about the rituals performed therein during the Sabbath. Luke also ties Jesus' programmatic speech delivered on a Sabbath in 4:16–30 with the healings and exorcisms that occur immediately afterwards on another Sabbath in Capernaum. In this way, Luke's readers witness the beginning of the unfolding of Jesus' ministry, summarized in his reading and exposition of Isaiah 61:1–2 and 58:6, as he delivers one man from demonic oppression, Peter's mother-in-law from her fever, and many other people afflicted by disease and evil spirits. For Luke, physical ailment stems from demonic forces. As argued in chapter 4, the supernatural dimension Luke ascribes to the generation of physical disease allows him to underscore the urgency and need for Jesus to combat such evil forces on the Sabbath. For Luke, the Sabbath day is *an* (but not the only) appropriate time for Jesus to proclaim eschatological liberation *and* to free the children of Israel from their oppression. Whether Luke actually thinks that his readers should emulate Jesus' Sabbath praxis is another question I return to at the conclusions of Part I and chapter 7.

Chapter 3

Plucking Grain on the Sabbath

"And Moses said: 'Eat it [i.e., the manna] today for the Sabbath is the day for the Lord. Today you will not find it in the field.' R. Zeriqah says: From here [i.e., Exod 16:25], we learn that there are three meals on the Sabbath."
(*Mekilta* Beshallah-Wayassa Parashah 4 on Exod 16:25)

"Said Rabbi Shimon in the name of Rabbi Simeon Hasida: 'In this world a person goes to pick figs [on the Sabbath], the fig doesn't say anything; but in the world to come a person goes to pick a fig on the Sabbath, and she cries and says: It is the Sabbath!'"
(*Midrash Psalms* 73:4)[1]

Matthew 12:1–8

Introduction

The first controversy over Sabbath keeping in the synoptic tradition focuses on the question of plucking grain on the Sabbath. The nature and topic of the controversy are rather unique, since all other disputes about Sabbath keeping in the synoptic gospels handle the issue of healing non-life-threatening conditions on the Sabbath day.[2] I begin my analysis with Mat-

---

[1] Translation of both rabbinic texts mine.
[2] Form critics classify this story as a controversy dialogue occasioned by either the conduct of Jesus or that of his disciples. So Rudolf Bultmann, *The History of the Synoptic Tradition* (trans. John Marsh; Oxford: Basil Blackwell, 1963), 16–17, 39. Robert C. Tannehill, "Varieties of Synoptic Pronouncement Stories," *Semeia* 20 (1981): 107, labels the episode as an "objection story." For Bultmann, the story was composed by the *ekklesia* as a means of defending their own Sabbath praxis by projecting it onto the persona of Jesus – a questionable point we shall deal with later. The results yielded by form criticism show that such stories do not accurately report historical incidents because of their form, polemics and one-sided portrait, generalizing tendencies, pre-redactional modifications, developments, and variants, depending which synoptic gospel is consulted. These stories may be "based on a true story," but they do not give us the full picture nor inform us about how the "reported" event "really happened." Like certain movie directors, the followers of Jesus felt free to replace and refurbish these stories into ever-newer narrated contexts according to their liking. The following scene is no less different. Opponents are depicted in a rather stereotypical fashion. In this case, the Pharisees stand in as the typical antagonists, keeping watch and preying over Jesus and his disciples. Note Sand-

thew's version of the story and then move to Luke. Nothing in either Matthew or Luke's account of this episode suggests that the Sabbath has been abrogated. Rather, the discussion revolves around *how* the disciples of Jesus should observe the Sabbath in the presence of their master Jesus and in light of his teachings and authority. Both Matthew and Luke report the episode especially to highlight Jesus' lordship, not to announce the abrogation of the Sabbath.

Literary Context

It is especially important to note the wider literary context in which this Matthean pericope appears. The division of canonical literature into chapters and verses should not deter one from reading Matt 12:1–8 (as well as the following Sabbath pericope in 12:9–14) in light of the immediate preceding verses (11:25–30), which serve as a sort of introduction to the theme of Sabbath keeping in Matthew.[3]

Matt 11:25–30 can be divided into two major units: vv. 25–27 and vv. 28–30.[4] In the first part, Jesus thanks the Father, using rather vague and

---

ers' cynicism: "Pharisees did not actually spend their sabbaths patrolling cornfields" ("Jesus and the Constraint of the Law," *JSNT* 17 [1983], 20). However, the scene is "believable," since Jews could walk on the Sabbath up to a certain distance, and so it is possible to imagine a controversy spontaneously arising between Jesus and the Pharisees one Sabbath in the fields adjacent to a Galilean town. Nevertheless, the portrayal here remains highly idealized. For one thing, the Pharisaic opponents *never* get to voice their counter arguments. Sven-Olav Back, *Jesus of Nazareth and the Sabbath Commandment* (Åbo: Åbo Akademi University Press, 1995), 90, holds onto the basic authenticity of the setting of the story. Cf. also W. D. Davies and Dale C. Allison, *The Gospel according to Saint Matthew* (3 vols.; ICC; London: T&T Clark, 1988–1997), 2:304, who defend the historicity of this episode, which they see as based on a tradition stemming from the life of Jesus.

[3] Matt 12:1–8 is closely linked to the next Sabbath controversy pericope (12:9–14), which is discussed in the following chapter. Within its broader literary context, Matt 12:1–8 probably belongs to the larger narrative block of Matt chs. 11–12. Here I will focus on the immediate literary context. See discussion in Yang, *Jesus and the Sabbath*, 141–61. Unlike Yang, I am not as confident in reading Matt 12:1–8 and 9–14 tightly with 12:15–21. The thematic and linguistic connectors between Matt 12:15–21 and the preceding two Sabbath controversies (12:1–14) are not as prominent as those in Matt 11:25–30, which may, among other things, function as an opening to these Sabbath stories. Matt 12:15–21 should probably be read in its own right and then more broadly with the rest of the gospel.

[4] Many scholars divide 11:25–30 into three subunits (vv. 25–26; v. 27; vv. 28–30). So Bultmann, *History of the Synoptic Tradition*, 159–60; Davies and Allison, *The Gospel According to Matthew*, 2:271–72; Joachim Gnilka, *Das Matthäusevangelium* (2 vols.; HTKNT; Freiburg: Herder, 1986), 1:432. For reasons of simplification and since Matt 11:25–27 is paralleled in Luke 10:21–22, I cut Matt 11:25–30 into two sections. Matt 11:28–30 is also partly matched by *Gos. Thom.* 90.

elusive language susceptible to different interpretations,[5] for having "hidden" (ἔκρυψας) certain "things" (ταῦτα)[6] from the "wise and the intelligent" (σοφῶν καὶ συνετῶν) and for having "revealed" (ἀπεκάλυψας) them to "infants" (νηπίοις). In v. 27, Matthew's Jesus affirms that "all things" (πάντα)[7] have been "handed down" (παρεδόθη) to him directly from the Father. No one except the Father's son and those who receive revelation (ἀποκαλύψαι) through the son can actually "know" (ἐπιγινώσκει) the Father. The language is purposefully cryptic throughout. In the second part, Jesus promises in the first person to give *rest* (ἀναπαύσω) to those who are "weary and carrying heavy burdens" (οἱ κοπιῶντες καὶ πεφορτισμένοι). Finally, Jesus invites his addressees to bear his "yoke" (ζυγός) and learn from him, promising that they will find "*rest*" (ἀνάπαυσιν) for their souls, as his yoke is "easy" (χρηστός) and his "burden" (φορτίον) "light" (ἐλαφρόν).

Whatever may have been the meaning of such esoteric statements in their pre-redactional stages, they do have some bearing for the interpretation of the subsequent two Sabbath dispute stories: not only do they precede the two Sabbath disputes recorded in Matthew, but they also contain vocabulary connected to the themes of rest and work that conceptually and semantically overlap with the institution of the Sabbath (ἀναπαύσω; ἀνάπαυσιν; κοπιῶντες). Furthermore, Matthew links 11:25–30 with the Sabbath dispute stories through the repetition of the prepositional phrase "at that time" (ἐν ἐκείνῳ τῷ καιρῷ; Matt 11:25 and 12:1).[8] Matthew intends with the repetition of the prepositional phrase to connect both sections thematically,[9] if not also chronologically.[10]

It is possible that Matthew understands the labels of "wise and intelligent" as representing the Pharisees and scribes who oppose Jesus' disciples

---

[5] Hubert Frankemölle, *Matthäus: Kommentar* (2 vols.; Düsseldorf: Patmos, 1997), 2:122.

[6] The nebulous reference to "these things" (ταῦτα) may be connected to the "mysteries of the kingdom of heaven" (Matt 13:11), including the secret messiahship of Jesus. So Charles H. Talbert, *Matthew* (Paideia Commentaries on the New Testament; Grand Rapids, Mich.: Baker Academic, 2010), 149. Perhaps, Matthew also thinks here of the words and works of Jesus (11:2, 19). So Yang, *Jesus and the Sabbath*, 154–55.

[7] The ambiguous "all things" probably points back to the preceding ταῦτα. See Davies and Allison, *The Gospel according to Matthew*, 2:279.

[8] This prepositional phrase is redactional appearing again only in 14:1.

[9] Davies and Allison, *The Gospel according to Matthew*, 2:305: "The phrase is not intended to supply chronological information but to serve as a thematic bridge." Cf. Frankemölle, *Matthäus*, 2:129–30.

[10] Cf. Carson, "Jesus and the Sabbath in the Four Gospels," 75; Yang, *Jesus and the Sabbath*, 143.

(i.e., the "infants"),[11] objecting to their manner of observing the Sabbath and imposing unnecessary burdens (explicitly held against the Pharisees in Matt 23:4, φορτία βαρέα) that interfere with the full enjoyment of the eschatological rest promised by Jesus.[12] According to Matthew, these Pharisees boast about the *traditions* of the elders (τὴν παράδοσιν τῶν πρεσβυτέρων; Matt 15:2) but remain ignorant about God's will. To emphasize this point, Matthew contrasts pharisaic tradition with the divine revelation that has been both *transmitted* (παρεδόθη) and *revealed* (ἀποκαλύψαι) to the son and his inner circle of followers.[13]

Matthew's Jesus invites *all* (πάντες) those who are weary (κοπιῶντες) and carrying heavy burdens (πεφορτισμένοι) to enter into his rest. The general form of this invitation welcoming all people to partake in this rest suggests that Matthew targets a larger audience of potential beneficiaries than a select, inner circle of disciples.[14] These weary and laden people belong neither to the class of the "wise" nor to healthy individuals who

---

[11] The "infants" probably represent the followers of Jesus. Luz, *Matthew*, 2:163, equates them with the *Am Haaretz*. He points to the usage of νήπιος in the LXX, which translates the Hebrew עולל ("infant") or פתי ("simple"). He also cites 4QpNah 3–4 iii:5 where the פתאי אפרים ("simple ones of Ephraim") represent people who do not belong to the Qumran sect and are led astray by the Pharisees. While Luz's interpretation may be correct, it requires some qualification. Arguably, Matthew may be in competition with the Pharisees in influencing the "crowds" (i.e., other "ordinary" non-Pharisaic Jews), but one must remember that the "common people" were not in constant conflict with the Pharisees or later rabbis. See corrective already in Oppenheimer, *The ʿAm Ha-aretz*, 2–9.

[12] So Davies and Allison, *The Gospel according to Matthew*, 2:275; Mayer-Haas, *Geschenk*, 437–38; Yang, *Jesus and the Sabbath*, 144. Since Matt 11:25–30 is also partly attested in Luke 10:21–22 and *Gos. Thom.* 90, we must not assume that this material was originally formulated against Pharisees. Nevertheless, at the Matthean level, this reading seems quite justified, given the pronounced polemics against Pharisees as well as the immediate juxtaposition of 11:25–30 with disputes between Jesus and Pharisees about Sabbath keeping. See Gnilka, *Das Matthäusevangelium*, 1:433–34, for a brief discussion on the history of tradition. In contradistinction to Yang, I wish to point out that *Matthew* contrasts the imposition of the "heavy" traditions of the Pharisees with the "easy" and "light" yoke/burden of Jesus. This does not mean that *Pharisees* (or other non-Pharisaic Jews for that matter) viewed their traditions as "burdensome," a problematic assumption that appears throughout Yang's work. If anything, the Pharisees could have objected that Jesus' yoke was heavier, since it theoretically required exceeding their own righteousness (5:20)! Yang states the like (more than once): "Nevertheless too many rules which were extremely meticulous regarding trivial areas of everyday life without emphasizing the fundamental significance of the sabbath would have inevitably caused extreme inconvenience, trouble, and sometimes even danger, and become burdensome" (96–97).

[13] Davies and Allison, *The Gospel according to Matthew*, 2:275.

[14] Jon Laansma, *I Will Give You Rest: The Rest Motif in the New Testament with Special Reference to Mt 11 and Heb 3–4* (WUNT 2.98; Tübingen: Mohr Siebeck, 1997), 241: "…a call to discipleship more than to disciples." Cf. Daniel J. Harrington, *The Gospel of Matthew* (SP 1; Collegeville, Minn.: Liturgical, 1991), 167.

stand in no need of a physician, but to the sick (Matt 9:12) and the "poor who have good news brought to them" (Matt 11:5).[15] All of these afflicted persons can enter into Jesus' rest if they chose to embrace his call. They are, at least in Matthew's eyes, wearied and overburdened (πεφορτισμένοι) by the Pharisaic interpretations of Torah praxis and the so-called traditions of the elders.[16] Matthew further alludes to this negative correlation between Pharisaic tradition and halakic encumbrance through the rare usage of the verb φορτίζω in the participial form, πεφορτισμένοι (11:28: "burdened"). This verb appears only twice in the synoptic writings (once in Matthew and once in Luke), although Matthew describes the traditions of the Pharisees with the related noun "burdens" (φορτία 23:4).[17]

Scholarly attention has centered on Matthew's paradoxical correlation of the terms "yoke" (ζυγός) and "burden" (φορτίον) with the epithets "easy" (χρηστός) and "light" (ἐλαφρόν). How can a yoke be "easy" and a burden "light"? Perhaps, part of the problem lies in our Western presuppositions and understandings of terms that did not sound entirely pejorative to ancient Jewish readers. True, words such as "yoke" and "burden" can often carry a negative connotation even in ancient Jewish literature, but at least the term "yoke" (Hebrew: עוֹל; Aramaic: נִיר; Greek: ζυγός) appears in positive light in various Jewish texts. Thus, in the book of Jeremiah (2:20, 5:5), Israel is rebuked for walking away from God's Law, for "breaking the yoke." Presumably, the author of this book believes that remaining under God's yoke can guarantee a more positive outcome for Israel. The book of Lamentations, a work ascribed to the prophet Jeremiah, declares in quite favorable terms that "it is good for one to bear the yoke in youth" (3:27). In *Pss. Sol.* 7:9, the people of Israel deliberately take it upon themselves to remain under God's yoke.[18] Finally, Sir 51:26 in many ways resembles Matt 11:29 when it admonishes its audience to put its neck under the yoke of wisdom (cf. Sir 6:30).[19]

---

[15] On the correlation between the "poor" in 11:5 with 11:25–30, see Laansma, *I Will Give You Rest*, 242.

[16] According to Yang, *Jesus and the Sabbath*, 157, many New Testament interpreters follow this line of interpretation. The Matthean passage, however, should not be reduced to a Pharisaic reading; Matthew also thinks of oppression and affliction in more general terms.

[17] Cf. Luke 11:46, which appears next to materials criticizing the Pharisees, but really only condemns the so-called "lawyers": "Woe also to you lawyers! For you load (φορτίζετε) people with burdens (φορτία) hard to bear, and you yourselves do not lift a finger to ease them." Cf. Gal 6:5; Acts 27:10; Herm. *Sim.* 9.2.4.

[18] Cf. *Pss. Sol.* 17:30, declaring that the nations will be under the yoke of the messiah. Zeph 3:9 (LXX) prophesizes about the day when all will be under God's yoke.

[19] Many commentators posit a relationship between Sir 51 and Matt 11:25–30. See Frankemölle, *Matthäus*, 125–29; Gnilka, *Das Matthäusevangelium*, 439; Harrington, *The Gospel of Matthew*, 169–70; Yang, *Jesus and the Sabbath*, 153–54, for further references

Many ancient Jews would not find the imagery of submitting to a "yoke" offensive or repulsive. As a chosen people, they willingly committed themselves to their special calling to serve the God of Israel. The real concern involves assessing the administration and demands of the authority controlling a given "yoke." Are they reasonable and fair? When Rehoboam rises to the throne of his father Solomon, the Israelite people beg him to lighten the hard service of his father and "his heavy yoke" (עֻלּוֹ הַכָּבֵד; LXX: ζυγοῦ αὐτοῦ τοῦ βαρέος) while promising to serve the new king should his demands prove reasonable (2 Chr 10:4).[20] The Israelites do not object to the idea of subservience, but voice their concern about overwhelming and unjust stipulations that might overburden their energy and resources. This is certainly how Josephus (*Ant.* 8:213) understands and rewrites this episode, claiming that the people requested from Rehoboam to be *easier* (χρηστότερον) on them than his father Solomon, whose yoke was heavy (βαρὺν ζυγὸν), while reaffirming their willingness to embrace servitude (ἀγαπήσειν τὴν δουλείαν) should the new king rule with kindness rather than fear (διὰ τὴν ἐπιείκειαν ἢ διὰ τὸν φόβον). The overlap between the Josephan passage and Matt 11:29–30 strikes the eye: Jesus' claims that his yoke (ζυγός) is *easy* (χρηστός), not heavy, and promises to be a "gentle and humble" (πραΰς καὶ ταπεινός) ruler (11:29).[21] Matthew envisages Jesus as harnessing his yoke with clemency, consistently applying the principle of mercy in his administration of the kingdom of heaven (Matt 9:13; 12:7; 23:23). In this way, Matthew believes that living under Jesus' yoke ultimately proves to be "lighter" and "easier" than bearing the supposedly unreasonable demands of the Pharisees.

A number of exegetes think that Matthew's yoke imagery refers primarily to Jesus' teachings and interpretation of the Torah.[22] Jesus' followers submit to his yoke through discipleship, by learning about his interpretation of the Torah (v. 29: μάθετε ἀπ' ἐμοῦ).[23] Later rabbinic passages em-

---

and discussion. For an alternative view, see Laansma, *I Will Give You Rest*, 250. Cf. the cautionary comments of Loader, *Jesus' Attitude towards the Law*, 200: "Matthew will have understood the allusion to wisdom in similar terms to the way it is used in Sirach, where wisdom is identified with Torah. It remains, however, at the level of occasional imagery, rather than of fundamental theology; otherwise its absence elsewhere is too difficult to explain."

[20] See also 2 Chr 10: 9, 10, 11, and 14.

[21] Cf. Matt 21:5 where Jesus compares himself to a humble (πραΰς) king.

[22] Celia Deutsch, *Hidden Wisdom and the Easy Yoke: Wisdom, Torah, and Discipleship in Matthew 11.25–30* (JSNTSup 18; Sheffield: JSOT, 1987), 42; Gnilka, *Das Matthäusevangelium*, 439–40; Hagner, *Matthew*, 1:324; Yang, *Jesus and the Sabbath*, 158.

[23] Cf. *Did.* 6:2: "the yoke of the Lord." Some understand "the yoke of the Lord" in the *Didache* as a technical term designating obedience to the Torah. See Jonathan A. Draper, "The Holy Vine of David Made Known to the Gentiles through God's Servant Jesus: 'Christian Judaism' in the *Didache*," in *Jewish Christianity Reconsidered*, 261–63.

ploy terms such as עול תורה ("the yoke of the Torah") or עול מצוה ("the yoke of the commandment") to denote voluntary submission to the observance of the Torah.²⁴ In fact, *m. Avot* 3:5 reveals remarkable similarities with Matt 11:28–30, promising concrete rewards to those who follow the Torah: "He that takes upon himself the yoke of the Law (עול תורה), from him shall be taken away the yoke of the kingdom and the yoke of worldly care." Like Matt 11:28–30, this rabbinic saying guarantees a certain refuge from oppression and daily struggles to those who attach themselves to the Torah. Matthew "commercially" competes with the Pharisaic school(s) by promoting an alternative, comprehensive package centered on the instructions, clement rulership, and persona of Jesus in and through whom the weary and heavy-laden can find rest.

Undoubtedly, Matthew also ascribes an eschatological dimension to the notion of rest announced in 11:25–30.²⁵ This should come as no surprise since several Second Temple sources express a yearning for collective eschatological restoration couched in primordial language stemming from the establishment of the Sabbath at creation.²⁶ Because the reference to eschatological rest in Matt 11:27 appears right before two episodes reporting disputes about Sabbath keeping, both sections might symbiotically illuminate one another: the idea of eschatological rest in Matt 11:25–30 conceptually sheds light on the subsequent Sabbath stories in Matt 12:1–14 just as the Sabbath stories themselves exemplify in concrete circumstances how the notion of eschatological rest plays out in the daily lives of Jesus and his followers. However, over-relating Matthew's concept of eschatological rest with the institution and observance of the weekly Sabbath should be avoided. Bacchiocchi essentially reduces Matthew's idea of eschatological rest to the notion of weekly Sabbath keeping.²⁷ But for Matthew, the reality of eschatological rest constitutes a much broader category and experience that can be enjoyed through communion with the teachings and the persona of Jesus *throughout the week*, not just on the

---

²⁴ *M. Ber.* 2:2; *Sifre Deut* Pisqa 344.

²⁵ Davies and Allison, *The Gospel according to Matthew*, 2:298: "…Jesus, the Messiah and bringer of the kingdom, offers eschatological rest to those who join him and his cause. This rest is not idleness but the peace and contentment and fullness of life that come with knowing and doing the truth as revealed by God's Son, who is always with his people."

²⁶ 2 *En.* 33:1–2 (this book is textually attested only in very late sources; see Andrei Orlov and Gabriele Boccaccini, eds., *New Perspectives on 2 Enoch: No Longer Slavonic Only* [Studia Judaeoslavica 4; Leiden: Brill, 2012], for a discussion of the new Coptic fragments as well as the dating of this work); *L.A.E.* 51:2; Heb ch. 4; cf. Isa 66:23.

²⁷ See his once popular *From Sabbath to Sunday*, 62. Notice there his triumphal and supersessionist contrast between the "rabbinical" mode of Sabbath keeping and "Christian" Sabbath observance.

Sabbath. Matthean disciples of Jesus enter into eschatological rest not only when they observe the weekly Sabbath according to Jesus' halakah. Rather, the application of Jesus' teachings and communion with his persona activate and guarantee continual access into an eschatological state of rest that also affects the very way in which the weekly Sabbath is kept, without, of course, abrogating its observance.[28] The subsequent two Sabbath pericopes (Matt 12:1–8 and 9–14) demonstrate how Matthew's concept of eschatological rest invades the human sphere and affects the Sabbath keeping of Jesus' disciples.[29]

Determining the Controversy

Determining what the controversy in the story on plucking grain actually involves from a halakic point of view is not a simple matter. Solving this problem is of primary importance, since it would allow for a more precise assessment of the synoptic authors' attitudes toward Sabbath observance. What are the Pharisees in the synoptic gospels really complaining about? Is it the disciples' alleged traveling on the Sabbath, the actual plucking of grains, both deeds, or something else? The Markan formulation (2:23) of the opening of this scene is quite ambiguous and curiously phrased: "as they made their way his disciples began to pluck heads of grain" (οἱ μαθηταὶ αὐτοῦ ἤρξαντο ὁδὸν ποιεῖν τίλλοντες τοὺς στάχυας). Some interpreters interpret the Greek participial phrase, τίλλοντες τοὺς στάχυας, circumstantially, viewing the main problem as involving the disciples' treading through the field. "To make way" (ὁδὸν ποιεῖν) would refer quite literally to "making way through the standing crop."[30] Some Jews would have allegedly objected to this act, because it would involve treading down furrows, analogous in some ways to performing agricultural operations, and could also cause unnecessary loss to the owners' fields.[31] Alternative-

---

[28] According to some later rabbinic traditions, the eschaton will be like a day that is always the Sabbath. See, for example, *b. Ber.* 57b (the pleasures of the Sabbath are one-sixtieth of the delights of the world to come).This does not mean that Matthew believes it is no longer necessary to keep the Sabbath, as if every day is now a Sabbath. Jesus has not yet returned in his full power. The eschatological era is *entering* into human history but not fully realized until the Parousia. In this interim period, the Torah continues to be observed, albeit in light of Jesus' teachings and ministry.

[29] Harrington, *The Gospel of Matthew,* 171, claims that Matt 12:1–8 and 9–14 are put forward as examples of the "light burden" imposed by Jesus.

[30] J. Duncan M. Derrett, *Studies in the New Testament Vol. I: Glimpses of the Legal and Social Presuppositions of the Author* (Leiden: Brill, 1977), 91.

[31] Derrett, *Studies in the New Testament*, 90–91, suggests that Jesus and his disciples were making a path in order to avoid the Sabbath limits. Many fields had pathways that ran through them, and one could use these paths to travel between villages without violating (at least, according to rabbinic halakah) the Sabbath limit of 2000 cubits. See

ly, some exegetes understand the reference to "making way" as a royal act forbidden for ordinary people to perform, but permissible for a king (*m. Sanh.* 2:4). This view maintains that no infringement of a particular Sabbath law occurred in this instance, but rather the transgression of a norm forbidden *on any day* to the *common people*, which in this episode happens to occur on a Sabbath.[32]

Others rightly dismiss this reading, arguing that ὁδὸν ποιεῖν can simply mean "to make a journey" rather than "to build a path," either reflecting a Latinism (*iter facere*) or a variation of ὁδόν ποεῖσθαι in the active voice (cf. LXX Judg 17:8), with the participial construction representing the main idea of the clause.[33] The most likely halakic infringement, then, would concern the act of plucking grain (τίλλοντες τοὺς στάχυας), not the movement of Jesus and his disciples through the fields.[34] Both Matthew and Luke clarify this halakic issue by deleting Mark's clumsy ὁδόν ποεῖσθαι, retaining and juxtaposing the act of plucking with the explicit reference to *eating* (Matt 12:1; Luke 6:1). The fact that in both Matthew and Luke the Pharisees' reproach immediately follows the reference to plucking and eating implies that both gospel authors understand the controversy as involving the act of harvesting food on the Sabbath rather than some other halakic transgression. This interpretation becomes even more evident when one notices that the Pharisees rebuke the behavior of Jesus' *disciples*: "Look, your disciples do what is not lawful to do on a Sabbath" (Matt 12:2)/ "Why are you doing (ποιεῖτε) what is not lawful on the sabbath?" (Luke 6:2) Since both Matthew and Luke only explicitly portray Jesus as going through the fields (Matt 12:1: ἐπορεύθη ὁ Ἰησοῦς/Luke 6:1: διαπορεύεσθαι αὐτὸν), although the movement of his disciples is surely implied, the reproach of the Pharisees, couched in the plural form, primarily criticizes the action committed by his disciples (Matt 12:1: "*they* began to pluck heads of grain and to eat"/Luke 6:1: "*his disciples* plucked some heads of grain, rubbed them in their hands, and ate them"). This is certainly how Matthew understands the Pharisaic rebuke, since in 12:1 he underlines the hunger Jesus' disciples experience (οἱ δὲ μαθηταὶ αὐτοῦ ἐπείνασαν).

Phillip Sigal, *The Halakhah of Jesus of Nazareth according to the Gospel of Matthew* (SBL 18; Leiden: Brill, 2007), 157 n. 44, for a brief discussion of the rabbinic evidence on this matter.

[32] Benjamin Murmelstein, "Jesu Gang durch die Saatfelder," *Angelos* 3 (1930): 118; Pierre Benoît, *Exégèse et théologie III* (Cogitatio fidei 30; Paris: Cerf, 1968), 236–37; Derrett, *Studies in the New Testament*, 94.

[33] Doering, "Sabbath Laws," 208–9; Gnilka, *Das Evangelium nach Markus*, 1:21 n. 16.

[34] See also the discussion in Édouard Delebecque, "Les épis 'égrenés' dans les synoptiques," *REG* 88 (1975): 134–35.

This interpretation rules out appending a second Sabbath infringement to the story, namely, that Jesus and his disciples traveled beyond the distance prescribed for the Sabbath (2000 cubits = c. 1 km).[35] First, as the subsequent analysis demonstrates, the rebuke of the Pharisees in both Matthew and Luke is best understood as a statement condemning the harvesting and eating of food that has not been set aside and prepared before the Sabbath. Second, a travel infringement would clash with the narrated coherence of the text: if Jesus and his disciples travel beyond the limited distance imposed on the Sabbath, then so do the Pharisees! Moreover, walking in itself is not forbidden on the Sabbath, provided one goes not beyond the Sabbath limits.[36] Finally, agricultural fields were often located adjacent to towns to prevent Jews from transgressing the Sabbath limits.[37]

Having dismissed these alternative explanations, how may one understand the issue of plucking itself? The Mosaic Torah allows the needy to glean with their hands grain from the fields owned by others in order to alleviate their hunger (Deut 23:35). If the disciples of Jesus were gleaning from other people's fields, presumably the controversy could have centered on the performance of such an act on the Sabbath, even if the Torah neither explicitly permits nor condemns performing such an act on the Sabbath. A few exegetes fancy that the phrase τίλλειν στάχυας refers not to the plucking of the *stalks* of grain but to the actual removal of grains from the ears of the plant.[38] The evidence brought forth, however, is ambiguous and inconclusive as Doering points out: "τίλλειν is used with the direct object denoting either the matter *being* plucked off or the matter *from which* things are plucked off."[39]

In any case, this philological hairsplitting would be of relevance only if the synoptic authors assume that Jesus' disciples have plucked grain from

---

[35] Luke is well informed about the halakah on the Sabbath limits (תחום שבת), since in Acts 1:12 he refers to the matter (σαββάτου ἔχον ὁδόν). By deleting Mark's awkward ὁδὸν ποιεῖν, Luke makes it clear that Jesus and his disciples have not trespassed the Sabbath limits. This deletion of Mark's phrase, along with other remarkable Jewish measurements used in Acts, suggests that *Luke* refrains from traveling on the Sabbath (see chapter 7 on the Sabbath in Acts).

[36] Doering, "Sabbath Laws," 214, citing *b. Eruv.* 30a–b; *m. Yoma* 6:4 f.; *m. Rosh Hash.* 2:5 for the limit of 2000 cubits, while pointing to the Qumranic distinction between 1000 cubits for normal walking and 2000 cubits for pasturing animals in CD 10:21; 4Q421 13:1; 4Q264a 1:1 (1000 cubits); CD 11:5; 4Q265 7:4 (2000 cubits). See further Doering, *Schabbat,* 145–54, 175 f., 228.

[37] See Doering, "Sabbath Laws," 214 n. 34 for references in ancient Jewish sources.

[38] Édouard Delebecque, "Les épis 'égrenés' dans les synoptiques," 135–42; Derrett, "Judaica in Mark," 90; Ceslas Spicq, "τίλλω," *TLNT* 3:380.

[39] Doering, "Sabbath Laws," 210. As Doering points out, if τίλλειν refers strictly to pulling grain from the ears of the plant, it would be tautological for Luke (6:1) to speak also of the rubbing of the ears of grain (ψώχοντες ταῖς χερσίν).

stalks of corn that have *already fallen on the ground*.⁴⁰ Such a scenario is envisaged in *m. Pesah.* 3:8 where some rabbinic sages rebuke the people of Jericho for eating on the Sabbath fruit that has fallen under a tree (cf. *t. Pesah.* 3:19, 21). The rabbis object to eating such food because the fruit may have fallen on the Sabbath itself and thus be forbidden.⁴¹ A non-rabbinic text, Damascus Document (10:22–23), grants permission to eat on the Sabbath from "that which is spoiling in the field" (האובד בשדה), a practice that would align itself closer to the custom of the people of Jericho than the halakah of the rabbinic sages.⁴²

Do the synoptic accounts refer to a scenario where Jesus' disciples only eat grain from stalks already lying and spoiling on the ground, an act similar to the practice of the people of Jericho and the halakic position advocated in CD? In other words, the Pharisaic reproach in the synoptic gospels would simply consist in specifying that such food items may have fallen on the Sabbath itself. Such a reading demands too fine a halakic analysis from polemical episodes originally created as idealized scenes probably envisaging a more deliberate rupture with traditional Sabbath keeping. Positing that the synoptic Pharisees object to the act of plucking *fresh* grain would fit better with the general tendency of such controversy stories. If we read this episode with this point in mind, it is easy to see how some Jews would have found this practice unacceptable. As noted above, CD 10:22 permits eating on the Sabbath only food that has been set aside and prepared be-

---

⁴⁰ Even Delebecque, "Les épis," 138–40, claims that neither Matthew nor Mark are interested in describing how the disciples acquire the ears of grain to begin with. He theorizes that the disciples have either plucked the entire stalk with the ear or stopped along their way in order to shear off with their fingers the ears on the stalks. According to Delebecque, Luke provides an answer to this question by adding the participial phrase "rubbing with their hands" (Luke 6:1). This participial phrase allegedly implies that the whole stalks have been pulled out, hanging outside of the disciples' hands as they rub the ears. But once again, how do the stalks end up in the disciples' hands to begin with? Are they already lying on the ground before the disciples pick them up?

⁴¹ See Lawrence H. Schiffman, *The Halakhah at Qumran* (SJLA 16; Leiden: Brill, 1975), 100; Doering, *Schabbat*, 155–57.

⁴² Probably this phrase should be understood as referring to food that was spoiling *on the ground*, not to fruit or vegetables still hanging on a tree or a plant as Louis Ginzberg, *An Unknown Jewish Sect* (Moreshet Series 1; New York: Jewish Theological Seminary of America, 1970), 59–60 assumes. See Schiffman, *The Halakhah,* 100; Doering, *Schabbat*, 156. Schiffman, *The Halakhah,* 100, views CD as mediating between the views of the Tannaim and the people of Jericho: "Apparently, the men of Jericho were not willing to abstain from eating these fruits on the mere possibility (*safeq*) that they had fallen off on the Sabbath. The sect [i.e., CD] took a midway position. It allowed the eating of the fruit if it had started to decay." Doering, *Schabbat,* 156–57, however, thinks Schiffman overinterprets the position advocated in CD: "Der Text läßt nicht erkennen daß die Früchte *bereits vor Sabbat* untergefallen sein müssen. Damit steht er der Position der 'Leute von Jericho' nahe, die am Sabbat die heruntergefallenen Früchte aßen."

forehand or produce perishing in the field, but certainly not fresh grain harvested or plucked from a plant on the Sabbath. Similarly, Philo claims that Jews should not cut any shoot, twig, leaf, or even pluck fruit on the Sabbath day (*Mos.* 2:22).[43] The evidence from Second Temple sources prohibiting the plucking of grain on the Sabbath, while slim, is complimented by later rabbinic passages.[44] Even if significant challenges persist for the modern interpreter in determining to what extent "ordinary" Jews would have agreed or disagreed with the retort of the Pharisees as voiced in the synoptic gospels, it is certainly reasonable to posit that at least some Jews would have objected to plucking grain on the Sabbath.[45]

---

[43] Some like Mayer-Haas, *Geschenk,* 159 n. 115, view Philo's statement as an ideal declaration and not indicative of actual Jewish praxis: for Philo, any human interference with creation on the Sabbath, including the removal of plants should in theory be forbidden. On the other hand, Doering believes that some kind of halakic practice among Diasporan Jews is reflected in Philo's statement. See Doering, "Sabbath Laws," 212.

[44] See Doering, "Sabbath Laws," 213, for pertinent rabbinic references.

[45] Doering, "Sabbath Laws," 213, favors viewing the rebuke of the Pharisees as representing a broadly shared opinion among many Jews, not just strict Pharisees. Nevertheless, Doering admits that not every Jew would have held such a position. On the other hand, Mayer-Haas, *Geschenk*, 159, finds it unlikely that the majority of the Jews of Jesus' time and environment would have maintained such a strict observance so as to forbid hungry travelers from plucking and rubbing grain on the Sabbath. Citing *m. Pesah.* 4:8, she thinks that the Mishnah discriminates between the practice of the simple people and the pious sages. She also claims that the rabbis themselves permitted reaping dry herbs for consumption as long as bare hands were used or only a small amount was reaped (*b. Shabb.* 128a). The latter passage, however, does not concern itself with reaping or plucking grain, but with plants that have been set aside *before the Sabbath* as animal feed (למאכל בהמה). This point has been misunderstood by many including Pierre Bonnard, *L'évangile selon saint Matthieu* (CNT 1; Neuchâtel: Delachaux & Niestlé, 1963), 172; Luz, *Matthew*, 2:181; Yang, *Jesus and the Sabbath*, 170 n. 133, among others. Neither the verb to "pluck" (תלש) nor "harvest" (קצר) appear in this rabbinic text, but the verb קטם, which means to "cut," "chop," or "lop," not "pluck." See Jastrow, "קטם," 1349. The verb קטם does not appear as one of the thirty-nine forbidden works in *m. Shabb.* 7:2. Actually, the *Gemara* in *b. Shabb.* 128a comments on mishnayot that have nothing to do with harvesting or plucking, but with the usage and movement of objects on the Sabbath that have already been set aside or stored. See Doering, *Schabbat,* 426–27, who also refutes the attempts of Sigal, *The Halakhah of Jesus of Nazareth*, 157–59 as well as of M. Casey, "Culture and Historicity: The Plucking of the Grain (Mark 2:23–28)," *NTS* 34 (1988):1–23, in exonerating the disciples of Jesus from any Sabbath violation (according to rabbinic standards). Sigal claims that since "plucking" (תולש) is not named as one of the forbidden labors (אבות מלאכות) in *m. Shabb.* 7:2, and even allowed for with qualification in *m. Shabb.*10:6, the disciples' action of plucking a small amount of grain on the Sabbath, performed in order to relieve their hunger, would not have been viewed as forbidden (by later rabbis), and is similar to permitted acts such as peeling an apple on the Sabbath. But according to *m. Shabb.* 7:2, "harvesting" (קוצר) is one of the thirty-nine labors forbidden on the Sabbath, which in *t. Shabb.* 9 [10]:17 is assigned with "plucking" (תולש) as one kind of labor, while in *y. Shabb.* 7:2 9c, 10a, it is classified as a

The Nob Incident

In defense of his disciples' behavior, Jesus refers to a biblical precedent involving David's flight from king Saul to the city of Nob where he obtains holy bread set aside as a rule for priestly consumption. Some modern commentators have made much, perhaps too much, of the supposed exegetical and logical inconsistencies embedded in the brief synoptic retelling and appropriation of the biblical story as reported in 1 Sam 21.[46] One of

---

sub-category of harvesting. According to *m. Shabb.* 10:6, the sages allow "plucking" from plants in pots without holes dug in the ground, while R. Shimon permits plucking from plants in pots with or without holes. The sages here, however, deliberate whether such pots should be viewed as belonging to the soil in which they are placed. It presupposes the prohibition of plucking or harvesting food on the Sabbath that grows directly from the ground. Finally, peeling an apple, as Doering notes, which has already been reaped, is a different matter than plucking plants bound to the ground.

[46] Meier, *Marginal Jew*, 4:276–79, exaggerates the significance of the supposed incongruities between 1 Sam 21:2–10 and Mark's usage of the story, which to a large extent would apply to Matthew and Luke as well. One of the conspicuous "contradictions" singled out involves the contrast between David's apparent *solitary* flight in 1 Sam 21 with the claim in the synoptics that other people accompanied David. Nevertheless, this problem is not as great as some imagine, since in 1 Sam 21:3 David speaks of other men he has hidden in a safe place. True, in 1 Sam David provides this information to evade Ahimelech's inquiry. However, the synoptic authors may not have viewed David's reply as a complete ruse, but believed that he did indeed secure some other men during his flight even while concealing from Ahimelech the true reason for his journey. According to 1 Sam 21:3, David asks for five loaves of bread, which he could have carried with him to give to his companions, at least from the synoptic point of view. Furthermore, all three synoptic authors explicitly state that *only David entered the sanctuary* (εἰσῆλθεν εἰς τὸν οἶκον τοῦ θεοῦ). The terse rendition of the episode allows the synoptic authors to envisage David giving the bread to his companions once he has left the sanctuary precincts. 1 Sam never claims that David ate the bread in the sanctuary. We do not know *when* this event occurs. The synoptic writers do not provide precise and detailed information about this episode. Their primary goal is to draw an analogy, not to provide a coherent retelling of the David story that will satisfy the critical acumens of modern scholars. Yang, *Jesus and the Sabbath*, 172, might be correct when he argues that the episode in 1 Sam neither denies nor confirms the presence of David's companions. Meier charges the Jewish followers of Jesus from Palestine for failing to read the David episode properly. However, this approach only transfers ignorance about the Jewish scriptures from the historical Jesus to the *Jewish* followers of Jesus without trying to understand the synoptic episodes on their own terms. Many also single out the error Mark commits by confusing Abiathar (Mark 2:26) for his father, Ahimelech (1 Sam 21:1). Mark also mistakenly refers to Abiathar as a "high priest." John P. Meier, "The Historical Jesus and the Plucking of Grain on the Sabbath," *CBQ* 66 (2004): 577, views this outcome as stemming from Mark's ignorance of the "Old Testament." Nevertheless, as Doering notes, the epithet "high priest" is found in Josephus, *Ant.* 6:242; *L.A.B.* 63:2; and manuscript C of *Tg. Jon.* 1 Sam 21:1. Regarding the name Ahimelech, this name is rendered "A*b*imelech" in the LXX and Josephus, and Mark could have easily confused the two. See Doering, "Sabbath Laws in the New Testament Gospels," 215 n. 38. Matthew and

the incongruities concerns the time setting in both episodes: there is no explicit reference in 1 Samuel that David comes to Nob *on the Sabbath*, raising questions about the legitimacy and solicitation of this biblical story as an appropriate precedent for the argumentation Jesus makes in the synoptic episode. A few commentators, however, find hints in 1 Samuel that may suggest a Sabbath setting for the story.[47] Thus 1 Sam 21:6 reads: "So the priest gave him the holy bread; for there was no bread there except the bread of the Presence, which is removed from before the LORD, to be replaced by hot bread on the day it is taken away" (המוסרים מלפני יהוה לשום לחם חם ביום הלקחו). According to Lev 24:8, the showbread was to be replaced on the Sabbath. Later on, certain rabbinic sages posited a connection between Lev 24:8 and 1 Sam 21:6, proposing a Sabbath setting for the Nob incident (*b. Menaḥ.* 95b; *Yalq.* §130 on 1 Sam 21:5). Nevertheless, this exegetical link only appears in much later rabbinic texts, while no synoptic author, including Matthew, singles out this element for comparative purposes even though they could have readily done so.[48]

What analogy then is Matthew trying to highlight between the two situations in order to justify the halakic "misdemeanor" committed by Jesus' disciples? First, Matthew adds to the Markan text that the disciples were *hungry* (12:1: ἐπείνασαν), thus solidifying the link between David's hunger (ἐπείνασεν) and that of Jesus' followers.[49] This connection also assists Matthew in relieving the disciples of Jesus from the charge that they capriciously pluck grain on the Sabbath simply to delight their greedy appetites, a possible misunderstanding of the episode the Markan version could have generated.[50] Mayer-Haas thinks that already Mark's version of the story presupposes an urgent situation, which would correspond in part to the

---

Luke have eliminated the name Abiathar from their gospels, revealing thereby their familiarity with 1 Sam 21.

[47] See already Murmelstein, "Jesu Gang durch die Saatfelder," 116.

[48] Correctly, Repschinski, *The Controversy Stories in Matthew,* 97 n. 20. Some argue the analogy would still prove deficient even if a Sabbath setting is presumed, as it would compare the infringement of consuming holy food assigned to priests with the transgression of a Sabbath regulation. See Doering, "Sabbath Laws," 215; D. M. Cohn-Sherbok, "An Analysis of Jesus' Arguments concerning the Plucking of Grain on the Sabbath," *JSNT* 1 (1979): 39.

[49] The analogy does not meet later *rabbinic* criteria to constitute a valid *gezerah shavah*. See Cohn-Sherbok, "An Analysis of Jesus' Arguments," 34–36.

[50] See Alberto Mello, *Evangelo secondo Matteo* (Magnano: Edizioni Qiqajon, 1995), 210; Juan L. Segundo, *El Caso Mateo: Los comienzos de una ética judeo-cristiana* (Colección "Presencia Teológica" 74; Santander: Editorial Sal Terrae, 1994), 161. I take Matthew's explicit reference to hunger as an indication of the special circumstances the disciples find themselves in. Contra Yang, *Jesus and the Sabbath,* 174–77, who does not think Jesus expects his disciples to fulfill the literal regulations of the Sabbath, and views the reference to hunger only as a "surface" analogy.

precedent in 1 Sam 21.[51] There is correspondence between David and Jesus' disciples' situations, however, only to a certain point. The scenario Jesus and his disciples find themselves in, as presented in all three synoptics, does not appear to be life-threatening. If human life were indeed at stake, the disciples' action would constitute a harmless misdemeanor even to many Jews who were more stringent in their Sabbath praxis. In addition, if Jesus and the disciples were fleeing for their lives, they could hardly have paused and afforded the luxury of engaging with the Pharisees in a halakic debate over forbidden and permitted works on the Sabbath. For the episode to become more credible at the narrative level, we must assume that Jesus and his followers were not facing any *imminent* danger.[52] Consequently, it seems preferable to view Matthew's argumentation as extending (rather than equating) the principle known in rabbinic parlance as פיקוח נפש ("saving a life") that allowed for the temporary suspension of the Sabbath in life-threatening situations. Matthew expands this principle to include less mitigating circumstances.

It is more challenging to establish further links between the David story and the synoptic episode besides the comparison between David's hunger and that of Jesus' disciples, which Matthew highlights more strongly than Mark.[53] Mathew seems to employ the Nob incident only in the most general manner: David and his followers in a certain instance (flight from Saul) experience hunger and break a regulation from the Torah (consummation of consecrated food); in a similar yet different instance, Jesus' disciples also experience hunger and transgress a Sabbath regulation (plucking grain). The synoptic authors, however, probably perceive one further important connection between both stories: the relationship between the figures of David and Jesus. As noted above, Matthew and Luke only explicitly refer to Jesus going through the fields, while claiming his disciples perform the actual plucking and eating of the grain. Nevertheless, the Pharisees in Matthew call upon Jesus to answer on behalf of his disciples: "Look, your disciples are doing what is not lawful (ὃ οὐκ ἔξεστιν) to

---

[51] Mayer-Haas, *Geschenk,* 162. But see Doering, "Sabbath Laws," 215.

[52] Mello, *Evangelo,* 210, however, maintains that for Matthew the hunger of the disciples falls under the category of פיקוח נפש. Luz, *Matthew,* 2:181, also leans towards this direction, claiming that the "rabbis regard hunger as life-threatening, and a life-threatening situation had always taken precedence over keeping the Sabbath commandment." True, life-threatening situations override the Sabbath, but hunger in itself does not. The rabbinic text (*m. Yoma* 8.6) cited by Luz does not support his point. The satiation of hunger in that passage is qualified: בולמוס (in Greek βούλιμος, Latin, *bulimus*) refers to a fierce, ravenous hunger, which presumably could be life-threatening for certain individuals.

[53] Bonnard, *L'évangile,* 172: "...le point de comparaison avec le geste des disciples est très lointain...."

do on the sabbath" (12:1).[54] Although Jesus is not directly complicit in the act of plucking, he remains complacent, and his authority is called into question. Ultimately, the master must clarify and justify the halakic orientation of his disciples. Probably, the synoptic authors wish to enhance Jesus' authority by correlating his figure with the greatest monarch of Israel. If David can consume and provide bread for his men, then Jesus too, by virtue of the christological credentials invested to him, can authorize his disciples to pluck grain from the fields on the Sabbath.[55]

Additional Matthean Arguments

Matthew strengthens his portfolio by bringing another argument to the table: the service the priests perform every Sabbath in the temple. Since 1 Samuel does not explicitly claim that David entered into the sanctuary on a Sabbath day, Matthew summons another scenario that relates more closely to the question of Sabbath keeping and even occurs in temple space. By pointing out that the priests work every Sabbath yet are not held guilty for profaning (βεβηλοῦσιν) its sanctity, Matthew hopes to justify the Sabbath praxis of Jesus and his disciples (12:5). *Prima facie*, the reference to the priestly administration in the temple seems more appropriate than the Nob incident to bolster Matthew's Jesus' argument: the priests, like the disciples of Jesus, "work" on the Sabbath. In addition, the reference to the priestly service on the Sabbath stems from the Mosaic Torah, not the books of the Prophets (12:5: ἐν τῷ νόμῳ).[56] Nevertheless, some argue that even this comparison is not entirely apt: whereas the priests *minister* on the Sabbath *within the temple* because they are *commanded* to do so, Jesus' disciples do not officiate as priests in any sanctuary, but simply harvest and consume food in broad daylight![57] The author of *Jubilees* would certainly not have agreed with the rationale of Matthew's argumentation:

---

[54] The phrase ὃ οὐκ ἔξεστιν appears in other Jewish legal contexts discussing which deeds are allowed or prohibited to perform on the Sabbath. See Doering, *Schabbat*, 450 n. 297, for references.

[55] For a christological correlation between David and Jesus, see Bonnard, *L'évangile*, 172; Boyarin, *The Jewish Gospels*, 60–70; Yang, *Jesus and the Sabbath*, 176.

[56] See Davies and Allison, *The Gospel according to Matthew*, 2:313, who claim that the David story belongs more to the realm of haggadah rather than halakah (categories that, of course, stem from the later rabbinic realms). Cf. Cohn-Sherbok, "An Analysis of Jesus' Arguments," 36; Repschinski, *The Controversy Stories in Matthew*, 98.

[57] But see Loader, *Jesus Attitude towards the Law*, 203: "It is the particular relation to the temple which makes priests' work on the sabbath appropriate. It is the particular relation to Jesus which, according to Matthew, makes what the disciples are doing on the sabbath appropriate." Cf. Klinghardt, *Gesetz und Volk Gottes*, 228–29, who suggests that both Matthew and Luke's reworking of Mark's pericope brings the discussion back to its supposed original discussion (found in Mark 2:23–26, before the alleged additions of

On the sabbath day do not do any work which you have not prepared for yourself on the sixth day so that you may eat, drink, rest, keep sabbath on this day from all work.... For great is the honor which the Lord has given Israel to eat, drink, and be filled on this festal day; and to rest on it from any work that belongs to the work of mankind except to burn incense and to bring before the Lord offerings and sacrifices for the days and the sabbaths. Only this (kind of) work is to be done on the sabbath days in the sanctuary of the Lord....(*Jub.* 50:9–11)[58]

For the author of *Jubilees*, offering sacrifices in the temple on the Sabbath would certainly not sanction plucking or cooking food that had not been set aside or prepared before the Sabbath. But against this potential counter argument Matthew has Jesus retort that "something greater than the temple is here" (12:6). As some commentators point out, the Greek term for "greater" appears in this verse in the neuter singular (μεῖζόν), not the masculine. The neuter form allows one to interpret this verse as pointing to the deeds and words of Jesus rather than his figure or persona.[59] Such a reading enjoys the benefit of agreeing in gender with the neuter noun ἔλεος ("mercy"), which appears right after in v. 7: "But if you had known what this means, 'I desire mercy and not sacrifice,' you would not have condemned the guiltless."[60] Here Matthew refers to Hos 6:6 in order to boost his case by connecting the concept and application of mercy with the mes-

---

2:27–28) that defended the right for missionaries to feed themselves on the Sabbath (through analogy with the ministry of the priests). The debate in Luke 6:1–5 would have more to do with the early mission of the *ekklesia* than the problem of Sabbath keeping. This hypothesis is attractive, since it accounts for the unique nature of the debate involved (all other Sabbath controversies in the synoptics deal with healing on the Sabbath). Etan Levine, "The Sabbath Controversy according to Matthew," *NTS* 22 (1975/76): 480–83, tries to show that Jesus appeals to the practice of reaping the *Omer* offering (first sheaves of barley), which was allowed by the rabbis on the Sabbath (see *m. Menah.* 10:1 f.). But why does Matthew (or any other gospel author) not explicitly refer to this matter?

[58] All translations of *Jubilees* are taken from James C. VanderKam, *The Book of Jubilees* (2 vols. Corpus scriptorum christianorum orientalium 510–511; Scriptores Aethiopici 87–88; Leuven: Peeters, 1989).

[59] Doering, *Schabbat,* 434; Luz, *Matthew,* 2:181; Frankmölle, *Matthäus,* 2:133; Saldarini, *Matthew's Jewish-Christian Community,* 129–31; Sigal, *The Halakhah of Jesus of Nazareth,* 161. Many commentators, however, applying a christological reading, tie "μεῖζόν" with the figure of Jesus. This christological reading connects v. 6 with v. 8 ("the Son of Man is lord of the sabbath"). So Banks, *Jesus and the Law,* 117; Antonio Rodríguez Carmona, *Evangelio de Mateo* (Bilbao: Desclée De Brouwer, 2006), 123; Yang, *Jesus and the Sabbath,* 179–82.

[60] Doering, "Sabbath Laws," 223 n. 72. Frankmölle, *Matthäus,* 2:132–33, suggests tying "something" with "these things" and "all things" (also in the neuter in Greek) mentioned in 11:25 and 27. It is undeniable that the christological argument eventually appears in this pericope but in the clearest way only at the very end when Jesus claims to be lord of the Sabbath (v. 8).

sage and mission of Jesus.[61] If the temple service overrides the Sabbath, how much more should "something greater," that is, the arrival of the messianic rule of clemency, justify Jesus' disciples' temporary breach of the Sabbath, especially since God desires mercy, not sacrifice. The argument resembles roughly the rabbinic *qal vahomer* although Matthew remains more interested in making general analogies rather than establishing rigorous and precise points of correspondence between two situations.[62]

Just as the book of Hosea does not abolish sacrifices, but begs Israel to demonstrate a proper *état d'esprit* when fulfilling cultic duties, so does Matthew encourage a different attitude toward Sabbath keeping without calling for its abrogation.[63] The application of the principle of mercy becomes a means for Matthew for assessing any halakic dilemma in which human needs such as hunger collide with Sabbath regulations. Matthew pleads, in the name of mercy, for a more compassionate consideration of basic human needs, for an expression of greater sensibility and a more lenient application of halakah than the one allegedly practiced by his Pharisaic detractors.[64]

Matthew's claim that something greater than the temple had arrived into Israel's sphere must have resounded with particular reverberation in the aftermath of 70 CE. Confronted with the cultic and spiritual vacuum left by the desolation of the temple, the rabbinic sages devised way to fill this void, employing Hos 6:6 to establish the study of the Torah and the practice of charity as acts more meritorious than offering sacrifices. According to rabbinic tradition, R. Yohanan b. Zakkai employed Hos 6:6 in order to comfort those morning the destruction of the temple, claiming that a means of atonement had become available in lieu of the temple, namely, "acts of charity" (גמילות חסדים).[65] Although Matthew cites Hos 6:6 in order to

---

[61] Hos 6:6 is an important verse for Matthew. See Matt 9:13 where it is solicited in order to justify Jesus' commensality with sinners. Cf. Matt 23:23. On this matter, see David Hill, "On the Use of and Meaning of Hosea VI. 6 in Matthew's Gospel," *NTS* 24 (1978): 107–19; Mayer-Haas, *Geschenk*, 445–48. Hos 6:6 is also used in rabbinic literature (e.g., *Avot R. Nat.* A 4) to show how works based on love rather than sacrifice atone for the sins of Israel. Whether the "historical Yohanan b. Zakkai" actually emphasized this ethical dimension, as some assume, is another matter. See Luz, *Matthew*, 2:34, 183.

[62] The Matthean *a minori ad maius* argument would not constitute a valid *qal vahomer* according to rabbinic logic. See Cohn-Sherbok, "An Analysis of Jesus' Arguments," 36–40.

[63] Luz, *Matthew*, 2:182: "God wants mercy *more* than sacrifice. Jesus does not intend to abolish the laws of sacrifice."

[64] Cf. Saldarini, *Matthew's Jewish-Christian Community*, 129.

[65] *Avot R. Nat.* A 4. Cf. *Avot R. Nat.* B 8–9; *Pirqe R. El.* "Horev," chs. 11, 16; *Yal.* §310 on Jeremiah 30 and §522 on Hosea 6. The sages tie the noun for mercy (חסד) in Hos 6:6 with the rabbinic term for acts of charity (גמילות חסדים). By no means am I trying to demonstrate that the historical R. Yohanan b. Zakkai uttered these words. See

justify a temporary breach of the Sabbath,⁶⁶ this statement may have assisted his readers in coping with the void left after 70 CE. Matthew's consolation is that someone with something greater than the temple has arrived to rule Israel through clemency. His reference and usage of Hos 6:6 to justify a particular halakic orientation that looks back to and beyond the temple fits perfectly within the spectrum of Jewish expressions and discourses we would expect to find at that time.⁶⁷

Matthew wraps up this Sabbath episode with a final claim that certainly would have stirred the hearts of those already belonging to his circle(s) but hardly convinced those outside the Jesus movement: "the Son of Man is lord of the sabbath" (12:8). Undoubtedly, this phrase means for Matthew that Jesus' lordship as the Son of Man ultimately determines the halakic orientation of his community.⁶⁸ In this way, Matthew also seeks to draw the reader's attention to the question of Jesus' messiahship. Matthew credits Jesus, as the Son of Man, for inaugurating the eschatological age in which the administration of mercy assists the distressed of the commonwealth of Israel. This point brings us back to the eschatological prelude in Matt 11:25–30. The weary and heavily laden now experience on the Sabbath day the eschatological alleviation promised by Jesus. Among Jesus' followers, can be found the needy and poor residents of the land of Israel, who on a regular basis, whether it be on a Sabbath or a normal weekday, experience hunger and other physical ordeals. These hardships reduce and even impede their ability to procure and prepare food before the Sabbath. Consequently, these have-nots can rightfully glean from the fields of others even on the Sabbath. In the dawning of a new eschatological era, it would be unfitting for anyone to suffer from hunger on the Sabbath day. Failure to reveal and share compassion in such circumstances lies in the hearts of those (Pharisaic) opponents, the "wise and intelligent," who wrongfully blame Matthew and his needy compatriots for the performance of such an act.⁶⁹

---

already Neusner's earlier work, *The Development of a Legend: Studies on the Tradition concerning Yohanan ben Zakkai* (StPB 16; Leiden: Brill, 1970), 113.

⁶⁶ Gnilka, *Das Matthäusevangelium,* 445: "Nicht der Tempel ist das eigentliche Thema der Perikope, sondern das Verhalten des Menschen am Sabbat."

⁶⁷ Cf. Reinhart Hummel, *Die Auseinandersetzung zwischen Kirche und Judentum im Matthäusevangelium* (BEvT 33; München: Chr. Kaiser, 1966), 97.

⁶⁸ The christological overtones of the title "Son of Man" can no longer be underestimated, certainly at the Matthean level, given the current consensus among many Second Temple Jewish specialists concerning the dating of the *Parables of Enoch* to the first century BCE. See Gabriele Boccaccini, ed., *Enoch the Messiah Son of Man: Revisiting the Book of Parables* (Grand Rapids, Mich.: Eerdmans, 2007).

⁶⁹ Segundo, *El caso Mateo,* 164–69, presents Matthew's argumentation as an attempt to solve an ethical dilemma to perform one of two noble tasks. Whether it be David, who

All of the previous observations should make it clear that Matthew is not interested in demonstrating that the eschatological transition announced by Jesus cancels Sabbath keeping altogether. Matthew's effort in multiplying justifications for this "transgressive" act (in the eyes of his opponents) reveals his ongoing concern for Sabbath keeping.[70] Matthew does not call for the abrogation of the Sabbath but for a reassessment of its *raison d'être*, for a more gracious disposition toward the physical needs of the poor, the weary and heavy-laden, and ultimately for a recognition of Jesus' messianic authority.

Luke 6:1–5

Literary Context

Before reporting the dispute over plucking grain on the Sabbath, Luke deals with the issue of fasting (5:33–39). The followers of John the Baptist as well as the Pharisees practice fasting on a regular basis, but Jesus' followers do not. Jesus accounts for the practice of his disciples by declaring it inappropriate to fast when the bridegroom is present with his guests for a wedding celebration (vv. 34–35). Luke's Jesus develops this point with a "parable": no one would sew a piece of new cloth onto an old garment; otherwise, the new patch would tear and not match the old garment (v. 36). Similarly, no one would put new wine into old wineskins; otherwise, the new wine would burst the old wine skins (v. 37). New wine obviously belongs in new wine skins (v. 38). Up until this point, Jesus' reply in Luke is straightforward (cf. Matt 9:14–17; Mark 2:18–22): it is not appropriate to mix the old with the new just as it is not fitting to fast during a wedding. The statement in Luke 5:39, however, which is unattested in Mark and Matthew, complicates matters somewhat when it declares: "And no one

---

must choose between saving his life or profaning the showbread, or the priests who must serve in the temple and "violate" the Sabbath, or finally the disciples of Jesus who must choose between resting on the Sabbath or suffering from hunger on a day designed for blessing and joy, Matthew employs all of these cases to demonstrate that the disciples are justified in their performance of a "lesser evil," that is, temporarily suspending the Sabbath to relieve human hunger.

[70] Correctly, Doering, *Schabbat*, 435–36; Saldarini, *Matthew's Christian-Jewish Community*, 131. Cf. Davies and Allison, *The Gospel according to Matthew*, 2:307. Contra Bonnard, *L'évangile*, 173: "Jésus…confirme la valeur du sabbat avant de le rendre caduc"; Juan Mateos and Fernando Camacho, *El Evangelio de Mateo lectura comentada* (Lectura del Nuevo Testamento; Madrid: Cristiandad, 1981), 119: "Jesús suprime la carga insoportable de la observancia del sábado y la Ley misma del descanso festive."

after drinking old wine desires new wine, but says, 'The old is good.'"[71] Right after this verse, Luke recounts the story about Jesus and the disciples plucking grain on the Sabbath.

The final statement in 5:39 has puzzled many commentators. Why would Luke include such a saying at the end of Jesus' reply to the question on fasting? *Prima facie,* the saying would seem to deter from Luke's main argument. Ancient cultures, after all, generally valued any custom or belief that was rooted in antiquity and regarded all novel phenomena and practices with suspicion. Jesus' opponents probably would have considered the abstinence of his disciples from fasting as an innovative practice. Not surprisingly, many commentators resort to interpreting Luke 5:39 as a sort of rebuke toward those who choose to hold on to older (read "Jewish") practices and fail to appreciate the new element in Jesus' teachings.[72] According to this understanding of the saying, Luke, in contradistinction to the rest of his peers from the Greco-Roman world, whether Jewish or Greek, would be underscoring the novel element in Jesus' message rather than seeking to root it in antiquity. Bovon understands the parable in this way, claiming that Luke deems the new element in Jesus' message to be irreconcilable with ancient Judaism: "Probably for Luke, the way of life introduced by Jesus is so new that one cannot simultaneously live as a Jew and as a Christian."[73] Bovon constructs a false dichotomy based on anachronistic notions. Luke is not opposing a Jewish way of living with a "Christian" lifestyle, as if these two were autonomous categories diametrically opposed to each other.[74] Luke and the other synoptic gospels present this debate as an *intra-Jewish* affair between different Jewish groups, whether they be disciples of John the Baptist, Pharisees, or followers of Jesus. "The issue is not about the gospel and the Law," as William Loader astutely notes, "but about the way of Jesus and the ways of the scribes and

---

[71] A parallel to Luke's statement appears in *Gosp. Thom.* 47, at the beginning of the discourse.

[72] Alfred Plummer, *The Gospel According to Luke* (5th ed.; ICC; Edinburgh: T&T Clark, 1989), 164–65: "while the first two (parables) show how fatal it would be to couple the new spirit of the Gospel with the worn out forms of Judaism, the third shows how natural it is that those who have been brought up under these forms would be unwilling to abandon them for something untried."

[73] *Luke 1*, 193. Bovon also interprets Luke's reference to old wine in a dual sense: in a negative way to symbolize the Jewish practice of fasting; in a positive way as representing a Christian lifestyle.

[74] The same criticism applies to a lesser extent to Salo, *Luke's Treatment of the Law,* 85: "The whole section also has the purpose of showing the impossibility of changing the direction of influences between Judaism and Christianity. Although some habits or ideas of the old may be part of the new, the reverse is inconceivable: Christianity will be destroyed if one attempts to bring its elements or cast it as a whole in the form of Judaism."

the Pharisees."[75] We could also add, "about the way of the disciples of John the Baptist."

Commentators such as Flusser,[76] Good,[77] and Mayer-Haas[78] read Luke 5:33–39 in a radically different way: Luke claims that the frequent fasts of the Pharisees and the disciples of John constitute the real innovation, since the Torah does not prescribe regular fasts.[79] This interpretation would fit nicely with Luke's overall scheme to describe the Jesus movement in terms of continuity with Judaism, indeed as the true bearer and fulfiller of its original, one might say, "ancient" mission and purpose. According to this understanding of the parable, Luke views the imposition of habitual weekly fasts, unattested in the Torah, as constituting innovative practice. It is the novel practice of regular and fixed fasting, symbolized by a new patch of cloth and new wine, that tears from the old garment and bursts the old wineskins, disrupting the celebration of the wedding. Alternative interpretations of Luke 5:39 abound,[80] and over-reading the parable by making too many associations concerning its symbols should be avoided.[81]

In any case, Luke is not trying to make definitive, long-term statements about the supposed incompatibility of Jesus' teachings with the observance of the Torah or even Pharisaic practice. After all, once the bridegroom, that is, Jesus, physically departs from the earthly sphere, his disciples revert to practicing fasting, much like the Pharisees and the disciples of John (Acts 13:2, 3; 14:23). The saying in 5:39 appears at the end of a pericope that has more to do with accounting for the behavior and non-fasting of Jesus' disciples in the *physical* presence of Jesus during his *earthly* ministry than in justifying a *contemporary* praxis that deviates from or categorically opposes Jewish customs and conventions. Indeed, the episode focuses

---

[75] Loader, *Jesus' Attitude towards the Law,* 311.

[76] David Flusser, "Do You Prefer New Wine?" *Immanuel* 9 (1979): 26–31.

[77] R. S. Good, "Jesus Protagonist of the Old, in Lk 5:33–39," *NovT* 25 (1983): 19–36.

[78] Mayer-Haas, *Geschenk,* 303.

[79] See Good, "Jesus Protagonist of the Old," 35.

[80] Loader, *Jesus' Attitude towards the Law,* 311, proposes irony for understanding the saying in 5:39: "Luke adds to the wine image the comment that no one drinking the old wine will want the new, because the old wine is better. This is good wine wisdom, but appears to be used ironically to explain the resistance of the Pharisees."

[81] On the interpretation of parables of the New Testament within their Jewish contexts (especially in light of rabbinic parables), see David Flusser, *Die rabbinischen Gleichnisse und der Gleichniserzähler Jesus* (Judaica et Christiana 4; Bern: Peter Lang, 1981); Harvey K. McArthur and Robert Morris Johnston, *They Also Taught in Parables: Rabbinic Parables from the First Centuries of the Christian Era* (Grand Rapids, Mich.: Academie Books, 1990); Brad H. Young, *Jesus and His Jewish Parables: Rediscovering the Roots of Jesus' Teaching* (Theological Inquiries; New York: Paulist Press, 1989); *The Parables: Jewish Tradition and Christian Interpretation* (Peabody, Mass.: Hendrickson, 1998).

more on the authority and figure of Jesus, the bridegroom, than on the issue of fasting. The same holds true for the subsequent pericope on plucking grain on the Sabbath. It does not appear in Luke's gospel in order to endorse the non-observance of the Sabbath. Rather, it illustrates how the Sabbath is to be observed and celebrated, not abrogated, in the *physical* presence of the bridegroom. In *Luke's* day, after the ascension of the bridegroom to his heavenly headquarters, many Jewish followers of Jesus continued to keep the Sabbath, and nowhere in Luke-Acts are such efforts condemned, in fact, they are even commended.[82]

Analysis

Luke presents the briefest account of the episode, with approximately ninety-two words, shorter than the corresponding versions in Mark (108 words) and Matthew (136 words).[83] Luke's version reveals remarkable similarities with its Markan counterpart, yet contains several modifications, some resulting from stylistic improvements, others more significant for assessing his attitude toward the Sabbath.[84] Because of its brevity, Flusser argues that the Lukan version contains the more primitive account of the event.[85] Flusser also points to a supposed halakic precision made in

---

[82] In Matthew's case, Repschinski, *The Controversy Stories in Matthew,* 88, claims that the parables of the cloth and the wine "argue for the incompatibility of the new and the old. In terms of Matthew's community this means that their status as the community of Jesus implies new ways of expressing itself. Fasting is one issue where such a re-organization becomes visible, and is consequently challenged by the opponents of the community. The two parables point out very strongly that the Matthean community represents something entirely new that cannot be fit into the categories that the opponents of Jesus was to apply." But on p. 87, Repschinski recognizes that the time of "mourning" (a motif missing in Luke) preferably refers to the time of the resurrection until the end of times (though he notes the inconsistency with Matt 28:20) when presumably even Matthew's "community" resumed observing fasts.

[83] Following the text of the *Novum Testamentum Graece* (Nestle-Aland 27th edition).

[84] See Mayer-Haas, *Geschenk,* 303–4, for a more detailed redactional analysis. One important difference, which many have noted, is Luke's precision that only *some* of the Pharisees (τινὲς δὲ τῶν Φαρισαίων) confront Jesus' disciples. This nuanced portrayal of the Pharisees differs from the generalizations found in Mark and Matthew. See Klinghardt, *Gesetz und Volk Gottes,* 228 and especially John A. Ziesler, "Luke and the Pharisees," *NTS* 25 (1978/79): 146–57.

[85] Flusser, *The Sage from Galilee,* 35. Flusser, like Robert Lindsey, often favors Luke over the other two synoptic gospels. He even posits an original proto-gospel written in *Hebrew,* which was subsequently translated into Greek and underwent further modifications. According to Flusser, Luke often preserves the Hebraic flavor of this proto-gospel. See Flusser, "Do You Want New Wine," 26; Robert L. Lindsey, *A Hebrew Translation of the Gospel of Mark* (Jerusalem: Dugith Publishers, 1973), 9–84. At other times, Flusser seems to have promoted a modified thesis of the synoptic problem that occasionally

Luke 6:1 concerning Jesus disciples' manner of handling the grain on the Sabbath: they *rub* the heads of grain with their *hands* (τοὺς στάχυας ψώχοντες ταῖς χερσίν). Flusser claims that the prevailing Jewish opinion of that time allowed for picking up fallen heads of grain and rubbing them between the *fingers* on the Sabbath. Citing a tradition from the Babylonian Talmud (*b. Shabb.* 128a), which allegedly refers to a Galilean practice of rubbing grain on the Sabbath even with one's *hands*, Flusser argues that some of the Pharisees reproach Jesus' disciples for behaving like Galileans. The Greek translator of the supposed original account, which, according to Flusser, was written in Hebrew, was unacquainted with these customs and added the statement about *plucking* grain on the Sabbath in order to make the scene more vivid. By doing so, the Greek translator "introduced the one and only act of transgression of the law recorded in the Synoptic tradition."[86]

Unfortunately, Flusser's argument proves unconvincing on several grounds. First, few have found Flusser's solution to the synoptic problem, namely, that there was an original Hebrew biography of Jesus' life subsequently translated into Greek, persuasive. Doering also notes that no evidence exists positing an early Galilean custom of rubbing ears with the hand from grain that was not gathered as fodder before the Sabbath.[87] The Talmudic passage, then, carries little weight for elucidating Luke's account of the Sabbath controversy.[88] Although Flusser presupposes that the Lukan account refers to the rubbing of grain that has fallen on the ground either before or even during the Sabbath, Luke never hints at such a halakic scenario. The Lukan phrase, "rubbed them in their hands," is simply a literary production penned by Luke to provide a more "realistic" account to the episode.[89]

---

favors Matthean priority. See Malcolm Lowe and David Flusser, "Evidence Corroborating a Modified Proto-Matthean Synoptic Theory," *NTS* 29 (1983): 25–47.

[86] Flusser, *The Sage from Galilee*, 35.

[87] See previous discussion on this matter in the section on Matthew's version of the story; Doering, "Sabbath Laws," 225–26; *Schabbat,* 426–27. As noted earlier, R. Judah discusses rubbing food that has been collected beforehand as animal fodder (*b. Shabb.* 128a).

[88] As Doering, "Sabbath Laws," 225, notes, citing Saul Lieberman, a key passage for elucidating *b. Shabb.* 128a is *t. Shabb.* 14[15]: 11. Lieberman suggests that the original debate in *t. Shabb.* 14[15]:11, full of textual-critical problems, concerned not the alternatives of "hands" vs. "fingers" but "fingers and hands" vs. "utensils," implying that all rabbinic sages agreed that Jews could rub grain with either their hands or fingers on the Sabbath. See Lieberman, *Tosefta ki-Fshutah* [in Hebrew] (10 vols.; 2d ed.; Jerusalem: The Jewish Theological Seminary of America/The Maxwell Abbell Publication Fund, 1992), 3:237.

[89] Doering, *Schabbat,* 437; Mayer-Haas, *Geschenk,* 304, refuting Hermann Aichinger, "Quellenkritische Untersuchung der Perikope vom Ährenraufen am Sabbat. Mk 2,23–28

Luke, unlike Matthew, does not explicitly mention the hunger of Jesus' disciples, but he does state that the disciples "ate" (ἤσθιον) the grains after plucking them. This explicit reference to eating, which is lacking in Mark, matches David's action, the king of Israel, who also "ate" (ἔφαγεν) from the showbread of the sanctuary (6:4). The connection in Luke, therefore, between David's hunger and that of the disciples of Jesus is more direct and to the point than in Mark: just as David was hungry when he entered the house of God and ate the bread of the Presence, so too Jesus' disciples one Sabbath experienced hunger and consumed some grain (6:3–4). Doering claims that Luke's deletion of the Markan phrase, "David was in need" (χρείαν ἔσχεν, Mark 2:25), means that Luke views *any* hunger as legitimately displacing the Sabbath.[90] But Matthew has also left out this Markan phrase, which both synoptic authors probably viewed as a superfluous element and deleted for stylistic reasons.[91] Moreover, Luke portrays this incident as a one-time event. He describes its one-time occurrence by employing the singular ἐν σαββάτῳ, instead of Mark and Matthew's plural τοῖς σάββασιν, and by substituting the Markan verbal imperfects and presents with aorists (εἶπαν instead of ἔλεγον in Luke 6:2; ἀποκριθεὶς and εἶπεν instead of λέγει in 6:3).[92] In this way, the Lukan narration reports a singular event rather than a reoccurring action that can be used to legitimize the satiation of greedy appetites under any circumstances on the Sabbath. Luke justifies this exceptional suspension of the Sabbath by anchoring it into a biblical precedent, David's flight from Saul, an incident that also occurred under unique and demanding circumstances. As Loader points out, by summoning the story about David, Luke seems to combine three arguments to justify the Sabbath praxis of Jesus' disciples: "appeal to scripture or scriptural precedent, appeal to the moral claim of human need and appeal to the example of an authority figure."[93]

After citing the David incident, Luke immediately proceeds to the christological argument: the Son of Man is lord of the Sabbath (v. 6). With this statement, Luke does not claim that the Sabbath has been abrogated. Rather, Jesus, as the Son of Man, has the authority to determine *how* the

---

par Mt 12, 1–8 par Lk 6, 1–5," in *Jesus in der Verkündigung der Kirche* (ed. Albert Fuchs; SNTU A1; Linz: A. Fuchs, 1976), 134, who thinks Luke is trying to highlight a further violation of the Sabbath.

[90] Doering, *Schabbat*, 436.
[91] Mayer-Haas, *Geschenk*, 306.
[92] The plural τοῖς σάββασιν can also refer to a single Sabbath (see *BDAG* 909), but Luke has intentionally used the singular form, ἐν σαββάτῳ, to signal the one-time occurrence of the event. Elsewhere (Luke 4:31 and 13:10), Luke employs the plural form when he wishes to emphasize a recurring habit (e.g., Jesus going to the synagogue on the Sabbath according to his custom).
[93] Loader, *Jesus' Attitude towards the Law,* 312.

Sabbath should be observed in his presence. In the Lukan horizon, the question of recognizing Jesus' lordship always stands more in the foreground than the issue of Sabbath keeping proper, which Luke does not oppose. The main reproach Luke holds against non-believing Jews in Jesus, in this case, *some* (not all) Pharisees, concerns their failure to recognize the messianic authority of Jesus that grants the right to his first disciples – those in the physical presence of their master – to suspend momentarily the Sabbath during a moment of physical need. To refuse alleviating such hunger may even constitute for Luke a "fast" – an unacceptable physical state to experience on the Sabbath, especially in the presence of the messianic bridegroom.[94] As long as the bridegroom is present, it is unfitting for Jesus' followers to experience any hunger or physical suffering, especially on the Sabbath day. "The days will come" though "when the bridegroom will be taken away from them, and then they will fast in those days" (5:35). After the death of Jesus, many disciples of Jesus began to fast, some on a weekly basis.[95] In the physical absence of their lord, some of Jesus' disciples "reverted" to upholding more conventional customs observed by other Jews. We should be careful, therefore, not to over-interpret this unique episode in Luke concerning a one-time incident that occurred in Jesus' physical presence as reflecting *Luke's* Sabbath praxis. It could well be that Luke understands this story more as an "anecdote" illustrating Jesus' authority during his earthly ministry than as an example to be emulated as far as Sabbath keeping is concerned. But even if this text does inform us about Luke's stance on Sabbath keeping, at best, it only provides a license to bypass the Sabbath in exceptional cases such as alleviating human hunger.

Excursus: Why Is Mark 2:27 Missing in Matthew and Luke?

Up until now, the most conspicuous variation to Mark's version on the plucking controversy, namely, the Matthean and Lukan deletion (?) of Mark 2:27, has not been addressed. Mark 2:27 declares: "the sabbath was made for humankind, and not humankind for the sabbath" (τὸ σάββατον διὰ τὸν ἄνθρωπον ἐγένετο καὶ οὐχ ὁ ἄνθρωπος διὰ τὸ σάββατον). The first part of this logion makes a positive statement, followed by an antithetical

---

[94] Fasting on the Sabbath is already forbidden in *Jub.* 50:13. Jodi Magness, *Stone and Dung, Oil and Spit: Jewish Daily Life in the Time of Jesus* (Grand Rapids, Mich.: Eerdmans. 2011), 90–96, however, argues that some Jews fasted on the Sabbath during the Second Temple period.

[95] See especially *Did.* 8:1. Cf. *Did.* 1:3; 7:4; Acts 13:2, 3; 14:23; *2 Clem.* 16:4; *Mart. Pol.* 7:2.

phrase in the second part of the sentence. A host of scholars accepts this logion as an authentic saying going back to the historical Jesus.⁹⁶ Originally, the saying appears to have emphasized the subordination of the Sabbath as a tool for the benefit of Jews, not its abrogation.⁹⁷ As an authentic Jesus saying, its primary addressees would have been Jews, not Gentiles, since Jesus' ministry was mainly directed to the house of Israel. The usage of terms such as "ἐγένετο" ("was made" or "became") and "ἄνθρωπος" ("human")⁹⁸ may echo the language of creation found in Genesis,⁹⁹ although Jesus would not have employed such terminology to formulate a universal statement about the pertinence of the Sabbath for Gentiles *à la* Philo (*Opif.* 89). The usage of the terms "humankind" or "any human" in connection with the Sabbath can appear even in the most exclusive works such as the book of *Jubilees* without addressing Gentiles in any way.¹⁰⁰ It is possible, however, that at the Markan level Gentile followers of Jesus applied this verse universally, viewing the Sabbath as a beneficial institution for all of humankind, not only Jews.¹⁰¹

Statements bearing a similar syntactic structure appear in Jewish literature such as 2 Macc 5:19: "But the Lord did not choose the nation for the sake of the holy place, but the place for the sake of the nation."¹⁰² A re-

---

⁹⁶ See Doering, *Schabbat,* 414–16 and especially F. Neirynck, "Jesus and the Sabbath. Some Observations on Mk II, 27," in *Jésus aux origines de la christologie* (ed. Jacques Dupont; BETL 40; Leuven/Louvain: Leuven University Press, 1975), 227–70, for references.

⁹⁷ Doering, *Schabbat,* 416 refers to it as a "Vorordnung des Menschen vor den Sabbat und Einordnung des Sabbat als eine dem Menschen dienende Institution." Back, *Jesus of Nazareth and the Sabbath Commandment*, 96–101, remains very pessimistic regarding the actual meaning of the dictum, since we do not have the original context for interpreting this "free-floating logion."

⁹⁸ Following the NRSV, I translate the Greek noun ἄνθρωπος with the gender inclusive "human," although the English word is misleading since it conveys a universal notion to the saying that is foreign to its original, exclusive thrust and context.

⁹⁹ Cf. John 1:3, 10; Heb 1:2; 11:3; Col 1:16. See also the LXX of Gen 2:4; Exod 34:20; Isa 48:7.

¹⁰⁰ See Doering, *Schabbat,* 418 n. 117: "Auch im Jub, das die Exklusivität der Sabbatbeobachtung Israels hervorhebt, gibt es Formulierungen wie 'Mensch' oder 'alles Flesch,' wobei stets die Zughörigkeit zum Volk Israel vorausgesetzt wird. Eine universalistische Interpretation des Sabbats ist für Jesus nicht erkennbar." See also Doering, *Schabbat,* 64 n. 104, commenting on *Jub.* 2:28 ("every man") and 2:30 ("any human"), which appear in reference to the Sabbath but clearly envisage its observance as relevant only for *Israel*.

¹⁰¹ Weiss, *A Day of Gladness,* 95, adopts a universal interpretation without distinguishing the redactional level of the saying from its original Palestinian setting.

¹⁰² *2 Bar.* 14:18: "And you said that you would make a man for this world as a guardian over your works that it should be known that he was not created for the world, but the world for him." 1 Cor 11:8–9: "Neither was man created for the sake of woman, but

markably similar claim to Mark 2:27 appears in Tannaitic literature: "To you the Sabbath is handed over, and you are not handed over to the Sabbath."[103] As with the Markan logion, the rabbinic saying also deals with Sabbath praxis and provides room for breaking the Sabbath under special circumstances such as circumcision or saving human life. However, unlike Mark, the rabbinic passage does not state that the Sabbath was *made* (ἐγένετο)[104] but *handed* (מסורה) to Israel. In addition, the rabbinic logion, at least as it appears in this section of the *Mekilta*, is exegetically connected to Exod 31:13 and 14, which explicitly refer to the Sabbath as a covenantal sign between Israel and God, taking the reader back to Sinai rather than creation.[105] Thus, the dictum in Mark points back to (restored) creation, while the rabbinic saying echoes covenantal language and the bestowal of the Torah at Sinai. Nevertheless, both sayings, within their original respective horizons, share the same presupposition regarding Sabbath observance as being incumbent upon the Jewish people only.[106] Finally, both sayings naturally assume an ongoing obligation for Jews to keep the Sabbath with neither statement declaring its abrogation. Instead both say-

---

woman for the sake of man" (καὶ γὰρ οὐκ ἐκτίσθη ἀνὴρ διὰ τὴν γυναῖκα ἀλλὰ γυνὴ διὰ τὸν ἄνδρα).

[103] *Mek.* Ki Tissa-Shabbeta Parashah 1: לכם שבת מסורה ואי אתם מסורין לשבת. Translation mine. Cf. *b. Yoma* 85b.

[104] Mayer-Haas, *Geschenk,* 167, states that despite the allusion to Gen 1 the verb ἐγένετο should not be translated in Mark 2:27 as "created," since references to the *creation* of the Sabbath are rare in Jewish literature. Admittedly, the verb γίγνεσθαι is occasionally used in the LXX as one of the verbs to express creation, though ποιεῖν and κτίζειν are more common. In Mark 2:27, ἐγένετο refers in general terms to the emergence of humanity and the Sabbath on the cosmic scene. Mark 2:27 uses neither κτίζειν nor ποιεῖν in reference to the creation of the Sabbath, even though it alludes to the Genesis creation account(s). See, however, *Midr. Psalms* 92 where the Sabbath is created (נברא).

[105] Doering, "Sabbath Laws," 217 n. 46 is unsure whether the saying at is appears in the *Mekilta* refers to the revelation of the Torah on Mount Sinai, since elsewhere the *Mekilta* employs מסר with the Sabbath without relating it to the bestowal of the Torah at Sinai.

[106] Doering, *Schabbat,* 418. As in the case with the logion found in Mark 2:27, Doering points out that the rabbinic language of the dictum, "the Sabbath is committed to your hands, not you to its hands," was not coined originally out of concern for Gentiles encroaching upon the sacred established relationship between Israel and Sabbath. Instead it stresses the priority of the people of Israel over the Sabbath. Nevertheless, the rabbinic formulation of the saying seems to presuppose the exclusive duty of Sabbath keeping for Israel alone. Thus, in *Mek.* Ki Tissa-Shabbeta Parashah 1, commenting upon the phrase in Exodus 31:13 ("it is a sign between you and me"), the *Mekilta* adds "and not between me and the nations of the world." For a further discussion on Sabbath keeping and Gentiles in Second Temple and rabbinic passages, see Isaac W. Oliver, "Forming Jewish Identity by Formulating Legislation for Gentiles," *JAJ* 4 (2013): 105–32.

ings plead to show understanding in certain circumstances when the Sabbath needs to be temporarily suspended.[107]

Certain Gentiles, however, with little knowledge about the Jewish background of such a saying could have easily misunderstood its content and interpreted it to mean that humans can override the Sabbath in any circumstances, à volonté. By applying a Greek, "humanistic" reading to the Markan logion, these Gentiles could make humankind the sovereign measuring yardstick for determining how the Sabbath should be observed. Such a humanistic perspective could in the end even call for the complete dismantlement of the Sabbath institution. The *Homo-Mensura* saying, ascribed to the pre-Socratic philosopher Protagoras, expresses this anthropocentric worldview: "Of all things the measure is man, of the things that are, that they are, and of the things that are not, that they are not."[108] In addition to transforming humans into the measure of all things, another saying, also ascribed to Protagoras, tends to relativize ethical situations, submitting them to further subjective human interpretation: "Although no one opinion is truer than another, one opinion may be better than another."[109] Such a relativistic, anthropocentric worldview, which grants humans considerable autonomy, could displace the theocentric orientation of Jesus' saying and promote an uncontrollable laxity toward Sabbath keeping that could eventually lead to its complete abandonment.[110]

Both Matthew and Luke may have deleted the saying in Mark in order to avoid such misunderstandings.[111] Alternative proposals, however, abound to account for the mysterious absence of the Markan logion in the gospels of Matthew and Luke. Some commentators prefer a textual-critical suggestion: the absence of the saying in Matthew and Luke belongs to a

---

[107] Mayer-Haas, *Geschenk*, 169: "Mk 2,27 selbst hat wie die Mekhilta zu Ex 31, 14 die Funktion, für eine sehr liberale Auslegung des Sabbatruhegebotes zu plädieren: Es handelt sich hier nicht um Halacha, sondern um ein Plädoyer." Cf. Doering, "Sabbath Laws," 217.

[108] Sextus Empiricus, *Adv. math.* 7:60: πάντων χρημάτων μέτρον ἐστὶν ἄνθρωπος, τῶν μὲν ὄντων ὡς ἔστιν, τῶν δὲ οὐκ ὄντων ὡς οὐκ ἔστιν. See also Plato's *Theaetetus* 152A. Cf. Francis Wright Beare, "The Sabbath Was Made for Man?" *JBL* 79 (1960): 32, who claims that Mark 2:27 "sounds more like Protagoras of Abdera." This is not entirely true, given the Jewish parallels highlighted above. See also Félix Gils, "Le sabbat a été fait pour l'homme," *RB* 69 (1962): 516–21.

[109] Cited in W. K. C. Guthrie, *The Greek Philosophers from Thales to Aristotle* (New York: Harper & Row, 1975), 69.

[110] Mayer-Haas, *Geschenk*, 165.

[111] Mayer-Haas, *Geschenk*, 171, thinks that Mark already tried to avoid this anthropocentric, lax reading of the saying by including the christological statement in 2:28: the Son of Man, that is, Christ, becomes the final authority for determining Sabbath observance, which remains in full force. Cf. Davies and Allison, *The Gospel According to Matthew*, 2:315.

number of so-called "minor agreements" between both gospels, indicating that both synoptic authors either used two different sources when composing this section[112] or had a different version of Mark at their disposal.[113] Some find this proposal of an additional source to the Markan episode superfluous and unnecessary, as many of the minor agreements between Matthew and Luke in this pericope can allegedly be accounted for as resulting from independent redaction designed to improve the language and thread of Mark's prose.[114] One also wonders why both Matthew and Luke would prefer the version of a hypothetical second source that would not have contained the saying found in Mark 2:27 to the Markan one. Finally, a Deutero-Markan hypothesis raises several perplexing questions regarding the development and formation of the Markan pericope.[115]

---

[112] Hans Hübner, *Das Gesetz in der synoptischen Tradition: Studien zur These einer progressiven Qumranisierung und Judaisierung innerhalb der synoptischen Tradition* (2d ed.; Göttingen: Vandenhoeck & Ruprecht, 1986), 117–19. According to Back, *Jesus of Nazareth and the Sabbath Commandment*, 73, Matthew and Luke used a parallel tradition that does not necessarily stem from Q.

[113] Aichinger, "Quellenkritische Untersuchung der Perikope vom Ährenraufen am Sabbat," 141–53; Andreas Ennulat, *Die "Minor Agreements": Untersuchungen zu einer offenen Frage des synoptischen Problems* (WUNT 62; Tübingen: Mohr Siebeck, 1994), 84.

[114] Some of the salient minor agreements between Matt and Luke in this pericope include: the absence of Mark's ὁδὸν ποιεῖν (Mark 2:23); the inclusion of ἐσθίειν (Matt 12:1) or ἤσθιον (Luke 6:1), εἶπαν and εἶπεν (Matt 12:2, 3; Luke 6:2, 3); the placement of ὃ οὐκ ἔξεστιν (Matt 12:2; Luke 6:2) before the word, "Sabbath"; the absence of χρείαν ἔσχεν (Mark 2:25) and the erroneous name and designation of Abiathar as high priest (Mark 2:26); the placement of ὁ υἱὸς τοῦ ἀνθρώπου at the end of the sentence in Matt 12:8 and Luke 6:5. Mayer-Haas, *Geschenk*, 306–7, thinks these similarities between Matthew and Luke result from independent redactional efforts. For example, the difficult "ὁδὸν ποιεῖν" has been erased because it complicates the interpretation of the text and is superfluous. Moreover, both Matthew and Luke may have wanted to avoid the impression that Jesus and his followers were travelling on the Sabbath. The common replacement of the aorist for the imperfect is also understandable from a narrative standpoint, given the one-time occurrence of the event. Matthew and Luke also remove the superfluous χρείαν ἔσχεν for stylistic reasons. The repositioning of ὃ οὐκ ἔξεστιν before "the Sabbath" clarifies the halakic issue at stake, eliminating the potential misunderstanding that the disciples committed an act forbidden on any weekday (see introduction above to section on Matt 12). The joint deletion of Abiathar is understandable: both Matthew and Luke know that this figure is not the correct priest in the Nob story. Finally, the repositioning of "the Son of Man" at the beginning of the final sentence stresses the christological dimension so dear to Matthew and Luke.

[115] Most scholars view the present form of the story in Mark 2:23–28 as a multi-layered pericope. One model suggests that Mark 2:25 f. and v. 28 are secondary additions, while 2:23, 24, 27 (and sometimes v. 28) are seen as traditional. So, Mayer-Haas, *Geschenk*, 307, 173–75. If so, Mark 2:27 could not have been added later into the Markan text, but would have been known to Matthew and Luke. A second model views 2:23–26

In the case of the gospel of Matthew, some suggest that Matthew prefers to appeal to Hos 6:6 (the argument of mercy) rather than the Markan saying because the former finds its basis in the Jewish scriptures.[116] Others opine that Matthew and Luke detect a *non sequitur* in Mark's text that could potentially detract from the unique claim of authority ascribed to the Son of Man over the Sabbath.[117] After all, it does not logically follow that Jesus, as Son of Man, is the lord of the Sabbath, if the preceding verse in Mark already announces its subordination to all of humanity. This supposed incoherence in Mark – humans rule over the Sabbath, "therefore" ("ὥστε") the Son of Man is also lord of the Sabbath – may have bothered both Matthew and Luke, leading them to remove the saying in Mark 2:27 from their texts. This suggestion, however, seems unlikely. The ὥστε and the καὶ in Mark 2:28 can just as easily be pointing back to 2:10 in order to show that the Son of Man has authority on earth to forgive sins and is lord of the Sabbath.[118]

Others point to the christological dimension both Matthew and Luke wish to highlight in this pericope: Jesus' authority as Son of Man ultimately determines how his followers observe the Sabbath in his presence. Both Matthew and Luke deem the christological argument to be the final and decisive criterion for dealing with controversies about Sabbath keeping. They therefore leave out the saying in Mark 2:27 in order to underline this christological dimension. There is, of course, no denying the centrality Jesus' messianic authority plays in *all* three synoptic writings. Consequently, this christological proposal inadequately accounts for Matthew and Luke's mutual deletion of Mark 2:27. In his version of the Sabbath dispute over plucking grain, Matthew inserts other arguments besides the christological one to strengthen his case, while even Luke supplies in his numerous other episodes about Jesus' Sabbath keeping rationalizations of a

---

as traditional, while vv. 27–28 were added later since they focus more on the person of Jesus and his role in a post-Easter context. So, for example, Collins, *Mark*, 201. The logion of 2:27, however, is not christological in itself and even enjoys Jewish parallels in form and content. Moreover, one would have to account for Matthew and Luke's inclusion of Mark 2:28 without 2:27 if indeed these two sayings were already combined as a couplet. One solution would be to posit that the redactor of the alleged Deutero-Markan text deleted v. 27 before it became available to Matthew and Luke. Such a variant, however, is not attested in any of the extant textual witnesses to Mark.

[116] Mello, *Evangelo secondo Matteo*, 221–22. Cf. John Nolland, *The Gospel of Matthew: A Commentary on the Greek Text* (NIGTC; Grand Rapids, Mich.: Eerdmans, 2005), 485.

[117] R. T. France, *The Gospel of Matthew* (NICNT; Grand Rapids, Mich.: Eerdmans, 2007), 462.

[118] Boyarin, *The Jewish Gospels*, 68; Loader, *Jesus' Attitude towards the Law*, 35.

halakic and ethical type that have little to do with Christology in order to justify Jesus' orientation toward the Sabbath.

Weiss has offered yet another explanation for the deletion of the Markan saying. First, he understands Mark 2:27 in universal terms:

> It stresses the gift of the Sabbath to humanity. Given the general openness to the Gentiles in the Gospel of Mark, it is quite possible that the author fully intended the universalistic thrust of the saying. This would indicate that the Jewish disagreements as to whether or not a Gentile could keep the Sabbath were somewhat familiar to the Christians. Here Mark is making a strong statement in favor of the universality of the Sabbath as a gift of God. It is clearly intended against those who would restrict its benefits exclusively to the Jews.[119]

Weiss suggests the universalistic thrust of the logion in Mark may have prevented both Matthew and Luke from reproducing it.[120] Weiss' proposal is intriguing, but why would an author like Luke, or even Matthew, with his so-called Great Commission to the Gentiles, discourage or even oppose Gentile observance of the Sabbath? Did the synoptic authors expect Gentiles to keep the Sabbath? I return to this matter later on this book, maintaining that Matthew and Luke do not oppose spontaneous and voluntary adoption by Gentiles of Jewish customs such as the Sabbath though they do not *require* non-Jews to observe them. They leave this matter up to Gentile followers of Jesus to decide on their own. It is questionable, therefore, whether the universal dimension supposedly lurking behind the saying in Mark 2:27 led Matthew and Luke to omit it from their gospels.

Finally, other commentators, such as Saldarini, point to the direction hinted at the beginning of this section. Saldarini believes that Matthew has removed the Markan logion because of the potential laxity it could have promoted vis-à-vis Sabbath keeping: "Readers of Matthew might subordinate Sabbath observance to a variety of human needs and desires, and that would undermine its status as a divine commandment incumbent on Israel."[121] The current dichotomy that still separates Matthew the faithful "Jewish Christian" from Luke the Gentile universalist should not deter us from seriously considering the possibility that the latter has also removed the saying in Mark for similar reasons.[122] Luke, just as much as Matthew,

---

[119] Weiss, *A Day of Gladness*, 95.
[120] Weiss, *A Day of Gladness*, 95.
[121] Saldarini, *Matthew's Christian-Jewish Community*, 131.
[122] F. Vouga, *Jésus et la Loi selon la tradition synoptique* (Le Monde de la Bible; Geneva: Labor et Fides, 1988), 50–52, suggests that Luke omits Mark 2:27 because the Law is no longer a live issue for him. Why then does Luke have more disputes about the Sabbath than any other gospel? I find Vouga's position untenable because of the strong interest Luke shows in the Law throughout both of his writings, including issues related to purity, dietary laws, and circumcision.

may have sensed the potential misunderstandings about the Sabbath the saying in Mark could engender.[123]

In the end, no proposal absolutely accounts for the absence of Mark 2:27 in Matthew and Luke. Ultimately, all of the suggestions outlined above rely upon arguments *e silentio*. Admittedly, for both Matthew and Luke, the christological dimension constitutes the final and definitive justification for the behavior of Jesus' (Jewish) disciples on the Sabbath. Yet the appeal to the christological credentials of Jesus cannot be taken as evidence for the abrogation of the Sabbath on the part of either gospel author.[124] While it is impossible to prove beyond doubt that both synoptic cousins "corrected" their "younger" Markan peer for the potentially slippery slope he left in his text, in the end, both Matthew and Luke have crafted their texts in ways that do not warrant breaking the Sabbath whenever human fancy dictates.[125]

Conclusion

Matthew boasts a rich repertoire of arguments on behalf of the Sabbath praxis of Jesus and his first followers. When citing the biblical precedent about David's consumption of priestly bread, Matthew, more than Mark, highlights the disciples' hunger. He also draws an analogy between the priests who serve in the temple on the Sabbath and the conduct of Jesus'

---

[123] Klinghardt, *Gesetz und Volk Gottes,* 228; Mayer-Haas, *Geschenk,* 307–8; Bear, "The Sabbath Was Made for Man?" 134, who, nevertheless, proceeds to state that the followers of Jesus did not keep the Sabbath. See Neirynck, "Jesus and the Sabbath. Some Observations on Mk II, 27," 241 n. 48, for further references. Wolter, *Das Lukasevangelium*, 235, however, prefers the christological argument, and rejects Mayer-Haas' reading as well as the deutero-Markan hypothesis. For him, the immediate juxtaposition of David and Jesus creates an *argumentum a comparatione* ("if David…how much more Jesus").

[124] Wolter, *Das Lukasevangelium*, 235: "Dass der Sabbat vom Menschensohn 'abgeschafft' ist, sagt Lukas nicht."

[125] Boyarin, *The Jewish Gospels,* 66, links Mark 2:27 with the David story in the following way to account for Matthew and Luke's deletion of the verse: "In short my suggestion is that a set of controversy arguments in favor of allowing violation of the Sabbath for healing (now an accepted practice) has been overlaid with and radicalized by a further apocalyptic moment suggested by the very connection with David's behavior. The David story itself can go either way. Just as the Rabbis chose to emphasize David's hunger and thus the life-saving aspect of the story, justifying other breaches of the law if a life can be saved (Palestinian Talmud Yoma 8:6, 45b), so did Matthew; Mark, by contrast, understanding the story as being about the special privileges of the Messiah, pushed it in the direction that he did. On this account, the reason for the absence of v. 27 in Matthew (and Luke) is that Mark's messianic theology was a bit too radical for the later evangelists."

disciples who, according to Matthew, abide in a reality greater than the temple itself. Finally, he cites an additional verse from scripture (Hos 6:6) to plea with his opponents to show mercy on the Sabbath in light of the unique circumstances affecting Jesus' disciples. A rich and robust portfolio indeed that combines halakic and christological argumentation.

Some take Luke's terse retelling of the same episode as an indication that he is no longer interested in the question of Torah observance. This is unlikely, since Luke includes three more disputes about Sabbath keeping – more Sabbath controversies than any other gospel. He saves his ammunition for subsequent episodes in his narrative. However, even below Luke's succinct retelling of this first Sabbath controversy lies a remarkably dense argumentation. Thus, the citation of the biblical precedent involving David substantiates the action of Jesus' disciples in a threefold way: it points back to scripture; it singles out the exceptional circumstances affecting both parties (hunger); it solicits a great figure from Israel's past, king David. In fact, the absence of Mark 2:27 in Luke's text encourages the reader to draw an immediate correlation between the figures of king David and Jesus the messiah. Luke, however, does not deploy the christological argument to make a generalizing claim announcing the abrogation of the Sabbath. He calls upon the authority of Jesus only to advocate a temporary breach with the Sabbath for the sake of alleviating human hunger. Finally, as suggested above, it is not entirely clear whether in Luke's eyes this episode functions as a model to be emulated, stipulating how Jewish followers of Jesus should observe the Sabbath. The story especially seeks to magnify Jesus' authority.

Chapter 4

Healing on the Sabbath

"And so Rabban Shimon ben Gamaliel would say: 'The House of Shammai says that one does not provide charity to the poor on the Sabbath in the synagogue even to marry an orphan boy and an orphan girl, and one does not negotiate a marriage between a husband and a wife, and one does not pray for the sick on the Sabbath. And the House of Hillel permits."
(*T. Shabb.* 16:22)[1]

Introduction

This chapter analyzes all of the remaining Sabbath controversies in the gospels of Matthew and Luke. All the disputes assessed here revolve around the issue of performing healings on the Sabbath. The ailments Jesus cures, as I will argue throughout this chapter, are of a non-fatal type. In other words, Matthew and Luke do not view them as life-threatening. My aim, therefore, is to assess how both synoptic authors go about justifying Jesus' actions, since some Jews would have opposed performing healings of this type on the Sabbath. I maintain that Luke offers an argumentation on behalf of Jesus' Sabbath praxis that is just as sustained, sophisticated, and Jewish as Matthew's presentation of this topic. The fact that Luke reports no less than three disputes about Jesus' healings, compared to Matthew's single report about the healing of a man suffering from a withered hand, shows that the question of Sabbath keeping and the Jewish Law in general remain important for him.

Healing the Withered Hand: Matt 12:9–14

Literary Context

Both Matthew and Luke follow Mark in including another clash over Sabbath keeping between Jesus and the Pharisees, which they place right after

---

[1] Translation mine.

the plucking of grain incident. Matthew links both episodes more closely than Mark by indicating that Jesus entered into a synagogue straight after leaving the grainfields: "he left that place (i.e., the grainfields) and entered their synagogue" (12:9).[2] In this way, Matthew conveys the impression that this new episode takes place on the same Sabbath as a sequel to the previous controversy over plucking grain.[3] By more tightly relating both pericopes, Matthew encourages reading the second incident in similar ways to the preceding one: the second episode builds upon the former, further demonstrating Jesus' application of the programmatic statement on rest announced in 11:25–30. In addition, the following episode, like the preceding Sabbath controversy, does not deal with a life-threatening situation but further develops the rationale for a particular orientation that warrants temporarily suspending the Sabbath in order to relieve human suffering.[4]

Analysis

Whereas Mark simply states that Jesus "entered the synagogue," Matthew specifies, once again, that Jesus entered *their* synagogue, signaling his sustained effort of demarcation and possible alienation from Pharisaic control and space.[5] According to Matthew, the Pharisees immediately

---

[2] As noted in the previous chapter, all Sabbath controversies in the synoptic gospels focus on Jesus' healings with the exception of the incident of the plucking of grain. Form critics such as Theissen have classified the following controversy over healing on the Sabbath as a "rule miracle," that is, a miracle story used to reinforce sacred prescriptions, in this case, the justification of the divine prescription to do good on the Sabbath. See Gerhard Theissen, *The Miracle Stories of the Early Christian Tradition* (trans. Francis McDonagh; Edinburgh: T&T Clark, 1983), 106. Tannehill, "Varieties of Synoptic Pronouncement Stories," 107, places the healing of the withered hand under the rubric of "objection stories," which brings it close to Bultmann's "controversy stories." Bultmann includes the story in his section of apophthegms containing a conflict/didactic saying occasioned by Jesus' healing. See Bultmann, *History of the Synoptic Tradition*, 12, 48. Bultmann firmly believes that the formation of such material took place in the "Palestinian Church," which formulated these healing stories in order to defend a particular Sabbath conduct. Bultmann maintains this is true even if the criticism in such stories is launched at Jesus rather than his followers, for the healing stories at the same time are meant to glorify him (48).

[3] Mark 3:1 states that Jesus went *again* into the synagogue, taking the reader's attention back to Mark 1:21 when Jesus entered the synagogue of Capernaum on a previous Sabbath. Likewise, Mark 3:1 states "and a man was there" (καὶ ἦν ἐκεῖ ἄνθρωπος), which matches Mark 1:23 (καὶ εὐθὺς ἦν ἐν τῇ συναγωγῇ αὐτῶν ἄνθρωπος). These features are the result of redactional activity. See Collins, *Mark*, 206.

[4] Cf. Frankemölle, *Matthäus*, 2:134.

[5] Luz, *Matthew*, 2:187, understands the possessive pronoun in a general sense as representing the synagogue of the Jews. Frankmölle, *Matthäus*, 2:135, argues that the pronoun refers here to the synagogue of the Pharisees. Cf. Runesson, "Rethinking Early

confront Jesus with their halakic reasoning, questioning the legitimacy of healing minor diseases on the Sabbath. Initially, their inquiry seems to provide a scholastic-legal flair to the entire pericope, as if the entire Matthean episode was merely recounting a halakic debate about a particular legal matter from the Torah, in this case healing on the Sabbath.[6] But little room for a fair debate between both parties is left in such stories that were primarily designed to exalt the authority of a particular figure above the caricatured and vilified attitude of the opponents. Thus, Matthew never grants the Pharisees an opportunity to voice their opinion about Jesus' reasoning and actions. A hostile atmosphere reigning over both parties persists throughout the pericope: the Pharisees supposedly raise their question only in order to find a way of accusing Jesus (v. 10: κατηγορήσωσιν). Their malevolent motives anticipate the end of the episode where Matthew, following Mark, claims that the Pharisees conspire together to get rid of Jesus (v. 14).[7]

As in the previous Sabbath dispute, Matthew seems unsatisfied with the rationale provided by Mark for justifying Jesus' Sabbath healing. According to the gospel of Mark, after curing the man with a withered hand in the synagogue, Jesus simply asks his opponents whether it is "lawful to do good or to do harm on the sabbath, to save life or to kill" (3:4). In the gospel of Matthew, however, Jesus presents a different type of question and argument: "Suppose one of you has only one sheep and it falls into a pit on the sabbath; will you not lay hold of it and lift it out?" (Matt 12:11) Matthew's Jesus then appends an *a fortiori* argument to his rhetorical

---

Jewish Christian Relations," 95–132, who maintains that Matthew envisages synagogues of Pharisaic association. France, *Gospel of Matthew,* 463, claims that "their synagogue" refers in this case to the synagogue in Capernaum.

[6] Davies and Allison, *The Gospel according to Matthew,* 2:328; Hummel, *Auseinandersetzung,* 44–45; Loader, *Jesus' Attitude towards the Law,* 205; Saldarini, *Matthew's Christian-Jewish Community,* 132. In Mark 3:2, the opponents watch to see if Jesus will do something wrong. In Matt 12:10, the Pharisees ask whether it is lawful (ἔξεστιν) to heal on the Sabbath. This formulation further links both Sabbath dispute stories in Matthew (Matt 12:2: οὐκ ἔξεστιν).

[7] See Davies and Allison, *The Gospel according to Matthew*, 2:318–19. Neither Matthew nor Luke contains the curious Markan reference to Pharisees and *Herodians* conspiring with each other against Jesus (Mark 3:6). At the narrative level, their conspiracy anticipates the passion of Jesus. Accusations, however, against Jesus' alleged Sabbath violations do not rise during his final trial in the synoptic tradition. Likewise, Pharisees are completely absent in the passion narratives, save for one incident in Matthew (27:62–66) that was surely generated by post-paschal polemics. The chief priests, Sadducees, and other Jerusalem authorities, along with the Romans, appear in the synoptics as the culprits responsible for Jesus' death, not the Pharisees. Yang, *Jesus and the Sabbath,* 209–14, insinuates that the Pharisees truly did conspire against Jesus' life because of his Sabbath keeping. From a historical point of view, such a position is untenable.

question: "How much more valuable is a human being than a sheep! So it is lawful to do good on the sabbath" (12:12). Only the last statement of Matt 12:12, ἔξεστιν τοῖς σάββασιν καλῶς ποιεῖν, parallels Mark's ἔξεστιν τοῖς σάββασιν ἀγαθὸν ποιῆσαι, although Matthew's statement appears postpositively as a conclusion to an argument (introduced by ὥστε), while Mark employs similar wording to initiate Jesus' rhetorical question.[8] Matthew's deployment of the *a fortiori* argument was already noted in the previous pericope where Jesus points to "something" greater than the temple entering into the historical-social sphere of Israel (12:6). The repetition of the *a fortiori* argument provides further symmetry to both pericopes and becomes the favorite form of argumentation deployed by Matthew in such settings.

The "medical" diagnosis in Matt 12:10 describes the person as suffering from a "withered hand" (χεῖρα ξηράν). The adjective ξηρός ("dry") can refer to physical conditions affecting humans and is translated variously in English with such terms as "withered," "lean," "haggard," "shrunken," or "paralyzed."[9] In this instance, "hand" probably denotes *pars pro toto* "arm."[10] In the LXX of 1 Kgs 13:4, Jeroboam's hand temporarily dried up (ἐξηράνθη) when he stretched it out (ἐξέτεινεν) to harm one of God's prophets. As a result of this divine punishment, Jeroboam was unable to move his hand (οὐκ ἠδυνήθη ἐπιστρέψαι αὐτήν).[11] In Matt 12:13, divine action reverses the paralyzing effects of such a condition. Jesus commands

---

[8] Probably the phrase καλῶς ποιεῖν should not be translated as "do good" but "do well," since καλῶς is adverbial. This phrase appears in the LXX as a translation for להיטיב. See Mayer-Haas, *Geschenk*, 452 n. 203; Doering, "Sabbath Laws," 236. Eric Ottenheijm, "Genezen als goed doen. Halachische logica in Mt 12, 9–14," *Bijdr* 63.3 (2002): 356–65, ties this adverbial phrase with the rabbinic category מעשים טובים ("good deeds"). For Ottenheijm, the Matthean approach follows the ethos of the House of Hillel: whereas the House of Shammai would oppose giving alms to the poor in the synagogue, matchmaking, and praying for the sick on the Sabbath, the House of Hillel would approve such practices (*t. Shabb.* 16 [17]:22). In a parallel passage, *b. Shabb.* 12a, such acts are known as "deeds of loving kindness" (גמילות חסדים) and belong to the category of "good deeds." Ottenheijm sees the healing in Matthew as relieving the man from his poverty and misery thereby unveiling how Jesus' act exemplifies the application of "good deeds" that are justifiable on the Sabbath. Even if Matthew does not couch Jesus' healing in nominal terms of "good deeds," he probably relates the adverbial καλῶς ποιεῖν with the concept of mercy previously mentioned in Matt 12:7. Ottenheijm's thesis is original and compelling.

[9] See "ξηρός," in *BDAG* and *LSJ*.

[10] Doering, "Sabbath Laws," 227; Mateos and Camacho, *El Evangelio*, 121: "En este contexto, donde el hombre ha de extenderlo (13), ha de interpretarse como 'brazo,' símbolo de la actividad."

[11] Cf. *T. Sim.* 2:12 where Simeon's "right hand was half withered for seven days" (ἡ χείρ μου ἡ δεξιὰ ἡμίξηρος ἦν ἐπὶ ἡμέρας ἑπτά) because of his anger toward his younger brother Joseph. Cf. LXX Hos 9:14; Zech 11:17; Mark 9:18; John 5:3.

the affected person to stretch out his hand (ἔκτεινόν σου τὴν χεῖρα). The immediate and obedient response of the man (καὶ ἐξέτεινεν) publicly confirms the efficacy of Jesus' healing powers and exalts his authority.

There is little indication in either Matthew or the other synoptic gospels that the physical ailment afflicting the man placed his life under jeopardy.[12] His disability, which impedes proper mobility, affects only *one* of the members of his body.[13] Presumably, from the perspective of the synoptic Pharisees, care for the man's hand can wait until another day, since his chronic condition presents no imminent health risks to his survival. Only this reading of the pericope, which presupposes the reticence among certain Jews to care for "minor" ailments on the Sabbath, adequately accounts from a halakic point of view for the Pharisees' objection voiced in the synoptics.[14] Despite the idealization of such stories, in my opinion, some historical and halakic credibility should be allotted to the opposition they recorded. Some, however, could argue that the *a fortiori* statement in Matthew would in fact point to a life-threatening situation. Does the *a fortiori* argument, after all, not construe an analogy between the life-

---

[12] Doering, "Sabbath Laws," 227; France, *Gospel of Matthew,* 464; Nolland, *The Gospel of Matthew,* 487.

[13] Mello, *Evangelo,* 220, cites the version of this story found in the *Gospel of the Hebrews,* which refers to the profession of the sick man, a stoneworker, in order to show how he is unable to make a living due to his condition. Mello argues that the condition afflicting the man affects not only his health but also his ability to bring bread to his house. The man is, therefore, unable to observe the positive aspect of Ex 20: 9–10 ("six days you shall labor") and enjoy the second part of the fourth commandment, namely, to rest on the seventh day. Cf. Luz, *Matthew*, 2:188–89.

[14] As noted in the introduction to chapter 2, an intimidating number of prominent scholars (to whom I owe a great deal of learning and respect) argue that Jesus did not perform any act contrary to the halakic conventions of his time. Thus, Flusser, *The Sage from Galilee,* 39, claims that "Jesus is never shown in conflict with current practice of the law." Similarly, E. P. Sanders and Margaret Davies, *Studying the Synoptic Gospels* (London: SCM, 1989), 157, conclude that the healing (at least in its Markan version) is superficial and artificial because saving human life would have been accepted among Pharisees. But does Mark view the situation of the man suffering from a withered hand as life-threatening? Similarly, Sanders, *Jesus and Judaism,* 266, states: "The Stories of healing on the Sabbath…also reveal no instance in which Jesus transgressed the Sabbath law." True, Jesus did not go against anything prohibited in the (written) Mosaic Torah. But what about contemporary halakah from the Second Temple Period? Cf. Vermes, *Jesus the Jew*, 25. Hyam Maccoby, *Early Rabbinic Writings* (vol. 3; Cambridge Commentaries on Writings of the Jewish and Christian World, 200 B.C. to A.D. 200; Cambridge: Cambridge University Press, 1988), 171, unconvincingly tries to show that these Sabbath controversies originally posited Jesus against the Sadducees. Later the *ekklesia* replaced the Sadducees with the Pharisees as the main opponents of Jesus. While most of these modern authors seem more concerned with uncovering the halakic stance of the historical Jesus, their comments prove equally pertinent for the consideration and understanding of the gospels at their redactional level.

threatening situation of a sheep caught in a pit with the supposedly and equally dangerous condition of the person suffering from a withered hand? For several reasons, however, this sort of analogical deliberation does not convince. First, Matthew seeks to justify in *broad* terms the right for Jesus to "do good" on the Sabbath rather than confine his compassionate intervention on the Sabbath only to situations where human life is under imminent danger. Thus, Matthew leaves out the Markan phrase ψυχὴν σῶσαι ("to save a life"; Mark 3:4), because he does not view the disability of the man as life-threatening. It should also be pointed out that an argument on behalf of saving life would have proven superfluous for many Jews of that time who accepted the priority of human life over against a strict observance of the Sabbath. Like the David story in the previous Sabbath controversy (Matt 12:3–4), Matthew's aim is not to construct an analogy of life-threatening proportions. He is not strictly comparing the life-threatening situation of a sheep caught in a pit with the chronic condition of a human suffering from a withered hand, just as he does not equate the life-threatening position David finds himself in with the circumstances of Jesus' disciples who are not running for their lives. Matthew, instead, solicits the practice of saving sheep on the Sabbath in order to show how humans should be *treated*: if certain Jews are willing on the Sabbath to save animals, then how much more should they deal with humans on the Sabbath with even greater care and sensibility. In other words, they should recognize Jesus' right to care on the Sabbath for less mitigating cases such as chronic illnesses, and, if we may draw from the previous pericope, to alleviate other physical needs such as human hunger.[15]

Moreover, Matthew may not even view the circumstances affecting the trapped sheep as imminently life-threatening. In contrast to Luke's version of the logion (14:5), which speaks of an animal trapped in a *well* (φρέαρ) – a life-threatening scenario indeed, depending on the depth of the waters – Matthew's form of the saying simply refers to a sheep caught in a *pit* (βόθυνον), suggesting that the sheep's life is not imminently at risk.[16] Consequently, some Jews, in this case, certain Pharisees, could legitimately maintain that the sheep be rescued only after the end of the Sabbath. Nevertheless, the sheep's owner, worried about the *damage* incurred upon his or her domestic property, might prove unwilling to delay the rescue until

---

[15] Saldarini, *Matthew's Christian-Jewish Community*, 132, argues that Matthew deems Mark's rhetorical question to be far too broad and imprecise. Since the crippled man is under no threat of dying, the principle of saving a life would not apply here. Rather we are dealing with a conflict between two principles of the Law: keeping the Sabbath and healing those in need. Cf. Segundo, *El Caso Mateo*, 66 f., for the development of Matthew's reasoning concerning this halakic and ethical dilemma.

[16] Nolland, *The Gospel of Matthew*, 488.

the following day. Matthew may be equating this concern for the sheep's welfare with Jesus' effort to relieve humans from their physical *affliction*. If this suggestion is correct, the *a fortiori* argumentation in Matthew seeks to convey the following point: if some Jews are ready to succor an animal on the Sabbath so as to prevent economic loss and thereby relieve the creature from its distress, how much more should they accept Jesus' right to relieve human suffering on the Sabbath.

Surprisingly, no Jewish text known to us from antiquity allows for lifting an animal out of a pit or well on the Sabbath.[17] Matthew's Jesus, however, seems to take this practice for granted, rhetorically addressing the issue to his opponents as if they would agree with his premises.[18] Were there any Jews in antiquity who would have helped domestic animals come out of a well or a pit on the Sabbath? The Damascus Document disapproves of such a practice, perhaps because some other Jews acted otherwise: "No one should help an animal give birth on the Sabbath; and if it falls into a well or a pit, he may not lift it out on the Sabbath" (CD 11:13–14).[19] A similar prohibition appears in 4Q265 (4QMisc Rules) 6:5–6: "Let no one raise up an animal which has fallen into the water on the Sabbath day."[20] Rabbinic tradition makes certain concessions on this issue. According to *t. Shabb.* 14:3, one can provide food for a domestic animal that has fallen into a well but may not actively seek to lift it out.[21] A similar and slightly more lenient view, which nevertheless falls short of permitting the direct hauling up of an animal on the Sabbath, appears in the Bavli: "If an animal falls into a dyke (אמת המים), one brings pillows and bedding and places [them] under it, and if it ascends it ascends" (*b. Shabb.* 128b).[22]

---

[17] Doering, *Schabbat*, 459; "Sabbath Laws," 231 f.

[18] Or is the Matthean Jesus addressing the crowd in the synagogue, who may share the same assumption, rather than the Pharisees?

[19] ואם תפיל <תפול> אל בור ואל פחת אל יקימה בשבת.

[20] אל יעל איש בהמה אשר תפול אל המים ביום שבת.

[21] בהמה שנפלה לתוך הבור עושין לה פרנסה במקומה בשביל שלא תמות.

[22] It should be pointed out that 4Q265 6:5–6, *t. Shabb.* 14[15]:3, and *b. Shabb.* 128b all discuss the scenario of an animal falling into a body of water, not a pit, which may or may not contain water. The scenario envisaged in these texts, therefore, is more severe than in Matthew, with an explicit concern, at least on the part of the rabbis, to save the life of the animal while safeguarding the sanctity of the Sabbath. Thus the fuller passage in *b. Shabb.* 128b reads: "Rab Judah said in Rab's name: If an animal falls into a dyke, one brings pillows and bedding and places [them] under it, and if it ascends it ascends. An objection is raised: If an animal falls into a dyke, provisions are made for it where it lies so that it should not perish. Thus, only provisions, but not pillows and bedding? – There is no difficulty: here it means where provisions are possible; there, where provisions are impossible. If provisions are possible, well and good; but if not, one brings pillows and bedding and places them under it. But he robs a utensil of its readiness [for use]? – [The avoidance of] suffering of dumb animals is a Biblical [law], so the Biblical

Because no known parallel from the extant sources corresponds to the presupposition voiced in Matthew, some modern interpreters attempt reading Matt 12:11 in such a way so as to conform it to rabbinic halakah. For example, Tomson claims that Matthew is not referring to the action of *lifting up* an animal out of a well, but is using "the exact halakhic expression that the animal may be *raised up*."²³ In other words, Matthew refers to the act of raising the animal to a *standing position*, or even placing some pillows and bedding under the animal to assist it in standing up, without going as far as pulling it out of the well. This is a clever reading, but applies too precise a halakic reading of rabbinic standards to a verse from Matthew that seems rather raw and generalizing in its halakic deliberation.²⁴ Such an interpretation of Matthew also grants too much credit to rabbinic sources and the documents discovered at Qumran as representing *all* of Jewish practice in Palestine during the first century CE. Moreover, the parallel saying to Matthew in Luke 14:5 does refer explicitly to the act of *lifting up* an animal out of a well, using the verb ἀνασπάσει ("draw" or "pull up") instead of Matthew's ἐγερεῖ.²⁵ Luke's choice of vocabulary does not reveal an ignorance about halakah due to his supposed Gentile background,²⁶ since 4Q265 6:5–6, which deals with the same scenario, also

---

law comes and supersedes the [interdict] of the Rabbis." As Doering points out, both the aforementioned passage from the Tosefta as well as the text from the Bavli advise the avoidance of actively hauling up a domestic animal on the Sabbath. See Doering, *Schabbat,* 459. Saldarini, *Matthew's Christian-Jewish Community,* 132–33, points to *t. Yom Tov* 3:2, which allows raising an animal on a festival day, as evidence that the matter of raising animals was not solved even one hundred years after Matthew. But the passage in the Tosefta discusses what one may do on a *festival day*, not the Sabbath proper. Rabbinic halakah tends to treat festival days more leniently than the Sabbath. See fuller discussion in chapter 5 treating the halakic problem involved in Jesus' burial supposedly occurring on a Passover falling right before a Sabbath.

²³ Tomson, *If This Be from Heaven,* 220; so also Eric Ottenheijm, "Genezen," 356.

²⁴ Doering notes that even the language in CD 11:13–14 אל יקימה ("he shall not lift it up") is ambiguous: does יקים (*hifil* third pers.) refer to "lifting out of" or only to "raising" an animal? Alternatively, should we read the verb in the *piel* form and translate it as "sustain," in conformance with the halakah in the *Tosefta* that allows one to supply food for the endangered animal without lifting it out of the well? See Doering, "Sabbath Laws," 233–34.

²⁵ See "ἀνασπάω," in *BDAG* and *LSJ*. The verb can be used to denote drawing water *out* of a well (Josephus, *Ant.* 2:259); to draw up with a hook (LXX Hab 1:15); to bring up and out of a den (LXX Dan 6:18); to draw one's sword *out* or *forth* (ἐκ χροὸς ἔγχος ἀνεσπάσατο; see references in *LSJ*). In Acts 11:10, the sheet Peter sees in his vision is drawn up to the sky (ἀνεσπάσθη εἰς τὸν οὐρανόν).

²⁶ Contra Tomson, *If This Be from Heaven,* 220: "Pulling up an animal is not, however, in keeping with the Jewish law, not even in the opinion of the later rabbis. On the other hand, in Matthew Jesus uses the exact halakhic expression that the animal may be *raised up* (Mt. 12.11). In comparison to this, 'Luke' betrays a lack of practical

refers to the act of lifting (יעל) an animal out of the water.²⁷ There is no need, therefore, to view Luke's formulation of the saying as a mistranslation or manifestation of his halakic ignorance, given the attestation in 4Q265. The usage of ἀνασπάσει in Luke 14:5 is perfectly understandable: the animal falls into a *well* (φρέαρ) rather than a (dry) pit (βόθυνον). It would only be natural for Luke to describe the act of lifting an animal *out* of the well, rather than merely raising it to a standing position, lest the creature drown in the water.²⁸

In conformance to the experiment adopted throughout this monograph, I suggest taking Matthew and Luke more seriously as retaining an alternative *Jewish* view regarding such matters.²⁹ Indeed, some suggest that Matt

---

knowledge of the Jewish law, in striking contrast to his otherwise so sympathetic attitude towards Jewry. *The author of Luke and Acts apparently did not have Pharisaic schooling and was probably not a Jew himself*"(emphasis Tomson's).

²⁷ The *hifil* of the verb עלה can denote bringing someone/something up and out of a lower place. Thus in Judg 5:13 some inhabitants from Judah bring Samson up from the rock (ויעלוהו מן־הסלע). Most unequivocal is the reference in Gen 37:28: "they drew Joseph up, *lifting him out of the pit*" (ויעלו את־יוסף מן־הבור). Cf. Ps 40:3; Jer 38:10, 13. See "עלה" in *HALOT* and *BDB*. In the LXX, the verb ἀνασπάω, which appears in Luke 14:5, can translate the *hifil* stem of the verb עלה. See, for example, Hab 1:15.

²⁸ Another attempt to conform Matthew's position with rabbinic halakah appears in Jan Joosten and Menahem Kister, "The New Testament and Rabbinic Hebrew," in *The New Testament and Rabbinic Literature*, 340–45, who suggest the Greek verb ἐγερεῖ in Matthew 12:11 would represent a mistranslation of a Hebrew *Vorlage* that contained the verb יקים, originally understood as a *piel* stem, meaning to "sustain," but misunderstood by the more commonly used *hifil* stem. This conjecture, however, reminiscent of the so-called Jerusalem School's preference for a Hebrew *Vorlage* to the synoptic tradition, goes against the "mainstream" assumption of positing an Aramaic substratum behind such sayings. Joosten and Kister also argue that in CD 11:14 אל יקימה (normally, translated as "he shall not lift it up") should be rendered "he should not sustain it." Most scholars, however, have understood יקים in CD 11:14 as a reference to lifting the animal out of the well. So Doering, *Schabbat,* 193–95; Florentino García Martínez and Eibert J.C. Tigchelaar, *The Dead Sea Scrolls Study Edition* (2 vols.; Brill: Leiden, 1997–1998), 1:569; Schiffman, *Halakhah,* 121 f.; Geza Vermes, *The Dead Sea Scrolls in English* (5th ed.; London: Penguin, 1997), 140.

²⁹ Cf. Frankemölle, *Matthäus*, 2:135. Yang, *Jesus and the Sabbath,* 203, who tends to accept the historicity of such controversy stories, suggests that Galilean Pharisees may have shared a more lenient view toward lifting animals out of wells/pits on the Sabbath, or that they did not object to other people performing such acts. If, however, the findings of form criticism are taking more seriously, it is understandable how such a logion may have loosely been reinserted into new and different contexts without a concern for accurately depicting the views of the opponents. It is indeed possible that most, or at least many, Pharisees would have objected to lifting an animal out of a well on the Sabbath. Gnilka, *Das Matthäusevangelium*, 1:448, suggests that Jesus' debate may be with more stringent Shammaites, but to the best of my knowledge no rabbinic passage alludes to a more lenient Hillelite position on this matter.

12:14 reflects a Palestinian rural custom embraced by poor Jewish farmers who were willing to save their animals on the Sabbath in order to prevent economic loss.[30] In line with this understanding, certain commentators favor reading "πρόβατον ἕν" in Matt 12:11 as "*one* sheep" rather than simply "*a* sheep," underscoring the poor economic conditions of Galilean farmers who for pragmatic reasons would have been more lax in this aspect of their Sabbath keeping.[31] There may even have been a biblical basis for such a practice, since passages such as Exod 23:5 and Deut 22:4 ordain helping an animal that is lying under a burden.[32]

These observations fit well with the overall concern Matthew shows for the "poor" (11:5), the "sick" (9:12; 11:5), and the "weary and heavy laden" (11:28). For Matthew, Jesus' healing of a sick and needy man is yet another manifestation of the rest promised to the weary and overburdened in 11:25–30. However, as in the previous case of the plucking of grain, Matthew's justification for Jesus' healing hardly translates into a full revoking of Sabbath observance. Matthew only defends Jesus' right on the Sabbath to intervene on behalf of the oppressed and suffering by combining an *a*

---

[30] Doering, *Schabbat*, 460; "Sabbath Laws," 234. Doering suggests that the argument in Matt 12:11 was directed at "Jewish Christians" in an inner-community debate over Sabbath practice, rather than at Pharisees, who, as far as the limited evidence allows, would not have consented with the presupposition voiced by Jesus in this passage. See Doering, *Schabbat,* 461. See also Luz, *Matthew*, 2:187, who makes an exegetical connection with the single sheep of the poor man mentioned in the "parable" of the prophet Nathan (2 Sam 12:3). Matthew is not condemning the Pharisees or the Jews for their supposed materialism, that is, being willing to save an animal to prevent economic loss, as some patristic (e.g., Jerome) and modern authors have claimed. Contra Mateos and Camacho, *El Evangelio,* 121 as well as Bonnard, *L'Évangile,* 176, following Adolf Schlatter, *Der Evangelist Matthäus* (2d ed.; Stuttgart: Calwer Verlag, 1933), 400: "Die traditionelle Ethik schätzte das Eigentum hoch, versagte dagegen dem Menschen die Liebe. Jesus dagegen schätzt den Menschen, nicht das Eigentum."

[31] Doering *Schabbat,* 461; Luz, *Matthew*, 187, claims that ἕν in Matthew is rarely used as an indefinite article, especially when placed *after* the noun as in Matt 12:14. Since Matthew refers to "seizing" (κρατήσει) one *sheep* (a small animal) rather than raising larger creatures such as cattle (בהמה; so CD; 4Q265, and rabbinic texts) with *instruments*, Martin Vahrenhorst, *"Ihr sollt überhaupt nicht schwören." Matthäus im halachischen Diskurs* (WMANT 95; Neukirchen-Vluyn: Neukirchener Verlag, 2002), 388 n. 33, suggests that Matthew presumes seizing a sheep with one's *hands*, an act that would presumably be permissible on the Sabbath. Once again, it is questionable whether Matthew is making such nuances, as he seems to be justifying a more "aggressive" breach with halakic practice. Unlike the rabbinic texts or CD, the phrasing in Matthew 12:11 seems to presuppose that "one *actively* takes the sheep out, i.e., that one does more than put padding and cushions under him" (Luz, *Matthew,* 187 n. 15).

[32] Cf. the aforementioned rabbinic passage from *b. Shabb.* 128b as well as *m. Shabb.* 18:2.

fortiori argument with a plea for showing mercy.³³ Once again, it seems that Matthew expands the boundaries of the concept known (in rabbinic literature) as פיקוח נפש to encompass the treatment of non-fatal illnesses.³⁴ According to Matthew, Jesus loosens but does not eliminate Sabbath restrictions. For example, he does not encourage Jews to earn their living or travel and take a cruise along the Mediterranean on the Sabbath (cf. Matt 24:20). Matthew's Jesus only loosens some aspects of Sabbath halakah in order to legitimize his right to bring eschatological rest by "doing well" (καλῶς ποιεῖν) and showing mercy (12:7) to the oppressed children of Israel.³⁵

Healing the Withered Hand: Luke 6:6–11

Analysis

Luke situates the healing incident on "another Sabbath" (ἐν ἑτέρῳ σαββάτῳ) instead of locating it like Matthew on the same Sabbath when Jesus' disciples pluck grain. This stylistic feature provides a greater sense of realism to the narrative, while simultaneously preserving a thematic link between both Sabbath pericopes. In general, Luke follows Mark's depiction of this incident, providing no further justification for Jesus' actions. Luke, however, opens the scene with Jesus *teaching* (διδάσκειν) in the synagogue, a pedagogical activity he enjoys mentioning when depicting the Sabbath praxis of the main protagonists in his two works, Jesus and Paul.³⁶ Luke also retains with some modification Mark's rhetorical question: "Is it lawful to do good or to do harm on the sabbath, to save life or to

---

³³ See Nolland, *The Gospel of Matthew*, 488, pointing to the comparison of humans with birds in Matt 6:26 ("Are you not of more value than they?") and Matt 10:31 ("you are of more value than many sparrows"). See also Mayer-Haas, *Geschenk*, 451.

³⁴ Doering, *Schabbat*, 453.

³⁵ Matthew's concept of "doing well," however, remains dramatically vague in its formulation and application. How does one concretely define and apply this principle in other cases? Cf. Bonnard, *L'Évangile,* 175: "…l'instruction du Christ matthéen apparaît à la fois libératrice et inquiétante; libératrice parce qu'elle subordonne toute pratique religieuse au service concret de l'homme dans la détresse; inquiétante car, généralisée, elle rendrait impossible toute vie d'Eglise organisée: il y a toujours un "bien" plutôt qu'un devoir religieux à accomplir." Cf. Loader, *Jesus' Attitude towards the Law*, 205.

³⁶ This leads Klinghardt, *Gesetz und Volkes Gottes*, 230, to suggest that the pericope is more concerned with Jesus' act of teaching than his healing activity, perhaps an exaggeration. Nevertheless, as I suggest at the conclusion to Part I, Luke may not have overly encouraged Jewish followers of Jesus to perform Sabbath healings, despite the multiple occurrences of such acts by Jesus in the gospel of Luke.

destroy it?" (Luke 6:9) But unlike in Mark, Luke's Jesus does not belligerently look at the surrounding Pharisees and scribes "with anger" because "he was grieved at their hardness of heart" (so Mark 3:5). In harmony with the more nuanced perspective on the Pharisees and their scribes in Luke, Jesus simply gazes "around them all" (6:10). Luke makes no mention of Jesus' anger (Mark 3:5: μετ' ὀργῆς) and grief over his adversaries' stubbornness and opposition (cf. Mark: συλλυπούμενος ἐπὶ τῇ πωρώσει τῆς καρδίας). Furthermore, Luke's Pharisees, though lacking *understanding* (ἀνοίας), do not conspire with each other in order to have Jesus *killed* (so Mark 3:6; Matt 12:14), but consider among themselves what they *might do with* or *about* him (6:11).[37]

Like the other synoptic authors, Luke does not claim that the life of the man suffering from a withered hand is in danger. In 6:1, however, Luke does specify that the afflicted man suffers from a disability on his *right* hand (ἡ χείρ αὐτοῦ ἡ δεξιά). In my opinion, this anatomical precision constitutes more than a literary element merely furnishing greater plausibility to the narrated scene.[38] Luke wishes to show that Jesus heals not just *any* random member of the human body, but the right hand, a bodily part essential for economic survival, particularly in an ancient society where most people earned their living through manual labor. In this way, Luke heightens the urgency and need for Jesus' intervention, seeking to present this Sabbath healing in more acceptable terms to those who might question its legitimacy.[39]

As noted above, Luke also preserves the central argument made by Mark's Jesus in the form of a rhetorical question:

Luke 6:9:
ἔξεστιν τῷ σαββάτῳ
ἀγαθοποιῆσαι ἢ κακοποιῆσαι,
ψυχὴν σῶσαι ἢ ἀπολέσαι;

Mark 3:4:
ἔξεστιν τοῖς σάββασιν
ἀγαθὸν ποιῆσαι ἢ κακοποιῆσαι,
ψυχὴν σῶσαι ἢ ἀποκτεῖναι;

The Lukan and Markan formulations of the saying are quite similar: the only changes involve Luke's shift of τοῖς σάββασιν to the singular τῷ σαββάτῳ, the "fusion" of ἀγαθὸν ποιῆσαι into ἀγαθοποιῆσαι, and the replacement of ἀποκτεῖναι ("to kill") with ἀπολέσαι ("to destroy"). The verb

---

[37] The Greek reads, τί ἂν ποιήσαιεν τῷ Ἰησοῦ, and is further discussed in the excursus below.
[38] Doering, "Sabbath Laws," 237.
[39] Wolter, *Das Lukasevangelium*, 237.

ἀπολέσαι, however, can also mean "to kill" or "to put to death."[40] The structure of the sentence resembles a *parallelismus membrorum*, in this case, a synonymous parallelism, characteristic of Hebrew poetry, though found sometimes in Jewish texts written in Greek and influenced by Semitic idiom. In this case, the idea expressed in the first phrase is repeated in the second. Thus, the first phrase, ἀγαθοποιῆσαι ἢ κακοποιῆσαι, is paralleled by the second phrase, ψυχὴν σῶσαι ἢ ἀπολέσαι. Each verbal member shares its equivalent in the sister phrase: "doing good" is matched by "saving life," while "doing evil" is connected to the idea of "destroying" or "killing." Within each phrase appears an antithetical formulation (ἀγαθοποιῆσαι is contrasted with its antonym κακοποιῆσαι; ψυχὴν σῶσαι with ἀπολέσαι). The form of the question highlights an absurd alternative that presumably no Jew would desire to embrace, namely, to commit evil acts or kill on the Sabbath.[41] The whole sentence is introduced by the phrase, ἔξεστιν τῷ σαββάτῳ, which appears in other Jewish passages dealing with halakic matters.[42]

The formulation of the Greek phrase, ψυχὴν σῶσαι, resembles and recalls the rabbinic concept of פיקוח נפש, the license provided for overriding the Sabbath in cases where the risk of losing human life is involved.[43] The parallel structure of the saying in Luke also equates saving human life with the larger and more general category of "doing good." The actual placement of the saying within an episode dealing with the healing of a non-life-threatening condition strengthens the argument that Luke views Jesus' healing acts as embodying and simultaneously expanding the application of the principle of פיקוח נפש. Healing a man's withered hand, like saving a

---

[40] "ἀπόλλυμι," BDAG. Mayer-Haas, *Geschenk*, 310, accounts for the switch of ἀποκτεῖναι to ἀπολέσαι as a Lukan attempt to create greater correspondence with the antonym σῶσαι.

[41] See Doering, *Schabbat,* 451–53, who argues that the saying contains no neutral ground: not doing good is like doing evil, not saving a soul is like killing. The antonym to "doing good" (e.g., healing) is "doing harm," just as the opposite of "saving a life" is "destroying" it. Therefore, one may heal on the Sabbath (=doing good), since the failure to do otherwise results in doing harm, which should not occur on the holy day of the Sabbath.

[42] See, for example, Josephus, *Ant.* 13:252 (οὐκ ἔξεστι δ' ἡμῖν οὔτε τοῖς σαββάτοις οὔτ' ἐν τῇ ἑορτῇ ὁδεύειν); Mark 2:24; John 5:10. For rabbinic parallels, see Doering, *Schabbat,* 450; Levy, "מותר," *WTM* 3:303 and "נתר," *WTM* 3:460.

[43] Since in Mark 8:35 ψυχὴν σῶσαι appears with the definite article ("For those who want to save their life will lose it"/ὃς γὰρ ἐὰν θέλῃ τὴν ψυχὴν αὐτοῦ σῶσαι ἀπολέσει αὐτήν), it does not militate against reading Luke 6:9 (or Mark 3:4) in light of the halakic background suggested by the Hebrew equivalents of פיקוח נפש and ספק נפשות. See Doering, "Sabbath Laws," 230. There is no need to read this verse soteriologically as Bovon, *Luke 1*, 203 and Mayer-Haas, *Geschenk*, 196. Cf. Nolland, *Luke*, 1:261: "…σῶσαι is here not at all theological."

human from fatal danger on the Sabbath, represents an instantiation of "doing good." According to Luke, both the deliverance of humans from imminent life-threatening situations and the healing of less grave ailments that impede and even threaten a person's economic survival are appropriate for Jesus to perform on the Sabbath.

While in the previous pericope Luke highlights the christological authority of Jesus (6:5), leading some to insinuate that the Sabbath is no longer of any importance for the third evangelist,[44] it is noteworthy that in this instance other arguments besides the christological criterion appear on behalf of Jesus' Sabbath praxis. Luke signals how Jesus heals the *right* hand of the man, enabling him not only to recover his physical health but also his social dignity and professional ability to earn a living. Luke's Jesus also appeals to the principle of doing good on the Sabbath by expanding the category of פיקוח נפש. Besides exalting Jesus' messianic credentials, the primary theme of this pericope, Luke seeks to make his lord appear more acceptable to Jews who hold on to rigorous standards of Sabbath observance.

Excursus: Luke 6:11 in Modern Translation

The translation of Luke 6:11 is too conspicuous not to warrant a momentary deviation from our inquiry on the Sabbath. This survey, in the end, will hopefully prove to be of some importance when I try to situate Luke and Matthew within their respective historical-social horizons in the concluding chapter of this book.

Most modern English translations render Luke 6:11 in the following way: "But they were filled with *fury* (ἀνοίας) and discussed with one another what they might do *to* Jesus" (NRSV; emphasis mine). For several reasons, however, I argue that my translation of the verse captures more accurately Luke's perspective on the Pharisees: "And they were filled with

---

[44] So Wolter, *Das Lukasevangelium*, 238–39. First, Wolter thinks that the statement in Luke 6:9 no longer focuses on the manner of observing the Sabbath. Next, Wolter leaps to the conclusion that the statement is interested in making a universal declaration in which the sacredness of the Sabbath is *de facto* suspended, since the content of Jesus' question can apply to any day of the week. Finally, Wolter places his interpretation of the saying within the wider "parting of the ways" process: the saying replaces an exclusive Jewish ethos with an inclusive ethic in which the differentiation between Jew and Gentile is abrogated. Wolter probably underestimates the halakic form of the saying Luke has chosen to preserve in this pericope. Furthermore, at least at the level of the narrative, the person Jesus heals on the Sabbath is presumably a Jew, not a Gentile. Finally, the newer models that suggest an ongoing interaction and overlap between Jews and Christians encourage reconsidering Luke's relationship with Jewish society.

want of understanding and discussed with one another what they *might* do *with* Jesus." This translation highlights the usage of the *potential* optative (ἂν ποιήσαιεν), which can connote the *contemplation* of what one *might* or *may* do rather than describe the actual fulfillment or execution of such deliberation. In harmony with this rendering, I do not interpret the usage of the dative τῷ Ἰησου in a purely adversative way ("against/to Jesus"), preferring instead to employ the prepositions "with" or "about."[45] For Luke, *some* of the Pharisees (cf. 6:1; 13:31; 19:39) fail to recognize Jesus' messianic credentials and continue to discuss among themselves what they should do about him – the debate remains open, and, unlike the other synoptic gospels, the Pharisees are not depicted in this instance as set on eliminating Jesus. Luke knows very well that the Pharisees have nothing to do with Jesus' execution. In fact, when the opportunity arises, some of them even protect him and his disciples (Luke 13:31; Acts 5:34; 23:9). In Luke's eyes, the Pharisees' initial attempt to find a way of accusing Jesus (6:7: ἵνα εὕρωσιν κατηγορεῖν αὐτοῦ) fails: since they are unable to find him guilty on any charges, they remain bewildered and full of thoughtlessness as what to do about him. Perhaps, only the *New Jerusalem Bible* and the *New Living Translation* convey this meaning somewhat more accurately in the English language: "the best way of dealing *with* Jesus" (NJB) or "what to do *with* him" (NLT).

Unfortunately, both of these versions translate ἄνοια with problematic terms such as "furious" or "wild with rage," respectively. Many other English versions of the Bible translate the Greek term in a similar way: "fury,"[46] "full of wrath,"[47] "rage,"[48] or even "mindless rage."[49] The same tendency occurs in French translations including renderings such as "fureur"[50] or "rage."[51] Other Latin-based languages follow the same trajectory: Italian ("rabbia,"[52] or "furore"[53]); Portuguese ("furor"[54]); Spanish ("furiosos"[55] or "furor"[56]). Likewise, Delitzsch's translation of the New

---

[45] Loader, *Jesus' Attitude towards the Law*, 313: "Luke omits Jesus' anger at the hardness of his opponents' hearts and the severity of their response. Instead of plotting to kill, they are portrayed as asking the question: 'What are we going to do with Jesus?'"

[46] *New Revised Standard Version*; *English Standard Version*. The *New International Version* and *Today's New International Version*: "furious."

[47] *The Bible in Basic English*.

[48] *Holman Christian Standard Bible*; *The New American Bible* ("enraged"); *The New American Standard Bible*; *New King James Version*.

[49] *New English Translation*.

[50] *Bible en Français Courant*; *Louis Segond*; *Traduction Œcuménique de la Bible*.

[51] *La Bible de Jérusalem*.

[52] *Nuovissima Versione della Bibbia*; *La Nuova Diodati*.

[53] *La Sacra Bibbia Nuova Riveduta*.

[54] *João Ferreira de Almeida, Revista e Atualizada*.

[55] *La Biblia de Nuestro Pueblo*.

Testament into Hebrew and the Salkinson-Ginsburg Hebrew edition employ the term חמה ("anger"). Similarly, some German translations render the Greek term with "sinnloser Wut" ("senseless rage")[57] or "blinder Wut" ("blind rage"),[58] although a few German versions of the New Testament correctly offer an alternative translation: "Unverstand" ("lack of judgment").[59] Many modern commentators also interpret the Greek term as expressing emotional anger.[60]

Perhaps, this consensus among modern translations stems from a harmonizing tendency to read Luke in light of the more stereotyped and negative portraits of the Pharisees found in Mark and especially Matthew. The *LSJ* lexicon does not provide a single entry or passage where ἄνοια means "fury," "rage," "madness," or the like. The *BDAG* lexicon translates ἄνοια in Luke 6:11 as "fury," but provides no evidence to back this point, save for a lone reference in *Papyrus Egerton* 2 line 51 where it states that Jesus "perceived their [i.e., of his opponents] *purpose*," (εἰδὼς τὴν [δι]άνοια [αὐτ]ῶν). The Greek word διάνοια, however, simply means, "purpose," "disposition," or "mind," and need not connote the intense emotions of fury or anger.

To justify interpreting ἄνοια in Luke 6:11 as referring to Jesus' anger, Bovon and others point to Plato, *Tim.* 86B where the Greek philosopher discusses two types of ἄνοια: "madness" (μανία) and "ignorance" (ἀμαθία).[61] However, there is no evidence to posit that Luke is thinking along platonic lines in this pericope. The fact that Luke uses elsewhere the term ἄγνοια ("ignorance"; Acts 3:17; 17:30) hardly proves that he intends with ἄνοια to denote the idea of "madness." In Luke's writings, the term ἄγνοια refers to the ignorance on the part of individuals who are yet uninformed about a certain matter,[62] while ἄνοια highlights a persistent senselessness or lack of understanding *even after* knowledge or proof is provided to a certain party on a particular issue (e.g., the messiahship of Jesus). In any case, as Wolter correctly points out, the correlation between Luke's ἄνοια and Plato's μανία is unfounded, since the Hellenistic literature writ-

---

[56] *Reina Valera* (1995).

[57] *Einheitsübersetzung der Heiligen Schrift.*

[58] *Die Bibel: Die Heilige Schrift des Alten und Neuen Bundes.*

[59] *Elberfelder Bibel revidierte Fassung; Münchener Neues Testament;* Schlachter, *Die Bibel* (2000). Cf. *Lutherbibel* (1545): "ganz unsinnig."

[60] See, for example, Bovon, *Luke 1,* 204: "blind fury."

[61] Bovon, *Luke 1,* 204; Fitzmyer, *The Gospel according to Luke,* 1:611.

[62] For example, the "Jews" in Jerusalem and from the Diaspora are unaware in Acts 3:17 of their supposed responsibility for the death of Jesus; the Gentiles of Athens in Acts 17:30 are ignorant about the true God of Israel.

ten around the time of Luke normally use ἄνοια in the sense of ignorance, not madness.[63]

Admittedly, Luke occasionally portrays some Pharisees in a negative light in both his gospel as well as the Acts of the Apostles, but they are criticized for their lack of understanding rather than their involvement in the deaths of Jesus and his disciples. In this respect, Flusser is certainly right in critiquing the traditional translation of ἄνοια in Luke 6:11, although, unlike Flusser, I take the Lukan wording as evidence for the *redactor's* attitude toward the Pharisees rather than reflecting a more primitive form of the episode.[64] In other words, Luke's nuanced portrait of the Pharisees and their interaction with Jesus and his followers is more credible but not necessarily historical. His more balanced description of the Pharisaic party, in comparison to Matthew, might even offer us a glimpse into his social world. I return to this point at the end of this monograph, suggesting that the differences between Matthew and Luke should be assessed more along the social-historical contexts they find themselves in rather than along theological lines, at least as far as the theme of Torah praxis is concerned, since they both agree on the necessity for Jewish followers of Jesus to continue observing the Jewish Law.

Healing the Crippled Woman: Luke 13:10–17

Literary Context

Luke includes two additional Sabbath controversies, unattested in any other gospel (13:10–21; 14:1–6). Both episodes appear within Luke's report about Jesus' itinerary (9:51–19:27) through Palestine and final pilgrimage up to Jerusalem. Mayer-Haas thinks this block of material relating Jesus' itinerary functions more intensely than other sections of Luke's gospel as a model of behavior for followers of Jesus to emulate.[65] Luke's readers, among other things, should follow Jesus' example by

---

[63] See Wolter, *Das Lukasevangelium*, 239, for references in Philo, Josephus, and other authors. See also J. Behm, "ἄνοια," 4:962–63.

[64] Flusser, *The Sage from Galilee*, 17 n. 41. Tomson, *If This Be From Heaven*, 155, 226, seems to follow Flusser in considering the Lukan version of the episode as more original. But cf. Doering, "Sabbath Laws," 237 and Mayer-Haas, *Geschenk*, 311.

[65] Mayer-Haas, *Geschenk*, 313. However, in the conclusions to Part I on the Sabbath, I argue that the Sabbath healings of Jesus as reported in the gospel of Luke do not necessarily reflect Lukan Sabbath praxis.

preaching and teaching in the synagogues on the Sabbath (13:10).[66] Interestingly, Luke brackets this healing episode with statements about Jesus' teaching activities:

A. Jesus teaches in the synagogue (v. 10)
B. Healing of the crippled woman (vv. 11–17)
C. Jesus teaches in parables (vv. 18–21)

Section A introduces the healing story in section B. Together they constitute a self-contained unit. Luke appends Section C to the healing story: the particle οὖν in v. 18, understood in the sense of "so" or "as had been said,"[67] resumes the narration and does not signal a new setting or episode.[68] On the other hand, Luke does not thematically connect the content of the parables on the mustard seed and the leaven in vv. 18–21 with the healing episode in vv. 11–17. If there is any thematic connection between the two, it occurs only at the most general level, relating Jesus' teaching about the kingdom of God with its demonstration through the healing of the crippled woman.[69] Here, Luke simply takes the opportunity to insert

---

[66] Loader, *Jesus' Attitude towards the Law*, 313, however, is skeptical about this point. But see Klinghardt, *Gesetz und Volkes Gottes*, 230–31. Cf. Luke 4:31 (Jesus teaching on the Sabbath in the synagogue of Nazareth); 6:6 (teaching in the synagogue of Capernaum) as well as 13:10; 19:47; 20:1; 21:37; 23:5 where Jesus teaches in Galilee, Judea, and especially the temple. The disciples of Jesus in Acts 5:25, 28, 42; 15:35; 18:11; 21:21; 21:28; 28:31 also follow Jesus' example. Moreover, Luke 13:10 is largely redactional. Notice the periphrastic construction (Ἦν δὲ διδάσκων) and the plural reference to the Sabbath (ἐν τοῖς σάββασιν), highlighting the frequency of such occurrences. Neirynck, "Jesus and the Sabbath. Some Observations on Mk II, 27," 230, thinks the pericope of Luke 13:10–17 is almost entirely redactional. Bultmann, *History of the Synoptic Tradition*, 12–13, who classifies this story as a controversy dialogue, claims that the pericope was built (in its pre-redactional stages) around the isolated saying of v. 15, while 17b stems from the editor, Luke. Many, however, have rejected Bultmann's reconstruction. See, for example, Fitzmyer, *The Gospel according to Luke*, 2:1010–11, who sees the story as deriving from "L." In any case, some redactional activity is surely detectable (e.g., some of the features in v. 10). Contra Yang, *Jesus and the Sabbath*, 257, who claims it impossible to distinguish between redactional and traditional features within this pericope.

[67] Luke uses οὖν in this sense in 3:7 in order to connect its content with v. 3. See "οὖν," *BDAG*.

[68] The particle οὖν should not be understood here in a causal way, "therefore" (NRSV). Cf. Fitzmyer, *The Gospel according to Luke*, 2:1016: "The Lucan setting for this comment of Jesus is still that of the synagogue of v. 10." Wolter, *Das Lukasevangelium*, 480, includes vv. 18–21 with vv. 10–17.

[69] Claiming that the parables in vv.18–21 provide "an interpretative key" to the healing episode is an exaggeration. Contra Robert F. O'Toole, "Some Exegetical Reflections on Luke 13, 10–17," *Bib* 73 (1992): 91. This sort of hermeneutics can lead to the claim that the kingdom of God is in fact the only theme of importance in the Sabbath pericope, that "sabbath observance was no longer a real issue for Luke and his readers," Yang,

some teachings of Jesus on the kingdom of God into his narrative. It is important for Luke to record the actual content of his master's teachings and to relate its delivery within synagogue space and sacred time. He goes beyond any gospel writer in this endeavor (cf. Luke 4:16). Luke's manner of resuming the narration also highlights Jesus' authority and complete control over the situation at hand: even after the controversial healing of the woman on the Sabbath and the ensuing, heated exchange with his opponents, Jesus confidently continues instructing his audience in the synagogue.

Analysis

The crippled woman in this episode suffers from a chronic illness that has lasted for eighteen years (v. 11). A nefarious "spirit" (πνεῦμα), an oppressive agent Luke explicitly ties to the satanic realm, is responsible for her prolonged affliction (v. 17).[70] After acknowledging her presence, Jesus summons the woman and announces her freedom from her weakness. Jesus' pronouncement appears in the perfect passive: "you have been set free (ἀπολέλυσαι) from your ailment" (v. 12). Some suggest that the impersonal form of this statement shows that Luke views God as the true source and author of the healing.[71] The perfect verbal form could also indicate that the healing occurs even before Jesus lays his hands on the woman (v. 13).[72] If this is true, the laying of the hands only represents a physical gesture on the part of Jesus confirming what God has already accomplished. In other words, the woman would already have the ability to stand on her own as Jesus announces her healing.

Some might argue that Luke's depiction of Jesus' healing on the Sabbath contains nothing scandalous from a halakic point of view. After all, Jesus merely announces the healing, but does not perform any *physical*

Jesus and the Sabbath, 259, following Stephen G. Wilson, *Luke and the Law* (SNTSMS 50; Cambridge: Cambridge University Press, 1983), 38–39.

[70] The overlap in Luke's "diagnosis" between physical ailment and demonic oppression has already been noted in previous chapters. In 4:39, Luke's Jesus "rebuked" (ἐπετίμησεν) the fever of the mother-in-law of Peter, the same verb used for rebuking people possessed by evil spirits (cf. 4:35). This overlap appears also in passages such as Luke 6:18 and 7:21 where people affected by diseases, plagues, blindness, or spirits are all said to have been "cured" (ἐθεραπεύοντο in 6:18). See also Acts 10:38: "he went about doing good and healing all who were oppressed by the devil." Cf. Acts 16:16: "spirit of divination" (πνεῦμα πύθωνα).

[71] François Bovon, *L'Évangile selon saint Luc* (4 vols; CNT. Deuxième série; Geneva: Labor et Fides, 1991–2009), 2:347, 356; Nolland, *Luke,* 2:724.

[72] Wolter, *Das Lukasevangelium,* 482: "Mit dem resultativen Perfekt...kündigt Jesus die Heilung nicht erst an...sondern er stellt fest, dass sie bereits geschehen ist." Similarly, Plummer, *The Gospel according to Luke,* 342.

labor forbidden on the Sabbath. I have already argued against this sort of halakic deliberation and hairsplitting, which tries to present the synoptic Jesus in complete conformity to the standards of Sabbath observance of all Jews of his time.[73] Luke's main goal, however, is to emphasize the authority and power of Jesus' *word* to heal and exorcize the sick. He is not concerned here in showing that the *manner* in which Jesus performs his healings on the Sabbath fully conforms to the halakic standards of his time, because, in any case, some ancient Jews would have contended with the very attempt, whether through verbal or physical means, to attend to non-life-threatening conditions on the Sabbath. As elsewhere in his gospel, Luke argues that Jesus is entitled on the Sabbath to heal ailments, whether they be fatal in nature or not.

This interpretation accounts for the rebuke voiced by the leader of the synagogue (ἀρχισυνάγωγος)[74] who cares less whether Jesus has only *uttered* but not physically performed the healing. His objection condemns Jesus for what has *de facto* occurred, that is, the treatment of a non-fatal condition on the Sabbath: "There are six days on which *work* (ἐργάζεσθαι) ought to be done; come on those days and be cured, and not on the sabbath day" (v. 14).[75] This reproach ascribed to the head of the synagogue reflects not a Lukan aberration or creation of a halakic straw man, but a genuine Jewish objection to attending to minor diseases on the Sabbath.[76]

In response to such criticism, Luke's Jesus does not content himself in reiterating his christological credentials, which could have roughly run along the following lines: "the Son of Man (i.e., Jesus) does whatever he pleases on the Sabbath because he is lord of the Sabbath" (cf. Luke 6:5).[77] Instead, Luke's Jesus points to the chronic condition of the lady and employs an argument formulated in a way to persuade Jewish hearts and minds: just as anyone (at least from Luke's perspective) would "on the sabbath *untie* (λύει) his ox or his donkey from the manger, and lead it away to give it water" (v. 15), so may a woman, a daughter of Abraham for that

---

[73] Cf. the reservations of Sanders, *Jewish Law from Jesus to the Mishnah*, 20: "I somewhat doubt that Luke was aware of this fine legal distinction – that the laying of hands was work – though in an actual debate in Palestine it would have been an important issue." Contrary to Sanders, I would not hesitate to affirm Luke's cognizance of such halakic intricacies. But Luke does not deliberate on such matters because he acknowledges that Jesus' act, namely, to heal on the Sabbath, does go against the halakic conventions of certain Jews of his time.

[74] The term appears in Luke 8:49; Acts 13:15; 18:8, 17.

[75] Surprisingly, the head of the synagogue addresses and reproaches the crowd, not only Jesus (v. 14). On this feature, see Klinghardt, *Gesetz und Volkes Gottes*, 231, 239.

[76] Cf. Doering, "Sabbath Laws," 240; Klinghardt, *Gesetz und Volkes Gottes*, 231–32.

[77] Klinghardt, *Gesetz und Volkes*, 231, correctly notes that Luke's Jesus does not resort to a christological argumentation here.

matter, whom Satan has bound for eighteen years, be *"set free"* (λυθῆναι) from her oppression on the Sabbath day (v. 16).[78] The analogy Luke construes here is more "logical" in its nature than literary or exegetical. Jesus does not quote a verse from scripture in rabbinic fashion, following the hermeneutical principle known as *gezerah shavah*.[79] No verse from the Pentateuch declares that one may untie an animal in order to feed and provide it with drink on the Sabbath. Rather, the repetition of the verb λύω in the Lukan episode establishes an analogy arguing that one accepted practice (i.e., untying domestic animals to provide them with drink on the Sabbath) justifies the application of a similar yet different (abstracted)

---

[78] According to *m. Shabb.* 7:2, "untying" (המתיר) belongs to one of the thirty-nine works prohibited on the Sabbath. But the Mishnah allows one to tie and untie certain knots on the Sabbath, those, as R. Judah puts it, that are not "long-lasting" (*m. Shabb.* 15:2: קשר שאינו של קימא). Though *m. Shabb.* 15:1 prohibits tying or untying (long-lasting) knots such as camel-drivers and sailors' knots, R. Meir allows any knot to be untied with *one* hand. *M. Shabb.* 15:2 allows a woman to tie up the slit of her shift or the strings of a hair-net or belt. R. Eliezer b. Jacob allows one to tie up a cattle (or tie a rope before the entrance of the stall) on the Sabbath lest they stray away (*m. Shabb.* 15:2). See further *t. Shabb.* 18:1 [17:20]. As Doering points out, since texts from Qumran do not deal with tying knots on the Sabbath but allow leading an animal up to 2000 cubits for pasturing (CD 11:5 f.; 4Q265 7:4 f.), it seems unlikely that such Jews would have left their cattle untied on the Sabbath. Neither do these passages appear to indicate a more lenient position toward "tying." Alternatively, tying/untying was not yet understood as a prohibited labor on the Sabbath. The rabbinic texts would reflect an initial systematization incorporating tying into its taxonomy of prohibited works. Concerning giving an animal water on the Sabbath, Doering points to a baraita in *b. Eruv.* 20b–21a that allows for pouring water in front of an animal so that it can drink on its own, although it forbids offering drawn water directly to the animal. See Doering, "Sabbath Laws," 241–42. Luke, however, simply employs a generalizing term, ποτίζει ("to give water"), and does not refer to drawing water from a well, assuming that Jews would somehow relieve the thirst of their domestic animals on the Sabbath. This does not mean that Luke knows nothing about halakah. The Qumranic evidence is also silent on the matter, and Jews may very well have untied their animals on the Sabbath in order to provide them with food and drink. The rulings in *m. Shabb.* 5:1–4 presuppose that Jews lead their animals into open spaces on the Sabbath, though these passages do not deal specifically with the issue of untying and feeding (but see the end of *m. Shabb.* 5:1). According to *m. Shabb.* 5:3, one may not tie camels together (one behind the other) on the Sabbath when leading them out. This ruling, however, may be due to other concerns unrelated to tying (e.g., appearing to lead animals to the marketplace for sale on the Sabbath). See *b. Shabb.* 54a.

[79] See Louis Jacobs and David Derovan, "Hermeneutics," *EJ* 9:25–27; Cohn-Sherbok, "An Analysis of Jesus' Arguments," 34–36. A prime rabbinic example of *gezerah shavah* involves the timing of the Passover offering. Should it be offered on the Sabbath (a day when work should be avoided)? The rabbis point to the usage of the word במועדו ("in its appointed time") both in regard to the Paschal lamb (Num 9:2) and to the daily offering (Num 28:2), the latter being offered on the Sabbath as well. The terminological correspondence leads the rabbinic sages to infer that the Paschal offering may be offered on the Sabbath even though work is normally forbidden on that day (*b. Pesah.* 66a).

"untying," freeing humans from sicknesses and demonic oppression on the Sabbath.

Jesus' reply to the head of the synagogue, besides drawing upon analogy, also contains a *qal vahomer*-like argument: if one may untie an ox or a donkey on the Sabbath in order to relieve it from its thirst, how much more should a daughter of Abraham experience freedom from her physical distress and satanic torment.[80] God, in Luke's eyes, certainly cares for a daughter of Israel as much as and even more than animals (cf. Luke 12:6–7, 27). Furthermore, Luke's Jesus presents the condition of the Israelite woman in far graver terms than a thirsty ox or donkey: the daughter of Abraham has been waiting for *eighteen years* to be relieved from the *bondage of Satan*; the ox or donkey, "mere" domestic animals, only suffer from *thirst* for *one day*. The length and severity of the woman's ailment more than justify Jesus' right to intervene on the Sabbath, all the more so since she enjoys special membership with the chosen people of Israel.

In highlighting the severity of the woman's condition, Luke also emphasizes the necessity, if not the obligation, for performing such a healing on the Sabbath through a wordplay with the Greek impersonal verb δεῖ: the head of the synagogue states that "there are six days on which work *ought* (δεῖ ἐργάζεσθαι) to be done" (v. 14), to which Luke's Jesus replies that the woman certainly "*ought* to be freed" (ἔδει λυθῆναι) from her bondage on the Sabbath day (v. 16).[81] Here, the head of the synagogue alludes to the commandment of the Sabbath in the Torah that orders Israel not only to rest on the Sabbath but also to work six days a week (Exod 20:9; Deut 5:13). Six days are allocated for performing work during which Jews may care for non-life-threatening ailments. Nevertheless, for the many reasons presented above (e.g., the superiority of humans over animals, the severity and duration of the condition), Luke's Jesus maintains that it is his responsibility to heal on the Sabbath day.

There may be yet another dimension to the argumentation offered by Jesus in this Lukan episode: by highlighting the length of the woman's condition, nothing less than eighteen years, the *Sabbath day* marks the *end* of this painful and prolonged process. Luke incorporates the Sabbath day into the theme of eschatological liberation and redemption proclaimed by Jesus during his inaugural address on the Sabbath in the synagogue of his hometown Nazareth (Luke 4:16–21). If for Philo the Sabbath is "the birthday of the world" (Philo, *Opif.* 89), for Luke it is a day celebrating rebirth for those children of Israel who experience through Jesus liberation from

---

[80] Doering, "Sabbath Laws," 241, speaks of a *tertium comparationis* ("to release") that was added to the initial implicit *argumentum a fortiori* in Luke 13:15–16.

[81] Wolter, *Das Lukasevangelium*, 484. Mayer-Haas, *Geschenk*, 320, also notes a further wordplay in the usage of ἔδησεν and ἔδει in v. 16.

satanic oppression and physical suffering. Luke does not go so far as to state that the Sabbath is the only or even the best day for Jesus to perform his healings and exorcisms, since Jesus carries out his healing ministry throughout the week. However, Luke certainly stresses that the Sabbath constitutes an appropriate time for Jesus to proclaim *and* bring liberation to the children of Israel. After all, the Torah itself portrays the Sabbath as a memorial commemorating Israel's redemption from her bondage to Egypt (Deut 5:15; cf. Exod 20:2). Luke, of course, does not explicitly cite this verse, nor does he fully tap on the scriptural resources at his disposal for developing a stronger symbolic and theological link between eschatological redemption and the institution of the weekly Sabbath.[82] Nevertheless, Luke lays several blocks for the construction of a particular Sabbath theology by having Jesus deliver his inaugural address on eschatological release on the Sabbath (4:16–30), by immediately describing in concrete terms how Jesus provides these eschatological benefits to Jews by healing and performing exorcisms on the Sabbath (4:31–39; cf. 6:1–11), and by adding a subsequent healing episode, unparalleled in any other gospel, in which a women encounters on the Sabbath her long awaited and desired *freedom* from demonic oppressors.[83]

Finally, in Luke, the Sabbath finds itself caught in an arena of ongoing *cosmic warfare* between the invasive kingdom of God as proclaimed by Jesus and the opposing forces of Satan. If satanic powers do not cease attacking and oppressing Israel on the Sabbath day, then God's incoming empire cannot and should not resist striking back. Ever since Maccabean times, certain Jews had acknowledged the necessity of momentarily suspending the Sabbath during times of human warfare. By analogy, we might add that Jesus' healings, which for Luke really just constitute a manifestation of divine power and providence, must also be carried out on the Sabbath. It is a matter of cosmic proportions involving a controversy between good and evil, a story about God's reign overcoming Satan's rule, not just a question of improving human welfare. Admittedly, Luke does not openly draw or develop an analogy between Sabbath halakah momentarily allowing Jews to engage in warfare and an eschatological theology that involves a cosmic confrontation. Nevertheless, he insinuates at several points through the usage of the passive voice that God is the one acting through Jesus to overcome ailments generated by satanic forces. For example, the usage of the passive voice in vv. 12 and 16 ("you are set free"/ ἀπολέλυσαι

---

[82] See Bovon, *Luc*, 2:351, who refers to the redefinition of the Sabbath here in terms of liberation, echoing the tradition about the Exodus from Egypt.

[83] Cf. Back, *Jesus of Nazareth and the Sabbath Commandment*, 137; Mayer-Haas, *Geschenk*, 321.

and "be set free"/ λυθῆναι) points in this direction.[84] Read in this light, for Luke, the main issue in such episodes lies in properly appreciating the cosmic controversy at hand as well as the divine source energizing and enabling Jesus to intervene rather than in questioning the ongoing validity of the institution of the Sabbath: will Jesus' opponents interpret his healing of ailments caused by satanic forces merely as a human act or even a satanically inspired performance (Luke 11:15–20)? Or will they see it as a miraculous deed originating from above and therefore legitimate for him to carry out on the Sabbath?[85] Luke rebukes his opponents, embodied here by the leader of the synagogue, mainly for failing to recognize the divine authority and special credentials granted to Jesus to carry out such actions, not for their insistence on keeping the Sabbath – a Jewish value Luke does not condemn but actually upholds.

The case Luke makes in 13:15–16 on behalf of Jesus' Sabbath praxis is rich and dense in its argumentation and logic.[86] Even though Luke primarily seeks to exalt Jesus' authority in such episodes, much of the line of reasoning on behalf of Jesus' Sabbath keeping stands independently from the question of recognizing his messianic credentials. Theoretically, some of its argumentation could be used in order to justify a certain orientation toward the Sabbath without believing in Jesus as the messiah. If Jews are willing to satiate the thirst of their domestic beasts on the Sabbath, then they should tolerate on the same day the healing and liberation of their Jewish kin from sickness and suffering, especially if the source of such distress stems from satanic forces. Moreover, in this particular case, a precious daughter of Israel has experienced a prolonged state of suffering, lasting several years, almost two decades. Luke contrasts her special status as a daughter of Abraham and her psychosomatic distress with the mere physical needs of domestic animals in order to justify Jesus' intervention on the Sabbath. All of this shows that Luke is not content in simply rehearsing Jesus' christological portfolio as the sole means for justifying his lord's behavior on the Sabbath. Even the messiah must account for his comportment when it deviates from normal conventions. The christological argument is the final argumentation composed of several additional ingredients brought to the table. Luke, therefore, amplifies Mark's repertoire on behalf of Jesus' Sabbath praxis just as much as Matthew does. In this instance, Luke's argumentation is just as "proto-rabbinic" in its halakic deliberation as Matthew's reasoning. Luke employs arguments that resem-

---

[84] The usage of ἀνωρθώθη (v. 13) may also imply that God restores the woman to her right posture.

[85] Cf. Mayer-Haas, *Geschenk*, 321, 330–31.

[86] The depth of Luke's argumentation is underappreciated. Wilson, *Luke and the Law*, 37, for example, dedicates a mere paragraph to this episode.

ble the *qal vahomer* and *gezerah shavah* principles found in later rabbinic debates, albeit in a more primitive and less sophisticated form. Like Matthew, Luke also solicits the practice of rural Jews in Palestine and elsewhere, who would come to the rescue of their domestic animals if they were trapped in wells (14:5) or needed to be fed and given water, in order to justify Jesus' healings on the Sabbath. Luke's defense of Jesus' Sabbath praxis, therefore, is just as halakic and robust as Matthew's presentation of the same topic.

Healing on the Sabbath in Pharisaic Space: Luke 14:1–6

Literary Context

This final Lukan episode reporting a controversy about Jesus' Sabbath praxis appears not long after the previous Sabbath incident on the healing of the crippled woman (13:10–17). After freeing that daughter of Abraham from her chronic condition, Luke's Jesus continues to deliver his instruction in the synagogue on the Sabbath, relating two parables about the kingdom of God (13:18–19: parable of the mustard seed; 13:20–21: parable of the leaven). In 13:22–30, Luke's Jesus resumes his journey up to Jerusalem, teaching along the way in the neighboring towns and villages. Luke then reports how some Pharisees warn Jesus about Herod's plot to remove his life. This remarkable gesture on their part appears only in Luke and conforms to the larger portrait of the Pharisees found elsewhere in Luke-Acts. One hardly needs to interpret their gesture as a mischievous act to mean that Luke's Pharisees did not really intend on saving Jesus' life but were cunningly trying to rid themselves of his presence in Judea.[87]

---

[87] Contra Adelbert Denaux, "L'hypocrisie des Pharisiens et le dessein de Dieu. Analyse de Lc. XIII, 31–33," in *L'évangile de Luc/The Gospel of Luke* (ed. F. Neirynck; 2d ed.; BETL 32; Leuven: Leuven University Press, 1989), 155–95; 316–21; Burton Scott Easton, *The Gospel according to St. Luke* (Edinburgh: T & T Clark, 1926), 221. Later on, Denaux acknowledges his overly negative portrayal of the Pharisees in Luke-Acts, but still holds on to the core of his thesis as far as Luke 13:31–33 is concerned. See "L'hypocrisie des Pharisiens," 316–21. Similarly, Plummer, *The Gospel according to St. Luke,* 348: "The Pharisees wanted to frighten Jesus into Judaea, where He would be more in the power of the Sanhedrin...."; Wolter, *Das Lukasevangelium*, 495, who first dismisses a "hypocritical" portrayal of the Pharisees, but nevertheless concludes that they are portrayed in a negative light because they fail to understand the true purpose of Jesus' journey up to Jerusalem: "Lukas will die Pharisäer hier nicht als um Jesu Überleben Besorgte; sondern als Ignoranten charakterisieren." The same reproach would then have to be held against the Jesus' disciples, who even after Jesus' death fail to understand the reason for his ascent to Jerusalem (cf. Luke ch. 24). Correctly, Fitzmyer, *The Gospel*

Luke's Jesus does not read any ulterior motives behind the Pharisees' warning but promptly proceeds to condemn Herod.

Despite this warning, Luke's Jesus reaffirms his intention to make it to Jerusalem, delivering a solemn prophecy against Jerusalem in anticipation of the fate awaiting him (vv. 32–35).[88] Our Sabbath pericope finally begins in 14:1 where Jesus finds himself dining on the Sabbath in the house of a leader of the Pharisees, signaling once again the social proximity Luke is willing to entertain between both parties. In the house of this prominent Pharisee, Jesus daringly heals a man suffering from dropsy. The narrative ideally portrays Jesus defending his act in a way that the Pharisees are unable to argue against him (vv. 2–6). After the healing, Jesus nonchalantly proceeds teaching, presumably within the same Pharisaic hospices where he has been welcomed as a guest (vv. 7–24). The content of his teaching, however, is not intricately tied to the healing episode. In many ways, the structure of this portion resembles the previous Sabbath episode in 13:10–17. In 13:10, Jesus enters a synagogue on the Sabbath (13:10); here, he finds himself in a Pharisee's house (14:1). In the synagogue, he heals a crippled woman (13:11: introduced by καὶ ἰδοὺ and a diagnosis of her condition) and then responds to his opponents; here, he heals a man suffering from dropsy (14:2: also introduced by καὶ ἰδοὺ accompanied by a description of the ailment) and anticipates his adversaries' objections. After healing the woman, Jesus resumes his instruction in the synagogue, teaching in parables (13:18–21); here, Jesus teaches in parables after curing the man's dropsy (14:7–24).[89]

Analysis

As noted throughout this chapter, Luke, in contrast to Matthew, is willing to present a more amicable disposition and even a commensality shared

---

according to Luke, 2:1030; Tomson, *If this be from Heaven . . .'*, 223; Ziesler, "Luke and the Pharisees," 149–50.

[88] But even 13:35 contains hope for the restoration of Jerusalem: "you will not see me *until* the time comes when you say, 'Blessed is the one who comes in the name of the Lord.'" Luke does not add the qualification that when this time comes it will be too late for Israel to repent. Luke has not given up on Jerusalem, but looks forward to the time when it will no longer be trampled upon by the Gentiles (cf. Luke 21:24; Acts 1:6). Correctly, Bovon, *Luc,* 2:406–7.

[89] Luke 14:1–6 also shares a number of resemblances with Luke 6:6–11 (the healing of the man with a withered hand), which Luke uses to compose this last Sabbath pericope. Both share similar openings (Semitic-like use of ἐγένετο followed by infinitive in 14:1/6:1; a reference to the entrance [ἐλθεῖν/εἰσελθεῖν] into the house of a Pharisee/synagogue on the Sabbath). In both episodes, Jesus is observed carefully by the Pharisees (αὐτοὶ ἦσαν παρατηρούμενοι αὐτόν/παρετηροῦντο δὲ αὐτὸν). Likewise, the saying in 14:3 may be based on 6:9.

between Jesus and certain Pharisees.⁹⁰ According to this passage (v. 1), Jesus' host is a prominent Pharisee, one who enjoys some kind of leadership role within his sphere of influence, "one of the leaders of the Pharisees" ("τινος τῶν ἀρχόντων [τῶν] Φαρισαίων").⁹¹ But despite the honorable reception on Jesus' behalf, Luke depicts the host-guest relationship with ambivalence and suspicion: as Jesus breaks bread with his Pharisaic hosts, they keep close watch over him (αὐτοὶ ἦσαν παρατηρούμενοι αὐτόν).⁹²

The sudden entrance of a new character introduces a new scene into this episode: "Just then (καὶ ἰδοὺ) in front of him, there was a man who had dropsy (ὑδρωπικὸς)" (v. 2). Luke does not present the condition of the man as life-threatening. Dropsy, also known as edema, refers generally to the abnormal accumulation of fluids beneath the skin or in the cavities of the body. This disease is well attested in classical medical literature as well as ancient Jewish texts.⁹³ While some ancient thinkers viewed dropsy as life-threatening,⁹⁴ Luke provides no indication in this case that the man's life is *imminently* at risk. The man's condition should be likened to previous non-fatal ailments affecting people whom Jesus heals on the Sabbath (e.g., the crippled woman and the man suffering from a withered hand). These individuals suffer from chronic, harmful conditions, which in due time might threaten the life of the person, were sudden deteriorating complications to present themselves and remain untreated. But by no means are they presented as imminently life-threatening so as to legitimize in the eyes of other Jews immediate intervention on the Sabbath. As in previous incidents, Luke simply reports another Sabbath healing of a non-life-threatening condition.

Before performing the healing, Jesus preemptively deploys a rhetorical question for the sake of his interlocutors, asking the legal specialists (νομικοὺς)⁹⁵ present as well as the Pharisees whether it is lawful to cure on the Sabbath. The question resembles Luke 6:9 in its rationale and structure:

---

⁹⁰ Cf. Lk 7:36; 11:37. The Pharisees are the presumed hosts throughout 14:1–24 (see vv. 7, 12, 15). While such portrayals may have coincided with the historical Jesus' attitude toward and interaction with the Pharisees, I take them to be redactional constructions.

⁹¹ Klinghardt, *Gesetz und Volkes Gottes,* 232–33, posits a correspondence with the ἀρχισυνάγωγος of Luke 13:10–17.

⁹² Cf. Luke 6:7: "The scribes and the Pharisees watched (παρετηροῦντο) him to see whether he would cure on the sabbath." Cf. Luke 20:20; Acts 9:24.

⁹³ See Bovon, *Luc*, 2:417–18, for references.

⁹⁴ For example, Diogenes Laertius 4:27.

⁹⁵ The term is used by Luke interchangeably with γραμματεύς to refer to an expert in Jewish law. Cf. Luke 7:30; 10:25; 11:45, 52. See Mayer-Haas, *Geschenk*, 333 n. 350.

Luke 6:9 (cf. Mark 3:4)
ἔξεστιν τῷ σαββάτῳ ἀγαθοποιῆσαι ἢ κακοποιῆσαι, ψυχὴν σῶσαι ἢ ἀπολέσαι;
(Is it lawful to do good or to do harm on the sabbath, to save life or to destroy it?)

Luke 14:3
ἔξεστιν τῷ σαββάτῳ θεραπεῦσαι ἢ οὔ;
(Is it lawful to cure people on the sabbath, or not?)[96]

The saying in Luke 6:9 is based on Mark 3:4, while the question in 14:3 may have been penned entirely by Luke. Both sayings open with the same impersonal third person singular form of the verb ἔξειμι (ἔξεστιν) and temporal reference (τῷ σαββάτῳ), accompanied by an infinitive verbal construction (ἀγαθοποιῆσαι/ψυχὴν σῶσαι/θεραπεῦσαι) and the conjunction ἤ. On the other hand, the question in Luke 14:3 is shorter than its counterparts in Mark 3:4 and Luke 6:9: there is no repetition of verbal phrases, and an infinitive verb appearing after the conjunction ἤ is totally lacking.[97] Instead, Luke 14:3 ends with the negative particle οὔ. Normally, the particle οὔ does not precede an infinitive even in Koine Greek, [98] and, in any case, no infinitive verb appears in the second clause of this verse. Luke 14:3, therefore, should be translated in the following way: "Is it lawful on the Sabbath to heal, or not [i.e., is it not lawful]?"

The question in 14:3 presents the reader not so much with a new argumentation as with a final recapitulation justifying Jesus' Sabbath praxis (6:1–11; 13:10–17). The question in 14:3 seems more confrontational than argumentative, more affirmative of what has already been proven and demonstrated than novel and substantial in its logic. Since it has already been shown in previous episodes that Jesus is right in "doing good" on the Sabbath, Luke has Jesus confront his Pharisaic interlocutors one last time about this matter. This is the final incident in Luke where Jesus performs a controversial act on the Sabbath. Now it is time for a final application and review of Jesus' message, a last opportunity to verify whether the Pharisaic adversaries have learned their lesson from previous incidents and to illustrate once and for all that Jesus' actions do not go against the Sabbath and its *raison d'être*.

---

[96] The formulation of the question is paralleled in other Jewish passages dealing with legal issues related to Sabbath keeping. See Doering, *Schabbat,* 450 n. 297 and Levy, "מותר," *WTM* 3:303 and "נתר," *WTM* 3:460, for further examples and rabbinic parallels. Some examples in Greek include *Ant.* 13:252 (οὐκ ἔξεστι δ' ἡμῖν οὔτε τοῖς σαββάτοις οὔτ' ἐν τῇ ἑορτῇ ὁδεύειν); Mark 2:24 (ἴδε τί ποιοῦσιν τοῖς σάββασιν ὃ οὐκ ἔξεστιν); Mark 3:4 (ἔξεστιν τοῖς σάββασιν ἀγαθὸν ποιῆσαι ἢ κακοποιῆσαι, ψυχὴν σῶσαι ἢ ἀποκτεῖναι). Cf. *Ant.* 3:251; 15:259; 20:268 and *J.W.* 6:423.

[97] In Luke 14:3 the conjunction ἤ is sharply disjunctive. See BDF §446; Wolter, *Das Lukasevangelium,* 502.

[98] A. T. Robertson, *A Grammar of the Greek New Testament in Light of Historical Research* (Leicester: Hodder & Stoughton, 1919), 1162.

The Pharisees neither conspire to kill Jesus nor argue with him despite his audacious provocation. Instead, they remain speechless (v. 4: οἱ δὲ ἡσύχασαν). Their silence, however, hardly means that actual, historical Pharisees would have consented to Jesus' actions. Luke's Pharisees have already been confronted with such a situation in previous episodes. Lost in their supposed folly or lack of understanding (Luke 6:11: ἄνοια), they remain unable to figure out what to make of this Jesus. Now, according to Luke, they recognize, at least silently, their inability to counter Jesus. Their silence, in Luke's eyes, implies a grudging consent or an irritated recognition of their failure to refute Jesus on this point.[99] Of course, this idealized portrayal of muted and defeated Pharisees only reveals *Luke's* belief in Jesus' successful rebuttal of his adversaries – not an actual report about events as they really happened. The silence of the Pharisees provides the Lukan Jesus with a *laissez-passer* for performing another healing on the Sabbath. Beyond all chutzpah, Luke's Jesus proceeds to heal an individual on the Sabbath day within the house of a prominent Pharisee! A rather rude guest! The Pharisees' emotional reaction to this instigation within their own space remains remarkably subdued. It is certainly hard to imagine Matthew ever portraying them in such a mellow manner.

Luke describes the performance of the healing in three simple acts: Jesus takes (ἐπιλαβόμενος), heals (ἰάσατο), and releases (ἀπέλυσεν) the sick person. The first verb, ἐπιλαβόμενος, is rather general in its thrust, conveying the impression that Jesus simply takes the man, perhaps by the hand, in order to heal him. As in the previous Sabbath pericope, where the woman bound by Satan is "released" (cf. ἀπολέλυσαι in 13:12; λύει and λυθῆναι in 13:15–16) from her suffering, here too, Jesus "releases" the man from his dropsy. Because of this parallelism, it seems unlikely that the verb ἀπέλυσεν should be understood only in a general sense to mean that Jesus sends the man away once he accomplishes the healing.[100] The man has also been literally released from his suffering, from the (demonic) source of torment that has kept him captive until now. A *double entendre* is at play here: Jesus both liberates and dismisses the man.[101] Thus, the "release" motif appears once again in the gospel of Luke: yet another member of the house of Israel experiences on the Sabbath the benefits of eschatological liberation announced by Jesus one Sabbath in the synagogue of Nazareth (4:16–21).

Until the very final episode dealing with a Sabbath healing, Luke seeks to defend Jesus' actions. To fulfill this aim, Luke brings an argument

---

[99] Cf. Fitzmyer, *Luke*, 2:1041: "But to be silent is to agree (especially when legal matters are the issue)."

[100] So Wolter, *Das Lukasevangelium*, 502, pointing to Luke 8:38 and Acts 19:40.

[101] Cf. Bovon, *Luc*, 2:421; Mayer-Haas, *Geschenk*, 338.

similar in some respects to Luke 13:15 where Jesus asks his audience whether they would not untie their ox or donkey on the Sabbath and lead it out to give it water. Here Luke's Jesus states: "If one of you has a child or an ox that has fallen into a well, will you not immediately pull it out on a sabbath day?" (14:5). A parallel form of this statement appears in Matt 12:11. The following table presents the contents of Matt 12:11, Luke 13:15 and 14:5 next to each other for the purpose of comparison:

Matt 12:11	Luke 13:15	Luke 14:5
τίς ἔσται ἐξ ὑμῶν ἄνθρωπος ὃς ἕξει πρόβατον ἓν καὶ ἐὰν ἐμπέσῃ τοῦτο τοῖς σάββασιν εἰς βόθυνον, οὐχὶ κρατήσει αὐτὸ καὶ ἐγερεῖ;	ἕκαστος ὑμῶν τῷ σαββάτῳ οὐ λύει τὸν βοῦν αὐτοῦ ἢ τὸν ὄνον ἀπὸ τῆς φάτνης καὶ ἀπαγαγὼν ποτίζει;	τίνος ὑμῶν υἱὸς ἢ βοῦς εἰς φρέαρ πεσεῖται, καὶ οὐκ εὐθέως ἀνασπάσει αὐτὸν ἐν ἡμέρᾳ τοῦ σαββάτου;
"Suppose one of you has only one sheep and it falls into a pit on the sabbath; will you not lay hold of it and lift it out?"	"Does not each of you on the sabbath untie his ox or his donkey from the manger, and lead it away to give it water?"	"If one of you has a child or an ox that has fallen into a well, will you not immediately pull it out on a sabbath day?"

All three sayings mention animals, although Luke 14:5 also contains the word "son" (υἱός). Matt 12:11 refers to a pit (βόθυνον), while Luke 14:15 mentions the word well (φρέαρ) and Luke 13:15 may also imply the presence of a well (or another source of water). Conceptually, the saying in Luke 14:5 resembles mostly Matt 12:11, since both of these verses refer to a creature that has fallen into a pit/well, while Luke 13:15 only deals with the alleviation of an animal's thirst by untying and leading it to a source of water. More than Matt 12:11, Luke 14:5 contains a ring of heightened urgency: a person would *immediately* (εὐθέως) draw up (ἀνασπάσει)[102] a son or an ox from a *well*. The usage of the word "well", instead of "pit" as in Matthew, further accentuates the predicament of the animal: the drowning waters threaten its life. Immediate action is required.[103]

In Matt 12:11, Jesus concludes the saying with *a minori ad maius* argument: "How much more valuable is a human being than a sheep!" (Matt 12:12a). The current Lukan version of the dictum, however, cannot employ a *qal vahomer*-like argument, since it also contains the word "son," which

---

[102] The verb ἀνασπάσει implies that the person will indeed draw the creature out of the well, not just lift it up to a standing position as the verb in Matthew may imply. This reading of Matthew, however, was rejected. See section above on Matt 12:11.

[103] Mayer-Haas, *Geschenk*, 348. However, I do not believe that Luke is arguing through this analogy that the man's condition is life-threatening.

eliminates the contrast between animals and humans.[104] Some scribes already noticed this problem and tried to replace the word "son" with "donkey" (ὄνος) or "sheep" (πρόβατον).[105] From a textual critical perspective, however, the reading of "son" is to be preferred: it is the *lectio difficilior* and enjoys a better textual attestation.[106] The particular usage of the word "son," instead of "man" or "human," also heightens the empathy particularly felt by a parent for a child in danger. As in the previous case on the *daughter* of Abraham, crippled because of a nefarious spirit (13:16), Luke's Jesus maintains that he must go about healing on the Sabbath other children of Israel afflicted by the evil powers of Satan.

The usage of the word "son" also furnishes the saying with a greater degree of halakic legitimacy based on what is known so far from the extant sources about Jewish praxis on this matter. As noted earlier,[107] the ancient halakic texts that do tackle the problem envisaged in Luke 14:5, assume, contrary to Jesus' rhetorical question, that one should *not* actively save an *animal* that has fallen into a pit or water on the Sabbath (e.g., CD 11:14; 4Q265 6:5–6). Other Jews, at least in later times, devised ways to bypass this problem partially by providing the animal with food or other implements that would enable the animal to survive that day or come out on its own (*t. Shabb.* 14:3; *b. Shabb.* 128b). But in cases involving a *human* who

---

[104] Contra Mayer-Haas, *Geschenk*, 344–45, 354, who speaks of Luke 14:5 as containing a *qal vahomer* argument.

[105] ὄνος: א K L Ψ, etc.; πρόβατον: D. The similarities between Matt 12:11 and Luke 14:5 have led some to posit a common source for both sayings, for example, Q. So, Back, *Jesus of Nazareth and the Sabbath Commandment,* 137; Neirynck, "Jesus and the Sabbath. Some Observations on Mk II, 27," 227. Fitzmyer, *The Gospel according to Luke*, 2:1039, maintains that "the wording is so different that v. 5 is better ascribed to 'L.'" Mayer-Haas, *Geschenk*, 351–53, argues against Q as being the source for Luke 14:5 and Matt 12:11. It is not essential for our purposes to determine the source nor the oldest form the saying. An Aramaic *Vorlage* has also been proposed for this saying. Doering, *Schabbat*, 458, thinks that the sayings in both Matthew and Luke represent two different translations of an Aramaic *Vorlage*, since the differences between both versions seem so great. Many exegetes view Matt 12:11/Luke 14:5 as containing an authentic saying of the historical Jesus. For a discussion of this issue, see Doering, *Schabbat*, 457–62. Joachim Jeremias and Matthew Black discuss the potential wordplay going on in the supposed Aramaic between the words ברא ("son"), בעירא ("cattle"), and בירא ("well" or "pit"). See Matthew Black, *An Aramaic Approach to the Gospels and Acts* (3d ed.; Oxford: Clarendon, 1967), 168–71; Joachim Jeremias, review of Matthew Black, *An Aramaic Approach to the Gospels and Acts, GGA* 210 (1956): 1–12.

[106] The word "son" may have been added to the saying sometime during its pre-Lukan transmission. See Wolter, *Das Lukasevangelium*, 503. Doering, *Schabbat*, 458–59, explains the intrusion of the word "son" by pointing to its supposed Aramaic *Vorlage*: originally, the saying only mentioned an ox (בערא) and a well (בירא) to which was added the phonetically similar ברא ("son").

[107] See section dealing with Matt 12:11.

falls into a body of water or a cistern, even the more stringent texts of Qumran allow for one to draw a person out, provided instruments are not used (presumably, because their usage would constitute "work"): "Any living human who falls into a body of water or a cistern shall not be helped out with ladder, rope, or tool" (CD 11:15–17).[108] The additional reference to a "son" in the Lukan saying could potentially appeal to the even more stringent wings of Jewish society: if one is not ready to save an animal on the Sabbath, he or she will at least save a human. It creates an *a pari* rather than an *a fortiori* argument: just as one would save an animal, or at least a child, on the Sabbath, so also can one heal a person on the Sabbath.[109] The analogy, however, is "quasi-logical," as a correlation exists only between the status of the creatures (i.e., humans) but not their corresponding situations. Luke's opponents could still argue that the necessity for healing a man suffering from dropsy does not prove as urgent as saving someone whose life is truly and imminently in danger. Consequently, the proposal to see here an extension of the principle of saving life on the Sabbath (פיקוח נפש) becomes once again attractive: if one would draw a human or even an ox out of a well on the Sabbath, why is it unlawful to heal non-life-threatening diseases of humans on the same day?

Once again, the Pharisees are supposedly "unable" to object to Jesus' argument and prevent him from acting. Luke plays with his words in this one-sided and idealized portrait: in v. 4, the Pharisees "were silent" (ἡσύχασαν), here they are "unable" (ἴσχυσαν) to answer back (v. 6). Since in Luke's eyes Jesus' Sabbath healings are perfectly legitimate, his lord can continue, according to his custom, to teach (in parables) with full confidence even within the home of a Pharisee where he has performed a questionable healing. This is how Luke chooses to end his saga on the question of Jesus and his Sabbath keeping. The only other time Jesus appears again in the third canonical gospel in a Sabbath setting occurs during his burial, "resting," as it were, in a tomb on that holy day, while his disciples faithfully observe the Sabbath according to the Law of Moses (23:56).

Conclusion

None of the controversy stories assessed in this chapter announces the abrogation of the Sabbath. The dispute centers always on the interpretation of the Law, on how to keep the Sabbath when human need conflicts with

---

[108] Similarly, 4Q265 6:6–8: "But if it is a man who falls into the water [on] the Sabbath [day], one shall extend his garment to him to pull him out with it, but he shall not carry an implement [to pull him out on the] Sabbath [day]."

[109] Cf. Fitzmyer, *Luke*, 2:1041.

its sanctity and observance. In reality, Matthew and especially Luke seem more interested in exalting the image of their central figure, in justifying Jesus' right to perform his healing ministry on the Sabbath in conformance with his call to fulfill his messianic duty during the dawn of the new eschatological age unfolding before Israel's eyes. If these stories do reflect the Sabbath practices of Matthew and Luke, at best, they only show how both of them would not have objected to treating minor illnesses on the Sabbath. Regardless of what one makes of this matter, it cannot be maintained that Luke is not interested in the Law when he recounts such stories. Luke reports more Sabbath healings than any other author but never presents in these episodes a presumptuous Jesus who stands aloof from halakic and Jewish sensibilities, sweepingly announcing the abolition of a central commandment of the Torah. Instead, Luke, like Matthew, combines eschatological-christological statements with halakic-ethical considerations in order to bolster Jesus' Sabbath praxis in ways that comply with the ethos of the Torah and imply its ongoing relevance for Jewish followers of Jesus.

Chapter 5

Burying on the Sabbath

"As Busy as a Jew on a Friday."
(Ladino Proverb)

Introduction:
Matt 27:57–28:1; Mark 15:42–16:2; Luke 23:50–24:1

The synoptic portrayals of Jesus' burial contain interesting information about the care for his body *before* and *after* the Sabbath.[1] Joseph of Arimathea, who graciously volunteers to attend to Jesus' burial, hurries to perform this duty before the arrival of the Sabbath. All three synoptic writers portray Joseph in a commendable way, as a pious Jew who simultaneously seeks to care for a corpse and respect the sanctity of the Sabbath. Likewise, all three synoptics authors, especially Luke, underscore the Sabbath observance of Jesus' female disciples who note the location of Jesus' burial but wait until after the Sabbath before visiting his tomb. This section of the so-called passion narrative contains nothing controversial about the Sabbath keeping of Jesus' disciples. Both Matthew and Luke approve of Joseph and Jesus' followers' pious efforts to keep the Sabbath even while endeavoring to care for Jesus' body. This portrait confirms the impression highlighted throughout this book that both Matthew and Luke continue to respect and observe the Sabbath as a holy day. It is easy to overlook the significance of these materials for discussing the synoptic perspectives on the Sabbath. Such neglect can create an unbalanced portrait about the topic by focusing only on the controversial episodes about Sabbath keeping. To counterbalance this tendency, I take the opportunity to assess this neglected material more closely, tackling along the way some of the historical and halakic conundrums surrounding Jesus' burial, which, from the synoptic

---

[1] I would like to thank professor Richard Kalmin for his input on my usage and treatment of some of the rabbinic passages cited in my paper, "Breaking Passover to Keep the Sabbath: The Burial of Jesus and the Halakic Dilemma as Embedded within the Synoptic Narratives," (paper presented at the annual meeting of the Midwest Region of the SBL, Bourbonnais, Ill., February 12, 2011), which is part of this chapter.

point of view, seems to have occurred on a Passover falling right before a Sabbath.

Breaking Passover to Keep the Sabbath? Chronological and Halakic Dilemmas

According to the synoptics, Joseph of Arimathea hurries to bury Jesus *before* the arrival of the Sabbath.[2] During a subsequent visit *after* the Sab-

---

[2] Mark 15:43 describes Joseph of Arimathea as a "respected member of the council (εὐσχήμων βουλευτής)," "also himself looking for the kingdom of God." The label "respected member of the council" is ambiguous, implying either membership with the local council in the otherwise unknown town of Arimathea or with the Judean council of Jerusalem. See Collins, *Mark,* 777. Luke seems to infer that Joseph belongs to the Jerusalem council although he makes sure to clarify that he is a "good and righteous man" who has nothing to do with their evil purposes and deeds (23:50–51). Luke does not view Joseph as a disciple of Jesus but as a friendly outsider, in some ways similar to certain Pharisees favorably disposed toward Jesus. This portrait reflects once again Luke's more nuanced attitude toward certain Jews (so often members of the Pharisaic camp) who speak and act on behalf of Jesus and his followers. Even if Luke does not explicitly designate Joseph as a Pharisee, he may have viewed him as such, since, according to Luke, Joseph is a member of the council and described in positive terms, acting on behalf of Jesus, much like the Pharisees who warn Jesus to be aware of Herod's evil intentions (13:31–33), or Gamaliel, another Pharisee, who convinces the Sanhedrin to release the apostles from custody (Acts 5:33–39), or finally the Pharisees who side with Paul against the Sadducees during his trial in Jerusalem (Acts 23:6–10). Cf. Nolland, *Luke,* 3:1163; Ziesler, "Luke and the Pharisees," 153–54.

Going against a Lukan Pharisaic identification of Joseph is the fact that Luke (as well as the other synoptic authors) does not describe Pharisaic involvement during the arrest and trial of Jesus (neither explicit Sadducean involvement for that matter, as Ziesler notes, suggesting that the trial had less to do with party affiliations than individuals presiding in their official, judicial functions). Consequently, Luke may think that no Pharisees presided during Jesus' trial or that some were present in the Sanhedrin but were favorably disposed towards Jesus. In Acts, Luke does view the Sanhedrin of Jerusalem as composed of Pharisees and Sadducees (5:34; 23:6). Therefore, the possibility is not ruled out that Luke imagines Joseph to be a good Pharisee. It certainly seems unlikely that Luke would have thought of Joseph as a chief priest (i.e., a Sadducee), given his portrayal of the chief priests' (presumably Sadducees) involvement in the arrest and trial of Jesus and his followers (Luke 9:22; 19:47; 20:1; 20:19; 22:2, 4; 22:52; 22:66; 23:4, 10, 13; 24:20; Acts 4:1–23; 5:17, 21, 24, 27, 33; 9:14, 21; 22:30, 23:1–5, 14; 25:2, 15; 26:10, 12). See also *Ant.* 20:200–203 where Josephus claims that the high priest Ananus had James, the brother of Jesus, stoned, prompting criticism against the priest by certain Jews who were very *scrupulous* in their law observance (περὶ τοὺς νόμους ἀκριβεῖς) – an epithet ascribed to the sect of the Pharisees in Acts 26:5. The infancy narrative in Luke portrays Simon in a similar way as Joseph, "righteous and devout," awaiting the consolation of Israel (2:25).

Matthew, unlike Mark and Luke, does not claim that Joseph of Arimathea is a respectable member of the council, but rather "a disciple of Jesus." This correction corre-

bath, some of Jesus' female disciples seek to provide further care for his body through anointment with spices. These chronological brackets reveal an acute awareness on the part of all three synoptic gospel authors that according to Jewish practice burials and purchases are not to be pursued on the Sabbath.[3] Nevertheless, some chronological and terminological terms used by the synoptic authors prove confusing and at times contradictory.

The problem begins in Mark 14:12 where Jesus and his disciples are said to have made the necessary preparations for the Passover meal, presumably on a Thursday, before the arrival of Friday at sunset (the weekday when Passover supposedly began that year): "On the first day of Unleavened Bread, when the Passover lamb is sacrificed, his disciples said to him, 'Where do you want us to go and make the preparations for you to eat the Passover?'"[4] (14:12) The preparation for the Passover meal occurs before Jesus' arrest. At some point after the meal, which presumably takes place on a Thursday night, that is, the beginning of Friday according to Jewish reckoning, Jesus is arrested, tried, and eventually executed (on Friday during daytime). Matthew and Luke follow Mark's timeframe, meaning that all three synoptic authors assume that Jesus was crucified *during* Passover, on the fifteenth of Nisan. All of this is puzzling for it would mean that Joseph of Arimathea requests from Pilate Jesus' body *on Passover* in order to bury it as "evening had come (ἤδη ὀψίας γενομένης),[5] and

---

sponds to Matthew's adamant opposition to the Pharisees and other Jewish members holding positions of leadership. Matthew cannot admit that Joseph of Arimathea is a Pharisee or a member of the Jewish council, but transforms him into a follower of Jesus. See Davies and Allison, *Matthew*, 3:649; Luz, *Matthew*, 3:577; Mello, *Evangelo*, 485.

[3] Doering, "Sabbath Laws," 252; Mayer-Haas, *Geschenk*, 228–31; Weiss, *A Day of Gladness*, 89–90.

[4] This time reference in itself is awkward. The disciples inquire about preparations for Passover on the first day of Unleavened Bread, which technically would be the fifteenth of Nisan, already the beginning of Passover. Nevertheless, Mark 14:12 states that this was the day on which the Passover lamb was sacrificed, which must mean the fourteenth of Nisan (cf. Exod 12:6). Josephus, *J.W.* 5:99, also refers to the feast of Unleavened Bread as arriving on the fourteenth month of Xanthicus (τῆς τῶν ἀζύμων ἐνστάσης ἡμέρας τεσσαρεσκαιδεκάτῃ Ξανθικοῦ μηνός). As France, *The Gospel of Matthew*, 981 n. 5, suggests, this linguistic usage may stem from the practice of removing leaven from houses on the evening that *began* the fourteenth of Nisan, that is, one day ahead of the official beginning of the feast (the fifteenth of Nisan). See, for example, *m. Pesah.* 1:1–3.

[5] ἤδη ὀψίας γενομένης could possibly be translated as "when evening was coming." This translation would cohere with Joseph's intent to bury Jesus before the arrival of the Sabbath. Elsewhere, however, Mark uses γενομένης to refer to the "arrival of a point in time rather than its approach" (Joel Marcus, *Mark* [AB 27–27A; New York: Doubleday, 2000–2009], 2:1070). See Mark 1:32; 4:17; 6:2, 21, 35, 47; 15:33. Nevertheless, Marcus and others point out that this word could refer not only to the time after sunset but also to the late afternoon, meaning the Sabbath had not yet begun. See also Gundry, *Mark*, 983; Mayer-Haas, *Geschenk*, 228–29. Notice the rabbinic usage of עם חשכה (literally, "with

since it was the day of Preparation (παρασκευή),[6] that is, the day before the sabbath" (15:42).

Apparently, Mark wants to underscore Joseph of Arimathea's concern to bury Jesus before the Sabbath begins. The synoptic description accords with what we know about Sabbath keeping as well as the Jewish preference for promptly burying a body, typically on the same day death is ascertained. However, the synoptic portrayal would imply that Jesus' burial takes place on Passover, also a holy day. Hooker phrases the problem succinctly: "it makes little sense for Joseph to avoid desecration of the sabbath by burying Jesus on another holy day."[7] Mark even claims that Joseph purchases a linen cloth, has Jesus' body brought down from the cross, wrapped, and then placed in a tomb, all of this presumably taking place on Passover (15:46). Ancient Jewish texts and archaeological sources confirm Mark's description about the practice of wrapping a body in cloth,[8] but the Markan timing of this action on a Passover, especially the reference to the unnecessary *purchase* of linen on a holy day is perplexing.

Some commentators such as Joel Marcus account for this dilemma by maintaining that the pre-Markan tradition situated Jesus' crucifixion on the day before Passover. In the pre-Markan tradition, the expression "the day of preparation" referred to the day of preparation *for Passover* (rather than the Sabbath), while the introduction of the temporal phrase "the day before Sabbath" in Mark 15:42 would stem from Mark's (clumsy) effort to bring the tradition into line with his own chronology.[9] This suggestion, however, does not explore or solve the halakic dilemma outlined above; it only assesses how Mark unsatisfactorily (at least from our perspective) sought to harmonize his pre-Markan materials with his own narrative.

Prima facie, it could be tempting to dismiss this problem by embracing harmonizing schemes such as Jaubert's ingenious theory about the supposed usage in the synoptic tradition of an Essene 364-day calendar ac-

---

darkness/nightfall"), which refers not to the actual arrival of sunset, but its imminent approach, in passages discussing which types of works may or may not be initiated right before the Sabbath (*m. Shabb.* 1:10, 11; 2:7).

[6] The word παρασκευή can refer either to the day of preparation before the Sabbath, that is, Friday (e.g., Josephus, *Ant.* 16:163; Mark 15:42; Luke 23:54), or the day of preparation before Passover (e.g., John 19:14).

[7] Hooker, *A Commentary on the Gospel according to St Mark,* 380. The problem is also pointed out by Doering, "Sabbath Laws in the New Testament Gospels," 252–53, but without providing any solution.

[8] Linen textiles found in the tombs of Ein Gedi from the Second Temple period have been identified as burial shrouds. See Rachel Hachlili, *Jewish Funerary Customs, Practices and Rites in the Second Temple Period* (Supplements to JSJ 94; Leiden: Brill, 2005), 466–67, 480–8. Wrapping the body in a shroud is also mentioned in John 11:44; *m. Kil.* 9:4; *m. Ma'as.* 5:12; *t. Ned.* 2:7.

[9] Marcus, *Mark,* 2:1070.

cording to which Jesus would have held Passover on Tuesday evening/beginning of Wednesday (Passover always falls on a Wednesday according to this calendar) and would have then been crucified on a Friday before the official Passover feast, which that year would have fallen on a Sabbath according to the lunar-solar calendar used by the temple authorities (as attested in the Johannine tradition).[10] Unfortunately, her theory seems almost too good to be true, and as Fitzmyer points out "rides roughshod over the long-accepted analyses of so many of the passage involved according to form-critical methods that it cannot be taken seriously."[11]

Some of the chronological contradictions in the pre-Markan, Johannine, and synoptic traditions might remain forever unsolved. However, the halakic dilemma discussed above still itches: were *all* of the synoptic authors so ignorant of Jewish custom so as to portray Joseph of Arimathea and the female disciples of Jesus rushing to keep the Sabbath only to break Passover unwittingly? It could well be, as the pre-Markan and Johannine traditions attest, that Jesus was crucified on a Friday, the day before Passover, which that year fell on a Sabbath, but a tendency had evolved in certain circles before or by the time of the composition of the synoptic gospels to date Jesus' last supper during Passover.[12] This development in the tradition may have created the following halakic dilemma, a contradiction in the synoptic narrative, which the synoptic authors did not fully anticipate, or were inadvertently "trapped" into, once they affirmed that Jesus' last meal had occurred on the eve of Passover: how does one care for the body of a

---

[10] Annie Jaubert, *La date de la Cène. Calendrier biblique et liturgie chrétienne* (Paris, Gabalda, 1957).

[11] Fitzmyer, *Luke*, 2:1379. France, *Matthew,* 981–85, also proposes a harmonizing scheme in which Jesus would have actually held an *anticipatory* Passover meal on the evening that began on the fourteenth of Nisan (rather than on the official date, the evening beginning the fifteenth of Nisan). Jesus organized this Passover meal because he sensed he would not make it to the official date when Passover would be celebrated. With France and others, we can at least agree that that the synoptic description of Jesus' burial as well as the Johannine tradition (cf. also *Gos. Pet.* 2:5, which also states that Jesus was crucified before the first day of Unleavened Bread) attest to a pre-gospel tradition that placed Jesus' crucifixion before Passover, making the Johannine account more historically reliable, or at least credible, *in this aspect* regarding the dating of events. Why else would the synoptic authors portray Joseph and the women as faithful Sabbath keepers, only to have them theoretically desecrate Passover? France's harmonizing proposal is also more appealing that Jaubert's in another regard: it at least derives from the text, while Jaubert imposes a foreign scheme upon the gospels for which no internal evidence exists.

[12] Earlier in Mark 14:1–2, the gospel writer claims that the chief priests and the scribes were conspiring to eliminate Jesus *two* days before Passover in order to avoid causing a riot among the Jewish people during the festival. Are there traces of tradition here that conform to the Johannine dating of events and place the arrest and execution of Jesus before Passover?

person who dies on a holy festival followed by a Sabbath, that is, during two successive holy days?[13]

According to Hooker, the Mishnah does not discuss what should be done with a corpse when two holy days fall on subsequent days.[14] Neither does tractate *Semahot*, also known as *Ebel Rabbati*, which describes halakot and customs related to mourning and burial, deal with the problem. The dating of this small tractate, which does not appear in the Mishnah, is contested. In his edition and translation of *Semahot*, Zlotnick argues for an early dating, toward the end of the third century CE.[15] Other rabbinic specialists, however, reject this early dating.[16] But given the paucity of ancient literary sources dealing with the topic of Jewish burial, it would be better to consider all of the potential evidence at our disposal, even those of a later rabbinic provenance.[17] The potentially late date of the *final* composition of *Semahot* does not exclude the possibility that it contains earlier traditions. As McCane notes, burial customs change very slowly over time:

> The important point here is only that *when it comes to the specific topic of death ritual,* the rabbinic sources – even though they are later than the early Roman period – have been shown to record information that generally conforms with the patterns evident in the material remains of early Roman Jewish burial customs. In addition, it is something of an anthropological commonplace that burial practices typically change only in response to significant alternations in the social structure. Theological ideas about death and the afterlife often are quite vague and fluid, but the public ritual process of death has a weight and mass all its own.[18]

---

[13] Hooker, *A Commentary on the Gospel according to St Mark*, 380: "Once again, it seems that Mark's narrative supports the Johannine dating of the crucifixion (according to which Passover coincided with the sabbath) rather than his own. It is true that he refers here to the following day as the sabbath, not as the Passover, but obviously he could not make the latter identification in view of his interpretation of the Last Supper."

[14] Hooker, *A Commentary on the Gospel according to St Mark*, 380.

[15] Dov Zlotnick, *The Tractate "Mourning"* (New Haven: Yale University Press, 1966), 4–9.

[16] David Kraemer, *The Meanings of Death in Rabbinic Judaism* (London: Routledge, 2000), 9–10.

[17] Besides a few references in Josephus (*J.W.* 1:673, 3:437; *Ant.* 15:196–200; *Ag. Ap.* 2:205) and early Christian literature, the rabbinic documents constitute the only other main *literary* source describing Jewish burial and mourning customs. From the Qumran literature, the Temple Scroll deals briefly with certain burial issues and purity concerns. See 11QT^a 48:11–14; 49:5–21; 50:5–9. The book of Sirach (22:11–12; 38:16–23), Tobit (chs. 2, 4, and 14), and the Epistle of Jeremiah (vv. 27, 32) also contain some brief references to mourning and burial customs. See Kraemer, *The Meanings of Death*, 14–22, for a discussion of these texts and other sporadic references in the Second Temple literature.

[18] Byron McCane, *Roll Back the Stone: Death and Burial in the World of Jesus* (Harrisburg, Pa.: Trinity Press International, 2003), 30–31.

McCane's statement carries weight only when extra-rabbinic evidence corroborates the reliability of a particular rabbinic description on Jewish burial. In addition, the rabbinic descriptions and prescriptions about burial – some of which may reflect rabbinic fantasy rather than actual praxis – need not represent the customs of *all* ancient Jews, which could have varied regionally. Nevertheless, some of the rabbinic descriptions about burial and mourning have been shown to overlap with the practice of other ancient Jews. Each rabbinic tradition, then, should be assessed on an individual basis instead of being discarded because of *a priori* academic prejudices. Tractate *Semahot* does indeed contain material pertinent, at least as a heuristic device, for exploring the halakic dilemma involved in burying Jesus on a Passover that falls before a Sabbath:

> Whosoever has buried his dead two days before the end of a festival must suspend mourning during the entire festival and then count seven days, the public paying their respects to him for five days after the festival. *If seven days before the end of a festival*, he should suspend mourning during the entire festival and then count seven days, the public not attending him at all after the festival (*Sem.* 7:5; emphasis added).[19]

This passage assumes that Jews could bury a corpse "seven days before the end of a festival" (שבעה ימים בתוך הרגל). The Hebrew word for festival here, רגל, can refer to the three major pilgrimage festivals, which Jews ideally attempted to celebrate in Jerusalem, namely, Passover, Pentecost, and the Feast of Tabernacles. Both Passover and the Feast of Tabernacles run for seven days.[20] Both the first (fifteenth of Nisan) and seventh day (twenty-first of Nisan) of Passover are considered days of "holy convocation" (Num 28:18: מקרא קודש), in rabbinic parlance, a *Yom Tov*, a day in which work is generally prohibited, save for the preparation of food (Exod 12:16) and a few other types of work.[21] According to Zlotnick and Lieberman, the Hebrew בתוך, which literally means "in the midst," should be understood here as "before the end of," referring to the *beginning* of a festival period.[22] Thus, were we to count back "seven days before the end

---

[19] English Translations of *Semahot* are taken from Zlotnick's edition.

[20] The Feast of Tabernacles also includes an "eighth day of solemn assembly" (Shemini Atseret).

[21] Yom Kippur is an exception, since according to Lev 16:31, it is a שבת שבתון, "a Sabbath of complete rest," during which no work can be done. By contrast, the Torah declares the other festivals merely as שבתון (Lev 23:24, 29), "a day of rest."

[22] Zlotnick, *The Tractate "Mourning,"* 128 n. 5. Zlotnick renders בתוך with the awkward English phrase "before the end of" (a festival) because of the linguistic parallelism with the previous halakot in *Semahot*. According to Lieberman, *Tosefta Ki-Fshutah*, 5:1252, בתוך should be מתוך, meaning here that they buried the person on the first day of the feast.

of Passover," it would bring us back to the fifteenth of Nisan.[23] A similar rabbinic assumption about burying a corpse on a festival day appears in the Babylonian Talmud:

> Abaye enquired of Rabbah: "What if one buried his dead during the festival (קברו ברגל)? Does the festival enter into his counting of the thirty days, or does the festival not enter into his counting of the thirty days?..." He [Rabbah] replied: "The [days of the] festival do not enter into the counting" (*b. Mo'ed Qat.* 19b).

Here Abaye, a fourth generation Babylonian Amora (c. 280–339 CE), inquires with his teacher Rabbah about a case where someone is buried on a festival day. Should that day be counted as one of the thirty days of mourning, known in Hebrew as *Sheloshim*, or should it not, since a festival day is normally not included in the counting of the first seven days of mourning (in Hebrew, *Shiva*)? One could argue that the chronological terminology used here is ambiguous: the talmudic passage only speaks of the possibility of burying someone *during* a festival (ברגל). Perhaps, *intermediate* days of a festival are meant here. Rabbinic halakah treats intermediate festival days more loosely than holy days of convocation (e.g., the first or last days of Passover). The following baraita, however, appearing in the same section of the Babylonian Talmud, refers in unequivocal terms to a burial occurring on a festival day:

> If one buried his dead at the beginning of the festival (קברו בתחילת הרגל) he counts seven days [of mourning] after the festival and his work is done by others....(*b. Mo'ed Qat.* 20a)

The reference to the *beginning* of a festival day, coupled by the command to count *seven* days of mourning after the festival, makes it clear that the scenario envisaged here involves burying a corpse on a festival day, for example, on the fifteenth of Nisan, the first day of Passover. Another passage from the same section of the Bavli reports that Rabin (fourth generation Palestinian Amora) claimed in the name of R. Johanan (second generation Palestinian Amora, died c. 279) that if one buried a dead person during the festival (קברו ברגל), that part of the festival should be counted into the first thirty days of mourning. The Bavli maintains that R. Eleazar (third generation Amora) held the same position on the matter, instructing his son R. Pedath to count the festival as part of the thirty days, "even if one buried his dead during the festival" (*b. Mo'ed Qat.* 20a). As noted

---

[23] And not the fourteenth of Nisan, which would be *eight* days before the end of the festival, that is, one day before the *beginning* of the festival. Cf. *Sem.* 7:4: "If he has buried his dead eight days before the festival, he may, if he wishes, cut his hair and wash his clothes on the eve of the festival. If he did not do so on the eve of the festival, he may not do so until the šĕlošim are completed."

above, the phrase "during the festival" remains somewhat ambiguous. Are only intermediate days of a festival assumed here? Probably not, since Shavuot, which is also a רגל, does not have any intermediate days. Non-intermediate days, then, are probably presupposed in the usage of the prepositional phrase "during the festival."[24]

These rabbinic injunctions are striking since a halakah from the Mishnah clearly states that the Sabbath differs from a festival day *only with regard to the preparation of food* (*m. Yom Tov* 5:2; *m. Meg.*1:5). The rabbinic sages allowed certain foods to be prepared on a festival day, but in many other aspects treated the festivals in the same way as the Sabbath. Perhaps, the aforementioned passages from the Bavli and *Semahot* attest to a yet another example of rabbinic laxity toward festival days in comparison to the weekly Sabbath.[25]

---

[24] *Sem.* 4:6 is very interesting: even a priest must become defiled on the *eve of Passover* (ערב פסחים) if one of his close relatives passes away. The text does not indicate, however, whether such rabbis think a priest should actually bury their relative on the eve of Passover. This passage recalls in some ways John 19:31 where the priests allegedly avoid entering Pilate's headquarters in order to avoid contracting ritual defilement that could disqualify them from eating the Passover meal. Presumably, a similar concern is imagined in this rabbinic passage. *Sem.* 4:6 continues: "In the case of all those of whom it is said that for them a priest should defile himself, it is not a matter of choice – it is mandatory. Rabbi Simeon says: 'It is a matter of choice.' Rabbi Judah says: 'It is mandatory.' It happened that the wife of Joseph the Priest died on Passover Eve, and he did not want to defile himself for her. The Sages thereupon pushed him down and defiled him against his will, while they said to him: 'It is not a matter of choice – it is mandatory.'" *Sem.* 4:7 continues its discussion regarding the priestly obligation towards funeral preparations and attendance: "How long does he defile himself for her? Rabbi Meir says: 'All that day.' Rabbi Simeon says: 'Up to three days.' Rabbi Judah in the name of Rabbi Tarfon says: 'Until the tomb is sealed.'" If we should read *Sem.* 4:7 in light of *Sem.* 4:6, it would mean that contact or at least proximity with a dead body is assumed well into Passover, since at least R. Simeon agrees that that a priest must defile himself up to three days after the person died, which inevitably encompasses the first day of Passover, as said person died on the eve of that holy day. Does this passage assume that the body could be buried on Passover? One cannot confidently derive that much information from this passage. The text may assume that Jews bury the person on the eve death is determined, as prompt burial before nightfall was the preferred practice among Jews. Alternatively, the passage might assume that *Gentiles* would take care of burying a Jew on a festival day (to be discussed below).

[25] Previously, I pointed out another lenient attitude of the rabbis with regard to lifting an animal out of a trap on a festival day (*m. Yom Tov* 3:2) – an act that the rabbis forbid on the Sabbath (see chapter 4 and the section dealing with Matt 12:9–14). The rabbis could treat festival days more leniently because the word מלאכה is used in the Mosaic Torah only with respect to the Sabbath (and the Day of Atonement). See David Instone-Brewer, *Feasts and Sabbaths: Passover and Atonement* (TRENT 2A; Grand Rapids, Mich.: Eerdmans, 2011), 2.

Some important qualifications are of order though. First, it should be noted that the rabbinic passages discussed above focus on how festival observance cuts off the mourning period.[26] Moreover, in his monumental commentary on the Tosefta, Lieberman provides a gloss *en passant* about the aforementioned passage from *Semahot*, claiming that *Gentiles* would bury the bodies of Jews on a festival day. Lieberman, however, does not include any references in rabbinic literature where such a qualification is made.[27] So far, I have come across three passages in the Bavli that do refer to such a scenario. In *b. Yom Tov* 6a (also mentioned in *b. Yom Tov* 22a), Rava (fourth generation Babylonian Amora) states that "on the first day of a Festival, [only] Gentiles may busy themselves with a corpse, [but] on the second day, Israelites may busy themselves with a corpse...." This statement, ascribed to Rava, stimulates further talmudic discussion. Mar Zutra (Babylonian Amora, died c. 417) argues that such a practice should occur only if the person has been dead for some time, presumably because of body decay and the call to respect the dead through prompt burial. Otherwise, the corpse should be left alone until the festival has passed. R. Ashi (Babylonian Amora, died c. 427), however, maintains that even if the body has not been lying around for a long time, burial should be performed immediately. This debate is interesting and comes closer to the scenario presumed in the synoptic gospels: here some Babylonian sages discuss what should be done to a corpse that could potentially remain unburied for two festival days, generating at least two differing positions, one preferring postponement (Mar Zutra), the other advocating prompt burial (R. Ashi).

Finally, in *b. Shabb.* 139a–b, a rabbinic parallel more analogous to the halakic problem embedded in the synoptic narrative emerges:

The citizens of Bashkar sent [a question] to Levi: "What about...a dead man on a Festival?" By the time he [the messenger] arrived [at Levi's home] Levi had died. Said Samuel to R. Menashia: "If you are wise, send them [an answer]." [So] he sent [word] to them...."Neither Jews nor Syrians [non-Jews] may occupy themselves with a corpse, neither on the first day of a Festival nor on the second." But that is not so? For R. Judah b. Shilath said in R. Assi's name: "Such a case happened in the synagogue of Ma'on on a Festival near the Sabbath, though I do not know whether it preceded or followed it, and when they went before R. Johanan, he said to them: 'Let Gentiles occupy themselves with him [the dead].'" Raba too said: "As for a corpse, on the first day of Festivals

---

[26] See also *b. Sanh.* 35a–36a, which discusses the impossibility of burying an executed man on the Sabbath and may treat festival days in the same way (see beginning of 36a).

[27] See Lieberman, *Tosefta Ki-Fshutah*, 5:1252 n. 26.

Gentiles should occupy themselves with him; on the second day of Festivals Israelites may occupy themselves with him...."[28]

In this passage, some people from Bashkar (i.e., Caskar, the chief town in the Mesene region on the right bank of the old Tigris) inquire about burying someone on a festival day. At first, the rabbinic reply categorically forbids this act as a preventive measure out of fear that the inhabitants of Bashkar will break a festival day in other aspects as well. Neither Jews nor Gentiles, therefore, may busy themselves with a corpse during the first and second days of a festival. Nevertheless, R. Judah b. Shilath reports a case that happened in the synagogue of Ma'on (a town near Tiberias) when a festival fell near the Sabbath. During that incident, R. Johanan instructed that Gentiles could occupy themselves with the burial of the dead person on the first day of a festival, while Jews could do so only on the second day.

Since these passages clearly indicate that Gentiles should perform burials for Jews in such circumstances, perhaps, following Lieberman, we should presuppose that all other pertinent rabbinic passages (e.g., the text from *Semahot* and the baraita in the Bavli) assume non-Jews as carrying out burials on festival days. Nevertheless, my main goal in soliciting later rabbinic passages lies not in proving the antiquity or popularity of the practices they mention as in illustrating how burials on festival days were at least conceivable to other ancient Jews, admittedly from a period after the final composition of the synoptic gospels.

How might these findings assist in assessing the halakic dilemma within the synoptic gospels? First, we should not assume that rabbinic practice reflected the customs of all Jews living in antiquity, especially those in the Diaspora – the milieu in which some of the synoptic gospels probably reached their final shape. It could be that some Diasporan Jews, during unusual circumstances, buried their dead on festival days even without the assistance of Gentiles. However, in the absence of literary and archaeological attestations, such remarks remain purely speculative.[29] Is it possible

---

[28] The follow passage from Yerushalmi, although it deals with the issue of burying someone on the eve of the Sabbath, not on a festival proper, is also noteworthy: "R. Helbo, R. Huna in the name of Rab: 'If the eighth day [after burial] coincided with the Sabbath, one gets a haircut on the eve of the Sabbath.' How is such a thing possible? [Was the deceased buried on the Sabbath? Surely not.]....R. Abun, 'Interpret [the earlier statement to deal with a case in which] the grave was sealed on the eve of the Sabbath at sunset.' How is such a thing possible? Said R. Aha, 'Interpret the case to speak of a burial in which Gentiles sealed the grave'" (*y. Mo'ed Qat.* 3:5 82a). Translation taken and adapted from Neusner's preliminary translation of the Yerushalmi.

[29] An epitaph from Hierapolis (Asia Minor), dated to the end of the second century or beginning of the third century CE, from the family tomb of a said P. Aelius Glykon and Aurelia Amia, contains an interesting reference to the donation of money for annual

that Matthew and Luke assume that *Gentiles* take care of Jesus' burial? Few clues point in this direction, although such a possibility remains open. The synoptic gospels (Matt 27:58–60; Mark 15:43–46; Luke 23:52–53) describe Jesus' burial in the singular, crediting Joseph of Arimathea for its execution. Nevertheless, a person of such rank would not have been willing or even capable on his own of performing all the physical actions required to dispose properly of a body (removing the body from the cross, wrapping it in cloth, transporting it to the tomb, rolling the stone on the tomb, etc.).[30] Probably, the synoptic authors imagine Joseph as *supervising* the burial process. None of the synoptic authors, however, indicates whether Jews or Gentiles participated in these actions.

More importantly, the exceptional circumstances surrounding Jesus' death should be duly noted in order to account for the "inadvertent" halakic dilemma embedded in the synoptic burial accounts. Many Jews may have well approved of the synoptic description of Joseph's behavior, given the less than ideal circumstances in which he has to act: which Jew in such extreme circumstances would want to leave a Jewish corpse hanging on a Roman cross during Passover as well as the Sabbath in the environs of the holy city of Jerusalem? Joseph's act may have appeared commendable to

---

grave ceremonies that apparently were to be celebrated on the Jewish festivals of Unleavened Bread and Pentecost. The full translation with Greek text and discussion of the epitaph can be found in Philip A. Harland, "Acculturation and Identity in the Diaspora: A Jewish Family and 'Pagan' Guilds at Hierapolis," *JJS* 57 (2006): 222–44. It reads: "This grave and the burial ground beneath it together with the surrounding place belong to Publius Aelius Glykon Zeuxianos Aelianus and to Aurelia Amia, daughter of Amianos Seleukos. In it he will bury himself, his wife, and his children, but no one else is permitted to be buried here. He left behind 200 denaria for the grave-crowning ceremony to the most holy presidency of the purple-dyers, so that it would produce from the interest enough for each to take a share in the seventh month during the festival of Unleavened Bread. Likewise he also left behind 150 denaria for the grave-crowning ceremony to the association of carpet-weavers, so that the revenues from the interest should be distributed, half during the festival of Kalends on eighth day of the fourth month and half during the festival of Pentecost. A copy of this inscription was put into the archives." Perhaps, this epitaph shows that certain Jews would have no problem with either collections of donations or grave ceremonies occurring on Jewish festival days such as the feast of Unleavened Bread. Unfortunately, the inscription does not allow to infer further whether Jews themselves would carry out such activities on festival days, let alone perform burials, a different matter altogether, although it might place them near grave sites at such sacred times (if the celebrations occurred within the vicinity of the cemetery).

[30] Acts 13:29 states in the plural that "they took him down (καθελόντες) from the tree and laid (ἔθηκαν) him in a tomb," whereas Luke 23:53 reads in the singular: "he [i.e., Joseph of Arimathea] took it down (καθελών), wrapped it in a linen cloth, and laid (ἔθηκεν) it in a rock-hewn tomb." The plural usage in Acts 13:29 shows that Luke believes other people assisted in burying Jesus.

Matthew and Luke's Jewish readers in yet another way. Deut 21:22–23 states:

> When someone is convicted of a crime punishable by death and is executed, and you hang him on a tree, his corpse must not remain all night upon the tree; you shall bury him that same day, for anyone hung on a tree is under God's curse. You must not defile the land that the LORD your God is giving you for possession.

To leave a corpse exposed on a cross for more than one day would lie in tension with the Mosaic command to remove and bury it promptly. Presumably, this injunction would be valid for *any* day of the week, not just Friday.[31] Joseph's piety, then, becomes all the more noteworthy when we fully appreciate the halakic, ethical, and political complexity confronting him: he wishes to remove the body on the very same day in order to avoid defiling the land and the unbearable shame of seeing a Jewish corpse hanging on a cross during a high holy day carrying strong "national" overtones; he also seeks to perform this duty before the arrival of the Sabbath, which would postpone prompt burial for even a longer time. In either case, a halakic-ethical dilemma emerges forcing a decision to either desecrate the holy land or a holy day. The latter option carries certain advantages: by exceptionally breaking Passover, Joseph can at least properly observe the upcoming Sabbath and prevent the land from becoming desecrated. Furthermore, the rest of the many Jews gathered in Jerusalem can resume their Passover and Sabbath keeping without enduring the shame of seeing of one of their fellow compatriots hanging dishonorably on a cross.

To what extent the synoptic authors were aware or even perturbed by this hypothetical scheme – one based on a contemporary reading of the synoptic tradition as the byproduct of an inconsistent meshing of divergent traditions – remains uncertain. If Mark thought that Jesus' burial occurred on a Passover, he may have clumsily arranged his narrative in one regard, namely, by having Joseph purchase a linen cloth on a holy day: theoretically, Joseph could have found a way to acquire a linen garment without buying it, regardless of the pressing circumstances or the hypothetical involvement of Gentiles.[32] This *may* explain why both Matthew and Luke

---

[31] Collins, *Mark*, 777. Cf. Josephus, *J.W.* 4:317: "…the Jews used to take so much care of the burial of men, that they took down those who were condemned and crucified, and buried them before the going down of the sun."

[32] Even Strack and Billerbeck, 2:834, in their tendentious dismissal of the halakic problems involved in dating Jesus' trial, execution, and burial on a Passover, admit that Mark's reference to Joseph's purchase remains puzzling. Joachim Jeremias, *The Eucharistic Words of Jesus* (trans. Norman Perrin; New York: Scribner, 1966), 74–79, attempts to read this passage in light of Mishnaic passages that allow for purchases of food on festivals (through pledged transactions that are then completed after the festival), speculating that items for burial, like food, would have been viewed as "items of necessity."

have deleted Mark's reference to purchasing: in their narratives, Joseph simply wraps Jesus in a linen cloth.[33] Likewise, the unique timing of Jesus' burial (on a Passover falling right before the weekly Sabbath) may have led both Matthew and Luke to delete any reference to the washing of Jesus' body, which, according to Jewish custom, is one of the most important acts to be performed on behalf of a dead person before burial. The pressing circumstances did not allow anyone to perform such actions on Jesus' behalf.[34] Matthew also says nothing about the anointing of Jesus' body (even after the Sabbath).[35] Quite interestingly, *m. Shabb.* 23:5 allows Jews on the Sabbath to "make ready all that is needful for the dead, and anoint it and wash it, provided that they do not move any member of it." Nevertheless, Matthew and Luke are aware of the exceptional and pressing circumstances of this case (two successive holy days during which the body would be exposed if not buried immediately). A logical outcome would be to describe the burial of Jesus in the most speedily manner without mentioning washing and anointing, because of Passover and the fast approach of the Sabbath.[36]

Jeremias, however, might be reading too much into the synoptic accounts. See the reservations of Derrett, *Studies in the New Testament*, 97.

[33] Some commentators like Collins, *Mark,* 778, think that Matthew and Luke have deleted this detail simply because it was superfluous. Cf. Davies and Allison, *Matthew,* 3:650, with regard to Matthew: "...it is no surprise that 'having bought' is absent: not only is the detail superfluous, but one might ask how Joseph can, if it is by now the Sabbath, buy anything." True, but what about buying a cloth and burying a body on Passover?

[34] Cf. Magness' remarks in *Stone and Dung,* 170 about the rush to bury Jesus: "When the Gospels tell us that Joseph of Arimathea offered Jesus a spot in his tomb, it is because Jesus' family did not own a rock-cut tomb and there was no time to prepare a grave – that is, there was no time to *dig* a grave, *not* hew a rock-cut tomb (!) – before the Sabbath."

[35] Mark and Luke, however, mention the intent on the part of the women to anoint Jesus' body on the third day. The *Gospel of Peter* explicitly refers to the washing of Jesus' body (*Gos. Pet.* 6:24), while the gospel of John (19:39–40) claims his body was anointed with spices, but does not mention washing. For Mayer-Haas, *Geschenk*, 228 n. 467, 233, the washing of Jesus' body is implied in the Markan narrative: since Joseph of Arimathea provides Jesus with a dignified burial, he would have had his body washed. Supposedly, Mark fails to mention the anointing of Jesus' corpse in order to highlight the previous scene in Mark 14:3–8. For further descriptions of Jewish burial practices, see Luz, *Matthew,* 3:578, referencing Samuel Klein, *Tod und Begräbnis in Palästina zur Zeit der Tannaiten* (Berlin: Itzkowski, 1908), 41–100. See also Gnilka, *Markus*, 2:334–37; Samuel Krauss, *Talmudische Archäologie* (Hildesheim: Olms, 1966), 2:54–82; Hachlili, *Jewish Funerary Customs*; Magness, *Stone and Dung*, 145–80; McCane, *Roll Back the Stone*.

[36] So Nolland, *Matthew*, 1231: "The burial account will combine minimal preparation of the body with a most dignified resting place. This is consonant with Joseph's making the most of a very limited window of opportunity." Shmuel Safrai, "Home and Family,"

Do Joseph and the Women Perform Work on the Sabbath?

A cursory reading of Mark could lead to the conclusion that Joseph buries Jesus on the Sabbath, since it is already evening (ἤδη ὀψίας γενομένης) when he requests permission for burial from Pilate (15:42). Matthew, however, deletes the word ἤδη, while the remaining words ὀψίας δὲ γενομένης (Matt 27:57) can be understood as referring to the late afternoon.[37] Matthew also omits Mark's explanatory phrase "it was the day of Preparation, that is, it was before the Sabbath" (ἐπεὶ ἦν παρασκευὴ ὅ ἐστιν προσάββατον), presumably because his readers would not need such clarification (unlike some of Mark's Gentile readers). Matthew's audience already knows that in a case where the Sabbath is fast approaching prompt action is required to guarantee proper burial.[38]

Unlike Matthew and Mark, Luke does not open his narration of Jesus' burial with chronological markers.[39] Instead, he simply states that Joseph of Arimathea approaches Pilate to request for Jesus' body, probably sometime on Friday afternoon. Only *after* Joseph performs these actions, does Luke refer to the approaching of the Sabbath: "it was the day of Preparation, and the sabbath was beginning" (23:54: ἡμέρα ἦν παρασκευῆς καὶ σάββατον ἐπέφωσκεν). This Lukan literary postponement, which mentions the day of Preparation and the incoming Sabbath only after Joseph buries Jesus, may actually serve as an opening for the subsequent unit describing the presence and actions of the women from Galilee (vv. 55–56) rather than as a conclusion to the preceding scene reporting Joseph's activities.[40] In other words, Luke's Joseph buries Jesus "well" before the beginning of the Sabbath, while the women who follow Jesus manage to prepare their spices right before the arrival of the Sabbath (23:56).

---

in *The Jewish People in the First Century* (eds. Shmuel Safrai and Menahem Stern; 2 vols.; Compendia rerum iudaicarum ad Novum Testamentum; Amsterdam: Van Gorcum, 1976), 2:776 n. 3: "It [i.e., the washing of the body] is possible that it was omitted because of the imminent approach of the Sabbath." See also the interesting point made by Kraemer (citing rabbinic sources) that until the third day Jews thought an individual could come back to life. On the third day, the soul would be struggling in its final attempt to leave the body. Oil would have been applied to sooth the anguished corpse up until the third day to ease this painful process. See Kraemer, *The Meanings of Death in Rabbinic Judaism*, 21, 84.

[37] See note above on its usage in Mark. Cf. Nolland, *Matthew*, 1227.

[38] So Mayer-Haas, *Geschenk*, 460.

[39] The Lukan precision, absent in Mark, that Arimathea is a "city of the Jews," does not prove that Luke is a Gentile. Contra Bovon, *Luc*, 3:395. Arimathea is an obscure name, its precise identification remaining unknown even to scholars. Because of its obscurity, Luke clarifies for his audience (Gentiles but also Diasporan Jews ignorant of its location) that this town is located in Judea and inhabited by Jews.

[40] So Fitzmyer, *Luke*, 2:1524.

Further proof for this interpretation might lie in Luke's employment of the verb ἐπιφώσκω in the imperfect rather than in the aorist or perfect, suggesting that when the women prepare the spices for Jesus' body, the Sabbath has not yet begun, but is *in transit, in the process of arriving*.[41] A compelling argument for this understanding of Luke appears in the *Gospel of Peter*. There, Joseph of Arimathea asks permission for burial from Pilate *before* the execution of Jesus. Pilate proceeds to request Jesus' body from Herod. The latter, however, assures Pilate that "even if no one had requested him, we would have buried him, since indeed Sabbath is dawning (ἐπεὶ καὶ σάββατον ἐπιφώσκει). For in the Law it has been written: The sun is not to set on one put to death" (*Gos. Pet.* 2:5). Here the verb ἐπιφώσκει describes the imminent *approach* of the Sabbath, not its arrival.[42] Luke, then, may have envisaged the following scenario: as the Sabbath approaches, the female disciples of Jesus witness the location where Jesus rests and then return to prepare spices and ointments, whereupon Luke explicitly declares – he is the only gospel writer to do so – that "on the sabbath they rested according to the commandment" (23:56: τὸ μὲν σάββατον ἡσύχασαν κατὰ τὴν ἐντολήν).[43] Luke's composition of this phrase highlights his ea-

---

[41] Similarly, Mayer-Haas, *Geschenk*, 363: "Luke 23, 54b weist auf den kurz bevorstehenden Beginn des Sabbats...das heißt, die Zeit der letzten Vorbereitungen war gekommen, der eigentliche Beginn des Sabbats stand aber noch bevor."

[42] The usage of ἐπιφώσκει in Luke and the *Gos. Pet.* resembles the rabbinic עם חשכה, which refers to the imminent (not actual) arrival of nightfall. The rabbinic sages debate under which circumstances certain works may be undertaken during this final window of opportunity before the arrival of the Sabbath (*m. Shabb.* 1:10, 11; 2:7). On the other hand, CD 10:14–16 adds an extra amount of time before the Sabbath officially begins when performing work is prohibited: "A man may not work on the { } sixth day from the time that the solar orb is above the horizon by its diameter." In rabbinic literature, this additional time before sunset that is added onto the Sabbath is known as תוספת שבת. See *b. Yoma* 81a–b; Joseph M. Baumgarten, "The Religious Law of the Qumran Community," [in Hebrew] *Qadmoniot* 30 (1997): 97.

[43] Daniel Boyarin, "'After the Sabbath' (Matt 28:1) – Once More into the Crux," *JTS* 52 (2001): 678–88, suggests Luke has gotten himself into a muddle here, since in v. 54 he refers to the beginning of the Sabbath, while in v. 56 he mentions the preparation of spices as presumably taking place on the Sabbath (or at least at the beginning of the Sabbath). However, does Luke see a narrow timeframe in which the women prepare the spices during the "gray" area of transition from Friday to the Sabbath? The reading of ἐπιφώσκω suggested above could allow for this interpretation. There would be no need, then, to follow Klinghardt's proposal that Luke has suddenly shifted from a Jewish to a Roman reckoning of time, meaning that the Sabbath for Luke starts only in the morning rather than the evening. Why should a sudden transition in reckoning abruptly occur within a pericope in which Luke is eager to portray the disciples of Jesus as Torah observant? See Klinghardt, *Gesetz und Volk Gottes*, 263–64. Alternatively, preparing spices for a corpse on Passover may have been viewed as permissible, given the following statement from the Mishnah: "they may make ready [on the Sabbath] all that is needful

gerness to illustrate that the Jewish followers of Jesus remain faithful in their observance of the Sabbath and the Torah in general.[44]

When Do the Women Visit Jesus' Tomb?

Considerable scholarly energy has been devoted to determining the exact timing of the women's visit to Jesus' tomb as reported in the synoptic gospels. Mark 16:1–2 contains a twofold description in which the women first purchase their spices for anointing Jesus' body, once the Sabbath is over (καὶ διαγενομένου τοῦ σαββάτου),[45] and then walk to Jesus' tomb "very early on the first day of the week, when the sun had risen" (λίαν πρωῒ τῇ μιᾷ τῶν σαββάτων...ἀνατείλαντος τοῦ ἡλίου). Matt 28:1 frames Mary Magdalene and Mary's visit to the tomb with a peculiar Greek phrase that has generated much debate: ὀψὲ δὲ σαββάτων τῇ ἐπιφωσκούσῃ εἰς μίαν σαββάτων.[46] The exegetical problem concerns determining the meaning of ὀψέ, which in theory can mean "late" or "after" (when functioning as a preposition followed by a genitive), as well as deciphering the unusual ἐπιφωσκούσῃ, which *BDAG* translates as "to grow towards or become daylight, shine forth, dawn, break, perhaps draw on."[47] If ὀψέ means, "late," and ἐπιφωσκούσῃ refers to the dawning of a new morning, then the

---

for the dead, and anoint it and wash it" (*m. Shabb.* 23:5). Why not also prepare spices even if they will be applied only after the Sabbath, as Jesus' body had to be rushed to Joseph's tomb? This matter may not have been viewed as such a big deal, given the less than favorable circumstances surrounding Jesus' death.

[44] Weiss, *A Day of Gladness,* 89, finds the appearance of the Lukan phrase "according to the commandment" surprising, "since usually he [i.e., Luke] is reluctant to mention the law and the commandments." Perhaps, the phraseology here stems from a tradition that emphasized the women's Torah piety. In any case, Luke finds it useful to retain this traditional formulation; it fits with his larger portrait of Jesus and his followers as faithful to the Torah and its stipulations. Even Weiss acknowledges later in his book that the "author of Luke/Acts repeatedly brings Jesus and Paul to the synagogue on the Sabbath and makes the point that attending the synagogue was their custom....This author clearly wishes to make the point, in particular about Paul, that he was an observant Jew" (171). Part of the problem probably lies in scholarly attempts to distinguish too neatly between the terms and concepts of "custom" and "law/commandment."

[45] J. Michael Winger, "When Did the Women Visit the Tomb?" *NTS* 40 (1994): 287, suggests that διαγενομένου τοῦ σαββάτου reflects a Semitic phrase, either the Aramaic נגהי חד בשבתא or the Hebrew אור לאחד בשבת.

[46] μίαν σαββάτων (literally, "first of the Sabbaths") is a Semitism, and refers to the first day of the week.

[47] *LSJ* points to only one Greek papyrus (*Plond* 1.130.39 from the first century CE) where the verb ἐπιφώσκω would carry this meaning of growing toward daylight, that is, dawn. Many of the other references cited therein come from the gospels.

Matthean chronology contains an inconsistency: it cannot be late in the Sabbath, if it is already Sunday morning.

Building on the work of the late George Foot Moore, Boyarin has recently solved the problem in a convincing way by pointing back to Hebrew and Aramaic phrases presumably standing behind the Judeo-Greek formulation found in Matthew's gospel.[48] A long time ago, Moore supposed Matt 28:1 contained a literal reproduction in Greek of a Jewish idiom that could be translated back either into Aramaic as באפוקי שבתא נגהי חד בשתא or into Hebrew as במוצאי שבת אור לאחד בשבת.[49] Accordingly, the Judeo-Greek phrase in Matthew translates as "at the end of the Sabbath, at the beginning of the first day."[50] The Greek τῇ ἐπιφωσκούσῃ would be nothing else than a rendition of the Hebrew אור ל or the Aramaic נגהי, both of which literally refer to "light," but point not to the dawning light of early sunrise, but to the beginning of the day at sunset (following the Jewish reckoning of time).[51] These Hebrew and Aramaic formulations are well attested in rabbinic literature, and their Greek counterpart in Matthew can be translated rather easily and smoothly back into its original Semitic idiom.[52] This would mean that for Matthew Mary Magdalene and Mary visit the tomb after the end of the Sabbath, that is, after sunset, in our modern parlance, on a Saturday night, rather than early Sunday morning.[53]

Matthew's phraseology leads Mayer-Haas to posit a possible weekly memorial commemorating the death and resurrection of Jesus on the part of Matthew and his group that would have taken place immediately after sunset on the Sabbath instead of the early hours of Sunday morning.[54] While such a practice is certainly conceivable, especially when viewed as an extension to the Sabbath keeping allegedly observed by Matthew and some of his readers, the insufficiency and nature of the literary evidence prevent one from building a solid case on behalf of this thesis. In any case, my primary aim is to stress the timing of the women's visit: it occurs *after* the Sabbath, underscoring the respect Jesus' followers ascribe to that holy day. Doering points out that even if we translate ὀψὲ σαββάτων as "late on

---

[48] Boyarin, "'After the Sabbath,'" 678–88.

[49] George F. Moore, "Conjectanea Talmudica," *JAOS* 26 (1905): 328.

[50] Boyarin, "'After the Sabbath,'" 688.

[51] Boyarin, "After the Sabbath," 685; Moore, "Conjectanea Talmudica," 327.

[52] According to Moore, "Conjectanea Talmudica," 325, the phrases במוצאי שבת or באפוקי שבתא always denote a period of time occurring after the end of the Sabbath.

[53] Those who want to translate ἐπιφωσκούσῃ as "dawning," that is, as a reference to Sunday morning, usually do so in order to harmonize Matthew with the other gospel accounts. To resort to a Hebrew or Aramaic background is not an act of despair as Luz, *Matthew,* 3:594 n. 39, maintains. As noted above, Matthew's wording is quite unique and translates easily back into Semitic idiom.

[54] *Geschenk,* 468.

the Sabbath," meaning that the women set out to Jesus' tomb when it is still the Sabbath, it would be problematic from a halakic point of view only if the women would have exceeded the Sabbath limit (2000 cubits) before sunset.[55] Matthew, then, portrays these followers of Jesus as strictly complying with Jewish practice: they refrain from traveling, purchasing, and burying a body on the Sabbath day.[56]

Luke essentially follows Mark's chronology,[57] stating that "on the first day of the week, at early dawn (τῇ δὲ μιᾷ τῶν σαββάτων ὄρθρου βαθέως), they came to the tomb, taking the spices that they had prepared." With the words ὄρθρου βαθέως (literally, "at deep dawn"), Luke means that the women arrive to the tomb very early Sunday morning, just before daybreak.[58] Thus, like Matthew (and Mark), Luke depicts the women as faithfully observing the Sabbath, waiting until that sacred day is over before making their way to the tomb.

Matthew's Polemics against the Pharisees and their Sabbath keeping

Right after recounting Jesus' burial, Matthew refers to a unique incident involving the Pharisees that surely reflects the polemics of his own day.[59] The episode begins in 27:62 when the chief priests and the Pharisees allegedly approach Pilate out of concern that Jesus' body might be stolen, imploring the Roman official to place guards at the tomb. According to Matt 27:62, this event takes place the day after Jesus' crucifixion, "on the next day, that is, after the day of Preparation" (τῇ δὲ ἐπαύριον, ἥτις ἐστὶν μετὰ τὴν παρασκευήν). Here, Matthew uses a circumlocution for the Sabbath, referring to it as the "next day," perhaps because even he knows that his polemical portrait is not entirely credible: would the Pharisees and the

---

[55] Doering, "Sabbath Laws in the New Testament Gospels," 252 n. 192. See *b. Shabb.* 150b–151b.

[56] Writing decades after the Holocaust, it is incredible to see Mateos and Camacho, *El Evangelio*, 282, state that "las dos mujeres...han observado el descanso judío; no han roto aún con la institución que ha crucificado a Jesús."

[57] Luke replaces Mark's λίαν πρωΐ with ὄρθρου βαθέως, while Mark's ἀνατείλαντος τοῦ ἡλίου is left out. In addition, Luke does not have the woman purchase spices right after the Sabbath, since he claims that they have prepared them right before the Sabbath.

[58] The Greek ὄρθρος βαθύς means early "dawn, just before daybreak." See "ὄρθρος," *LSJ*.

[59] The incident appears only in Matthew. The sudden intrusion of the Pharisees, who, otherwise, remain absent from the passion narrative, stems from Mathew's wider polemics against that particular group. See Davies and Allison, *The Gospel according to Matthew,* 3:652–53.

chief priests really be busying themselves on the Sabbath with the supervision of Jesus' body?[60] Matthew may also be insinuating that the Pharisees and the chief priests not only request guards to watch over Jesus' body, but also accompany them to the tomb on the Sabbath: "So they went with the guard and made the tomb secure by sealing the stone" (27:66: οἱ δὲ πορευθέντες ἠσφαλίσαντο τὸν τάφον σφραγίσαντες τὸν λίθον μετὰ τῆς κουστωδίας). In the Greek, the verbs "went" (πορευθέντες), "secured" (ἠσφαλίσαντο) and "sealed" (σφραγίσαντες) all appear in the plural. The prepositional phrase μετὰ τῆς κουστωδίας suggests some people accompany the guard. Probable candidates who belong to this escort would be the chief priests and Pharisees mentioned in the preceding verse. The prepositional phrase μετὰ τῆς κουστωδίας appears at the end of the sentence, after the participial verb σφραγίσαντες, possibly indicating that the chief priests and Pharisees even assist with the sealing of the tomb. Matthew's language may be purposefully ambiguous, subtly deprecating his opponents by portraying them as Sabbath transgressors.[61]

Conclusion

Both Matthew and Luke portray Joseph of Arimathea and the women from Galilee as pious Jews attentively caring for Jesus' body while simultaneously seeking to honor the Sabbath: Joseph ensures that Jesus receives a proper burial before the arrival of the Sabbath; the female disciples rest on the Sabbath and wait until after sunset before visiting the tomb. More openly than any other synoptic writer, Luke signals the Torah observance of the female disciples of Jesus by explicitly referring to their Sabbath keeping (23:56).[62]

Are Matthew and Luke cognizant of the halakic dilemma embedded in their narratives, namely, that by painting Jesus' admirers as pious Sabbath keepers, they also indirectly and unwittingly present them as transgressors of the feast of Passover? It might be telling that they both leave out Mark's reference to Joseph purchasing a garment for Jesus' body. Perhaps, they believe that in spite of the pressing circumstances Joseph was nevertheless

---

[60] See Davies and Allison, *The Gospel according to Matthew*, 3:653 n. 54.

[61] But see Mayer-Haas, *Geschenk*, 462–63, for an alternative view. Cf. *y. Mo'ed Qat.* 3:5 82a where the rabbis presuppose that sealing a tomb on the eve of the Sabbath at sunset is forbidden.

[62] Loader, *Jesus' Attitude towards the Law*, 357: "Luke alone, among the evangelists, makes a point of emphasising their Torah observance (23:56). It is as relevant to emphasise this at the end of Jesus' life as it was at the beginning, because obedience to Torah and sharing Israel's hopes are fundamental values which Luke's Jesus and Luke assume."

able to avoid buying such an item on a holy day. I pointed to several rabbinic traditions envisaging the possibility of performing burials on Passover, although the assumption running in many of these passages is that Gentiles should always be the ones carrying out such work. The rabbinic evidence invites us to consider the possibility that many Jews may well have approved of Joseph's efforts, as reported in the synoptics. For various halakic and ethical reasons, they knew well that there were times when a burial had to be carried out even on a festival day like Passover, particularly if it happened to fall right before a Sabbath. We cannot, therefore, charge the synoptic writers of being ignorant about halakic matters simply because their narratives date Jesus' burial on a Passover. The social-political circumstances surrounding Jesus' death were sufficiently drastic, at least in the eyes of Jesus' admirers, to call for a momentary suspension of the Torah in order to guarantee his proper burial.

Indeed, there is so little we will ever know about the last hours surrounding Jesus' life, partly because some of the embarrassing features surrounding his death may have been suppressed from the complex and evolving traditions that came to be included in the canonical gospels. Undoubtedly, scholars will continue to debate about the social, political, and religious factors leading to Jesus' arrest and eventual death. Were the Roman authorities the sole ones who wished to have Jesus executed because they viewed him as a political threat? Alternatively, did some of the Jewish authorities of Jerusalem (not the Jewish people!), namely, the priestly elite and members of the Sanhedrin of that time, in conjunction with Pilate, seek to have Jesus eliminated? According to *m. Sanh.* 11:4, in certain circumstances a person sentenced to death could be brought before the Great Court in Jerusalem and be executed even on a festival day. *M. Sanh.* 6:5 also states that the Sanhedrin forbade those executed for violating Jewish Law from being buried in family tombs or burial grounds. Did the Sanhedrin in Jerusalem, with the assistance of the Romans, condemn Jesus to death on religious grounds and have him executed on Passover? And did those Jesus disciples who created the traditions assessed above try to hide some of the shameful features about their master's demise, seeking, among other things, to grant him a noble burial by claiming that a prominent Jew of the Sanhedrin had Jesus placed in his own tomb? Perhaps, some of these questions and considerations could explain why the synoptic gospels conceal traces that suggest the historical Jesus was crucified and buried on a Passover: the priestly elite believed Jesus acted in some way against the temple, and, consequently, had him executed on Passover with the assistance of the Romans who also perceived his act as a political threat to the maintenance of Roman rule and order in the unsettling Judean region. In response, the followers of Jesus would have sought to highlight

Jesus' innocence and to develop a narrative that awarded him a burial worthy of the devotion they thought all should pay him.[63]

These difficult, delicate, and controversial questions cannot receive their proper treatment in this book.[64] On the other hand, Matthew and even

---

[63] See further John Dominic Crossan, *Who Killed Jesus? Exposing the Roots of Anti-Semitism in the Gospel Story of the Death of Jesus* (San Francisco: HarperSanFrancisco, 1995), 160–63; Martin Hengel, *Crucifixion in the Ancient World and the Folly of the Message of the Cross* (trans. John Bowden; Philadelphia, Minn.: Fortress, 1977), 19, 83, 90; McCane, *Roll Back the Stone,* 89, who highlight the embarrassing features about Jesus' burial that have apparently been removed from the canonical gospels. Magness, *Stone and Dung,* 164–72, however, argues against this position, maintaining that the "Gospel accounts of Jesus' burial appear to be largely consistent with the archaeological evidence" and that the "source(s) of these accounts were familiar with the manner in which wealthy Jews living in Jerusalem during the time of Jesus disposed of their dead." I full heartedly agree with Magness that the sources (I would add the authors) of the synoptic gospels reveal an accurate understanding about halakah related to Jewish burial and Sabbath keeping. Accurate knowledge about Jewish customs, however, as Magness herself acknowledges, does not demonstrate or confirm the historicity of the events reported in the gospels. Furthermore, Magness seems unaware of the halakic problem involved with burying Jesus on a Passover. So I still wonder whether the synoptic writings (and/or the sources behind such materials) are not hiding something embarrassing about Jesus' death, namely, that because he was tried (on a Passover?) by the Sanhedrin for "violating" Jewish Law by attacking the temple establishment, he was not allowed to be buried in a family tomb or burial ground. Magness (pp. 165–66) thinks that Jesus was crucified for crimes committed against the Roman Empire, not by the Sanhedrin for violating Jewish Law. She claims Romans used crucifixion as a means for punishing rebellious provincials, while the Mishnah speaks of four modes of execution (stoning, burning, decapitation, and strangulation), none of which include crucifixion. But even she indirectly admits (p. 167) that some scholars view the meaning of "strangulation" (and "hanging") in some ancient Jewish sources as referring to the usage by Jews of crucifixion as a means of execution. Furthermore, I am not at all certain that we can eliminate any endeavor on the part of the temple authorities to have Jesus eliminated. True, they needed Roman consent to have Jesus executed, but the Roman authorities themselves may have perceived Jesus as a political threat. It is difficult indeed to know what really happened on the ground two thousand years ago, but there is little doubt that the *synoptic* portrayal is accurate in its description of Jesus' burial *from a halakic perspective.*

[64] The Johannine portrait positing that Jesus died on a Friday that was *not* a Passover may *in this instance* prove more credible from a historical point of view than the synoptic presentation of the events. Some, however, place Jesus' trial on Passover. So, for example, Jeremias, *The Eucharistic Words of Jesus,* 74–79; John J. Hamilton, "The Chronology of the Crucifixion and the Passover," *Churchman* 106.4 (1992): 334–35; Str-B, 2:822–34. Speaking against such a position are the following arguments: 1) The priests, along with the Roman authorities, could have very well postponed their decisions regarding Jesus' fate until *after* Passover had passed, just as Herod had Peter arrested but intended to wait until *after* Passover before decreeing a final sentence (Acts 12:4). 2) Josephus speaks of the exemption accorded by Romans to Jews from appearing before Gentile courts on the Sabbath (*Ant.* 16:163). Does it not seem even more unlikely that *Jews*

Luke could be portraying the Jerusalem authorities in a negative light by emphasizing their involvement in the arrest and trial of Jesus *on a Passover*.[65] This process comes to the foreground in Matthew with regard to the question of Sabbath keeping, as the Pharisees, along with the chief priests, dishonor the sanctity of this holy day by occupying themselves with the supervision of Jesus' body (27:62). By contrast, the disciples of Jesus desist from taking care of his body during the Sabbath.[66]

In conclusion, to this chapter, I find little to object with in Weiss' remarks concerning the presentation of the Sabbath in the synoptic narratives about Jesus' burial, although I argue at the end of Part I of this monograph that neither Matthew nor Luke expect or demand *Gentile* followers of Jesus to observe the Sabbath:

> Taken together, these three reports of the burial show no awareness of any Sabbath controversies. They reflect the views of Christians who are unaware that Sabbath observance is a questionable practice. It would seem, therefore, that when the story of the Sunday morning anointing became part of the Passion Narrative, and as such became part of the gospel story, the Christian communities that embedded them in the tradition saw no problem with Sabbath observance. In fact, it could be argued that these Christians wished to show the women (and themselves) as observant of the Sabbath. In the Matthean account, the redactional elaboration argues that Christians are better Sabbath keepers than the Pharisees.[67]

---

would require their compatriots to appear before a Jewish court on a festival day? 3) Other passages from early rabbinic literature prohibit trials from being conducted on the Sabbath or a festival (even on the eve of a festival; see, e.g., *m. Sanh.* 4:1). 4) Even in *m. Sanh.* 11:4, R. Judah disagrees with R. Akiba about whether a criminal should be brought to Jerusalem to be executed on a festival day.

[65] Luke's critique would only concern the chief priests, not the Pharisees, who remain completely absent from his passion narrative.

[66] So Weiss, *A Day of Gladness*, 89: "By this means, he shows the Pharisees to be in flagrant violation of the Sabbath while, by contrast, the Christian women, who were rather anxious to anoint Jesus' body, wait until after the Sabbath to go about their business (28:1). This is a common device, used repeatedly by Josephus, by means of which the observance of those not expected to be observant is highlighted against the nonobservance of those who are presumed to be observant in order to show the piety of the former group."

[67] Weiss, *A Day of Gladness*, 89–90.

Chapter 6

Traveling on the Sabbath in Matthew

"So they made this decision that day: 'Let us fight against anyone who comes to attack us on the sabbath day; let us not all die as our kindred died in their hiding places.'"
(1 Maccabees 2:41)

Introduction

As is well known, Matt 24:20 contains an intriguing statement, which is absent in Mark and Luke, about fleeing on the Sabbath: "Pray that your flight may not be in winter or on a sabbath." Matt 24:20, which is based on Mark 13:18, contains some redactional features penned by Matthew himself, including the reference to the Sabbath day. In fact, I will argue that this verse marks an important and sudden shift in the eschatological discourse and sequences of events outlined in Matthew's "Little Apocalypse" that directly addresses and exhorts Matthew's readers. This reading will strengthen the thesis upheld by those who think that Matthew objects to traveling on the Sabbath and is open to this possibility only under special circumstances.

Literary Context and Analysis

Matt 24:1 opens with Jesus' disciples glamorously expressing their admiration over the monumental splendor and structure of the temple in Jerusalem. With prophetic doom, however, Jesus warns them that "not one stone will be left here upon another; all will be thrown down" (v. 2). Jesus' disciples express interest in hearing more about their master's message of fire and brimstone, wondering "when will this be" (πότε ταῦτα ἔσται) and inquiring about the sign of his coming (τὸ σημεῖον τῆς σῆς παρουσίας) and "the end of the age" (συντελείας τοῦ αἰῶνος). Matthew's formulation of the disciples' question is expressly different from its Markan counterpart. In Mark 13:4, the disciples simply ask: "When will this be, and what will be the sign that all these things are about to be accomplished?" The Markan version focuses more tightly on the previous statement pronounced by

Jesus against the temple. Matthew, on the other hand, reformulates the question in a more general way that prophetically gazes beyond the immediate horizons of the destruction of the temple. He is not only interested in announcing the downfall of the temple, by his time, a fulfilled event, but also in foretelling the end-time events that will immediately precede the Parousia.

The different formulations between Matthew and Mark may be accounted for if, like many scholars, we date the gospel of Matthew after 70 and locate Mark within a time-span running during or immediately after the first revolt (c. 66–73 CE). In response to the destruction of the temple, Matthew's eschatological scope focuses ever more on the latter day events preceding the Parousia, hoping for the speedily return of Jesus.[1] From Matthew's post-70 perspective and experience, the prophecies delivered by Jesus must refer to events that encompass *both* the destruction of the temple as well as the subsequent end-time and Parousia. In other words, Matthew would have understood some of the contents of Matt 24 as fulfilled prophecy, providing him and his readers with firm assurance that the remaining unfulfilled events reported therein would also crystallize just as the former did. This observation is significant, since verse 20 with its reference to the Sabbath, so I argue, belongs in the eyes of Matthew to the realm of *unfulfilled prophecy*, yet to materialize in the days immediately preceding the Parousia.

A brief outline of the remaining contents leading to v. 20 will further illustrate this point. After delivering his sober warning about the eventual demise of the temple, Jesus predicts the arrival of false christs (vv. 4–5) and the increased occurrence of wars (v. 6). The clarification made at the end of v. 6, namely, that such things must indeed take place but do not in themselves mark the actual end of time, suggest that for Matthew the events announced in vv. 4–6 have already begun to take place.[2] The prophetic forecast in v. 7 on the violent confrontations between foreign nations and the increase in natural disasters only signals "the beginning of birth pangs" (v. 8). This eschatological gloss suggests that Matthew also

---

[1] Despite the delay of the Parousia, Matthew still expects the end to come soon. Scholars who think Matthew has de-eschatologized his gospel because of the delay of Jesus' return (some five decades or so, assuming Matthean composition toward the end of the first century) as well as his "developed" ecclesiology, simply overlook the fact that religious movements can organize themselves and still remain apocalyptic for sustained periods of time. The Qumran community provides a nice equivalent (organized and structured community but intensely apocalyptic). I side with scholars like David Sim, *Apocalyptic Eschatology in the Gospel of Matthew* (SNTSMS 88; Cambridge: Cambridge University Press, 1996), who see Matthew as imminently eschatological.

[2] Sim, *Apocalyptic Eschatology*, 162; Thompson, "An Historical Perspective on the Gospel of Matthew," 248–49.

views the events prophesied in v. 7 as unfolding in his own day.³ Verses 9–13 address internal experiences among Jesus' followers, which Matthew probably views as partly fulfilled prophesy still reeling out in his own time. According to these verses, Jesus' followers will continue to experience suffering, persecution, even death, and hatred at the hands of the Gentiles (v. 9).⁴ Likewise, many false prophets will continually lead others astray in an age of degeneration in which lawlessness flourishes and love declines.⁵ The promise of salvation extended to those who prove faithful until the end exhorts Matthew's readers to remain steadfast as the end draws nearer (v. 13). In the meantime, Matthew's Jesus claims that the gospel of the kingdom "will be being preached" (κηρυχθήσεται) in the whole world as a witness to the Gentiles. Then the end will finally come (v. 14). Undoubtedly, Matthew knows that the worldwide proclamation of the gospel has already begun in his own day, but views this endeavor as an ongoing project that has not yet been completed.⁶

Matt 24:15 is significant. Here Jesus warns his followers of the "desolating sacrilege standing in the holy place" (τὸ βδέλυγμα τῆς ἐρημώσεως ἑστὸς ἐν τόπῳ ἁγίῳ), which is recorded in the book of Daniel. This phrase also appears in Mark 13:14 but its meaning in its Markan context remains unclear, particularly because of Mark's peculiar and ungrammatical juxtaposition of a masculine participle, ἑστηκότα ("set up"), with the neuter noun, βδέλυγμα ("abomination"). Those who favor a pre-70 dating for Mark understand the masculine participle as referring to a *person* (e.g., the

---

³ Sim, *Apocalyptic Eschatology*, 162; Thompson, "An Historical Perspective on the Gospel of Matthew," 248–49.

⁴ Matthew's phrase, "you will be hated by all the nations (ὑπὸ πάντων τῶν ἐθνῶν) because of my name," which is unattested in Mark, draws attention to his Jewish outlook toward the world in which there exist two kinds of people, Jews and Gentiles, the latter often, but not always, hostile to the Jewish people. Incidentally, Luke's apocalyptic discourse proves equally Jewish in this respect. Luke is the only gospel author who states that "Jerusalem will be trampled on by the Gentiles, *until* the times of the Gentiles are fulfilled" (21:24). I take this verse to mean that Luke blames the Romans for destroying the temple and looks forward to the restoration of Israel after the cup of the Gentiles is filled.

⁵ Certain exegetes tie these false prophets of "lawlessness" with those announced in Matt 7:15–23. See Sim, *Apocalyptic Eschatology*, 164–65. Nevertheless, others contest this association. See Hagner, *Matthew*, 1:182; David Hill, "False Prophets and Charismatics: Structure and Interpretation in Matthew 7:15–23," *Biblica* 75 (1976): 327–48; Foster, *Community, Law, and Mission*, 146.

⁶ Hence, my preference for translating κηρυχθήσεται with the unaesthetic "will be being preached," rather than "will be preached." Matthew is obviously not saying that the disciples will first experience persecution and deception by false prophet and *then* preach the gospel to the nations. Rather, both processes overlap and exist next to each other until the end of time. The preaching of the gospel, like many other events in Matt 24, is an ongoing process.

Roman Emperor Claudius or an antichrist figure) rather than an event.[7] Matthew, however, must have understood this verse as referring to the destruction of the temple in 70 CE. His correction of Mark's ungrammatical masculine participle into the neuter (ἑστός) strongly suggests that he views the "abomination" as referring to an event, mainly the destruction of the temple in 70, rather than a person. Luke certainly ties Mark's reference to the abomination of the temple with its destruction (Luke 21:20), and there is no reason to see why Matthew could not have done likewise.[8] In other words, for Matthew, this verse describes fulfilled prophecy. Likewise, the warnings in vv. 16–19 address the first generation of Jesus' followers, those who either knew him personally or lived in pre-70 times. Here Jesus warns his first followers who are in *Judea* to flee to the mountains (v. 16).[9] "The one on the housetop must not go down to take what is in the house," (v. 17), while "the one in the field must not turn back to get his coat" (v. 18). Matthew's Jesus pities the plight of those living in *those days*, that is, during the *past* (by Matthew's time) events of 66–73 CE:

---

[7] See Lloyd Gaston, *No Stone on Another: Studies in the Significance of the Fall of Jerusalem in the Synoptic Gospels* (NovTSup 23; Leiden: Brill, 1970), 27–28; Willi Marxsen, *Mark the Evangelist: Studies on the Redaction History of the Gospel* (Nashville, Tenn.: Abingdon, 1969), 180–82; B. H. Streeter, *The Four Gospels* (London: Macmillan, 1924), 492–93. Those who view Mark as written shortly after 70 read 13:14 as referring to the destruction of the temple in 70. So Timothy J. Geddert, *Watchwords: Mark 13 in Markan Eschatology* (JSNTSup 26; Sheffield: Sheffield Academic Press, 1989), 206–7; Rudolf Pesch, *Das Markusevangelium* (2 vols.; Wege der Forschung 411; Darmstadt: Wissenschaftliche Buchgesellschaft, 1979), 2:291–92. Other interpretations certainly exist. See discussion in Collins, *Mark,* 608–12; Marcus, *Mark,* 889–91.

[8] Gnilka, *Das Matthäusevangelium,* 2:322 and Sim, *Apocalyptic Eschatology,* 158, deny reading Matt 24:15 as a reference to the destruction of the temple. I think the destruction of the temple was too great an event for Matthew to gloss over. Sim suggests that Matt 24:6–7a alludes to the events of the Jewish War of 66–70 CE. I find this very unlikely. The verses are so terse and general to be taken as such. Furthermore, I see no explicit evidence in Matt 24 regarding an antichrist figure. Matthew only talks of false *prophets* and false *christs* (in the plural), not of one single figure who opposes the true Christ. Sim also seeks to interpret Matt 24:15–28 as pointing only to future events, while the previous verses (4–14) would speak of fulfilled events or those in the process of being accomplished. I suggest, however, that until verse 19 Matthew refers primarily to fulfilled and unfolding events. Only in verse 20 does Matthew truly shift his prophetic gaze to the future. In this way, Matthew provides an answer to the double question raised by Jesus' disciples in Matt 24:3 about the destruction of the temple *and* the Parousia.

[9] The geographical specification of Judea as the site of exodus signals the limited territorial reach of the danger foretold here, which corresponds roughly to the circumstances of 66–73 CE, a revolt that affected mainly Palestine and particularly Judea and Jerusalem. Contra Gnilka, *Das Matthäusevangelium,* 2:323, who wants to read the flight from Judea to the mountains as a generalizing motif (i.e., unrestricted to Judea), since he views 24:15–20 as referring primarily to *future* events.

"Woe to those who are pregnant and to those who are nursing infants in those days (ἐν ἐκείναις ταῖς ἡμέραις)!" (v. 19)

However, for Matthew, v. 20 would no longer refer to the days when the temple stood in Jerusalem, but to the great(est) tribulation (θλῖψις μεγάλη) *yet* to occur *after* 70 CE and immediately before the eschaton.[10] Here, Jesus advises his, or better, *Matthew's* audience to "pray that *your flight* (ἡ φυγὴ ὑμῶν) may not be in winter *or on a sabbath* (μηδὲ σαββάτῳ)" (v. 20), "*for* (γὰρ) *then* (τότε) there *will be* (ἔσται) great suffering, such as has not been from the beginning of the world until now, no, and never will be" (v. 21). I suggest that Matthew's audience would have detected a shift of prophecy in verse 20, reading it along with the following verses as referring to an event in the (near) future concerning their own flight and plight. In other words, they would have understood the preceding vv. 15–19 as addressing Jesus' first circle of disciples, some of whom experienced the dreadful events of 66–73, while v. 20 would describe a future scenario they would witness.

The NSRV renders the beginning of v. 21 as, "for *at that time* there will be great suffering," interpreting the keyword τότε as relating itself to the events narrated previously in vv. 15–19. Nevertheless, τότε can also be translated as "then," or better, as "thereupon" or "thereafter," introducing a subsequent event, in this case, events occurring after the destruction of the Temple.[11] This understanding of τότε seems more accurate not only because of its juxtaposition with a verb in the future, ἔσται, but also because of the linkage provided by the postpositive γὰρ in v. 21. Read in this way, v. 20 reports not a *fait accompli* but functions as an exhortation directly addressing the Matthean audience, a trial yet to happen in the not-too-distant-future. For Matthew's readers, the conjunction "δὲ" in v. 20, read disjunctively as "but," could have also subtly signaled such a transition. Nevertheless, it is especially the inclusion of "your flight," with its switch

---

[10] Matthew has added to Mark's statement the adjective μεγάλη to signal the unique and dreadful tribulation yet to occur that will outmatch the terrible events of 66–73 CE as well as all previous trials and persecutions.

[11] See "τότε," in *BDAG*. English translations that render τότε as "then" include the *English Standard Version*; *New American Standard Bible*; *New English Translation*; *New International Version, New Jerusalem Bible*. *The New Living Translation* curiously leaves out the translation of τότε. Matthew's substitution of Mark's αἱ ἡμέραι ἐκεῖναι (Mark 13:19) with τότε not only eliminates the awkward Markan phrase "those days will be a tribulation," but may also suggest a shift in time. If Matthew wanted to retain Mark's timeframe, he could have rephrased Mark's αἱ ἡμέραι ἐκεῖναι simply into ἐν ἐκείναις ταῖς ἡμέραις. Nevertheless, Matthew opts for his favorite adverb τότε (appearing ninety times in Matthew), which marks here a transition to a subsequent event.

from the third to the second person,¹² that would have caught their attention.¹³ As they recalled the distress of their predecessors (maybe even some of them had lived through the events of 66–73 CE), they were to hope that during the great tribulation their flight would not be further disrupted by the inconvenient timing of the winter season or the weekly Sabbath.¹⁴

This proposed reading of vv. 20–21 fits nicely with the subsequent material in vv. 22–31, all of which make pronouncements about future events to occur during the great days of tribulation. Thus, v. 22, with its chilling assessment that "if those days had not been cut short, no one would be saved" could point to a series of events yet to happen during the end of time. Some of Jesus' Jewish followers had survived the aftermath of 70, but an even worse tribulation was yet to come, which, thankfully, God would mercifully cut short.¹⁵ If some believed that the destruction of the temple marked the final tribulation and wondered why the Parousia had not yet occurred, they were mistaken in their prophetic interpretation: the greatest tribulation was still to come. In this way, Matthew could reread Mark in light of contemporary events in such a way that made Jesus' prophecy sound perfectly coherent, relevant, and reliable, reaffirming thereby the promise of the second coming. This reading of Matt 24, I might add, fits well with contemporary Jewish understandings of eschatological events. Thus, the book of *2 Baruch* – written around the same time as Matthew – warns that an even greater tribulation than the destructions of the first and second temples will come upon the world:

For after a short time, the building of Zion will be shaken in order that it will be rebuilt. That building will not remain; but it will again be uprooted after some time and will remain desolate for a time.... We should not, therefore, be so sad regarding the evil which has come now, but much more (distressed) regarding that which is in the future.

---

¹² Verses 16–19 speak in the third person, "those in Judea must flee," "the one on the roof," and so on (the previous usage of the second person in v. 15 should be understood as addressing Jesus' first disciples, *the audience in the narrative*, not Matthew's readers).

¹³ The NRSV does not translate the adversative particle δέ. The *New American Standard Bible* renders the conjunction: "*But* pray that your flight will not be in the winter, or on a Sabbath"

¹⁴ David Sim, *Apocalyptic Eschatology*, 157: "The addition of the sabbath reference makes no sense at all if the flight is an event of the past and the day of flight is already established; clearly here Matthew is thinking of an event which has yet to take place. This means that all the material in the immediate context of this verse, Matthew 24:15–28, seems to pertain to the future and not to the past." As noted earlier, I doubt whether for Matthew future predictions begin already in v. 15. Nevertheless, both Sim and I understand verse 20 as referring to future time.

¹⁵ Alternatively, those who prefer to read v. 22 as pointing to the past events of the Jewish War argue that Matthew thinks God shortened the time-span of those terrible days to guarantee the survival of Jesus' followers.

For greater than the two evils will be the trial when the Mighty One will renew his creation (*2 Bar.* 32:2–7).[16]

This passage from *2 Baruch* looks at the tragic past of Israel, the two terrible destructions of the temple of Jerusalem, yet maintains that an even greater trial will occur when God renews creation. In a similar fashion, *m. Sot.* 9:15, which was written after the destruction of the Second Temple, expresses great pessimism about the time leading up to the coming of the messiah to the point of acknowledging that only the heavenly Father can be trusted during this time of great tribulation:

With the footprints of the Messiah presumption shall increase and dearth reach its height; the vine shall yield its fruit but the wine shall be costly; and the empire shall fall into heresy and there shall be none to utter reproof. The council-chamber shall be given to fornication. Galilee shall be laid waste and Gablan shall be made desolate; and the people of the frontier shall go about from city to city with none to show pity on them. The wisdom of the Scribes shall become insipid and they that shun sin shall be deemed contemptible, and truth shall nowhere be found. Children shall shame the elders, and the elders shall rise up before the children, *for the son dishonoureth the father, the daughter riseth up against her mother, the daughter-in-law against her mother-in-law: a man's enemies are the men of his own house* [Mic 7:6]. The face of this generation is as the face of a dog, and the son will not be put to shame by his father. On whom can we stay ourselves? – on our Father in heaven.

It is, therefore, very possible, in light of the Jewish traditions cited above, which are nearly contemporaneous to Matthew, that Matt 24:20 could be understood by its author and audience as referring to a future trial rather than the destruction of the temple in Jerusalem in 70.

Verses 24–26 repeat and mirror some of the motifs announced earlier in vv. 4–5: false christs and prophets will arise in those (final) days seeking to mislead even the elect. The destruction of the temple was preceded by the appearance of false prophets and christs; this phenomenon will persist even during the final, greater tribulation. In v. 27, the announcement of the Parousia finally appears. The return of the Son of Man will be like lightning in the sky, flashing from east to west. After the great tribulation, "the sun will be darkened, the moon will not give its light, the stars will fall from heaven, and the powers of heaven will be shaken" (v. 29). In the midst of these cosmic wonders and natural disasters, the sign of the Son of Man will finally appear: "Then (τότε) the sign of the Son of Man *will appear* (φανήσεται) in heaven, and then (τότε) all the tribes of the earth *will mourn* (κόψονται), and they will see 'the Son of Man coming on the clouds of heaven' with power and great glory." The NRSV has suddenly switched its translation of τότε to "then" instead of "at that time," perhaps

---

[16] Translation taken from Charlesworth's edition of the so-called Old Testament Pseudepigrapha.

because its translators view this verse, in contradistinction to v. 20, as pointing to a future event. The literary symmetry, however, between v. 20 and v. 29 should not be overlooked: in both cases, τότε is followed by a verb in the future, which could, according to Matthew's understanding, both point to an unfulfilled event.

With reasonable confidence, then, we may view v. 20 as marking the beginning of material describing Matthew's outlook about the eschatological future, when the great tribulation would occur and the Parousia finally crystallize. This reading of Matt 24 would further strengthen the thesis positing that the phrases "your flight" (ἡ φυγὴ ὑμῶν) and "or on a Sabbath" (μηδὲ σαββάτῳ), which are unique to Matthew, are indeed redactional.[17] Matthew uses the particle μηδὲ no less than eleven times[18] and enjoys forming pairs with conjunctions.[19] The supplemental possessive phrase "your flight" directly exhorts the audience reading this text. Finally, the explicit reference to the Sabbath shows that even Matthew's followers would have wished to avoid fleeing on the Sabbath, presumably because they continued to observe this day by honoring its sanctity.

Matt 24:20 and Modern Scholarship

The plethora of modern interpretations on Matt 24:20 will surely impress, if not overwhelm, any contemporary reader. It is hard to resist stating that part of the reason for the generation of so many takes on Matt 24:20 has been due to a certain malaise among some with entertaining the idea that Matthew and other followers of Jesus would have remained committed to the Torah to the point of feeling uncomfortable with the idea of traveling on the Sabbath. Not surprisingly, some have sought to downplay the relevance of Matt 24:20 by shifting the generation of such material back to primitive "Jewish Christian" stages that addressed Torah observant followers of Jesus who stood at the fringes of the Jesus movement. Others have devised novel and unconvincing ways of bypassing this material.

One position contends that the reference to the Sabbath in Matt 24:20 underscores a fear on the part of Matthew of antagonizing other Jews (i.e., non-followers of Jesus) who might persecute his community were they to flee on the Sabbath. For example, the late Matthean scholar, Graham Stanton, maintained that the Matthean community did not keep the Sabbath strictly and therefore "would not have hesitated to escape on the Sabbath;

---

[17] Cf. Doering, *Schabbat,* 402; Gnilka, *Matthäus,* 2:320, 323; Mayer-Haas, *Geschenk,* 455.

[18] 7x in Luke; 6x in Mark.

[19] Banks, *Jesus and the Law,* 103 n. 1.

however, it knows that in so doing they would antagonize still further some of its persecutors."[20] There is nothing, however, in the immediate literary context and even in the rest of Matt 24 that legitimates such a reading. Overall, Matt 24 does not reveal a concern for a persecution on the part of the Jews because of differing halakic practices, focusing more often on Gentile persecution and the wars between the nations (24:6, 7, 9, etc.). Moreover, Stanton's conception of a milder Matthean attitude toward the issue of traveling on the Sabbath may be dismissed on the grounds that many other ancient Jews would have fled on the Sabbath were their lives under threat.[21]

Others argue that the reluctance to flee on the Sabbath stems from the more challenging logistics presented on such a holy day, since the gates, stores, and other basic services would have been shut on the Sabbath, complicating access to provisions and other items needed for immediate departure.[22] This view is problematic for several reasons. Luz even finds it amusing: "Of course: on the Sabbath the stores are closed and the busses are not running!"[23] In times of war and tribulation, conditions for securing flight might prove difficult and chaotic on any given day. Moreover, if many Jews of that time would have been willing to flee on the Sabbath in order to save their lives, what would have prevented them from exceptionally providing certain services in order to facilitate imminent withdrawal? In any case, during times of war and extreme distress, people can hardly

---

[20] Graham Stanton, *A Gospel for a New People* (Edinburgh: T&T Clark, 1992), 205. Before Stanton, but with unfortunate anti-Semitic language, see Gerhard Barth, who, following in the footsteps of Emanuel Hirsch, *Die Frühgeschichte des Evangeliums* (2 vols.; Tübingen: J. C. B. Mohr, 1941), 2:313, blissfully spoke of the "dangers from the side of the hate-charged Jews; 'a Christian congregation fleeing on the Sabbath would have been as recognisable in Palestine as a spotted dog.' The severe tension between Church and Judaism in Matthew's Gospel would make this addition intelligible" (Gerhard Barth, "Matthew's Understanding of the Law," in *Tradition and Interpretation in Matthew*, 92). Similarly, Walter Grundmann, *Das Evangelium nach Matthäus* (THKNT; Berlin: Evangelische Verlagsanstalt, 1968), 506; Mateos and Camacho, *El Evangelio*, 237; Leon Morris, *The Gospel according to Matthew* (Grand Rapids, Mich.: Eerdmans, 1992), 605. For a critique of Stanton's position, see E. K. C. Wong, "The Matthean Understanding of the Sabbath: A Response to G. N. Stanton," *JSNT* 44 (1991): 3–18.

[21] Doering, *Schabbat*, 402 n. 25.

[22] Banks, *Jesus and the Law*, 102; Craig L. Blomberg, *Matthew* (NAC; Nashville, Tenn.: Broadman, 1992), 358; Carson, "Jesus and the Sabbath in the Four Gospels," 74; Robert Horton Gundry, *Matthew: A Commentary on His Handbook for a Mixed Church under Persecution* (2d ed.; Grand Rapids, Mich.: Eerdmans, 1994), 483; John P. Meier, *Matthew* (Collegeville, Minn.: Liturgical Press, 1990), 284; Yang, *Jesus and the Sabbath*, 238–41. Some of these interpreters, such as Carson (and to some extent Yang) make no diachronic distinction between sayings attributed to the historical Jesus, traditional material, and the redactional layers of the gospels.

[23] Luz, *Matthew*, 3:197 n. 131.

afford the luxury to delay their flight by collecting provisions for traveling.[24] The flight from Judea described in the preceding verses certainly does not envisage time for "packing suitcases": "the one on the housetop must not go down to take what is in the house; the one in the field must not turn back to get a coat" (24:17–18).

The presence of redactional features in Matt 24:20 particularly challenges those who have argued (more in the past) for a Gentile Christian authorship and audience for Matthew. If the Sabbath is no longer of any relevance and Matthew's gospel is written for Gentiles, why is Matthew still reminiscing about Sabbath keeping?[25] For this reason, some try to bifurcate the gospel of Matthew at this juncture into pre-"Jewish Christian" and Matthean layers. Luz is one prominent exegete who favors this approach, reading Matt 24:20 as pertinent for earlier "Jewish-Christian churches" but not the Matthean community. But even Luz struggles with embracing his position, which only transfers the halakic and exegetical problems involved to an earlier period without properly addressing them:

> Whether we assume that problem for the Matthean churches or for Jewish Christian churches that earlier had expanded the Markan text must remain an open question. For me the latter, even though it involves taking refuge in a pre-Matthean tradition, is more easily understandable than is a summons from Matthew to his own church, for based on what Jesus (or Matthew) taught the church quite openly about the Sabbath in 12:1–14, it really had no need to be anxious about violating the Sabbath commandment in emergencies.[26]

We should note, however, that while Matthew's Jesus justifies in 12:1–14 the momentary suspension of the Sabbath in instances where human welfare is at stake (e.g., hunger or illnesses), the concern to keep the Sabbath in all its other aspects, for example, as a day of rest and cessation from weekly labor, remains in full force for Matthew. The desire to honor the sanctity of the Sabbath by respecting its traveling restrictions constitutes a *separate* halakic issue from healing or alleviating hunger on the Sabbath. Presumably, if there were no pressing need to travel on the Sabbath, Matthew, like many other observant Jews, would have refrained from such practice. Obviously, in life-threatening circumstances Matthew would not

---

[24] Cf. Davies and Allison, *The Gospel according to Matthew*, 3:350: "Surely one could flee for a day without provisions; and v. 16 implies distance from cities."

[25] See Strecker, *Weg*, 32, who argued that v. 20 was originally part of a "Jewish Christian" apocalyptic; Rolf Walker, *Heilsgeschichte im ersten Evangelium* (FRLANT 91; Göttingen: Vandenhoeck & Ruprecht, 1967), 86: an irrelevant anachronism. Some like Yang, *Jesus and the Sabbath,* 235, even speculate (without providing any proof) that the saying in its Matthean form goes back to the historical Jesus. This position seems untenable in light of the discussion above on the historical dating, literary context, and redactional elements embedded in Matt 24.

[26] Luz, *Matthew*, 3:198.

oppose traveling on the Sabbath in order to save human life even though he could still wish that such a scenario take place on another day because it would be particularly unfitting to undergo emotional distress and physical hardship on a holy day designed for Jews to experience rest and peace. The Sabbath should be a "palace in time," to solicit Abraham Joshua Heschel's well-known imagery, a sanctuary and refuge from all danger and hardships, not a day when Jews desperately flee for their lives.[27]

On the other end of the scholarly spectrum exists a tendency to portray Matthew as being more zealous in his Sabbath keeping than his Jewish contemporaries. Saldarini declares that Matthew and his community take their Sabbath observance so seriously that their commitment to Torah observance would not "allow them to flee the dangers and horrors of the end of the world because journeys are not allowed on the Sabbath."[28] Along similar yet different lines, Mayer-Haas, following Wong, thinks that Matt 24:20 addresses the conservative wing of the Matthean community, which observes the Sabbath even more stringently than their Pharisaic competitors.[29] She thinks evidence for the existence of such strict observers can be deduced from the materials Matthew draws from Q (e.g., Matt 23:23 concerning the practice of tithing in a meticulous way analogous to Pharisaic observance). Matthew's prayer, therefore, is that these conservative followers of Jesus will not find themselves in an end-time scenario where they will have to decide between keeping the Sabbath (by not fleeing) or remaining part of the rest of the Matthean community on flight during the final tribulation. Mayer-Haas takes the preceding section (24:9–14) as evidence for inner-community schism, particularly v. 12: "And because of the increase of lawlessness (ἀνομίαν), the love of many will grow cold."[30]

But if Matt 24:9–14 hints at inner-community tensions, it could be attacking a *liberal*, if not antinomian, stance toward the Law, not a strict, meticulous approach to Torah observance. In 24:12, Matthew's Jesus describes and condemns a situation of law*lessness*. The intrusion of the theme of lawlessness seems to be tied with the appearance of false prophets who are leading many astray (v. 11). Not a few scholars have tied these

---

[27] Abraham Joshua Heschel, *The Sabbath: Its Meaning for Modern Man* (New York: Noonday, 1997), 12.

[28] Saldarini, *Matthew's Christian-Jewish Community*, 126. So too Mello, *Evangelo*, 420.

[29] Wong, "The Matthean Understanding of the Sabbath," 17: "To 'pray that your flight may not be…on a Sabbath' implies that at least some of the members of the Matthaean community (probably some of the conservative Jewish Christians who still behave according to their tradition) would hesitate to flee on a Sabbath, even though their lives were thus in increased danger."

[30] Mayer-Haas, *Geschenk*, 458.

false prophets with those found in Matt 7:15–23.[31] There, Matthew's Jesus describes the false prophets as ravenous wolves wearing sheep's clothing, warning his audience to test them by their fruits (vv. 16–20). One day these false prophets, along with other sinners, will face judgment: "On that day many will say to me, 'Lord, Lord, did we not prophesy in your name, and cast out demons in your name, and do many deeds of power in your name?' Then I will declare to them, 'I never knew you; go away from me, you evildoers (οἱ ἐργαζόμενοι τὴν ἀνομίαν; Matt 7:22–23).'" The NRSV translates the phrase οἱ ἐργαζόμενοι τὴν ἀνομίαν simply as "evildoers." A literal rendition of the Greek, however, would be "workers of lawlessness," which could link Matt 7:15–23 with Matt 24:11–12 more closely where the themes of false prophecy and lawlessness reappear. Such false prophets cannot represent strict Torah observant Jews. They perform deeds of *lawlessness*. In other words, while Matt 7:15–23 and 24:11–12 may reflect intra or inter-polemics occurring in Matthew's time and milieu, these passages do not inform us about "conservative" and "liberal" branches of the Matthean community that differ in their halakic stringency toward the Sabbath and other Mosaic commandments. If anything, the lawless ones may represent other followers of Jesus who do not belong to Matthew's community and do not observe the ritual aspects of the Torah at all.

Matt 24:20 does not address a more conservative wing of the Jesus movement, but reveals Matthew's own attitude toward the Sabbath. Nevertheless, Mayer-Haas and Wong are probably correct in suggesting that this verse applies only to a certain segment of Matthew's readers. I would suggest, however, that it would be better to divide Matthew's audience more along ethnic lines, between Torah observant Jewish followers of Jesus, who do continue to observe the Sabbath, and Gentile followers of Jesus, whom Matthew does not expect or call upon to keep the Sabbath day. While it is impossible to prove such a thesis, given the state of the evidence, and while we should be cautious not to superimpose any scheme onto a text, I suggest that a bilateral ecclesiology[32] or a halakic *Doppelgleisigkeit*[33] as found in the book of Acts, which clearly differentiates

---

[31] See references in Sim, *Apocalyptic Eschatology*, 164–67. Others are skeptical about this identification. See Foster, *Community, Law, and Mission*, 146.

[32] The term used by Mark Kinzer in his *Postmissionary Messianic Judaism: Redefining Christian Engagement with the Jewish People* (Grand Rapids, Mich.: Brazos Press, 2005).

[33] David Flusser and Shmuel Safrai, "Das Aposteldekret und die Noachitischen Gebote," in *"Wer Tora vermehrt, mehrt Leben." Festgabe für Heinz Kremers zum 60. Geburtstag* (eds. Edna Brocke and Hans-Joachim Barkenings; Neukirchen-Vluyn: Neukirchener Verlag, 1986), 173, who cite the works of the English deist John Tolland and Moses Mendelssohn, maintaining that segments within the early Jesus movement af-

between Jews and Gentiles in so far as their obligations toward Mosaic legislation are concerned, particularly in its ritual aspects, may best account for addressing Matthew's simultaneous affirmation of the Torah (for Jews) and his openness toward evangelizing Gentiles (without imposing upon them circumcision or full conversion into Judaism).

Conclusion

The literary, eschatological, and halakic contexts of Matt 24:20 show that Matthew addresses (Jewish) readers from his audience when he exhorts them to pray that their flight during the end of times not take place on a Sabbath. Like most of his Jewish contemporaries, Matthew would have aspired to honor the sanctity of the Sabbath under normal circumstances. However, the preservation of human life momentarily supersedes the Sabbath during times of war and other fatal disasters. In such circumstances, Matthew agrees to flee on the Sabbath in order to save human life, but this does not mean that he *welcomes* such a scenario. He would rather observe the Sabbath in full peace and serenity. His Jewish readers, therefore, are to *pray* (not avoid fleeing altogether as some claim) that the great tribulation fall not on a Sabbath.[34]

Conclusion on Sabbath Keeping in Matthew and Luke

Matthew's Sabbath Repertoire

In the two main pericopes (plucking of grain and healing of the withered hand) that do deal with disputes over Sabbath keeping, Matthew reworks and enlarges Mark's repertoire of arguments on behalf of Jesus' actions. First, Matthew prefaces both episodes with the theme of eschatological rest (11:25–30). This organization of the narrative material can engender a particular theology of the Sabbath that interprets it symbolically in eschatological terms. Nevertheless, I have warned against over-interpreting Matt 11:25–30 in light of the weekly institution of the Sabbath. Matt 11:25–30 refers to a state of eschatological rest that can be accessed not only on the

---

firmed an ongoing and full attachment to the Law on the part of Jewish followers of Jesus while not imposing such demands upon Gentiles.

[34] By comparing the Sabbath with the winter season, Matthew intends to show that both periods are unfavorable moments for fleeing from danger, albeit for different reasons: fleeing in the winter poses several environmental threats and physical hardships; fleeing on the Sabbath psychologically and spiritually unsettles those who would have wished to observe this day properly. Cf. Doering, *Schabbat,* 402 n. 25.

Sabbath day but anytime throughout the week. It is primarily because of his call to fulfill his eschatological duties that Matthew's Jesus relates differently to certain aspects of Sabbath keeping. In order to accomplish his mission to bring the kingdom of heaven down on earth, Matthew's Jesus must cure the sick and assist the weary even on the Sabbath day.

For this end, the Matthean Jesus appeals to the principle of mercy (Matt 12:7), a prominent theme in the gospel of Matthew (cf. 9:13; 23:23). Mercy and leniency must be shown to the poor and the suffering on the Sabbath day. In addition, Matthew cites scriptural antecedents to justify Jesus' exceptional behavior, including the David story (12:3–4), which also appears in Mark and Luke, and more particularly the service of the priests in the temple on the Sabbath (12:4–6). Matthew enjoys employing the *a fortiori* argument: "How much more valuable is a human being than a sheep!" (12:12) But Matthew uses the *a fortiori* argument only in the most general way, loosely comparing biblical precedents and other scenarios with the situation of Jesus and his disciples. He seems to extend the application of the principle of פיקוח נפש to justify the healing of less serious conditions such as chronic illnesses.

Matthew's Jesus, however, does not go so far as to justify *any* breach with the Sabbath. Only two kinds of departures from conventional Sabbath keeping arise in Matthew's gospel: plucking grain to alleviate human hunger and healing chronic, non-life-threatening diseases. In Matthew's Jesus' eyes, these two deviations from conventional standards of observance are completely legitimate since they ameliorate the condition of the weary and overburdened, acts intimately linked with his mission to bring eschatological rest to Israel. In the presence of their master, the hungry and needy followers of Jesus cannot experience want or suffering, but are to enjoy eschatological satisfaction and restoration, particularly on the Sabbath, a day designed for all of Israel to partake in such blessings.

Matthew's own way of keeping the Sabbath, however, would not have radically differed from the rest of Jewry in other respects. This point becomes evident when Matt 24:20 is fully appreciated within its literary, eschatological, and redactional frameworks. In the previous section, I argued that this text addresses the situation of Matthew's readers rather than the first generation of Jesus' followers. This finding shows that Matthew and his readers, like many Jews in antiquity, refrained from traveling on the Sabbath unless it would have proven absolutely necessary. The depiction of Joseph of Arimathea, for Matthew, a disciple of Jesus, as well as of Mary Magdalene and Mary as faithful Sabbath keepers (Matt 27:57–28:1) strengthens the supposition that in most aspects Matthew's manner of observing the Sabbath would have been similar to that of his Jewish contemporaries.

Luke's Sabbath Repertoire

In his gospel, Luke retains the Sabbath settings Mark frames for the various episodes on Jesus' healings and exorcisms, but repositions them in his narrative in ways that serve his theological purposes. Thus, Luke's Jesus performs the exorcism in the synagogue of Capernaum (4:31–37) as well as the healing of Peter's mother-in-law (4:38–39) and the masses (4:40–41) only after he has delivered his ambitious sermon in the synagogue of Nazareth on a Sabbath (4:16–30). Luke composes new material and reorganizes events reported in Mark's gospel in order to illustrate how the marvelous deeds accomplished in 4:31–41 embody the eschatological manifesto proclaimed by Jesus in 4:16–30. At this juncture of his narrative, Luke sees no need to distract his readers with polemics regarding Sabbath keeping. He is most set on reporting the outpouring of the blessings of Jesus' ministry upon Israel rather than entangling himself in halakic controversy.

When controversies do arise, Luke's repertoire on behalf of Jesus' Sabbath praxis proves just as rich as Matthew's. Ultimately, for Luke, as for Matthew, the christological criterion and recognition of Jesus' authority constitute the final word in any debate about Sabbath keeping. Even so, Luke, like Matthew, solicits arguments of a semi or non-christological texture to justify his messiah's approach to the Sabbath. Like Matthew and Mark, he cites the David story (6:3–4) and appeals to the principle of doing good and saving life on the Sabbath (6:9). In addition, he removes (so does Matthew) the logion found in Mark 2:27 in order to avoid subjective interpretations on Sabbath keeping that this statement could engender. The two special Sabbath pericopes in the gospel of Luke (13:10–17 and 14:1–6) contain a host of additional arguments on behalf of Jesus' praxis, showing that the Sabbath remains a pressing concern for its author.[35] Here, Luke imports a rich cluster of ethical, halakic, and eschatological arguments to defend an approach to Sabbath keeping that could almost stand on its own apart from the question of Jesus' messiahship. In both episodes, the Lukan Jesus appeals to contemporary Jewish practice (e.g., the custom on the Sabbath of untying an animal to relieve it from its thirst; lifting an animal out of a well to save its life) to justify the treatment of chronic diseases on the Sabbath (13:15; 14:5). Luke also accentuates the gravity of human ailments (without equating them with life-threatening conditions) in order to legitimize Jesus' healings. Children of Israel who suffer from long-term conditions that affect their lives on a daily basis, sometimes for

---

[35] Klinghardt, *Gesetz und Volk Gottes*, 225: "Hier zeigt sich bereits, daß Lk nicht *nolens volens* traditionelles Material nur einfach übernimmt, sondern daß er an diesem Problem ein eigenes Interesse hatte."

years, can surely partake of divine, restorative blessings on the Sabbath day, especially if Jewish practice allows for the physical alleviation and deliverance of "mere" animals. Luke further stresses this point by drawing attention to the satanic source responsible for such conditions (4:35, 39, 13:16; 14:4). In such circumstances, Jesus cannot passively stand on the sidelines during the Sabbath while Satan's powers continue to afflict God's people. In the dawning of God's reign, the children of Israel must experience immediate and complete liberation from demonic oppression, even if it requires intervention on the Sabbath.

Besides these justifiable and momentary suspensions of the Sabbath, Luke argues nowhere else for a comprehensive and lawless approach toward the Sabbath that would dismiss its observance altogether. In this respect, it is vital to notice what Luke is *not* saying in his gospel. Luke does not roundly declare that Jewish followers of Jesus may now completely abandon Sabbath observance because of the dawning of a new era of *Heilsgeschichte*. For Luke, Jewish followers of Jesus are not free to earn their wages on the Sabbath, to build or repair their houses, plant and water their gardens, or engage in any other unnecessary exertion unrelated to Jesus' ministry of healing and restoration as announced in Luke 4:18–21. A tradition found in Codex Bezae, which is inserted after Luke 6:4, could be making such sweeping claims when it states: "On the same day, having seen someone working on the Sabbath, he [i.e., Jesus] said to him, 'Human, if you know what you are doing, you are blessed; if you do not know, you are cursed and a transgressor of the Law.'"[36] One could infer from this passage that *any* type of work is permitted on the Sabbath, provided one "knows" what he or she is doing. However, Luke does not make such generalizing statements that exalt human reasoning above divinely ordained institutions, choosing instead to restrict instances of Sabbath transgressions to acts of healing and alleviation that confirm Jesus' authority and lordship.

Thus, in most aspects, it is possible that Luke's Sabbath praxis, like Matthew's, would have appeared quite ordinary to the eyes of other Jews. Quite significantly, in his account of Jesus' burial, Luke is even more concerned than Matthew in portraying the women who followed Jesus

---

[36] Author's translation. On this passage, see Back, *Jesus of Nazareth and the Sabbath Commandment*, 145–47; Ernst Bammel, "The Cambridge Pericope: The Addition to Luke 6:4 in Codex Bezae," *NTS* 32 (1986): 404–26; Joël Delobel, "Luke 6,5 in Codex Bezae: The Man Who Worked on Sabbath,'" in *À cause de l'évangile. Études sur les synoptiques et les Actes offertes au P. Jacques Dupont, O.S.B., à l'occasion de son 70e anniversaire* (Lection divina 23; Paris: Cerf, 1985), 453–77; J. Duncan M. Derrett, "Luke 6:5D Reexamined," *NovT* 37.3 (1995): 232–48; Doering, *Schabbat*, 438–40; Nicklas Tobias, "Das Agraphon vom 'Sabbatarbeiter' und sein Kontext: Lk 6:1–11 in der Textform des Codex Bezae Cantabrigiensis (D)," *NovT* 44.2 (2002): 160–75.

from Galilee to Jerusalem as faithful Sabbath keepers. Luke is the only gospel to state explicitly that the women rested on the Sabbath "according to the commandment" (23:56). Luke also enjoys highlighting Jesus' regular attendance and teaching in the synagogue on the Sabbath (4:16, 31; 6:6; 13:10). Luke is not simply portraying Jesus as a missionary or evangelist when he states that Jesus attended the synagogue on the Sabbath "according to his custom" (4:16).[37] It would be a grave mistake to take this phrase as an indication that Luke is interested in attending the synagogue only to "convert" Jews, while Sabbath keeping in itself no longer holds any intrinsic value. A preemptive citation from Luke's Paul, who also regularly attends the synagogue on the Sabbath according to the book of Acts, illustrates this point: "I [i.e., Paul] have done nothing against our people or the customs of our ancestors" (Acts 28:17). If Luke does not believe in the necessity for Jewish followers of Jesus to observe the customs of their ancestors, including the Sabbath, in other words, if there is no intrinsic value in maintaining fidelity to the Torah other than to entice Jews to "Christianity," then Luke can be charged with the most blatant of evangelistic hypocrisy. How could he with a straight face claim that his Paul, or any of the other Jewish followers of Jesus for that matter, had done nothing against the customs of their ancestors if they were teaching "all the Jews living among the Gentiles to forsake Moses," and persuading them "not to circumcise their children or observe the customs [e.g., the Sabbath]"? (Acts 21:21) It is most natural to see in this statement a desire by Luke to dismiss such accusations and affirm the centrality of Torah observance for Jewish followers of Jesus. Luke expresses concern for the preservation of Jewish identity within the Jesus movement through the perpetuation of Torah observance, and hardly teaches his audience to play the Jew merely for the sake of proselytizing.

Matthean and Lukan Sabbath Theologies Compared

Like Matthew who inserts a cardinal speech of Jesus (Matt 11:25–30) before two Sabbath pericopes (12:1–14), Luke also places in his narrative an important sermon delivered by Jesus during the Sabbath (4:16–30) right before its concrete application on another Sabbath day (4:31–41). While Matthew expresses Jesus' pivotal message in terms of "rest" for the weary and overburdened, Luke's favorite concept is the theme of "release" or liberation:

---

[37] See further arguments in chapter 2.

Matt 11:25–30	Luke 4:16–30
Literary setting: before the Sabbath controversies on the plucking of grain (12:1–8) and the healing of the withered hand (12:9–14).	Literary setting: before two miracles performed on the Sabbath, an exorcism in Capernaum (4:31–37) and the healing of Peter's mother-in-law (4:38–39).
Key Word: "Rest"	Key Word: "Release"
Beneficiaries: The weary and overburdened	Beneficiaries: Captives

Both Matthew and Luke organize their narratives in such a way that Jesus ministers on the Sabbath immediately after delivering a programmatic message about his distinctive mission. Each author further connects the Sabbath with Jesus' mission by employing vocabulary that recalls some of the rich symbols and messages associated with the Sabbath. Thus, Matthew chooses the motif of "rest" (ἀνάπαυσις), which naturally connects itself with the concept of Sabbath rest found in the Jewish scriptures.[38] Luke, on the other hand, prefers the concept of "release" (ἄφεσις), which announces the eschatological arrival of the sabbatical year of the jubilee (cf. Lev 25:10). The concept of liberation from captivity is also related to the institution of the weekly Sabbath, since it commemorates, among other things, Israel's freedom from her captivity in Egypt (cf. Deut 5:15). Luke highlights the motif of release in his Sabbath pericopes, demonstrating how Jesus' healings and exorcisms constitute powerful acts of liberation from Satan's captivity. A table recording these instances further illustrates this point.

---

[38] Cf. LXX of Gen 2:1–3; Exod 16:23; 20:11; 23:12; 31:15, 17; 35:2; Lev 16:31; 23:3, etc.

> Luke 4:18 (citing Isa 61:1): "to proclaim *release* (ἄφεσιν) to the captives."
> Luke 4:18 (citing Isa 58:6): "to let the oppressed go *free* (ἐν ἀφέσει)."
> Luke 13:12: "Woman you are *set free* (ἀπολέλυσαι) from your ailment."
> Luke 13:15–16: "Does not each of you on the sabbath *untie* (λύει) his ox or his donkey from the manger, and lead it away to give it water? And ought not this woman, a daughter of Abraham whom Satan *bound* (ἔδησεν) for eighteen long years, be *set free* (λυθῆναι) from this bondage on the sabbath day?"
> Luke 14:4: "So Jesus took him and healed him, and *sent* him *away* (ἀπέλυσεν)."
> Acts 13:38: "Let it be known to you therefore, my brothers, that through this man *forgiveness* (ἄφεσις) of sins is proclaimed to you."

Luke uses a number of words (ἄφεσις, λύω, ἀπολύω) to express the themes of liberation and forgiveness from sins that could potentially highlight the Sabbath as a day commemorating Israel's freedom from captivity. He reinterprets and connects this theme with Jesus' redemptive work to announce and carry out Israel's liberation from satanic oppression and human transgression. The composition and rearrangement of several episodes in his narrative, the repetition of pertinent vocabulary and particular motifs, as well as the multiplication of Sabbath pericopes about Jesus' healings provide a rich cluster of material that suggest a particular Lukan theology and understanding of the Sabbath. But obviously for Luke (and Matthew), the Sabbath is not the *only* day when Jesus' ministry affects and blesses the children of Israel, since such dynamic activity persists and permeates throughout Israel during the week without interruption. Nevertheless, both Matthew and Luke connect Jesus' ministry with various themes related to the institution of the Sabbath and its rich symbolic universe in order to legitimate Jesus' orientation toward the Sabbath.

Matthean and Lukan Sabbath Praxis

Can anything else be inferred in further detail about Matthew and Luke's attitude toward and manner of observing the Sabbath? I have already argued that neither of the two announces the abrogation of the Sabbath and suggested that their Sabbath keeping would have largely conformed to "ordinary" standards of observance. These observations should not be underestimated. In contrast to other (nearly) contemporaneous authors, neither Matthew nor Luke argues *against* the observance of the Sabbath. Comparing Matthew and Luke with the works of *Barnabas* or the letters of Ignatius can illustrate this point. When *Barnabas* states that Jewish practices such as the Sabbath have indeed been abolished (2:5–6), and then tries to dissuade his audience from observing the Sabbath in favor of commemorating the eighth day (15:9), he goes well beyond what Matthew or Luke ever claim in any part of their works. Similarly, Ignatius' dismissal of Sabbath keeping in favor of the observance of the Lord's day (*Magn.* 9:1) will not be found in either Matthew or Luke.[39]

Beyond the reasonable assumption that Matthew and Luke affirm Sabbath keeping and observe that day much like their fellow Jews (e.g., refraining from traveling, from earning their living, from burying their dead, etc.), it is difficult to make any further observations about their Sabbath praxis, given the genre and state of the literary evidence at our disposal. A methodological fallacy to be avoided would consist in reading every Sabbath tradition within Matthew and Luke as a clear mirror reflecting their world and daily life even though the compositional-critical approach, adopted in this book, embraces viewing such literature as original products of their final authors. To put it bluntly, a gospel text *can* contain passages that report about a *prior* event that does *not* reflect contemporary practice. After all, the gospels do purportedly contain traditions, however theologized and modified, about a certain historical figure and events that *precede* the period when such documents received their final shape. During their sustained periods of transmission, modification, and development, spanning roughly from the historical Jesus to the final gospel redactors, certain materials may have no longer come to play an integral role in informing a particular kind of praxis, even if the gospel writers chose to retain these traditions in their writings for diverse reasons. Probably, only *reoccurring* motifs and features, unique to either gospel, can more firmly inform contemporary readers about a distinctive perspective on observing the Sabbath (e.g., healing minor diseases). In all other aspects, given the early historical period dealt with here (end of first century/beginning of

---

[39] Some, however, date the letters of Ignatius toward the 140s or the latter half of the second century CE. See Timothy David Barnes, "The Date of Ignatius," *ExpTim* 120 (2008): 119–30; Reinhard Hübner, "Thesen zur Echtheit und Datierung der sieben Briefe des Ignatius von Antiochen," *ZAC* (1997): 44–72; Thomas Lechner, *Ignatius Adversus Valentinianos? Chronologische und theologiegeschichtliche Studien zu den Briefen des Ignatius von Antiochen* (Supplements to Vigiliae Christianae 47; Leiden: Brill, 1999). With the majority of scholars, I assume that Ignatius contrasts the Lord's *day* (κυριακὴν), that is, Sunday, with the Sabbath keeping (σαββατίζοντες) of Jews on *Saturday*. Some interpreters in an attempt to eliminate any trace of Christian Sunday worship from the first century (and the beginning of the second century CE), argue that Ignatius is contrasting a certain *way* of observing the Sabbath (i.e., the supposedly "legalistic" Jewish manner) with the Christian way of keeping the *same* day. See, for example, Bacchiocchi, *From Sabbath to Sunday*, 213–17; Fritz Guy, "The Lord's Day in the Letter of Ignatius to the Magnesians," *AUSS* 2 (1964): 1–17; Richard B. Lewis, "Ignatius and the Lord's Day," *AUSS* 6 (1968): 46–59; Kenneth Strand, "Another Look at the 'Lord's Day' in the Early Church and in Rev. 1:10," *NTS* 13 (1965): 174–81. Given Ignatius' penchant for clearly constructing and contrasting his version of Christianity from Judaism (*Phld.* 6:1; *Magn.* 8:1; 10:3), I find this position unconvincing. Cf. Richard Bauckham, "The Lord's Day," Pages 221–50 in *From Sabbath to Lord's Day*.

second century CE) in which the so-called "parting of the ways" had not yet fully occurred, it seems reasonable to assume that Matthew and Luke would have observed the Sabbath day in the same way as many other Jews did, although this assumption is based in part on an argument from silence, as the authors never directly speak about themselves and their own manner of living.

A long time ago, Bultmann had suggested that the controversy Sabbath dialogues were formulated already in their pre-redactional stages in order to defend the Sabbath practice of the *ekklesia* in Palestine.[40] After all, the Pharisees in such traditions occasionally question Jesus for the practice of *his disciples*, wondering, for example, why *they* pluck grain on the Sabbath (Matt 12:2; Luke 6:2). With respect to healings, however, accusations are always directly launched at Jesus in the synoptic gospels. Bultmann accounts for this feature by stating that the Sabbath healings "make it necessary for the attack to be directed against Jesus himself, for the healings are at the same time miracles meant to glorify him."[41] If Bultmann's thesis is correct, it would mean that certain followers of Jesus in Palestine practiced healings on the Sabbath and developed these idealized stories in order to defend themselves against the accusations of their opponents.

Yet Bultmann's assertion that such stories reflect a community practice has been called into question by certain scholars. As Back forthrightly observes: "there is no methodological necessity to assume that the Sabbath practice of a community must be reflected in Sabbath stories which are transmitted by that community."[42] In other words, even if Jesus performed

---

[40] Bultmann, *The History of the Synoptic Tradition,* 16; 48; Tannehill, "Varieties of Synoptic Pronouncement Stories," 102, 107, 111; Maria Trautmann, *Zeichenhafte Handlungen Jesu. Ein Beitrag zur Frage nach dem geschichtlichen Jesus* (FB 37; Würzburg: Echter, 1980), 280, detects three interests the community held in relating such stories: the justification of Jesus' transgressive acts, the legitimization of Christian practice, and the affirmation of Jesus' authority.

[41] Bultmann, *The History of the Synoptic Tradition*, 48.

[42] Back, *Jesus of Nazareth and the Sabbath Commandment,* 64. With respect to Matthew, Repschinski, *The Controversy Stories in the Gospel of Matthew*, 63, phrases the problem very well: "In the controversy stories the attitudes of the gospel of Matthew with regard to the Jewish leaders are most tangible. A redaction-critical examination of these stories reveals the particularly Matthean interest in the Jesus' quarrels with the Jewish leaders. In other words, if authors like Strecker and Meier are right in their 'historicizing' view of the gospel's relationship with Judaism, the redaction-critical analysis ought to reveal that the Matthean interest in these stories lies in the tradition about Jesus' conflict with the Jewish leaders rather than in an updating of these stories for the purposes of illuminating the community's struggle with such opponents. On the other hand, should the redaction focus on an interpretation of these stories with a view towards their applicability to the community, such a historicizing view fails. In this case, it is much more likely that the conflict between Jesus and his opponents finds its continuation in a con-

healings on the Sabbath, it does not necessarily follow that the first post-Easter disciples, the *Urgemeinde* that developed such stories about Jesus' acts, continued such a practice in the physical absence of their master. To further illustrate his point, Back points to the controversy about fasting during which the disciples of John the Baptist and the Pharisees inquire with Jesus about why *his disciples* do not regularly fast (Matt 9:14–17; Mark 2:18–20; Luke 5:33–39). It seems unlikely that the non-fasting of a post-Easter community is reflected in such passages, since the abstinence from fasting is justified by an appeal to the physical presence of Jesus, the bridegroom.[43] In addition, evidence from the early work known as the *Didache* points to the subsequent practice or resumption of regular fasting among certain followers of Jesus, confirming the impression that once the bridegroom had indeed left the wedding party (Matt 9:15; Mark 2:20; Luke 5:35), the praxis of Jesus' disciples could revert to forms that resembled more or less that of other Jewish groups: "And let not your fasts be with the hypocrites, for they fast on the second day (i.e., Monday) and the fifth day (i.e., Thursday) of the week (σαββάτων). But fast on the fourth day (i.e., Wednesday) and on the day of preparation (παρασκευήν; i.e., Friday)" (*Did.* 8:1).[44] Interestingly, some scholars tie the reference in the *Didache* to the "hypocrites" with Matthew's Pharisees, since the same polemical epithet appears in Matthew to describe such people.[45]

Naturally, these observations regarding the pre-redactional stages of the tradition could apply to the time and realms of Matthew and Luke. More specifically, this could mean that the Sabbath pericopes in both gospels need not mirror the actual practice of their final authors and readers. For a variety of reasons, some of Matthew and Luke's readers could have even refrained from performing Sabbath healings (of minor diseases), either because they were no longer in the physical presence of their master or wanted to avoid causing further conflicts with their fellow Jews. The ab-

---

flict between the community of the gospel and the successors of the opponents of Jesus. These controversy stories, then, express part of the life experience of the Matthean community. These redaction-critical conclusions would also have important consequences for the analysis of the social setting of the entire gospel." Repschinski opts for the latter option in the case of Matthew. Indeed, this seems to be the case. See below.

[43] Back, *Jesus of Nazareth and the Sabbath Commandment*, 64.

[44] Author's translation.

[45] For a different opinion, see Aaron Milavec, *The Didache: Faith, Hope, and Life of the Earliest Christian Communities, 50–70 C.E.* (Mahwah, N.J.: Newman, 2003), 301–4. If this passage from the *Didache* can be linked to Pharisees, it is interesting to note that the proper way of fasting outlined here sets itself apart from the practice of other Jewish groups only in chronological terms. Interestingly enough, rabbinic traditions prescribe fasting on the second and fifth days of the week during times of drought (*m. Ta'an.* 1:4; 2:9; cf. Luke 18:12).

sence of any Sabbath healings in the book of Acts could be taken in this direction, highlighting Luke's primary interest in magnifying the authority of Jesus rather than justifying a contemporary Sabbath praxis that would depart from prevailing Jewish conventions. It could be that Luke is more set on historicizing and justifying Jesus' approach to the Sabbath in the context of his eschatological mission rather than encouraging Jewish followers of Jesus of his own day to observe the Sabbath in a radically different way than their non-Christian peers.

On the other hand, Repschinski has made a compelling case, through a remarkable form and redactional-critical analysis, to read the controversy stories in Matthew as reflecting the actual practice of Matthew and his "community." As he amply demonstrates, the manner in which Matthew develops the Markan pericopes at his disposal shows that the *Sitz im Leben* of many of the controversy stories was very much part of the life of the "Matthean community."[46] Matthew is not simply content to state that Jesus has authority (neither is Luke), but seeks to buttress Jesus' claims by anchoring them in the Jewish scriptures and Law.[47] The harsher polemical tone against the Pharisees seems to confirm this impression. Moreover, "Matthew also redacts the stories to reflect more clearly that the conflict is not just between Jesus and his opponents, but that it involves Jesus' disciples as well." All of this shows that Matthew is not simply repeating his sources, but appropriating and remodeling traditions that probably reflect a social situation marked by conflict with the Pharisees in a post-70 setting.

An important ecclesiological question about Sabbath keeping and Jewish-Gentile relations also requires some consideration. It is probable that Matthew and Luke only expected *Jewish* followers of Jesus to observe the Sabbath, although they allowed but did not demand Gentiles to observe this day. Some could argue that the distinctions between Jew and Gentile within the Jesus movement, in so far as Torah praxis is concerned, would not apply in Matthew and Luke's case, meaning that both writers required Jew and Gentile alike to observe (or neglect) the Mosaic stipulations in an identical manner. However, in the Acts of the Apostles, Luke clearly presupposes a distinction between Gentiles and Jews as far as Torah praxis is concerned: Jewish followers of Jesus are expected to keep the Torah in its entirety, while Gentiles are only required to observe certain Mosaic commandments – the Sabbath not being incumbent upon the latter. I further develop this thesis in the following chapters dealing with food laws and circumcision.

In the case of Matthew, the question proves more challenging to settle, since he did not write a second volume to his gospel equivalent to Luke's

---

[46] Repschinski, *The Controversy Stories in the Gospel of Matthew*, 104.
[47] Ibid., 344.

Acts where we could have gathered more information about his halakic expectations for Gentile followers of Jesus, unless some of the traditions in the *Didache* can complement our understanding of Matthew's position on this matter. *Did.* 6:2–3, for example, encourages Gentile followers of Jesus to "bear all the yoke of the Lord" and with regard to food matters to observe what they are able. This approach is not too different from the Apostolic Decree, as recorded in Acts, which seeks not to overburden Gentiles with observing Mosaic commandments. Whatever one makes of the relationship between the *Didache* and Matthew, it is possible that Matthew, like many (but not all) Jews, would have at least welcomed the *voluntary* observance of the Sabbath among Gentiles, given his openness to the Gentile mission.[48]

---

[48] See chapter 12 on circumcision where I further discuss Torah observance in Matthew among non-Jews in light of the mission to the Gentiles. In contradistinction to the *book of Jubilees* (2:19–21) or *certain* (often later) rabbinic traditions (*Mek.* Ki Tissa-Shabbeta Parashah 1 on Exod 31:12f.; *b. Yoma* 85b; *b. Sanh.* 58b; *Gen. Rab.* 11:8; *Exod. Rab.* 25:11; *Deut. Rab.* 1:21) that argue that Sabbath keeping is *only* for Jews, Josephus (*Ag. Ap.* 2:282–284) and Philo (*Opif.* 89) actually boast of its universality and seem to have no qualms with Gentiles attending the synagogue on the Sabbath. Even in the case of the rabbinic tradition, which should not be viewed as a monolithic whole, Hirshman has suggested identifying a "universalist" stream within the Tannaitic literature, which he ascribes to the school of R. Ishmael. This school of thought viewed the whole Torah as available to the nations of the world, saw the conversion of Gentiles to Judaism in a positive way, and even encouraged non-Jews to observe Jewish rituals without converting. Overall, I find Hirshman's thesis convincing except for his claim that this school of Tannaim was *actively* proselytizing non-Jews. See Marc G. Hirshman, "Rabbinic Universalism in the Second and Third Centuries," *Harvard Theological Review* 93 (2000): 101–15; *Torah for the Entire World* [in Hebrew] (Tel Aviv: Ha-Kibbutz ha-Me'uhad, 1999) as well as my forthcoming "Forming Jewish Identity by Formulating Legislation for Gentiles."

Chapter 7

The Sabbath in the Acts of the Apostles

"Now these laws they are taught at other times, indeed, but most especially on the seventh day, for the seventh day is accounted sacred, on which they abstain from all other employments, and frequent the sacred places which are called synagogues, and there they sit according to their age in classes, the younger sitting under the elder, and listening with eager attention in becoming order."
(Philo, *Prob.* 81)

Introduction

The book of Acts contains some precious jewels of information that can complement our appreciation of Luke's perspective on the Sabbath. Quite significantly, Luke records no controversy in Acts over Jesus' disciples' observance of the Sabbath. This "discrepancy" with the gospel of Luke, which contains the *greatest* amount of controversy stories about Jesus' Sabbath praxis, is accounted for at the end of this chapter. Along the way, I also highlight Luke's remarkable usage of Jewish concepts and terminology to describe and organize his narrative, which underlines not only his familiarity with the world of the synagogue but also his respect for the institution of the Sabbath.

Respecting the Sabbath Limits: Acts 1:12

Literary Context

Often some of the most significant aspects concerning a writer's background and audience can appear in the most casual of comments. The first reference to the Sabbath in the book of the Acts seems to represent such a case. It appears at the beginning of the book, in the prologue to Acts, which recalls in many ways the opening of the third gospel. The numerous literary problems that plague the prologue of Acts cannot be discussed here.¹ The primary goal in this section is to rehearse its main features in order to demonstrate where v. 12 actually fits within the opening of Acts.

Luke opens Acts by referring to his first work, the gospel he had previously written, and then briefly summarizes the last days of Jesus on earth from his resurrection until his final "take off" to heaven (v. 2).² In v. 3, Luke refers to multiple post-crucifixion epiphanies of Jesus to his disciples that last for forty days. Upon his departure, Jesus commands his disciples to remain in Jerusalem in anticipation of the baptism of the spirit (vv. 4–5). The disciples of Jesus then ask a question that has startled much of secondary scholarship so accustomed to viewing Luke as a Roman friendly Gentile Christian:³ "Lord, is this the time when you will restore the kingdom to Israel?" (1:6). Here, the disciples of Jesus wonder whether the time has finally arrived for *Israel's* restoration.⁴ Their question has rightly been interpreted as expressing hope for Israel's national liberation from the yoke of Roman occupation.⁵ On the other hand, the prevailing judgment that views the question of disciples as representing a *misunderstanding* of the gospel message is hardly hinted at by Luke.⁶ The oblique answer pro-

---

[1] In Acts 1:1, Luke refers to the first work he composed (τὸν πρῶτον λόγον) and addresses the same Theophilus mentioned in Luke 1:3. Scholars continue to debate about the actual ending of the prologue. Pervo, *Acts*, 34, favors viewing all of 1:1–14 as constituting the prologue, since technically only v. 15 contains new material, while the previous verses partly overlap with the end of the gospel of Luke. I. Howard Marshall, *The Acts of the Apostles: An Introduction and Commentary* (Grand Rapids, Mich.: Eerdmans, 1980), 55, sees v. 5 as marking the end of the prologue. C. K. Barrett, *The Acts of the Apostles* (ICC; 2 vols.; Edinburgh: T&T Clark, 1994), 1:61–62, at first seems to consider v. 8 as the ending of the introduction, but then opts for v. 14. Joseph A. Fitzmyer, *The Acts of the Apostles* (AB 31; New York: Doubleday, 1998), 191, considers only the first two verses as part of the prologue.

[2] Verse 2 presupposes an ascension, which is repeated in vv. 9–11. These repetitions create some confusion with Luke 24:50–53, which could be taken to mean that Jesus' ascension occurred on the same evening when the empty tomb was discovered. All sorts of theses, which can be found in the standard commentaries, arise in order to account for this problem and will not deter us here.

[3] Franz Mussner, *Apostelgeschichte* (NEBNT 5; Würzburg: Echter, 1984), 16: "klingt überraschend und fast seltsam."

[4] Jervell, *Die Apostelgeschichte*, 113–14, ties the disciples' question with the previous promise of the spirit. After the baptism of the spirit, the disciples wonder whether the restoration of Israel will finally occur. Luke's answer is that the outpouring precedes the full restoration of Israel.

[5] Frederick F. Bruce, *Commentary on the Book of Acts* (NICNT; Grand Rapids, Mich.: Eerdmans, 1968), 38: "The apostles maintained their interest in the hope of seeing the kingdom of God realized in the restoration of Israel's national independence."

[6] Contra Barrett, *Acts*, 1:76: "It is nearer to the truth to say that Luke uses the question to underline the non-nationalist character of the Christian movement...."; Bruce, *Commentary on the Book of Acts*, 38: "Instead of the political power which had formerly been the object of their ambitions, a power far greater and nobler would be theirs"; Hans

vided in Acts simply advises the disciples not to worry about calculating

---

Conzelmann, *Acts of the Apostles* (trans. James Limburg et al; Hermeneia; Philadelphia: Fortress, 1987), 7: "The question about the 'restoration" of the kingdom to 'Israel' provides the foil for both the promise of the Spirit and the universalism announced in vs 8."

In which way, however, is the question misguided? If there is an implicit rebuke to the disciples' question, it has nothing to do with their concern regarding the restoration of Israel, but its *timing*. In Luke, Jesus and his disciples are on the same page regarding the restoration of Israel. In the meantime, the disciples should not speculate about the "when," but focus on *how* this process will play out. Marshall, *The Acts of the Apostles*, 60, bifurcates a single Jewish-Lukan agenda into two separated issues that are actually interrelated: "This [i.e., the disciples' question] may reflect the Jewish hope that God would establish his rule in such a way that the people of Israel would be freed from their enemies (especially the Romans) and established as a nation to which other peoples would be subservient. If so, the disciples would appear here as representatives of those of Luke's readers who had not yet realized that Jesus had transformed the Jewish hope of the kingdom of God by purging it of its nationalistic political elements. Another possibility is that Luke's readers might think that the 'times of the Gentiles', during which Jerusalem was to be desolate, ought now to be coming to an end and giving place to the coming of the kingdom...." Correctly, Le Cornu and Shulam, *A Commentary on the Jewish Roots of Acts,* 1:15: "Jesus' answer to the Apostles does not delegitimate their question but merely places it beyond the scope of human knowledge"; Jervell, *Die Apostelgeschichte*, 114, "Es wird nicht danach gefragt, ob das Reich für Israel wiederhergestellt werden soll, denn das ist selbstverständlich. Dies wird ja auch in der Antwort Jesu nicht korrigiert"; Loader, *Jesus' Attitude towards the Law,* 381–82. Cf. Serge Ruzer, "Jesus' Crucifixion in Luke and Acts: The Search for a Meaning vis-à-vis the Biblical Pattern of Persecuted Prophet," in *Judaistik und neutestamentliche Wissenschaft,* 174: "This passage...clearly indicates that the author does not wish to abrogate the hope for Israel's redemption, which seems to be presented as having also political overtones."

The question in v. 6 and the subsequent answer are entirely compatible with expectations voiced *only* in Luke concerning the restoration of Israel: "They [those in Judea] will fall by the edge of the sword and be taken away as captives among all nations; and Jerusalem will be trampled on by the Gentiles, *until the times of the Gentiles are fulfilled* (ἄχρι οὗ πληρωθῶσιν καιροὶ ἐθνῶν; Luke 21:24)." The end of Jewish suffering will come after the time of the Gentiles, some of whom are now beginning to join the cause initiated by a band of Jewish followers emanating from Jerusalem, the very target and victim of Roman oppression and trampling. Other similar hopes of restoration for Israel are also voiced in Luke: "Blessed be the Lord God of Israel, for he has looked favorably on his people and redeemed them" (ἐποίησεν λύτρωσιν τῷ λαῷ αὐτοῦ; Luke 1:68); "At that moment she came, and began to praise God and to speak about the child to all who were looking for the *redemption of Jerusalem*" (λύτρωσιν Ἰερουσαλήμ; Luke 2:38). Cf. Luke 1:16 and 1:54–55; 2:25 (the "consolation of Israel"); 24:21 ("we had hoped that he was the one to redeem [λυτροῦσθαι] Israel"). The Hebrew equivalents גאולת ישראל and חרות ישראל to the term λύτρωσις ("redemption") appear on Jewish coins from the two Jewish Revolts against Rome. While Luke was certainly no zealot calling for followers of Jesus to *bear arms* against Rome, there is no need to exclude from the generic term λύτρωσις a hope for the eventual dismantlement of Rome and the restoration of Israel. Cf. Flusser, *The Sage from Galilee*, 126–27.

"the times or periods (χρόνους ἢ καιροὺς) that the Father has set by his own authority" (1:7). In the meantime, they are supposed to serve as Jesus' witnesses, setting out from Jerusalem to Judea, Samaria, and beyond. In this way, Jesus turns their attention away from the end of time "to the end of the earth" (1:8: ἕως ἐσχάτου τῆς γῆς).[7]

After this final commission, the disciples witness the "rapture" of their master (vv. 9–11). The author of Acts then reports how the disciples of Jesus "returned to Jerusalem from the mount called Olivet, which is near Jerusalem, a sabbath day's journey away (σαββάτου ἔχον ὁδόν)." Verses 13–14 signal a new unit in the narrative that describes the prayer and vigil of the disciples upon their return to Jerusalem. Acts 1:12 serves as a transitional verse that links both units (vv. 9–11 and vv. 13–14):

Ascension of Jesus (1:9–11)
Return of the Disciples to Jerusalem (1:12)
The *Ekklesia* in Jerusalem (1:12–14)

Redactional Analysis

Many scholars have correctly detected the redactional character of v. 12.[8] As noted above, Luke has composed this verse in order to tie the previous section, vv. 9–11, which possibly contains some traditional material,[9] with the following one (vv. 13–14). Most of the words and constructions in v. 12 are well attested in other passages from the gospel of Luke:

---

[7] The author of Acts assumes that the commission to go to the "ends of the earth" includes Gentile outreach. Daniel R. Schwartz, "The end of the ΓΗ (Acts 1:8): Beginning or End of the Christian Vision?" *JBL* 105.4 (1986): 669–76, thinks "earth" here means "land of Israel." Luke, however, is probably mimicking the LXX. The phrase echoes the LXX of Isa 49:6, which speaks of God's servant bringing light to the nations, salvation to "the ends of the earth" (ἕως ἐσχάτου τῆς γῆς). Possibly, the eschatological vision in Luke-Acts includes not only the gathering of those in exile, but also the Gentiles who are expected to come from their countries to Jerusalem in order to worship the God of Israel. See Le Cornu and Shulam, *Jewish Roots of Acts,* 1:23. I suggest that it is along these lines that we should understand Luke's vision for Israel's restoration. It is subversive in that it seeks to conquer Rome through "proselytizing," convincing as many Gentiles to serve the God of Israel and the true lord Jesus to form a reconstituted Israel that will eventually take over the world. Cf. *Pss. Sol.* 8:15 where Rome comes from the end of the earth (ἀπ' ἐσχάτου τῆς γῆς) to conquer Jerusalem. In Acts, the disciples go forth from Jerusalem and "attack" Rome, thereby reversing the axis of conquest, threatening through the dissemination of the gospel to take over the very last frontiers of the Roman Empire. Rome is *not* the center of the world for Luke. Rather, the word of God goes out of Zion to the ends of earth. Jerusalem lies at the center to which Luke always points back.

[8] So already Conzelmann, *Acts of the Apostles,* 7, who, nevertheless wonders whether the reference to "a Sabbath day's journey" stems from tradition. This terminology, however, is clearly redactional as demonstrated below.

[9] Barrett, *The Acts of the Apostles,* 1:62, acknowledges traces of Lukan style.

τότε: The adverb of time occurs no less than twenty-one times in Acts, fifteen times in Luke. Only the gospel of Matthew (90x) surpasses Luke in its usage (cf. *Barn.*: 13x; Herm. *Sim.*: 10x; Herm. *Vis.*: 3x; Herm. *Mand.*: 3x; John: 10x; *Diog.*: 7x; Mark: 6x; 1 Cor: 6x; *Did.*: 4x; Gal: 3x; Heb: 3x; Ign. *Rom.*: 2x; Ign. *Eph.*: 1x; *1 Clem.*: 1x; *2 Clem.*: 1x; Pol. *Phil.*: 1x; *Mart. Pol.*: 1x; Rom: 1; 2 Cor: 1x; Col: 1x; 1 Thess: 1x; 2 Thess: 1x; 2 Pet: 1x).

ὑπέστρεψαν εἰς Ἰερουσαλήμ: These three words appear verbatim in Luke 2:45 (καὶ μὴ εὑρόντες ὑπέστρεψαν εἰς Ἰερουσαλὴμ ἀναζητοῦντες αὐτόν). The indicative aorist active third person plural ὑπέστρεψαν (from ὑποστρέφω) appears rarely in early Christian literature, but is attested in Luke (5x) and Acts (5x). Likewise, Luke prefers the Hebraicizing form of Jerusalem (Ἰερουσαλήμ; Luke: 27x; Acts: 37x; Matt: 2x; Pauline writings: 7x; Revelation: 3x; Hebrews: 1x; *1 Clem.*: 1x) to the traditional Hellenistic form Ἱεροσόλυμα (Luke: 3x; Acts: 11x; compared to Matt: 9x; Mark: 7x; John: 4x; Gal: 3x). In this instance, Ἰερουσαλήμ should be considered redactional.[10]

ἀπὸ ὄρους τοῦ καλουμένου Ἐλαιῶνος: the prepositional phrase finds an almost perfect match in Luke 19:29 (πρὸς τὸ ὄρος τὸ καλούμενον Ἐλαιῶν) and Luke 21:37 (εἰς τὸ ὄρος τὸ καλούμενον Ἐλαιῶν). The differences between both examples result from the usage of different prepositions and cases (genitive vs. accusative), while the noun ὄρος is anarthrous in Acts 1:12.[11] Luke 21:37 is especially interesting: it refers to Jesus' custom of teaching in the temple (a leitmotif in Luke) and his subsequent, periodical withdrawals to the Mount of Olives. In Acts 1:12, the disciples "mimic" this movement: they descend to Jerusalem from the Mount of Olives, and eventually find themselves praying and teaching in the temple. In the New Testament, the juxtaposition of the Mt. of Olives with the attributive τοῦ καλουμένου/τὸ καλούμενον also occurs only in Luke (though paralleled in Josephus).

ὅ ἐστιν ἐγγὺς Ἰερουσαλήμ: The Hebraicizing Ἰερουσαλήμ, which Luke prefers, appears again. The remaining words (ὅ ἐστιν ἐγγὺς) are too common to designate them with any particular redactional labels. Nevertheless, they seem to have been composed by the author to inform his (Diasporan) audience about the topography of Jerusalem.

σαββάτου ἔχον ὁδόν: The phrase is unattested in the writings now contained in the New Testament and Apostolic Fathers. Nevertheless, Luke employs similar language elsewhere to describe traveling distances: "Assuming that he was in the group of travelers, they went a day's journey (ἡμέρας ὁδὸν)" (Luke 2:44).[12]

---

[10] According to Wehnert, *Die Reinheit*, 34–35, the shift in usage of both forms in Luke-Acts is not random. Luke uses Ἰερουσαλήμ in direct speeches that are delivered by Jews, followers of Jesus or so-called God-fearers. By contrast, the pagan Festus uses the profane form Ἱεροσόλυμα. In indirect speech, Ἰερουσαλήμ also prevails. In the narrative parts, the distribution of both forms is unequal: the Hebraicizing Ἰερουσαλήμ appears 14x between 1:12 and 12:25, while Ἱεροσόλυμα appears 13x between 8:1 and 25:7. Especially noteworthy is the consistent usage of Ἱεροσόλυμα in the reports about Paul's journeys. Since, according to Wehnert, the descriptions of Paul's missionary itinerary for the most part go back to tradition, the supposition that the term Ἱεροσόλυμα stems predominantly from tradition, while Ἰερουσαλήμ is redactional, seems likely in his eyes.

[11] A similar anarthrous formulation appears in Josephus, *Ant.* 20:169: πρός ὄρος τό προσαγορευόμενον ἐλαιῶν; εἰς τὸ ἐλαιῶν καλούμενον ὄρος (*J.W.* 2:262); κατὰ τὸ Ἐλαιῶν καλούμενον ὄρος (*J.W.* 5:70).

[12] Luke uses the unusual ἔχον where one would have expected ἀπέχειν to describe the distance between Jerusalem and the Mt. of Olives Cf. Luke 24:13: "Now on that same

The numerous Lukan traits noted above strengthen the proposal to see Acts 1:12 as entirely redactional, including the last phrase referring to the distance traveled by the disciples, a Sabbath's walk.[13] Although the reference to the Mt. of Olives may reflect a traditional recollection that located Jesus's ascension at such a spot, its wording, including the clarification regarding its distance from Jerusalem, is thoroughly Lukan in style. Even if one would argue that the specification, "a Sabbath day's journey," is traditional rather than redactional, which seems unlikely, it is quite remarkable that the author of Acts retains this language and feels no need to clarify its meaning for his readers.

Interpretation

The redactional analysis has demonstrated that the author of Acts has composed this verse through the casual usage of Jewish terms to describe the topography of Jerusalem. Quite significantly, Luke feels no need to clarify this Jewish jargon for his readers. This observation indicates that Luke's audience is sufficiently familiar with Jewish terminology and halakah related to the Sabbath limits (תחום שבת), but not intimately acquainted with the topography of Jerusalem and its surroundings, since Luke has to inform them about the precise distance between the Mount of Olives and Jerusalem.

The phrase, σαββάτου ἔχον ὁδόν, refers to the limit for traveling on the Sabbath. According to Exod 16:29 (cf. Jer 17:21–27), during the Sabbath each Israelite was supposed to remain in his or her "place" (מקום) and not leave it. Early rabbinic halakah eventually interpreted the Hebrew term for "place" in Exod 16:29 as a reference to the city or settlement (by linking it with the private domain) where one lives, allowing for Jews to walk up to 2000 cubits (c. 1km) beyond the city limits on the Sabbath, while texts from Qumran permitted one to journey only 1000 cubits.[14] Josephus de-

---

day two of them were going to a village called Emmaus, about seven miles from Jerusalem (ἀπέχουσαν σταδίους ἑξήκοντα ἀπὸ Ἰερουσαλήμ)." Luke uses the conventional measurement of stadia here because the journey from Jerusalem to Emmaus is longer than the limit allowed for on the Sabbath. This unique usage of ἔχον is not entirely unprecedented though, as it appears in *Periplus Mar. Erythr.* 37. Cf. Barrett, *The Acts of the Apostles*, 86.

[13] Josef Zmijewski, *Die Apostelgeschichte* (RNT; Regensburg: Friedrich Pustet, 1994), 73; Mayer-Haas, *Geschenk*, 378.

[14] *M. Eruv.* 4:3, 7; 5:7; *b. Eruv.* 51a; CD 10:21, 11:5; cf. *Tg. Ps.-J.* Exod 16:29. Qumran texts do allow for grazing animals up to 2000 cubits. See discussion on the Sabbath limits in Doering, *Schabbat*, 87–94; 145–54; 228; 270; 295–99; 353; 376; 429; 493; 532; 569. There are different ways of measuring 2000 cubits, all approximating 1 km. For references and discussion of different measurements of the "cubit," see Arye Ben David, *Talmudische Ökonomie: Die Wirtschaft des jüdischen Palästina zur Zeit der Mischna*

clares that Jews would not travel on the Sabbath but does not provide any measurement regarding a fixed limit in distance (*Ant.* 13:252; 14:226). Nevertheless, Luke's casual reference to the distance of the Sabbath limits in Acts 1:12, without providing further clarification, indicates that by the end of the first century CE the limit of 2000 cubits was well known among many Jews.[15]

It is worthwhile noting that, in both the *Jewish Wars* and *Antiquities*, Josephus also describes the distance between Jerusalem and the Mount of Olives. However, unlike Luke, Josephus does not employ Jewish idiom in order to explain the topography of Jerusalem to his Greco-Roman readers. Thus, in *J.W.* 5:70, Josephus places the Roman legions who encamped during the First Jewish Revolt at the distance of *six stadia* from Jerusalem (ἐξ τῶν Ἱεροσολύμων σταδίους) somewhere along the Mount of Olives (κατὰ τὸ Ἐλαιῶν καλούμενον ὄρος). In his later work, *Jewish Antiquities*, Josephus uses the same terminology claiming that the Mount of Olives lies about five stadia away from Jerusalem (*Ant.* 20:169).[16] The similarities and significant differences in terminological usage between Josephus and Luke are remarkable. Both authors write in Greek somewhere along the Mediterranean basin and have Gentiles (but also Jews) in mind as forming part of their readership. Likewise, both authors write to an audience that does not enjoy a firsthand knowledge of the topography of Jerusalem, although one employs language understandable to an "international" audience, while the other uses particular Jewish idiom for describing time and space.

The particular measurement employed in Acts means that its author and audience understand such Jewish parameters and find them sufficiently meaningful to describe their surroundings. Luke's usage of Jewish idiom does not mean that he "is concerned to depict the apostles as Christians still observant of their Jewish obligations," if we mean by this that Luke

---

und des Talmud Vol. 1 (Hildesheim: Olms, 1974), 344; Doering, *Schabbat*, 146, 154; Asher S. Kaufmann, "Determining the Length of the Medium Cubit," *PEQ* 116 (1984): 120–32; Rudolf Pesch, *Die Apostelgeschichte* (2 vols.; EKKNT 5; Zurich: Benziger, 1986), 1:80; Gerhard Schneider, *Die Apostelgeschichte* (2 vols.; HTKNT 5; Freiburg im Breisgau: Herder, 1980–1982), 1:205 n. 59; Str-B 2:590–94.

[15] Doering, *Schabbat,* 154. Modern measurements confirm a distance of about 1 km between the Mount of Olives and Jerusalem, which roughly corresponds to the distance of 2000 cubits, regardless of the ancient standard of measurement employed (see previous footnote).

[16] The different measurements in Josephus, five vs. six stadia, can be explained in the following manner: *Ant.* 20:169 does not refer to the actual distance between Jerusalem and the Mount of Olives but to the *location* of the Roman encampment, while *J.W.* 5:70 describes the distance between the mount and the city. See Conzelmann, *Acts of the Apostles*, 9; Doering, *Schabbat*, 154; Eb. Nestle, "Zu Acta 1:12," *ZNW* 3 (1902): 247–49.

thinks Jesus' disciples witnessed their lord's ascension on a Sabbath.[17] There is no indication that Jesus' ascension occurred on a Sabbath in Acts. Luke claims in Acts 1:3 that Jesus showed himself to his disciples "during forty days" (δι' ἡμερῶν τεσσεράκοντα).[18] If we read this verse in light of Luke 24:1, which states that Jesus rose early on the first day of the week, a forty-day count until Jesus' final departure would not fall on a Sabbath as the following table shows:[19]

Sunday: Resurrection (day 1)	Monday (day 2)	Tuesday (day 3)	Wednesday (day 4)	Thursday (day 5)	Friday (day 6)	Sabbath (day 7)
Sunday (day 8)	Monday (day 9)	Tuesday (day 10)	Wednesday (day 11)	Thursday (day 12)	Friday (day 13)	Sabbath (day 14)
Sunday (day 15)	Monday (day 16)	Tuesday (day 17)	Wednesday (day 18)	Thursday (day 19)	Friday (day 20)	Sabbath (day 21)
Sunday (day 22)	Monday (day 23)	Tuesday (day 24)	Wednesday (day 25)	Thursday (day 26)	Friday (day 27)	Sabbath (day 28)
Sunday (day 29)	Monday (day 30)	Tuesday (day 31)	Wednesday (day 32)	Thursday (day 33)	Friday (day 34)	Sabbath (day 35)
Sunday (day 36)	Monday (day 37)	Tuesday (day 38)	Wednesday (day 39)	Thursday: Ascension (day 40)	Friday (day 41)	Sabbath (day 42)

According to this chart, which, for the purposes of illustration, reads Luke 24:1 and Acts 1:3 in literal sequence, Jesus' departure would have taken place on a Thursday, not on a Sabbath. Whether Luke would have read his narrative in such a rigid sequence is another question. As Pervo correctly notes, the reference to a Sabbath journey in Acts 1:12 is "merely a rough measure of distance, not an indication that the incident occurred on a Saturday."[20] Pervo adds that through the employment of Jewish measurement the "characters and narrative are firmly located in a world of Torah ob-

---

[17] So Fitzmyer, *The Acts of the Apostles*, 213. I agree with Fitzmyer that Luke is generally concerned in portraying the followers of Jesus as Torah observant, but in this passage there is no indication that the disciples' walk from the Mt. of Olives to Jerusalem takes place on a Sabbath.

[18] The use of διά with the genitive of time describes "time within which." See Fitzmyer, *Acts,* 203; BDF § 223.1.

[19] Cf. Barrett, *The Acts of the Apostles*, 1:86.

[20] Richard I. Pervo, *Acts*, 46 n. 51. See Mayer-Haas, *Geschenk*, 379 n. 506.

servance."[21] This statement, while true, can be further exploited. The "holy measurement"[22] used in Acts 1:12 provides more than just a literary "background" describing Jewish scenery for the entertainment of a Gentile audience. Not only are the characters and narrative inscribed within a world of Torah observance, but also *the author and the readers* of Acts are familiar with these Jewish landmarks and find these categories meaningful for dividing and describing their space and time.

These observations could possibly be taken one step further, once the custom of over reading Luke-Acts in a predominantly Greek and Gentile Christian environment is set aside: could this description indicate that *Luke* respects the Sabbath limits?[23] Such a suggestion should no longer seem so outrageous, especially when serious attention is given to Luke's thorough usage of Jewish chronological and geographical measurements elsewhere in Acts, particularly in his report of Paul's itinerary. Stökl Ben Ezra has pointed to an important feature concerning Luke's usage of the Jewish calendric system, arguing that Luke observed Yom Kippur.[24] During Paul's final journey to Rome, the author of Acts refers to Yom Kippur in order to situate the itinerary of the apostle to the Gentiles: "…we came to a place called Fair Havens, near the city of Lasea. Since much time had been lost and sailing was now dangerous, because even *the Fast* had already gone by, Paul advised them…." (Acts 27:8–9). Scholars largely agree that the fast (τὴν νηστείαν) mentioned here refers to the festival of Yom Kippur.[25]

---

[21] Pervo, *Acts,* 46. Zmijewski, *Die Apostelgeschichte*, 75, sees the reference to the Sabbath limits only as an attempt by Luke to underline in a solemn way the return of the disciples to Jerusalem, which marks the beginning of the "age of the church."

[22] Otto Bauernfeind, *Die Apostelgeschichte* (THKNT 5; Leipzig: A. Deichert, 1939), 23: "heiligen Maßes."

[23] I do not share the reservations of Turner, "The Sabbath, Sunday, and the Law in Luke/Acts," in *From Sabbath to Lord's Day*, 124: "From 1:12 we may deduce nothing about early church Sabbath theology and little more about their Sabbath practice." The very usage of such terminology is telling for assessing the Jewishness of Luke-Acts.

[24] Stökl Ben Ezra, "'Christians' Observing 'Jewish' Festivals of Autumn," in The Image of the Judaeo-Christians in Ancient Jewish and Christian Literature, 53–73; *The Impact of Yom Kippur on Early Christianity: The Day of Atonement from Second Temple Judaism to the Fifth Century* (WUNT 163; Tübingen: Mohr Siebeck, 2003).

[25] Stökl Ben Ezra, *The Impact of Yom Kippur on Early Christianity*, 215: "Commentators are unanimous in interpreting ἡ νηστεία as referring to the fast of Yom Kippur. The word νηστεία appears with complete neutrality in the context, without polemical or pejorative accretions. In the same way, a modern Jew would understand a friend saying in late summer that he will return 'after the holidays' as meaning at the end of Sukkot. We can therefore assume that the attitude of Luke and his addressees to the fast of the Day of Atonement was to that of a revered and observed festival." Earlier on, the reference to Yom Kippur in Acts 27:9 led Edward Carus Selwyn, *St. Luke the Prophet* (London: Macmillan, 1901), 37 n. 1, to conclude that its author was Jewish: "None but a Jew would use this expression."

The casual manner in which Yom Kippur appears in this passage is quite striking, leading some commentators, who see a close relationship between the author of Luke-Acts and Paul, to deduce that Paul observed Yom Kippur.[26] But this reading of Acts, as is often the case, looks back into the pre-70 era in order to gather what precious kernel may be found about the first generation of Jesus' followers while overlooking its significance for understanding Luke's world. Given the employment, or at least retention, of a Jewish calendric reference for describing a secular problem, one natural exegetical reflex would be to posit that Luke observed the Day of Atonement.[27]

This hardly constitutes the only instance in Acts where Luke brackets Paul's traveling with Jewish chronological parameters. In Acts 20:6, Luke reports that Paul and his companions set sail from Philippi only *after* the end of the festival of Unleavened Bread.[28] Similarly, in Acts 20:16, Luke's Paul decides to sail past Ephesus, because of his concern to arrive in Jerusalem in time for Pentecost. In fact, the whole book of Acts is permeated with Jewish chronology, referring multiple times to Paul's visits to various

---

[26] Conzelmann, *Acts of the Apostles*, 216; James D. G. Dunn, *The Acts of the Apostles* (Narrative Commentaries; Valley Forge, Penn.: Trinity Press International, 1996), 338; R. P. C. Hanson, *The Acts in the Revised Standard Version* (The New Clarendon Bible; Oxford: Clarendon Press, 1967), 245; Eugène Jacquier, *Les Actes des apôtres* (EBib 18; Paris: J. Gabalda, 1926), 726; Le Cornu and Shulam, *The Jewish Roots of Acts*, 2:1443.

[27] Stökl Ben Ezra, "'Christians' Observing 'Jewish' Festivals of Autumn," 62. The fact that Acts 27:9 is located within the so-called "we-sections" of the book does not deter from this argument. Stökl Ben Ezra points to the weakness of this counterargument: it would mean that the author blindly copied from his source without modifying it for his audience. Contra Reidar Hvalvik, "Paul as a Jewish Believer – According to the Book of Acts," in *Jewish Believers in Jesus: The Early Centuries* (ed. Oskar Skarsaune and Reidar Hvalvik; Peabody, Mass.: Hendrickson Publishers, 2007), 143. n. 115, who thinks Stökl Ben Ezra over interprets Acts 27:9. Hvalvik mentions three possible readings for Acts 27:9. 1) It was taken from a tradition holding no special interest for Luke; 2) it is editorial and shows Luke's interest in depicting Paul as a pious Jew; 3) it is historical. The first suggestion is hardly convincing, since Luke could have easily edited his material if such a chronological parameter was meaningless. The second suggestion fails to address fully *why* Luke is portraying Paul in such a manner. Even if the third suggestion were correct, we would still have to discern why Luke retains such a reference in such a casual way.

[28] Following Jervell, *Die Apostelgeschichte*, 499, such time references constitute more than a mere dating of events. Luke does not just enjoy outlining his narrative according to Jewish feasts, but ties them to the central character of his work, Paul. This certainly means that Luke viewed Paul as a Passover keeper but it also could indicate that he kept the festival. Moreover, if Luke is indeed the author of the "we passages," as some continue to argue (e.g., Wolter, *Das Lukasevangelium*, 8), he would have kept Passover and other Jewish festivals with Paul during their mutual excursions (to the extent that such reports reflect historical reality).

synagogues throughout the Diaspora on the Sabbath. Quite significantly, Luke *never* portrays Paul as setting out to travel on the Sabbath or on other Jewish festivals; neither does he ever speak of such events in pejorative terms when employing them to organize his narrative. These observations suggest that Luke himself also honored the Sabbath limits. Hopefully, this argument will become more compelling in the subsequent sections of this chapter.[29]

Visiting the Synagogue at Antioch of Pisidia

Key Verses

13:14: "...but they went on from Perga and came to Antioch in Pisidia. And on the sabbath day they went into the synagogue and sat down."
13:27: "Because the residents of Jerusalem and their leaders did not recognize him or understand the words of the prophets that are read every sabbath, they fulfilled those words by condemning him."
13:42: "As Paul and Barnabas were going out, the people urged them to speak about these things again the next sabbath."
13:44: "The next sabbath almost the whole city gathered to hear the word of the Lord."

Literary Context

In Acts 13:14, Luke makes his first explicit reference to Paul attending a synagogue on the Sabbath day, although the apostle to the Gentiles already appears in synagogue space in previous passages (9:20; 13:5). While these earlier sections in Acts do not explicitly refer to a Sabbath setting, Luke probably presupposes such a timeframe, given his penchant elsewhere for timing Paul's delivery of the gospel at such a suitable moment when larger crowds would presumably attend the synagogue in order to hear the reading and exposition of the scriptures.[30]

---

[29] In addition to these references, we should notice Luke's depiction of Jesus' submission to Jewish rhythms of life: Luke 2:41–42: "Now every year his parents went to Jerusalem for the festival of the Passover. And when he was twelve years old, they went up as usual for *the festival*"; 2:21–22: "*After eight days* had passed, it was time to circumcise the child; and he was called Jesus, the name given by the angel before he was conceived in the womb. When *the time came for their purification* according to the law of Moses, they brought him up to Jerusalem to present him to the Lord" (2:22). Cf. the circumcision of John the Baptist: "*On the eighth day* they came to circumcise the child, and they were going to name him Zechariah after his father" (1:59). Cf. Luke 4:16; 23:56.

[30] Probably a Sabbath setting is also presupposed in the subsequent chapter (14:1), when Paul visits the synagogue of Iconium.

Acts 13:14, 27, 42, and 44 appear within a much larger section, beginning in v. 13 and ending in v. 52. Verses 13–52 in turn belong to an even larger block of material reporting Paul's "first missionary journey." Beginning in 13:1, Paul and Barnabas are dispatched on their first mission by the *ekklesia* of Antioch (Syria) and first travel to the island of Cyprus (13:4–12). After their stay in Cyprus, Paul and Barnabas sail to Perga, in the province of Pamphylia (Asia Minor), and eventually reach Pisidian Antioch (v. 14a). Upon their arrival, they visit the local synagogue on the Sabbath day. Next follows a lengthy description of Paul's preaching and interaction with the local synagogue and populace, which can be outlined in the following way:

Arrival in Pisidian Antioch (14)
   First Sabbath Reference (14b)
Synagogue Service (15–16a)
   Reading of the Law and the Prophets (15a)
   Call for Exhortation (15b)
   Paul's Initiative (16a)
Paul's Sermon (16b–41)
   History of Israel from the Exodus to David (17–23)
   Ministry of John the Baptist (24–25)
   Death and Resurrection of Jesus (26–31)
     Second Sabbath Reference (27)
   Announcement of the Fulfillment of Scriptures (32–37)
   Proclamation of Israel's *Release* from Sins (38–39)
   Solemn Warning (40–41)
Reception and Rejection of Paul and Barnabas in Antioch (42–52)
   Third Sabbath Reference: Invitation to Preach on the Following Sabbath (42)
   Jews and Proselytes Becomes Followers of Jesus (43)
   Fourth Sabbath Reference: Second Sabbath Visit to the Synagogue (44)
   Confrontation with the "Jews" (45–51)
   Joy of the Disciples (52)

The sermon (according to v. 15, a "word of exhortation"), purportedly delivered by Paul, is not historical.[31] It shares many parallels with the sermons of Peter (Acts chs. 2, 3, and 10), Stephen (ch. 7), and especially, for our purposes, with the sermon of Jesus delivered on the Sabbath in the synagogue of Nazareth (Luke 4:16–30).[32] Paul's sermon begins with a brief recounting of Israel's history (vv. 17–23) from the Exodus to king David, according to Luke, an ancestor of Jesus, as well as the ministry of

---

[31] Pervo, *Acts*, 334: "The speech fully exposes the unhistorical character of the missionary speeches in Acts. Although it purports to be a speech of Paul in a Diaspora synagogue, even a superficial reading indicates that the sermon is directed to the readers of the book rather than to the dramatic audience, which would have found much of it confusing and/or unintelligible."

[32] Pervo, *Acts,* 334.

John the Baptist (vv. 24–25). In paradoxical way, Jesus has brought deliverance to Israel through his unexpected death, but the Lukan Paul insists this tragic event conforms to the divine plan outlined long ago in scripture. Moreover, the resurrection demonstrates that Jesus has indeed been entrusted with a special mission of redemption (vv. 26–31). Within this unit appears the second Sabbath reference: Luke's Paul claims that those living in Jerusalem and their rulers, not recognizing Jesus nor the words of the prophets, *which are read every Sabbath* (τὰς φωνὰς τῶν προφητῶν τὰς κατὰ πᾶν σάββατον ἀναγινωσκομένας), fulfilled divine will despite themselves by condemning Jesus to death (v. 27). The following verses (32–37) contain a series of proof texts that seek to tie these events with prophecy and divine providence.[33]

In vv. 38–39, Paul announces the "release" (ἄφεσις) of Israel from her sins (ἁμαρτιῶν): Israel can now be "made right"/"released" from all it was unable to fulfill in the Law of Moses (ἀπὸ πάντων ὧν οὐκ ἠδυνήθητε ἐν νόμῳ Μωϋσέως δικαιωθῆναι), should it collectively recognize Jesus' messiahship (v. 39). The very brief language employed here echoes some of the themes found in Pauline theology. Luke tersely ties the Jesus event to the announcement of forgiveness/release from sins but does not elaborate on this topic.[34] On the other hand, the reference to ἄφεσις picks up a favorite theme of Luke already announced during Jesus' "inaugural address" in Nazareth (Luke 4:18–21) where the term is used in a different sense referring more to the idea of deliverance from bondage and suffering rather than forgiveness of sins. Nevertheless, here, as in Luke ch. 4, the Sabbath day and synagogue space become temporal and physical vehicles that allow Jesus and his messenger, Paul, to proclaim a new jubilary age of freedom promising deliverance from both sin and suffering. The final two verses of Paul's sermon (vv. 40–41) end with a solemn warning to heed to his message.

After the "homily," the synagogue members entreat both Paul and Barnabas to return the following Sabbath (εἰς τὸ μεταξὺ σάββατον) for a further presentation (v. 42). Once they leave the synagogue, a train of many Jews and devout proselytes (πολλοὶ τῶν Ἰουδαίων καὶ τῶν σεβομένων προσηλύτων)[35] follows Paul and Barnabas. It seems that from Luke's per-

---

[33] Ps 2:7; 16:10; Isa 55:3.

[34] LeCornu and Shulam, *Jewish Roots of Acts,* 1:739–743, read vv. 38–39 in light of 11Q Melchizedek, a text announcing the release from bondage to sin. See Jervell, *Die Apostelgeschichte*, 361, who links the forgiveness of sins with the enthronement of Jesus. Verses 38–39 cannot be taken as evidence that the Law is no longer relevant for Luke. The Torah still plays an important role, if anything, to signal and preserve Israel's identity. So Jervell *Die Apostelgeschichte*, 361; Klinghardt, *Gesetz und Volk Gottes*, 108.

[35] In this instance σεβομένων προσηλύτων may refer to full "converts" (involving circumcision in the case of males), given the juxtaposition here of the participle with the

spective, these individuals have become followers of Jesus, because Paul and Barnabas persuade them to remain in the grace of God (ἔπειθον αὐτοὺς προσμένειν τῇ χάριτι τοῦ θεοῦ).[36] Up until this point, no controversy over Paul's message and missionary activity emerges. Only on the following Sabbath (τῷ δὲ ἐρχομένῳ σαββάτῳ), when Luke hyperbolically claims that almost the whole city gathered at the synagogue, do "the Jews,"[37] allegedly out of jealousy over the attraction of the Gentile crowds, interrupt and confront Paul and Barnabas.[38] In response to such opposition, the two ambassadors of Jesus announce their intent to bring their message to the Gentiles (vv. 46–47).[39] While this declaration enthralls the Gentiles (v.

---

noun. These people appear to constitute part of the addressees in vv. 16 and 26. There, the terms φοβούμενοι τὸν θεόν probably refer to full converts as well, since they are addressed as belonging to the brothers and descendants of Abraham (13:26: Ἄνδρες ἀδελφοί, υἱοὶ γένους Ἀβραὰμ καὶ οἱ ἐν ὑμῖν φοβούμενοι τὸν θεόν). On the following Sabbath, Luke claims synagogue attendance had reached its full capacity (13:44). This time Luke surely envisions the presence of Gentiles (v. 48). Elsewhere (16:14, 17:4, 17 and 18:7), σεβόμενοι probably refers to Gentiles. The other term, φοβούμενος, can designate non-Jews who sympathize with Jewish customs and society (10:22; 10:35; 13:16; 13:26; 27:17). Robert S. MacLennan and A. Thomas Kraabel, "The God-Fearers – A literary and Theological Invention," *BAR* 12 (1986): 47–53, argue that these terms should not be understood in a rigid, technical sense (depending on the literature or inscription, they may refer to Jews or even "pagans" who have nothing to do with Judaism). In addition, their sympathy to Jewish society should not always be reduced to religious interests. At times, their support for the local Jewish community may stem from economic, civic, political, and social interests. Nevertheless, it is undeniable that a number of non-Jews felt attracted to the customs and beliefs of Jews throughout the Roman Empire as evidenced in both Greco-Roman and Jewish literature.

[36] Cf. Acts 11:23: "When he came and saw the grace of God (τὴν χάριν τοῦ θεοῦ), he rejoiced, and he exhorted them all to remain faithful to the Lord (προσμένειν τῷ κυρίῳ) with steadfast devotion"; 14:22: "There they strengthened the souls of the disciples and encouraged them to continue in the faith" (ἐμμένειν τῇ πίστει). The usage of the verb πείθω in the sense of persuading appears prominently in Acts (13:43, 18:4; 19:8, 26; 26:28; 28:23).

[37] I hope address the problematic usage of "the Jews" in a second book I would like to write on Luke-Acts. Needless to say, "the Jews" cannot refer here to all the Jewish populace of Pisidian Antioch, since Paul and Barnabas have already gained some of them along with their devout proselytes to their cause. Luke presents a divided Jewish audience: some side with Paul and Barnabas; others oppose them.

[38] This pattern, which is repeated in 17:1–5, probably shows that many Jews in the Diaspora were concerned about the social-political repercussions the public success of the gospel among Gentiles could bring upon their local communities. Cf. Klinghardt, *Gesetz und Volkes Gottes,* 235. Wolfgang Stegemann, *Zwischen Synagoge und Obrigkeit: Zur historischen Situation der lukanischen Christen* (FRLANT 152; Göttingen: Vandenhoeck und Ruprecht, 1991), 97–110.

[39] This declaration does not mean that Paul and Barnabas no longer preach to Jews, since immediately after their departure from Pisidian Antioch, they enter into another synagogue in Iconium and speak to both Jews and Greeks (14:1). The same observations

48), "the Jews," according to Luke, succeed in convincing the "devout women of high standing" (τὰς σεβομένας γυναῖκας τὰς εὐσχήμονας)[40] and the leaders of the city (τοὺς πρώτους τῆς πόλεως) to drive Paul and Barnabas out of the city (v. 50).[41] Paul and Barnabas are now forced to move out

---

apply to the evangelization of the Gentiles: Paul has already received his call to preach to the Gentiles prior to this occasion (9:15), and certain Gentiles have already heard the good news (e.g., Cornelius). No radical transition occurs here in the narration of Acts whereby Luke fully gives up on the Jews and now only gazes at the Gentile horizon. The outreach to the Gentiles, which is already anticipated in 1:8, does not occur because of the Jewish rejection of the Gospel. It belongs to God's predetermined design that had been set from the beginning of time. Cf. Mayer-Haas, *Geschenk*, 381–82: Pesch, *Die Apostelgeschichte,* 2:47: "keine Absage an die Judenmission."

[40] These women are probably of non-Jewish origin, since "the Jews" incite them. So Barrett, *The Acts of the Apostles,* 1:659. On other prominent women joining the Jesus movement in Acts, see 16:14; 17:4, 12, 34. See also Shelly Matthews, *First Converts: Rich Pagan Women and the Rhetoric of Mission in Early Judaism and Christianity* (Stanford, Calif.: Stanford University Press, 2001).

[41] Luke's reference to the alleged "jealousy" of the "Jews" is charged with polemical texture and obviously only conveys *his* (subjective) perspective on a delicate and complicated issue concerning Jewish-Gentile relations in the Roman Empire. From a historical perspective, I find helpful for the elucidation of the conflicts reported in Acts between disciples of Jesus and other Diasporan Jews to adopt some of the ideas presented by Paula Fredriksen, "What 'Parting of the Ways'?: Jews, Gentiles, and the Ancient Mediterranean City," in *The Ways That Never Parted*, 35–63. Briefly stated, the Romans had granted certain privileges to the Jewish people, among others, the right to practice their customs without having to participate fully in the polytheistic and imperial cults (e.g., by offering sacrifices) of the mainstream culture. However, these privileges were contingent on the care of the Jews not to offend the customs of the other surrounding peoples whose limited tolerance could disintegrate if Jews successfully and visibly turned Gentiles into monotheists. Many of the so-called God-fearers in the first century continued to participate in local polytheistic cults and other idolatrous acts that were forbidden to Jews. It was in the interest of the Jews, therefore, not to demand that these Gentiles give up those practices.

By contrast, the radical Jewish Jesus movement demanded that non-Jews fully give up idolatry and become exclusive monotheists. This act provoked many non-Jews and subverted the delicate social status quo existing between Jews and Gentiles, particularly in times of conflict (e.g., during and after the first Jewish Revolt, the time when Luke and Acts were written). This explains why said "Jews" in Acts repeatedly attempt to clarify their position to the local civil authorities by distancing themselves from the Jesus movement and claiming that they do not endorse the subversive actions generated by such zealous messianism. This model also accounts for Luke's resentment toward other Jews for not fully embarking on his project. He is bewildered by the fact that "the Jews" are not rejoicing at the good news announced by the Jesus movement: despite the Roman occupation, Israel still has a Davidic king who is enthroned in heaven. Moreover, God has demonstrated his faithfulness to Israel by raising Jesus from the dead. A new era is proclaimed under the heavenly reign of Jesus granting Israel release from sins. Finally, Israel will reachieve its liberation and supremacy as many Gentiles gradually free themselves from the yoke of idolatry and their wicked ways and join Israel in serving the one

of Antioch and subsequently make their way to the neighboring Iconium. Nevertheless, Luke, true to his optimistic spirit, ends this section on a triumphant note: "the disciples were filled with joy and the Holy Spirit" (v. 52).[42]

Interpretation

In this rather large pericope, the author of Acts reveals his remarkable familiarity with the services held on the Sabbath in the Diasporan synagogue through his description of many of features including the customary "reading of the law and the prophets" (τὴν ἀνάγνωσιν τοῦ νόμου καὶ τῶν προφητῶν), the presence of the synagogue officials (οἱ ἀρχισυνάγωγοι), as well as the delivery of a word of exhortation (λόγος παρακλήσεως). The practice of reading the Jewish scriptures on the Sabbath is well attested in Philo (*Somn.* 2:127; *Prob.* 81–83; *Legat.* 156–157, 311–313) and Josephus (*Ant.* 16:43 and *Ag. Ap.* 2:175). In *Somn.* 2:127, Philo refers to acts that parallel many of the features mentioned in Acts 13: sitting down in the synagogue (Philo: καθεδεῖσθε ἐν τοῖς συναγωγίοις; Acts 13:14: ελθόντες εἰς τὴν συναγωγὴν τῇ ἡμέρᾳ τῶν σαββάτων ἐκάθισαν); the reading of scriptures (Philo: τὰς ἱερὰς βίβλους ἀναγινώσκοντες; Acts 13:15: τὴν ἀνάγνωσιν τοῦ νόμου καὶ τῶν προφητῶν); a message of exposition or exhortation (Philo, in terms of philosophical exposition of scripture: διαπτύσσοντες καὶ τῇ πατρίῳ φιλοσοφίᾳ διὰ μακρηγορίας ἐνευκαιροῦντές τε καὶ ἐνσχολάζοντες; Acts 13:15, in terms of exhortation for the Jewish people: λόγος παρακλήσεως πρὸς τὸν λαόν).[43] The term used for designating the synagogue officials (οἱ ἀρχισυνάγωγοι) appears in Acts 18:8, 17; Luke 8:49; 13:14 (in the singular) and is also attested in inscriptions.[44] It seems to correspond to the Hebrew term ראש הכנסת (e.g., *m. Sotah* 7:7, 8). Luke's rich description provides precious information on synagogue life during the end of the first century CE.[45]

---

true God and lord Jesus. In a sense, Luke is disappointed that his form of Judaism is more zealous and "Jewish" than that of his compatriots. Too many of them, from his perspective, have become complacent with the status quo with Rome and are "jealous" because of the success of the Jesus movement among Gentiles.

[42] This is the positive way in which the author of Acts will also choose to end his entire work, claiming that Paul, despite his ejection from Jerusalem and imprisonment in Rome, continued without hindrance to proclaim the gospel in all openness and confidence (28:31).

[43] Cf. *Prob.* 81–83, referring to the gathering, sitting, reading, and allegorical teaching of scripture in the synagogues every seventh day.

[44] Lee Levine, *The Ancient Synagogue: The First Thousand Years* (2d ed.; New Haven, Conn.: Yale University Press, 2005), 415–27.

[45] Levine, *The Ancient Synagogue*, 116: "Much has been written about the historical reliability of Acts – from the more skeptical to the largely accepting. Theological agen-

More significantly for this analysis, Luke's descriptions of Sabbath synagogue services reveal his own acquaintance and (former?) interaction with this environment. This becomes apparent through Luke's sustained portraits of Jesus and Paul's visits to synagogues on the Sabbath in which literary parallels and structural patterns emerge. Thus, Acts 13:13–52 matches in many ways Luke 4:16–30. Both passages begin with similar openings. In Luke 4:16, Jesus comes to Nazareth (ἦλθεν εἰς Ναζαρά) and enters the synagogue on the Sabbath according to his custom (εἰσῆλθεν κατὰ τὸ εἰωθὸς αὐτῷ ἐν τῇ ἡμέρᾳ τῶν σαββάτων εἰς τὴν συναγωγὴν); in Acts 13:14, Paul and Barnabas arrive in Antioch of Pisidia (παρεγένοντο εἰς Ἀντιόχειαν) and visit the local synagogue (ελθόντες εἰς τὴν συναγωγὴν τῇ ἡμέρᾳ τῶν σαββάτων ἐκάθισαν). Both passages refer to the reading of the scriptures. In Luke 4:16–17, Jesus stands and reads from the book of Isaiah (ἀνέστη ἀναγνῶναι καὶ ἐπεδόθη αὐτῷ βιβλίον τοῦ προφήτου Ἡσαΐου . . .), while in Acts apparently the local members, perhaps, the ἀρχισυνάγωγοι, read from the Law and the Prophets (v. 15: τὴν ἀνάγνωσιν τοῦ νόμου καὶ τῶν προφητῶν). In Acts 13:27, Luke refers again to the reading of the scriptures on the Sabbath (τὰς φωνὰς τῶν προφητῶν τὰς κατὰ πᾶν σάββατον ἀναγινωσκομένας).[46] Finally, while delivering their sermons (Luke 4:23–27/Acts 13:40–41), both Luke's Jesus and Paul anticipate the rejections they experience at the local synagogue.

These literary correspondences suggest that all of the verses in Acts 13 referring to the Sabbath (13:14, 27, 42, and 44) are redactional. They might even open a window into the redactor's own world and experience: Luke has regularly attended the synagogue, knows of the customary readings and exposition of scripture, and interprets this material christologically for his readers. Equally remarkable is the assumption on Luke's part that his readers also know a great deal about synagogue life, as he feels no need to explain such features to them.

Finally, in contradistinction to the portrayal of Jesus' Sabbath practice in the gospel of Luke, no controversy arises here over the Sabbath practice of the Jewish disciples of Jesus (i.e., Paul and Barnabas). While the Lukan Jesus announces the "release to the captives and recovery of sight to the blind" (Luke 4:18), and then immediately proceeds to perform healings

---

das aside, one may assume that the specific events reported, especially those relating to the synagogue, are largely credible. The author was certainly familiar with the Jewish Diaspora and wrote for Christian Diaspora communities. It is hard to imagine that he would invent accounts for a population that knew a great deal about the synagogue, its workings, and Paul's activities." The main force of Levine's statement lies in underscoring Luke's familiarity with the synagogue world, not the historical reliability of his depiction of Paul's visits, speeches, and interaction with such an environment, which must be demonstrated on an individual basis.

[46] Cf. Acts 8:30; 15:21; Luke 24:27.

and exorcisms on the Sabbath (Luke 4:31–39; cf. 6:1–11; 13:10–17; 14:1–6), Luke's Paul only proclaims Israel's release from its sins (Acts 13:38–39) and refrains throughout Acts from performing any controversial act on the Sabbath. This dissonance between Luke and Acts discourages hastily equating Jesus' Sabbath praxis as portrayed in the gospel of Luke with the Sabbath observance practiced by the author of Luke-Acts. In Acts, the controversy between followers of Jesus and other Jews focuses on the apparent success of the dissemination of the gospel, particularly among Gentiles, not the question of Sabbath keeping. By contrast, in the gospel of Luke, controversy centers on Jesus' unique authority and how this affects his manner of observing the Law. However, as the narration gradually shifts from the persona of Jesus in the gospel of Luke to his followers in Acts, polemics regarding Sabbath practice completely disappear. In Acts, the Jewish followers of Jesus simply appear as characters who are thoroughly familiar with the normal protocols carried out on a regular Sabbath day in the realm of the synagogue. From Luke's perspective, the only reproach that can be held against them is their persistent endorsement and proclamation of the gospel, which is entirely rooted in the Torah and the Prophets.

Reading Moses on the Sabbath: Acts 15:21

Literary Context

Acts 15:21, purportedly "one of the most difficult verses in the New Testament,"[47] appears at the heart of Acts, in a chapter reporting the so-called Jerusalem Council, a gathering brought to order (at least according to Luke) because of the controversy regarding the circumcision of Gentiles (15:1). The matter is fully resolved among the apostles, so Luke would have his readers believe, once James, the brother of Jesus and head of the *ekklesia* in Jerusalem, delivers his approval in a speech that has been dubbed in German a *Miniaturrede* (15:13–21).[48] The speech itself, characterized (with the exception of v. 20b) by a strong usage and mimesis of the language of the Septuagint that appears so prominently in the gospel of Luke and Acts, is thoroughly redactional.[49] The intriguing statement about

---

[47] Martin Dibelius, *Studies in the Acts of the Apostles* (trans. Mary Ling; London: SCM Press, 1956), 97.

[48] Eckhard Plümacher, *Lukas als hellenistischer Schriftsteller. Studien zur Apostelgeschichte* (SUNT 9; Göttingen: Vandenhoeck & Ruprecht, 1972), 47.

[49] The very citation of the Gentile friendly LXX version of Amos 9:11–12, which is placed in the mouth of James, makes it more than likely that the speech has largely been

the Sabbath appears at the end of James' discourse on the "Apostolic Decree." This decree proclaims that Gentiles should abstain only "from things polluted by idols and from fornication and from whatever has been strangled and from blood" (15:19–20).

Redactional Analysis

Μωϋσῆς: The proper noun appears ten times in Luke, twenty times in Acts. It is used in this passage in reference to the Torah (cf. Luke 16:29, 31).[50]

ἐκ γενεῶν ἀρχαίων: Probably, the prepositional phrase is entirely redactional, as γενεά is frequently used by Luke (Luke: 10x; Acts: 5x), while ἀρχαῖος also appears in the genitive plural in Luke 9:8 (προφήτης τις τῶν ἀρχαίων), which itself is a Lukan rewording of Mark 6:15 (προφήτης ὡς εἷς τῶν προφητῶν). This same construction appears again in Luke 9:19 (cf. Mark 8:27/Matt 16:14 where ἀρχαίων is absent). Earlier in Acts 15:7, the construction ἀφ' ἡμερῶν ἀρχαίων appears in the mouth of Peter, also a Lukan composition.

κατὰ πόλιν: The usage of the preposition κατὰ plus the accusative reflects Lukan style (Luke: 37x; Acts: 74x). Besides a few attestations in Titus 1:5; Ign. *Rom.* 9:3 and *Mart. Pol.* 5:1, the combination of κατὰ with the noun πόλις in the accusative appears mainly in Luke and Acts (Luke 8:1, 4; Acts 15:36; 20:23; 24:12; κατὰ πόλεις also only in Luke 13:22). Thus, in Luke 8:1, Jesus goes through cities and villages *proclaiming* and announcing the kingdom of God (κατὰ πόλιν καὶ κώμην κηρύσσων καὶ εὐαγγελιζόμενος τὴν βασιλείαν τοῦ θεοῦ). In Acts 15:21, Moses is *proclaimed* in every city (κατὰ πόλιν τοὺς κηρύσσοντας αὐτόν).[51] In Acts 15:36, after the conclusion of the so-called Jerusalem Council, Paul and Barnabas decide to go through every city in which they had announced the word of the lord (κατὰ πόλιν πᾶσαν ἐν αἷς κατηγγείλαμεν τὸν λόγον τοῦ κυρίου).

ἐν ταῖς συναγωγαῖς: The synagogue is a favorite locale in Luke-Acts. The prepositional phrase ἐν ταῖς συναγωγαῖς appears four times in Acts (9:20; 13:5; 15:21; 24:12) and three times in Luke (4:15; 11:43; 20:46).

κατὰ πᾶν σάββατον: This construction appears only in Acts (13:27; 18:24). As noted earlier, Acts 13:27 is also redactional (see previous section).

ἀναγινωσκόμενος: a favorite Lukan term referring to the reading of the Jewish scriptures (cf. Luke 10:26; Acts 8:30; 13:27). 15:21b largely resembles a phrase from Acts 13:27:

---

redacted by Luke. Amos 9:12, as cited in Acts 15:17, refers to Gentiles in a positive way, prophesying how many of them will one day seek the God of Israel. The MT of Amos 9:12, however, contains a rather hostile reference concerning the nations, which the LXX has euphemized. It seems very unlikely that James, an Aramaic speaking Jew, would have recited the LXX in Greek at a gathering in Jerusalem. The harmonizing tendency of the speech as well as its Septuagintal style, so characteristic of Luke, point towards redaction (save for 15:20). See Wehnert, *Die Reinheit*, 41.

[50] There is no need to interpret Luke's reference to "Moses" as Daniel Schwartz, "The Futility of Preaching Moses (Acts 15, 21)," *Bib* 67 (1986): 280–81, does, claiming that Luke is relativizing the divine origin of the Law with the usage of this nomenclature.

[51] Wehnert, *Die Reinheit*, 46, suggests that the usage of κηρύσσοντας may in this instance be traditional, since normally Luke uses it as term denoting the proclamation of Jesus as the Christ, whereas here it refers more broadly to instruction derived from the Jewish tradition (cf. Gal 5:11).

τὰς φωνὰς τῶν προφητῶν τὰς κατὰ πᾶν σάββατον ἀναγινωσκομένας (13:27).
κατὰ πᾶν σάββατον ἀναγινωσκόμενος (15:21b).

Conclusion: the number of salient Lukan features points to the thorough redaction of 15:21.

Interpretation

One of the major challenges lies in determining in what sense the conjunction γὰρ links v. 21 with the previous statements in either v. 19 or v. 20. What does James, or for our purposes, the author of Acts, mean with his declaration that Gentiles should not be troubled (v. 19), but only avoid the pollution of idols, sexual immorality, strangled meat, and blood (v. 20), "since" (γὰρ) Moses has (ἔχει)[52] those who proclaim him every Sabbath in the synagogues? Some time ago, Trocmé suggested connecting v. 21 exclusively with v. 19, maintaining that both verses stem from a same source, while v. 20 is a Lukan addition.[53] This suggestion seems unlikely, since James' *Miniaturrede* is so thoroughly marked by Lukan composition. As Pervo correctly notes, "nothing from v. 16 through v. 20 makes a satisfactory link. Verse 20 wins by default."[54]

Following the many interpreters who tie v. 21 with its immediate antecedents in v. 20, I suggest, among the plethora of proposals, to highlight the apologetic dimension inherent within this connection.[55] By composing

---

[52] The translation of ἔχει in the present (so NASV) is to be preferred to the NRSV, which reads, "Moses *has had* those who proclaim him." For Luke, the reading of the scriptures in the synagogue is as an ongoing and present reality.

[53] Étienne Trocmé, *Le livre des Actes et l'histoire* (Paris: Presses Universitaires de France, 1957), 160–61.

[54] Pervo, *Acts*, 378. Schwartz, "The Futility of Preaching Moses (Acts 15, 21)," 276–81, does not view Acts 15:21 as explaining v. 20. He points to the difficulty among commentators in explaining why only some Mosaic requirements are adopted and not others. Many commentators, however, have pointed to Lev 17–18 as the proper background for understanding the Apostolic Decree in Acts 15:20. Wehnert has recently solidified this proposal by pointing to the Targumic evidence (this is fully addressed in Part II of this monograph). Schwartz claims: "James means only that since long and widespread Jewish experience shows that Gentiles will not (by and large) accept Mosaic law, a Christian attempt to impose it upon Gentiles (whether already converted or contemplating it) would be futile" (279). I do not think that Luke's James has given up on the Gentiles because of previous failures. If we accept this argument, Luke should also have given up requesting Gentiles to abandon idolatry and polytheism, since Jewish experience has experienced failure in this area as well.

[55] Vaguely formulated by Haenchen, *The Acts of the Apostles*, 450: "It gives the justification for the immediately preceding verse 20...." Similarly, Conzelmann, *Acts of the Apostles*, 120: "Perhaps the verse intends to substantiate the *decree*." A concise summary of a number of proposals can be found in Schwartz, "The Futility of Preaching Moses," 276–81.

v. 21, Luke not only expresses his concern over the problem of Torah praxis among Gentiles, but also reveals his concrete knowledge about the operation of synagogue institutions scattered across the Mediterranean basin. Quite possibly, he has several fronts in mind when composing v. 21 (and much of Acts for that matter): 1) Gentile and Jewish followers of Jesus who have nearly or completely abandoned observing the Torah 2) Jewish followers of Jesus (and maybe some other Jews) who demand Gentiles to observe all of the Torah (including circumcision) 3) non-Christian Jews and certain Jewish followers of Jesus who not only suspect but also accuse segments within the Jesus movement of leading their Jewish compatriots away from the Torah (Acts 21:21; 28:17). This Jewish suspicion probably arose because of the extensive fellowship occurring in certain circles between Jewish and Gentile followers of Jesus. In response, Luke composed v. 21 and tied it with the so-called Apostolic Decree (part of his solution to this complicated problem) in order demonstrate how the apostolic decision is firmly grounded in the Torah of Moses. The Apostolic Decree is necessary to follow, so Luke's James argues, because it is anchored in the Mosaic Torah, which is read aloud every week in the synagogue.[56] Gentile followers of Jesus are to follow this rigorous set of demands (e.g., abandoning idolatry) – they are not entirely dispensed from observing the Torah – that go beyond what other (non-Christian) Diasporan Jews expected from Gentile God-fearers, who for understandable social, economic, and political reasons continued to engage in idolatrous activity even while attending the synagogue.

Unfortunately, besides revealing his acquaintance with the Sabbath services held at an average Diasporan synagogue, Luke provides no other information in Acts 15:21 on the question of Sabbath observance proper. Perhaps, he assumes with this verse that Jewish and Gentile followers of Jesus can readily and easily attend their local synagogue every Sabbath and listen to the reading of the Law of Moses. However, even this assumption cannot be used to show that Luke *requires Gentile* followers of Jesus to keep the Sabbath.[57] The commandments contained in the Apostolic Decree, which are incumbent upon non-Jews, revolve mainly around moral issues, certain purity laws, as well as dietary practices that can allow for Jews and Gentiles to interact freely and extensively with one another.

---

[56] Jervell, *Die Apostelgeschichte*, 399: "Nicht nur Jakobus, sondern vor allem Mose verbürgt die Autorität des Dekrets."

[57] This is the direction that Bacchiocchi, *From Sabbath to Sunday,* 145–48, leans toward, but even he seems to acknowledge (albeit without distinguishing between redactional and traditional layers) at this point that the evidence speaks primarily in favor of Jewish followers of Jesus keeping the Sabbath. Of course, from Luke's perspective, the question of whether *Jews* should keep the Sabbath is entirely affirmative, since he assumes that they will keep the Torah *in toto*.

Sabbath keeping does not fall within the immediate circumference of Luke's concern for improving Jewish-Gentile relations, because a Gentile neglect of Sabbath observance need not in principle deter a practicing Jewish follower of Jesus from continuing to honor that holy day.[58] Nevertheless, given the willingness and great sacrifice demonstrated by Gentile followers of Jesus to worship the God of Israel by abandoning idolatry, it is possible that some of them might have also voluntarily chosen to observe the Sabbath.[59] Such a spontaneous embrace of Jewish customs among Gentile followers of Jesus should not be surprising, since Sabbath keeping was popular among Gentiles during this period of history.[60] Luke may have even welcomed Sabbath celebration among non-Jews, interpreting their observance of the fourth commandment as an expression of their release from idolatry and commitment to the God "who made the heaven and the earth and the sea and all that is in them" (Acts 14:15).[61] In any

---

[58] The absence of the Sabbath within the Apostolic Decree can hardly be taken as evidence for Sunday observance. Rordorf, *Sunday*, 219, interprets the silence of the Sabbath with the Apostolic Decree as "the most eloquent proof that the observance of Sunday had been recognized by the entire apostolic Church and had been adopted by the Pauline Churches." Similarly, Jewett, *The Lord's Day*, 56–57: "The fact that we find no hint of such [i.e., debate over the Sabbath], especially at the Jerusalem Council (Acts 15), indicates that in this matter the entire apostolic church, including the Jewish party, was in agreement. First-day worship, then, was not a Pauline invention." These observations are all beside the point. Luke needs to be replaced in his Jewish context and compared with other Jewish authors who deal with the question of which Torah commandments are incumbent upon Jews and not Gentiles. Like many other Jews of his time, Luke discriminates between both ethnic groups as far as their Mosaic obligations are concerned.

[59] Mayer-Haas, *Geschenk*, 368, sees Sabbath keeping as presupposed by Luke, presumably for Jew and Gentile alike, since it belongs to the legislation of the Ten Commandments: "Für den Autor der Apostelgeschichte ist die christliche Sabbatobservanz offensichtlich kein Thema, wobei er aber nirgendwo durchblicken läßt, daß Christen das Dekaloggebot der Sabbatruhe nicht praktizieren (sollen), so daß die Schlußfolgerung, für seine Adressaten sei dieses Gebot längst in Vergessenheit geraten, auf keinen Fall die Sachlage trifft. Eher handelt es sich bei dem Schweigen der Apostelgeschichte um die stillschweigende Anerkennung des hohen Stellenwertes, den das Sabbatgebot als Identitätszeichen des Judentums auch unter den Heidenchristen der lukanischen Gemeinde noch besaß." My unease with this proposal concerns the singling out of the Ten Commandments as a distinctive corpus of legislation enjoying a higher degree of authority and pertinence among Jews and Gentiles for which the evidence in Luke-Acts does not speak. Luke only signals the supremacy and universality of the "moral" commandments contained in the Decalogue (cf. Luke 18:20). Accordingly, the ritual commandment to keep the Sabbath only concerns Jewish followers of Jesus.

[60] See Introduction to chapter 1 of this book for a brief discussion of primary and secondary sources.

[61] This phrase, which appears in Acts 14:15, where Paul and Barnabas attempt to dissuade the non-Jews of Lystra from worshiping them as gods, is taken from the fourth commandment on the Sabbath as it appears in the LXX (Exod 20:11) although it might

case, Acts 15:21 may at least indicate that that Luke is not *opposed* to Gentile followers of Jesus (and certainly not Jewish followers of Jesus!) keeping the Sabbath.⁶²

Worshiping Outdoors on the Sabbath: Acts 16:12–15

Literary Context

This passage, which belongs to the so-called "we sections," appears within a wider unit (16:11–40) reporting Paul's visit to Philippi. During their stay, Paul and his crew make contact on the Sabbath (τῇ τε ἡμέρᾳ τῶν σαββάτων) with a local group of women at a place of prayer (προσευχὴν). One of these women, Lydia, a worshiper of God and a dealer of purple cloth, becomes a follower of Jesus and is baptized along with the rest of her household. Later on during his extended time in Philippi, Paul expels a spirit of divination (πνεῦμα πύθωνα) from a slave-girl (16:16–18). This exorcism does not seem to take place on a Sabbath even though v. 16 indicates that Paul first encountered this girl on his way to the προσευχὴν, the same place where he met Lydia on a previous Sabbath. Ancient Jews, however, did not attend their places of prayer or synagogues only on the Sabbath. Furthermore, according to v. 18, Paul frees the slave-girl from demonic possession only after she hassles him "for many days" (ἐπὶ πολλὰς ἡμέρας). The vague chronological formulation does not clearly indicate whether Paul performs this exorcism on a Sabbath or on some other day of the week, though we note the complete absence of any explicit reference to healings or exorcisms occurring on the Sabbath throughout Acts.

Analysis

The recurring motif of introducing Paul (and his entourage) into a synagogue of the Diaspora on the Sabbath day appears once again in Acts.

---

also have been inspired by LXX Ps 145:6 (the whole Psalm with its promise of healing and restoration for the blind and oppressed would have particularly pleased Luke). Luke has Paul and Barnabas recite this phrase, which is embedded in the Sabbath commandment, in order to dissuade non-Jews from practicing idolatry (cf. Acts 4:24; 17:24), though he never explicitly calls upon Gentiles to observe the Sabbath as a celebration of creation or expression of their liberation from idolatry. I would like to thank Anthony Kent for pointing me to these passages in Acts and their possible pertinence for addressing the question of Sabbath observance in Luke-Acts.

⁶² For more on Jewish attitudes toward Gentiles keeping the Sabbath, see my "Forming Jewish Identity by Formulating Legislation for Gentiles."

However, a slight variation to this literary pattern catches the reader's eye: instead of entering a synagogue (συναγωγή), the locale Luke normally mentions in Acts, Paul searches for a "place of prayer" (προσευχὴν) outside the gates of the city, somewhere near the river. The word προσευχὴν can designate a place of gathering for Jews. Thus, 3 Macc 7:20 refers to the dedication of a site as a place of prayer (τόπον προσευχῆς). Likewise, in his *Life* (280), Josephus refers to assembling in a place of prayer (συναγόμενον ἤδη τὸ πλῆθος εἰς τὴν προσευχήν).[63] Epigraphical and papyrological documents also attest to the usage of *proseuche* in reference to a synagogue building, particularly in the region of Egypt.[64] Some ancient sources indicate a preference among Jews in the Diaspora for building their synagogues near the sea.[65] Josephus (*Ant.* 14:258) records the following decree made on behalf of the Jews of Halicarnassus: "We have decreed, that as many men and women of the Jews as are willing so to do, may celebrate their Sabbaths, and perform their holy offices, according to Jewish laws; and may make their places of prayer at the seaside" (τὰς προσευχὰς ποιεῖσθαι πρὸς τῇ θαλάττῃ). The reason for setting up prayer sites along the seaside is not entirely clear. Some scholars suggest Jews viewed the sea as a suitable location for performing purification rites.[66] Others speculate that certain Jews met outside the city gates in order to avoid confrontations with non-Jews.[67] Also unclear is whether the term *proseuche* refers in this instance to an actual building or to a more informal place of gathering,

---

[63] Cf. Josephus, *Ag. Ap.* 2:10; Philo, *Flacc.* 41, 45, 122; *Legat.* 152.

[64] Levine, *The Ancient Synagogue*, 127: 53% of the occurrences concerning Diaspora synagogues refer to a *proseuche*. The term is almost exclusively used in Hellenistic Egypt, the Bosphorus, and Delos, which account for almost all of the evidence for the Diaspora during the first century CE. For further discussions on the *proseuche*, see Levine, *The Ancient Synagogue*, 151–59.

[65] Levine, *The Ancient Synagogue*, 106.

[66] Cf. *Letter of Aristeas* 305, which speaks of the custom of all the Jews to wash their hands in the sea and pray to God; *Sib. Or.* 3:591–593: "For on the contrary, at dawn they lift up holy arms toward heaven, from their beds, always sanctifying their flesh [or "hands" depending on the manuscript] with water...." Cf. *Sib. Or.* 4:165: "wash your whole bodies in perennial rivers." The smaller number of ritual baths (*miqvaot*) discovered in Galilee in comparison to Judea may be due to the presence of the Sea of Galilee, which served as a site for ritual immersion. See Magness, *Stone and Dung*, 16–17. For the practice of hand washing before praying as evidenced in the archaeological finds of Diasporan synagogues, see Anders Runesson, "Water and Worship: Ostia and the Ritual Bath in the Diaspora Synagogue," in *The Synagogue of Ancient Ostia and the Jews of Rome* (eds. Birger Olsson et al.; Stockholm: P. Astroem, 2001), 115–29.

[67] Zmijewski, *Die Apostelgeschichte*, 607, who thinks that the Jews in Philippi constituted a small group seeking to avoid confrontation because of the supposed anti-Jewish sentiment prevalent in that city.

perhaps in the open air.⁶⁸ In the absence of any reference to the reading of scriptures on the Sabbath, which Luke loves to highlight, probably an informal gathering in the outdoors should be envisioned here.

According to Acts 16:13, Paul and his comrades exit from the city gate and go to the river (ἔξω τῆς πύλης παρὰ ποταμὸν). Many commentators identify this river as the Gangites, which lies at about 2.4 km from Philippi.⁶⁹ The distance covered during a roundtrip to the river and back to the ancient city of Philippi would have been about five kilometers, well beyond the Sabbath journey limits (c. 1 km).⁷⁰ Because of this halakic dilemma, Lemerle and Festugière suggest the nearer creek, Crenides, which is located right next to the occidental gate, as the location for the gathering.⁷¹ This proposal is appealing, as it would conform to Luke's intention to portray Jewish followers of Jesus as honoring the Torah, in this case, by respecting the Sabbath limits.⁷² As noted above in the analysis of Acts 1:12, Luke clearly knows about the halakah concerning the Sabbath limits, which, according to his measurement, roughly corresponds to the distance between Jerusalem and the Mount of Olives (c. 1 km).⁷³

---

⁶⁸ Tertullian, *Ad nationes* 1:13, mentions the *orationes litorales* of the Jews. In his *De jejunio adversus psychios* 16, he talks of Jews praying in the open air after the destruction of their temple. Mayer-Haas, *Geschenk*, 376, following Stegemann, *Zwischen Synagoge und Obrigkeit*, 211–14, thinks that in this instance the term does not refer to an established building, but to a secret site, since the ambassadors of Jesus have to look for a place outside the city gates and only find women gathered there.

⁶⁹ See Fitzmyer, *The Acts of the Apostles*, 585.

⁷⁰ The problem is noted by Le Cornu and Shulam, *Jewish Roots of Acts*, 2:879, but with the mere subsequent remark that its location "may reflect the importance of washing in relation to prayer."

⁷¹ Paul Lemerle, *Philippes et la Macédoine orientale à l'époque chrétienne et byzantine* (Bibliothèque des Écoles françaises d'Athènes et de Rome 158; Pairs: É. de Boccard, 1945), 23–27. Lemerle adds another argument against identifying the river as the Gangites: "il est inutile de supposer que la proseuque était à une si grande distance, quand les Juifs de Philippes, qui habitaient la ville même (c'étaient des commerçants ou des artisans, non des agriculteurs ou des propriétaires terriens), trouvaient beaucoup plus près ce qu'ils cherchaient" (25). See also A. J. Festugière, review of Paul Lemerle, *Philippes et la Macédoine orientale à l'époque chrétienne et byzantine*, *RB* 54 (1947): 132–33.

⁷² Or should we assume Luke's ignorance of the topography of Philippi? This would be unlikely if Luke is the author of the "we sections," meaning that he would have visited Philippi. On the other hand, the Greek παρὰ ποταμὸν could mean that the place of prayer lies somewhere near the river, but within the Sabbath limits. This reading, however, could be ruled out by v. 15, if Lydia's baptism occurred on the same day, implying that the location of the prayer site lay right next to a river.

⁷³ Is it possible that some Jews did not strictly observe the Sabbath limits? Perhaps some Jews in the Diaspora did walk beyond the limit but did not travel long distances on the Sabbath. In two passages (*Ant.* 13:252: οὐκ ἔξεστι δ' ἡμῖν οὔτε τοῖς σαββάτοις οὔτ' ἐν τῇ ἑορτῇ ὁδεύειν; *Ant.* 14:226: μήτε ὁδοιπορεῖν ἐν ταῖς ἡμέραις τῶν σαββάτων), Josephus refers to the prohibition of traveling on the Sabbath, but does not mention the Sabbath

Luke ascribes to Lydia the label of "worshiper of God" (σεβομένη τὸν θεόν), which on its own may not be taken as decisive evidence for her Gentile background, since elsewhere in Acts the term σεβόμενοι seems to refer to Jews or proselytes (those who have undergone full conversion).[74] But probably Lydia is a Gentile, since other pious non-Jews, who are affiliated in various ways to their local Jewish communities, appear prominently throughout Acts and often become members of the Jesus movement. The Roman centurion Cornelius, "a devout man who feared God" (10:2: εὐσεβὴς καὶ φοβούμενος τὸν θεόν), best exemplifies such Gentiles who gravitate toward the Jewish people and their customs.[75] Since Luke refers elsewhere to prominent Greek women who join Paul's movement (17:12; cf. 13:50), perhaps Lydia should be viewed as a Gentile sympathizer of Judaism.[76]

Like many other Gentiles in Acts, Lydia regularly attends the synagogue/prayer place on the Sabbath without hesitation (cf. 14:1; 18:4). Admittedly, Luke portrays Lydia attending the Jewish prayer site at Philippi on the Sabbath *before* her baptism and entrance into the Jesus movement. Nevertheless, the passage may still reflect Luke's openness to the ongoing possibility for Gentiles to attend the synagogue on the Sabbath even after their incorporation into the Jesus movement. Nowhere does Luke hint that after their baptism Gentiles are forbidden from observing, voluntarily and spontaneously, Jewish customs such as the Sabbath. As for Luke's Paul, a Jewish follower of Jesus, he appears once again in the

---

limits. In *Mos.* 2:214, Philo assumes that Jews may go out on the Sabbath from "the gates to some quiet spot, that they might pray in some retired and peaceful place" (πυλῶν γὰρ ἔξω προελθόντες τινὲς εἰς ἐρημίαν, ἵν' ἐν τῷ καθαρωτάτῳ καὶ ἡσυχάζοντι εὔξωνται). Like Josephus, he does not refer to the Sabbath limits. Quite interestingly, Philo's description would seem to correspond to the scenario envisaged in Acts 16:13: Some Jews in the Diaspora did seek places for prayer outside the city gates, although we do not know how far they went. Philo's passage should not be taken as evidence that Diasporan Jews did not refrain at all from traveling on the Sabbath. Even the pagan sources reveal that Jews did not travel long distances on the Sabbath (Tibullus, *Carmina*, I, 3:15–18; Ovid, *Remedia Amoris* 219; see Stern, *Greek and Latin Authors*, 1:319, 349). Doering, *Schabbat*, 354, 570, cautiously leaves the question open.

[74] See section above discussing its usage in Acts 13. Probably in Acts 13:43, σεβομένων προσηλύτων refers to full converts (involving circumcision in the case of males). In 13:16 and 26, φοβούμενοι τὸν θεόν quite possibly refers to full converts as well. In 16:14; 17:4, 17 and 18:7, σεβόμενοι most likely designates Gentiles, while the term φοβούμενος is also employed in reference to non-Jews who sympathize with Jewish customs and society (10:22; 10:35; 13:16; 13:26; 27:17).

[75] Cf. Acts 17:4 where Luke mentions "a great many of the devout Greeks" (τῶν σεβομένων Ἑλλήνων πλῆθος πολύ) in the synagogue of Thessalonica, whom Paul eventually wins over to his cause.

[76] Cf. Jervell, *Die Apostelgeschichte*, 422.

traditional pattern found elsewhere in Acts, searching, as many other Jews would probably do upon their arrival in a new town in the Diaspora, for a local Jewish synagogue.

More Sabbath Services in the Synagogue
Acts 17:2 and 18:4

Literary Context

Acts 17:2 and 18:4 repeat a pattern that should by now seem rather familiar (cf. Luke 4:16–30; Acts 13:14, 27, 42, 44; 16:12). They add little new information about Luke's attitude toward the question of Sabbath keeping, although they do underscore his desire to portray Paul as a pious Jew interacting on the Sabbath with his compatriots within synagogue space.[77] Within the narrative of Acts, only the geographical settings shift, while the outline emphasizing Paul's habitual visit to the synagogue on the Sabbath (as well as his eventual ejection) remains intact. Thus, in Acts 17:1, Paul finds himself in Thessalonica where he preaches for three consecutive Sabbaths in the local synagogue (v. 2). The same routine occurs: initial success followed by Jewish opposition (v. 4). The "Jews," for understandable social-political reasons, accuse Paul of "turning the world upside down" and of acting against Caesar's decree by claiming no other king but Jesus (vv. 6–7).

Behind this polemical description probably lurks a historical reflection of a complex social-political dynamic that persisted in Luke's day: Jews, as a minority group in the wider Greco-Roman Diaspora, feared the potential repercussions the burgeoning Jesus movement could bring upon themselves partly because of the visible and popular gravitation of non-Jews from their ancestral polytheistic practices to the exclusive beliefs and practices of Judaism. Understandably, the local Jews sought to dissociate themselves from this radical messianic movement. This historical reconstruction accounts for the eventual expulsion of Paul and Silas (v. 10). In Acts 18:1, the pattern repeats itself again: Paul visits the synagogue of Corinth on the Sabbath (v. 4) and enjoys initial success. In this case, even

---

[77] To these two verses, may be added Acts 18:24–28 as well as 19:1–20 (see especially v. 8), which also presume synagogue attendance on the Sabbath, although the seventh day is not explicitly mentioned. In the former passage, a Jew named Apollos as well as two other Jewish followers of Jesus, Priscilla and Aquila, attend the synagogue and preach about Jesus. In Acts 19:8, Paul spends three months at the synagogue of Ephesus, reasoning with the local members about the kingdom of God. Probably Acts 17:17 (visit to the synagogue of Athens) also presupposes a Sabbath setting.

the head of the synagogue, Crispus, becomes a follower. Nevertheless, Paul ultimately encounters opposition (vv. 12–17).[78]

Redactional Analysis

Part of the language of Acts 17:2 repeats verbatim the wording in Luke 4:16, thereby creating a parallelism between Jesus and Paul that was already detected and appreciated in the section of this chapter dealing with Acts 13:

κατὰ δὲ τὸ εἰωθὸς τῷ Παύλῳ εἰσῆλθεν πρὸς αὐτοὺς καὶ ἐπὶ σάββατα τρία διελέξατο αὐτοῖς ἀπὸ τῶν γραφῶν (Acts 17:2)
καὶ εἰσῆλθεν κατὰ τὸ εἰωθὸς αὐτῷ ἐν τῇ ἡμέρᾳ τῶν σαββάτων εἰς τὴν συναγωγὴν καὶ ἀνέστη ἀναγνῶναι (Luke 4:16).

Luke has redacted these verses, which create symmetry between Jesus and Paul's actions. The common redactional features include the usage of the verb εἰσῆλθεν as well as the construction κατὰ τὸ εἰωθὸς followed by the dative (τῷ Παύλῳ/ αὐτῷ). Just as Jesus "according to his custom" (κατὰ τὸ εἰωθὸς) "entered" (εἰσῆλθεν) the synagogue of Nazareth "on the Sabbath day" (ἐν τῇ ἡμέρᾳ τῶν σαββάτων), so also Paul "entered" (εἰσῆλθεν) the synagogue in Thessalonica "according to his custom" (κατὰ τὸ εἰωθὸς). Likewise, just as Jesus read and preached from the prophet Isaiah (Luke 4:16–21), in a similar way, Paul reasoned from the Jewish scriptures with the synagogue members of Thessalonica for three Sabbaths (ἐπὶ σάββατα τρία διελέξατο αὐτοῖς ἀπὸ τῶν γραφῶν).[79]

In Acts 18:4, Luke repeats this motif, having Paul discuss every Sabbath in a local synagogue of Corinth in an attempt to convince both Jews and Greeks alike (διελέγετο δὲ ἐν τῇ συναγωγῇ κατὰ πᾶν σάββατον ἔπειθέν τε Ἰουδαίους καὶ Ἕλληνας). The prepositional phrase, κατὰ πᾶν σάββατον, is also a Lukan composition, appearing only in Acts (13:27; 18:4). The reference to Paul's discussion in the synagogue (διελέγετο δὲ ἐν τῇ συναγωγῇ) matches the previous depiction in 17:2 where the same apostle also discusses with the Jews citing scripture (τρία διελέξατο αὐτοῖς ἀπὸ τῶν γραφῶν). Both Acts 18:4 and 17:2, then, are literary Lukan products *par*

---

[78] In verses 12–17, Paul is brought before the proconsul of Achaia, Gallio, before whom the "Jews" present their case against him. Most interesting is Luke's portrayal of the issue from the Roman perspective: Gallio remains indifferent toward the controversy, pointing to the intra-Jewish nature of the debate, which he claims should be solved among the Jews themselves.

[79] ἐπὶ σάββατα τρία should be translated here as "on three Sabbaths," and not "for three weeks." Even though the latter translation is a possible one, it seems less likely, given the recurring pattern in Acts depicting Paul preaching in the synagogues on the Sabbath day. Correctly, Barrett, *The Acts of the Apostles,* 2:809; Haenchen, *The Acts of the Apostles*, 507.

excellence. Besides providing a setting for Paul's engagement with local Jewish communities from the Diaspora, these verses portray him, once again, as a Jew who is thoroughly comfortable with the synagogue habitat, intensely dedicated to spreading the gospel message among Jewish compatriots and Gentile sympathizers alike.[80]

When Do the Followers of Jesus "Break Bread"? Acts 20:7–12

Literary Context

The final passage in Acts on the Sabbath is set within the city of Troas, located in the northwest corner of Asia Minor (v. 6). The wider literary setting, which belongs to the so-called "we sections" reporting Paul's final return to Palestine, contains a number of remarkable chronological features that divide time in a Jewish manner. These include the reference to Paul's departure from Philippi to Troas *after the feast of Unleavened bread* (20:6), the setting of the Eucharist in Troas *on the first day of the week* (20:7), and the apostle's intent on arriving in Jerusalem *before Pentecost* (20:16). In the midst of these events, a miracle story about the "resuscitation" of a certain Eutychus, which has apparently been inserted into this "we section,"[81] momentarily interrupts the literary flow of the narration (vv. 7–12) on Paul's journey back to Jerusalem.

Analysis

The main item of interest for this inquiry concerns the Jewish formulation of the chronological setting of this miracle story: ἐν δὲ τῇ μιᾷ τῶν σαββάτων,[82] literally, "on the one of the Sabbaths," that is, on a Sunday.[83]

---

[80] Jervell, *Die Apostelgeschichte*, 433: "als Jude und Missionar."

[81] Some commentators like, Pervo, *Acts*, 506, view vv. 7–12 as a Lukan creation, inspired by the LXX. Others, like Barrett, *The Acts of the Apostles,* 2:943–44, see traces of tradition here, albeit with some redactional touches: "It gives the impression of being a free piece of tradition which Luke had some reason to connect with Troas (perhaps he heard it there) and interpolated into the record of the journey."

[82] Cf. Luke 24:1; Mark 16:2; John 20:1, 19. See also Luke 18:12: "I fast twice a week (δὶς τοῦ σαββάτου); I give a tenth of all my income."

[83] Some view the chronological introduction in Acts 20:7 as traditional and intrinsically tied to the narrative. See Zmijewski, *Die Apostelgeschichte*, 725. Given Luke's ample usage of such chronological terms to divide his narrative, a strong case for its redactional status could also be made. In either case, this type of chronological formulation perfectly suits Luke's preference for employing Jewish language to structure his narrative.

Such language would be comprehensible only to individuals with some basic acquaintance with the Jewish system of enumerating and dividing time.[84] The whole phrase corresponds to the Hebrew באחד בשבת.[85] Luke's manner of dividing time would have earned him the commendation of the Tanna R. Isaac who purportedly said: "Do not count in the way that others count, but count for the sake of/in reference to (לשם) the Sabbath."[86]

Because of the Jewish texture of the opening to this section, some scholars posit that Luke depicts Paul and the disciples in Troas breaking bread on the evening/night of Saturday, since according to Jewish reckoning the day begins in the evening rather than the morning (Gen 1:5; Exod 12:18; Lev 23:32, etc.).[87] If the words, "to break bread" (κλάσαι ἄρτον), are technical terms designating the celebration of the Eucharist,[88] this could mean that, according to Luke, Paul and the disciples at Troas observed this rite immediately after the Sabbath, as an extension of their Sabbath keeping.

Other commentators, however, who posit the usage of Roman reckoning in this pericope, maintain that Luke refers to a Sunday service extending

---

[84] This Jewish enumeration of the days of the week was employed for a while in certain Christian circles. See Eduard Lose, "σάββατον," *TDNT* 7:32, for references. Louse's dated treatment contains some problematic comments, including his interpretation of *Did.* 8:1 (Αἱ δὲ νηστεῖαι ὑμῶν μὴ ἔστωσαν μετὰ τῶν ὑποκριτῶν νηστεύουσι γὰρ δευτέρᾳ σαββάτων καὶ πέμπτῃ ὑμεῖς δὲ νηστεύσατε τετράδα καὶ παρασκευήν), as an unqualified contrast between "Christian" and "Jewish" fasts. The passage only chronologically (through the usage of Jewish language) distinguishes Jewish (-Christian) fasting from Jewish (-Pharisaic?) fasting.

[85] *M. Ta'an.* 4:1; *Mek.* Beshallah-Wayassa Parashah 1; *b. B. Qam.* 82a.

[86] *Mek.* Yitro-BaHodesh Parashah 7. Author's translation. In the same passage from the *Mekilta*, R. Eleazar ben Hanina ben Hezekiah, commenting on the command in the Torah, "Remember the Sabbath to keep it holy," declares that one should start remembering the Sabbath day already from the "first day of the week" (מאחד בשבת) onward.

[87] Bacchiocchi, *From Sabbath to Sunday*, 101–111; Fitzmyer, *The Acts of the Apostles*, 668–69; LeCornu and Shulam, *The Jewish Roots of Acts*, 2:1105–7; Mayer-Haas, *Geschenk*, 379–80; H. Riesenfeld, "Sabbat et jour du Seigneur," in *New Testament Essays. Studies in Memory of Thomas Walter Manson* (ed. A. J. B. Higgins; Manchester: Manchester University Press, 1959), 210–18; Reinhart Staats, "Die Sonntagnachmittaggottesdienste der christlichen Frühzeit," *ZNW* 66 (1975): 224–63.

[88] Bacchiocchi, *From Sabbath to Sunday*, 101–11, argues against the technical understanding of the terms κλάσαι ἄρτον. However, his systematic attempt to sanitize the New Testament from any reference to Sunday commemorations raises suspicion. His position seems untenable, since *Did.* 14:1 as well as Ignatius, *Ephesians* 20:2 (assuming this work is not pseudepigraphic and dates from the beginning of the second century) appear to employ the verb as a technical term for the Eucharist. If Acts is a work written by the end of the first century, there is no gap in time between the former and the latter works. Nevertheless, see J. Behm, "κλάω," *TDNT* 3:728–29.

well into Monday morning.[89] In support of their thesis, some of these interpreters point to the usage of the Greek ἐπαύριον (translated by them as "tomorrow") in 20:7 and compare it with such passages as Acts 4:3 and 23:31–32. Since in the latter two passages the terms ἐπαύριον/αὔριον appear in conjunction with the evening or the night, they argue that Luke conceives of time in Acts 20:7 according to Roman standards. Otherwise, the usage of such language would be redundant, since, according to Jewish tradition, the evening or nighttime already marks the arrival of a new day. Consequently, there would be no need for Luke to mention ἐπαύριον/αὔριον unless he conceives of the beginning of a new day according to a Roman reckoning of time.

This argument, however, carries limited weight once we realize that ἐπαύριον/αὔριον can also mean "on the next morrow," that is, the next *morning* rather than the next day.[90] Such an understanding of ἐπαύριον/αὔριον can readily elucidate the aforementioned passages in Acts. Thus, in Acts 4:3, when Luke states that the chief priests had Peter and John arrested and placed in custody "until the next day" (εἰς τὴν αὔριον), he means with this temporal phrase that the apostles were imprisoned "until the next morning," "since it was already evening" (ἦν γὰρ ἑσπέρα ἤδη). The same applies for Acts 20:31–32: the Roman soldiers accompany Paul during the night to Antipatris (v. 31), while the horsemen travel on with him on the next morning (τῇ δὲ ἐπαύριον).

This interpretation can also make good sense of the events related in 20:7–12. The followers of Jesus could have gathered (συνηγμένων, related to the noun "synagogue") on a Saturday evening/night, that is, the beginning of Sunday according to Jewish reckoning. This would have been a convenient time for Jesus' followers to come together, especially if they were already enjoying each other's company during the Sabbath day, perhaps, first in the synagogue and then in their private homes (20:7).[91] With the arrival of sunset, Sabbath traveling restrictions would no longer

---

[89] Klinghardt, *Gesetz und Volk Gottes,* 261–64; Rordorf, *Sunday,* 196–205, allows for both possibilities but then prefers a setting during Sunday evening because of his reading of the evidence from Pliny (*Ep.* 10:96). On the problematic usage of Pliny's letter for elucidating Acts 20:7, see Klinghardt, *Gesetz und Volk Gottes,* 262 n. 12.

[90] Bacchiocchi, *From Sabbath to Sunday,* 103–4; Klinghardt, *Gesetz und Volk Gottes*, 262 n. 14: "Gemeint ist hier: nächster Lichttag (nicht Kalendartage); ἐπαύριον ist der folgende Tag im Gegensatz zur Nachte." Louis Pirot and Albert Clamer, *La Sainte Bible: Texte latin et traduction française d'après les textes originaux avec un commentaire exégétique et théologique* (12 vols.; Paris: Letouzey, 1946), 11:276. According to Liddell-Scott, "αὔριον," is akin to ἠώς ("morning" or "dawn") and ἐς αὔριον means "on the morrow or till morning."

[91] Or maybe only in their private homes because of the tensions between Jews and followers of Jesus.

impede the Lukan Paul, a Torah observant Jew, from parting to his next destination.[92] Accordingly, he would have taken one last opportunity to speak until midnight (μέχρι μεσονυκτίου) with those assembled in Troas before his departure the next morning (τῇ ἐπαύριον). In 20:11, Luke states that Paul "continued to converse with them until dawn (ἄχρι αὐγῆς); then he left."[93] The prepositional phrase ἄχρι αὐγῆς could mean that, according to Luke, Paul did indeed fulfill his intent, mentioned earlier in v. 7, to leave the following morning (μέλλων ἐξιέναι τῇ ἐπαύριον) rather than the following calendar day.

Klinghardt, however, views the usage of μέχρι μεσονυκτίου in Acts 20:7 as proof that Luke conceives of time according to the Roman mode of reckoning, since the prepositional phrase would signal a point in time rather than a time span. While Jewish reckoning traditionally divides the night into three parts or "watches" (6–9; 10–2; 2–6), Roman time separates it into four night watches (6–9; 9–12; 12–3; 3–6).[94] Klinghardt believes that the prepositional phrase, μέχρι μεσονυκτίου, refers to the beginning of the *custodia tertia* ("third watch"), which starts at midnight.[95] It remains

---

[92] Bacchiocchi, *From Sabbath to Sunday,* 106, citing F. J. Foakes-Jackson: "Paul and his friends could not as good Jews start on a journey on a Sabbath; they did so as soon after it as was possible, v. 12 at dawn on the 'first day' – the Sabbath having ended at sunset." Note Bacchiocchi's subsequent triumphalist and anti-Judaic twist on this matter: "The restraints of the Sabbath did no longer apply and both Jewish (as Paul and Timothy) and Gentile Christians could freely engage in social and spiritual activities. The weakness of this observation is that it implies that Christians observed the Sabbath according to restrictive rabbinical conceptions. Such a view hardly harmonizes with the positive and spiritual understanding of the Sabbath we find in the Gospels" (*From Sabbath to Sunday,* 106). Another problem with Bacchiocchi's portrait lies in his presupposition that all writers of the New Testament expected both Jewish and Gentile followers of Jesus to refrain from traveling on the Sabbath. By contrast, I argue throughout this work that Luke and Matthew only demanded Jewish followers of Jesus to observe the Sabbath.

[93] The hapax legomenon αὐγή ("light," "light of the sun," or "daylight") probably acquired the meaning of "dawn" in later times, overlapping with ἕως/ἠώς in Koine Greek. It is still used with the meaning of "dawn" in Modern Greek. See Carl Darling Buck, *A Dictionary of Selected Synonyms in the Principal Indo-European Languages* (Chicago: University of Chicago Press, 1949), 993; Pierre Chantraine, *Dictionnaire étymologique de la langue grecque* (Klincksieck, 2009), 131. A similar usage appears in *PMag. Leid. W.* 11.35.

[94] See Fitzmyer, *The Gospel According to Luke,* 2:988. Lam 2:19 mentions a first watch (ראש אשמרות), Judg 7:19 a middle watch (האשמרת התיכונה), Exod 14:24 and 1 Sam 11:11 a morning watch (אשמרת הבקר). Apparently, the division of the night into three parts was standard in Mesopotamia. See A. Stiglmair, "לילה\ליל," *TDOT* 7:533–42.

[95] *Gesetz und Volk Gottes,* 263–64, citing the grammarian from the third century CE, Censorinus, *De Die Natali* 24, who divides the time preceding midnight in the following manner: after the evening (*vesperum*) and twilight (*crepusculum*), follow the time of lighting the lamps (*luminibus accensis*), bedtime (*concubium*), the "dead of night" (*nox intempesta*), the time before midnight (*ad mediam noctem*), and midnight (*media nox*).

uncertain, however, whether we can make such precise inferences from the few chronological referents mentioned in this passage. On its own, the usage of μεσονύκτιον may not demonstrate a Roman division of time at all, since the term also appears in Luke's beloved LXX as a translation of חצי הלילה/לילה חצות, "midnight" – a Hebrew construct well attested in the Jewish scriptures.[96] In addition, it is possible that with the term μεσονύκτιον Luke does not envisage a specific night "watch" but conceives of a more fluid time span, "sometime in the middle of the night" (as in Acts 27:27: μέσον τῆς νυκτός).[97] Indeed, if a specific timeline should be sought for in Acts 20:7, its structure might conform to a tripartite division following Jewish reckoning:

Ἐν δὲ τῇ μιᾷ τῶν σαββάτων (v. 7a) → μέχρι μεσονυκτίου (v. 7c) → τῇ ἐπαύριον (v. 7b)/ἄχρι αὐγῆς (v. 11)
[Sometime] on the first day of the week (c. 6–9?) → until sometime in the middle of the night (c. 9–2?) → until dawn (c. 2–6?)[98]

Elsewhere Luke clearly refers to the tripartite Jewish way of dividing the night:

Be like those who are waiting for their master to return from the wedding banquet, so that they may open the door for him as soon as he comes and knocks. Blessed are those slaves whom the master finds alert when he comes; truly I tell you, he will fasten his belt and have them sit down to eat, and he will come and serve them. If he comes during the middle of the night (ἐν τῇ δευτέρᾳ), or near dawn (ἐν τῇ τρίτῃ φυλακῇ), and finds them so, blessed are those slaves. But know this: if the owner of the house had known at what hour the thief was coming, he would not have let his house be broken into. You also must be ready, for the Son of Man is coming at an unexpected hour. (Luke 12:36–40)

The Greek terms ἐν τῇ δευτέρᾳ and ἐν τῇ τρίτῃ φυλακῇ surely point to the second and third watches of a tripartite division of the night, as such an understanding makes best sense of this passage, which exhorts its audience to remain faithful to the very last hours of the night even if the Son of Man tarries. A Roman reckoning of time would have necessitated mentioning

---

[96] See LXX Judg (A) 16:3 (2x); Judg (B) 16:3; Isa 59:10; Ps 118 (119): 62.

[97] Possibly, μεσονύκτιον is used in Luke 11:5 to refer loosely to the "middle of the night," rather than a specific Roman watch starting at 12:00. This is how *The English Bible in Basic English* and *The New Jerusalem Bible* render the term ("middle of the night," instead of "midnight"). So too, the French *Louis Segond* and the *Traduction Œcuménique de la Bible* ("au milieu de la nuit"); German: "mitten in der Nacht" (*Herder*). Cf. Exod 11:4 ("About midnight [כחצת הלילה] I will go out through Egypt"); Acts 16:25 ("About midnight [Κατὰ δὲ τὸ μεσονύκτιον] Paul and Silas were praying and singing hymns to God").

[98] Alternatively, following the Roman model, the timeline of the pericope would look like this: sometime on Sunday (v. 7a) → until midnight on Sunday (v. 7c) → until Monday morning (vv. 7b and 11).

the *fourth* watch in order to refer to the dawning hours of the night.⁹⁹ Luke, however, feels no need to modify this material to confirm it to the Roman chronological system of enumeration. In chapter 5 of this book, I underscored Luke's usage of Jewish reckoning to provide a timeframe for Jesus' burial: with the Sabbath fast approaching (ἐπέφωσκεν), Joseph of Arimathea hastens to have Jesus' body buried before sunset (Luke 23:54). In this instance, Luke clearly sees the Sabbath day as beginning in the evening. In the case of Acts 20:7, might we not equally assume that Luke conceives of Saturday evening as marking the end of the Sabbath and the beginning of Sunday?¹⁰⁰

In a few other places, Luke also ties *daylight* hours with the rhythms of Jewish daily life. Thus in Acts 3:1, Luke states that "Peter and John were going up to the temple at the hour of prayer, at three o'clock in the afternoon (ἐπὶ τὴν ὥραν τῆς προσευχῆς τὴν ἐνάτην)" (Acts 3:1). The Greek literally reads "at the hour of prayer, the ninth [hour]." As daylight time was divided from sunrise to sunset into twelve parts or hours,¹⁰¹ the ninth hour would occur sometime in the afternoon, the time when the *Tamid* offering was offered in the temple.¹⁰² At this time of the afternoon, certain Jews would also offer their daily prayers (Dan 9:21; Jud. 9:1).¹⁰³ A similar phenomenon probably occurs in Acts 10:2–4 where Luke portrays the Gentile Cornelius as a man of prayer (v. 2) who receives a vision at the ninth hour of the day as an answer to his petitions from the God of Israel (vv. 3–4). Quite possibly, Luke wishes to portray Cornelius as offering his

---

⁹⁹ Wolter, *Das Lukasevangelium,* 426; cf. Bovon, *Luc,* 2:294; Nolland, *Luke,* 702; Plummer, *The Gospel according to St. Luke,* 331. Contra Str-B 1:689.

¹⁰⁰ Staats, "Die Sonntagnachmittaggottesdienste der christlichen Frühzeit," 247, even argues that the start of the day in the evening should be presupposed throughout Luke-Acts because of the clear Jewish reckoning appearing in Luke 23:54. Klinghardt, *Gesetz und Volk Gottes,* 263, however, argues that both Jewish and non-Jewish reckonings appear in Luke 23:54–57: the switch from Jewish reckoning in 23:54 to Roman reckoning occurs in 23:55–56 where Luke describes the women's preparation of spices (a form of "work" happening on the Sabbath, since sunset had supposedly already arrived) and then highlights their observance of the Sabbath. In order to solve this inconsistency, Klinghardt suggests that Luke depicts the women as beginning to keep the Sabbath only in the morning (according to Roman reckoning). This reading, however, was rejected in chapter 5. The proposal is problematic on several accounts: it requires a sudden and unexpected shift from Jewish to Roman reckoning of time within the same pericope; it fails to account for the possible halakic dilemma embedded with this episode (the women perform work on Passover, also a holy day); external evidence does not support the claim that some Jews viewed the Sabbath as beginning at sunrise rather than sunset.

¹⁰¹ See "ὥρα," BGAD.

¹⁰² Josephus, *Ant.* 14:65; 3:237; *m. Ber.* 4:1; cf. Exod 29:39; Num 28:3–4, 8; Ezek 46:13–15.

¹⁰³ Barrett, *The Acts of the Apostles,* 1:178; Fitzmyer, *The Acts of the Apostles,* 277; Marguerat, *Les Actes des apôtres,* 117; Pervo, *Acts,* 99.

prayers in synchrony with the services in temple of Jerusalem, a time when other Jews might have also taken the same opportunity to do likewise.[104] By employing such chronological references, Luke consciously seeks to date various episodes in his narrative according to Jewish rhythms and routines (e.g., daily prayer, offering of sacrifices, etc.).

On the other hand, a couple of passages in Acts do manifestly point to a Roman division of nighttime. According to Acts 12:4, when King Herod had Peter imprisoned, he appointed "four squads of four soldiers to guard him" (τέσσαρσιν τετραδίοις στρατιωτῶν φυλάσσειν αὐτόν). The placement of four distinct squads, each containing four guards, corresponds to the Roman practice of assigning each squad the duty of watching over the prisoner during one of the four "watches" of the night.[105] In Acts 23:23, Luke might equally presuppose a Roman division of nighttime when he refers to a Roman tribune ordering two centurions to "leave by nine o'clock tonight (ἀπὸ τρίτης ὥρας τῆς νυκτός) for Caesarea with two hundred soldiers, seventy horsemen, and two hundred spearmen." The reference to nine o'clock (i.e., the third hour of the night) would correspond to the beginning of the second Roman watch of the night (9–12). But in both of these instances, Roman watches are in play, so they hardly prove to be counterarguments to the thesis arguing that Luke generally prefers using Jewish reckoning to divide time and organize his narrative. This interplay between Roman and Jewish reckonings in Acts is clarified when we notice that Luke consistently employs Jewish schematization for dating religious (daily prayers, temple sacrifices, Sabbath, etc.) and even "secular" events (e.g., the call for vigilance in Luke 12:38; Paul's itinerary) while reserving the usage of Roman reckoning for the occasional depiction of Roman customs and personalities (the Roman-like night watch of the Herodian guards, the Roman soldiers accompanying Paul to Caesarea).

Such an interchange between Jewish and Roman ways of dividing time should not seem so striking, since it is attested in other Jewish writings from this period. Thus, Josephus refers to the fourth watch even when

---

[104] Marguerat, *Les Actes des apôtres*, 374. Cf. Luke 23:44–46 where Jesus' death occurs around the ninth hour of the day, coinciding with the daily *Minhah* service in the temple. However, see Acts 10:9 (Peter praying at the sixth hour of the day, not a normal time for Jewish prayer). Barrett, *The Acts of the Apostles,* 1:505: "Probably we should be content with the thought that for Luke apostles were men who prayed more frequently than most." Henry J. Cadbury, "Some Lukan Expressions of Time (Lexical Notes on Luke-Acts VII)," *JBL* 82 (1963): 272–78, opines that some of these time references simply coincide with the ways ancient people, who did not have watches or clocks, loosely referred to time in the most general manner ("morning," "midday," "mid-afternoon," etc.).

[105] Haenchen, *Acts of the Apostles,* 382; Wolter, *Das Lukasevangelium*, 462. Philo is aware of this practice (*Flacc.* 111: τινα τῶν ἐν τοῖς τετραδίοις φυλάκων).

retelling biblical stories (*Ant.* 5:223; cf. *Ant.* 18:356). Surprisingly, Josephus seems to assume a Jewish tripartite division of time when describing the Roman siege of Jerusalem (*J.W.* 5:510). Even Matthew, viewed as the most Jewish gospel by many, divides the night into four watches: "And early in the morning (τετάρτῃ δὲ φυλακῇ τῆς νυκτὸς) he came walking toward them on the sea" (Matt 14:25). The appropriation of Roman parameters to date events should not mislead the contemporary reader into thinking that Jews such as Josephus, Philo, and Matthew did not reckon that *sacred* Jewish days (e.g., Sabbath, Passover, etc.) started in the evening toward sunset (Josephus, *J.W.* 4:582; Matt 28:1). In later rabbinic passages, the sages also discuss among themselves whether the night is divided into three or four watches (*t. Ber.* 1:1; *b. Ber.* 3a; *p. Ber.* 1:9 2d) even while assuming that a sacred day such as the Sabbath begins in the evening. Probably the most striking rabbinic "parallel" to our passage in Acts appears at the very beginning of the first tractate of the Mishnah:

> Whence do they read the *Shema* in the evening (בערבית)? From the hour when the priests enter to eat their *Terumah* until the end of the first watch (אשמורה הראשנה) – the words of R. Eliezer. But the sages say: until midnight (עד חצות). Rabban Gamaliel says: until the pillar of dawn rises (עד שיעלה עמוד השחר). (*m. Ber.* 1:1)

Like the pericope in Acts 20:7–12 (Ἐν δὲ τῇ μιᾷ τῶν σαββάτων → μέχρι μεσονυκτίου → τῇ ἐπαύριον/ἄχρι αὐγῆς), three divisions appear in this discussion about the proper timing for reciting the *Shema* during the evening: evening/first watch → midnight (עד חצות = μέχρι μεσονυκτίου) → dawn (עד עמוד השחר = ἄχρι αὐγῆς). We also note that the Mishnah first discusses the recitation of the *Shema* during the evening (rather than the morning), as it works under the assumption that a halakic day (such as the Sabbath or a holy day) normally begins at sunset, not sunrise.[106] The view that a halakic day begins in the evening does not prevent the Mishnah from employing the term "midnight" in its discussion, regardless of whether three (Jewish) or four (Roman) night watches are to be presupposed in *m.*

---

[106] The biblical source governing the organization of this section of the Mishnah is Deut 6:7 ("Recite them…when you lie down and when you rise.") In this verse, the act of lying down precedes rising, implying that the day begins in the evening, not the morning. Consequently, the Mishnah begins by discussing the recital of the *Shema* in the evening before discussing its recital during the morning (*m. Ber.* 1:2). Cf. *m. Hul.* 5:5 and its discussion of יום אחד in Gen 1:5 and Lev 22:28. On the other hand, with respect to the handling of sacrifices and offerings, some rabbinic passages seem to incorporate the following night as part of the preceding day. Thus, *m. Zevah.* 6:1 allows eating a meal offering up until the midnight following the preceding daylight (see Lev 7:15). 4Q394 (4QMMT^{a+b}) 3–7 i interprets Lev 7:15 differently to mean that the following midnight is part of a new halakic day. See Elisha Qimron and John Strugnell, eds., *Discoveries in the Judaean Desert X, Qumran Cave 4, V, Miqsat Ma'ase Ha-Torah* (Oxford: Clarendon Press, 1994), 150.

Ber. 1:1.¹⁰⁷ The rabbinic evidence illustrates how ancient Jews could view the evening as marking the beginning of a halakic day even while dividing the night according to four Roman watches.¹⁰⁸

All of these findings show that even if certain scholars are correct in their assertion regarding a Roman division of nighttime in Acts 20:7, they have only demonstrated that point, nothing more. Luke, like other Jews, could still have conceived of Sunday as beginning when the sun had set on Saturday evening even if he was referring in Acts 20:7 to the division of the night according to Roman standards. The chronological proximity of Sunday to the Sabbath, a sacred day in the Jewish rhythm of life, as well as the Jewish formulation (ἐν δὲ τῇ μιᾷ τῶν σαββάτων) employed in Acts suggest that Luke viewed Saturday night as marking the beginning of the first day of the week.

Remarkably, before and after Acts 20:7, Luke places Paul's itinerary within a Jewish timeframe: Paul travels *after* the feast of Unleavened Bread (20:6), attempts to reach Jerusalem *before* Pentecost (20:16), and later on resumes his final voyage to Rome *after* Yom Kippur (21:9).¹⁰⁹ Quite significantly, Paul is *never* portrayed in Acts as setting sail *on* the Sabbath – his itinerary seems to be planned as best as possible around this sacred day.¹¹⁰ A closer look at Luke's portrayal of Paul's journey from

---

¹⁰⁷ The *Gemara* in the *Bavli* (*b. Ber.* 3a–b) on this portion of the Mishnah discusses whether there are three or four watches in a night. The rabbinic position, however, that seeks to support four watches by "anchoring" its argument in scripture is rather tenuous.

¹⁰⁸ See the comments on Mishnah *Nedarim* made by Solomon Zeitlin, "The Beginning of the Jewish Day during the Second Commonwealth," *JQR* 36 (1946): 410: "...Rabbi Jochanan lived in Palestine where the Graeco-Roman civilization prevailed. In the Roman calendar the day began with mid-night and the Jews who spoke Greek followed the Roman custom, just as Jews today, who speak the vernacular language of the countries where they live use the general calendar. Although Sabbath begins with the preceding evening, nevertheless in the vernacular language of the Jews they speak of Friday night....The sages in the Talmud when the referred to the "day" as a standard of time measurement put the night before the day. When they spoke of a day of importance, as one for work, study, etc. they put the day first, since in actual life the day takes precedence over the night as regards activity."

¹⁰⁹ Acts 21:9, of course, cannot be taken to mean that Luke's Paul avoided traveling on Yom Kippur, since he was a prisoner awaiting trial in Rome and traveling on a Roman vessel that had just been shipwrecked. Rather, the reference to Yom Kippur is used to frame the narrative, showing how the festival still holds meaning for Luke. See the section above dealing with the analysis of Acts 1:12.

¹¹⁰ See Doering, *Schabbat*, 99–101, for a halakic analysis of the issue of traveling by sea on the Sabbath. Apparently, *Jub.* 50:12 prohibits *any* traveling on the sea that might extend into the Sabbath. This would imply that certain Jews did indeed undertake long sea journeys during the week that continued into the Sabbath. The rabbinic literature reveals a more flexible position than *Jubilees*. For example, *m. Shabb.* 16:8 and *m. Eruv.* 4:1–2 assume the presence of Jews on ships during the Sabbath. The real question for the

Philippi to Troas may further illustrate this point. As Paul sails from Philippi after the feast of Unleavened Bread (20:6), he reaches Troas in five days (ἄχρι ἡμερῶν πέντε). Upon his arrival, he spends seven days in Troas (ἡμέρας ἑπτά). If we assume that Paul partakes of the Eucharist with the congregation of Troas on a Saturday evening/Sunday morning and count back seven days, the count reaches back to a Sunday. As Paul is said to have arrived to Troas after a five-day journey from Philippi, a further five-day count backwards would bring us to a Wednesday. The chart presents this hypothetical (and artificial) reconstruction of Paul's itinerary.[111]

---

rabbis concerns how many days *before* the Sabbath one may embark on a sea journey that could potentially extend into the Sabbath. In *Sifre Deut* Pisqa 203, Shammai the Elder declares that one should set sail for a long journey on the Mediterranean at least three days before the Sabbath. For a short journey, one may set sail in less than three days before the Sabbath. *Midr. Tann.* on Deut 20:20; *y. Shabb.* 1:8 4a; *t. Shabb.* 13:13 and *b. Shabb.* 19a grant even greater leniency (for legal reasons) in the case of long journeys on the sea. Of course, these passages represent rabbinic opinions on the matter. It is uncertain how other Jews would have acted in such scenarios. One thinks of the journey of Philo to Rome from Alexandria reported in his *Legatio ad Gaium* (180) or even of Josephus' journey to Rome as described in his *Life* (13–16). Unfortunately, neither of these texts provides relevant halakic details. However, many Jews inevitably found themselves traveling on the sea during the Sabbath for a variety of reasons. Josephus does refer to the prohibition of traveling on the Sabbath (*Ant.* 13:252; 14:226), but perhaps his statements should be taken as evidence that Jews were not to *set out* on sea journeys during the Sabbath. Pagan sources also refer to a Jewish abstinence from traveling on the Sabbath (Tibullus, *Carmina*, I, 3:15–18; Ovid, *Remedia Amoris* 219; see Stern, *Greek and Latin Authors*, 1:319, 349). However, the question of *setting out* on a journey on the Sabbath must be properly distinguished from the issue of voyages that extend into the Sabbath. It seems safe to posit that many Diasporan Jews would have tried in varying degrees to plan their trips around the Sabbath whenever possible, with many avoiding embarking on a long journey at least by Friday afternoon. See further Doering, *Schabbat*, 101, for the positions of Samaritans, Karaites, and Falashas.

[111] It is doubtful whether Luke would have ever wanted his audience to read his narrative in the "accurate" way suggested in the timetable above. According to Acts 21:4, Paul spent seven days in Tyre with the local followers of Jesus. Likewise, in 28:14, Paul also spent seven days with local members in Puteoli. This conspicuous repetition of the stock number, seven, should deter one from searching for accurate itinerary reports within Acts. Luke uses chronological figures in a very fluid way to tie the loose ends of his narrative.

Sunday	Monday	Tuesday (End of Unleavened Bread) (Acts 20:6a)	Wednesday Departure from Philippi: 1st day of journey (Acts 20:6b)	Thursday 2nd day of journey	Friday 3rd day of journey	Saturday 4th day of journey
Sunday 5th day of journey: arrival and 1st day in Troas (Acts 20:6b)	Monday 2nd day in Troas	Tuesday 3rd day in Troas	Wednesday 4th day in Troas	Thursday 5th day in Troas	Friday 6th day in Troas	Saturday 7th day in Troas: departure right after the Sabbath (20:6c, 7, 11)
Sunday Departure from Troas	Monday					

The table only illustrates how Luke *may* have envisioned the timetable of Paul's journey, since accuracy in the reporting of such events should not be expected, while loose indicators such as "after the Feast of Unleavened Bread" need not imply that Paul actually left Philippi on the very next day after the festival.[112] However, even with these caveats in mind, Luke's consistent portrayal of Paul and possibly of himself (depending on whether he should be viewed as the author of the "we-passages") as never setting out to travel on the Sabbath remains noteworthy. In the broadest terms possible and regardless of what one makes of the timing of the celebration of the Eucharist in Troas, Luke's Paul chooses to sail from Philippi after Passover and leave Troas after the Sabbath.[113]

---

[112] Barrett, *The Acts of the Apostles,* 2:952; Bruce, *The Book of Acts,* 424; Le Cornu and Shulam, *Jewish Roots of Acts,* 2:1103. The alternative attempt to place Paul's departure from Troas on a Monday (meaning he celebrates the Eucharist on a Sunday), has Paul arriving at that same city on a Tuesday. The preceding five-day journey from Philippi would have begun on a Friday. In any case, Paul would not have sailed on a Sabbath (even when the days are not counted inclusively). Nevertheless, all such calculations remain conjectural and artificial even if they derive from chronological features contained within the narrative.

[113] In favor of Klinghardt's thesis for a Roman division of the night into four watches, should we understand the reference in 20:8 to the lighting of lamps as well as Eutychus' drowsiness as pointing to the Roman time referents of lighting the lamps (*luminibus accensis*) and bedtime (*concubium*)? Still, this would only prove that Luke divides nighttime in this instance according to Roman standards. The question whether he conceives of Saturday evening as marking the commencement of Sunday is another matter.

Conclusion

Three salient features arise from the analysis of the Sabbath in the book of Acts: 1) Luke knows about the halakah dealing with the Sabbath limits and probably even refrained from traveling on the Sabbath; 2) he is familiar with the *déroulement* of Sabbath services in the synagogue 3) he avoids portraying Paul and other Jesus followers as performing questionable acts (e.g., healings) on the Sabbath.

Regarding the first point, Luke reveals his firm halakic knowledge about the Sabbath limits through his composition of Acts 1:12. This verse, penned entirely by Luke, hangs not merely as a literary ornament conferring a Septuagint-like flavor or Jewish "background" to the narration of Acts, but illustrates how meaningful the usage of Jewish terminology remained for Luke and his readers.[114] Luke's superimposition of Jewish chronology throughout his narrative might even suggest that he himself avoided traveling on the Sabbath. Not only did Luke choose to employ a host of Jewish chronological signposts at various junctures of his narrative (e.g., references to daily sacrifices in the temple, the time of daily prayers,

---

Luke 24:30 with its reference to Jesus breaking bread with the disciples of Emmaus, presumably occurring on a Sunday evening, might strengthen the thesis that Luke's Paul also celebrated the Eucharist in Troas at the same time on another Sunday. Commentators, however, seem divided on this issue. Some detect Eucharistic hints in Luke 24:30; others see parallels with Jesus' last meal but think Luke 24:30 lacks some key Eucharistic features. For a eucharistic reading, see Bovon, *Luc,* 4:447; Fitzmyer, *Luke,* 2:1559. Cf. Nolland, *Luke,* 3:1206 and Wolter, *Das Lukasevangelium,* 785. In the case of the gospel of John, a Sunday evening setting for the Eucharist has also been suggested, given the double repetition of post-resurrection appearances to the disciples on a Sunday, one in the evening (20:19–23), the other not specified (20:26). See discussion in Raymond Brown, *The Gospel according to John* (2 vols.; AB 29–29A; Garden City: Doubleday, 1966–1970), 2:1019–20. On the other hand, in Matt 28:1 Mary Magdalene and Mary visit Jesus' tomb on a *Saturday night* (see chapter 5). Does this reference point to a celebration of the Eucharist among Matthew's circle on a Saturday night? In any case, even if Luke thinks that Paul celebrated the Eucharist on a Sunday evening, it would not deter from the main argument of this section, namely, that Luke normally conceives of time in a Jewish manner (besides those sole instances where Roman figures are involved) and portrays Paul as honoring the Sabbath. Even while arguing for a Sunday-Monday setting in Acts 20:7, Klinghardt suggests that the Sabbath remained relevant for Luke and his readers. Klinghardt believes that the Sabbath continued to function as a day of worship for Luke during which his circle partook of synagogue service, while Sunday provided them with an occasion to enjoy a more intimate communion. See Klinghardt, *Gesetz und Volk Gottes,* 264.

[114] The reference to the Sabbath limits (2000 cubits) does not appear in the Septuagint, neither in Exod 16:29 nor in Num 35:4–5, where one might have expected to detect its intrusion. Luke, therefore, is not simply mimicking the LXX when composing Acts 1:12, but revealing his knowledge of *contemporary* Jewish praxis.

Jewish festivals such as Passover, Pentecost, the Day of Atonement, etc.), but he also went out of his way to depict his primary protagonist in Acts, Paul, as an observant Jew who refrained from undertaking journeys on sacred occasions. Thus, in Acts, Luke's Paul travels after the feast of Unleavened Bread, leaves Troas after the Sabbath, and attempts to arrive to Jerusalem in time to celebrate Pentecost. Luke's deletion (Luke 6:1) of Mark's awkward ὁδὸν ποιεῖν (Mark 2:23) in the pericope dealing with the issue of plucking grain on the Sabbath might also confirm this impression: Luke removes Mark's gloss not only for stylistic reasons but also in order to clarify that Jesus and his disciples did not travel on the Sabbath.[115] All of these findings might suggest that Luke himself kept the Sabbath, refraining like many other ancient Jews from traveling on that holy day.

The second finding confirms a picture already anticipated in the first chapter: Luke's thorough acquaintance with the atmosphere of the Diasporan synagogues and the services held therein on the Sabbath. Like Luke's Jesus (Luke 4:16–30; cf. Luke 4:31), the Paul of Acts enters synagogue space on a regular basis each Sabbath in order to proclaim the good news allegedly announced in the Jewish scriptures (Acts 13:14, 27, 42, 44; 15:21; 16:13; 17:2; 18:4). It would be a mistake to reduce Luke's depiction of Paul (and Jesus') synagogue attendance on the Sabbath as a mere evangelistic device. This reductionist reading seems unlikely given the absence in Acts of any negative statement about the Sabbath and its observance. The controversies that inevitably arise on the Sabbath between Luke's Paul and the local Jewish members of the various synagogues dispersed throughout the Mediterranean regions concern not the question of Sabbath keeping but the acceptance of the gospel with all of its unsettling social-political ramifications for Jew and Gentile alike living in the Roman Empire.

Because of Luke's sustained depictions of Jesus and his followers visiting the synagogue on the Sabbath, commentators such as Klinghardt suggest Luke's circle(s) continued to attend their local synagogue(s) on the Sabbath. After all, Luke depicts the synagogue as the main locale for the reading of Jewish scripture accompanied by a messianic interpretation of its contents. On the other hand, the synagogue also turns into an arena of unfortunate contention where followers of Jesus clash with other Jews and eventually experience rejection and alienation from this familiar environment. We might say that Luke and many of his readers would have continued attending the synagogue each Sabbath were the rest of the Jews more favorably disposed toward the reception of their ideology. For understandable reasons, however, especially in a post-70 atmosphere of ongoing

---

[115] See chapter 3 for further discussion about this Markan gloss and its elimination in both Matthew and Luke.

political tensions between Jews and Romans, many Jews living as a minority within the wider Greco-Roman world found themselves unable to embrace the radical messianism the followers of Jesus proclaimed. This social-political complexity leads to the conjecture that some of Luke's readers may have resorted to meeting on the Sabbath in their own private settings where they also celebrated the Eucharist either on Saturday evening, as an extension to their Sabbath worship, or on the following Sunday.[116] Others still might have continued to attend their local synagogue (responses may have varied depending on regional location) in their ongoing desire to belong to their local Jewish communities and to win their Jewish fellows to the cause of the gospel.[117]

In any case, ejection from the local synagogue need not translate into rejection of the Sabbath institution. Followers of Jesus could have continued to observe and celebrate this day in their own assemblies, and the interest in the Sabbath Luke continually shows in both of his writings suggests that this institution continued to play an important role in the lives of many members of the Jesus movement. Furthermore, it should be stressed that Luke does not attempt to dissuade his audience from keeping the Sabbath or attending the synagogue. In contradistinction to (Pseudo?) Ignatius and *Barnabas*, Luke does not seek to dissuade Gentiles, let alone Jewish followers of Jesus, from keeping the Sabbath. While the Sabbath does not figure in the set of apostolic demands Luke expects non-Jews to observe (see section above on Acts 15:21), he presupposes that Jewish followers of Jesus will continue to respect this institution and even depicts the Jewish protagonists of his writings as faithful Sabbath keepers. This

---

[116] Cf. Klinghardt, *Gesetz und Volk Gottes*, 266: "Bei Lk existieren beide Veranstaltungen nebeneinander her und haben jeder seine eigene Funktion. Der sonntägliche Gottesdienst findet 'im Haus' statt, Teilnehmer sind Glieder der Gemeinde. Der synagogale Gottesdienst dagegen besaß eine größere Öffentlichkeit. Die hier stattfindende christliche Missionspredigt erreicht nichtchristliche Juden und wohl auch Heiden."

[117] Given Luke's accentuation of synagogue attendance, the Sabbath day may have been observed more as a day of *worship* rather than a day of *rest* (cessation from labor) among Lukan *Gentile* followers of Jesus. On the other hand, Luke would have encouraged *Jewish* followers of Jesus to continue observing the Sabbath as a day of rest. McKay, *Sabbath and Synagogue*, 13–14; 18–19; 24; 41–42, makes a firm distinction between the notions of Sabbath observance and Sabbath worship. Stronger evidence exists in the Jewish sources for viewing the Sabbath as a day of rest rather than a day of worship at the turn of the era. However, after 70 CE firm evidence does appear for Sabbath worship (a day set aside for the reading of scripture and prayer in the synagogue) – Acts, among other books, providing documentation for such a phenomenon. Cf. Pieter W. van der Horst, "Was the Synagogue a Place of Sabbath Worship before 70 C.E.?" in *Jews, Christians, and Polytheists in the Ancient Synagogue* (ed. Steven Fine; Baltimore Studies in the History of Judaism; London: Routledge, 1999), 18–43.

halakic and ecclesiological distinction is perfectly understandable, for a Gentile exemption from observing the Sabbath need not entail a Jewish neglect of the same institution. The question of observing the Sabbath is an entirely different matter than the issue of table fellowship between Jews and Gentiles, which naturally necessitates that Gentiles respect the dietary customs and other concerns of Torah observant Jews during such interaction. On the other hand, Jews can continue to observe the Sabbath even while Gentiles remain free to choose how they relate to this institution.[118] The ecclesiological distinction made by Luke between Jew and Gentile as far as their Torah obligations are concerned will become more apparent in Parts II and III of this book where the Apostolic Decree and the issue of circumcision receive their proper treatments.

The third and final point concerning the absence of Sabbath controversies in Acts, while constituting an argument *e silentio*, suggests that Luke did not oppose Sabbath observance among followers of Jesus and even affirmed its perpetuation. In Acts, none of the central protagonists performs healings or exorcisms on the Sabbath. Only two of the pericopes assessed above refer to performances of miracles, but these occur outside a Sabbath timeframe (Acts 16:18; 21:7–12). This portrayal in Acts stands in conspicuous contrast to the numerous healing-exorcism episodes occurring on the Sabbath in the gospel of Luke, which holds the record among all gospels for reporting Sabbath controversies. As I proposed earlier, it could be that the disputes over the Sabbath as reported in Luke seek more to justify *Jesus'* right to heal and do right on the Sabbath, given his call and duty to fulfill his eschatological mission and prove his messianic credentials, rather than to promote a Sabbath praxis that radically departs from "normative" conventions. At best, Luke, like Matthew, is arguing about *how* the Sabbath should be observed, not affirming its abrogation.

These observations raise important methodological questions for compositional-critical approaches that might too hastily read the gospel literature as a transparent window reflecting from every angle the world and practice of the gospel authors. A teleological tendency to posit simple,

---

[118] Esler, *Community and Gospel,* 116, is one of the few commentators to have noticed this distinction (though he assumes that Jewish followers of Jesus had to forsake their ethnic identity when sharing meals with Gentiles): "To make sense of Luke's attitude to the sabbath it is necessary to have regard to the social and religious context of his community. Although it was essential to the unity of Christian communities in the Diaspora that Jews forsake their ethnic identity to the extent of dining with Gentiles, this was not the case with sabbath observance. Nothing in principle prevented Jewish Christians observing the sabbath, and Gentiles, whom Luke portrays as exempted from virtually all of the requirements of the Mosaic law by virtue of the Apostolic Council in Acts 15, continuing to work on that day." See also the conclusion of my treatment on the Sabbath in Matthew and Luke in chapter 6.

linear developments that depict the Jesus movement as always and everywhere moving inevitably away from Judaism and its practices should be avoided.[119] The fact that neither Paul, Peter, James, nor any other character in Acts performs healings of minor diseases or any other objectionable act on the Sabbath might illustrate how willing Luke was to accommodate to contemporary Jewish sensibilities for the sake of the gospel and the preservation of Jewish identity within the *ekklesia*. On the other hand, it seems that Matthew's reports of Sabbath controversies might reflect a particular stand, voiced in more aggressive and polemical terms against non-Matthean Jews, that did indeed allow for the treatment of minor diseases on the Sabbath. Repschinski's thorough treatment of this matter in Matthew, through the usage of form and redactional-critical methods, is compelling.[120] This impression is strengthened in the subsequent part of this book dealing with hand washing, where it seems as if Matthew strongly disagrees with the necessity to observe this rite, while Luke, once again, proves to be less polemical and accommodating on such matters.

---

[119] Cf. the criticism made by Klinghardt, *Gesetz und Volkes Gottes,* 241 n. 1, against a simple, inevitable, and linear development from a strict Sabbath observance to its complete disintegration among early Christians.

[120] See conclusion in chapter 6.

Part II

Food Laws in Matthew and Luke-Acts

Chapter 8

Food Laws in Matthew

"R. Hisda said to R. Huna, There is [a Baraitha] taught that supports your contention: [The verse,] 'And every creeping thing that creepeth upon the earth [is a detestable thing; it shall not be eaten],' includes insects found in liquids that have been passed through a strainer. The reason [then that they are forbidden] is because they had passed through a strainer, but had they not passed through a strainer they would be permitted."
(B. Hull. 67a)

Food Laws and Jewish Identity in Antiquity

In addition to Sabbath keeping, Jewish dietary practices served as another distinctive marker of Jewish identity in antiquity that could (and still can) regulate Jewish-Gentile relations in a very restrictive way.[1] The origins of

---

[1] Technically, the term kosher, which literally means "fit" or "appropriate," can encompass a wider set of issues unrelated to food. In this chapter, the focus is on the dietary dimension of kashrut. The noun derives from the Hebrew root כשר, which appears only three times in the Hebrew scriptures (Esth 8:5; Qoh 10:10; 11:6), and even then with no connection whatsoever to food. See Gene Schramm, "Meals Customs," *ABD* 4:648–50; Harry Rabinowicz and Rela Mintz Geffen, "Dietary Laws," *EJ* 5:650–59. But see Magness, *Stone and Dung*, 19–20 as well as Guy D. Stiebel, "'Meager Bread and Scant Water' – Food for Thought at Masada," in *Halakhah in Light of Epigraphy* (eds. Albert I. Baumgarten et al.; Journal of Ancient Judaism Supplements 3; Göttingen: Vandenhoeck & Ruprecht, 2011), 299–301, for the discussion of four ostraca from Masada bearing the inscription "fit (כשר) for the purity of hallowed things." For this inquiry, I use the terms "food laws," "kashrut" (an anachronism), and "dietary laws" interchangeably. The term "dietary laws" should not lead one to perceive anachronistically this legislation as "medical" or hygienic prescriptions seeking to promote a healthy and balanced diet. Mary Douglas, "Impurity of Land Animals," in *Purity and Holiness: The Heritage of Leviticus* (eds. Marcel J. H. M. Poorthuis and Joshua Schwartz; Jewish and Christian Perspectives Series 2; Brill: Leiden, 2000), 45: "The text itself specifically says that the rules are made for the people of Israel; what is designated as unclean for them is not unclean for the whole of humanity. Thus the rules of impurity are not a way of promoting a universal hygienic principle or pronouncing a general health warning. Nowhere in either book [i.e., Leviticus and Deuteronomy] is it ever said that the foods that are forbidden are bad for the health." Consequently, I prefer using the pair pure/impure rather than clean/unclean to avoid the impression that such practices were observed by ancient Jews merely for preserving hygiene and health. Following Milgrom, *Leviticus*, 1:732, the terms

the Jewish food laws will probably remain obscure forever, although this reality has certainly not dissuaded scholars from continually providing diverse and creative theories about their genesis.[2] In any case, it is unquestionable that by the Second Temple period such legislation came to play an integral role in signaling and setting the Jewish people apart from other ethnic groups. By the first century CE, probably many Jews were following the injunctions found in Lev 11 and Deut 14, refraining from eating animals deemed "impure," that is, non-kosher or forbidden.[3] Creatures prohibited for Jewish consumption include, among others, camels, pigs, and hares (Lev 11:5–7), but also fish with no fins or scales (Lev 11:9), birds of prey, such as eagles and vultures (Lev 11:13), and all reptiles and insects, save for certain locusts (Lev 11:20–23). The legislation in Leviticus designates some of these forbidden creatures as "impure" (טמא) and dubs others as "detestable" or "abominable" (שקץ). Leviticus 11 ascribes the term שקץ to certain marine creatures (v. 10), birds (v. 13), flying insects (v. 23), and reptiles (vv. 41–44), but not to quadrupeds and the eight vermin creatures (vv. 29–38), which are labeled instead as טמא.

The term "impure," when used in reference to non-kosher creatures, carries a special connotation: it refers to a *perpetual* or permanent type of "impurity." Contrary to other temporal forms of ritual impurity, which can be reversed, the "impurity" of non-kosher animals cannot be removed. These creatures remain impure *forever*.[4] Baptizing a pig will never make it kosher! Consequently, it might be preferable to describe non-kosher animals as *forbidden*, rather than "impure," and kosher animals as *permitted*,

---

pure/purity are defined negatively: they refer to the absence of impurity, however defined. Cf. Sanders, *Jewish Law from Jesus to the Mishnah*, 137: "I shall not attempt a positive definition of 'purity'. It is simple to define 'impurity,' and so we shall proceed by the *via negativa*: purity is the absence of impurity." The usage of the pair pure/impure to describe the permitted and forbidden foods in Lev 11/Deut 14 carries a whole set of other problems, however, generating an unfortunate confusion between kashrut and purity laws. It is imperative though to distinguish these two realms, conceptually and halakically. More on this below.

[2] For a summary of various proposals, see Milgrom, *Leviticus*, 1:718–36. For a convenient summary on the history of interpretation of Lev 11/Deut 14, see Jirí Moskala, *The Laws of Clean and Unclean Animals of Leviticus 11: Their Nature, Theology, and Rationale (an Intertextual Study)* (Adventist Theological Dissertation Series 4; Berrien Springs, Mich.: Adventist Theological Society Publications, 2000), 15–111. For a structuralist approach, see Jean Soler, *Sacrifices et interdits alimentaires dans la Bible. Aux origines du Dieu unique* (Paris: Hachette, 2004), 13–29.

[3] John M. G. Barclay, *Jews in the Mediterranean Diaspora: From Alexander to Trajan (323 BCE–117 CE)* (Edinburgh: T&T Clark, 1996), 434–37; But see Kraemer, "Food, Eating, and Meals," 403–19; *Jewish Eating and Identity*, 123–45, who suggests that some ancient Jews disregarded kashrut.

[4] Milgrom, *Leviticus*, 1:648.

rather than "pure," to avoid misunderstandings and mixtures of two different halakic systems (i.e., kashrut and purity).⁵ Indeed, touching or even consuming non-kosher animals dubbed "detestable" (שקץ) does not render one ritually impure, at least according to Leviticus 11.⁶ For example, touching or even eating a fish without scales would not defile a person, although such an act would certainly be frowned upon, for, according to Lev 11, forbidden fish are "detestable" (though not "impure").⁷

---

⁵ Boyarin, *The Jewish Gospels*, 113: "While all Jews are forbidden always to eat pork, lobster, milk and meat together, and meat that has not been properly slaughtered, only some Jews, some of the time, are forbidden to eat kosher food that has become contaminated with ritual impurity. While in English they are sometimes confused, the system of purity and impurity laws and the system of dietary laws (kashrut) are two different systems within the Torah's rules for eating….One of the biggest obstacles to this understanding has been in the use of the English words 'clean' and 'unclean' to refer both to the laws of permitted and forbidden foods and to the laws of pollution or impurity and purity. These translate two entirely different sets of Hebrew words [*muttar* vs. *tahor*]. It would be better to translate the first by permitted and forbidden and use clean and unclean or pure and impure only for the latter set."

⁶ Maccoby, *Ritual and Morality*, 69: "Only the carcases of land animals cause impurity. Creatures of the sea and the air even when forbidden for food do not cause impurity. Even among land creatures, there are some categories of forbidden food that do not cause impurity, notably insects." Similarly, Milgrom, *Leviticus*, 1:656, claims that שקץ refers to animals whose ingestion is forbidden but do not defile through contact or consumption, whereas טמא refers to animals that in addition to being forbidden as food also defile through contact (when dead). Mary Douglas, "Impurity of Land Animals," 33–45, argues that Deuteronomy, unlike Leviticus, no longer makes a difference between the two terms, at least terminologically: what is unclean is abominable and what is abominable is unclean. Could this imply that some Jews during the Second Temple period thought that the consumption of any forbidden animal was in some sense defiling? More on this below.

⁷ On the other hand, eating certain forbidden animals that are labeled as "impure" or touching their *carcasses* can defile. See, for example, Lev 11:3, which considers forbidden quadrupeds such as camels and pigs as defiling: "Of their flesh you shall not eat, and their carcasses you shall not touch; they are *unclean* unto you." See also Lev 11:39–40 with respect to the impurity conveyed by touching or consuming the carcasses of *permitted* quadrupeds. The eight vermin (when dead) are notoriously singled out for their ability to spread impurity (Lev 11:29–38), but these are exceptional critters among the "swarming creatures" (שרץ), since they are considered טמא (Lev 11:29). *Living* non-kosher animals, however, do not convey impurity. In other words, touching a live pig would not convey impurity. See Maccoby, *Ritual and Morality*, 67. Yair Furstenberg, "Defilement Penetrating the Body: A New Understanding of Contamination in Mark 7.15," *NTS* (2008): 195, states: "The only biblical case in which impurity is transmitted solely through ingestion is the consumption of 'swarming creatures' in Lev 11.43–44. However, since these creatures do not otherwise convey impurity, it seems that the impurity attributed to them is only an expression of the fact that they are considered abominable and that their consumption is prohibited. Furthermore, unlike in Lev 17.15, there are no purification procedures that ameliorate the defilement." This is not entirely true. Even forbidden land creatures that do not "swarm," such as camels, convey impurity

It should also be noted that many Jews did (and still do) not expect Gentiles to observe such legislation. Most of the Jewish food laws, save for the abstinence from consuming blood, were never viewed as *universally* binding, both in the Torah and in subsequent Jewish history.[8] The end of Lev 11 only exhorts the *people of Israel* to keep kosher, for only they are called to be a *holy* nation (vv. 44–45; cf. Deut 14:2).[9] Maccoby states:

> What the dietary laws and the ritual purity laws have in common is that they form part of the priestly code laid down in the Torah for the Israelites as a priest-nation. It is significant that none of these laws is included in the Ten Commandments, or in any of the lists which were made from time to time (notably the rabbinic Seven Noahide Laws) to express basic human morality. Neither the dietary laws (*kashrut*) nor the purity laws were regarded as obligatory for non-Israelites. Nations or peoples castigated in the Bible for immorality (the generation of the Flood, the people of Sodom, the Canaanites) were never accused of breaches of purity, but only of basic morality.[10]

The Mosaic injunction against the consumption of blood is an exception, since Noah and his descendants received the commandment to "not eat flesh with its life, that is, its blood" (Gen 9:4).[11] This commandment appears again in Lev 17, where Moses instructs both the house of Israel and resident aliens to refrain from eating blood, "for the life of the flesh is in the blood" (vv. 10–11; cf. vv. 12, 14). Instead, before consuming meat,

---

if their dead bodies are touched or consumed. Nevertheless, Furstenberg rightly notes, as others before him, that the Mosaic Torah prescribes no method to remove this kind of impurity. It seems, then, that we are dealing with a different form of impurity, more akin to "moral impurity," as Klawans, *Impurity and Sin*, 31, claims, following David Z. Hoffmann, *Das Buch Leviticus* (2 vols.; Berlin: Poppelauer, 1905), 1:303–5. Eating a forbidden animal is tantamount to committing a grave sin, morally defiling the person. Accordingly, Israel must avoid this type of impurity by maintaining its sanctification through the abstinence of forbidden foods.

[8] The Tannaim make this point explicit. See Rosenblum, *Food and Identity*, 68–73, for a discussion of pertinent passages in the *Sifra*.

[9] Contra Moskala, *The Laws of Clean and Unclean Animals of Leviticus 11*, who ahistorically reads Lev 11 in light of the Genesis creation narratives to posit the universality of kashrut, when in reality *those* responsible for the composition of both Lev 11 and the Genesis creation account assume that this legislation applies only to Israel.

[10] Maccoby, *Ritual and Morality,* viii.

[11] Milgrom, *Leviticus*, 1:705: "God's command to Noah and his sons takes the form of a law – the first in the Bible, the first to humanity. And the blood prohibition is the quintessential component of this law. It is the divine remedy for human sinfulness, which hitherto has polluted the earth and necessitated its purgation by blood....Man's nature will not change; he shall continue sinful (Gen 8:22), but his violence need no longer pollute the earth if he will but heed one law: abstain from blood....Man must abstain from blood: human blood must not be shed and animal blood must not be ingested. In the Priestly scale of values, the prohibition actually stands higher than the Ten Commandments. The Decalogue was given solely to Israel, but the blood prohibition was enjoined upon all humankind; it alone is the basis for a viable human society."

both the Israelite and the foreigner abiding in the holy land must "pour out its blood and cover it with earth" (Lev 17:13; cf. Deut 12:16, 23). According to Lev 17:10, the God of Israel will cut off any person who consumes blood. Jews from the Second Temple period onwards continued to show interest in these regulations, some, like the author of *Jubilees* (7:28–33), becoming increasingly obsessed with abstaining from consuming and handling blood (cf. *1 En.* 7:5; 98:11; CD 3:6; 12:14; Philo, *Spec.* 4:123; *Jos. Asen.* 8:5). In fact, as many have correctly argued, the prohibition against consuming blood, which appears as a universal commandment in the so-called Apostolic Decree, is based largely on Lev 17.[12]

The centrality kashrut played in shaping Jewish identity during the Second Temple period cannot be underestimated. At times, its practice served as a test for expressing one's fidelity to Jewry and ancestral Jewish traditions. This issues emerges already in the Maccabean period, if not earlier, when Jews in Palestine were compelled "to sacrifice swine and other unclean animals...to make themselves abominable by everything unclean and profane" (1 Macc 1:47–48; cf. 1:62). The book of 4 Maccabees relates graphic stories glorifying those Jewish men and women who courageously

---

[12] More on this matter in chapter 11 dealing with Acts 15. In the rabbinic discussion on Noahide Laws, the rabbis interpret the command against eating blood, as far as its application for Gentiles is concerned, as a call for not eating an animal *while it is still alive*, in rabbinic terminology, אבר מן החי ("a limb from a live creature"). In other words, from the rabbinic perspective, Gentiles *can* consume meat with its blood, as long as the animal is already dead prior to consumption. They are not obliged to slaughter the animal ritually by following the laws of *shehitah* so as to drain the blood sufficiently. See Klaus Müller, *Tora für die Völker: Die noachidischen Gebote und Ansätze zu ihrer Rezeption im Christentum* (Studien zu Kirche und Israel 15; Berlin: Institut Kirche und Judentum, 1994), 131, as well as the discussion in chapter 11.

Other Jewish dietary regulations include the prohibition against eating certain kinds of fat of kosher animals (Lev 3:17; 7:23–25) as well as the sciatic nerve (Gen 32:33). The threefold repetition not to "boil a kid in its mother's milk" (Exod 23:19; 34:26: Deut 14:21) was taken by the rabbis to mean that Jews could not eat dairy products with meat at the same meal. While these rabbinic discussions are very early, apparently going back to the Houses of Shammai and Hillel (e.g., *m. Hul.* 8:1), it is probable that many Jews in antiquity, especially those living in the Diaspora, did not observe this custom. So, Kraemer, *Jewish Eating and Identity*, 36–37. Philo, *Virt.* 143–144, reads the Mosaic prohibition against boiling a kind in its mother's milk, literally. Nevertheless, it is possible that by the first century CE other Jews from Judea besides those affiliated with the Houses of Shammai and Hillel were refraining from mixing dairy with meat. See Sanders, *Judaism: Practice and Belief,* 217. The silence in non-rabbinic Judean sources may stem from the state of the evidence. For example, 4Q251 (4QHalakha A) 12 line 5 could possibly be referring to a halakah about boiling a kid in the mother's milk. Unfortunately, the fragmentary nature of this document does not allow further determination. See Lawrence H. Schiffman, "Laws Pertaining to Forbidden Foods in the Dead Sea Scrolls," in *Halakah in Light of Epigraphy*, 71–72.

endured torture rather than submit to the temptation of eating pork (4 Macc 5:2, 6; 6:15).[13] Even many Hellenistic Jews, like the author of the *Letter of Aristeas* and Philo of Alexandria, who applied an allegorizing hermeneutic to their reading of Jewish scriptures, affirmed the importance of observing kashrut and appreciated the great task it served in forming and preserving a distinctive Jewish identity (e.g., *Let. Arist.* 151; Philo, *Spec.* 4:95–131; cf. 3 Macc 3:4).

The observance of kashrut governed to a large extent the nature of Jewish-Gentile interaction in antiquity. As Schramm points out, "the effects of practicing kashruth, from a socioreligious standpoint, are clear: the strictures of kashruth make social intercourse between the practicing Jew and the outside world possible only on the basis of a one-sided relationship, and that is on the terms of the one who observes kashruth." Classical authors from antiquity reveal their awareness, sometimes in a hostile manner, of the social barriers such dietary practices could create between Jews and non-Jews. In hyperbolic fashion, Tacitus blames the Jews for regarding "as profane all that we hold sacred; on the other hand, they permit all that we abhor" (*Historiae* V, 4). In this same section, Tacitus, who singles out the Jewish abstention from pork, grudgingly claims that "the Jews are extremely loyal toward one another," and "sit apart at meals" (V, 5).[14] Likewise, Apollonius Molon (first century BCE) labels Jews as misanthropes, accusing them for their unwillingness to associate with others (Josephus, *Ag. Ap.* 2:148, 258).

These Greco-Roman reports should not all be taken at face value, given their polemical tendencies, even though they do indirectly confirm the prominent role kashrut played in forming and preserving Jewish identity in antiquity. The classical sources should also not nourish the misconception that ancient Jews, particularly those in the Diaspora, did not dine or interact at all with non-Jews.[15] Many ancient Jews did interact in various de-

---

[13] Cf. Philo, *Flacc.* 96.

[14] In *Legatio ad Gaium* 360, Philo recalls the embarrassing situation he found himself in, along with a Jewish delegation from Alexandria, when they were questioned by the Roman emperor regarding the reason for their abstention from eating pork. The question is said to have raised the mocking laughter of Philo's adversaries present during this awkward encounter.

[15] The comments made by Leonard Victor Rutgers in his article, "Archaeological Evidence for the Interaction of Jews and non-Jews in Antiquity," *AJA* 96 (1992): 101–18, although mainly descriptive of the third and fourth centuries of the Common Era, are also pertinent for considering Jewish-Gentile relations in the Diaspora during the time Luke composed his writings. Rutgers highlights the significant exchange and interaction between Jews and non-Jews as evidenced in sarcophagi, lamps, amulets, and art. Commenting on Jewish neighborhoods in Rome, Rutgers states: "In Rome, one of the centers of Jewish settlement was in *Transtiberim*, present-day Trastevere, Augustus's *regio* XIV. This piece of land, located on the left side of the Tiber and outside the *pomerium*, attract-

grees and avenues with non-Jews, and occasionally, under the proper conditions, were even willing to *eat with them*.[16] Freidenreich assembles and assesses a range of literary sources from Alexandria that suggest its Jewish population did not refrain from eating with Gentiles, provided the food offered at their tables were permitted for Jewish consumption.[17] *The Letter of Aristeas* (182–186) presents Jewish guests eating at the table of a Gentile king, but underscores the fact that the king's staff prepared the meal to suit the dietary concerns of the Jews. Likewise, Philo asserts that Jews and Gentiles assembled and feasted together during an annual celebration of the translation of the LXX (*Mos.* 2:41–42). Finally, 3 Maccabees reports without reservation the celebration of the deliverance of the Jews in Alexandria in a way that presumes Jews and Gentiles feasting together (6:30, 34, 40).

This point cannot be underestimated and is connected to the debate about Jewish purity laws in general. Sanders has argued extensively against the notion that most ancient Jews generally dissociated themselves from Gentiles because of a supposedly intrinsic impurity ascribed in Judaism to non-Jews.[18] More recently, Maccoby,[19] Klawans,[20] and Hayes[21] have further developed and strengthened this thesis.[22] These scholars make the

---

ed foreigners from all over the world, making it Rome's most cosmopolitan district. As a study of the relationship between the available soil and known *vici* reveals, the area was densely populated and the ration of the spacious *domus* to the uncomfortable *insulae* was the lowest anywhere in the city. Thus ancient Trastevere was the setting for an urban life that, like some cities in the Orient today, was hectic and noisy....The living conditions in Trastevere being what they were, Jewish families could hardly avoid communicating with neighbors having radically different religious preferences" (116–17). In his later work, *Making Myths*, 126, however, Rutgers observes that physical proximity or even regular contact is not sufficient for reducing tension between groups.

[16] See already Yehezkel Cohen, "Attitude to the Gentile in the Halacha and in Reality in the Tannaitic Period," [in Hebrew] (Ph.D. diss., Hebrew University, Jerusalem, 1975); Peter J. Tomson, *Paul and the Jewish Law: Halakha in the Letters of the Apostle to the Gentiles* (CRINT 3; Jewish Traditions in Early Christian Literature 1; Assen, Netherlands: Van Gorcum, 1990), 230–36; Sanders, "Jewish Association with Gentiles and Galatians 2:11–14," in *The Conversation Continues: Essays on Paul and John Presented to J. Louis Martyn* (eds. Robert Fortna and Beverly Gaventa; Nashville, Tenn.: Abingdon, 1990), 177–88; *Jewish Law from Jesus to the Mishnah*, 282; *Judaism: Practice and Belief*, 75, 216.

[17] Freidenreich, *Foreigners and Their Food,* 32–34.

[18] Sanders, "Jewish Association with Gentiles," 185.

[19] *Ritual and Morality,* especially pp. 8–12.

[20] Klawans, *Impurity and Sin*.

[21] Hayes, *Gentile Impurities and Jewish Identities*.

[22] For an alternative view upholding Alon Gedalyahu's thesis about intrinsic Gentile impurity, see Vered Noam, "The Gentileness of the Gentiles": Two Approaches to the Impurity of non-Jews," in *Halakhah in Light of Epigraphy*, 27–42.

distinction between what may be called "moral impurity" and "ritual impurity."[23] According to Hayes, moral impurity "arises from the commission of certain heinous sins (murder, idolatry and specified sexual sins). This impurity is not conveyed to others, nor is it subject to rites of purification. It does, however, defile the sinner himself, the land, and the sanctuary and incurs severe punishment."[24] Ritual impurity, on the other hand, "is a highly contagious, generally impermanent condition, resulting from primary or secondary contact with certain natural and often unavoidable processes and substances (e.g., corpses, genital flux, and scale disease)."[25] Hayes argues that contracting ritual impurity is not viewed as sinful: "The primary consequence of ritual impurity is that the defiled person or object is disqualified from contact with sancta. Ritual impurity, which is not in itself sinful, can be conveyed to persons and is removed by rituals of purification."[26]

These observations are important but require some qualification and further considerations. Kazen has demonstrated that some Second Temple Jews of an expansionist tendency toward preserving purity did view certain types of skin diseases (misleadingly dubbed "leprosy") as resulting from

---

[23] Hayes, *Gentile Impurities and Jewish Identities*, 27, adds yet a third category, "genealogical impurity." A thorough discussion of the use of the terms "moral" and "ritual" *tout court* is a desideratum. I do not wish through the use of such terminolgy to perpetuate unwittingly the tendency to bifurcate the Law of Moses into two artificial realms, subordinating its "ceremonial" or "ritual" aspects to its supposedly greater and loftier "moral" contents (often equated or reduced in Christianity to the Ten Commandments). See the brief discussion of the traditionally pejorative use of the term "ritual purity" among New Testament scholars in Sanders, *Jewish Law from Jesus to the Mishnah*, 137. The *Mekilta* captures the important value, appreciated by many Jews of the Second Temple period onwards, of observing the Torah in its *totality*. Commenting on Exod 21:1 ("*And* these are the ordinances . . ."), the *Mekilta* (Mishpatim-Neziqin Parashah 1) wonders why the Torah states here "*And* these" (ואלה) instead of simply stating "these" (אלה). The answer given is that the conjunctive *vav* connects what precedes (the Ten Commandments and the altar) with what follows (civil ordinances): both set of laws were given at Sinai. While the Ten Commandments enjoyed a certain prominence in ancient Judaism, many Jews certainly did not neglect observing the "lesser," ritual commandments. A similar perspective can be found in both Matthew and Luke. In Matthew, Jesus condemns the Pharisees for tithing mint, dill, and cumin, while neglecting the "weightier matters of the law" (justice, mercy and faith). Jesus, nevertheless, adds a caveat often overlooked: "It is these you ought to have practiced *without* neglecting the others." Similarly, Luke 11:42. Despite the problems involved in using the terms "ritual" and "moral," I still find these categories useful for discussing purity matters. Kazen, *Jesus and Purity Halakhah*, 200–261, suggests speaking of an "inner" and "outer" (im)purity for elucidating the historical Jesus' perspective on purity.

[24] Hayes, *Gentile Impurities and Jewish Identities*, 5.
[25] Ibid.
[26] Ibid.

sinful behavior or divine punishment and avoided coming into contact with people suffering from abnormal bodily discharges.[27] Impurity acquired through menstruation or corpse impurity was probably viewed differently, as it was tightly connected to natural processes of the human cycle of life. However, those Jews embracing an expansionist tendency probably also avoided acquiring these forms of impurity whenever possible.[28] The question is whether ancient Jews would have viewed the Mosaic legislation governing ritual purity as applicable to non-Jews. According to some experts of early Judaism, ancient Jews did not think that Gentiles had to observe the ritual system of purity/impurity as outlined in Lev 12–15. These regulations only concern(ed) the holy people of Israel. On the other hand, Gentiles were held accountable for committing cardinal sins such as murder, idolatry, and sexual immorality, acts that fall under the rubric of moral impurity.[29] Still, some Jews (e.g., Essenes) did consider Gentiles to be ritually and intrinsically impure, while others might have avoided contact with non-Jews partly out of disgust toward their bodily discharges, blood, foods, corpses, and other objects, even if they knew Gentiles were not obliged to observe ritual purity.

Furthermore, Kraemer and Freidenreich have argued that some Jews from the Second Temple period avoided eating food prepared by Gentiles even if the food items served at the table were permitted.[30] Freidenreich notes that much of the literature discouraging Jewish-Gentile table fellowship or the consumption of food prepared by Gentiles stems from Judea. According to the book of Daniel, Daniel avoids eating the "royal rations of food and wine" (Dan 1:8). There may well be the concern here that the wine offered in the king's court was previously used for idolatry, but the issue of idolatry does not account for Daniel's abstention from the rest of the food offered by the king. The term used in Hebrew for food, פתבג, is not further qualified, and it could include permitted ingredients for Jewish consumption such as bread and other kosher food items. The most economical explanation for Daniel's avoidance of such food would be that some ancient Jews avoided eating food *prepared by Gentiles*. The very act of Gentiles preparing the food transforms it into non-Jewish food prohibited for Jews to eat. Hence, Daniel requests only to eat vegetables and water, food items that have not been processed by Gentiles.[31] The same view

---

[27] Kazen, *Jesus and Purity Halakhah,* 109–17, 147–56.
[28] Ibid., 181–84.
[29] Hayes, *Gentile Impurities and Jewish Identities*, 22–23.
[30] Kraemer, *Jewish Eating and Identity,* 26–29; Freidenreich, *Foreigners and Their Food,* 35–38.
[31] Cf. Josephus, *Life* 14, reporting on Jewish priests imprisoned in Rome who only eat figs and nuts. Likewise, the diet of the "weak," as described in Rom 14:1–2, who only eat vegetables might also refer to a similar concern over Gentile foods. 2 Macc 5:27 men-

might appear in other sources such as the book of Tobit. In Tob 1:10–13, Tobit boasts of not eating the food of the Gentiles, without providing further qualification. Kraemer comments on this passage: "He condemns his compatriots for eating *gentile* food....So the trouble is not with the substance of the food, but with the fact that the food is the food of gentiles."[32] The book of Judith also exhibits a concern for food prepared by a foreigner. Consequently, Judith consumes food prepared by Jewish hands, albeit while sharing a meal with a Gentile (12:1–2).[33]

There is no need, however, to posit that these texts express a concern for consuming food prepared by Gentiles because of ritual contamination. With respect to Daniel 1, Freidenreich notes:

> Efforts to ascribe impurity-based concerns to Daniel's behavior stem from the misinterpretation of his desire not to 'defile himself [*yitga'al*]' in terms of circumstantial impurity. This term is consistently associated in the Hebrew Bible with impurity resulting from offensive behavior – which is to say the performance of a prohibited actions – rather than with the occurrence of a natural or unavoidable event. In this case, the action is the consumption of the king's food, and the resulting defilement is unrelated to the purity status of the food or its preparers. Daniel does not believe that eating the king's food is prohibited because the food is polluted; he believes such food is defiling because its consumption is prohibited.[34]

This is certainly a possible interpretation, and, as I note in chapter 11 dealing with Jewish food laws and the so-called Apostolic Decree, the term ἀλίσγημα, which is related to the verb ἀλισγέω, the Greek word used to translate יתגאל in Dan 1:8, refers to food offered to idols. Thus, *one* of the primary obstacles impeding the fostering of Jewish-Gentile relations revolved around "moral" concerns, especially the issue of idolatry (cf. *Jub.*

---

tions how Judah and his band only eat herbs in the wilderness in order to avoid defilement. Freidenreich, *Foreigners and Their Food,* 36–37, maintains that Judah, like Daniel, adheres to a prohibition against food cooked by foreigners (I would add even food prepared by other Jews, those who have "Hellenized" too much in the eyes of the author). Thus, an Essene, excluded from his community but still bound by oaths, resorts to eating grass until he perishes (*J.W.* 2:143). Perhaps, the Essenes distrust the food of all other Jews as ritually impure. We might also note John the Baptist's diet of *wild* honey (Matt 3:4/Mark 1:6; see end of this chapter dealing with food laws in Matthew). Note 4 Bar 7:38: Jeremiah offers figs to his people and teaches them to avoid the pollutions of the Gentiles of Babylon; *Ascen. Isa.* 2:11: Isaiah eats "wild herbs."

[32] Kraemer, *Jewish Eating and Identity,* 27.

[33] Cf. Additions to Esther C 14:17: "And your servant has not eaten at Haman's table, and I have not honored the king's feast or drunk the wine of libations" (NRSV). In contrast to the Hebrew book of Esther, the abstinence from eating at a Gentile table is highlighted. See Freidenreich, *Foreigners and Their Food,* 28.

[34] Freidenreich, *Foreigners and Their Food,* 36.

22:16).[35] In addition, many Jews, including some those in the Diaspora, avoided *extensive* Jewish-Gentile interaction out of concern of assimilation and forsaking their ancestral customs. Others chose not to eat with Gentiles simply because they were Gentiles; these strict Jews employed and ascribed various concepts of impurity that underscore their desire to refrain from interacting with Gentiles. Upholding Jewish food laws assisted in maintaining a clear demarcation between Jews and Gentiles on a daily basis and solidified Jewish communal identity.

The distinctions between moral and ritual impurity, on the one hand, and the Jewish dietary system of kashrut, on the other, must, therefore, be fully appreciated in order to comprehend Matthew and Luke's perspectives on Jewish food laws. One final quotation from Hayes will suffice to underscore the importance of this point:

> Some scholars cite texts that refer to Jewish abstention from Gentile foods as evidence of a Gentile ritual impurity. However, the biblical laws of *kashrut* (and their postbiblical development) are sufficient to explain this abstention, and one need not resort to a theory of Gentile impurity. In other words, Jews most likely objected to Gentile food on the grounds that it was nonkosher rather than on the grounds that it was ritually defiled by contact with Gentiles.[36]

Many have conflated kashrut and purity partly because the Torah occasionally employs the same terminology of (im)purity to describe both systems: "The food laws may be considered to be purity laws, since forbidden food is called 'impure' (e.g. Lev 11:4). They deserve separate treatment, however, because impure foods are strictly prohibited; they are not only 'impure', they are 'abominable' (e.g. Lev 11:10), and there is no rite of purification in the Bible, either for impure food or for the person who eats it."[37]

Food Laws in Matthew and Luke-Acts: Preliminary Observations

By distinguishing and exploring kashrut and (im)purity, I hope to offer a more precise and nuanced understanding of Matthew and Luke's stance on

---

[35] The rabbinic sources also exhibit a concern for idolatry, but this is not the only impediment against Jewish-Gentile commensality. Intermarriage, assimilation, and the status of Gentiles *tout court* also present major obstacles. See Kraemer, *Jewish Eating and Identity*, 68–69; Rosenblum, *Food and Identity*, 92.

[36] Hayes, *Gentile Impurities and Jewish Identities*, 49.

[37] Sanders, *Jewish Law from Jesus to the Mishnah*, 24.

the issue of food laws.[38] Throughout Part II of this book, I focus on Matthew and Luke's attitude toward dietary laws, viewed as a salient marker of Jewish identity,[39] rather than on other issues related to purity, although it is impossible to ignore the treatment of the latter category. Indeed, many passages that have previously been taken as evidence for a supposed abrogation of kashrut really only inform us about the opinions of the gospel writers on matters related to ritual and moral (im)purity.[40] To put it bluntly, I am more interested in treating the following questions: did Matthew and Luke instruct their Jewish and/or Gentile readers to consume pork? Did they think that Jewish and Gentile followers of Jesus could consume meat with its blood? How did they envision Jewish-Gentile table fellowship in light of their views on Jewish food laws? I maintain throughout this inquiry that neither the gospel of Matthew nor Luke-Acts announces the end of the Jewish dietary system. Luke in particular addresses the *moral*

---

[38] While the three systems of "impurity," ritual, moral, and dietary, can be distinguished we should not be too orthodox in our categorizations. Cf. Kazen, *Jesus and Purity Halakhah,* 210–11: "They all overlap to some degree....Lev 11 about clean and unclean animals, i.e. edible and non-edible meat, transmutes into a discussion about animal carcasses and their defilement by contact (v 24ff). The issues of eating is still present, and ends the section (v 41, 47), but the emphasis has shifted to a type of impurity which is transferred in the same way, and requires the same type of purifications, as do the bodily impurities of Lev 12–15. Within the system of bodily impurity (Lev 12–15; Num 19) there is little which deviates, but the isolation of the 'leper' (Lev 13:45–46, and possibly that of the *zab* and the and the corpse-impure, if Num 5 is taken into account), must have been to some degree stigmatizing, which is evidenced by the view of discharges and 'leprosy' mentioned above (i.e. Miriam's punishment, etc.). There is thus at least a hint for a moral connotation. Finally, the system of defiling immorality in the *Holiness Code* (Lev 18; 20) overlaps with the other two systems, including the prohibition of sex during menstruation (Lev 18:19; 20:18; cf. 15:24) in the midst of discussions about serious sexual sins, and a reference to the distinction between clean and unclean food (Lev 20:25; cf. 11:46–47)."

[39] This is how Deines, "Das Aposteldekret – Halacha für Heidenchristen oder christliche Rücksichtnahme auf jüdische Tabus?" 323–98, tackles the issue of the Apostolic Decree. However, our conclusions differ.

[40] On other purity concerns in Luke-Acts, see Bart J. Koet, "Purity and Impurity of the Body in Luke-Acts," in *Purity and Holiness: The Heritage of Leviticus* (eds. Marcel J. H. M. Poorthuis and Joshua Schwartz; Jewish and Christian Perspectives Series 2; Brill: Leiden, 2000), 93–106, who argues that Luke depicts Jesus and other figures in Luke-Acts as law-abiding and conscious of purity regulations. See also Eric Ottenheijm, "Impurity between Intention and Deed: Purity Disputes in First Century Judaism and in the New Testament," in *Purity and Holiness: The Heritage of Leviticus*, 105: "It seems to us that Luke depicts Jesus as even more attuned to purity than the other Gospels. Maybe this reflects a different attitude towards purity in the community for which he writes." For an alternative view on Jesus' attitude toward purity, see Christian Grappe, "Jésus et l'impureté," *RHPR* 84 (2004): 393–417, building on the work of Klaus Berger, "Jesus als Pharisäer und frühe Christen als Pharisäer," *NovT* 30 (1988): 231–62.

purification of Gentile followers of Jesus and how this transformation affects Jewish-Gentile relations and commensality. But the observance of kashrut is presumed throughout Matthew and Luke-Acts, although I suggest that both authors, while expecting Jews to continue observing their dietary laws *in toto*, only required Gentiles to do so in a limited way and under certain circumstances for the sake of promoting Jewish-Gentile *koinōnia*.

A note should be made here about the selection of passages analyzed in Matthew and Luke-Acts. Those passages dealing with the miraculous feeding of the multitudes, which appear in all four canonical gospels, have been left out of this study. The symbolic nature and form of such stories invite so many interpretations that impede one from deriving any concrete information about the question of kashrut. Matt 14:13–21 contains an account relating a feeding of five thousand men (besides women and children according to Matthew's "counting"), while Matt 15:29–39 refers to a second feeding of four thousand (following Mark 6:30–44 and 8:1–10, which also mention two feedings). In the first feeding reported by Matthew, *five* loaves of bread and two fish are multiplied to nourish the populace (14:17), with *twelve* extra baskets of food miraculously remaining after the feeding (v. 20). But in the second feeding, which in many ways resembles the first one, Matthew speaks of *seven* loaves and a few fish (15:34) as well as *seven* remaining baskets (v. 37). By contrast, Luke only reports one feeding (9:10–17: five loaves, two fish, five thousand people, and twelve extra baskets).[41]

The Jewish numerology (e.g., seven and twelve) and the different number of feedings (two in Matthew and Mark, one in Luke) have led scholars to conjure up a host of interpretations about their possible symbolical meanings. According to Davies and Allison, many equate the five loaves with the five books of Moses and the two fish with the psalms and the prophets or the apostles and the gospel.[42] For some, the twelve baskets represent either the twelve tribes or the twelve apostles.[43] The seven baskets have at times been associated with the Gentiles (cf. the seven Noahide Laws; the seven men appointed to take care of the Hellenists in Acts 6:3).[44] If we were to follow this allegorizing approach, could the two Matthean feedings and the singular account in Luke mean that Matthew believes in

---

[41] The gospel of John (6:1–15) also reports only one feeding (five loaves, two fish, five thousand fed, and twelve baskets).

[42] Davies and Allison, *The Gospel According to Saint Matthew,* 2:489.

[43] See already Origen, *Comm. Matt.* 11:3.

[44] However, the basis in Jewish tradition for attaching the number seven with the Gentiles is rather weak. The seven men appointed to take care of the Hellenists in Acts 6:3 do not represent Gentiles, but simply the Hellenist yet Jewish (in contrast to the Hebrew) contingent of the early *ekklesia*.

separate table fellowships (whether for the Eucharist or other meals), one for Jews (symbolized by the twelve baskets), the other for Gentiles (symbolized by seven baskets), while Luke advocates only one table fellowship where both Jews and Gentiles commune together eating non-kosher food?[45] This seems unlikely and demands too much from such texts.

Because of its references to seven loaves and seven baskets, Deines suggests that the second feeding in Matthew creates a "kind of table fellowship between Jews and Gentiles, with the disciples serving the tables (cf. Acts 6:2)."[46] However, even if Deines' suggestion were true, such a social phenomenon should not prove so astonishing, since non-Christian Jews certainly could devise ways for dining with non-Jews, and the menu of the miraculous feeding in Matthew only mentions bread and fish, hardly items that go against a kosher diet (provided the fish have fins and scales). Even if eucharistic features are embedded within the feeding accounts of Matthew and Luke, we cannot infer from this that both gospel authors dismiss the importance of observing Jewish food laws.[47] Jewish and Gentile followers of Jesus could very well have celebrated the Eucharist together even while honoring kashrut during such encounters.

Consequently, in my treatment of the gospel of Matthew, I deal mainly with the analysis of one key passage in Matthew, 15:1–20, although I do search for traces of kashrut in other Matthean passages. In reality, Matt 15:1–20 only reports a debate between Jesus and the Pharisees about washing hands before eating, an issue concerning ritual purity, not food laws, which are never condemned throughout Matthew's gospel. Luke does not even retain Mark's story about the controversy of washing hands before meals, although he refers to a similar incident, which nevertheless does not

---

[45] The Lukan deletion of the doublet may simply stem from stylistic reasons: why repeat a feeding story twice, if they resemble each other so much? See Fitzmyer, *The Gospel according to Luke*, 2:762. The absence of the second feeding in Luke also stems from his "great omission" of a block of Markan materials. Bovon, *Luke 1*, 353, is surprised at the Lukan absence of the second feeding found in Mark, "since both the setting and this version in a Gentile region and the symbolic number of seven baskets of leftover pieces point to the Gentile church, which is a special concern of Luke."

[46] Roland Deines, "Not the Law but the Messiah," in *Built upon the Rock: Studies in the Gospel of Matthew* (eds. Daniel M. Gurtner and John Nolland; Grand Rapids, Mich.: Eerdmans, 2008), 69.

[47] A eucharistic dimension has been ascribed to the feeding pericopes, a possibility surely to be reckoned with at least in the case of Matt 14:13–21. Scholars, however, also detect spiritual, moral, soteriological, eschatological, social, and ecclesiological dimensions in these stories. The multiplicity of interpretations speaks for itself, showing how difficult it is to extract from these passages precise information about Matthew and Luke's views on kashrut and table fellowship between Jews and Gentiles. For a summary of the history of interpretation on these feedings stories, see Dale and Allison, *The Gospel according to Saint Matthew*, 2:480–85; Luz, *Matthew*, 2:312–13.

systematically oppose the observance of kashrut or even the maintenance of ritual purity (11:37–41). In Luke's case, I also show that his account about the commission of the seventy-two disciples (10:1 ff.) does not contain "proof" about a supposed abrogation of Jewish food laws, contrary to what some New Testament commentators have recently claimed. Finally, I assess two major sections in Acts, Peter's vision of the impure animals and his encounter with Cornelius (chs. 10 and 11) as well as the much-debated Apostolic Decree (Acts 15). Both of these passages, I argue, address the question of the moral impurity of Gentiles, while presupposing the observance of kashrut on the part of Jesus' Jewish followers and even to a certain degree of Gentile disciples of Jesus, particularly when they commune with the Jewish branch of the *ekklesia*.

Hand Washing before Eating: Matt 15:1–20

Literary Context

Matthew essentially follows Mark's order of narration as the following table shows:

Mark	Matthew
6:30–44: First feeding of the crowds	14:13–21: First feeding of the crowds
6:45–52: Jesus walks on water	14:22–33: Jesus walks on water
6:53–56: Healing in Gennesaret	14:34–36: Healing in Gennesaret
7:1–23: Hand washing before meals	*15:1–20: Hand washing before meals*
7:24–30: Syrophoenician Woman	15:21–28: Syrophoenician Woman
7:31–37: Healing of deaf-mute person	15:29–31: Mass healings[48]
8:1–10: Second feeding	15:32–39: Second feeding

In both Matthew and Mark, the controversy on hand washing is preceded and followed by feeding stories (as well as other miraculous accounts). Furthermore, the story of Jesus' encounter with a Gentile woman from Tyre occurs immediately after the controversy on hand washing. Noteworthy is the verbal exchange between Jesus and the Syrophoenician woman employing food imagery to describe Jewish-Gentile relations: Jesus expresses his initial reluctance to act on behalf of a non-Jew, claiming it unfair that children's food be given to dogs; the woman responds by argu-

---

[48] Matthew replaces Mark's story on the healing of a deaf mute with the report about Jesus healing many sick people. This substitution has little to do with Matthew's desire to highlight Jesus' ministry to the Gentiles as Gundry, *Matthew,* 317, suggests. Matthew's distaste for some of the "magic" features and the messianic secret in Mark is well known (see chapter 2 on the Sabbath and Matthew's deletion of Mark's episode on exorcism). See further Allison and Davies, *The Gospel according to Matthew,* 2:561.

ing that even dogs may eat from the crumbs that fall under the table (Matt 15:26–27; Mark 7:27–28). Marcus has argued that in the gospel of Mark the first multiplication of food represents a feeding of a Jewish populace (five loaves representing the Torah of Moses; twelve baskets, the twelve tribes of Israel), while the second multiplication represents a feeding of Gentiles, which occurs in the environs of the Gentile populated region of Decapolis (8:31).[49] Marcus believes that Mark's literary placement of the hand washing controversy in the midst of such materials is not accidental, and that the sweeping statement allegedly abolishing Jewish food laws in Mark 7:19b means that Jews and Gentiles in the *ekklesia* may now freely eat together unimpeded by such exclusionary measures.[50]

These observations do not apply to Matthew, while scholars will now have to contend with the possibility that even Mark 7:19b does not declare the end of kashrut.[51] First, Matthew has removed the generalizing statement in Mark 7:19b.[52] Second, it is unlikely that the second multiplication in Matthew symbolizes a feeding of the Gentiles.[53] Even if this were true, a feeding of the Gentiles need not be interpreted as a Matthean abolishment of the Jewish food laws. In terms of *Heilsgeschichte,* it could simply symbolize a new phase of divine interaction in which Gentiles are spiritually fed with the message of the good news once the Jews have received their opportunity to partake of such nourishment. Even as the Gentiles were provided with the opportunity to hear and receive the gospel, the Jewish followers of Jesus of Matthew's milieu could very well have persisted in their faithful observance of food practices as outlined in the Torah of Moses.[54]

---

[49] Marcus, *Mark,* 1:458.

[50] Ibid.

[51] Boyarin, *The Jewish Gospels*, 121, provides an alternative reading of Mark 7:19b, interpreting it not as a declaration announcing that all foods are *permitted* (i.e., kosher), but as rejecting a Pharisaic extension of purity laws beyond their original biblical foundations. See also Kinzer, *Postmissionary*, 54–58, who, noting the heuristic import of *Pesiq. Rab Kah.* 4:7 (cf. *Num. Rab.* 19:8), suggests that Mark's statement applies to the *Gentile* audience he addresses in his gospel rather than Jewish followers of Jesus. Cf. James Dunn, *Jesus, Paul and the Law* (Louisville: Westminster John Knox, 1990), 45, viewing Mark 7:19b as "designed to point out or serve as a reassurance to Gentile believers that the Jewish food laws were not obligatory for them" (but see Dunn on p. 38).

[52] Or did Matthew have another version of Mark that did not contain this statement?

[53] Dale and Allison, *The Gospel according to Saint Matthew,* 2:563–64; Luz, *Matthew,* 2:344–46. Donald A. Hagner, *Matthew* (WBC 33A–B; Dallas, Tex.: Word Books, 1993–1994), 2: 419, 452, however, views the second feeding as foreshadowing the blessing of the Gentiles.

[54] Davies and Allison, *The Gospel according to Saint Matthew,* 2:517, conclude that there is no obvious thematic link between 15:1–20 and the surrounding material.

Literary Structure

Matt 15:1–20 can be separated into two major parts, which are really three:[55]

I. 15:1–9
II. 15:10–20
    A. 10–11
    B. 12–20

The shifting audiences within the narrative have governed to a large extent the decision to separate this pericope into two (or three) sections. In section I, Jesus addresses *Pharisees and scribes* from Jerusalem who question Jesus regarding his disciples' neglect of the "traditions of the elders," since they do not wash their hands before eating (v. 1). The reply given in vv. 2–9 to the Pharisees and scribes' objection does not touch on the particular issue of washing hands, but deals with the larger issue of the so-called "traditions of the elders." In the first part of section II (vv. 10–11), the Matthean Jesus briefly addresses the *crowds* (v. 10) before interacting with *his disciples* (vv. 12–20). In section II, Matthew's Jesus finally addresses the question of washing hands before eating (vv. 11 and 17–20). In fact, in the entire pericope, only the contents in vv. 2, 11, and 17–20 deal more closely with the issue of washing hands before eating, while the rest of the pericope relays polemical material directed against the teachings and behavior of the Pharisees in general.

Halakic Analysis: Hand Washing before Meals

Before assessing the (ir)relevance of this pericope for comprehending Matthew's attitude toward kashrut, it is necessary to discuss briefly some of the halakic issues concerning hand washing before meals. The terse formulation of the question voiced by the Pharisees in Matt ch. 15 appears to contain several assumptions about this custom: (1) impure hands can carry impurity separately from the rest of the body; (2) impure hands can defile (kosher) food; (3) such food can in turn defile the rest of the body upon ingestion; (4) hand washing should be performed before *any* meal (not just on special and festive occasions or when setting food aside for priests); (5) Pharisees wash their hands before eating; (6) Pharisees expect other Jews (in this case, the followers of Jesus) to uphold this practice, which belongs to the halakic corpus known as the "traditions of the elders."

---

[55] So Davies and Allison, *The Gospel according to Saint Matthew*, 2:516: "drawn-out objection story with three scenes."

Unfortunately, when one turns to the relevant, extant sources on the topic of hand washing, whether from the Second Temple or rabbinic literary corpora, the picture becomes very complicated at several levels. First, the Mosaic Torah only calls for *priests* to wash their hands and feet before offering *sacrifices* (Exod 30:18–21; 40:31). Lev 15:11, however, records a special regulation for persons suffering from an abnormal discharge (הזב): "All those whom the one with the discharge touches without his having rinsed his hands in water shall wash their clothes, and bathe in water, and be unclean until the evening." This passage assumes that a person suffering from an abnormal discharge can indeed defile other people by touching them with his or her unwashed wands. Besides these meager references, the question of hand washing remains conspicuously absent in the Torah and in the rest of the books now contained in the Hebrew Bible.

In non-canonical sources, some passages mention the custom of hand washing among Jews in the *Diaspora*. However, this evidence does not explicitly tie hand washing with eating food.[56] Thus, the *Letter of Aristeas* (305) claims that it is the custom of all Jews to wash their hands in the sea (ἔθος ἐστὶ πᾶσι τοῖς Ἰουδαίοις ἀπονιψάμενοι τῇ θαλάσσῃ τὰς χεῖρας), but this act precedes prayer (ὡς ἄν εὔξωνται πρὸς τὸν θεόν) and the reading of scrip-

---

[56] Eyal Regev, "Non-Priestly Purity and Its Religious Aspects according to Historical Sources and Archaeological Findings," in *Purity and Holiness*, 225–29, claims that Diasporan Jews ate *common* food in purity (229). The evidence he adduces, however, is not conclusive. The Book of Tobit 2:9 and the passages from Philo point only to bathing after corpse impurity and sexual relations, but do not discuss hand washing before eating ordinary food. In *Let. Aris.* 306, the author provides a rationale for this practice in the Diaspora: "'What is their purpose in washing their hands while saying their prayers?' They explained that it is evidence that they have done no evil, for all activity takes place by means of the hands." Commenting on this passage, Susan Haber, *"They Shall Purify Themselves": Essays on Purity in Early Judaism* (ed. Adele Reinhartz; SBLEJL 24; Atlanta: Society of Biblical Literature, 2008), 174, claims that the purported reason given here for hand washing concerns not ritual purification, but moral purity. She holds that since sin is regarded as ritually defiling, it may be removed through the ceremony of hand washing. It is uncertain, however, whether this passage makes such a statement. It only declares that hand washing is (symbolic) evidence or *testimony* (μαρτύριον) that such persons are morally upright before God when they engage in prayer and the reading of scripture. Whether the rite itself of hand washing plays a role in removing moral sin remains an open question.

ture, not eating.⁵⁷ Similarly, the *Sibylline Oracles* 3:591–93 indicates that Jews wash their hands before praying.⁵⁸

For the practice of hand washing in Palestine, some of the Qumranic evidence refers to the immersion of the entire body before eating (1QS 5:16; 4Q514).⁵⁹ Some of the earliest rabbinic traditions contain halakic debates (purportedly between Shammaites and Hillelites) about hand washing for the preparation and setting aside of food for *priests*.⁶⁰ According to the Mosaic Torah, the priests are supposed to consume their food in purity in the temple. No Mosaic commandment, however, explicitly demands that food offered by lay people to the priests remain in constant purity until its conferral to priestly hands. On the other hand, certain rabbinic discussions reveal a concern for harvesting and transporting such food with pure hands. Because these rabbinic debates question the very need for preserving the purity of food harvested and set apart by lay people for priests, Sanders wonders whether Pharisees (insofar as such rabbinic discussions between the two Houses can be taken as representing Pharisaic views) would have washed their hands before eating *common* food.⁶¹ Many of these rabbinic passages, of course, imagine a pre-70 setting when the temple in Jerusalem was still in operation. But what about post-70 Pharisaic practice? Sanders claims that even in the rabbinic traditions of the post-

---

⁵⁷ See chapter 7 dealing with Acts 16:12–16 for references on synagogues built next to rivers or seas, possibly because of their location near natural water that Jews used for ablutions. Sanders, *Jewish Law from Jesus to the Mishnah,* 270, proposes that Philo believed Jews could carry out certain rites in the Diaspora and become pure from certain impurities (e.g., corpse impurity) in spite of their distance from the temple.

⁵⁸ Perhaps, the practice of hand washing in the Jewish Diaspora may have stemmed from surrounding non-Jewish custom. See Furstenberg, "Defilement Penetrating the Body," 193–94; Haber, *They Shall Purify Themselves,* 174; Walter Burkert, *Greek Religion* (trans. John Raffan; Cambridge, Mass.: Harvard University Press, 1985), 75–84.

⁵⁹ See Roger P. Booth, *Jesus and the Laws of Purity: Tradition History and Legal History* (JSNTSup 13; Sheffield: University of Sheffield, 1986), 161.

⁶⁰ For example, *m. Tehar.* 9:5 (preparation of olives of priestly due: if one crushes olives with impure hands, the olives are defiled); cf. *m. Tehar.* 10:4 (the two Houses debate when to wash hands in connection to producing wine, whether before putting the grapes in the press, following the Shammaites, or only when actually separating the priestly portion of the wine). See Sanders, *Jewish Law from Jesus to the Mishnah,* 228; Furstenberg, "Defilement Penetrating the Body," 185–86, for different views on this matter.

⁶¹ For example, *m. Bik.* 2:1, states that hand washing should be performed for all heave offerings and first fruits, apparently assuming this halakah applies only to food offered to priests. *M. Hal* 1:9 also seems to presuppose that hand washing before common meals is not required. See further Chaim Milikowsky, "Reflections on Hand-Washing, Hand-Purity and Holy Scripture in Rabbinic Literature," in *Purity and Holiness,* 149–62. Furstenberg, "Defilement Penetrating the Body," 176–200, however, argues throughout for an expansionist practice among Pharisees (and other Jews) of hand washing before common meals. Similarly, Kazen, *Jesus and Purity Halakhah,* 86–88.

70 era complete uniformity on this matter did not exist.⁶² Consequently, he suggests that some Pharisees might have washed their hands only during sacred meals held on the Sabbath and festivals but not before common meals.⁶³

To further complicate the picture, we should note that hands can only acquire a second-degree impurity, at least according to rabbinic halakah, meaning that impure hands cannot directly defile common food, since secular (dry) food items also only acquire an impurity to the second degree.⁶⁴ According to this rabbinic perspective, the discussion in Matt ch. 15 would almost seem meaningless.⁶⁵ Nevertheless, Furstenberg and others

---

⁶² For example, Sanders points to *t. Ber*. 5:13, which states that washing hands before a meal is optional, but after a meal mandatory. Cf. *T. Ber.* 5:26 . Nevertheless, Sanders, *Jewish Law from Jesus to the Mishnah,* 230, acknowledges that *t. Ber*. 5:13 only records a discussion concerning the *timing* of the hand washing (before or after a meal), not a questioning of the necessity of observing such a rite.

⁶³ Sanders, *Jewish Law from Jesus to the Mishnah,* 248.

⁶⁴ Cf. Friedrich Avemarie, "Jesus and Purity," in *The New Testament and Rabbinic Literature*, 267–68. A handy summary of the rabbinic differentiation of degrees of impurities is available in Booth, *Jesus and the Laws of Purity*, 186–87. Briefly stated, impure hands, which can only contract second degree impurity apart from the rest of the body, cannot *directly* defile solid *Hullin* (common food) because such food is only susceptible to first or second degree impurity. According to this systematization, an object acquires an impurity one degree lower than the source of its impurity. For example, a source carrying a second-degree impurity makes another object impure only to a third or fourth degree (or "remove"). Since hands can only contract an impurity (independently from the rest of the body) of a second degree it cannot make another object also only susceptible to a second degree impurity, impure. Instead, the second degree impure hands render such an object (in Matthew's case, common food) "unfit" (פסול). An unfit object, however, cannot defile another object. In other words, some ancient rabbis would not hold that common food rendered unfit by impure hands of a second degree could in turn defile the rest of the body of a person who ingested such food. On the other hand, second degree impure hands can directly defile *liquid Hullin* (liquids such as water and oil, מכשירין, become impure to the first degree after entering into contact with second degree impurity). But, as Booth points out, the question of the Pharisees in Matthew refers to washing before *eating*, not drinking. Nevertheless, impure hands can defile solid *Hullin indirectly* if the hands enter into contact with liquid and then touch solid *Hullin*. Since, as Furstenberg, "Defilement Penetrating the Body," 184, notes, most people in antiquity ate without cutlery, wet impure hands may indeed have been a real problem during the consumption of common meals. To what degree this complex and systematized gradation of impurity applies to the halakic scenario envisaged in Matthew remains open to debate. Cf. Kazen, *Jesus and Purity Halakhah,* 77–78 n. 225 and his criticism of Booth's understanding of the term "unfit."

⁶⁵ We might further note that if the whole body were impure, hand washing would not remove the impurity of the rest of the body, since the hands, along with rest of the body would carry a first-degree impurity, which is only removable through bodily immersion. Booth, Jesus and the Laws of Purity, 187: "…the Pharisaic question urging handwashing is not credible on this basis, because there was no reason to wash the hands when the

before him have noted that liquids, when exposed to a second-degree impurity, enter themselves into a state of first-degree impurity. In turn, anything that comes into contact with the liquids, in our case common food, becomes ritually impure to the second degree. Most importantly, a person who eats this contaminated food becomes impure to the same level, and not to a degree below, as is normally the case.[66] Alternatively, Deines posits that Pharisees during the first century viewed hands as susceptible to first-degree impurity, meaning that they could make common food impure, which in turn could defile the rest of the human body. Later on, the Tannaim would have decreed a more lenient halakic approach, claiming that hands could only acquire second-degree impurity.[67] Finally, it could be that the complex system of graded purity, as attested later in the rabbinic literature, did not exist in the first century, so that hands could defile food directly, especially when moist.[68]

Despite Sanders' reservations about this matter, many New Testament commentators have assumed that Pharisees did strive to eat all of their

---

whole body was presumptively defiled with a more serious impurity." Booth, however, might be relying too heavily on the rabbinic evidence to reconstruct the practices of Pharisees and other Jews living during the first century. Cf. John C. Poirier, "Why Did the Pharisees Wash their Hands?" Journal of Jewish Studies 47 (1996): 226: "If we approach the pericope, however, without any preconceived notions about what handwashing ultimately signifies, the natural link between handwashing and the concern for the food purity reappears. The Pharisees washed their hands in order to maintain the purity of their food, so that impure food not enter their body. While this simple dynamic has not eluded all scholars, some write as if the pericope's connection between handwashing and food concerns requires special pleading. I must admit, this sounds strange to someone who was reared always to wash before eating."

[66] Furstenberg, "Defilement Penetrating the Body," 185 n. 22, citing *m. Tehar.* 2.2, which states that eating food that is impure to the second degree makes a person impure to the same degree.

[67] Roland Deines, *Jüdische Steingefäße und pharisäische Frömmigkeit: Ein archäologisch-historischer Beitrag zum Verständnis von Joh 2,6 und der jüdischen Reinheitshalacha zur Zeit Jesu* (WUNT 2.52; Tübingen: Mohr Siebeck, 1993), 299 n. 474.

[68] Furstenberg, "Defilement Penetrating the Body," 185: "An early source (from the Second Temple Period) describes this same result without articulating the system of degrees of impurity. In *m. Taharoth* 9.5 we read: 'He who crushes olives with impure hands defiles them.' The liquid on the crushed olives transfers impurity from the hands to the olives. *MTaharoth* 10.4 also connects hand impurity with the susceptibility of liquids to defilement." Cf. Jacob Neusner, *History of the Mishnaic Law of Purities* (22 vols; SJLA 6; Leiden: Brill, 1976), 13:144, 202–5, pointing out that the complex system of grades of impurity is known to us only in post-Temple sources from Yavneh. See also Thomas Kazen, *Issues of Impurity in Early Judaism* (ConBNT 45; Winona Lake, Ind.: Eisenbrauns, 2010), 115–16, who shows that there was some degree of differentiation and gradation in the purity system during the Second Temple period albeit not as clean and neat as later systematizations.

meals in a state of purity, in priestly imitation of the temple service.[69] Today experts on ancient Judaism are also affirming the notion that washing hands before meals was widespread albeit for different reasons.[70] Archaeological evidence confirms the impression that hand washing was widely practiced in Palestine, at least in Judea. Deines even tries to make a case for a widespread practice of hand washing among Jews of Palestine before common meals, spearheaded by none other than the Pharisees. The material data he singles out includes a number of stone vessels, including pitchers with handles, which were presumably used for hand washing.[71] Some Jews viewed stone vessels as impermeable to impurity (e.g., *m. Kel.* 10:1), and so the usage of stone vessels would have facilitated maintaining ritual purity.[72] Deines is also highly critical of Sanders' interpretation and usage of the rabbinic evidence, pointing to mishnaic passages where hand washing before common meals is presupposed (e.g., anonymous halakah in *m. Hag.* 2:5; cf. *m. Yad.* chs. 1–2).[73] Apparently, for Deines, there would

---

[69] Partly under the influence of Jacob Neusner, *The Idea of Purity in Ancient Judaism* (SJLA 1; Brill: Leiden, 1973). Sanders and others have criticized Neusner for over-relating purity practices with the temple. See Haber, *They Shall Purify Themselves,* 164 n. 14; John C. Poirier, "Purity beyond the Temple in the Second Temple Era," *JBL* 122 (2003): 247–65; Sanders, *Jewish Law from Jesus to the Mishnah,* 232. See especially Furstenberg, "Defilement Penetrating the Body," 193–94 and Kazen, *Issues of Impurity,* 117–19 for a critique against the notion that hand washing originated as an endeavor to emulate the priests in the temple.

[70] Furstenberg, "Defilement Penetrating the Body," 194, thinks Jews appropriated this practice from foreign custom and observed it out of hygienic and ritual concerns.

[71] For a discussion of the archaeological findings, see Deines, *Jüdische Steingefäße,* 39–165, especially p. 52 (illustration of a pitcher with handle, possibly used for ritual of hand washing), pp. 161–64, and p. 180. See also Magness, *Stone and Dung,* 17–21. Some take such archaeological findings as evidence that Jews washed their hands before consuming common meals. So James H. Charlesworth, *The Historical Jesus* (Nashville, Tenn.: Abingdon, 2008), 88; Regev, "Non-Priestly Purity and Its Religious Aspects," 232 n. 25; Avemarie, "Jesus and Purity," 265. Regev thinks that the sheer size of the archaeological findings points toward a general use of these vessels, not only for handling sacred food (e.g., heave offerings) but also ordinary food (pp. 232–33). But see the reasonable qualifications made by Kazen, *Issues of Impurity,* 114–15, on the interpretation of the archaeological evidence. See also Jonathan L. Reed, "Stone Vessels and Gospel Texts: Purity and Socio-Economics in John 2," in *Zeichen aus Text und Stein: Studien auf dem Weg zu einer Archäologie des Neuen Testaments* (eds. Stefan Alkier and Jürgen Zangenberg; Texte und Arbeiten zum neutestamentlichen Zeitalter 42; Tübingen: Francke Verlag, 2003), 381–401.

[72] On the other hand, the Dead Sea sectarians appear to have viewed stone implements as permeable to impurity. See Milgrom, *Leviticus,* 1:674, referencing CD 12:15–18; 11QT^a 49:13–16; 50:16–17. For further discussion of pertinent Jewish passages, see Deines, *Jüdische Steingefäße,* 168–246; Magness, *Stone and Dung,* 70–74.

[73] See his criticism of Sanders in *Jüdische Steingefäße,* 269–74. Here the thorny problem of methodological approaches to rabbinic evidence fully emerges. Whereas Sanders,

have been a widespread practice of hand washing before common meals in the first century CE, later attenuated by the rabbinic sages.[74]

In light of these findings, at least three possible scenarios on the issue can be imagined for elucidating the controversy in Matthew: (1) Matthew, like Mark, depicts a controversy that reflects more accurately Diasporan rather than Judean practice;[75] (2) Jews of the first century in Palestine generally washed their hands before handling food; (3) Only particular groups (e.g., certain Pharisees) sought to handle their food in constant purity and promoted their expansionist tendencies among the common people. Out of the three possibilities, the first option seems the least likely, while an intermediate position lying somewhere between the second and third options proves the most likely. Speaking against option one is the complete absence of any evidence directly associating the Diasporan practice of hand washing with eating.[76] Although the Jewish practice of hand washing may have originated from non-Jewish custom, there is no need to posit that Mark and Matthew have invented a story reflecting the habits of the Jewish Diaspora rather than Palestinian halakah. Mark and Matthew, for one thing, explicitly tie hand washing with eating, and while Mark may have colored his pericope with Diasporan pastels, this process seems less likely for Matthew who probably wrote in a milieu more affiliated with and attuned to Palestinian praxis. The advantage with options two and three is the serious consideration, which certainly must be qualified, it grants to Matthew and Mark as Jewish sources providing information about ancient halakah. Furthermore, the archaeological evidence brought

---

following Neusner, ignores the relevance of many of the anonymous material in the Mishnah, finding their dating elusive, Deines, like Epstein, is willing to entertain the notion that these anonymous passages retain older traditions. For Epstein's historical reconstruction of the earliest strata of the Mishnah, see his *Introduction to Tannaitic Literature,* 377–78. Kazen, *Jesus and Purity Halakhah,* also critiques Sanders extensively throughout his book.

[74] Deines, *Jüdische Steingefäße,* 272 n. 567 and 569; 299 n. 474.

[75] So Sanders, *Jewish Law from Jesus to the Mishnah,* 261–62; Meier, *Marginal Jew,* 4:402: "In fact, it is possible (though hardly provable) that the practice of handwashing before meals, along with certain other purity practices, first arose in the Diaspora, perhaps as a compensatory or substitutive observance for Jews who would not have had ready access to the Jerusalem temple and its purificatory rituals for lengthy periods. Since it is likely that Mark and Matthew composed their Gospels outside Palestine in the post-70 period, their portraits of Judaism may well have been influenced by Diaspora practices with which they were acquainted." Poirier, "Why Did the Pharisees Wash their Hands?" 217–33, suggests that the Diasporan custom of hand washing may have influenced Palestinian Jewish practice.

[76] However, Marcus, *Mark,* 1:441, states: "And if Jews washed their hands before or during prayer, and prayed before eating, then they would have washed their hands before eating."

to the forefront by Deines and others, which speaks on behalf of a Palestinian custom of washing hands before meals, cannot be underestimated.[77]

Fortunately, for the inquiry of this chapter, which is more devoted to the question of kashrut, the tortuous subject of hand washing before meals need not be fully resolved.[78] Only sufficient acquaintance with the matter and its questions is necessary when assessing statements in Matt 15 that could potentially have bearings on understanding the issue of consuming forbidden food items such as pork or blood. It should be noted that the custom of hand washing before meals by no means enjoyed the same status as the repeated injunctions in the Mosaic Torah against ingesting non-kosher food, which most Jews observed in antiquity and did not argue about.[79] Some Jews would have probably viewed the failure to wash hands before eating common meals as a minor halakic offense in comparison to the much weightier issue of ingesting forbidden meats such as pork – a true test of fidelity to Jewish identity. Finally, as the following analysis of the pericope shows, Matthew, more clearly than Mark, distinguishes the issue of hand washing before meals from the topic of kashrut.

Redactional Analysis

In the opening to his pericope, Matthew follows Mark, albeit with some stylistic differences, providing a setting in which Pharisees and scribes

---

[77] I do not adhere to Deines' claims regarding Pharisaic normative authority in the Second Temple period. The archaeological evidence needs further assessment, as much of it seems to stem from Jerusalem and Judea. Shimon Gibson, "Stone Vessels of the Early Roman Period from Jerusalem and Palestine: A Reassessment," in *One Land – Many Cultures: Archaeological Studies in Honour of Stanislao Loffreda* (eds. G. Claudio Bottini, Leah Di Segni, and L. Daniel Chrupcala; Jerusalem: Franciscan, 2003), 302, states: "The widespread distribution of these vessels, however, in so many different contexts, both urban and rural, supports the notion that they were not actually used by any one particular socio-economic or religious group within Judaism." But Magness, *Stone and Dung,* 70, notes that "the largest number of stone vessels seem to come from sites in Jerusalem, and most of the workshops found so far are located in Jerusalem's environs." How might Magness' observations affect our understanding of Jesus' attitude toward hand washing? Could it be that in Galilee, Jesus' "home state," the concern for ritual purity was not as intense as in Judea? See Vermes, *Jesus the Jew,* 52–57. Kazen, *Jesus and Purity Halakhah,* 277–85, searching for distinctive Galilean approaches to purity, concludes that Galilean practice was generally conservative and oriented toward Jerusalem.

[78] Compare the resignation of Milikowsky, "Reflections on Hand-Washing, Hand-Purity and Holy Scripture in Rabbinic Literature," 149: "The questions relating to purity of the hands in rabbinic literature are manifold, and many of them are probably insoluble...."

[79] Later rabbinic passages recognize this subordination: "washing of hands for non-sacred food is not prescribed by the Torah" (*b. Shabb.* 52b).

come down from Jerusalem to question Jesus.[80] The opening does not report a historical event involving Jesus and Pharisees "as it really happened" (although it is possible that the historical Jesus did neglect washing hands before eating). In Matthew's day, the story may have served as a polemic against Pharisees of the post-70 era, even if the latter were not centered in Jerusalem at that time.[81]

Matthew immediately jumps into the controversy between the Pharisees and Jesus over the issue of washing hands before eating food.[82] He com-

---

[80] Stylistic differences in v. 1 include Matthew's frequent usage of τότε (Matt: 90x; Mark: 6x; Luke: 15x); προσέρχονται (also a Matthean favorite: 52x in Matt; 6x in Mark; 10x in Luke) instead of Mark's συνάγονται (see already Willoughby C. Allen, *The Gospel according to S. Matthew* [3d ed.; ICC; Edinburgh: T&T Clark, 1977], 31, 163); τῷ Ἰησοῦ for Mark's πρὸς αὐτόν; Mark's qualified τινες τῶν γραμματέων has been generalized into γραμματεῖς, possibly to identify them more closely with the Pharisees (so Hagner, *Matthew*, 2:430); deletion of Mark's ἐλθόντες; addition of λέγοντες. The whole reshaped sentence in 15:1 bears the stamp of Matthew's pen. Cf. Matt 9:14 (Τότε προσέρχονται αὐτῷ οἱ μαθηταὶ Ἰωάννου λέγοντες) with Matt 15:1 (Τότε προσέρχονται τῷ Ἰησοῦ ἀπὸ Ἱεροσολύμων Φαρισαῖοι καὶ γραμματεῖς λέγοντες).

[81] The opening to this scene is not entirely reliable from a historical point of view. Would Pharisees in a pre-70 setting really travel all the way from Jerusalem to Galilee in order to inspect whether Jesus and his followers performed hand washing? What authority, in any case, would such Pharisees have in a pre-70 setting? Bultmann, *History of the Synoptic Tradition*, 39–40, reminds us that such stories contain ideal constructions. They may reflect a historical reminiscence involving the first followers of Jesus (even Jesus himself) but relate these happenings in an ideal way in which Jesus triumphantly refutes the Pharisees who are never given the opportunity to voice a counterargument. As soon as these Pharisees from Jerusalem appear on the literary scene (v. 1), they immediately vanish from the narration. Cf. Sanders, *Jesus and Judaism*, 265: "The extraordinarily unrealistic settings of many of the conflict stories should be realized: Pharisees did not organize themselves into groups to spend their Sabbaths in Galilean cornfields in the hopes of catching someone transgressing (Mark 2.23f.), nor is it credible that scribes and Pharisees made a special trip to Galilee from Jerusalem to inspect Jesus' disciples' hands (Mark 7.1f.)." However, Back, *Jesus of Nazareth and the Sabbath Commandment*, 55, finds it unlikely that the Pharisees' presence in such stories is the result of Markan redaction, since Pharisees were not Mark's contemporary adversaries. Rather, Back correctly maintains that the Pharisees were present in the pre-Markan tradition, since there is very little evidence for a strong presence of Pharisees in the Diaspora. These historical problems, of course, are not the focus of this analysis. It is possible that at the redactional level Matthew's report of such a debate reflects an actual *Auseinandersetzung* with the Pharisees of his own day. Cf. Eduard Schweizer, *Das Evangelium nach Matthäus* (NTD 2; Göttingen: Vandenhoeck & Ruprecht, 1981), 212: "Er gestaltet das Ganze formal stärker zu einem Streitgespräch um, wie es nach 70 n. Chr. sicher oft zwischen pharisäischen und christlichen Schriftgelehrten geführt wurde." See also Repschinski, *The Controversy Stories in the Gospel of Matthew*, 163.

[82] Literally, the Pharisees and scribes ask why Jesus' disciples do not wash before eating *bread* (ἄρτον). The Greek noun can mean either "bread" or "food" in general. See "ἄρτος," *BDAG*. There is late evidence suggesting that bread occupied a special position

pletely leaves out Mark's explanation concerning Pharisaic and Jewish purity practices (Mark 7:2–4), because they would prove superfluous for his more informed Jewish audience, perhaps even a bit disproportionate, as Mark claims that all Jews washed their hands before eating.[83]

Matthew phrases the breach with Pharisaic practice in stronger terms than Mark. Instead of accusing the disciples of Jesus for not "walking according to the traditions of the elders" (Mark 7:5),[84] in Matthew, the Pharisees and scribes blame them for transgressing (παραβαίνουσιν) their traditions. This language allows Matthew's Jesus to accuse the Pharisees in turn for transgressing (παραβαίνετε) the "commandment of God" (v. 3: τὴν ἐντολὴν τοῦ θεου).[85]

The reply given by Matthew's Jesus in vv. 3–9 focuses not on the specific question of hand washing but on a wider set of issues involving the observance of the so-called "traditions of the elders" (παράδοσιν τῶν πρεσβυτέρων). In this section, Matthew significantly reorganizes and modifies Mark's material in order to form a double antithesis (cf. v. 2 with v. 3) whose climax erupts in vv. 7–9.[86] Instead of beginning with the citation from the book of Isaiah, as Mark does, Matthew has Jesus first point out some of the inconsistencies and skewed prioritizations supposedly embedded within Pharisaic thought and tradition. Seemingly annoyed at their inquiry, Matthew's Jesus retorts by throwing the blame back at the Phari-

---

in relation to hand washing (*b. Hag.* 18b). However, given the general presentation of Matthew's pericope (as well as Mark's), it seems unlikely that he intends with this noun a restrictive rather than general connotation. On this question, see Booth, *Jesus and the Laws of Purity*, 121–22.

[83] Mark's parenthetical explanation stems from his need to explain Jewish (or Judean) praxis to a Gentile audience. Sanders, *Jewish Law from Jesus to the Mishnah,* 261–62, claims that Mark is exaggerating the prevalence of hand washing among Jews, that he is a Gentile from the Diaspora who only has outside knowledge about Judaism. Nevertheless, we have noted that many scholars have recently affirmed the popularity of hand washing at the time of Jesus. Mark's "exaggeration" then would not reflect a faulty knowledge of Judaism. Cf. Marcus, *Mark,* 1:440–41 and especially Boyarin, *The Jewish Gospels*, 111–17, who affirms that Mark in fact displays a very accurate knowledge about Jewish halakah.

[84] The Greek οὐ περιπατοῦσιν κατὰ (Mark 7:5) may reflect a Semitism (הלך, whence the noun halakah finds its derivation). So already P. M.-J. Lagrange, *Évangile selon saint Matthieu* (4th ed.; Paris: Librairie Lecoffre, 1927), 301.

[85] Matthew also describes the impurity of the hands with the adjective ἄνιπτος (v. 21: ἀνίπτοις χερσίν; cf. *m. Hul.* 2:4: ידים מסאבות) instead of Mark's κοιναῖς χερσὶν, possibly for stylistic reasons, since in v. 2, Jesus' disciples are said to not wash (νίπτονται) their hands before eating. Or does he deliberately avoid Mark's technical expression to soften the clash with the Jewish purity system? Cf. Peter Fiedler, *Das Matthäusevangelium* (Theologischer Kommentar zum Neuen Testament 1; Stuttgart: W. Kohlhammer, 2006), 278 n. 28.

[86] Allen, *Gospel According to S. Matthew,* 163–64.

sees: "And why do you break (παραβαίνετε) the commandment of God for the sake of your tradition?" (15:3) The formulation of the question essentially resembles the Pharisees' inquiry, except Matthew's Jesus accuses his opponents in stronger terms: the Pharisees transgress the commandment of God for the sake of their traditions (τὴν παράδοσιν ὑμῶν). If the Pharisees uphold the antiquity of their traditions (they originate from the elders) and seek to promote and impose their observance beyond the Pharisaic sphere, Matthew's Jesus reduces their importance by denying their ancestral origins, insinuating that they are merely Pharisaic inventions or innovations ("your" traditions instead of traditions of the "elders").[87]

Matthew's main objection to Pharisaic praxis involves what he sees as a misplaced prioritization of values. In his opinion, the Pharisaic teaching can lead others to transgress the commandments found in the Mosaic Torah. The Pharisees, of course, would have viewed this matter quite differently. Probably, they would have seen their traditions as properly applying the real substance and intent of the Torah, functioning, to use rabbinic imagery, as a protective fence against unwanted transgression (cf. Avot 1:1). Matthew, nonetheless, insists that the Pharisees disregard divine mandate: "For God said, 'Honor your father and your mother,' and, 'Whoever speaks evil of father or mother must surely die'" (15:4). Here, Matthew's Jesus recalls two important commandments related to honoring one's parents found in the Torah (one from the Decalogue: Exod 20:12/Deut 5:16; the other from Exod 21:17, the transgression of which technically leads to death). Whereas Mark describes Moses as the announcer of such commandments (Μωϋσῆς γὰρ εἶπεν), Matthew substitutes the human subject with God (ὁ γὰρ θεὸς εἶπεν) to further highlight the clash between Pharisaic precepts and divine imperative (v. 4).

In concrete terms, the Pharisees allegedly disregard divine commandments because they teach (v. 5: ὑμεῖς δὲ λέγετε) their comrades to withhold from their parents whatever possession they previously set aside as an offering for God. Whereas Mark uses the Hebrew term "Qorban" (κορβᾶν from קרבן), "that is, an offering to God" (Mark 7:11: ὅ ἐστιν δῶρον), Matthew speaks simply of a δῶρον (Mat 15:5).[88] This halakic matter can hardly

---

[87] Cf. Albert I. Baumgarten, "The Pharisaic Paradosis," *HTR* 80 (1987): 74, 77, who suggests that the Pharisees would have ascribed antiquity to their traditions. In Mark, Jesus refers to the traditions of the elders as the "traditions of humans" (τὴν παράδοσιν τῶν ἀνθρώπων). This appellation blends with the previous citation in Mark from Isaiah with its reference to "human precepts" (ἐντάλματα ἀνθρώπων). Matthew instead seeks to create an immediate, direct correspondence between the Pharisees' question and Jesus' opening reply.

[88] The term δῶρον is regularly used in the LXX to translate the Hebrew קרבן.

receive its appropriate treatment here,[89] but contrary to the custom of hand washing, the practice of vows enjoys a strong Mosaic foundation.[90] Briefly stated, Matthew seems to refer to the practice of setting aside through the pronouncement of a vow a profane object, property, or other possession as (or as if it were) an offering to the temple or God. Apparently, once the vow had been made, a person was obliged to fulfill his or her resolution as the following commandment in Deut 23:21–23 states: "If you make a vow to the LORD your God, do not postpone fulfilling it; for the LORD your God will surely require it of you, and you would incur guilt....Whatever your lips utter you must diligently perform, just as you have freely vowed to the LORD your God with your own mouth."[91]

Given the scrupulous Mosaic prescriptions concerning the fulfillment of vows (e.g., Num 30), Baumgarten suggests that the historical Pharisees would have released persons from vows in only very limited circumstances. The Jesus of Matthew and Mark rebukes Pharisees for requiring a son to fulfill his vow even at the cost of depriving his parents from material welfare. Apparently, in the eyes of Matthew's Jesus, such vows should be considered invalid ab initio.[92] In this case, Matthew seems to accuse the Pharisees for teaching people to uphold one commandment of the Torah at the cost of breaking another, probably more cardinal, commandment stemming from the same source of divine legislation: honoring one's parents.[93] In this way, so Matthew argues, the Pharisees, because of their

---

[89] See Albert I. Baumgarten, "*Korban* and the Pharisaic *Paradosis*," *JANES* 16–17 (1984–85): 5–17; Meier, *Marginal Jew*, 4:378–84.

[90] Gen 28:20–22 (Jacob vows to tithe his belongings if God will bless him); Lev 27:2, 8; Num 30. Cf. Judg 11:30 (tragic story of Jephthah), and so on.

[91] Second Temple sources relevant for the discussion of such vows include, among others, CD 16:14–20; Philo, *Hypoth.* 7:358; Josephus, *Ant.* 4:73; *Ag. Ap.* 1:167; tractate *Nedarim* (e.g., *m. Ned.* 1:4; 2:5; 4:6; 5:6, etc.). An important inscription from an ossuary dating from the first cent. BCE from Jebel Hallet et-Turi bears the word "Qorban": "Everything that a person will find to his profit in this ossuary is an offering (Qorban) to God from the one within it." See Baumgarten, "*Korban* and the Pharisaic *Paradosis*," 6, 17, 16; Joseph Fitzmyer, "The Aramaic Qorban Inscription from Jebel Hallet et-Tur and Mark 7:11/Mt 15:5," *JBL* 78 (1959): 60–65. Baumgarten interprets this inscription to mean that the items within the ossuary were to be treated as if they were an offering to God, rather than implying that they actually belonged to God. Marcus, *Mark*, 1:445, thinks that a similar understanding should be presumed in Mark 7:11: the person declaring an item as Qorban intends not to offer it to God, only to remove it from secular use.

[92] Baumgarten, "*Korban* and the Pharisaic *Paradosis*," 16. Perhaps, from Matthew's viewpoint, undertaking vows should be avoided all together, since swearing oaths is completely discouraged (5:33–37, cf. 23:16–22). So France, *The Gospel of Matthew*, 581.

[93] Cf. Meier, *Marginal Jew*, 4:379, with respect to the stance of the historical Jesus: "Apparently Jesus operated at least implicitly with the conviction that there were certain fundamental commandments and institutions in the Mosaic Torah that overrode or annulled any secondary obligations or institutions that came into conflict with them." In

traditions (διὰ τὴν παράδοσιν ὑμῶν), invalidate the word of God (v. 6: τὸν λόγον τοῦ θεοῦ).⁹⁴ They focus on the elaboration of the system of ritual purity, but overlook how their traditions lead to far greater transgressions such as dishonoring one's parents.⁹⁵

Matthew saves the last three verses of this first section (vv. 7–9; in Mark they appear at the beginning of Jesus' discourse) for the end of Jesus' speech, probably as his "punch line," since their content derives from scripture (Isa 29:13). Matthew opens this portion with an epithet he employs no less than eleven times in his gospel in the vocative plural, "hypocrites" (ὑποκριταί), always in reference to the Pharisees and the scribes.⁹⁶ Apparently, Matthew thinks Isa 29:13 actually contains a prophecy against the Pharisees: "Isaiah prophesied rightly about you when he said" (15:7).⁹⁷ The citation of the passage, which faithfully follows Mark's wording (7:6–

---

their defense, perhaps the Pharisees could have argued that the fulfillment of a vow was more important than honoring one's parents, since the vow was made to *God*. Fulfilling divine will supersedes all obligations, even those toward family members.

⁹⁴ Matthew's rephrasing in 15:6 of Mark's language creates greater symmetry with his previous statement in 15:3. Matthew's διὰ τὴν παράδοσιν ὑμῶν in 15:6 (instead of Mark's superfluous τῇ παραδόσει ὑμῶν ᾗ παρεδώκατε) corresponds to 15:3. Both verses highlight the antithesis Matthew wishes to signal: διὰ τί καὶ ὑμεῖς παραβαίνετε τὴν ἐντολὴν τοῦ θεοῦ διὰ τὴν παράδοσιν ὑμῶν; (15:3)/ καὶ ἠκυρώσατε τὸν λόγον τοῦ θεοῦ διὰ τὴν παράδοσιν ὑμῶν (15:6). Surprisingly, Matthew does not retain Mark's καὶ παρόμοια τοιαῦτα πολλὰ ποιεῖτε ("And you do many things like this"; Mark 7:13), which surely could have served his polemical interests. Fiedler, *Das Matthäusevangelium*, 279, following Hummel, *Auseinandersetzung,* 47, thinks that this elimination of Mark's phrase allows Matthew to focus exclusively on the Pharisaic approach to vows, thereby indirectly recognizing the wider authority of the Pharisees in other matters of Torah interpretation (cf. Matt 23:2–3, 23).

⁹⁵ Matthew seems to reproach the Pharisees for *insufficiently* releasing people from observing vows when it clashes with the observance of greater ethical commandments, not for their abuse in finding legal loopholes to rid themselves from observing vows. Contra H. Lesêtre, "Vœu," *DB* 5:2445: "En cas de nécessité, on en était quitte pour faire accomplir par un ou autre la chose qu'on s'était interdite. *Nedarim*, v, 6. C'est contre ces abus que Notre-Seigneur protesta, en déclarant que la loi de Dieu devait avoir le pas sur les traditions humaines." The Pharisaic approach to vows should not be completely assimilated into the more "liberal" rabbinic stance on this matter, one that sought to interpret loosely the language of vows to bypass them in various ways (see e.g., *m. Ḥul.* 8:1, permitting one who vowed not to benefit from meat to derive benefit from fish or grasshoppers). Unfortunately, this passage in Matthew (and Mark) has historically generated Christian anti-Jewish sentiments. See discussion in Luz, *Matthew,* 2:331.

⁹⁶ Cf. Mark 7:6: περὶ ὑμῶν τῶν ὑποκριτῶν, the only appearance of the word hypocrite in that entire gospel. In Luke, the epithet appears three times, *never* as an adjectival reference to the Pharisees (Luke 6:42; 12:56; 13:15), although Luke 12:1 does warn about the hypocrisy (ὑπόκρισις as an abstract noun) of the Pharisees.

⁹⁷ Cf. 1QpHab 10:6–11:2.

7),⁹⁸ is based on the text of the LXX.⁹⁹ Matthew brings this Isaian passage to the forefront in order to complete his antithetical discourse. Within this scriptural citation appears the key word καρδία ("heart"), which shows up two more times in Matt 15:18–19. The noun χεῖλος ("lip"), also from Isa 29:13, finds its equivalent in the subsequent section of the Matthean pericope where the word "mouth" (στόμα) appears no less than four times (vv. 11, 17, and 18). The passage from Isaiah highlights a point that will be elaborated later on in this analysis: the Pharisees concern themselves with honoring God with their "lips" (v. 8), in this incident, with food that enters their mouth (vv. 11 and 17), at the cost of neglecting and controlling the more important bodily organ, the heart, from which all kinds of evil and immoral thoughts emanate and materialize once they are vocally pronounced through the mouth (cf. v. 19). From Matthew's perspective, the Pharisees' hearts remain far from God, as they focus on teaching "human precepts" (v. 9: ἐντάλματα ἀνθρώπων) rather than uplifting "the commandment of God," (15:3: τὴν ἐντολὴν τοῦ θεοῦ).

Up until this point, the lengthy discourse delivered by Matthew's Jesus concerns itself not with the specific issue of hand washing, let alone with eating forbidden meats, but with contrasting the traditions of the Pharisees with the word or commandment of God (τὴν ἐντολὴν τοῦ θεοῦ/τὸν λόγον τοῦ θεοῦ) inscribed in the Torah.¹⁰⁰ Were we to formulate Matthew's position on the issue of food laws, based solely on this speech, a logical conclusion would be to posit the ongoing necessity of observing such practices, since, like the commandments concerning honoring one's parents (Exod 20:12, Deut 5:16, and Exod 21:17), the prohibition against eating impure meats and blood finds its basis in the same source of divine legislation. Possibly, Matthew would only suspend the observance of kashrut in extreme circumstances where serious ethical considerations would be involved. But the discussion in Matthew, so far, has concerned itself more with critiquing Pharisaic approaches to the Law of Moses that lead to transgressing its cardinal commandments, with pointing out the inconsistencies allegedly inherent within Pharisaic tradition as well as the suppos-

---

⁹⁸ Save for the slight emendation of οὗτος ὁ λαὸς (Mark 7:6) to ὁ λαὸς οὗτος (Matt 15:8).

⁹⁹ See Stendahl, *The School of St. Matthew*, 56–58; Meier, *Marginal Jew*, 4:369–76.

¹⁰⁰ In Matthew, ἐντολή refers to commandments found within the Law of Moses. Cf. Matt 19:17; 22:36, 38, 40, possibly 5:19. Deciphering the meaning of τὸν λόγον τοῦ θεοῦ proves more challenging, since it appears only in this instance within the entire gospel of Matthew. Here it seems to be used interchangeably with τὴν ἐντολὴν τοῦ θεοῦ, since the Pharisees are accused of nullifying a commandment (to honor one's parents) written in the Torah. Elsewhere, λόγος can be used to refer to the teachings of Jesus on the Torah. Thus, in 15:12, the disciples warn Jesus that the Pharisees might be offended with his "word" (τὸν λόγον), which is closely related to the "word of God."

edly distorted Pharisaic prioritization of ritual concerns at the cost of neglecting the weightier matters of the Torah.

The second major section (vv. 10–20) begins with Matthew's Jesus summoning the crowd for a special address (vv. 10–11).[101] Matthew signals the importance of the words about to be delivered by Jesus through the call to "listen and understand" (ἀκούετε καὶ συνίετε). The crowd hears a saying that more specifically addresses the question raised by the Pharisees at the beginning of the pericope regarding hand washing before meals, although only the disciples of Jesus have the opportunity of appreciating its meaning more fully, once they deliberate with their master (vv. 12–20): "It is not what goes into the mouth that defiles a person, but it is what comes out of the mouth that defiles" (15:11). Mark's version of the saying reads: "There is nothing outside a person that by going in can defile, but the things that come out are what defile" (7:15). In order to minimize the radical ramifications such a saying could generate, Matthew first denies Mark's claim that nothing (οὐδέν) coming from the outside may defile a person. He also restricts the application of the saying to matters related to the consumption of ritually contaminated (kosher) food by eliminating Mark's ἔξωθεν ("from outside"), which could possibly be taken to refer to other external impurities that "enter" a person (e.g., corpse impurity).[102]

---

[101] Matthew reworks Mark's description of Jesus summoning the crowd. He deletes Mark's πάλιν (in Mark 26x; Matt: 16x, only four of which come from Mark; see Allen, *Gospel according to S. Matthew*, xx); replaces ἔλεγεν with εἶπεν; shortens Mark's ἀκούσατέ μου πάντες καὶ σύνετε to ἀκούετε καὶ συνίετε.

[102] In Matt 23:27, Matthew's Jesus presupposes the defiling force of corpse impurity. Also in 23:25–26, Matthew thinks that internal purity takes *precedence* over external purity. See Luz, *Matthew,* 2:332. Of course, corpse impurity does not literally "enter" a person in the same sense that food would penetrate the human body through digestion, although it is telling that corpse impurity can enter uncovered vessels (Num 19:5). This might explain why Matthew has deleted Mark's generalizing ἔξωθεν, although even the Markan formulation focuses on food entering the body. According to Maccoby, *Ritual and Purity,* 158, not even ritual impurity conveyed through ingestion of contaminated foods actually "enters" the body: "No one ever claimed that the purpose of ritual purity was to prevent impurities from entering the body. On the contrary, it was held that ritual impurity never penetrates beyond the surface of the body. Even impurities incurred through eating forbidden food do not cause impurity to the interior of the body, only to the exterior." But the Markan and Matthean sayings do presume that purity can indeed penetrate the body. Cf. Furstenberg, "Defilement Penetrating the Body," 189 n. 33. Kazen, *Jesus and Purity Halakhah,* 219–22, discusses "inner" and "outer" impurity as close alternatives to "moral" vs. "ritual" impurity. Within a "Hebrew anthropology," "the innermost part of the body is seen as the seat of good and evil, the seat of purity and impurity. 'Morality' is located in the body, and purification from evil thoughts and acts is in a sense perceived as a purification of the innermost parts of the body" (221). By deleting Mark's ἔξωθεν, Matthew does not fully deny the force of "outer impurity" (i.e., ritual impurity) to defile the body.

Instead, Matthew narrows the focus of the saying by referring to things that enter a person through the mouth (εἰς τὸ στόμα). The focus in Matthew is about contaminated kosher food throughout.

Some, however, argue that Matthew's "anatomical" precision, τὸ στόμα, implies that even forbidden food such as pork, seafood, or blood are now permitted, since Matthew claims that what enters the mouth cannot defile.[103] Matthew, however, is hardly embarking on such a revolutionary project. He knows that the legislation prohibiting the consumption of forbidden meats and blood belongs to the "commandment/word of God," which is found in the Torah. He crafts the saying within a context that is confined in its opening and conclusion to the issue of washing hands before the consumption of common meals. The inclusion of the word "mouth" enables Matthew to highlight this organ not only as a physical passageway for food but especially as a vocal tunnel leading from the heart, the seat of potential evil thoughts and emotions, to the external world where wicked inclinations materialize into sinful utterances and acts, thereby defiling the person in a moral sense (cf. vv. 17–19). The content coming out of the mouth, this (τοῦτο), so Matthew emphasizes, is what (really) defiles a person.[104]

In the last part of the pericope (vv. 12–20), Jesus exchanges thoughts with his narrower circle of disciples. Unlike Mark, the disciples in Matthew do not first inquire about the meaning of Jesus' provocative saying, but express their worry over the offense it could create among the Phari-

---

[103] So France, *The Gospel of Matthew*, 583: "But the principle of externally contracted defilement is well illustrated by the Levitical food laws (Lev 11; cf. also 17:10–16), and it is this principle which Jesus is here setting aside, no less explicitly in Matthew's rather smoother version than in Mark's"; Grundmann, *Das Evangelium nach Matthäus*, 372: "…es gibt keine unreine speise….Damit gewinnt der Mensch Freiheit im Umgang mit der Natur und im Verkehr mit anderen Menschen. Die Israel von seiner Umwelt trennende Verfassung…ist aufgehoben"; Gundry, *Matthew*, 305–6; Meier, *The Vision of Matthew*, 100–104; Schweizer, *Das Evangelium nach Matthäus*, 211: "Dennoch hätte er V. 11 nicht schreiben könnten, wenn er die alttestamentlichen Speisegebote noch als verbindlich angesehen hätte."

[104] See the discussion in Davies-Allison, *Gospel according to Matthew*, 2:527–31, arguing essentially that Matthew's form of the saying comes close to the historical Jesus' view. What matters above all is the heart, even though such a hyperbolic statement does not set aside the food laws. Just as the prophetic tradition could state, "I desire mercy, not sacrifice" without seeking to set aside the cultic system, so the statement in Matthew highlights the priority of ethical matters above the application of ritual commandments. Commenting on a passage from the *Mekilta*, which states, "It is not the place that honors the person but the person who honors the place," Davies and Allison add (2:531): "If this were found not in a rabbinic document but in the gospels and regarded as an isolated saying of Jesus, would some scholars not consider it a radical attack on the temple and OT conceptions of sacred space?" Cf. Fiedler, *Das Matthäusevangelium*, 279–80.

sees.[105] This concern with Pharisaic sensibilities is completely absent in Mark. Its exclusive manifestation within Matthew may point to a more acute friction sensed by the author and his circles with contemporary Pharisees actively present in their own locale. The reply provided by Matthew's Jesus is also missing in Mark. Its content contains a general polemic exclusively launched against Pharisaic leadership (vv. 13–14). Theoretically, it could have been interpolated into almost any other section in Matthew where Jesus clashes with Pharisees. Here, Matthew's Jesus reassures his disciples not to worry about the Pharisees' reaction. They are foreign plants that will one day be uprooted (v. 13), the "blind leading the blind," guiding others into peril (v. 14).[106]

Peter's request that Jesus clarify his "parable" brings the discussion in Matthew back to the topic of purity.[107] Mark does not single out Peter from the rest of the disciples; Matthew, on the other hand, presents him as the inquirer.[108] Matthew's Jesus seems annoyed at Peter and, by extension, at all of the disciples for their inaptitude in comprehending his message: "Are you also still without understanding?" (v. 16)[109] He adds a "physiological" clarification about the previous statement made in v. 12: "Do you not see that whatever goes into the *mouth* enters the *stomach*, and goes out into the sewer?" (v. 17)[110] By contrast, "what comes out of the *mouth* proceeds from the *heart*, and this is what defiles" (v.18). The point of origination and final destination are contrasted in these two verses. The mouth func-

---

[105] In Mark 7:17, the setting shifts when Jesus leaves the crowd and enters a house (καὶ ὅτε εἰσῆλθεν εἰς οἶκον ἀπὸ τοῦ ὄχλου); in Matt 15:12, this movement does not occur. Rather, Matthew introduces the transition with his favorite τότε ("then"), whereupon the disciples approach Jesus and express their concern about the potential reaction of the Pharisees.

[106] Cf. Matt 23:16, 17, 19, 24, 26. The attempt by Schweizer, *Das Evangelium nach Matthäus*, 212–13, to interpret this content as a rejection of all of Israel is unconvincing. The blame is exclusively cast against the Pharisees for their alleged failure in properly leading the Jewish people.

[107] The word "parable" refers to the saying pronounced to the crowd in 15:12, not to the preceding polemical words leveled against the Pharisees in vv. 13–14, since Jesus' answer to Peter further clarifies the question regarding hand washing and impurity (vv. 16–20). Contra Schweizer, *Das Evangelium nach Matthäus*, 212–13.

[108] Is he simply speaking on behalf of the disciples? In Gal 2 as well as in Acts chs. 10, 11, and 15, Peter is singled out in matters dealing with purity laws, either to be reprimanded (by Paul in Galatians) or properly instructed on such issues (as in Acts). Could Matthew have intentionally inserted Peter into this pericope because of the prominence and usage of his figure in such discussions? On the figure of Peter and the Torah in Matthew, see Sim, *The Gospel of Matthew and Christian Judaism*, 200–212.

[109] In 15:16, Matthew replaces Mark's οὕτως ("in this manner," "so") with ἀκμὴν ("still"), possibly signaling an ongoing debate in his own time regarding such matters.

[110] Once again, Matthew deletes Mark's ἔξωθεν in order to demarcate the discussion more clearly around impurity in so far as it affects kosher food.

tions as a passageway, a two-way street through which material and immaterial objects enter and exit. What enters the mouth only passes through the stomach and eventually ends up in the latrine;[111] what exits the mouth originates from the heart and defiles the person. More than that, it can harmfully affect other humans, since "out of the heart come evil intentions, murder, adultery, fornication, theft, false witness, slander" (v. 19).[112]

As stated earlier, Matthew's portrayal of the mouth in this pericope as an orifice transporting both food and verbal utterance should not lead the modern interpreter into thinking that the observance of food laws has been forsaken. Here, the mouth is especially and literally viewed as an *oral* cavity tightly related to another key organ that has nothing to do with food, the heart. It is particularly the moral dimension of impurity that Matthew seeks to highlight when he brings such anatomical imagery to the foreground, not to suggest that kashrut no longer enjoys a place within the Jesus movement. For Matthew, both organs, the mouth and the heart, are rich symbols that convey important pedagogical and kerygmatic lessons. Thus, during his temptation, Matthew's Jesus cites from Deut 8:3: "One does not live by bread alone, but by every word that comes from the mouth of God" (Matt 4:4). This citation is completely missing in Mark, while Luke (4:4) only cites the first phrase of the Deuteronomic saying, not including the second phrase with its key references to the action of "coming out" (ἐκπορευομένῳ) and the organ "mouth" (στόματος), both of which appear in Matt 15:11, 18. Matthew thereby emphasizes the need to attend not only to physical needs but especially the word of God (cf. Matt 15:6: τὸν λόγον τοῦ θεοῦ). Similarly, before delivering the so-called beatitudes, Matthew's Jesus open his *mouth* to teach (5:2: ἀνοίξας τὸ στόμα αὐτοῦ ἐδίδασκεν) his audience about his message. By contrast, in his version of

---

[111] Instead of Mark's ἐκπορεύεται, Matthew uses the verb ἐκβάλλεται to describe the exit of food into the sewer. The verbal replacement probably has to do with Matthew's intent to highlight the theme of speech as Gundry, *Matthew*, 308, suggests.

[112] Matthew's list of vices (15:19) is shorter than Mark's (7:21–22: 12 items) containing only six or seven items (if the first item is to be considered as standing on its own): διαλογισμοὶ πονηροί, φόνοι, μοιχεῖαι, πορνεῖαι, κλοπαί, ψευδομαρτυρίαι, βλασφημίαι. By reducing Mark's more extensive list, Matthew is hardly claiming that *only* the Ten Commandments are the mandatory portion of the Torah Jewish followers of Jesus should observe, even though his list of vices approximates the contents of the second tablet of the Decalogue. Contra Schweizer, *Das Evangelium nach Matthäus*, 212. Not all of the commandments from the Decalogue are included in this list (e.g., idolatry, Sabbath, and covetousness). Moreover, some of the items do not correspond to the Decalogue: neither πορνεῖαι nor βλασφημίαι appear in the LXX of Exod 20 and Deut 5. Rudolf Schnackenburg, *Matthäusevangelium* (2 vols; Die Neue Echter Bibel; Würzburg: Echter, 1985–1987), 1:143, ties βλασφημίαι with 12:31, 34, 36. Francis Wright Beare, *The Gospel according to Matthew* (Oxford: Basil Blackwell, 1981), 339, sees Matthew's list as a scribal creation reducing the number of vices to the symbolic number seven.

the beatitudes, Luke does not refer to the delivery of Jesus' speech in such terms (6:20). Quite significantly, Matthew's Jesus accuses the Pharisees elsewhere for their supposed hypocrisy when he vehemently attacks them, stating: "You brood of vipers! How can you speak good things, when you are evil? For out of the abundance of the heart the mouth speaks" (Matt 12:34; cf. Luke 6:45). Matthew, then, uses the mouth in a special way to convey important theological lessons.[113]

Conspicuously missing from Matthew's pericope is Mark's sweeping claim that Jesus "declared all foods clean" (Mark 7:19b). Instead, Matthew ends the discussion with a declaration restricted to the theme of hand washing before eating: "but to eat with unwashed hands does not defile" (15:20). In this way, Matthew begins and closes this extended pericope with a focus on the topic at hand, namely, hand washing before meals. Matthew limits the halakic relevance of the saying pronounced by Jesus in v. 12, which is repeated and elaborated in vv. 17–20, to a discussion on a particular issue related to Pharisaic praxis rather than to a commandment of Mosaic (or divine) legislation. As noted above, Matthew further subdues the radicalizing force of Jesus' saying as found in Mark by denying the claim that *nothing* entering from the outside can defile a person (Matt 15:12). Even though Matthew adds the word, "mouth," to this saying, which, taken out of its Matthean context, could mistakenly promote the consumption of forbidden meats such as pork, the observations made above suggest he does so more in order to highlight the immoral functions such an organ can perform in concert with the heart where wicked thoughts germinate. Read as an ensemble, nothing in this pericope suggests that Matthew abrogates the observance of the food stipulations enounced in Lev 11/Deut 14 or the prohibition against eating blood as commanded in Gen 9, Lev 17, and Deut 12.[114]

---

[113] Other significant verses could be pointed out, including Matthew's citation of Psa 78:2 (unattested in the other canonical gospels): "I will open my mouth to speak in parables; I will proclaim what has been hidden from the foundation of the world" (13:34). Cf. Matt 18:16; 21:16. Pertinent verses describing the heart include: "Blessed are the pure in heart, for they will see God"(Matt 5:8; missing in Luke); "But I say to you that everyone who looks at a woman with lust has already committed adultery with her in his heart" (Mat 5:28); "Take my yoke upon you, and learn from me; for I am gentle and humble in heart, and you will find rest for your souls" (Matt 11:29); Cf. Matt 6:21; 9:4; 13:15, 19; 18:35; 22:37; 24:48.

[114] Correctly, Davies and Allison, *The Gospel according to Saint Matthew*, 2:517; Fiedler, *Das Matthäusevangelium*, 278, boldly argues that Matthew has Jesus clash with Pharisaic interpretation only on this point even while affirming their authority on other matters (cf. Matt 23:2–3); Frankemölle, *Matthäus*, 2:201–2; Gnilka, *Das Matthäusevangelium*, 26–27; Hagner, *Matthew*, 2:432; Harrington, *The Gospel of Matthew*, 231; Marcus, *Mark*, 1:446; Saldarini, *Matthew's Christian-Jewish Community*, Sim, *The Gospel of Matthew and Christian Judaism*, 135; Wolfgang Wiefel, *Das Evangelium nach*

Pigs, Dogs, Gnats, and Camels: Matt 7:6 and 23:24

Key Verses

Matt 7:6: "Do not give what is holy to dogs; and do not throw your pearls before swine, or they will trample them under foot and turn and maul you."
Matt 23:24: You blind guides! You strain out a gnat but swallow a camel!

Literary Context

Both sayings appear in different literary settings within Matthew but are analyzed together because of their mutual usage of imagery of non-kosher animals. The first saying (7:6) belongs to a larger block of teachings delivered by Matthew's Jesus during the so-called Sermon on the Mount (chs. 5–7). In its immediate literary setting, the saying appears right after a set of material warning against judging others (7:1–5). Right after the saying, Matthew's Jesus exhorts his audience to trust in divine provision (7:7–11).

Matthäus (THKNT; Leipzig: Evangelische Verlagsanstalt, 1998), 284: "von Speise ist nicht die Rede!" Even if Matthew, following Mark, no longer views forbidden meats as intrinsically "impure," this need not mean that he no longer observes the Jewish food laws. After all, other Jews could reach the same conclusion even while upholding the observance of such practices. The discussion between R. Yohanan b. Zakkai and a non-Jew regarding the red heifer (from admittedly much later rabbinic sources: *Pesiq. Rab Kah.* 4:7; *Num. Rab.* 19:8) illustrates this point: A Gentile accuses Jews of sorcery because they perform the rite of the red heifer, which involves burning the animal, pounding it into ashes, and sprinkling some of the ashes with water upon an impure person in order to remove corpse impurity. R. Yohanan points out that non-Jews practice similar rites such as the burning and sprinkling of roots upon a person tormented by an evil spirit. By analogy, R. Yohanan b. Zakkai argues that a Jewish person can be delivered from the "spirit of impurity" acquired through contact with a corpse. Apparently, this answer satisfies the non-Jew, but R. Yohanan's own disciples demand a better reply. Surprisingly, R. Yohanan declares that a corpse does not have the power in itself to defile, nor does the mixture of water with the ashes of the red heifer actually purify a person, rather, citing Num 19:2, the commandment regarding this purification rite is a viewed as a "a statute of the law that the LORD has commanded" (אשר־צוה חקת התורה יהוה). In other words, Jews should still observe purity laws even if impurity is bereft of an inherent ability to defile a person. Interestingly enough, according to the rabbinic mindset, the commandments governing forbidden meats belong to the category of "statutes" (חוקים) ordained by God: they are to be kept regardless of their rationale (cf. *b. Yoma* 67b). In the writings of Philo and *Aristeas,* appears an allegorizing and ethicizing process of Jewish dietary laws that seems to deny the intrinsic impurity of forbidden meats even while upholding the observance of such legislation. Contrary to the extreme allegorizers condemned by Philo or the author of *Barnabas* who took the next logical step in his allegorizing tendencies by abandoning Jewish dietary practices all together, Philo and the author of *Aristeas* held onto the observance of kashrut (see my discussion on Peter's vision of impure meats in chapter 10).

The saying is sandwiched, therefore, in between two rather straightforward themes: judging others (7:1) and trusting God (7:7). The reason for the placement of v. 6 at such a juncture is elusive and cannot assist in deciphering the meaning of this cryptic saying.[115] The symbolic content of this independent saying invites several interpretations. The precise meaning and usage of this saying among Matthew's readers, therefore, eludes us.[116]

As for the second saying, it appears within a notoriously antagonistic chapter of Matthew, unequaled in its invective against the Pharisees. Ironically, Matt 23 commences with a recognition of Pharisaic authority and instruction (vv. 2–3a), only to accuse Pharisees for failing to live up to their own teachings (v. 3b) because of their supposed hypocritical tendencies (vv. 4–7). Matthew then demands a more honest and humble display from his followers (vv. 8–12).[117] The invective against the scribes and the Pharisees reaches its climax in the subsequent "seven woes" pronounced by Matthew's Jesus (vv. 13–33):

First Woe: Closing the Kingdom of Heaven (v. 13)
Second Woe: Making Pharisaic "Proselytes" (v. 15)
Third Woe: Misusage of Oaths (vv. 16–22)
Fourth Woe: Neglect of the Weightier Matters of the Law (vv. 23–24)
Gnat-Camel Saying (v. 24)
Fifth Woe: Purifying the Outside, Neglecting the Inside (vv. 25–26)
Sixth Woe: Whitewashed Tombs (vv. 27–28)
Seventh Woe: Murder of the Prophets (vv. 29–33)

---

[115] However, see M. D. Goulder, *Midrash and Lection in Matthew* (London: SPCK, 1974), 265–66, who links v. 6 with vv. 1–5. So too, Davies and Allison, *Gospel according to Matthew,* 2:674: "Having warned his audience about judging others, Matthew now adds a 'gemara' in order to counteract an extreme interpretation of 7.1–5: if there must not be too much severity (vv. 1–5), there must at the same time not be too much laxity (v. 6)." These are possible interpretations, but somewhat imaginative. Cf. Bonnard, *L'Évangile,* 97, who refers to the saying as a "parole énigmatique" that is linked neither to what precedes or follows. Similarly, Luz, *Matthew,* 1:354: "This logion is a puzzle. Even its symbolic meaning is uncertain; its application and its sense in the Matthean context are a complete mystery."

[116] H. D. Betz, *The Sermon on the Mount: A Commentary on the Sermon on the Mount, Including the Sermon on the Plain (Matthew 5:3–7:27 and Luke 6:20–49)* (Hermeneia; Minneapolis: Fortress, 1995), 494–96.

[117] Matt 23:2–3 has generated a plethora of interpretations. See Mark Allan Powell, "Do and Keep What Moses Says (Matthew 23:2–7)," *JBL* 114 (1995): 419–35, for a useful summary and critique of various positions. Powell's own suggestion that Matthew's Jesus only recognizes the authority of the Pharisees because of their knowledge and control of the *contents* of scripture is questionable. Matthew himself evinces his literary capabilities and knowledge of scriptures throughout his compositional enterprise. Perhaps he was even a scribe. Furthermore, it is debatable to what extent the Pharisees would have monopolized the reading and exposition of the Jewish scriptures in the synagogues of Palestine.

The saying about the gnat and the camel appears in between the fourth and fifth woes, at the heart of this dire diatribe against the Pharisees. The saying either concludes the fourth woe or begins the fifth one, or better, it serves as a transitory verse thematically linking both woes and vividly illustrating how the Pharisees allegedly overlook more important issues because of their obsession with ritual matters. The fourth woe deals with the question of tithing mint, dill, and cumin (23:23), while the previous third woe condemns the Pharisaic approach to the practice of oaths. Immediately after the fourth woe, Matthew's Jesus criticizes the Pharisees for washing the outside of vessels while failing to clean the inside. In the sixth woe, Matthew's Jesus attaches Pharisaic immorality with the chief of impurities, corpse impurity. The saying about the gnat and the camel, then, appears in the midst of a treatment on a variety of matters stemming from what may be called, for lack of a better word, the "ritual" aspects of the Torah. The deployment of this material, I suggest, while directed against the immoral attitude and outlook of the Pharisees, may presuppose the ongoing importance of observing the dietary and purity systems of the Jewish Law among Matthew and his readers.

Analysis

The precise theological meaning of the enigmatic saying in Matt 7:6 cannot be determined. Nonetheless, Matthew's selection of a saying couched in Jewish terms and symbols as a means of conveying an important belief to his audience is remarkable.[118] First, one should note the attempts to translate the saying back into Aramaic.[119] The probable Semitic back-

---

[118] Besides the attempt to tie it to its immediate literary context, a host of other suggestions exists (anti-Gentile statement; general proverb; pronouncement against Christian apostates, and so on). See standard commentaries. I completely fail to see how with this saying "Jesus transcends the old Rabbinic restriction in Mt 7:6 and describes the majesty of the Gospel in a new way" (Otto Michel, "κύων," *TDNT* 3:1102). A variant form of the first saying (7:6) is attested in the *Gospel of Thomas* 93: "Don't give what is holy to dogs, for they might throw them upon the manure pile. Don't throw pearls [to] pigs, or they might...it [...]" (translation of *Thomas* taken from Patterson-Meyer in Robert J. Miller, ed., *The Complete Gospels* [rev. and enl. ed.; San Francisco, Calif.: HarperSanFrancisco, 1994). The concluding phrase in Matthew, "or they will trample them under foot and turn and maul you," is lacking in Thomas. Luz, *Matthew,* 2:354, thinks Matthew's version of the saying is the oldest. Davies and Allison, *Gospel according to Matthew,* 1:674, think the *Gos. Thom.* preserves a version independent of Matthew. Gundry, *Matthew,* 123, sees the saying in Matthew as entirely redactional, working under the assumption that the *Gos. Thom.* is secondary.

[119] An Aramaic retroversion, however, does not succeed in pinpointing the exact meaning of the saying within its Matthean setting. Some posit a supposed Greek mistranslation of the Aramaic terms קדישא ("ring"), misunderstood as קדשא ("what is holy") and rendering the Greek τὸ ἅγιον. See discussion in Luz, *Matthew,* 1:354.

ground of the saying underscores its provenance from Jewish lore, which could be used in a variety of settings to draw particular moral lessons.[120]

The saying in Matt 7:6 also echoes a halakic concern that scavenger animals such as dogs might eat sacred food or sacrificial offerings.[121] 4QMMT^d 2:2–3 declares that "[one should not let] dogs [enter the ho]ly [camp] [because they might eat some of the b]ones from the te[mple with] the flesh on [them]." A rabbinic halakah, largely corresponding to the first part of the logion in Matt 7:6, states: "All animal-offerings that have been rendered *terefah* may not be redeemed, since animal-offerings may not be redeemed in order to give them as food to the dogs" (*m. Tem.* 6:5).[122] Equally interesting is the following rabbinic prohibition: "They may not rear fowls in Jerusalem because of the Hallowed Things....None may rear swine anywhere. A man may not rear a dog unless it is kept bound by a chain" (*m. B. Qam.* 7:7). The command to keep a dog bound by a chain appears close to the halakah forbidding the raising of fowls (chickens) in Jerusalem on account of the "Holy Things" (הקשדים; cf. τὸ ἅγιον in Matt 7:6), that is, sacrificial food.[123] Apparently, the ban against raising chickens in Jerusalem, which are, after all, kosher animals, also stems from a preoccupation that they might eat sacrificial remains.[124] A fragment from the Dead Sea Scrolls (11QT^c 3:2–5), which also forbids people from raising chickens in Jerusalem, confirms this point.[125]

While Mesopotamian and especially Greco-Roman cultures appreciated dogs,[126] ancient Jewish tradition preserves a predominantly negative atti-

---

[120] Cf. Wiefel, *Das Evangelium nach Matthäus*, 145, who considers the saying "als selbständig umlaufendes Weisheitswort jüdischer Provenienz"; Gnilka, *Matthäusevangelium*, 1:258: "einen sehr jüdisch geprägten Satz." See also Bultmann, *Synoptic Tradition*, 107. Huub van de Sandt, "'Do Not Give What Is Holy to the Dogs' (Did 9:5D and Matt 7:6A): The Eucharistic Food of the Didache in Its Jewish Purity Setting," *VC* 56.3 (2002): 223–46, argues that *Did.* 9:5d, which only contains the reference to throwing holy things to dogs, is more primitive than Matthew and derives from a Jewish expression from that time.

[121] Magness, *Stone and Dung*, 51–52.

[122] Cf. *b. Tem.* 30b. See Gnilka, *Das Matthäusevangelium*, 1:258.

[123] Sandt, "'Do Not Give What Is Holy to the Dogs,'" 231.

[124] Chickens, like dogs, could also transmit impurity by entering into contact with other impure items. See Danby, *The Mishnah*, 342 n. 2, commenting on *m. B. Qam.* 7:7 and its ban on raising chickens in Jerusalem because they were "liable to pick out a lentil's bulk of a dead creeping thing, so conveying uncleanness to houses."

[125] See Elisha Qimron, "Chickens in the Temple Scroll (11QTc)," [in Hebrew] *Tarbiz* 54 (1995): 473–76. Cf. Magness, *Stone and Dung*, 47.

[126] For a brief discussion of Greco-Roman sources, see Christian Hünemörder, "Hund," *DNP* 5:755–58: dogs represent faithfulness (Homer, *Od.* 17:291; Pliny. *Nat.* 8:143, etc.), intelligence/wisdom (Xenophon, *Oec.* 13:8; Aristotle, *Hist. an.* IX; 1; Pliny, *Nat.* 8:147; Plutarch, etc.). Loyal people were positively compared with dogs (Aeschylus, *Ag.* 607; 896; Aristophanes, *Eq.* 1023). Dogs were used for medicinal-magical purposes

tude toward the canine species, especially ownerless dogs (e.g., Ps 59:7, 15).[127] Dogs feed off animal carcasses and human corpses.[128] They even attack passersby (Ps 22:17). Goodfriend notes that because "canines were associated in the Israelite mind with the indiscriminate consumption of blood (a forbidden substance even if its source was a permitted animal)," they were expelled from anything related to sacrifice and sancta.[129] The term dog is often employed as an insult, particularly in the literature covering the lives of Israel's monarchs (1 Sam 17:43; 24:14; 2 Sam 9:8; cf. 2 Sam 3:8; 16:9; 2 Kgs 8:13). Quite interestingly, the term is often employed against Gentiles, the most pertinent passage appearing nowhere else than in Matt 15:26 (and Mark 7:27) where Jesus disparagingly replies to the Syrophoenician woman, "it is not fair to take the children's food and throw it to the dogs" (cf. Phil 3:2; Rev 22:15). Sim even interprets Matt 7:6 along with 15:26 and 13:45–46 (where the kingdom of heaven is likened to pearls) as evidence that Matthew was not actively involved in a Gentile mission.[130]

(Plin. *Nat.* 29:99–101). For Mesopotamia, see Edwin Firmage, "Zoology," *ABD* 6:1143–44: dogs played a role in rituals performed for the removal of impurity and disease in both Anatolia and Mesopotamia. Often in these rites, dogs were associated with young pigs. Dogs along with pigs were also used in the ritual of Lamaštu-exorcisms; images of dogs were used in Hittite rituals designed to exorcise evil spirits from royal palaces. One thinks also of the canine representation of the Egyptian god Anubis. Joshua Schwartz, "Dogs in Jewish Society in the Second Temple Period and in the Time of the Mishnah and Talmud," *JJS* 55 (2004): 250: "Dogs were quite popular in the Graeco-Roman world." On pp. 251–53, Schwartz claims that Romans were "mad" about dogs, but those most fond of dogs were the Persians who even venerated them.

[127] Alfred Ely Day, "Dog," *ISBE* 1:980–81; Jehuda Feliks, "Dog," *EJ* 5:733. For domestic dogs, see Tob 5:16; 11:4. The Hebrew Bible, however, does not always portray dogs in a negative light. See Geoffrey D. Miller, "Attitudes towards Dogs in Ancient Israel," *JSOT* 32 (2008): 487–500.

[128] 1 Kgs 14:11; 16:4; 21:19, 23; 23:38.

[129] Elaine Adler Goodfriend, "Could *Keleb* in Deuteronomy 23:19 Actually Refer to a Canine?" in *Pomegranates and Golden Bells: Studies in Biblical, Jewish, and Near Eastern Ritual, Law, and Literature in Honor of Jacob Milgrom* (eds. David P. Wright et al.; Winona Lake, Ind.: Eisenbrauns, 1995), 395–96.

[130] Sim, *The Gospel of Matthew and Christian Judaism*, 237–39. Reservations toward sharing the Torah with Gentiles occasionally appear in rabbinic literature (e.g., *b. Hag.* 13a; *b. Ketub.* 111a). Occasionally, the term dog is also used in a derogative way to deride Gentiles (*b. Avod. Zar.* 46a; *b. Meg.* 7b, etc.). These attestations cannot be used indiscriminately to posit a systematic, rabbinic reluctance to share the Torah with non-Jews. Hirshman, "Rabbinic Universalism in the Second and Third Centuries," 101–15; *Torah for the Entire World*, identifies a "universalist" stream within the Tannaitic literature, which he ascribes to the school of R. Ishmael. This school thought the Torah should be made available to the nations of the world and welcomed the conversion of Gentiles into Judaism.

The derogatory reference to filthy and non-kosher dogs appears in Matt 7:6 in conjunction with another nefariously impure animal, the pig. This is not the only passage where dogs and pigs appear next to each in Jewish tradition in a negative light. In fact, Schwartz maintains that there is a patent connection between dogs and pigs within certain rabbinic texts as exemplified in the following saying attributed to R. Eleazar: "the one who raises dogs is tantamount to the one who raises pigs."[131] Classical sources single the Jewish abstention from eating pork above all other impure animals.[132] This Jewish abstention stands in stark contrast to the widespread consumption and appreciation of pork among Greeks and Romans, particularly those living in Rome.[133] Pigs were also one of the most commonly sacrificed animals in the Roman Empire.[134] Not surprisingly, ancient Jewish literature exalts the abstention from consuming or sacrificing pigs as a fundamental expression of loyalty to Judaism,[135] and the rabbinic sages eventually associated the very image of the pig with Rome itself.[136]

Could the very solicitation of such images of non-kosher animals, so repulsive to Jewish taste, be used as evidence for a Matthean affirmation of kashrut? It is possible that if Matthew found such creatures disgusting, he would also not have eaten them.[137] Presumably, the Matthean logion would enjoy its fullest rhetorical effect among readers who kept kosher, although the saying by itself does not prove that Matthew kept the Jewish dietary laws. After all, other "Christian" documents also retained and employed such imagery for various purposes. We have already noted the parallel in *Did.* 9:5, which prohibits certain persons from participating in the Eucha-

---

[131] *T. B. Qam.* 8:17, translation from Schwartz, "Dogs in Jewish Society," 269. See his comments on the passage and other pertinent rabbinic references on p. 269 n. 125.

[132] Jordan D. Rosenblum, "'Why Do You Refuse to Eat Pork?' Jews, Food, and Identity in Roman Palestine," *JQR* 100 (2010): 95–110.

[133] Thus, Varro (c. 30 BCE) wonders: "Who of our people [i.e., Romans] cultivates a farm without keeping swine? (*Rust.* 2.4.3)" (translation taken from Rosenblum). By contrast, the rabbinic sages express their repugnance against swine with the following saying: "None may rear swine anywhere" (*m. B. Qam.* 7:7).

[134] Rosenblum, "'Why Do You Refuse to Eat Pork?'" 97.

[135] 1 Macc 1:44–50; 2 Macc 6:18–7:42; 4 Macc 5; Philo, *Flacc.* 95–96; Josephus, *Ant.* 12:253; 13:243.

[136] *Avot R. Nat.* A 34; *Lev. Rab.* 13:5; *Eccl. Rab.* 1:9. See Str-B 1:449–50 and especially, Rosenblum, "'Why Do You Refuse to Eat Pork?'" 100–110.

[137] Davies and Allison, *The Gospel according to Saint Matthew*, 1:675, capture some of the significance of the use of such language: "In Mat 7.6 this rule, by virtue of its new context, becomes a comprehensive statement about the necessity to keep distinct the realms of clean and unclean."

rist.[138] In its current literary setting, the parallel logion in the *Gospel of Thomas* (93) might articulate how the mysteries of the kingdom are to remain hidden from outsiders, without implying for the compilers of this document that the observance of Jewish food laws is still in force.[139] The author of *Barnabas* (ch. 10) even allegorizes the impurity of the forbidden animals in Lev 11 to convince his readers that they should not observe kashrut at all. Nevertheless, there are no such abrogating tendencies in Matthew, and even the allegorizing process in *Barnabas* might evince an effort on the part of its author to dissuade other followers of Jesus from persisting in the literal observance of the Mosaic legislation.[140]

In addition, the saying in Matt 23:24, which also contains its pair of non-kosher animals, a gnat and a camel, might indirectly speak on behalf of Matthew's observance of kashrut. As noted above, this logion appears right after the denunciation of Pharisaic scruples over tithing mint, dill, and cumin (23:23). The criticism in Matthew, however, concerns not so much the tithing of such plants but an over-preoccupation with such matters at the cost of neglecting more important issues, "the weightier matters of the law" (τὰ βαρύτερα τοῦ νόμου), such as justice, mercy, and faithfulness: "It is these you ought to have practiced *without neglecting the others*" (Mat 23:23b; emphasis mine). The import of this statement as a hermeneutical key for understanding Matthew's overall perspective on the Torah should not be underestimated.[141] This statement concerns not only the narrower question of tithing but also Matthew's approach to the ques-

---

[138] Nevertheless, an affirmation of the observance of kashrut may find some indirect support in *Did.* 6:2–3. See Draper, "The Holy Vine of David Made Known to the Gentiles through God's Servant Jesus: 'Christian Judaism' in the *Didache*," 257–84.

[139] Cf. 2 Pet 2:22: "It has happened to them according to the true proverb, 'The dog turns back to its own vomit,' and, 'The sow is washed only to wallow in the mud.'" See also *Papyrus Oxyrhynchus* 840: "You have washed yourself in these running waters where dogs and pigs have wallowed day and night" (2:7). On the halakic features of papyrus 840, see Ze'ev Safrai and Chana Safrai ז״ל, "Papyrus Oxyrhynchus 840," in *Halakhah in Light of Epigraphy*, 255–82. Cf. François Bovon, "*Fragment Oxyrhynchus 840*, Fragment of a Lost Gospel, Witness of an Early Christian Controversy over Purity," *JBL* 119 (2000): 705–28.

[140] See, for example, Mimouni, *Le judéo-christianisme ancien*, 191, who thinks that *Barnabas* was written to a "Jewish Christian" audience.

[141] Cf. Kinzer, *Postmissionary*, 59–60, who ties this verse with Matt 5:19 ("whoever breaks one of the least of these commandments, and teaches others to do the same, will be called least in the kingdom of heaven"): "What is most remarkable about Matthew 5:19 and 23:23, however, is that both texts affirm that attentive obedience to the weightier/greater commandments should not lead to violation or neglect of the lighter/lesser commandments."

tion of the Jewish Law in all of its aspects, ethical and ritual.[142] Matthew does not oppose in absolute terms the observance of commandments so often labeled (with negative overtones) as "ceremonial," "cultic," or "ritual," over against the higher and loftier "moral law." On the contrary, he affirms their observance so long as they do not take precedence over ethical concerns. The same argument holds true for Luke who retains a similar statement: "But woe to you Pharisees! For you tithe mint and rue and herbs of all kinds, and neglect justice and the love of God; it is these you ought to have practiced, without neglecting the others" (11:41). I see no basis, therefore, for perpetuating a false dichotomy that uses the same statement on tithing as evidence for Matthew's affirmation of the Torah, on the one hand, and Luke's abrogation of the Jewish Law, on the other:

> The next step is taken then by Luke for whom in all probability the commandment to tithe has become obsolete along with all ritual commandments (Acts 10). For his Gentile Christian readers – and for almost all Gentile Christian readers of the later centuries – the commandment to tithe cooking herbs becomes something strange and bizarre, and the scribes and Pharisees become its representatives.[143]

Strangely, the same attestation can be read in one gospel as an affirmation of the practice of tithing and other ritual commandments while understood in the exact opposite way in another text. In my opinion, this contradictory reading of the same statement results from presuppositions concerning the supposed Jewish-Christian vs. Gentile-Christian texture of Matthew and Luke-Acts that has governed largely their interpretation.

No Mosaic regulation explicitly requires Jews to tithe herbs such as mint, dill, and cumin.[144] In Deut 14:23, only grain, wine, oil, and flocks are explicitly mentioned. However, Lev 27:30 ("All tithes from the land, whether the seed from the ground or the fruit from the tree") and Deut 14:22 ("a tithe of all the yield of your seed that is brought in yearly from the field") could have led some scrupulous Jews to infer that even herbs should be tithed.[145] The Pharisaic concern to tithe herbs reflects an effort to

---

[142] Hagner, *Matthew,* 2:670, seems to restrict the import of the phrase, "not forsaking the others," to the practice of tithing. David E. Garland, *The Intention of Matthew 23* (NovTSup 52; Leiden: Brill, 1979), 140, represses the significance of Matt 23:23b to "an earlier tradition which cannot be pressed too far theologically." Correctly, Loader, *Jesus' Attitude towards the Law,* 241: "This confirms the impression that Matthew assumes the validity of Torah and its application, even in areas such as tithing."

[143] Luz, *Matthew,* 2:125.

[144] For tithing in the Second Temple period, see Sanders, *Jewish Law from Jesus to the Mishnah,* 44–48; Schürer-Vermes, 2:263–65.

[145] See *m. Ma'as.* 1:1. In *m. Ma'as.* 4:5, dill is specifically mentioned along with other herbs. Cumin appears as tithable in *m. Dem.* 2:1, although some rabbinic sages treat certain herbs as "wild" and consequently non-tithable. Cf. *m. Hul.* 1:6 with respect to the tithing of sweet and bitter almonds.

carry out the commandment of tithing all agricultural products, even those that do not clearly fall under the category of "produce," in a meticulous way. Despite their commendable efforts, the Pharisees, so Matthew claims, overlook the weightier matters of the law. In the words of a catchy, proverbial saying, they "strain out a gnat but swallow a camel!" Has Matthew penned this dictum, drawn it from a source, or borrowed it from a thesaurus of Jewish proverbs? A wordplay in the probable Aramaic *Vorlage* of this saying occurs between the words "gnat" (קלמא) and "camel" (גמלא).[146] Matthew has introduced the saying with the polemical vocative, ὁδηγοὶ τυφλοί ("blind guides"), in order to condemn Pharisees for causing other Jews to transgress the Torah.[147] However, the logion could be easily used or inserted in a variety of settings to illustrate or make a (moral) point. In Luke's diatribe of woeful sayings against the Pharisees and lawyers (11:39–52), this logion is missing entirely. Perhaps, Matthew himself added and adapted the logion from a "lexicon" of Jewish sayings in order to express his point more vividly.[148] In any case, Matthew employs the saying to denounce the allegedly misguided Pharisaic superimposition of "ritual" practices upon "moral" concerns. Once again, for the proverb to carry its full weight, an ongoing abhorrence toward consuming forbidden creatures such as gnats and camels might be presupposed not only on the part of the Pharisees, the target of criticism, but also on the part of Matthew and his readers.

According to the Jewish dietary system, both the gnat and the camel are non-kosher animals. Lev 11:20 states: "All winged insects that walk upon all fours are detestable to you." Only certain types of locusts were permissible for consumption (Lev 11:21–22). Lev 11:4 and Deut 14:7 explicitly single out the camel as one of the quadrupeds forbidden for consumption. It is the largest impure animal living in the region of Palestine. The gnat, on the other hand, represents the smallest of impure creatures. Pharisees, like some other Jews, would have strained out gnats from their drinks (e.g., wine) with a sieve or other device in order to avoid consuming such forbidden insects.[149] Surprisingly, some rabbinic passages actually allow Jews

---

[146] Cf. saying in *b. Shabb.* 12a, "If one kills vermin on the Sabbath, it is as though he killed a camel" (הורג כינה בשבת כאילו הורג גמל).

[147] Cf. Luz, *Matthew,* 2:125.

[148] Luz, *Matthew,* 2:122, seems certain that the saying (apart from the address of "blind leaders") is pre-Matthean, going back to Q(Mt), but provides no argument. Nevertheless, he conjectures that the saying was not originally part of the fourth woe but was inserted into Q. The question is whether such a saying was coined by the earliest followers of Jesus or was simply borrowed from a common stock of Jewish sayings reappropriated by Matthew with the aim of condemning Pharisees.

[149] Maccoby, *Ritual and Morality,* 71. On filtering wine, see, for example, *m. Shabb.* 20:2; *b. Hul.* 67a.

to consume gnats found in liquids. In fact, some of these passages even condemn the practice of straining out gnats as "heresy."

> [And as to] gnats which are [found] in wine and vinegar, lo, these are permitted. [If] he strained them [out of the wine or vinegar], lo, these are forbidden. R. Judah says, "One who strains wine and vinegar, and one who recites a blessing for the sun [*t. Ber.* 6:6] – lo, this is heresy.[150]

Similarly, in *b. Hul.* 67a, a baraita forbids eating "every creeping thing that creepeth upon the earth" (Lev 11:41), including "insects found in liquids that have been passed through a strainer," the reason being that during the process of straining the creeping creature (either insects or worms) might have "crept," that is, "crawled" on the strainer (e.g., on the twigs used to filter the liquid) and thereby become a "creeping thing that creepeth upon the earth." Before the act of straining, the rabbis view the insect or worm as having always lived in the liquid and never crept on the earth. They therefore consider such insects or worms permitted for consumption.[151] On the other hand, as Magness notes, whereas Lev 11:41–44 forbids the consumption of creatures that creep (or "swarm") on the earth, the *Damascus Document* seems to prohibit even land-based creatures that swarm *in the water*. "No one may defile himself (ישקץ) with any creature or creeping thing by eating them: from the larvae of bees to any living creature that crawls in the water" (CD 12:11–13).[152] "Apparently, some Jewish groups of the late Second Temple period, including the Qumran sect, understood the legislation in Leviticus as prohibiting the consumption of all swarming creatures in water – not just fish without fins and scales but land-based swarming creatures such as insects and larvae as well."[153]

In Lev 11, among the swarming creatures only the eight vermin listed in Lev 11:29–30 are deemed "impure" (וזה לכם הטמא בשרץ השרץ). This is how the rabbis also understood the matter, not viewing insects or worms as impure but merely "detestable" (שקץ). Magness, however, argues that the Qumran sect took a more stringent position, viewing all swarming creatures that were forbidden for consumption as "impure."[154] Sanders had initially understood Lev 11:33–36 as referring primarily to insects, that they could defile vessels and liquids and were viewed by ancient Jews as

---

[150] *T. Ter.* 7:11. Translation taken from Magness, *Stone and Dung*, 35–36.

[151] See notes on *b. Hul.* 67a in the Soncino translation.

[152] This passage from CD, however, has its textual difficulties. See Schiffman, "Laws Pertaining to Forbidden Foods," 66–67.

[153] Magness, *Stone and Dung*, 35, also pointing to the remains of ancient food items infested with insects and their larvae that were found in excavations at Masada, illustrating how food preservation was a common problem for Jews during the Second Temple period.

[154] Magness, *Stone and Dung*, 34.

one of the main carriers of impurity.[155] Nevertheless, Maccoby has since then provided a corrective on this matter, arguing that Lev 11:33–36 refers (at least according to the rabbinic understanding) only to the eight categories of vermin singled out in Lev 11:29–30. In other words, dead insects do not render vessels, moist food, and liquids impure; only the eight vermin do.[156] Indeed, Sanders later changed his mind in his subsequent book on Jewish halakah.[157]

Is it likely that the group(s) standing behind the Damascus Document would have viewed all swarming creatures as ritually defiling? If this were true, then probably all their vessels and liquids would acquire impurity on a regular basis because of the many (dead) insects ("swarming creatures of the air") that would inevitably invade their residences in ancient, hot Palestine. Might it not have been more practical for them to declare all swarming creatures, including land-based swarming creatures such as worms, larvae (frequently found in foodstuffs such as fruit) and gnats (technically not a creature that "swarms in the water," but nevertheless residing in liquids such as wine) as *forbidden* for consumption rather than *defiling* (i.e., rendering something or someone ritually impure)? I believe the passage Magness cites (CD 12:11–13, 19–20) is open to such an interpretation. CD 12:11, following the language of Lev 11:44, only states that a person should not make his or her soul *detestable* (אל תשקצו איש את נפשו), but Magness seems to understand the verb תשקצו in the sense of *defiling*, that is, to render impure. Magness argues that the "Qumran sect" would have objected to the consumption of gnats found in liquids in contrast to some of the rabbinic sages. But if the "Qumranites" considered insects found in water to be defiling, would they not have to discard the entire drink (along with the vessel containing it, depending on what material it was made out of) rather than simply strain the gnats and then drink the liquid, assuming gnats could occasionally be found *dead* in the liquids ancient Jews strained? As Magness correctly argues, the saying in Matt 23:24 reflects a halakic controversy over the issue of consuming small insects that inevitably found their way into liquids such as wine and vinegar. However, the Matthean saying makes better sense against a halakic backdrop that views gnats in liquids simply as *forbidden* rather than *impure*. Otherwise, would straining not prove to be a futile exercise, since the gnats (and other insects), if dead, would render the liquids they inhabited impure as well? In other words, some ancient Jews would strain gnats from

---

[155] Sanders, *Jewish Law from Jesus to the Mishnah*, 138.
[156] *Ritual and Morality*, 69.
[157] *Judaism: Practice and Belief,* 520 n. 17.

their drinks simply because these creatures were not permitted for consumption.[158]

Matthew hyperbolically (and unfairly) accuses the Pharisees, as they busy themselves in filtering out insects from their drinks, for eating camels, the largest forbidden animal in the region of Palestine. In concrete terms, this would amount to tithing herbs while failing to tithe more obvious food items such as cereal. But, once again, Matthew employs the proverb to critique the Pharisaic (over-?) preoccupation with ritual matters while ignoring the "big camel in the room," namely, the practice of justice, mercy, and faithfulness. I would suggest that the very usage of the Jewish saying might presuppose the abstinence on the part of Matthew and some of his readers from eating non-kosher animals such as camels.[159] While Matthew may not have condemned Jews for failing to exert themselves rigorously in tithing all agricultural items (e.g., herbs) and consistently refraining from consuming little bugs caught in their liquids, he would certainly have upheld tithing produce in general and observing the basic, undisputed stipulations of kashrut (e.g., avoiding eating pork, camels, etc.).

As an ensemble, the two very Jewish sayings assessed above that refer to impure animals, ranging from dogs to pigs, gnats to camels, underscores Matthew's acquaintance and appreciation of a repertoire of Jewish proverbs and lore. These sayings might also point to Matthew's affirmation of the observance of the Jewish food laws. Much of secondary scholarship, obsessed with determining the precise theological meaning of such sayings, has forgotten to assess the significance of the very appropriation of such Jewish metaphors and symbols. Camels, dogs, gnats, and pigs repre-

---

[158] Correctly, Maccoby, *Ritual and Morality*, 71. Perhaps, some Jews thought that by eating forbidden insects trapped in liquids they were defiling themselves in a "moral" or "inner" sense, because they believed such an act seriously compromised with the observance of kashrut. I would like to thank Jodi Magness for kindly sharing some of her thoughts with me on this whole issue.

[159] Alternatively, one could posit a greater distance between Matthew and his readers and the halakic presuppositions embedded in this saying: *they,* that is, the Pharisees, strain gnats but eat camels, which are forbidden for them (but not for us). I find this reading less compelling. The saying is certainly mocking Pharisees, but the usage of the Jewish vocabulary and themes as well as the juxtaposition of Matt 23:24 with the preceding statement in v. 23, suggest an ongoing affirmation of the ritual aspects of the Torah. Douglas R. A. Hare, "How Jewish is the Gospel of Matthew?" *CBQ* 62 (2000): 271, downplays the import of v. 23: "Similarly, 23:23 must not be taken as proof that Matthew and his readers rigorously tithed their garden herbs and expected Gentile converts to do the same. Rather than demanding such observance, the saying radically diminishes the importance of such scrupulous tithing by hyperbolically subordinating it to ethical concerns in the attached saying, 'You blind guides! You strain out a gnat but swallow a camel!' (23:24)." Perhaps Matthew does not expect Gentiles to tithe their produce, but what about Jews?

sent not just allegorized symbols used by Matthew to make a theological point. They may point to a real disgust shared by Matthew and his readers toward consuming such creatures. At the very least, Matthew employs imagery of animals forbidden by the Jewish dietary system in order to draw analogies that he thinks his audience will find meaningful.

Non-Kosher Food in Impure Vessels: Matt 23:25–26

Literary Context

The final text in Matthew, which deals in part with food laws, appears in the same literary context as the previous passage assessed above (Matt 23:24).[160] As the fifth woe in Matthew's anti-Pharisaic diatribe, it appears right after the proverbial saying on the gnat and the camel. It is, therefore, also surrounded by material discussing ritual aspects of Torah praxis: oaths, tithes, food laws, and corpse impurity. These observations on the literary context should already deter one from viewing the contents of the fifth woe as merely reflecting hygienic concerns rather than ritual matters.[161]

Interpretation

The passage is of some relevance for the discussion of kashrut as it contains a reference to the purification of utensils, drinking vessels, and dishes that were used for the consumption of food and liquids. Indeed, this passage presents a borderline case between the systems of ritual impurity and kashrut that should warn against being too orthodox in dividing the Torah into ritual, moral, and dietary realms, since in reality the occasional terminological and conceptual overlap between these spheres occurs.[162] Thus, in the midst of a chapter dealing with forbidden, non-kosher animals, Lev 11:29–35 treats the topic of impurity acquired through contact with the dead bodies of certain creatures:

These are unclean for you among the creatures that swarm upon the earth: the weasel, the mouse, the great lizard according to its kind, the gecko, the land crocodile, the lizard, the sand lizard, and the chameleon. These are unclean for you among all that swarm; whoever touches one of them when they are dead shall be unclean until the evening. And anything upon which any of them falls when they are dead shall be unclean, whether an

---

[160] Matt 23:25–26 shares a parallel in Luke 11:39–41, which is discussed in the next chapter.

[161] Contra Hyam Maccoby, "The Washing of Cups," *JSNT* 14 (1982): 3–15.

[162] Kazen, *Issues of Impurity in Early Judaism,* 153–56.

article of wood or cloth or skin or sacking, any article that is used for any purpose; it shall be dipped into water, and it shall be unclean until the evening, and then it shall be clean. And if any of them falls into any earthen vessel, all that is in it shall be unclean, and you shall break the vessel. Any food that could be eaten shall be unclean if water from any such vessel comes upon it; and any liquid that could be drunk shall be unclean if it was in any such vessel. Everything on which any part of the carcass falls shall be unclean; whether an oven or stove, it shall be broken in pieces; they are unclean, and shall remain unclean for you.

The first part of this lengthy passage lists the eight "swarming" (שרץ)[163] creatures (mice, lizards, etc.) that convey impurity not only through ingestion but also through touch (when dead). These eight creatures would often find their way into houses and, because of their rather small size, could frequently end up inside vessels.[164] Their corpses could render vessels impure, but also wet foodstuffs. Vessels and food were more likely to incur impurity from such swarming things than any other source.[165] The rabbis frequently discuss scenarios where vessels acquire impurity through such contact (e.g., *m. Kel.* 8:18; 9:3; 10:9). Hence, the utility of stone vessels, at least for those who considered them immune to impurity, for preventing such contamination.[166] Vessels could also contract impurity from sources other than the eight vermin, including a human corpse (Num 19:14–15; 31:19–23) and a person suffering from a genital discharge (Lev 15:4, 12).

The major exegetical difficulty with Matt 23:25–26 lies in the apparent distinction made between the "inside" (τὸ ἔξωθεν/τὸ ἐκτός) and "outside" (ἔσωθεν/τὸ ἐντός) of a vessel. Such a distinction is also presupposed in *m. Kel.* 25:1 (cf. *m. Kel.* 25:7): "In all vessels an outer part and an inner part are distinguished." The saying in Matthew, however, further assumes that the inner and outer parts of vessels enjoy some kind of autonomy when it comes to the contraction of impurity: apparently, the outside of a vessel can become impure without necessarily defiling its inside (or vice versa). Yet (what came to be) the predominant rabbinic perspective views the *interior* part of a vessel as determinative with respect to impurity: "If a vessel's outer part was rendered unclean by [unclean] liquid, its inner part, rims, hangers, and handles remain clean. But if its inner part becomes

---

[163] According to Milgrom, *Leviticus*, 1:655, שרץ includes more generally all small creatures that go about in shoals and swarms, insects that fly in clouds, such as gnats and flies, and small creatures such as weasels, mice, and lizard that are low on the ground. Only the corpses of the eight swarming creatures, however, convey impurity.

[164] See Milgrom, *Leviticus*, 1:671.

[165] Maccoby, *Ritual and Morality*, 74: "The 'creeping things' are animals that were often found in houses, and their dead bodies were not infrequently found inside vessels. Impurity was incurred by humans and vessels more often from 'creeping things' than from any other source. This accounts for the fact that in the rabbinic literature the 'creeping thing' or *sheretz* is regarded as the paradigm case or archetype of impurity."

[166] Deines, *Jüdische Steingefäße*, 180.

unclean the whole is unclean" (*m. Kel.* 25:6). At least according to this ruling from the Mishnah, the saying in Matthew would prove meaningless: if the inside is impure and affects the whole vessel, the inside will always be washed "first."[167]

In response to this problem, Neusner suggests that prior to 70 CE the Shammaite position maintained that the outer part of a vessel could remain pure even if its interior was impure. For Neusner, the saying in *m. Kel.* 25:1, 7, "in all utensils an outer and an inner part are distinguished," does not explicitly declare that the impurity of the inside automatically affects the status of the outside, implying that before the completion of the Mishnah the inner and outer sides of a vessel were viewed as autonomous parts. In the post-70 developments of rabbinic Judaism, the Hillelite position solidified, claiming the inside as determinative for establishing the impurity of a vessel as a whole. From this perspective, the saying in Matthew becomes meaningful. Neusner not only seriously considers the gospel literature as a source about Jewish halakah but also provides a way for comprehending the halakic substance undergirding the saying in Matthew.[168] The opinion voiced by Jesus in Matthew, then, would seem to presuppose the priority of cleansing the interior of a vessel, positioning itself more closely to the Hillelite view. The statement in Matthew would indirectly denounce the Shammaite prioritization of purifying the outer parts of a vessel, although Matthew uses it primarily to condemn Pharisaic hypocrisy.

The statement in Matthew does not deny that the eight vermin cannot render the interior of a vessel impure. It only denounces a skewed prioritization that comes very close to the point made earlier about hand washing

---

[167] In many cases, such vessels would undergo complete immersion, making the distinctions between inside and outside, in so far as purification is concerned, pointless. See *m. Mikw.* 5:6; 6:2. Cf. Maccoby, "The Washing of Cups," 5, who, failing to discuss *m. Kel.* 25:6, probably exaggerates his point: "It is unquestionable that there was only one way of washing ritually-unclean vessels, whether wholly or partly unclean: to immerse them totally in the water of the *Miqveh*." On p. 12 n. 2, he cites Maimonides, *Mishneh Torah, Mikw.* 1:1. But *m. Kel.* 25:6 states: "If [unclean] liquid fell on to the bases, rims, hangers, or handles of vessels that have a receptacle, they need but to be dried (מנגבן) and they are clean."

[168] Jacob Neusner, "First Cleanse the Inside: The 'Halakhic' Background of a Controversy-Saying," *NTS* 22 (1976): 487–88: "Now when we are told, 'First cleanse the inside,' what can be the state of the law? Granted, we have a moral teaching about the priority of the inner condition of a person. Yet for that teaching to be tied to the metaphor of the purity-rule about the distinction between the inside and the outside of a cup as determinative of the condition, as to purity, of the cup as a whole, what shall we make of the instruction first to clean the inside of the cup?...For the metaphor to be useful, therefore, it must be addressed to people who either do not first of all clean the inside, or for whom the priority of the inside of the utensil is moot."

before meals (Matt 15:11, 17–20) and the distinction between the internal/moral and external/ritual realms of purity. Thus, in 15:11, 17–20, Matthew emphasizes the defiling power of evil thoughts coming from the *inside* of a person's heart above the external contamination acquired through eating with impure hands; in 23:25–26, the inner parts of vessels symbolize the Pharisees' hearts, which are allegedly filled with greed and self-indulgence.

Quite remarkably, the subsequent verses (vv. 27–28) to 23:25 also express this theme in a similar way:

καθαρίζετε τὸ <u>ἔξωθεν</u> τοῦ ποτηρίου καὶ τῆς παροψίδος, <u>ἔσωθεν δὲ γέμουσιν</u> ἐξ ἁρπαγῆς καὶ ἀκρασίας (v.25).

<u>ἔξωθεν</u> μὲν φαίνονται ὡραῖοι, <u>ἔσωθεν δὲ γέμουσιν</u> ὀστέων νεκρῶν καὶ πάσης ἀκαθαρσίας (v.27).

<u>ἔξωθεν</u> μὲν φαίνεσθε τοῖς ἀνθρώποις δίκαιοι, <u>ἔσωθεν δέ</u> ἐστε μεστοὶ ὑποκρίσεως καὶ ἀνομίας (v. 28).

These verses employ the same distinctive language that separates the outer from the inner (ἔξωθεν/ἔσωθεν).[169] The outside appears welcoming and clean. But Matthew claims that the Pharisees are full (γέμουσιν) of moral impurities on the inside: according to v. 26, they are filled with greed and self-indulgence; according to vv. 27–28, with hypocrisy and lawlessness. Defilement contracted from a human corpse represents one of the highest degrees of ritual impurity possible, requiring the sprinkling of water mixed with the ashes of the red heifer as a procedure for purification (Num 19:11–22) no longer executable after the destruction of the temple.

The polemical declarations in 23:27–28 that compare Pharisees with impure tombs and bones, like so many of the Jewish metaphors singled out in this chapter, become particularly pertinent if the readers know and accept such halakic categories about kashrut and purity. If Matthew mocks the Pharisees for resembling whitewashed tombs, he does so because, arguably, he still holds onto to Jewish notions concerning corpse impurity. Modern readers should not forget that the spirit of this metaphor was originally linked with the flesh and bones of a concrete Jewish system of praxis appropriated by Matthew to ridicule his opponents in sarcastic and polemical ways. This derision of Pharisaic praxis might also imply an ongoing appreciation and concern on Matthew's part to observe the entire Torah in a proper way. Matthew is certainly not openly refuting the necessity for Jews to purify vessels defiled by the dead bodies of impure vermin. He deploys such imagery only to blame his opponents for focusing on external (ritual) matters while overlooking the weightier, inner (or moral) commandments of the Torah. Nothing in this passage speaks against the con-

---

[169] On the importance of "inner" and "outer" impurity in Matt 23:25–28, see Kazen, *Jesus and Purity Halakhah*, 223–28.

tinual observance of kashrut, which like many other purity matters, remains in full force for Matthew.

Conclusion

No passage surveyed in this chapter suggests a Matthean abrogation of kashrut. The controversy in Matt 15:1–20 about hand washing before meals is nothing more than that, a debate about ritual purity, not dietary laws, even if Matthew includes the word "mouth" into the key statement found in 15:11, 17:

> When Jesus says there that it is not "what goes into the mouth that defiles a man, but what comes out of the mouth, this defiles a man" (11), he is not deprecating the laws of kashruth and abrogating them but resisting the halakhic innovations of the Pharisees, which these wish to impose as traditions of the elders. With respect to the hand-washing ritual before eating, the Evangelist surely has the upper hand historically. Rabbinic literature is still at some pains hundreds of years later to justify this relatively new (and apparently sectarian) practice.[170]

Elsewhere in this chapter (Matt 7:6, 23:24, 25–26), I have searched for traces that might indirectly affirm Matthew's observance of kashrut.[171] The

---

[170] Boyarin, *Borderlines,* 251–52 n. 125.

[171] Another passage that could possibly have some bearing on our understanding of kashrut in Matthew would be the description of John the Baptist's diet of wild honey and locusts (Matt 3:4; cf. Mark 1:6). While sectarian law mandated that locusts be cooked alive (either with fire or water) before being eaten (CD 12:14–15), rabbinic halakah allowed Jews to eat live or dead locusts (*t. Ter.* 9:6). Magness, *Stone and Dung,* 39, notes: "It seems unlikely that John followed sectarian law and ate only locusts that he caught alive and then cooked, as such an exceptional practice presumably would have been noticed and mentioned in the Gospel accounts." James A. Kelhoffer, "Did John the Baptist Eat like a Former Essene? Locust-Eating in the Ancient Near East and at Qumran," *DSD* 11 (2004): 293–314, asserts that the gospel accounts do not describe John eating specific types of locusts because they "were not intended primarily for an audience that was concerned with the finer details of kashrut. Especially in light of Mark 7:1–23//Matt. 15:1–20, which dispense with such requirements, this observation may come as no surprise" (p. 314). Kelhoffer's latter point can certainly not be maintained for the gospel of Matthew. Remarkably, both Mark and Matthew claim that John ate *wild* honey. As Magness remarks, this description reflects John's ascetic lifestyle *and* his concern for maintaining purity, as he only consumed wild rather than processed food (pp. 39–40). Cf. 2 Macc 5:27: "But Judas Maccabeus, with about nine others, got away to the wilderness, and kept himself and his companions alive in the mountains as wild animals do; they continued to live on what grew wild, so that they might not share in the defilement." John's lifestyle has been compared to Bannus' (Josephus, *Life* 11). See Hermann Lichtenberger, "The Dead Sea Scrolls and John the Baptist: Reflections on Josephus' Account of John the Baptist," in *The Dead Sea Scrolls: Forty Years of Research* (eds. Devorah Dimant and Uriel Rappaport; STDJ 10; Leiden: Brill, 1992), 340–46.

evidence, while suggestive, at the very least shows how meaningful and useful the appropriation of Jewish imagery from the worlds of kashrut and purity remains for Matthew and his readers. It is possible that Matthew proverbially mocks Pharisees for swallowing camels because he refrains from eating such forbidden animals. Likewise, if he believes that pigs and dogs symbolize filth and immorality, then it is possible that he also finds them disgusting as food. If he metaphorically condemns Pharisees for cleaning the outside of their vessels, while neglecting their inside, it is possible that he also believes that impure creatures such as the eight vermin can defile bowls and other kinds of dishes. Matthew's rich and persistent solicitation of symbols from the world of Jewish praxis for the development of spiritual and theological reflection may also inform us about his observance of the Torah.

Chapter 9

Food Laws in Luke

"Do not neglect to show hospitality to strangers, for by doing that some have entertained angels without knowing it."
(Hebrews 13:11)

Introduction

Two pericopes in the gospel of Luke necessitate careful analysis for the investigation of the question of kashrut: Luke 11:37–41, a pericope that really deals with purity matters, not kashrut, and Luke 10:1–11, reporting the commission of the seventy-two, which has been understood by some as granting the right for Jewish followers of Jesus to eat *whatever* their Gentile hosts serve them, including non-kosher food. I will argue that in 11:37–41 Luke, more consistently and clearly than Matthew, only argues against a misguided prioritization of ritual matters over against ethical concerns while presupposing the ongoing observance of kashrut and even approving the Jewish endeavor to keep purity laws. The commission to the seventy-two in 10:1–11, which admittedly contains a (secondary) universal dimension to it, does not encourage Jews to eat forbidden food. Luke's emphasis throughout this pericope centers on the right for Jesus' itinerant messengers to receive their pay when they visit a new home or town. This includes accepting the food and lodging offered to them by their hosts, but Luke's main point is not to declare that Jewish followers of Jesus may eat *anything* presented before them.

Perfecting Pharisaic Purity: Luke 11:37–41

Literary Context

Luke does not retain Mark's story about the controversy of hand washing, but he does report an incident that is quite similar, albeit without retaining most of the material and argumentation found in Mark 7:1–23.[1] Luke places his story within a reoccurring setting so peculiar to his gospel: during a meal at the house of a Pharisee (cf. Luke 7:36; 14:1–6). Potential for constructive dialogue between both parties, however, quickly vanishes in a pericope that contains some of the direst statements in Luke against (some) Pharisees (vv. 39–52; cf. 12:1). After Jesus deliberates on the washing of vessels, he delivers no less than six woes: three against Pharisees (vv. 42–44), three (harsher) ones against the lawyers (vv. 46–52). Luke, therefore, does not always depict the Pharisees in a positive way, even if he generally remains more balanced and favorable toward the Pharisaic party than any other gospel writer does. In addition, Luke does not go out of his way to compose this material because of an acute Matthean-like anger against the Pharisees. Some of the content mentioned here overlaps with Matt 23 and was probably taken and readapted from a source.[2] Indeed, already in its pre-redactional stages, some of this polemical material was probably crafted and directed against Pharisees.[3] Luke has retained this anti-Pharisaic material but not composed it. And even at the

---

[1] The Lukan deletion of Mark 7:1–23 belongs to the so-called "Great Omission" of material from Mark 6:45–8:26. The reasons proposed for this omission are legion. Some suggest Luke had a different version of Mark before him. Others claim Luke chose to omit this material from his gospel for a variety of other reasons: 1) stylistic (Mark's gospel was too lengthy; desire to avoid doublets, etc.); 2) Luke believed the mission to the Gentiles began during "the time of the church," not during Jesus's earthly ministry; 3) Luke transposed some of the Markan themes to Acts; 4) Luke disagreed with Mark's supposed abrogation of the Law. For a summary of the discussion, see Michael Pettem, "Luke's Great Omission and His View of the Law," *NTS* 42 (1996): 35–54. Pettem essentially develops Jervell's thesis (*Luke and the People of God*, 145), maintaining that for Luke God's Law was valid for Jews. While I am highly sympathetic to both Pettem and Jervell's thesis, I find reason number 2 more likely: Luke is consistent about postponing encounters with Gentiles until the book of Acts. While he does not retain Mark 7:1–23, he includes a very similar story that almost makes the same point as Mark (and Matthew). Finally, it is not entirely evident that Mark cancels the dietary laws in the controversy story about hand washing. Therefore, we cannot automatically operate under the assumption that Luke's "Great Omission" stemmed from a disagreement with Mark's supposed abrogation of the Law, although it could be that Luke was unsatisfied with the way Mark presented the whole matter, fearing misunderstandings Mark's gospel could potentially generate.

[2] I will hardly engage here in the tedious task of determining the original listing and wording of the woes as found within the hypothetical Q, only point out some of the redactional Lukan features that are embedded within Luke 11:37–41. Kazen, *Jesus and Purity Halakhah*, 224, argues that Luke 11:39b–44 contains less redactional changes than Matthew.

[3] Baumgarten, "The Pharisaic *Paradosis*," 72, has even suggested that some of the anti-Pharisaic materials in the gospels (e.g., in Matt 15 and Mark 7) are of pre-Christian origin.

climax of his anti-Pharisaic outburst, Luke critiques not so much the Pharisees as a collective group, but certain Pharisees, including *Pharisaic followers of Jesus*, the "Christian Pharisees" we discover later in Acts who refuse to interact with Gentiles unless they become Jews.[4]

Given the rather exceptional outburst of Luke's Jesus against the Pharisees, it is not surprising to see the latter at the end of this chapter seeking to find something reprehensible they can hold against him (11:53–54). Here too, some translations have misrendered Luke's portrait of the Pharisees.[5] For Luke, the Pharisees are not set on *eliminating* Jesus, even though they do try "to press exceedingly and question him concerning many things" (δεινῶς ἐνέχειν καὶ ἀποστοματίζειν αὐτὸν περὶ πλειόνων), "lying in wait for him to catch *something* out of his mouth" (ἐνεδρεύοντες αὐτὸν θηρεῦσαί τι ἐκ τοῦ στόματος αὐτοῦ).[6] In the end though, the Pharisees are unable to reprove Jesus or find anything objectionable about his teachings or behavior (cf. Luke 6:11 and 14:6). Instead, they remain speechless and unable to counterargue (14:1–6), thereby confirming, at least in Luke's eyes, the legitimacy and authority of Jesus' teaching and ministry.[7]

Redactional Analysis

Luke has penned the opening to this scene.[8] The Semitic, or better, Septuagint-like style employing ἐν τῷ followed by the infinitive is surely compositional (cf. 2:27; 3:21; 9:34, 36; 14:1; 19:15; 24:30; Acts 11:15). Furthermore, commensality between Pharisees and Jesus appears only in Luke. Thus, in Luke 7:36, a member of the Pharisees (τις τῶν Φαρισαίων) asks

---

[4] Here I find myself agreeing with Jack T. Sanders, *The Jews in Luke-Acts* (Philadelphia, Pa.: Fortress, 1987), 179–80, who claims that the Pharisees in Luke are surrogates for Torah observing Jewish followers of Jesus of his own day. I believe this can *occasionally* be the case as in Luke 11:37–41. See Ziesler, "Luke and the Pharisees," 147–48, who underlines the significance of "Christian Pharisees" in Acts.

[5] See especially the excursus in chapter 4 dealing with the mistranslation of Luke 6:11.

[6] Translation mine. The pronoun indefinite accusative neuter singular τι should be linked to the infinitive θηρεῦσαί. The object of the Pharisees is not *Jesus* but *what* he says. This is quite understandable since Jesus has just reproved them regarding their teachings and behavior. Consequently, they search for something objectionable in his teachings. Many translations render δεινῶς ἐνέχειν as "furious attack on him" (*New Jerusalem Bible*) or "to be very hostile toward him" (NRSV). In reality, Luke's Pharisees press Jesus for further answers to use as counterarguments against him. Cf. LXX Ezek 14:7 (ἐγὼ κύριος ἀποκριθήσομαι αὐτῷ ἐν ᾧ ἐνέχεται ἐν αὐτῷ). See "ἐνέχω," *TLNT* 2:3–5; Wolter, *Das Lukasevangelium*, 437.

[7] See Part I of this book where I deal with Luke 6:11 and 14:5.

[8] Josef Ernst, *Das Evangelium nach Lukas* (RNT; Regensburg: Friedrich Pustet, 1993), 286; Nolland, *Luke*, 2:663. Kazen, *Jesus and Purity Halakhah*, 277, however, thinks the setting is traditional.

Jesus to eat with him (ἐρώτα αὐτὸν ἵνα φάγῃ μετ᾽ αὐτοῦ); here, a Pharisee also asks Jesus to dine with him (ἐρωτᾷ αὐτὸν Φαρισαῖος ὅπως ἀριστήσῃ παρ᾽ αὐτῷ). In v. 38, Luke highlights the Pharisaic host's surprise at seeing (ἰδὼν ἐθαύμασεν) Jesus disregard washing before eating in his own house. The usage of ἐβαπτίσθη is ambiguous. Does Luke draw from tradition? Does the verb refer to hand washing or to full immersion before eating? I return to this issue below. In any case, it is likely that Luke has composed this verse in its entirety, basing himself in part on the opening in Mark 7 to the controversy on hand washing.[9]

The reply provided by Jesus (vv. 39–41), for Luke, "the Lord" (ὁ κύριος), finds its direct parallel in Matt 23:25–26. Notable is Luke's elimination of the woe formula (Οὐαὶ ὑμῖν), which introduces this same saying in Matt 23:25. That the saying originally did contain a woe formula seems likely, since it appears in Matt 23:25 and the other six woes in Luke 11:42, 43, 44, 46, 47, and 52. Besides the absence of this formula, Luke 11:39 bears great resemblance with Matt 23:25.[10]

In the following two verses, however, the compositional creativity of Luke reemerges. The epithet, ἄφρονες ("foolish" or "without reason"), which opens v. 40, reflects more properly what Luke holds against some Pharisees: their (supposed) senseless inability in comprehending the essence of purity and righteousness.[11] It is quite tempting to see all of the rhetorical question in v. 40 as stemming from Lukan composition, but the saying is also attested in the *Gos. Thom.* 89,[12] though missing in Matthew, so it must be traditional. Still, the usage of the verb ποιέω in the forms of ποιήσας (among the synoptics, attested in this form only in Luke) and ἐποίησεν, which echo the language of creation, would certainly have suited

---

[9] Besides Luke 11:38, within the New Testament ἰδὼν ἐθαύμασεν appears only here and in Acts 7:32 (ἰδὼν ἐθαύμαζεν; cf. Rev 17:6: ἐθαύμασα ἰδών). Remarkably, the Pharisee is only "surprised" at Jesus' neglect for washing before meals, not angry or furious at Jesus for showing such apathy. Cf. Wolter, *Das Lukasevangelium*, 431.

[10] Absent in Luke is Matthew's epithet ὑποκριταί, which the latter often uses against the Pharisees. How to account for πίνακος and πονηρίας (in Matt, παροψίδος and ἀκρασίας)? Do they stem from a different version of the hypothetical Q allegedly available to Luke?

[11] Besides Luke 11:40, the epithet appears in 12:20, but nowhere else in the synoptic gospels (cf. Rom 2:20; 1 Cor 15:36; 2 Cor 11:16, 19; 12:6, 11; Eph. 5:17; 1 Pet 2:15). It is used in the Jewish sapiential tradition (e.g., Prov 1:22; 10:21; 14:18; 17:12; 21:20; 22:3; 27:12; Job 34:36; Wis 3:12; 5:4) as well as in classical literature (e.g., Epictetus, *Discourses* 3.22.85; 4.10. 23). Luke's selection of this epithet conforms to his usage of ἀνοίας ("without understanding") in Luke 6:11 to describe the Pharisees' lack of understanding.

[12] "Don't you understand that the one who made the inside is also the one who made the outside?" (*Gosp. Thom.* 89) In the contrast to Luke, the *Gospel of Thomas* reverses the inside-outside contrast.

Luke's interests regarding the discussion of purity issues between Jews and Gentiles as reflected later in Acts (see interpretation below).

Compositional activity is also perceptible in the concluding remarks made in v. 41.[13] The coordinating conjunction, πλὴν (here bearing the meaning of "but"), appears no less than fifteen times in Luke and four times in Acts (Matt: 5x; Mark: 1x). The reference to "charity" (ἐλεημοσύνην) carries special significance for Luke (cf. Luke 12:33; Acts 3:2, 3, 10; 9:36; 10:2, 4, 31; 24:17).[14] In Acts, Cornelius, a Jewish friendly Gentile, stands out for his charitable acts toward the Jewish community (Acts 10:2, 4, 31). With the (dis?)advantage of hindsight, we could read the final phrase in Luke 11:41 – "and see, everything will be clean for you (καὶ ἰδοὺ πάντα καθαρὰ ὑμῖν ἐστιν)" – in light of the concerns voiced later by Luke in Acts. Quite remarkably, the Cornelius episode is embedded within a larger discourse on the impurity of Gentiles during which Peter receives a troubling vision regarding the impure animals who allegorically represent Gentile followers of Jesus. God commands Peter (in a vision) to eat impure animals now deemed pure (Acts 10:15: ἃ ὁ θεὸς ἐκαθάρισεν).[15] In my opinion the references to commensality (here, between Jesus and Pharisees; in Acts, between Gentile and Jewish followers of Jesus), purity (here, the moral impurity of the Pharisees; in Acts, the moral impurity of Gentiles), and charity (here, the Pharisaic neglect to do so; in Acts, the praise for Cornelius' charitable deeds) justify reading Luke 11:37–41 in light of Acts. In the following analysis, I offer, preemptively, an interpretation of the Lukan periscope read in light of Acts that will receive further treatment in the next chapter dealing with the Cornelius episode.

Interpretation

As noted above, the controversy story in Luke occurs in a setting where one (not all) Pharisee(s) (ὁ Φαρισαῖος) and Jesus argue about Torah matters as they share a meal. Once again, it should stressed that Luke does not view the Pharisees as a monolithic group systematically opposed to or even

---

[13] Nolland, *Luke*, 2:664, views Luke 11:41 and Matt 23:26 as variants of a single tradition, although he acknowledges Luke's recasting of the saying in light of his own interests.

[14] As Kazen, *Jesus and Purity Halakah*, 226 n. 109, points out, the word "charity" also appears in *Gosp. Thom.* 6 and 14. However, its practice appears there in a negative light: "and if you give to charity, you will harm your spirits" (14). It is not certain that its occurrence in *Gosp. Thom.* confirms the traditional status of Luke 11:41 as Kazen argues (pointing also to Matt 6:1–4, which is not attested in Luke). I favor seeing Luke 11:41 as entirely redactional, although Matt 6:1–4 shows that there were other traditions criticizing the "hypocrites" for not properly practicing charity.

[15] As I will argue in the next chapter, for Luke, the vision is really about Jews and Gentiles, *not* Jewish food laws.

divorced from the Jesus movement. For Luke, scores of Pharisees belong to the Jesus movement, including none other than Paul himself, whom Luke portrays as an *ongoing* Pharisee even after his "conversion" experience: "Brothers, I *am* a Pharisee (ἐγὼ Φαρισαῖός εἰμι), a son of Pharisees. I am on trial concerning the hope of the resurrection of the dead" (Acts 23:6).[16] In addition, Luke refers to members of the "sect" of the Pharisees who are believers in Jesus (τινες τῶν ἀπὸ τῆς αἱρέσεως τῶν Φαρισαίων πεπιστευκότες) and demand that Gentile males become circumcised in order to be saved (15:5).[17] The so-called Apostolic Decree, which, according to Luke, was drafted in response to this controversy and is intimately intertwined with the issue of Gentile impurity, contains a legislation proposing an acceptable manner of entertaining table fellowshipping between Jewish and Gentile followers of Jesus in which the practice of kashrut and purity is not discarded. Consequently, it should come as no surprise to imagine Luke pondering about this ongoing debate as he composes this section of his gospel.

The Pharisee seems surprised at Jesus' disregard for washing (ἐβαπτίσθη) before eating.[18] In the controversy on hand washing, Matthew does not employ the verb βαπτίζω, which literally means to "immerse" and often refers in the canonical gospels to the ritual of baptism practiced by John the Baptist and the followers of Jesus. Interestingly, the verb appears in Mark 7:4 (καὶ ἀπ' ἀγορᾶς ἐὰν μὴ βαπτίσωνται οὐκ ἐσθίουσιν) to mean that certain Jews immerse themselves or dip their hands in water before eating, or that they wash the food they purchase from the market prior to consumption.[19] In *J.W.* 2:129, Josephus claims that the Essenes wash their entire bodies before eating. Qumranic texts also refer to this practice (1QS

---

[16] I do not read this statement merely as an opportunistic declaration on the part of Luke's Paul to avoid punishment during his hearing before the Sanhedrin. Rather, Luke consciously portrays Paul in Pharisaic colors because he wants to show how the apostle to the Gentiles continues to remain a pious Jew who identifies with the most remarkable of Jewish parties. This reading conforms to some of the final words voiced by Luke's Paul at the end of Acts: "Brothers, though *I had done nothing against our people or the customs of our ancestors*, yet I was arrested in Jerusalem and handed over to the Romans" (28:17; emphasis mine). This declaration is not made just for rhetorical effect. It belongs to Luke's systematic attempt to reinscribe Paul as a Pharisaic Jew who remains faithful to the customs of the elders.

[17] The term "sect" is not entirely appropriate to describe the Pharisaic party. See, among others, Sanders, *Jewish Law from Jesus to the Mishnah*, 241, who reserves the term "sect" for groups that cut themselves off from mainline Jewish society.

[18] In contrast to Matthew's controversy on hand washing, Luke depicts Jesus, rather than his disciples, as disregarding this practice. The focus in Luke is always more upon the figure and authority of Jesus.

[19] This is how the NRSV understands the Greek: "and they do not eat anything from the market unless they wash it."

5:16; 4Q514), but there is no direct evidence confirming that Pharisees did the same. The gospel of Matthew suggests that certain Pharisees only washed their hands right before eating. However, it is possible that some Pharisees, upon returning from the market or a crowded area, would immerse themselves in water as Mark's gospel seems to indicate.[20] *M. Hag.* 2:5 claims that "for [the eating of food that is] unconsecrated or [Second] Tithe or Heave-offering, the hands need but to be rinsed; and for Hallowed Things they need to be immersed" (מטבילין; cf. Mark 7:4: βαπτίσωνται). This halakah refers to the practice of dipping the hands in water. Some scholars identify water basins at Masada and Jerusalem as *mikvaot* used for immersing hands.[21] Others, however, think these basins served for washing one's feet. This is possible, since Jews normally performed hand washing by pouring water from a vessel. Consequently, there would have been no need to design a small basin to carry out such a deed, which in addition would require people to lean down to dip their hands, not the most pragmatic way of fulfilling such a rite.[22] Luke's usage of the verb βαπτίζω, then, refers either to the dipping of hands into a vessel or to the immersion of the entire body in a ritual pool. Maybe Luke knew of a branch of Pharisees who immersed themselves before eating, much like some Essenes.[23]

The reply given by Luke's Jesus does not address the specific issue of washing before meals but the cleansing of cups and plates. Nonetheless, as I noted in my analysis of Matt 23:25–26, the cleansing of vessels appears in the legislation about kashrut in Lev 11. Thus, Lev 11:32 states: "And anything upon which any of them [i.e., the eight vermin] falls when they are dead shall be unclean, whether an article of wood or cloth or skin or sacking, any article that is used for any purpose; it shall be dipped into water, and it shall be unclean until the evening, and then it shall be clean." The position advocated in Luke's statement, as far as the observance of Jewish food laws is concerned, shows itself to be no less different from

---

[20] See Booth, *Jesus and the Laws of Impurity*, 200. Cf. *M. Hag.* 2:7 and especially *y. Shev.* 6:1 36c as well as Albert I. Baumgarten's comments on this latter passage in "Graeco-Roman Associations and Jewish Sects," in *Jews in a Graeco-Roman World* (ed. Martin Goodman; Oxford: Clarendon Press, 1998), 93–111 (pp. 103–5).

[21] Asher Grossberg, "The *Miqva'ot* (Ritual Baths) at Masada," in *Masada VIII: The Yigael Yadin Excavations 1963–1965* (eds. J. Aviram et al.; Jerusalem: Israel Exploration Society, 2007), 118–21. Cf. Yoel Elitzur, "Ritual Pools for Immersion of Hands," [in Hebrew] *Cathedra* 91 (1991): 169–72.

[22] Safrai and Safrai, "Papyrus Oxyrhynchus 840," 260–62.

[23] Baumgarten, "Graeco-Roman Associations and Jewish Sects," 103, favors reading Luke 11:38 as a reference to full body immersion and takes this statement as evidence of Pharisaic practice. The singular and passive form of ἐβαπτίσθη, coupled by the absence of any reference to the noun, "hands," speaks on behalf of his thesis. Perhaps, Luke envisions Jesus arriving from a public space where he could have acquired impurity and then entering into the Pharisee's house.

Matthew's. Luke, like Matthew, makes no sweeping declaration against the observance of Jewish food laws. He only criticizes some Pharisees for their allegedly misplaced priorities, employing the inner-outer antithetical contrast also present within Matthew. In Luke, however, the antithetical attack is aimed more directly at the Pharisees: "Now you Pharisees clean the outside of the cup and of the dish, but inside *you* (ὑμῶν) are full of greed and wickedness" (11:39). The Lukan switch to direct discourse in the second phrase of this statement marks the transition more strongly than in Matthew from the realm of ritual praxis to the supposedly immoral behavior of the Pharisees. The reference to greed (ἁρπαγή) coincides with Luke's claim elsewhere concerning the Pharisees' supposed love of money (16:14). But nowhere in this pericope does Luke try to dissuade Jews from honoring their ancestral traditions.

These comments also apply to the subsequent reply provided in vv. 40–41. Luke does not quarrel with the Pharisees over their devotion to ritual matters, but blames them for failing to care for the inner purity of their hearts. The same one who *made* the "outside" *also* (καὶ) made the "inside" (v. 40). The subject of the verb ποιήσας/ἐποίησεν should be understood here, as elsewhere in Luke-Acts, in reference to the divine creator, the one "who made (ὁ ποιήσας) the heaven and the earth, the sea, and everything in them" (Acts 4:24).[24] "From one ancestor he made (ἐποίησέν) all nations to inhabit the whole earth" (Acts 17:26). Luke looks back to creation as he ponders about the purity issues that continue to cause friction between Gentile followers of Jesus, certain Jewish disciples of Jesus, and even non-"Christian" Jews of his time. Those who refuse to dine or interact with Gentile believers because of their alleged moral impurity (or simply because they are Gentiles), fail to perceive "all the signs and wonders that God has done (ἐποίησέν)…among the Gentiles" (Acts 15:12; cf. 15:4; 21:19). These Pharisaic followers of Jesus (and perhaps even non-"Christian" Pharisees) fail to recognize that God has indeed purified the inner beings of such Gentiles, endowing them with the sacred spirit, which attests to their renunciation of morally defiling practices associated with the nations (idolatry, sexual immorality, etc.) that inhibit Jews from interacting with non-Jews more freely (cf. Acts chs. 10–11). Luke is frustrated with a *certain* Jewish contingent within and perhaps also outside the *ekklesia* that refuses to interact with Gentile followers of Jesus.[25]

---

[24] Cf. Acts 17:24: "The God who made (ὁ ποιήσας) the world and everything in it"; Acts 7:50: "Did not my hand make (ἐποίησεν) all these things?"; Acts 14:15: "the living God, who made (ἐποίησεν) the heaven and the earth and the sea and all that is in them." Cf. Luke 1:49, 51, 68; 8:39; Acts 2:22, 36; 14:27.

[25] Luke, as I argue, in the next chapter, is *not* arguing that *all* Gentiles are morally pure. Only those who have become followers of Jesus are pure, for only these have truly

Quite cleverly and daringly, Luke transfers the moral impurity, normally attributed to Gentiles, back on to such Jews: the Pharisaic followers of Jesus opposed to Jewish-Gentile fellowship are the ones full of "greed and wickedness" (Luke 11:39), not the Gentile believers such as Cornelius who practice charity. Many texts from the Dead Sea Scrolls associate the love and misuse of wealth with moral defilement.[26] The moral defilement of the Pharisees acquired through their supposed misuse and love for money stands in contrast with the charitable practices of Gentile followers of Jesus as exemplified through the archetypical Cornelius (Acts 10:2, 4, 31). Once said Pharisees will fully recognize the marvelous acts of the creator (on behalf of the nations) and practice charity (ἐλεημοσύνην), then indeed all things (πάντα) will be pure for them (Luke 11:41). Luke does not overtly introduce here the theme of the moral purification of the Gentile followers of Jesus. He, more than any other gospel author, is careful to keep the theme of the mission to the Gentiles out of his gospel narrative until the book of Acts. Nevertheless, here he subtly reverses the status of *certain* Jews (those who exemplify the attitude of the "extreme" Pharisee) and *certain* Gentiles (those who have fully abandoned idolatry and follow Jesus) by claiming that the former stand in need of the same purification the latter have experienced. In Luke's eyes, such Pharisees, who are champions in ritual matters, fall short in the preservation of moral purity. Once they devote their attention to moral purity, then their purity will truly become complete.

My reading of 11:41 – "and see, everything will be clean for you" – goes against the perception that sees this verse as denying the observance of the Jewish purity system and even the practice of Jewish food laws.[27]

---

abandoned idolatry and other immoralities and have received the sacred spirit. The categories of pure and impure remain in force for Luke, even if he rejects an intrinsic (rather than imputed) conception of impurity.

[26] CD 6:15; 8:5; 1QS 4:19; 1QpHab 8:10–13 and 12:7–10.

[27] Recently, Pervo, *Acts,* 269–70, 283; Previously, Blomberg, "The Law in Luke-Acts," 60; Turner, "The Sabbath, Sunday and the Law in Luke/Acts." 111. If Klawans, Hayes, and Maccoby are right in their assertion that Jews did not view Gentiles as intrinsically and ritually impure, then Nolland, *Luke,* 2:665, who does rightly point out that in this pericope Luke thinks more about Gentile (and I would add Jewish) followers of Jesus than actual (non-"Christian") Pharisees, misunderstands the issue when he states that because "of his right relationship to God...Cornelius could not be contaminated by his disregard of Jewish ritual purity requirements and, therefore, in turn could not contaminate Jewish Christians who shared table fellowship with him." The point is that Cornelius, or any other Gentile for that matter, could not become ritually contaminated nor contaminate other Jews because of a disregard of the Jewish ritual purity system, since many Jews understood such legislation to be binding upon Jews only, not Gentiles. Rather, Jews (to varying degrees) were mainly concerned with the *moral* impurity of Gentiles, because of their association with idolatry, polytheism, and other "immoral"

This Lukan pericope does not go beyond anything Matthew claims in his own work about the supposed abrogation of Jewish food laws. Luke only criticizes a Pharisaic *neglect* of attending to moral issues, in this case almsgiving, not their pious devotion to the Torah. Like Matthew, Luke has Jesus note: "it is these you ought to have practiced [i.e., justice and love], *without neglecting the others*" (Luke 11:42; emphasis mine). Like Matthew, there is no need to restrict the application of such a statement in Luke as only addressing the observance of tithing.[28] Finally, as in the case of Matthew, Luke might assume in his critique of Pharisaic praxis that one should avoid, when possible, the "father of impurities," corpse impurity: "Woe to you! For you are like unmarked graves, and people walk over them without realizing it" (11:44).

In addition, when we place the saying in Luke regarding charity and purity within its wider Jewish matrix, its content sounds far less radical than previously thought. Thus, in Tob 12:9, the author makes no less a radical statement regarding the far-reaching effects of almsgiving: "For almsgiving (ἐλεημοσύνη) saves from death and purges away (ἀποκαθαριεῖ) every sin. Those who give alms will enjoy a full life." Like Luke, the book of Tobit promises purity from all sins to those who practice charity. The overlap in terminology and concepts between both passages is quite striking, and several other ancient Jewish texts encourage the practice of almsgiving, promising similar rewards couched in language of purification and atonement.[29] For Luke, almsgiving is an antidote for (reified) Pharisaic greed and evil propensities. There is no need, therefore, to view Luke as categorically opposing the practice of kashrut or even ritual purity. His main critique against certain Pharisees centers on the themes of moral corruption, the neglect of inner contemplation and purification as well as the practice of justice and love, and an obsession with ritual matters that forbids commensality.

---

ways, and the potential apostasy from Judaism extensive interaction with non-Jews could generate. Alternatively, Luke disagrees with those Jews of an expansionist tendency who attributed an intrinsic and permanent impurity to Gentiles (e.g., certain Essenes). By emphasizing their purification and sanctification (via the sacred spirit), Luke affirms the possibility for Jews and Gentiles to partake of the same meals.

[28] Because of its moralizing tendency, Codex Bezae has left out the saying, presumably because of an unease with the implications this statement holds for the ongoing relevance of upholding ritual laws.

[29] "As water extinguishes a blazing fire, so almsgiving atones for sin" (Sir 3:30). Cf. Sir 29:12; 40:24; Tob 4:10; *b. B. Bat.* 9a, 10a, 19b; *b. Sukkah* 49b; *b. Ketub.* 68a; *Lev. Rab.* 34:8.

The Commission of the Seventy-Two: Luke 10:1–11

Literary Context

The opening prepositional phrase, μετὰ δὲ ταῦτα ("after these things"), in 10:1, ties this pericope with the preceding materials in 9:51–56 and vv. 57–62. The majority of scholars view 9:51 as marking a new stage in the macrostructure of Luke's gospel. Now Luke's Jesus begins his journey to Jerusalem, which will span several chapters.[30] Discussions about the literary macrostructures of Luke cannot occupy the center of attention here, but looking at the immediate literary vicinity one can notice several ways in which Luke has tied 9:51–56 with 10:1–11. In both pericopes, Jesus sends out messengers before him as he heads toward Jerusalem: in 9:52, he sends some disciples to Samaria; in 10:1, to towns and other places of Jewish provenance.[31] When visiting Samaritan territory, Jesus' emissaries experience rejection, and, in 10:1–11, Luke further develops this theme of rejection, particularly in vv. 10–11 and later on in vv. 12–16 where the resistance of the Galilean towns toward the gospel are contrasted with the more open attitude of non-Jewish cities such as Sodom, Tyre, and Sidon.[32] The positive attitude Luke attributes to the inhabitants of these Gentiles cities should not be exaggerated though, since the same material also appears in Matthew and possibly originates from a source Luke accessed. The Gentile-Jewish contrast serves to heighten the condemnation of certain Jewish segments that remain closed to the cause of the gospel while indirectly hinting at a future Gentile mission readers will fully discover in the book of Acts.

Luke has also connected 9:57–62, which contains three short anecdotes on discipleship, with 10:1–11. In the first story (9:57–58), a certain person approaches Jesus expressing his desire to become his disciple. The sober response Jesus delivers highlights the material sacrifices demanded by such discipleship: "Foxes have holes, and birds of the air have nests; but the Son of Man has nowhere to lay his head" (v. 58). In the second inci-

---

[30] Charles H. Talbert, *Reading Luke: A Literary and Theological Commentary on the Third Gospel* (Reading the New Testament Series; New York: Crossroad, 1986), 114–19, sees 19:44 as marking the end of this major unit. Wolter, *Das Lukasevangelium*, 364–68, brackets 9:51–18:34 as one literary unit.

[31] In the Greek, the link between 9:52 and 10:1 is more evident through the repetition of καὶ ἀπέστειλεν...πρὸ προσώπου αὐτοῦ ("and he sent...before his face").

[32] The reference to Sodom also recalls the theme of hospitality in Luke 10:1–11: when the angels visited Sodom (Gen 19), only Lot received them, while the rest of the city mistreated them. Those who do not welcome Jesus' messengers emulate the attitude of Sodom and therefore resist divine will. See Wolter, *Das Lukasevangelium*, 381.

dent, Jesus invites someone else to become his disciple. In response to this offer, this person first requests permission to bury his father before following him. Jesus, however, categorically denies him this request, famously declaring: "Let the dead bury their own dead" (v. 60).[33] Finally, a third person requests Jesus to bid his household farewell before becoming his disciple, but Luke's Jesus remains equally uncompromising: "No one who puts a hand to the plow and looks back is fit for the kingdom of God" (v. 62). Quite possibly, these anecdotes on discipleship also contain links with 10:1–11, since the seventy-two messengers adopt a life of simplicity and utter commitment to the cause of the kingdom of heaven. As they embark on their missionary journey, they are to commanded to "carry no purse, no bag, no sandals" (10:4), but to depend on the hospitality offered to them in the houses and towns that welcome them (10:7, 8). In this way, they replicate the itinerant, homeless lifestyle of Jesus, the Son of Man, who also has no house to dwell in.

Besides the connections signaled above with the two immediate preceding pericopes (9:51–56, 57–62), much of the theme, structure, and wording of the commission to the seventy-two resembles the first commission to the twelve (9:1–6, 10). Most obvious connectors include terminology used to describe both commissions (καὶ ἀπέστειλεν αὐτοὺς in 9:2/10:1) and the proclamation of the kingdom of God (9:2/10:9, 11) as well as the symbolic numerology (twelve vs. seventy-two). By referring to *other* (ἑτέρους) individuals in the second commission, Luke may also be hinting at the first commission to the twelve. There were "others" besides the twelve whom Luke's Jesus commissioned, although this gloss may also be pointing back to the more immediate literary context in which Jesus sends out messengers to Samaria (9:52). In the first commission, Jesus grants power to the twelve to expel demons and heal the sick (9:1). Even if no explicit mention of such "superpowers" appears in the second commission, they are clearly presupposed in 10:9 as well as in the report in 10:17–20. In the first commission, the twelve also report back to their master about their sojourn, although Luke does not contain (or compose) a record relating their experience. In both commissions, Jesus forbids his disciples to travel with any luggage or unnecessary belongings (9:3/10:4). Both commissions also expect Jesus' messengers to abide in the same house or town (implied in 9:4; commanded and elaborated in 10:7, 8). Finally, both commissions contain materials instructing the disciples on how to handle acceptance and rejection in towns where they announce the gospel (e.g., the symbolic act of shaking the dust off one's feet in 9:5/10:11).

---

[33] Probably, Jesus refers to *secondary* burial (ליקוט עצמות) of a deceased person, when Jews of the Second Temple period would gather the bones of their beloved and place them in ossuaries for reburial. See Evans, *Jesus and the Ossuaries*, 13.

Together, the reoccurring literary and thematic correspondences between Luke 10:1–11 and 9:51–62 as well as 9:1–6, 10 mirror a progression delineated in further detail in the book of Acts. The commission in Acts 1:8 outlines the dissemination of the gospel, beginning in Jerusalem and Judea and then spreading into Samaria, eventually reaching the very ends of the earth. Working under the assumption that the same author composed both Luke and Acts, it would be perfectly reasonable to posit that the first commission of the twelve in Luke symbolizes the mission to the Jews living in Palestine, while the scavenging into Samaritan territory in Luke 9:51–56 hints at the mission to the Samaritans in Acts 8,[34] and the final commission to the seventy-two, with its contrast between Galilean-Jewish and Gentile towns (Luke 10:12–16), points to the eventual proclamation of the gospel to the nations.

Redactional Features

As the previous analysis of the literary context to this pericope already suggests, Luke has penned the opening prepositional phrase in v. 1, "after these things" (μετὰ δὲ ταῦτα), in order to link it with the previous two sections of his narrative (9:51–56 and vv. 57–62).[35] Other distinctive Lukan features within v. 1 include Luke's employment of the title, κύριος, which he uses more than any other synoptic writer (Luke: 70x; Acts: 81x; Matt: 42x; Mark: 16x), particularly in reference to Jesus. Luke has also inserted the number "seventy/seventy-two," which is probably inspired by the story of the seventy-two translators of the Septuagint.[36] Not only is such a number entirely absent in both Mark 6:6b–13 and Matt 10:1–14, which only report the commission to the twelve, but also no other gospel writer besides Luke refers to two commissions. The fact that Luke avoids doublets elsewhere in his gospel makes the repetition of two commissions

---

[34] Jonathan Bourgel, "'On both sides of the borderline': The portrayal of the Samaritans in the Third Gospel," (paper presented at The Eighth Congress of the Société d'Études Samaritaines, Erfurt, Germany, July 15–20, 2012), makes a compelling argument that Luke's perspective on the Samaritans is entirely Jewish, marked by a positive yet ambivalent attitude toward this group, which reflects a transition occurring after 70 in the Jewish attitude toward the Samaritan people (from a purely negative to a more favorable perspective). I thank Jonathan for sharing a copy of his paper with me.

[35] Luke uses the prepositional phrase μετὰ δὲ as a transitional signpost throughout Luke-Acts (with the demonstrative pronoun οὗτος: Luke 1:24; 9:28; 18:4; Acts 15:36; 21:15; without the demonstrative: Acts 13:15; 15:13, 36; 20:1, 6; 24:1; 24:24; 28:11, 17). Cf. also Luke 5:27; 12:4; 17:8; Acts 7:7; 13:20; 15:16; 18:1: "μετὰ ταῦτα." Fitzmyer, *The Gospel according to Luke,* 2:845, calls it "a stereotyped Lucan transitional phrase." Cf. Bovon, *Luc,* 2:51.

[36] Some entertain the possibility that the number was present in Q. See Hans Klein, *Das Lukasevangelium* (KEK 1.3; Göttingen: Vandenhoeck & Ruprecht, 2005), 372.

all the more conspicuous. It seems reasonable, then, to view all of v. 1 as a Lukan composition introducing the entire pericope.³⁷

Scholars generally view the statements within 11:2–11 (as well as vv. 12–16) as containing traditional material, at times even preserving its content in better sequence than Matthew.³⁸ Consequently, distinguishing redactional activity from traditional material proves more difficult in this case than in v. 1. Verse 7 contains the first command of key interest with its reference to eating and drinking (ἐσθίοντες καὶ πίνοντες τὰ παρ' αὐτῶν) the food a host offers in the house (ἐν τῇ οἰκίᾳ) where the itinerant preacher momentarily resides. Some see this material as traditional, possibly stemming from Q.³⁹ In v. 8, the text shifts its direction to the *city* (εἰς ἣν ἂν πόλιν) and the command to eat appears once again in slightly different wording: ἐσθίετε τὰ παρατιθέμενα ὑμῖν (v. 8b). Some scholars view the phrase in v. 8b as redactional, while others opt for a traditional ascription.⁴⁰ The parallel saying in *Gosp. Thom.* 14 could suggest that Luke 10:8

---

³⁷ In greater redactional detail: ἀνέδειξεν is rare (among synoptic writers, used only here and in Acts 1:24 in this form); Luke includes ἑτέρους ("others"), probably to show that other laborers besides the twelve were and are still needed for the harvest (10:2); καὶ ἀπέστειλεν αὐτοὺς is found in 9:1, creating further symmetry between both commissions; ἀνὰ δύο (or the redundant ἀνὰ δύο δύο, depending on the textual witnesses) is probably based on Mark 6:7 (there: δύο δύο), which Luke leaves out from the first commission; for πᾶσαν πόλιν. Cf. Acts 15:36; τόπον might stem from Mark 6:11; πρὸ προσώπου αὐτοῦ sends the reader back to 9:52; the usage of ἤμελλεν is quite common in Luke-Acts (7:2; 9:31; 19:4; Acts 12:6; 16:27; 27:33); the whole phrase οὗ ἤμελλεν αὐτὸς ἔρχεσθαι also points back to 9:51.

³⁸ Bovon, *Luc,* 2:51; Fitzmyer, *The Gospel according to Luke,* 2:842; Klein, *Das Lukasevangelium,* 373.

³⁹ Bovon, *Luc,* 2:51, views the phrase, "eating and drinking what they provide," as traditional, since it provides a necessary gloss for the verb "remain" at the beginning of v. 7, justifying the rights of the itinerant preacher to obtain a salary as outlined in v. 7b.

⁴⁰ For further discussions see Klein, *Das Lukasevangelium,* 373 n. 17; Paul Hoffmann, *Studien zur Theologie der Logienquelle* (2d ed.; NTA 8; Münster: Aschendorff, 1972), 281: a Lukan composition. Jens Schröter, *Erinnerung an Worte Jesu: Studien zur Rezeption der Logienüberlieferung in Markus, Q und Thomas* (WMANT 76; Neukirchen-Vluyn, 1997), 187–92, provides a very useful summary on the different positions concerning the origins of 10:8. The weakness of his argument (overly interested in questions of origins and redaction at the cost of overlooking the pertinent Jewish sources and matrices involved) lies in his disinterest in interpreting the saying in Luke (as well as 1 Cor 10:27, critical for his evaluation of the matter) in light of halakic considerations. This leads him to view Luke 10:8 as a Lukan "Aufhebung der Speisevorschriften" (p. 187) without further qualification (see also p. 192 where he speaks of an "Aufhebung der trennenden Wirkung jüdischer Vorschriften"). In my opinion, Schröter presents some important arguments that slightly favor viewing Luke 10:8 as a Lukan insertion (whether it is a Lukan redaction remains open though, given the parallel in *Gosp. Thom.* 14), but need not be interpreted as an abrogation of kashrut, let alone purity laws. Rather, Jewish disciples of Jesus in Luke's day are to eat the *kosher* food presented to them without

is traditional, unless dependency on Luke is to be suspected in this case on the part of the *Gospel of Thomas*.[41] The phrase also bears great resemblance with 1 Cor 10:27 (πᾶν τὸ παρατιθέμενον ὑμῖν ἐσθίετε), save for the key adjective πᾶν ("all" or "every"), which is missing in Luke and of some significance for assessing the question of food laws in this pericope.

Regardless of whether Luke composed this phrase or simply copied it from a source, the twofold repetition in vv. 7 and 8b to accept food offered by the welcoming host must be accounted for. Even if they are redactional, they hardly provide firm evidence for Luke's dismissal of Jewish food laws. Nolland suggests the repetition of the phrase in v. 8b could simply be stylistic: "In Luke's source, the juxtaposition of what to do in connection with houses was probably abruptly juxtaposed with the material on towns. Luke provides a bridge with his repetitive 'eat what is put before you.'"[42] Arguably, one could maintain that Luke probably means with 10:8b that Jesus' disciples in his own day can accept food prepared by Gentiles in their homes. However, this accommodation need not entail a total abrogation of kashrut, as I argue below.

---

questioning its provenance. By doing so, they do not *consciously* eat food offered to idols. This interpretation would align itself with Tomson's view of 1 Cor 10:27 in his book *Paul and the Jewish Law,* which unfortunately Schröter does not interact with. Risto Uro, *Sheep among the Wolves: A Study of the Mission Instructions of Q* (AASF.DHL 47; Helsinki: Suomalainen Tiedeakatemia, 1987), 69, on the other hand, claims: "In general, Luke takes a respectful attitude towards Jewish ritual law, and a statement like 10.8b would be easier to understand as a saying deriving from the source of the evangelist than as his own formulation." I agree with Uro's view on Luke's attitude toward the Law. Nevertheless, I think that even if we posit Luke 10:8 as a Lukan composition, it can still be integrated into his rather positive stance towards the Jewish Law.

[41] The saying in the *Gosp. Thom.* reads: "When you go into any region and walk about in the countryside, when people take you in, eat what they serve you and heal the sick among them." The resemblances with Luke 10:8 and 9a are obvious: the hospitality offered by the people, the reference to eating what is offered, and the call to heal the sick. A noticeable difference includes the reference to visiting a region and any of its districts in the *Gosp. Thom.* rather than a "town." More conspicuous is the additional statement attached in *Gosp. Thom.* declaring, "after all, what goes into your mouth will not defile you; rather, it's what comes out of your mouth that will defile you." The link between both statements in *Gosp. Thom.* might be a mnemonic device as Kazen, *Jesus and Purity Halakhah*, 228, points out. In any case, Luke does not tie these two statements together. In fact, he does not even retain Mark's statement about the ritual inability of foods to contaminate. Luke's rationale for accepting food offered by a host is closely tied to the right for the preacher to receive his/her *salary*, as stated in 10:7.

[42] Nolland, *Luke*, 2:553.

Interpretation

Many New Testament scholars take the reference to the number seventy or seventy-two, understood as an allusion to Gentiles, coupled by the twofold repetition to eat the food served by the hosts, as evidence that Luke has discarded Jewish food laws.[43] Several observations, however, call into question the validity of such a position, which is built upon a pericope whose thematic focus and horizon certainly lie elsewhere.

First, the universal thrust so often attributed to this pericope, based in part on the symbolism presumed to lie behind the numbers "seventy" or "seventy-two," is not so evident and prominent as one might first think. Textual considerations complicate the matter: the textual tradition is divided, some manuscripts read "seventy" (ἑβδομήκοντα), others "seventy-two" (ἑβδομήκοντα δύο).[44] Scholars have turned, therefore, to the internal evidence in an attempt to determine the original reading. Wolter, for example, argues for an original reading that contained ἑβδομήκοντα δύο, which was subsequently changed to ἑβδομήκοντα. The digit δύο was dropped either because of scribal oversight or in an attempt to link the pericope with Jewish traditions that viewed the number seventy as representing the nations (*1 En.* 89:59; 90:22, 25; *Jub.* 44:34, etc.).[45] This suggestion more readily explains the textual process of scribal mutation, although it remains possible, though less likely, that the original reading contained "seventy" and was subsequently altered to "seventy-two" in order to confirm it with the list of the nations as found in the Septuagint text of Gen 10 (depending on how one counts the number of nations enlisted therein) or the number of

---

[43] Deines, "Das Aposteldekret," 332; Georges Gander, *L'Évangile pour les étrangers du monde: Commentaire de l'Évangile selon Luc* (Lausanne, 1986), 514; Pervo, *Acts*, 269–70; Talbert, *Reading Luke*, 117. Cf. Ernst, *Das Evangelium nach Lukas*, 253: "In der Wiederholung der Essenanweisung spiegeln sich die Schwierigkeiten, die sich für die judenchristlichen Missionare an den Tischen der Heiden oder Heidenchristen ergaben. Der beherrschende Gedanke liegt jedoch in dem Fortschreiten der Verkündigung vom Haus zur Stadt, die im Verständnis des Lk den Öffentlichkeitscharakter der missionarischen Verkündigung verdeutlicht."

[44] ἑβδομήκοντα δύο (𝔓75 B D 0181, etc.); ἑβδομήκοντα (א A C D L W Θ Ξ Ψ, etc.).

[45] Wolter, *Das Lukasevangelium*, 376–77; Joel B. Green, *The Gospel of Luke* (NICNT; Grand Rapids, Mich.: Eerdmans, 1997), 409 n. 28. Jozef Verheyden, "How Many Were Sent according to Lk 10,1?" in *Luke and His Readers: Festschrift A. Denaux* (eds. Adelbert Denaux et al.; BETL 182; Leuven: Leuven University Press, 2005), 193–238, points to Greco-Roman literature that often employs the number seventy to refer to a closed, complete group or entity. Nevertheless, as Wolter argues, this observation does not prove that Luke originally included the number seventy in his pericope. If anything, it might explain how in the process of transmission the number seventy-two was changed by (non-Jewish) scribes in conformance with Greco-Roman concepts. Bruce Metzger, "Seventy or Seventy-Two Disciples?" *NTS* 5 (1959): 299–306, remains uncertain about the original reading, leaving the question open to either possibility.

translators of the Septuagint, according to the *Letter of Aristeas* (50, 307), seventy-two.[46] This latter scenario seems less likely though, given the symbolic prominence of the number seventy deeply enrooted in Jewish tradition by the time of Luke (*1 En.* 10:12; *Jub.* 11:20; *4 Ezra* 14:46, etc.).

Many have precipitately identified either textual reading with the so-called Table of Nations in Genesis 10. Supposedly, the lists in the Masoretic text and Septuagint refer to seventy and seventy-two nations, respectively. However, according to Wolter's counting, the lists in the Masoretic text and the Septuagint refer to seventy-*one* and seventy-*three* nations.[47] Much depends on how one counts the list of names in Gen 10. The Masoretic text enumerates seventy-one descendants of Shem, Ham, and Japheth, perhaps even seventy-two, if one views the Asshur mentioned in Gen 10:11 as a descendant of Nimrod and as a separate individual from the Asshur mentioned later in Gen 10:22 as a son of Shem.[48] The late post-Talmudic work, *Halakot Gedolot* (c. 8th cent. CE), contains a list and computation of the Table of Nations with a sum adding up to seventy: not only the Asshur of Gen 10:11 (understood as the son of Nimrod) but also the Philistines (10:14) are left out from its reckoning, possibly to conform the list with the Jewish tradition that views the number seventy as a fixed quantity identifiable with the nations.[49] Concerning the list in LXX, seventy-three names are indeed recorded therein albeit with the repetition of Cainan (unattested in the MT) in 10:22 (as a son of Shem) and in 10:24 (as a son of Arpachshad and consequently a *grandson* of Shem).[50] Could the repetition of the name Cainan have been viewed as superfluous by ancient Jews, leading them to compute a total of seventy-two instead of seventy-three nations in Gen 10? Later Christian authors such as Augustine counted

---

[46] Cf. Klein, *Das Lukasevangelium*, 375 n. 30.

[47] Wolter, *Das Lukasevangelium*, 376.

[48] The NRSV understands the first Asshur in Gen 10:11 as referring to the *land of Assyria* rather than a person: "From that land he [i.e., Nimrod] went into Assyria." Other translations (e.g., *Jewish Publication Society*; *New Jerusalem Bible*), however, seem to understand Asshur as representing a person: "out of the land went forth Asshur." The Hebrew text (מן־הארץ ההוא יצא אשור) invites both readings. Ancient Jewish translations (see Targumim and LXX) offer both possibilities as well.

[49] See discussion of text in Samuel Krauss, "Die Zahl der biblischen Völkerschaften," *ZAW* 19 (1899): 5–7. Krauss suggests that *Halakot Gedolot* chooses to include Nimrod in the reckoning instead of Asshur because Nimrod founded Babylon while Asshur was merely one of his descendants. The Philistines are subsumed under the Caphtorim of Gen 10:14 (cf. Deut 2:23; Amos 9:7). Krauss thinks the computation of Gen 10 in *Halakot Gedolot* stems from earlier times.

[50] Incidentally, Cainan appears in the genealogy of Luke as a son of Arphachshad (3:36).

seventy-three names in Gen 10 but concluded that these persons only represented seventy-two nations to conform it to tradition.[51]

Because Wolter opts for the textual variant of seventy-two as the original reading and since the version of the Table of the Nations in the LXX technically contains seventy-three names, he concludes that Luke does not conceive of a universal proclamation of the gospel in the pericope on the second commission. Wolter claims that Luke looks back to the first commission of the twelve when writing this section. After all, seventy-two is a divisible of twelve, and Luke's Jesus does send out his disciples in pairs (thirty-six in total). Consequently, Wolter dismisses assigning any particular symbolism to the number seventy-two in this Lukan pericope, which, as he points out, is explicitly tied for the first time with the nations only by Irenaeus (*Haer.* 3.22.3) at the end of the second century CE.[52]

Wolter's thesis is extremely enticing. It would strengthen the argument proposed in this chapter by further restricting the second commission to a Jewish context. Luke 10:1–11 would prove itself irrelevant for the discussion on Jewish food laws since it only envisions a mission to Jews in Jewish territory. However, Wolter's restrictive reading of Luke 10:1–11 does not fully convince. When the second commission is read in light of the stories in Acts regarding the proclamation of the gospel to Jews, Samaritans, and Gentiles, it becomes very likely that a mission to the Gentiles is already envisaged in the gospel of Luke. This stands true regardless of which textual reading one opts for and despite the fact that both the MT and the LXX technically contain seventy-one and seventy-three names, respectively. As noted earlier, the tradition of seventy as representative of the nations was well attested in Luke's day. Thus, in *1 En.* 89:59, seventy shepherds are assigned to care for the seventy sheep that represent the nations (cf. *1 En.* 90:22, 25). In the book of *Jubilees,* the author explicitly refers to the seventy Gentile nations (44:34). Later rabbinic and targumic passages, some possibly deriving from earlier sources, also retain this

---

[51] *De civitate Dei* XVI, 3. See discussion of text and other medieval Christian reckonings in Krauss, "Die Zahl der biblischen Völkerschaften," 7–11.

[52] Wolter, *Das Lukasevangelium*, 377. Cf. Uro, *Sheep among the Wolves,* 64: "It is not impossible that Luke tied no specific reference or symbolic meaning to 'seventy (two)' and simply chose the number as a suitable 'round' number between twelve and the 120 brethren of Acts 1.15. The difference between 120 and 70 (72) gave room enough for the rest of Jesus' followers and relatives who did not take part in the mission of Lk 10 or joined his circle after that. If Luke, nevertheless, thought symbolically in Lk 10.1, the most obvious association would be with the figures 12 and 120, both determined by the notion of the twelve tribes of Israel. This could be the case, especially if the reading "seventy-two" is more original."

ascription in various forms.⁵³ The number seventy, therefore, would symbolize the nations regardless of how one computes the Table of the Nations in Gen 10.

Concerning the possible, if not plausible, original reading of seventy-two, the evidence from the *Letter of Aristeas* cannot be ignored, particularly for an author like Luke who relies on and draws so heavily from the Septuagint.⁵⁴ Luke probably knew about the legend concerning the origins of the LXX, that seventy-two elders allegedly translated the Hebrew scriptures into Greek.⁵⁵ According to *Let. Arist.* 46–50, six elders from each of the twelve tribes of Israel were commissioned to translate the Hebrew scriptures into Greek. To the author's delight, these seventy-two linguists succeeded in completing their translation in the serendipitous span of seventy-two days (*Let. Arist.* 307). While the author of the *Let. Arist.* does not explicitly tie this number with the nations (neither does Luke), he evinces throughout his work a concern for presenting Judaism in ways more palatable to Greek tastes and interests. Finally, despite the mechanical computations of the Table of Nations offered by Wolter for the MT and LXX, we could imagine, though it is impossible to prove, first century Jews rounding off the number of names contained in Gen 10 to either seventy or seventy-two, depending on the version of the list lying before them.⁵⁶

A universal thrust lurking behind Luke 10:1–11 (and vv. 12–24), therefore, seems probable, and Luke would have most likely viewed its contents as instructing itinerant preachers on how to carry out "missionary" work even among non-Jews in Gentile territory.⁵⁷ Some have pointed out that

---

⁵³ *M. Sheqal.* 5:1; *Midr. Tann.* on Deut 32 (seventy nations equated with the seventy members of Jacob's household); *Lev. Rab.* 2:4; *Pesiq. Rab Kah.* 28:9 (God created seventy nations); *B. Sukkah* 55b (seventy bulls offered representing the nations); *Tg. Ps.-J.* Deut 32:8.

⁵⁴ On Luke and the *Letter of Aristeas* see Sidney Jellicoe, "St. Luke and the Seventy-Two," *NTS* 6 (1960): 319–21 as well as his subsequent article "St. Luke and the Letter of Aristeas," *JBL* 80 (1961): 149–55.

⁵⁵ The fact that Josephus paraphrases extensively from *Let. Arist.* (see his *Ant.* 12:11–118) shows that the work, or at least the story regarding the translation of the LXX, was well known in Luke's day.

⁵⁶ We should note that in his retelling of the translation of the Septuagint, Josephus switches between the usage of "seventy" and "seventy-two" (*Ant.* 12:57, 86, 107). It is not surprising, therefore, to see the same confusion occurring within the textual tradition of Luke.

⁵⁷ Talbert, *Reading Luke*, 117: "From such a survey we can see the evangelist has used this section not only to foreshadow the Gentile mission of the church, but also to give certain instructions and guidance that would be needed at the time the gospel was written (e.g., payment of missionaries; eating of any food set before them; balance in one's concern for power in ministry and for one's own relationship with God)." Luke

Luke regularly avoids including doublets in his narrative (e.g., the elimination of the two feeding accounts in Mark), unless he sees a good reason to do so. The inclusion of two commissions, therefore, which is unattested in any other gospel, must be accounted for. Reading the number seventy-two as hinting toward the eventual outreach to the Gentiles, or at least pointing to an expedition into the Greek speaking Jewish Diaspora, best accounts for Luke's indulgence in including two commissions in his gospel.[58] This interpretation stands even if at the narrative level Jesus sends the seventy-two only into *Jewish territory*. Luke knows well that Jesus did not extensively interact with Gentiles during his earthly ministry. Therefore, he only hints at this universal dimension in his gospel narrative, while deliberating more fully on the topic in his second book.

How then do vv. 7 and 8 affect the discussion on Jewish food practices if they indirectly address non-Jewish settings? First of all, we should note that Luke hardly concentrates on the issue of kashrut when he has Jesus announce in v. 7 that his emissaries are to accept the food and drink offered to them by their welcoming hosts. The rationale given for this injunction focuses on the right of the worker to receive his or her salary: "for (γὰρ) the laborer deserves to be paid" (10:7).[59] The postpositive conjunction γὰρ might connect this phrase not only to the preceding instruction to eat and drink but also to the previous order to *remain in the house* where the itinerant preacher is welcomed. In other words, the "salary" (μισθός), the term Luke employs here, encompasses both "room and boarding."[60]

22:35–36 does not deter from this reading. In that passage, Jesus delivers his "correction" only in a dire situation right before his incumbent death. Contra France, *The Gospel of Matthew,* 386.

[58] The numbers seventy and seventy-two are associated with other entities besides the nations of the world. In the MT, Jacob's household contains seventy members (Gen 46:27; Exod 1:5; Deut 10:22); according to the LXX and Acts 7:14, seventy-five (except for LXX Deut 10:22: seventy members). In Num 11:25, God sends his spirit upon seventy elders of Israel. Interestingly enough, two additional men, Eldad and Medad, also receive this spirit (Num 11:26), adding to a total of seventy-two persons who are spiritually endowed. Is there a connection between the commission of the seventy-two disciples of Jesus and the seventy-plus-two individuals who receive the spirit in the book of Numbers intended to relate Jesus with the greatest prophet of Jewish tradition, Moses? Luke also shows great interest in the theme of the baptism of the spirit. Some like Luke Timothy Johnson, *The Gospel of Luke* (Sacra pagina Series 3; Collegeville, Minn.: Liturgical, 1991), 170, favor this interpretation and see the Gentile allusion only as secondary.

[59] Cf. Loader, *Jesus' Attitude towards the Law*, 326: "10.7 justifies the instruction by arguing that a labourer deserves to be paid. That is the focus, not food purity issues."

[60] In the commission to the twelve, Matt 10:10 (cf. *Did.* 13:2) states: "for laborers deserve their *food*" (τροφῆς). Probably, the term implies entitlement to other benefits as well, including lodging. Cf. 1 Cor 9:14–18; 2 Cor 11:7–11. 1 Tim 5:18 contains the same wording as Luke: ἄξιος ὁ ἐργάτης τοῦ μισθοῦ αὐτοῦ.

Gospel workers deserve compensation for the ministry they provide and should not hesitate to enjoy the hospitality offered by their hosts. On the other hand, those laboring on behalf of the gospel should not hop from house to house nor abuse the generosity of their hosts, but remain in the abode where they first obtain lodging. In other words, Jesus' laborers are to embrace a simple and undemanding lifestyle exemplified through their humble and grateful acceptance of the food and lodging offered to them.[61] The core of the instructions given in 10:7, then, focuses on host-guest protocols, on outlining the proper comportment laborers of Jesus are to embody as well as justifying their right to receive a salary in exchange for their ministry.[62]

What about the repetition of this injunction in 10:8? At the narrative level, we could interpret it to mean that the messengers of Jesus who visit *Jewish* homes should not worry whether the food or drink served before them surpasses all halakic reproach with regard to ritual impurity or tithing. For example, 10:8 might warrant overlooking whether the food offered by the Jewish host has been properly tithed[63] or prepared in a vigorous state of ritual purity (e.g., washing hands beforehand).[64] On the other hand, we should presuppose at the narrative and historical level that the Jewish hosts would not serve forbidden meats (e.g., pork), since, presumably, most Jews in Palestine would have honored the fundamentals of kashrut. Alternatively, the statement in v. 8 could simply be repeating the theme already announced in v. 7, namely, that the guest representing Jesus and proclaiming God's kingdom should rightfully accept, albeit in an

---

[61] Ernst, *Das Evangelium nach Lukas*, 253: "Der Bote soll nicht über Gebühr fordern, sondern mit dem zufrieden sein, was ihm vorgesetzt wird." Cf. Gander, *L'Évangile pour les nations du monde*, 527: "…en orient, l'hospitalité est sacrée, et l'on n'y admettrait pas que l'on méprise l'hospitalité d'une demeure pour lui en préférer une autre, après avoir usé de la première." Wolter, *Das Lukasevangelium*, 379: "Die zweite Weisung in 7b…kann für sich genommen als Aufforderung verstanden werden, sich den jeweiligen häuslichen Möglichkeiten anzupassen (im Sinne von: 'stellt keine Ansprüche, sondern begnügt euch mit dem, was man euch gibt')."

[62] The material in this section of Luke should be compared with *Did.* 11–13, which deals extensively with itinerant apostles, prophets, and the like, as well as host-guest relations.

[63] However, see Luke 11:42. The rabbinic tractate *Demai* deals extensively with the topic of foods whose tithing remains doubtful.

[64] Loader, *Jesus' Attitude towards the Law,* 326: "In 10:8 food purity issues may be in mind. Here the instruction would not be permission to eat non kosher foods, since the setting is within Israel. Luke will deal with food issues in Acts. The injunction here in a Jewish setting does, however, reflect a setting of priorities which could come into conflict with any requirement not to eat untithed food or wrongly prepared food. As such it probably reflects a contrast with Pharisaic interpretation, rather than with the Law itself."

exemplary and reasonable manner, the food and hospitality offered by the host.[65]

When assessing how Luke would have applied this text in his own day within a Diaspora setting, we should not hastily jump to the conclusion that he thinks Jews can eat *any* food offered to them by a Gentile host. This certainly might be the impression conveyed when consulting certain modern mistranslations of both vv. 7 and 8. For example, the NRSV translates v. 7 (ἐν αὐτῇ δὲ τῇ οἰκίᾳ μένετε ἐσθίοντες καὶ πίνοντες τὰ παρ' αὐτῶν) in the following manner: "Remain in the same house, eating and drinking what*ever* they provide" (emphasis mine).[66] The Greek text, however, need not be understood in this way. As Nolland remarks, the "Lukan statement lacks the vital πᾶν, 'everything,' which would justify comparison with 1 Cor 10:27."[67] In any case, even if Luke 10:8b (ἐσθίετε τὰ παρατιθέμενα ὑμῖν) does bear any relationship with 1 Cor 10:27 (πᾶν τὸ παρατιθέμενον ὑμῖν ἐσθίετε), it could still be addressing primarily the issue of eating food offered to idols, not the consumption of non-kosher animals, as seems to be the case in 1 Cor 10:28.

In addition, we should consider the possibility that Luke distinguishes between Jewish and Gentile followers of Jesus and their obligations vis-à-vis the Torah when entering a pagan house. Such a distinction is clearly presupposed later on in the book of Acts during the promulgation of the so-called Apostolic Decree, which assumes that Jewish followers of Jesus continue to observe the Torah *in toto* while only demanding Gentile believers to follow a smaller set of commandments. Accordingly, were Jewish followers of Jesus to enter a Gentile home, they were not to ask about the provenance of the *kosher* food set before them. Luke would not have envisaged Jewish followers of Jesus compromising with the fundamentals of kashrut by accepting to eat pork. In the case of Gentile followers of Jesus visiting the house of a non-believer, they were perhaps allowed to consume non-kosher meat, provided they did not compromise with the Apostolic Decree by knowingly eating food offered to idols before their hosts.

---

[65] Cf. Sir 31:16: "Eat what is set before you like a well brought-up person (φάγε ὡς ἄνθρωπος τὰ παρακείμενά σοι), and do not chew greedily, or you will give offense." Sira's phrase, φάγε τὰ παρακείμενά σοι, resembles Luke's, ἐσθίετε τὰ παρατιθέμενα ὑμῖν, although Ben Sira discusses more directly the theme of table etiquette. The phrase in Ben Sira, nonetheless, illustrates how Luke's statement should not be taken *a priori* as relativizing the observance of kashrut.

[66] Similarly, the *New International Reader's Version* translates v. 7 as "eat and drink *anything* they give you" (emphasis mine). Likewise, the New Living Translation renders v. 8 (ἐσθίετε τὰ παρατιθέμενα ὑμῖν) as "eat whatever is set before you."

[67] Nolland, *Luke*, 2:553.

As noted in the introduction to chapter 7 of this book, some Jews in antiquity were ready to eat with non-Jews, provided the latter respected the basics of kashrut. The *Letter of Aristeas*, with its reference to the seventy-two translators and outlook toward the non-Jewish world, envisages such a scenario by depicting the king in Alexandria hosting a banquet in which both Jews and Gentiles participate, albeit by respecting Jewish dietary restrictions (181–188). Other Jewish works, such as the book of Judith (12:19), also presuppose commensality between Jews and Gentiles in exceptional cases, without implying a departure from observing kashrut.[68] Sanders has perspicaciously argued that in certain cases Jews in the Diaspora did not refrain from acquiring meat, oil, and wine handled by Gentiles.[69] The idea, therefore, of a Jewish messenger of Jesus eating at the house of a Gentile even while respecting the main scruples of kashrut should be seriously considered as a halakic possibility Luke envisages even though other contemporary Jews of a stricter tendency would have objected to such a move because of various concerns over purity and idolatry, anxiety toward extensive contact with foreigners, or, in extreme cases, simple and unqualified disgust toward Gentiles.

If we may momentarily survey the reports in the Book of Acts of visits by Jewish followers of Jesus into non-Jewish houses, we can find further substantiation to back this point. Remarkably, the Gentiles houses Jewish disciples of Jesus visit in Acts are usually composed of non-Jews who are already affiliated in some way with their local Jewish communities or at least share some knowledge about the beliefs and practices of the Jewish people.[70] The episode reporting Peter's visit to Cornelius' house serves as

---

[68] Cf. *M. Avod. Zar.* 5:5.

[69] Sanders, *Judaism: Practice and Belief,* 216; 520 n. 216. See also Magness, *Stone and Dung*, 39, for the discussion on imported amphoras and fish bones in Herodian palaces of Jerusalem, Masada, Jericho, and the Herodium. These findings show that Roman fish sauces were popular among some Jews (e.g., the Jerusalem elite) in Palestine who were willing to consume *Gentile* products imported from as far as Spain. See also her discussion on p. 57 on a wide range of imported wares such as jars (containing Gentile wine!) in Jewish Quarter Mansions of Jerusalem from the Heriodian Period, showing that some Jews of Palestine, at least among the Judean elites, were willing to consume imported goods produced by Gentiles. On the other hand, other Jews objected not only to consuming such products but also handling Gentile vessels (unless they underwent purification) because of their contact with non-kosher food and association with idolatry. See Noam, "The Gentileness of Gentiles," 33–41, for a discussion of the rabbinic concept of גיעולי גוים and its possible antecedents in the Second Temple period. We should note thought that Jews treated (kosher) fish more leniently than other meats, because fish were generally not suitable for Greek or Roman sacrifice. So Jordan D. Rosenblum, "Kosher Olive Oil in Antiquity Reconsidered," *JSJ* 40 (2009): 356–65 (362 n. 16), citing *m. Avod. Zar.* 2:7.

[70] Esler, *Community and Gospel*, 71.

a prime example illustrating this point. As a devout Gentile who fears the deity of the Jews, Cornelius, even before joining the Jesus movement, supports his local Jewish community (through charity) and embraces certain Jewish practices and beliefs (e.g., prayer to the God of Israel; Acts 10:2). Given Cornelius' more than favorable disposition toward Judaism, it is very likely that Luke envisions him accommodating to Jewish customs and sensibilities, having kosher food made ready and available to Peter, the Jewish apostle. Quite significantly, Luke never claims that Peter eats forbidden food when he visits the Roman centurion, and the episode, as I argue in the next chapter, shares intimate thematic and literary links with the so-called Apostolic Decree – a legislation containing important instructions for administrating a proper Jewish-Gentile *Tischgemeinschaft*.

The same observations apply to Paul's visits to non-Jewish homes elsewhere in the book of Acts. Thus, in 16:15, Paul stays in Lydia's household, but Luke describes her as a "worshiper of God' (σεβομένη τὸν θεόν). She is, therefore, already acquainted with and sensitive toward Jewish mores and able to accommodate to the special needs of a Jewish guest. Interestingly enough, she bids Paul and his entourage to remain in her house only *after* her baptism. This pattern corresponds to the sequence of events reporting Peter's encounter with Cornelius: the Jewish apostle also resides in the Cornelius' house only after the Roman centurion receives the sacred spirit and baptism through water – proof for Luke that the morally impure status of Gentile followers of Jesus has indeed been eradicated. In Acts 16:34, Paul and Silas spend one night and share a meal in Philippi at the house of the local jailer who apparently does not enjoy any prior affiliation with the local Jewish community (at least Luke does not mention such a relation). However, in this case as well, Paul and Barnabas share a meal with his family only after his household receives baptism. Even here, Luke in all probability presupposes that Paul and Silas respect the basics of kashrut during their table fellowship with their newly purified Gentile pupil.

In 17:5, Paul and Silas spend time in the house of a certain Jason who suddenly and abruptly appears in the narrative. Little is known about this character, although some exegetes try to tie him with the Jason mentioned in Rom 16:21. The latter Jason is a Jew, since Paul describes him as a "fellow countryman" (συγγενής). In any case, the Jason of Acts enjoys some kind of affiliation with the Jewish community of Thessalonica: it is in the synagogue of that city that Paul and Silas succeed in attracting initial interest among local Jews and especially Gentiles sympathetic toward Judaism (17:4). Later on in 18:7, when Paul visits Corinth, he enters into the house of a certain Titius Justus, a "worshiper of God," whose house lies right next to a synagogue. During Paul's time in Corinth, even Crispus, the head of the synagogue, becomes a follower of Jesus (18:8).[71] Certainly, Luke would not imagine such a prominent Jewish "convert" eating pork and lobster with Paul and another God-fearer in a house located right next to a Jewish synagogue of Corinth.[72] Overall, it is quite impressive that Luke never declares anywhere that, during their commensality with non-Jews, Peter, Paul, Barnabas, Silas, or any other prominent Jewish member of the *ekklesia* consumed forbidden meats. This absence can be fully accounted for when we realize that Luke esteems that Gentiles who are sympathetic to Judaism and the Jesus movement should accommodate to the dietary restrictions of Jewish followers of Jesus in accordance with the spirit of the Apostolic Decree.

Very little indeed in Luke 10:1–11 speaks on behalf of an abrogation of kashrut. At the narrative level, the pericope describes a commission within Jewish borders, focusing on instructing itinerant emissaries proclaiming the arrival of the kingdom of God, not the abrogation of food laws. Even when conceding the secondary, universal dimension hinted at within the second commission to the seventy-two, nothing in the pericope suggests a dismantlement of kashrut. Jewish-Gentile interaction in the Greco-Roman Diaspora could occur in a variety of ways, and Luke provides and develops elsewhere his own solution for a *modus operandi* between both parties that does not demand Jews to forsake their ancestral customs. The strength of my reading of Luke 10:1–11 lies in its consideration of the various manners in which Jews could interact with their non-Jewish interlocutors, its compliance with the wider Lukan perspective about the ongoing importance of the observance of the Torah for Jewish followers of Jesus, and its appreciation of Luke's vision of Jewish-Gentile relations within the *ekklesia*.

---

[71] Right before entering Titius Justus' house, Paul shakes (ἐκτινάσσω) off the dust from his clothes in response to Jewish opposition. This act echoes the command in Luke 9:5 and 10:11 to shake the dust off from one's feet when a particular town rejects Jesus' emissaries. The passages in Luke, however, refer to wiping dust off one's *feet*, while Luke 10:11 employs a different Greek verb to describe the action (ἀπομάσσω), although Luke 9:5 uses ἀποτινάσσω, which is not far from ἐκτινάσσω. Cf. Acts 13:51; Mark 6:11.

[72] In 20:7, 21:4, and 28:14, Paul fellowships with individuals who are already believers, and so we might equally imagine (from Luke's perspective) such people accommodating to Jewish custom. In 21:8, 16, Paul spends time in the houses of Jewish followers of Jesus who live in Jewish territory (Paul of Caesarea, one of the "seven" from Acts 6:5; Mnason, probably also a Jewish disciple) and most likely observe kashrut. As a prisoner awaiting trial before Caesar, Paul boards a ship, guarded by Roman soldiers, and partakes of bread: "he took bread; and giving thanks to God in the presence of all, he broke it and began to eat" (27:35). Even in such unique circumstances, nothing is said regarding Paul indulging in eating forbidden meats (cf. 27:38, which refers to wheat aboard the ship).

Conclusion

Some scholars claim that Luke no longer cares about the observance of dietary laws. I have not found evidence to back this claim. Instead, Luke draws similar conclusions as Matthew, not even condemning the Pharisees for maintaining ritual purity, probably even affirming their stance on such matters, but criticizing them for neglecting ethical issues, particularly the observance of almsgiving. I suggest an interplay occurs in the gospel of Luke with an important theme developed later on in the book of Acts where Luke praises Gentile followers of Jesus for their practice of charity, a confirmation of their newly acquired moral purification. Indeed, the Pharisees Luke condemns in 11:37–41 may be surrogates for certain Jewish followers of Jesus of his own day who refuse to interact with Gentile believers because of purity concerns or simply because Gentiles are not Jewish. Luke condemns these "Christian Pharisees" (cf. Acts 15:5) for their exclusive attitude and even daringly throws the impurity they ascribe to Gentile believers back on them. Once they will practice almsgiving and be more considerate of the moral purification they stand in need of, then their purity will be complete (Luke 11:41).

As for the other main pericope analyzed in this chapter (10:1–11), there is little indeed that can speak on behalf of an abrogation of kashrut. At the most, it might suggest that Jewish followers of Jesus are to overlook the provenance of *kosher* food offered to them in the houses they reside (and this would have offended certain Jews who opposed consuming food *prepared* by Gentiles), while Gentile followers of Jesus are to refrain from knowingly consuming food offered to idols. In any case, the main point concerning food Luke develops in this pericope, as stated in 10:7, is the justification of Jesus' emissaries to receive their salary in exchange for their service on behalf of God's kingdom.

Chapter 10

The Cornelius Incident

"A gentile once brought fish to Rabban Gamaliel. He said, 'They are permitted but I have no wish to accept them from him.'"
(Mishnah, Yom Tov 3:2)

Introduction

For many New Testament scholars, the extended pericope, covering almost two chapters of Acts (10:1–11:18), which reports Peter's vision and his encounter with Cornelius, constitutes *the* proof text for Luke's abrogation of Jewish dietary regulations. As one prominent scholar of Luke-Acts roundly puts it, Peter's vision "effectively marks the end of dietary regulations for Christians."[1] This perspective runs deep in the history of scholarly research and is rooted in patristic literature.[2] Others, however, do not subscribe to this traditional perspective and argue that the vision of Peter really concerns Gentiles, not food. In the following chapter, I will try to solidify this position by drawing from the best of secondary scholarship on the question of kashrut and purity regulations, carefully distinguishing between both issues in order to demonstrate that Luke only announces the moral purification of Gentile followers of Jesus, not the euthanization of keeping kosher. I will continue here to read Acts as a Jewish text, placing it next to other Jewish documents that discuss food laws (*Letter of Aristeas,* Philo, 1 Macc, 4 Macc, etc.) in order to argue that Luke does not announce the end of the Jewish dietary regime. In fact, Luke does not even deny the validity of the Jewish purity system; he only seeks to reformulate some of its regulations in order to accommodate for the Gentile influx into

---

[1] Joseph B. Tyson, "Acts 6:1–7 and Dietary Regulations in Early Christianity," *PRSt* 10 (1983): 146. Similarly Bruce, *The Book of the Acts,* 218–19; Marguerat, *Les Actes des apôtres,* 406: Jewish food laws are abolished, but Luke partially holds onto these ideals in Acts 15. Nevertheless, I will argue that Acts 15 presupposes the ongoing observance of kashrut *in toto* (for Jewish followers of Jesus). Pervo, *Acts,* 269, treats kashrut and Jewish purity regulations indiscriminately. Previously, Sandmel, *Anti-Semitism,* 88: "...Jewish food prohibitions and the prohibition of eating improper food with Gentiles were nullified."

[2] Cf. Cyril of Alexandria, *Contra Julianum* 9:318–319.

the *ekklesia*. He does so by declaring the moral purification of Gentile believers and rejecting the inherent profaneness ascribed to them by other Jews.

Literary Context

Luke's description of the encounter between Peter and Cornelius appears at a logical and critical point within the intended sequence of his narrative. The missiological program, outlined in the commission of Acts 1:8 (from Jerusalem to Judea, Samaria, and eventually the ends of the earth) and already hinted at in Luke's gospel,[3] so far, has been carefully executed by his major protagonists. After Jesus' ascension to his royal, heavenly headquarters, the disciples faithfully follow their master's orders, first testifying to those many Jews gathered in Jerusalem during the festival of Pentecost (2:1–42) and then gradually moving beyond this geographical perimeter, reaching Samaria (8:5–25) where Philip preaches to the Samaritans, many of whom accept his message. Luke justifies this novel and questionable (for certain Jews) outreach toward Samaritans by having Peter and John lay hands upon the Samaritan disciples in order that they might receive the spirit (8:14–17) – a gift thus far granted solely to Jews within the narration of events in Acts.

Luke continues to stretch the regional borders the gospel message reaches through his description of a curious encounter between Philip and an Ethiopian eunuch who had come to worship in Jerusalem (8:26). The eunuch's relationship to Judaism remains unclear. Luke does not refer to him as a Jew by birth, and his status as a eunuch would have excluded him from the "assembly of the LORD" (Deut 23:1). But Luke certainly knows the prophetic verses from the book of Isaiah (56:3–7) that promise fuller integration of foreigners and eunuchs into Israel and the temple cult.[4]

---

[3] See previous chapter dealing with the commission of the seventy-two (Luke 10:1–11).

[4] Although Luke does not explicitly refer to Isa 56:3–7 in this pericope, the eunuch does read a passage from Isaiah that is not far away from this passage (53:7, 8). Furthermore, Luke certainly knows the last phrase of Isa 56:7, which he cites in part in his gospel (19:46). Luke also claims that the eunuch went to Jerusalem in order to worship there (Acts 8:27: ὃς ἐληλύθει προσκυνήσων εἰς Ἰερουσαλήμ). I suggest Luke claims, in line with the ethos of Isa 56:3–7 and against Ezek 44:6–7, that non-Jews do indeed have the right to participate more fully in the temple cult (though the temple no longer stood in Luke's day). Luke's position also stands in opposition to MMT (Section B 60–62), which excludes sacrificial offerings of Gentiles from the temple and prohibits sexually deformed or mutilated people from entering the congregation of Israel. Later in Acts 21:28 and 24:6, Luke's Paul is accused of having profaned the temple by alleged bringing a

When read within the ensemble of the narration in Acts, it becomes clear that this story serves Luke's theological and teleological mission to inscribe a process of gradual dissemination of the gospel into the history of the *ekklesia* that will eventually reach the Gentiles *en masse*. In some ways, the episode recounting the Ethiopian's conversion seems even more audacious than the Cornelius episode, especially if Luke views the former as a castrated non-Jew! The key difference, however, between both stories lies in the *continuous interaction* accorded to Cornelius with Jewish followers of Jesus. By contrast, Philip and the Ethiopian eunuch *instantly* depart and return to their respective homelands.[5] Moreover, the encounter between Philip and the eunuch occurs privately with no one to witness the event, whereas Cornelius' baptism enjoys a public audience, witnessed by several Jews and Gentiles. Finally, Philip does not *enter* the house of a non-Jew. Rather, the encounter occurs outdoors, in a deserted place, somewhere on a dirt road lying between Jerusalem and Gaza (8:26). Luke, therefore, presents a sort of precedent to a Gentile conversion before relating the Cornelius episode and the ramifications conversions of Gentiles will bring for Jewish-Gentile relations within the Jesus movement. He treads a path but develops its theme only when he presents his readers with the story about Peter's extensive stay in a Gentile home – a public encounter unique enough to arouse suspicion among certain Jews.[6]

Luke, then, has gone through considerable efforts in shaping his narrative so as to prepare his readers for what he sees as a monumental transition in the thus far, short-lived history of the earliest *ekklesia*: the proclamation of the gospel to non-Jews. Henceforth, contact with Gentiles will become commonplace within the narrative, and Luke will continuously clarify how such an opening toward the non-Jewish world by no means calls for a Jewish desertion of Torah observance (21:21; 25:8,10; 28:17). In fact, Luke has intimately tied the Cornelius incident with central questions related to Torah praxis: he will have Peter refer to the Cornelius episode as a precedent when the apostles meet in Jerusalem to discuss the

---

Gentile into premises presumably forbidden to them. True, there was a Gentile court accessible to non-Jews, but the charge insinuates that Paul had brought a Gentile beyond this space into the court reserved for Jews only. Luke never fully denies that Paul committed this controversial act because he believes Gentiles are not inherently profane (see discussion below). Cf. George Brooke, "Luke-Acts and the Qumran Scrolls: The Case of MMT," in *Luke's Literary Achievement: Collected Essays* (ed. Christopher M. Tuckett; JSNTSup 116; Sheffield: Sheffield Academic Press, 1995), 72–90, who argues that Luke insists that "all should have their proper place in the worship of God" (85).

[5] Cf. Barrett, *The Acts of the Apostles*, 2:421.

[6] The story of the eunuch and Philip may stem from a source, which Luke deemed appropriate to insert at this stage of his narrative, although he gives thematic primacy to Peter's encounter with Cornelius. See Barrett, *The Acts of the Apostles*, 2:421–22.

question of Gentile circumcision and the eventual proclamation of the so-called Apostolic Decree (15:7–11). Furthermore, as will be shown, questions related to Torah praxis lurk behind Luke's extensive narration of the Peter-Cornelius encounter. To appreciate the compatibility Luke sees between Gentile outreach and Jewish observance of the Law is to comprehend his aim to justify a mission to the Gentiles that aligns itself with Jewish concerns and halakah.

Literary Structure

I. Cornelius' Vision (10:1–8)
   A. Cornelius, the Pious Gentile (vv. 1–2)
   B. Cornelius' Vision (vv. 3–6)
   C. Cornelius' Compliance (vv. 7–8)
II. Peter's Vision (10:9–16)
   A. Peter, the Pious Jew (vv. 9–10)
   B. Peter's Vision (vv. 11–12)
   C. Peter's Non-Compliance (vv. 13–16)
III. Encounter between Peter and Cornelius' Embassy (10:17–23)
   A. Arrival of Cornelius' Embassy (vv. 17–18)
   B. Peter's Compliance (vv. 19–20)
   C. Hosting Cornelius' Embassy (vv. 21–23a)
IV. Encounter between Cornelius and Peter (10:23b–43)
   A. Cornelius and Peter Meet (vv. 23b–27)
      1. Journey to Caesarea (v. 23b)
      2. Entrance into Caesarea (vv. 24–26)
      3. Entrance into Cornelius' house (v. 27)
   B. Cornelius and Peter Talk (vv. 28–43)
      1. Peter's Pronouncement (vv. 28–29)
      2. Cornelius' Report (vv. 30–33)
      3. Peter's "Sermon" (vv. 34–43)
V. Baptism of Cornelius' Household (10:44–48)
   A. Baptism of the Spirit (vv. 44–46a)
   B. Baptism with Water (vv. 46b–48a)
   C. Hosting Peter (v. 48b)
VI. The Jerusalem Report (11:1–18)
   A. Judean Inquiry (vv. 1–3)
   B. Peter's Report (vv. 4–17)
   C. Judean Jubilation (v. 18)[7]

There are direct correspondences between parts I and II. In both parts, Luke describes Cornelius and Peter in pious terms: Cornelius is a particularly devout man who fears God, gives alms to the people of Israel, and prays (δεόμενος) constantly; Peter, for his part, goes up on a rooftop to pray

---

[7] Haenchen, *The Acts of the Apostles*, 358–59, neatly divides this extended pericope into seven scenes. I prefer to combine scenes four and five (10:23b–33 and 10:34–43) into one unit.

(προσεύξασθαι). As a recompense for their pious efforts, both Cornelius and Peter receive visions. Cornelius promptly obeys the orders given to him by the angel, sending out emissaries to Joppa in search of Peter. However, the literary symmetry between both episodes suddenly ceases: Peter, unlike Cornelius, refuses to comply with the orders he receives in his vision. Even though a heavenly voice commands him thrice to eat from the animals set before him, Peter refuses to obey. Deines concludes that the threefold command to eat what is impure implies that Luke no longer expects purity and kosher laws to be kept. Why else would Luke allow such a pointed repetition to subsist within his narrative?[8] This claim may be dismissed with the observation that Peter's persistently refuses to obey the command no less than three times, making his abstinence from eating forbidden foods all the more striking. Peter daringly refutes the heavenly voice – no small feat – and *never* partakes of the food presented before him, even though he hungers on top of a roof in hot Palestine at the hour of lunchtime. Instead, the rupture in literary symmetry and Peter's repeated refusal to obey the heavenly voice stimulate the reader to seek for a meaning of the vision that lies elsewhere than in the literal realm of kashrut. Like other prophetic or apocalyptic visions recorded in the Hebrew Bible and the Jewish tradition, Luke's Peter's vision is *symbolic* and requires further interpretation.

In part III, Cornelius' scouts finally arrive in Joppa and succeed in finding Peter's location. Only now as the perplexed Peter deliberates over the meaning of the vision he has just witnessed, does he comply with a different order given by the spirit, namely, to welcome Cornelius' men without passing judgment upon them. Accordingly, Peter invites Cornelius' men to enter (εἰσκαλεσάμενος) into the house where he is temporarily residing, entertaining them as his guests (ἐξένισεν). Thus, for the first time in Acts, Gentiles enter into a Jewish home and enjoy table fellowship with Jews as the verb ἐξένισεν implies. In addition, it could be that these Gentiles spend the night in the Jewish home where Peter temporarily resides, since only on the following day do they set out with the apostle on their journey to Caesarea. In this way, Luke subtly introduces the first step toward a Jewish-Gentile encounter that will shortly repeat itself within a non-Jewish home.

This progression continues in part IV as Cornelius' servants and Peter travel toward Caesarea. When Peter enters (εἰσελθεῖν) into Caesarea (vv. 24–26), he first meets an eager and humble Cornelius outside of his house. Proximity and intimacy with non-Jews increase as Peter continues to approach non-Jewish space (v. 27: εἰσῆλθεν), this time, the very house of Cornelius where he will stay for several days (v. 48). More intimate and

---

[8] Deines, "Das Aposteldekret," 331 n. 26.

substantial exchange now occurs between both parties within the house of the Roman centurion, with Peter delivering his first pronouncement regarding the new anthropological understanding he has acquired concerning non-Jews. This statement, like the command previously delivered to him through the spirit (v. 20), clarifies the true meaning of the vision he has seen earlier: it concerns humans, specifically Gentile followers of Jesus and their former impurity (v. 29). Cornelius in turn delivers his report about his "supernatural" encounter with an angel, leading Peter to affirm the moral of the vision a second time (vv. 34–35) and to deliver his testimony about Jesus (vv. 36–43).

In part V, the exceptional happens: Gentiles for the first time receive the gift of the spirit – an endowment exclusively reserved up until this point in Acts for Jews and certain "semi-Jews" such as the Samaritans. Not even the pious Ethiopian eunuch is said to have benefited from this spiritual privilege. After the spirit falls freely and generously upon the Gentile household, Peter proposes to commemorate this unique event through the baptism of water (vv. 46b–48a). Thereafter, Luke timidly insinuates that Peter spends several days within the house of the Gentile follower of Jesus (v. 48b).

Finally, Peter must confront his Judean compatriots from the Jerusalem headquarters, who hear rumors about his extensive stay in a Gentile household (11:1–3). Luke has Peter repeat in briefer terms the events already narrated for the reader in ch. 10 (11:4–17). The retelling of the Jewish-Gentile encounter signals the fundamental importance Luke ascribes to this formative event. Luke's Peter will briefly refer to it again during the Jerusalem council (15:7–9). Like Paul's "conversion," related no less than three times in the book of Acts (ch. 9; 22:6–21; 26:9–20), Luke recounts thrice Peter's own "conversion," that is, his adoption of a new perspective vis-à-vis Gentiles (ch. 10; 11:4–17; 15:7–9).[9] This threefold repetition, *during which kashrut is never explicitly denied*, underscores the theological importance the Cornelius episode holds for Luke.

Redactional Analysis

Many posit at least two pre-Lukan sources employed by the author of Acts in his retelling of the Cornelius incident. Thus, Dibelius distinguished long ago between an original narration reporting the conversion of Cornelius and a separate account recounting Peter's vision. For Dibelius the latter account announces the abrogation of Jewish food laws, while the former in

---

[9] Cf. Barrett, *The Acts of the Apostles,* 1:491.

its original, pristine form simply reported the conversion of a Gentile household.[10] Many have followed in Dibelius' footsteps, viewing Luke as an author who has ably fused two different traditions together to form one meta-story regarding the mission to the Gentiles and their incorporation into the *ekklesia*. For example, after his detailed redactional analysis, Weise concludes that Luke has reworked a written tradition whose content included Cornelius' vision, the commission of his messengers, the instruction of the spirit to Peter, the encounter between Peter and the centurion, Cornelius' report about his vision, and the spirit falling on Cornelius' household as well as their baptism through water. Luke would have introduced from another source of traditional material the vision of Peter (10:9–16) along with 10:28, 29a and 11:2 f. He would also have composed the speeches in 10:34–43 and 11:5–17, the related declarations in 10:22, 24b, 33b and 11:4, the pious characterizations of Cornelius (10:2, 4, 22, 31), the reference to Peter's companions (10:23b, 45; 11:12b), and the transitional and concluding verses in 11:1; 10:48b, and 11:18. Finally, he would have thoroughly reworked those parts reproduced from the traditional materials at hand.[11]

Wehnert, who roughly follows such a reconfiguration of sources, thinks that the traditional material recounting Peter's vision originally justified the abrogation of the food laws as found in Lev 11 and Deut 14:3–20 by seeking to eliminate the distinctions between pure and impure animals, either by alluding to the creation account (Gen 1:20–25) or the animals kept by Noah in the ark (Gen 6:20). Luke, however, would have allegorized this vision and shifted the focus away from kashrut and animals to the purification of human beings. The Lukan interpretation of Peter's vision and the Cornelius episode, therefore, would not have affirmed the abrogation of food laws, but only focused on the purity of Jews and Gentiles.[12] Others, however, who employ a structural analytical approach, resist dissecting the narration in Acts chs. 10–11 into distinct sources, criticizing the conclusions reached through traditional usages of form criticism.[13] Thus, for Klinghardt, Acts 10 and 11 present a consistent and unified unit that should not be divided into different sources or traditions.[14] In any case, concerning Luke's understanding of the pericope, Klinghardt

---

[10] Dibelius, *Studies in the Acts of the Apostles*, 109–22.

[11] Alfons Weiser, *Die Apostelgeschichte* (2 vols.; Ökumenischer Taschenbuch-Kommentar zum Neuen Testament 5.1–2; Gütersloh: Gütersloher Verlagshaus Gerd Mohn, 1982–1985), 1:262.

[12] Wehnert, *Die Reinheit*, 75–76; see especially 75–76 n. 85.

[13] See brief discussion and references in Klinghardt, *Gesetz und Volk Gottes*, 211–13.

[14] Klinghardt, *Gesetz und Volk Gottes*, 211: "konsistente Größe...die nicht in verschiedene Quellen oder Traditionen aufgeteilt werden kann."

in the end reaches the same conclusion as Wehnert, declaring that Jewish food regulations have not been abolished by Luke in Acts.[15]

In many ways, the analysis of sources and diachronic developments proves not so vital for this inquiry, which is more set on the outlook of the author of Acts in a post-70 setting. It would be tempting to embrace Wehnert's thesis regarding Luke's allegorization of a vision that originally abrogated Jewish food laws, since it would show all the more how far Luke is willing to reverse a process of de-Judaization within the *ekklesia*, in so far as Torah praxis is concerned. Nevertheless, perhaps even in the pre-Lukan traditions recounting Peter's vision, the thematic focused involved Jewish-Gentile fellowship (with *whom* one might eat) rather than kosher food (*what* one might eat).[16]

Given the complexity of the issue regarding the sources Luke uses in this section, it might be wiser to focus on chs. 10–11:18 as a whole, highlighting Luke's view on food laws in what has been dubbed "the largest narrated unit of the Acts of the Apostles."[17] What the preceding analysis of the literary context and structure of Acts 10–11:18 underscores is Luke's undeniable appropriation of the Cornelius episode, which he has significantly developed by repeating its contents and placing it at a critical juncture within his narrative interconnected with other key events in Acts (e.g., the Jerusalem Council).[18] All of these findings underline Luke's continual and profound interest in the contents and subject matter embedded in this pericope.

The Insignificance of Simon the Tanner[19]

For many New Testament commentators, the reference in Acts to Peter's temporary lodging in Joppa with a certain Simon, a tanner by profession (9:43; cf. 10:6, 32), points toward a dismissal of matters related to Jewish purity in the book of Acts. Those who embrace such a view incorporate this rather casual statement into a wider meta-narrative that announces in Acts not only the end of the Jewish purity system but also the abrogation

---

[15] Klinghardt, *Gesetz und Volk Gottes*, 212.

[16] Cf. Schneider, *Die Apostelgeschichte*, 2:62.

[17] Weiser, *Die Apostelgeschichte*, 2:251: "der längsten Erzähleinheit in der Apg."

[18] Even Klinghardt, *Gesetz und Volk Gottes*, 211 n. 13, who otherwise resists discerning between tradition and redaction at this point, recognizes that the repetition in Acts 11:1–18 must be redactional.

[19] The following section appeared in "Simon Peter Meets Simon the Tanner: The Ritual Insignificance of Tanning in Ancient Judaism." *New Testament Studies* 59 (2013): 50–60. I have since then added a few more references to primary sources in the footnotes of this section.

of Jewish food laws (i.e., kosher laws). Thus, the reference to Simon Peter's stay in the house of Simon the tanner would subtly pave the way in the narrative of Acts for the end of Jewish purity and dietary regulations supposedly announced in the subsequent pericope reporting Peter's vision and his encounter with the Gentile Cornelius. Essential to this thesis is the claim that ancient Jews despised the occupation of tanning because of the ritual impurity allegedly contracted through this trade. Although Strack and Billerbeck did not declare that tanning was ritually defiling, their biased observations against Judaism led other scholars to think so, once they claimed that the reference to Peter's stay in the house of Simon the tanner revealed his "inner freedom from Pharisaic regulations."[20] In any case, many commentaries on Acts and entries in biblical dictionaries and encyclopedias describe the profession of the tanner as ritually defiling.[21] A

---

[20] Str-B 2:695: "seine innere Freiheit von den pharisäischen Satzungen." Cf. Martin Hengel, *Acts and the History of Earliest Christianity* (trans. John Bowden; London: SCM Press, 1979), 93: "The fact that in Joppa he stayed with a tanner who was despised because of his unclean trade (9.43) is another indication of Peter's broad-mindedness." I do not know if Hengel drew his ideas about the supposed impurity of Jewish tanning and Peter's "liberalism" (as he states on p. 93) directly from Strack and Billerbeck, but at least Weiser, *Die Apostelgeschichte*, 1:245, does reveal his indebtedness to them when he states: "Da das Gerberhandwerk bei den Rabbinen als unrein galt, sehen *Bill*. II 695; Stählin: Apg 146 u.a. im Aufenthalt des Petrus beim Gerber Simon bereits die freiere Haltung des Petrus vorbereitet, von der in Kap. 10 f. die Rede sein wird." Weiser assumes that the rabbis deemed tanners impure. Does he misunderstand Strack and Billerbeck or is he primarily under the influence of Stählin? Weiser immediately proceeds to dismiss the relevance of Peter's sojourn in Simon the Tanner's house for the interpretation of Acts 10. Nevertheless, his statement show that he thinks tanning was ritually defiling. Gustav Stählin, *Die Apostelgeschichte* (NTD 5; Göttingen : Vandenhoeck & Ruprecht, 1980), 146, declares: "Sein Gastgeber (vgl. zu 21,16 f.) ist wieder ein Simon, 'Simon der Gerber' genannt...vielleicht soll aber mit der Erwähnung seines, von allen in der Apg. genannten Gewerben (vgl. 16, 14; 18, 3; 19, 24) am wenigsten geachteten Handwerks, der als unrein geltenden Gerberei, auf die folgende Geschichte (10, 14!) vorausgewiesen werden."

[21] So Adolf von Harnack, *The Acts of the Apostles* (trans. John Richard Wilkinson; Crown Theological Library 27; London: Williams & Norgate, 1909), 85: "tanning was an uncleanly trade"; Bruce, *Commentary on the Book of Acts,* 213 n. 68: "Peter's lodging with such a man was a mark of his increasing emancipation from ceremonial traditions." Similarly, William Neil, *Acts* (NCBC; Grand Rapids, Mich.: Eerdmans, 1981), 316; John Philipps, *Exploring Acts: Volume One Acts 1–12* (Chicago: Moody Press, 1986), 193; J. C. Trever, "Tanned, Tanner," *ISBE* 4:726: "The NT story of Peter's sojourn in Joppa with Simon, the tanner (Acts 9–10), implies that Peter had taken a step beyond the Jewish community with the Christian Gospel"; S. A. Cartledge, "Tanner, Tanning," *IDB* 4:516: "The fact that Peter was willing to stay with Simon was an indication of at least the beginning of a more liberal attitude on the part of Peter toward such ceremonial matters"; Kenneth D. Litwak, "Tanner, Tanning" *The New Interpreter's Dictionary of the Bible* (Nashville, Tenn.: Abingdon Press, 2006–2009), 5:470, who states without further quali-

recent commentary on Acts perpetuates this traditional understanding, claiming that Peter's stay in the residence of a Jewish tanner anticipates the "revolution" about to occur in Cornelius' house: the end of all separations imposed by Jewish purity regulations in the Christian regime.[22] Talbert's comments on the matter will suffice to summarize this point of view before providing an alternative reading to the rabbinic passages cited by him:

> On the other hand, that Peter resides "a long time in Joppa with Simon, a tanner" (v. 43), is very significant. Because Lev 11:39–40 pronounces unclean anyone who touches the carcass of even a clean animal, a tanner (even a Jewish one) would be perpetually unclean.[23] Being a tanner, therefore, was one of the trades a father should not teach his son (*m. Ketubim* 7:10; *b. Kiddushin* 82a Bar.). The rabbis said that tanneries could not be within fifty cubits of a town (*m. Baba Bathra* 2:9); that even if a tanner's wife agreed before marriage to live with him, he must put her away if she could not stand her circumstances after marriage (*m. Ketuboth* 7:10); that a synagogue building could not be sold for use as a tannery (*m. Megillah* 3:2). If Peter lives with a Jewish tanner over a period of time, it means that he has already come to the position that the cleanliness laws do not apply to Jews and to those who associate with them.[24]

A closer examination of the ancient Jewish sources and a proper understanding of the Jewish purity system, however, do not support this view. As long as a Jewish tanner could refrain from handling *carcasses* of kosher animals, contraction of ritual impurity – certainly no crime for many ancient Jews – could be avoided. The Mosaic Torah describes at least two types of carcasses: the *nevelah* (often translated as "an animal that has died on its own") and the *terefah* (an animal torn by a wild beast). Contact with such carcasses of kosher animals could transmit ritual impurity but contact with dead bodies of kosher animals that were ritually slaughtered would *not* transmit ritual impurity. Otherwise, as Miller points out, even priests would be more (ritually) impure than normal Jews because of their continual contact with slaughtered animals for the temple sacrifices![25] But even

---

fication that under "the Mosaic law, touching a dead thing made one unclean. Therefore, a tanner would have been almost perpetually unclean."

[22] Marguerat, *Les Actes des apôtres*, 357.

[23] Here Talbert assumes that Gentiles were bound by the ritual purity laws of Judaism and could become ritually defiled. However, as pointed out in the introduction to chapter 8 of this book, many specialists on ancient Judaism have argued against this understanding. See Hayes, *Gentile Impurities and Jewish Identities*, 19–22; 66–7, 142–44; Klawans, *Impurity and Sin*, 43–44, 48, 97; Maccoby, *Ritual and Morality*, 8–12.

[24] Charles H. Talbert, *Reading Acts: A Literary and Theological Commentary on the Acts of the Apostles* (Reading the New Testament Series; New York: The Crossroad Publishing Company, 1997), 104.

[25] Chris A. Miller, "Did Peter's Vision in Acts 10 Pertain to Men or the Menu?" *BSac* 159 (2002): 304. Cf. the statement made by Philo (*Spec.* 1:151) *in positive terms* regard-

with respect to the handling of carcasses of pure animals, rabbinic traditions, at least, maintain that only their *flesh* could transmit ritual impurity. Thus, *Sifra* Shemini Parashah 10:3–6 (cf. *m. Hul.* 9:1, 4), commenting on Lev 11:39 ("If an animal of which you may eat dies, anyone who touches *its carcass* shall be unclean until the evening"), states:

> "Its carcass" (בנבלתה): Not the bones and not the sinews and not the horns and not the hooves....[These parts of the carcass do not convey impurity when they are detached from the carcass]
> "Its carcass": Not hides (עור) that do not have on them flesh the size of an olive.[26]

This Tannaitic text claims that bones, sinews, horns, and hooves, when detached from a carcass, do not convey ritual impurity. It then goes on to discuss the case of hides, claiming that as long as they do not contain flesh attached to them that exceed the size of an olive, no carrion impurity is conveyed to the one handling them.[27] This rabbinic concession stems from the failure within the Mosaic Torah itself to tie in unequivocal terms the contraction of ritual impurity with the handling of carcasses of pure (i.e., kosher) animals.[28] In fact, certain rabbinic passages go as far as allowing Jews to handle the carcasses of *non-kosher* animals, provided this occurs

---

ing the priests who receive as a compensation for their priestly service the *skins* of the burnt offerings brought to them in the temple of Jerusalem.

[26] Author's translation. A baraita in *b. Hul.* 117b makes the same declaration: בנבלתה ולא בעור שאין עליו כזית בשר. See further Rashi on Lev 11:39; Milgrom, *Leviticus*, 1:682.

[27] Cf. *M. Hul.* 9:4: "If there remained an olive's bulk of flesh [of a carcass] on the hide and a man touched a shred of it that jutted forth, or a hair on the opposite side, he becomes unclean."

[28] As Milgrom acutely observes, certain regulations within the Pentateuch originally only forbade contact with carcasses of *impure* (i.e., non-kosher) animals (e.g., the carcass of a pig). Thus, Lev 5:2 states: "Or when any of you touch any *unclean* thing – whether the carcass of an *unclean* beast or the carcass of *unclean* livestock or the carcass of an *unclean* swarming thing – and are unaware of it, you have become unclean, and are guilty" (NRSV; emphasis mine). In this passage, the prohibition of touching carcasses only applies to animals that are by definition perpetually impure, that is, forbidden for consumption (cf. Lev 7:21). Interestingly enough, Lev 7:24 forbids the *consumption* of the *nevelah* or *terefah* of a pure animal, but allows Israelites to use their fat for any other purpose. Deut 14:21 even assumes that a Jew can touch a *nevelah* of a kosher animal (without contracting ritual impurity?): "You shall not eat anything that dies of itself; you may give it to aliens residing in your towns for them to eat, or you may sell it to a foreigner" (Deut 14:21). How does a Jew give or sell an animal that dies of itself to a Gentile without touching it? See Milgrom, *Leviticus*, 1:703. On the other hand, passages in the Mosaic Torah reveal that an Israelite could contract ritual impurity through contact with a carcass of either kosher or non-kosher animals (Lev 11:8, 39–40), although even such contraction of impurity was not a viewed by many Jews as a terrible, sinful act but a reality of daily life.

not on a festival day when a Jew would visit the temple.²⁹ Even a work such as the Temple Scroll, with its extreme concern for preserving ritual purity, recognizes the right for Jews to handle hides of kosher animals (ritually slaughtered). It only forbids Jews to bring hides of animals into Jerusalem that have not been slaughtered in the holy city: "If you slaughter it in my temple, it (the skin) will be clean for my temple; but if you will slaughter it in your cities, it will be clean for your cities" (11QTᵃ 47:15–17).³⁰

I have not come across one single rabbinic passage either from those cited in Strack-Billerbeck or from my own searches using the Bar Ilan Responsa database that views the profession of tanning as ritually defiling. Borrowing from the Greek language (βυρσεύς), rabbinic literature often employs the term בורסי for describing the trade, the same word that appears in Acts.³¹ The term בורסקי (from βυρσική), which refers to the tannery itself, is also attested (e.g., *m. Shabb.* 1:2). A closer examination of the rabbinic evidence shows that the rabbis generally despised this occupa-

---

²⁹ *Sifra* Shemini Pereq 4:8–9, commenting on the phrase "and their carcass you shall not touch" (ובנבלתם לא תגעו), which appears in Lev 11:8 in reference to the carcasses of forbidden animals such as pigs, maintains with a *qal vahomer* argument that lay Israelites can touch the carcasses of non-kosher creatures, since they are allowed to touch human corpses, which convey the highest degree of impurity. How much more the carcasses of forbidden animals whose impurity is less severe. The rabbis, of course, are not denying that such carcasses do indeed defile. Nevertheless, they understand that the Mosaic Torah does not view the contraction of ritual impurity as a sin as far as the handling of *common* food and objects is concerned. On the other hand, the conscious interaction with holy realms and objects, while ritually defiled, is strongly denounced in the Torah. Consequently, the same passage in the *Sifra* makes the qualification that one should avoid contracting ritual impurity during festival times when ordinary Jews could find themselves in the holy space of Jerusalem and its temple. See Rashi and his commentary on Lev 11:8. Possibly, 4Q397 (4QMMTᵈ) 3:11–13 with 4Q398 (4QMMTᵉ) 2–3:1–3 also forbid someone who has touched the skin of a *nevelah* from approaching sacred food or the temple. These texts, however, are very fragmentary. Of equal relevance is the statement in *m. Hul.* 9:2 declaring that even the hides of forbidden animals such as pigs or the eight vermin (Lev 11:29–30), the latter notoriously known for their ability to defile, when tanned, become pure (וכולן שעיבדן או שהילך בהן כדי עבודה טהורין). See also *m. Shabb.* 5:4 (usage of the skin of a hedgehog).

³⁰ Cf. 4Q394 3–10 (4QMMTᵃ) 2 (3–7ii): 2–4, which is very fragmentary but might contain a similar position as the Temple Scroll. Later, the Temple Scroll claims that the skin and bones of a carcass of a *forbidden* animal can transmit impurity (11QTᵃ 51:4–5). See further Magness, *Stone and Dung*, 42–43, for a discussion of this passage and other pertinent texts. A passage in Josephus, *Ant.* 12:146, forbids bringing the flesh or skins of *forbidden* animals (e.g., horses, mules, asses, leopards, foxes, or hares) into the holy city of Jerusalem.

³¹ Other terms used in rabbinic literature to describer tanners include עבדן and the less common צלעין. For references and discussion of these terms, see the still very useful Krauss, *Talmudische Archäologie*, 2:259–63.

tion because of the filth and strong stench associated with the work. Perhaps, they also looked down at this vocation because of its low social-economic standing. In other words, certain Jews found this vocation unattractive for *hygienic* reasons, because of its *uncleanliness*, that is, its filthiness or foul smell, not because of the ritual impurity allegedly involved. With these proper distinctions in mind, the reason for the rabbinic distaste toward tanning can be properly appreciated. When the rabbinic sages condemn tanning, they *never* point to ritual defilement as a reason for despising this trade.

For example, *m. Ketub.* 7:10 rules that Jews may compel a male tanner to divorce his wife if the latter can no longer endure living with her husband, not because of the ritual impurity associated with this trade, but because of the *physical deformities* (מומים) the husband acquires probably through his rough work.[32] Similarly, in *b. Hag* 7b, tanners, along with scrapers and coppersmiths, are exempted from appearing at the temple during pilgrimage festivals, not because of their ritual impurity, but because, as the Gemara explicitly states, of their unpleasant odor, which prevents them from going up with other persons (forming a separate group to go up to the temple is forbidden according to rabbinic halakah). In both of these passages, when the rabbis discriminate against tanners, they explicitly justify their halakic prejudices independent from considerations concerning ritual impurity.

---

[32] Perhaps also because of the foul smell and the filth involved. In the same passage, coppersmiths, among others, are also compelled to divorce their wives, not because of their ritual impurity, but because of the nature of the coarse work involved (cf. Sira 38:28: "So too is the smith, sitting by the anvil, intent on his iron-work; the breath of the fire melts his flesh, and he struggles with the heat of the furnace"). The mishnaic passage also cites the "gatherer" (המקמץ) who presumably collected dog, pig, and even human feces for the treatment of hides. Nevertheless, many Jews did not view feces of humans as ritually defiling (Milgrom, *Leviticus,* 1:767; Christine Hayes, *The Emergence of Judaism: Classical Traditions in Contemporary Perspective* [Minneapolis: Fortress, 2011], 36; Maccoby, *Ritual and Morality,* 30), and Jews of the Second Temple period used vessels made out of animal dung, some considering such vessels to be even immune to ritual impurity. See Magness, *Stone and Dung,* 75–76, for a discussion of the archaeological findings and literary sources. As far as we know, no Jew viewed animal dung as impure (see, for example, Ezekiel 4:15; *m. Shabb.* 4:1). Essenes, however, considered human feces (but not urine) to be ritually defiling (Josephus, *J.W.* 2:147; 11QT^a 46:15). In *b. Ber.* 25a, a baraita states: "A man should not recite the Shema in front either of human excrement or excrement of pigs or excrement of dogs when he puts skins in them." This halakah, however, does not claim that excrement (human or animal) is impure, as the Gemara to that section makes clear, only that it is *demeaning* or disrespectful to pray in such a setting. We should also note a late rabbinic text that acknowledges the usage of dog feces for tanning hides used for Torah Scrolls, tefillin, and mezuzot. See *Kallah Rabbati* 7:1. I would like to thank Jodi Magness for sharing some of her thoughts with me on this matter.

Elsewhere, the rabbis reveal a *moral* disdain for tanners. Thus, a baraita cited in *b. Qidd.* 82a forbids tanners from becoming a high priest or a king. But tanners are not the only workers singled out in this passage. Several other professionals do not qualify, including goldsmiths, carders, handmill cleaners, peddlers, wool-dressers, barbers, launderers, and bath attendants. In this same baraita, the rabbis place all of these professions under one common denominator: any man who engages in any of these trades supposedly possesses an immoral character because of his extensive interaction with women during work hours. Hence, the rabbis explicitly state that such people are exempt from serving as a high priest or king *not* because they are *unfit* (לא משום דפסילי), but because their vocations are demeaning, literally, "worthless" (זילי). In this passage, we learn about ancient patriarchal misogyny, not ritual impurity.

Regarding tanneries, one passage (*m. Meg.* 3:2) forbids a synagogue from being sold for use as a tannery. Once again, the concern here is not with ritual impurity but with the need to honor the sanctity of the synagogue. In other words, it would be demeaning to sell a synagogue if it were known that it would subsequently be transformed into a tannery. Such an act would reveal a lack of respect on the part of Jews for the synagogue.[33] Concerning the location of tanneries, some rabbis thought they should lie fifty cubits outside a city on its eastern side (e.g., *m. B. Bat.* 2:9) only because of the unpleasant smells emitted from such working places, not their inherent impurity.[34] In any case, references to tanneries lying outside cities also appear in non-Jewish literature. Thus, Artemidorus (c. 2nd cent. CE; *Oneirocritica,* 1.51) says that dreaming of tanning hides "is ill-omened for all. For the tanner handles dead bodies and lives outside the city."[35]

A passage like *b. B. Bat.* 21b does not view tanning as ritually defiling or even professionally reprehensible. In fact, this passage does not even

---

[33] Pinhas Kehati, *The Mishnah* (23 vols.; Jerusalem: Department for Torah Education and Culture in the Diaspora of the World Zionist Organization, 1987–1996), 5:34: "so that it will not seem that they are belittling the sanctity of the synagogue, as if they do not desire it, for it is of no account in their eyes (*Rashi*)"; Chanoch Albeck, *Shishah Sidre Mishnah* (6 vols.; Jerusalem: Bialik, 1952–1959), 2:362.This mishnah also forbids synagogues from being sold for use as bathhouses, as locales for immersion (טבילה), or as urinals (human urine, as pointed out earlier, was not viewed as ritually defiling).

[34] Because the prevailing winds in Palestine blow from the north-west, if a tannery was located on the westside, its unbearable stench would make its way into a town lying eastward. See Albeck, *Shishah Sidre Mishnah,* 4:123.

[35] Translation taken from Robert J. White, *The Interpretation of Dreams: The Oneirocritica of Artemidorus* (Park Ridge, N.J.: Noyes, 1975), 43. For non-Jewish references on tanners, see E. Beurlier, "Corroyeur," *DB* 2:1027–29.

concern itself with the halakic disrepute of tanners but with social-economic issues:

> A man may open a shop next to another man's shop or a bath next to another man's bath, and the latter cannot object. Because he can say to him, "I do what I like in my property and you do what you like in yours?" – On this point there is a difference of opinion among Tannaim, as appears from the following Baraitha: "The residents of an alley can prevent one another from bringing in a tailor or a tanner or a teacher or any other craftsman, but one cannot prevent another [from setting up in opposition]."

The baraita cited in this section of the Talmud allows local Jews to prevent tanners, or other artisans and professionals for that matter, from *another town* from moving into their neighborhoods in order to open businesses that already exist in the area. The preoccupation here seems to revolve around the social-economic unrest such commercial competition could bring to the local habitants. Nevertheless, the baraita and the ensuing discussion in the Gemara recognize the right for *local* residents to open up their businesses, including tanneries, even if such shops already exist in the neighborhoods they live in. This passage contains no negative pronouncement against the profession of tanning proper. If anything, it pragmatically recognizes the prevalence and need for tanners, given the useful and highly demanded products they manufacture.[36] *M. Shabb.* 1:2 even assumes that Jews regularly enter tanneries without condemning them for undertaking such normal and necessary transactions.[37] Indeed, the positive contributions of tanners should not be underestimated. They produced leather, which in turn was necessary for the production of harnesses, sandals, and even straps for tefillin, certainly no profane object! Furthermore, the preparation of animal skin was also essential for the production of parchment, the very surface upon which Jewish scribes inscribed the sacred letters of the Torah.[38]

---

[36] In *b. Pesah.* 65a, this social-economic reality is recognized: "The world cannot exist without a perfume maker and without a tanner." Cf. Sir 38:32, commenting upon the professions of the smith, potter, artisan, and the like, states: "Without them no city can be inhabited."

[37] Krauss, *Talmudische Archäologie*, 2:626 n. 82, cites *m. Shabb.* 1:2, along with *Sifre Deut* Pisqa 258; *b. Ber.* 22b and 25b, as proof that tanneries were "unrein." In reality, none of these passages makes such a claim. *M. Shabb.* 1:2 only states that one should not enter a tannery (or a bathhouse) if it is near the time of the afternoon prayer, presumably because transactions therein could delay the Jewish person from praying at the proper time. The same mishnah also commands Jews not to sit down before the barber nor to begin a meal or decide a legal suit near the time of prayer. None of this has to do with purity.

[38] See Josephus, *Ant.* 12:89–90. The processing of skin was important for the production of many other applications (*m. Kel.* 26:5; *m. Shabb.* 4:2: keeping food warm). See further Krauss, *Talmudische Archäologie,* 2:259 and R. Reed, *Ancient Skins, Parchments and Leathers* (London: Seminar Press, 1972), 86–88. On p. 94, Reed highlights the

Simon the tanner, therefore, probably did not find himself more often in a state of ritual impurity than other ordinary Jews. In any case, acquiring occasional ritual impurity, in the event that Jewish tanners would sometimes use hides that may have had some flesh from carcasses (animals not ritually slaughtered) of kosher animals attached to them, would not have been viewed as a sinful act among many ancient Jews, especially since they belonged to the poorer strata of society and would have understandably committed such acts in order to earn their living.[39] A simple immersion

---

honorable contribution to society on the part of Jewish tanners, but unfortunately thinks that the profession was ritually defiling (without citing one text to prove his point), and finally gets carried away when he states that "the New Testament statement that Peter was living with a tanner (Acts ix, 43) is probably an indication of how far, by aligning himself with the Gentiles and Christians, he had moved away from Jewish orthodoxy." He is also mistaken in claiming that Jews generally avoided processing skins and preferred that Gentiles handle this work. At least during the Middle Ages many Jews worked as tanners. See M. Lamed, "Leather Industry and Trade," *EJ* 12:574–77. We also know of at least one rabbinic sage who was a tanner (*b. Shabb.* 49 a–b; without any negative comments pronounced against the trade). The only passage Reed cites to justify his point is taken from *m. Shabb.* 1:8, which hardly speaks on behalf of a Jewish preference for Gentile handling of skins. The passage concerns itself with *Sabbath* halakah: a Jew may not give a hide to a Gentile tanner on a Friday (not on the Sabbath as Reed misinterprets this passage) if there is not enough time before sunset for the work to be completed. This halakah only forbids Jews to have Gentiles begin a work on a Friday that will continue into the Sabbath. Therefore, the passage tells us nothing about a general Jewish reluctance to engage in tanning.

[39] John Barclay raises a very important question when he asks me whether there is any information about who took the skin/hide off an animal in antiquity. Was it the job of a tanner or was it done before the hide arrived to a tannery? I can only offer some preliminary remarks on this issue based in part on Krauss' observations (the recent *Oxford Handbook of Jewish Daily Life in Roman Palestine* [Oxford: Oxford University Press, 2010], does not deal specifically with tanning). Krauss, *Talmudische Archäologie*, 2:259, first remarks that in peasant economies skins of animals, whether domestic or wild, must have been readily available to people who skinned them themselves for personal use as rugs, covers, and so on (see *m. Kel.* 26:8: hides belonging to a household; *b. Shabb.* 79a: distinguishing between dressed and undressed hides). Nevertheless, many of the local people would probably have handed their hides to tanners for further processing and resale. Some rabbinic passages presume this practice (e.g., *m. Shabb.* 1:8: handing a hide to a Gentile tanner). Most importantly, Krauss claims that it was the trade of professional *handlers*, who probably also flayed the animals, to provide tanners with hides: "Noch ehe das Fell zum Gerber kam, war es Gegenstand des Handels von Leuten (sie hießen גלדאי), die mitunter so zahlreich in einem Orte ansässig waren, daß man eine Gasse nach ihnen benannte. Vielleicht haben wir die berufsmäßigen Abdecker oder Schinder in ihnen zu erkennen, die wegen des üblen Geruches, den ihre Ware verbreitete, nur unter sich und außerhalb der Stadt wohnen durften" (pp. 259–60). If Krauss is correct, it would mean that tanners would normally not have dealt with the process of slaughtering and flaying animals, which would have been done beforehand, either by farmers, hunters, traders, or by other people. This would mean that tanners would normally not have to handle *car-

in a body of fresh water would have sufficed to recover ritual purity. For Simon the tanner, this would merely require a short walk out of his house for the occasional dip in the Mediterranean Sea, since he lived in the coastal city of Joppa.[40] Quite strikingly, *t. Ohal.* 18:2 theorizes about tanneries outside the land of Israel as shelters where purity can be more readily guaranteed because of their location near seas or rivers. Thus, R. Shimon states: "'I can feed the priests pure food in the tannery of Sidon and those that are in the cities of Lebanon because they are near the sea or the river.'"[41] In light of this passage, Peter's stay at a house near the sea could almost be taken as evidence of the Jewish apostle's concern for maintaining ritual purity, the exact contrary of what has been affirmed by much of secondary scholarship!

---

casses, making the contraction of impurity even less likely. On the other hand, depending on the quality of the work of the flayer, some flesh could have still adhered to the hide and made it impure if the hide stemmed from a carcass (and the flesh exceeded the size of bulk of an olive, at least according to rabbinic standards). I imagine that tanners could also slaughter and flay the animals on certain occasions, but probably they focused on their professional specialization: dressing hides. On a rabbinic discussion about how much of the skin from a carcass must be flayed in order to not convey ritual impurity, see *m. Hul.* 9:3. In a personal communication, Michael Greene, from Bradley University, points out that the open air market of Madrid, called "El Rastro" ("the trail"), is located near the site of earlier abattoirs and tanneries (the "Ribera de Curtidores," in English, the "Riverside of Tanneries"). Apparently, its name derives from the trail of blood that marked the path from the slaughterhouses to the tanneries.

[40] Cf. *m. Mikw.* 5:4: "All seas are valid as an Immersion-pool (*Mikweh*)."

[41] Author's translation: אמר ר' שמעון יכולני להאכיל את הכהנים טהרות בבורסקי שבצדון ושבעירות שבלבנוב מפני שסמוכין לים או לנהר. Krauss, *Talmudische Archäologie*, 2:260, refers to this passage as "eine alte positive Nachricht von einer Gerberei." This intriguing passage has some textual problems. See Saul Lieberman, *Tosefeth Rishonim: A Commentary* [in Hebrew] (4 vols.; New York: The Jewish Theological Seminary of America, 1999), 3:153–54. Although the discussion is purely theoretical, it is telling that this Toseftan passage initially considers tanneries as a convenient location for maintaining purity because of their location near bodies of natural water. Cf. *m. Ohal.* 18:6: "If a man went through the country of the gentiles in hilly or rocky country, he becomes unclean; but if by the sea or along the strand he remains clean. What is 'the strand'? Any place over which the sea rolls during a storm." It is surprising, therefore, to see in his translation of this Toseftan passage, Walter Windfuhr, *Die Tosefta: Band 6, Seder Toharot. 8. Heft, Ahilot/Negaim* (eds. Gerhard Kittel and Karl H. Rengstorf; Stuttgart: W. Kohlhammer, 1956), 327 n. 10, triumphantly declare (citing Rengstorf) that "Apg 9, 43 berichtet von einem längeren Aufenthalt des Petrus im Hause eines Gerbers Simon in Joppe (Jaffa) – ein angesichts der Reinheitsvorschriften offenbar für traditionell-fromme Juden höchst anstößiges Verhalten, deshalb aber nicht weniger bemerkenswert als Zeichen der Freiheit der jüdischen Christen von der Tradition!" Referencing *m. Shabb.* 1:2 and *m. B. Bat.* 2:9, Windfuhr claims that tanning was ritually defiling. However, as I argued above neither of these two passages speaks of such a thing.

But this is not the point the author of Acts seeks to make. At best, the reference to Simon's vocation might show a willingness on the part of certain followers of Jesus to associate with people of a lower social standing.[42] At the redactional level, the reference to Simon the tanner probably stems from tradition, as most New Testament commentators admit, the epithet, "tanner," assisting in distinguishing one Simon from the other more significant Simon Peter.[43] Finally, in the post-70 era when the author of Acts composed his writings, all Jews lived in a perpetual state of ritual defilement, making the alleged ritual impurity ascribed by many New Testament scholars to tanners a matter of even lesser halakic and theological significance.

The insignificance, then, of Simon's profession is twofold: it tells us nothing about a laxity on the part of Peter or the author of Acts toward ritual purity, let alone kashrut. On the other hand, it might inform us about the insignificant social-economic standing of certain Jewish members who joined the Jesus movement.

Cornelius: Righteous Gentile among the Nations

The Cornelius pericope opens with praise for the pious devotion of the Roman centurion toward the Jewish people and their ancestral ways. For Luke, Cornelius is not just any Gentile, but a "devout" man (εὐσεβὴς; cf. Acts 10:7) who fears the God of the Jews (φοβούμενος τὸν θεὸν) with his *entire* household (σὺν παντὶ τῷ οἴκῳ αὐτοῦ). Cornelius is one of those sympathizing, God-fearing Gentiles who attend their local Jewish synagogue, to be numbered with the many non-Jews who worship the God of Israel among the nations (Acts 10:35: ἐν παντὶ ἔθνει ὁ φοβούμενος αὐτὸν). He and his "philosemitic" household are acquainted with the essential mores of Judaism. Consequently, Luke holds them in higher esteem than he does the average Gentile.[44] Already in the opening to this key story,

---

[42] Because of the low status associated with the profession and their limited rights during the Middle Ages, many Jews worked as tanners. See Lamed, "Leather Industry and Trade," 12:574–77.

[43] Correctly, Schneider, *Die Apostelgeschichte*, 2:53 n. 67. Simon was one of the most common Jewish names in antiquity. See Margaret. H. Williams, "Palestinian Jewish Personal Names in Acts," in *The Book of Acts in Its Palestinian Setting* (ed. R. Bauckham; vol. 4 of the *The Book of Acts in Its First Century Setting,* ed. B. W. Winter; Grand Rapids, Mich.: Eerdmans, 1995), 93. It would seem rather odd for Luke to invent this character out of thin air for no reason. Hence, most commentators view this reference as part of tradition, but as Barrett, *Acts of the Apostles,* 1:486, points out, the traditional status of the name and profession does not prove the historicity of the event.

[44] Cf. Loader, *Jesus' Attitude towards the Law,* 368.

Luke strives to show that the non-Jewish space Peter will enter into contains Gentile members who are entirely sympathetic towards and knowledgeable about Judaism.

With this aim in mind, Luke continues to praise the qualities of Cornelius by highlighting his generosity toward the Jewish people: the Roman centurion gives alms in generous proportions to the Jewish community (ποιῶν ἐλεημοσύνας πολλὰς τῷ λαω). This description recalls in many ways Luke's portrayal in his gospel of another Roman centurion who also loves the people of Israel (ἀγαπᾷ τὸ ἔθνος ἡμῶν) and even assists with the edification of a synagogue (τὴν συναγωγὴν αὐτὸς ᾠκοδόμησεν), probably through monetary donations, much like the almsgiving of Cornelius (Luke 7:5).[45] It also points back to the preceding pericope concerning Tabitha, a woman "full of good works and charity" (Acts 9:36: πλήρης ἔργων ἀγαθῶν καὶ ἐλεημοσυνῶν).[46] In fact, this juxtaposition of "good works" with "charity" illustrates how the practice of the latter is really just the outer manifestation of a much broader devotion to the God of Israel.[47] Luke's reference to "almsgiving," therefore, should not be reduced to the material dimension of philanthropy. It conceptually overlaps with the broader category and practice of "righteousness" (צדקה/δικαιοσύνη).[48]

The inclusion of almsgiving as one of Cornelius' pious qualities in a pericope devoted to questions of purity and Jewish-Gentile contact is by no means accidental. As noted in the previous chapter, Luke has already inserted this feature into another debate about the ritual purity of vessels and washing before meals (Luke 11:37–41). Concerning that gospel passage, I argue that Luke might have had in mind "Christian Pharisees" of his own day, certain Jewish followers of Jesus similar to those who will shortly reprove Peter for entering into a Gentile house and dining with

---

[45] Quite interestingly, this praise for the Roman centurion's devotion to Jewish society is missing in Matthew (ch. 8). Moreover, Luke goes through greater efforts than Matthew does to keep a certain distance between the Roman centurion and Jesus: in the gospel of Luke, Jewish elders request on behalf of the Roman centurion Jesus' assistance, while in the gospel of Matthew the centurion enters into direct contact with Jesus. One could say that Luke's portrait is more "Jewish" than Matthew's account, since he shows greater sensitivity in depicting this Jewish-Gentile encounter.

[46] Luke also singles out Paul for his efforts in delivering donations when visiting Jerusalem (24:17). Cf. Acts 3:2, 3, 10.

[47] Cf. Klinghardt, *Gesetz und Volk Gottes,* 213.

[48] LXX of Prov 21:21: ὁδὸς δικαιοσύνης (MT: צדקה) καὶ ἐλεημοσύνης (MT: חסד) εὑρήσει ζωὴν καὶ δόξαν ("A way of righteousness and mercy [or almsgiving] will find life and glory"; translation mine). Tob 12:12: "Prayer with fasting is good, but better than both is almsgiving (ἐλεημοσύνης) with righteousness (δικαιοσύνης)." *B. B. Bat.* 10a: "Rabbi Eleazar used to give a *Perutah* [i.e., coin] to the poor and immediately pray. He said: 'for it is written, "I will see your face *in righteousness* (בצדק) [Ps 17:15]'" (translation mine).

non-Jews (Acts 11:2). Perhaps, Luke is also concerned with certain non-"Christian" Jews, particularly those in the Diaspora (cf. Acts 21:21; 28:17), who are suspicious of Jewish-Gentile interaction among disciples of Jesus, precisely because they hear that some Jews have abandoned their ancestral traditions. As outsiders to the Jesus movement, these Diasporan Jews fail to appreciate the unique qualities Luke ascribes to the Gentile disciples who are flocking into the *ekklesia*: they are sympathetic toward Judaism and practice virtuous, charitable deeds. For Luke, their *moral* purity is irreproachable, since they are fully committed to the God of Israel and perform good deeds central to the ethos of Judaism.[49] In fact, in Luke's eyes, it is the purity of his Jewish adversaries that is found wanting, since they allegedly do not practice the ethical cardinals required by their own tradition: when they will finally practice almsgiving, that is, righteousness, then their purity will become complete – in both the ritual and moral domains "everything will be clean" for them (Luke 11:41).

Luke's Cornelius also *prays* constantly to the God of Israel (δεόμενος τοῦ θεοῦ διὰ παντός). The theme of prayer appears so prominently in Acts that it would require a major deviation from the topic at hand in order to receive proper treatment.[50] At several major crossroads within Acts, the disciples of Jesus receive a divine revelation, a wondrous sign or miracle in response to their constant prayers. Thus already at the beginning of Acts, the disciples in Jerusalem receive the gift of the spirit in response to their constant prayers (1:14–16). This phenomenon repeats itself in Acts 4:31: after the disciples pray, they receive the sacred spirit and begin to speak the word of God in all boldness. In 8:15, Peter and John pray for the spirit to come upon the Samaritans. There are several other pertinent references within Acts,[51] but the novel element at this stage of the narrative consists in portraying a *Gentile* who prays and reaps heavenly benefits and shares the privilege normally accorded to other Jews of seeing a vision (ὅραμα), in Cornelius' case, an angelic apparition occurring around the ninth hour of the day.[52] The noun ὅραμα appears ten other times in Acts,

---

[49] According to Sir 3:30, almsgiving even atones for sins, and Luke's reference to Cornelius' practice of almsgiving serves to highlight the centurion's moral purity.

[50] The description of constant prayer recalls Anna's practice in the temple where she prays night and day (Luke 2:37).

[51] Acts 6:4, 6, 8:22, 24; 9:11, 40; 16:25, and so on.

[52] The reference to the timing of the revelation may not be accidental as it coincides with the hour at which offerings were presented in the temple of Jerusalem. Cf. Jdt 9:1. For Daniel K. Falk, "Jewish Prayer Literature and the Jerusalem Church in Acts," in *The Book of Acts in Its Palestinian Setting* (ed. Richard Bauckham; vol. 4 of the *The Book of Acts in Its First Century Setting,* ed. Bruce W. Winter; Grand Rapids: Eerdmans, 1995), 274 and Le Cornu and Shulam, *Jewish Roots of Acts,* 1:553, the declaration made by the angel concerning Cornelius' prayers (and charity) as having "ascended as a *memorial*

always in reference to a revelation transmitted to *Jews*.⁵³ Cornelius is the only non-Jew in Acts privileged with such a heavenly encounter. Moreover, the angel who appears to him *enters* (εἰσελθόντα πρὸς αὐτὸν) into his house, anticipating and preparing the way for Peter to do likewise when he visits the Roman centurion on the following day (10:24, 27). If a holy and pure angel of God (ἄγγελον τοῦ θεοῦ) can visit the house of a righteous Gentile, why not also a Jew?

Throughout this pericope, Luke continues to underscore Cornelius' devotion to Jewish tradition (e.g., 10:22). The repetition of Cornelius' Judaic credentials constantly reminds the reader that Peter is not interacting with the average Gentile. Despite his contemptible profession in the eyes of some Jews, particularly after the devastation of 70 CE, this Roman centurion proves to be righteous and God-fearing, appreciated by the *entire* Jewish *ethnos* (this is Lukan hyperbole). Luke also describes other members of Cornelius' entourage in similar terms: one of the messengers sent to Peter, also a soldier like Cornelius, is a devout (εὐσεβῆ) person (10:7). These positive traits, signaled by Luke, pave the way for Peter's eventual entry into Cornelius' house.

Peter's Vision: A Story about Gentiles, Not Food

Like Cornelius, Simon Peter receives a vision in response to his prayers, albeit at a different hour of the day: around noontime, in the heat of the day.⁵⁴ Not surprisingly, Peter is hungry at this hour and desires to eat (v. 10). The knowledge that his hosts are preparing him a meal (παρασκευαζόντων δὲ αὐτῶν) downstairs almost conditions Luke's Peter to

---

(μνημόσυνον) before God" recalls the description of offerings in the temple (אזכרה: Exod 28:29; Lev 2:2, 9, 16; 6:8).

⁵³ Acts 7:31 (Moses); 9:10 (Ananias); 9:12 (Paul); 10:17, 19; 11:5; 12:9 (Peter); 16:9, 10; 18:9 (Paul). Cf. Matt 17:9 (Jewish disciples of Jesus); Gen 15:1 (Abraham); Gen 46:2 (Jacob); Exod 3:3 (Moses); Num 12:6 (prophet of Israel); Dan 1:17; 2:19; 7:1, 7, 13, 15; 8:2, 13, 15, 17, 26, 27; 10:1 (Daniel and three friends). The king Nebuchadnezzar represents an exception although the dreams he sees do not come as a *response* to his prayers (Dan 2:1, 7, 26, 28, 36).

⁵⁴ Perhaps, we hear a distant echo of Abraham's own angelophany at the Oaks of Mamre, which occurs also around midday, "during the heat of the day" (MT Gen 18:1: כחם היום), that is, around noontime (LXX Gen 18:1: μεσημβρίας). Incidentally, Paul's own epiphany on the road to Damascus occurs at midday (see Acts 22:6: μεσημβρίαν). There is no need here to conform the timing of Peter's prayer to later rabbinic rhythms of prayer. For Luke, the major protagonists in Acts pray constantly and spontaneously throughout the day, not always in conformance to a fixed timeframe. Contra Str-B 2:699: "So kann man das Gebet des Petrus um die sechste Stunde (= mittags 12 Uhr) als vorzeitiges Mincha gebet erklären"; Le Cornu and Shulam, *Jewish Roots of Acts,* 1:558.

dream and fantasize about food. His resistance to indulge himself even in a vision proves all the more striking, given the hour and heat of the day as well as the hunger he is experiencing. Luke deploys these references concerning the timing and setting of Peter's vision to draw attention to the apostle's commendable abidance to kashrut, leaving the reader even more curious about the true meaning and import of the vision.

Before him, Luke's Peter beholds the sky opening and an "object" (σκεῦός) unfolding like a large linen cloth, lowered by its four corners upon the earth (τέσσαρσιν ἀρχαῖς καθιέμενον ἐπὶ τῆς γῆς). The reference to the four corners represents the world and already points toward the real application of this vision.[55] On the canopy, Peter finds *all* (πάντα) kinds of "quadrupeds" (τετράποδα), "reptiles" (ἑρπετά), and "birds" (πετεινά). This enumeration recalls passages from the creation account such as Gen 1:24, but also the list of pure and impure animals as delineated in Lev 11 and Deut 14. The Greek noun τετράποδα corresponds to the Hebrew בהמה, four-footed land animals, some but not all of which were viewed as forbidden for consumption. Only those four-footed land animals who divide a hoof into split hooves and chew the cud are permitted for consumption (Lev 11:3), while other animals who lack one or both of these characteristics are forbidden (Lev 11:4–7). The NRSV restricts too much the meaning of the Greek ἑρπετά by translating it as "reptiles." In the context of kashrut, it should refer more broadly to all "swarming" creatures, since it renders the Hebrew שרץ, a term denoting small creatures that go about in shoals and swarms, including insects that fly in clouds, such as gnats and flies, as well as land creatures such as weasels, mice, and lizards that creep low on the ground.[56] According to Lev 11, almost all swarming creatures are forbidden for consumption. Eight particular types of swarming creatures are especially singled out, capable of conveying impurity by ingestion and touch when they are dead (11:29–38). On the other hand, four types of locusts/grasshoppers are permitted for eating (Lev 11:22). Concerning birds, the Mosaic legislation sets no clear, comprehensive parameters, although birds of prey are often singled out as impure.[57]

Before this astounding sight, Luke's Peter hears a "voice" (φωνή) commanding him to "kill and eat." The voice is of heavenly, if not divine, provenance, as the answer of Peter in 10:14 implies: "by no means,

---

[55] Rev 7:1; Isa 11:12; Job 37:3.

[56] Milgrom, *Leviticus*, 1:655. Other versions such as the *New American Standard Bible* offer the more comprehensive term "crawling." In Greek, ἑρπετόν usually refers to *creeping* animals such as reptiles and serpents. But in the LXX, the term also encompasses certain winged insects (Lev 11:20).

[57] Already noted in the *Letter of Aristeas* (145–147). *M. Hul.* 3:6 discusses whether pure birds must have a crop, a gizzard that can easily be peeled off, and an extra talon.

Lord."⁵⁸ Luke's Peter understands the heavenly command in the most comprehensive way, sanctioning the consumption of *any* animal standing on the canopy: "By no means (μηδαμῶς), Lord, for I have never eaten anything that is profane or unclean (κοινὸν καὶ ἀκάθαρτον)" (10:14). In Luke-Acts, the adverb μηδαμῶς appears only here and once again in Acts 11:8. In the LXX, it often (but not always) renders the Hebrew חליל(ה. One thinks of Gen 19:7, where Abraham "bargains" with God over the fate of Sodom and Gomorrah, stating: "Far be it from you (μηδαμῶς/חללה) to do such a thing, to slay the righteous with the wicked, so that the righteous fare as the wicked! Far be that from you (μηδαμῶς/חללה)!" (Gen 18:25). It is Ezekiel's reply, however, that bears the greatest similarity with the answer given by Peter in Acts.⁵⁹ In Ezek 4:9–12, God orders Ezekiel to bake and eat some bread after cooking it over human dung as a symbolic act: "Thus shall the people of Israel eat their bread, unclean (טמא/ἀκάθαρτα), among the nations to which I will drive them" (v. 13). Ezekiel categorically refuses participating in such a disgusting act: "*By no means* (μηδαμῶς), *Lord* (κύριε) God of Israel, behold my soul has not been defiled with impurity and I have not eaten what has died of itself or what has been torn by a wild beast since my birth until now, nor has any stale flesh entered into my mouth."⁶⁰ In both scenarios, God orders a Jew to commit an act that is reprehensible and "impure." Both denials are phrased in a similar tone, containing overlapping vocabulary (μηδαμῶς/κύριε) and thematic links (impurity, food), suggesting a dependence of the wording in Acts upon Ezekiel.

Peter's response has confounded many scholars who rationalize how he should have simply selected a *pure* animal for consumption since *all* crea-

---

⁵⁸ Elsewhere, Luke clearly refers to the heavenly/divine status of this voice, describing it as φωνὴ κυρίου (Acts 7:31) or φωνὴ ἐκ τοῦ οὐρανοῦ (11:9; cf. Acts 9:4; Luke 9:35). In Jewish tradition, God and voice are easily identifiable with each another: Gen 3:8 (τὴν φωνὴν κυρίου τοῦ θεου), 10; τὴν φωνὴν κυρίου τοῦ θεου (Deut 18:16); Ps ch. 29; Isa 66:6; Mic 6:9.

⁵⁹ Cf. 1 Sam 12:23; 20:2, 9; 22:15; 24:7; 26:11; Jonah 1:14; Jdt 8:14; Tob 10:8; 2 Macc 7:25; 15:2, 36.

⁶⁰ My translation of the verse as it appears in the LXX. Ezekiel refuses to use *human* refuse, but not animal dung: "See, I will let you have cow's dung instead of human dung" (Ezek 4:15). Cf. James A. Patch, "Dung; Dung Gate," *ISBE* 1:996: "Ezek 4:12, 15 will be understood when it is known that the dung of animals is a common fuel throughout Palestine and Syria, where other fuel is scarce....There was no idea of uncleanness in Ezekiel's mind, associated with the use of animal dung as fuel (Ezek 4:15)." Cf. Emil G. Hirsch and Immanuel Benzinger, "Fuel," *JE* 5:525–26; Luke 13:8. As noted earlier, animal dung was not viewed as impure in ancient Judaism.

tures, both pure and impure, were lying in front of him on the canopy.⁶¹ However, Luke is not interested in engaging Peter and the heavens in a battle over semantics. Luke is more eager to move on to the moral of the vision, which really concerns people, rather than delay in portraying Peter trying to outwit a divine mandate that declares (in a vision) all foods to be pure.⁶² In this way, Luke chooses to present a Peter who refuses to imply in any way, even in a vision, that he would eat non-kosher animals.

This is not the first or last time in Jewish tradition that a human figure will resist a divine mandate to commit an act that presumably involves transgression. The prime example in Ezekiel 4:14 has already been noted, which might have even inspired the wording of Peter's reply in Acts 10:14 and 11:8. Deut 13:2–4 commands Israel not to listen to false prophets who have dreams claiming that one should worship false gods. While some (later) traditions concede that a heavenly voice (בת קול) may in certain instances establish a halakah,⁶³ the rabbis remain wary of any prophetic appeal to revelation for establishing legal decisions, let alone a deviation from the Torah.⁶⁴ "It is not in the heavens" (לא בשמים היא), citing Deut

---

⁶¹ See, for example, Barrett, *The Acts of the Apostles,* 1:508: "Again, why should Peter, with all living creatures before him, take for granted that he was being told to slaughter and eat an unclean animal? Why should he not pick out a clean, permitted one?"

⁶² One thinks of the rabbinic midrash (*Gen. Rab.* 55:7) on Gen 22:2 concerning an even more controversial divine command given to Abraham: "Take your son, your only son Isaac, whom you love, and go to the land of Moriah, and offer him there as a burnt offering on one of the mountains that I shall show you." The rabbinic midrash has Abraham engage in a debate of semantic "clarification" with God concerning this outrageous command: "And [God] said: 'Please take your son.' He [i.e., Abraham] said to him: 'Two sons I have [Isaac and Ishmael]. Which son?' He said to him: 'Your only one.' He said to him: 'This one is an only one to his mother and this one is an only one to his mother.' He said to him: 'The one whom you love.' He said to him: 'Are there limits to the bowels' [meaning: is there a limit to love, since I love both of my sons]?' He said to him: 'Isaac'" (translation mine; "God" has been masculinized in my translation only to replicate a literal rendition of the ancient text). Luke, of course, does not choose such a semantic route. Instead, he highlights Peter's categorical *refusal* to comply with an even more ambiguous and less outrageous demand, that of eating forbidden food in a vision.

⁶³ *B. Ber.* 51b; *b. Rosh. Hash.* 14b; *b. Eruv.* 6b–7a, 13b; *b. Pesah.* 114a; *b. Yevam.* 14a.

⁶⁴ Louis Isaac Rabinowitz, "Prophets and Prophecy," *EJ* 16:581–82: "The Talmud interprets the verse (Lev. 27:34) 'these are the commandments which the Lord commanded Moses for the children of Israel in Mount Sinai,' to mean that 'henceforth a prophet may make no innovations' (Shab. 104a). 'The prophets neither took away from, nor added to, aught that is written in the Torah, save only the commandment to read the *megillah* and even for that they sought biblical sanction (Meg. 14a). In conformity with this view, in the chain of tradition with which tractate *Avot* opens, the prophets appear merely as the tradents of the Torah of Moses, the successors to the elders after Joshua, and the predecessors of the men of the Great Synagogue."

30:12, is the famous response given to R. Eliezer b. Hyrcanus who appeals to heavenly communication as a means for justifying his halakic decision during the famous rabbinic debate over the impurity of the oven of Akhnai (*b. B. Metzi'a* 59b; *b. Pesah.* 114a). Of course, the historical contexts and social settings of Luke and the rabbis are "worlds apart." Nevertheless, such traditions, whether from Second Temple or rabbinic sources, illustrate how "reasonable" Peter's refusal to comply with a controversial command sent from above would appear to an audience familiar with Jewish tradition. After all, others prominent figures prior to Peter, such as Ezekiel or even Abraham, had bargained, questioned, or even refused to heed to divine commands they deemed questionable.

None of the subsequent interpretations of the visions made in this very extensive Lukan pericope ever claim that kashrut has been abrogated. Rather than providing an immediate and explicit interpretation of the vision, as attested in other contemporaneous (apocalyptic) Jewish literature of his time (e.g., *2 Bar.*; *4 Ezra*), Luke momentarily and skillfully delays this literary process. This artistic postponement allows Luke to augment the suspense for his readers, leaving them even more eager to discover the true significance of the vision.[65] Peter's bewilderment signals to Luke's readers that the meaning of the visions must lie elsewhere than in a literal application of its stipulations. Unlike some interpreters who easily conclude that the meaning of this vision clearly refers to eating non-kosher food, Luke's Peter remains "greatly puzzled," "completely at loss" (διηπόρει) at what to make about the sight he has just witnessed (10:17).

But even while avoiding revealing instantaneously the true import of the vision, Luke already and cleverly points toward its proper comprehension by coinciding Peter's bafflement with the arrival of Cornelius' messengers: "suddenly the men sent by Cornelius appeared. They were asking for Simon's house and were standing by the gate" (10:17). Luke already hints here at the theme of Jewish-Gentiles relations, not the kosher industry: the hermeneutical key to unlocking the interpretation of the dream lies right at the doorsteps of Simon the tanner's house. As Luke continues to highlight Peter's puzzlement (repeated a second time in 10:19 with the verb διενθυμέομαι, "to ponder"), the "spirit" (τὸ πνεῦμα) guides the Jewish apostle in the right direction towards understanding the vision: "Look, three men are searching for you. Now get up, go down, and go with them without hesitation; for I have sent them" (vv. 19–20). As Luke's Peter draws nearer to Gentiles, he gradually draws nearer to a proper comprehension of the vision. It will only be in the house of Cornelius that he will

---

[65] On the rhetorical and literary skills of Luke in this episode, see Miller, "Peter's Vision in Acts 10," 311.

finally understand its full significance: "God has shown me that I should not call *anyone* profane or unclean" (v. 28; cf. v. 34).

Distinguishing between Gentile Impurity and Profaneness

A challenging exegetical question concerns the interpretation of the twofold description in 10:14 to eat what is "profane or unclean" (NRSV), in Greek, κοινὸν καὶ ἀκάθαρτον. The NRSV has translated καὶ as "or," and many commentators follow this trajectory.[66] Haenchen even understands the construction as a hendiadys to mean, "I have never eaten anything impure."[67] In other words, there would be little or no connotative distinction between κοινὸν and ἀκάθαρτον.[68] Luke would have employed both adjectives simply for emphasis. This understanding of both terms is not without merit since by the Second Temple period the term κοινός had come to acquire in certain contexts a meaning synonymous with ἀκάθαρτος. In the LXX, the term ἀκάθαρτος translates the Hebrew טמא ("impure"), precisely the word used to describe forbidden meats in Lev 11/Deut 14 (Lev 11:4, 6, 7; Deut 14:7, 10, 19, etc.). Κοινός, on the other hand, which literally means "common" or "profane" is not used in the LXX in reference to forbidden meats. In addition, the LXX consistently uses the adjective βέβηλος or the verb βεβηλόω rather than κοινός or κοινόω to translate the Hebrew חל ("common" or "profane") and חלל.[69]

If in the Septuagint the term ἀκάθαρτος is reserved for describing what is impure or forbidden, while βέβηλος refers to the profane, in the book of 1 Maccabees, κοινός suddenly emerges in certain passages in reference, it

---

[66] Barrett, *The Acts of the Apostles*, 1:488; Fitzmyer, *The Acts of the Apostles*, 453, 455; Johnson, *The Acts of the Apostles*, 181, 184.

[67] Haenchen, *The Acts of the Apostles*, 357–59.

[68] Inspired by Ezek 4:14, Delitzsch's renders in his Hebrew translation of the New Testament κοινὸν καὶ ἀκάθαρτον as פגול וטמא. The term פגול, however, in the Pentateuch refers to sacrificial meat that has become desecrated because it has not been handled or eaten within its specified time (Lev 7:18; 19:7; translated in LXX as μίασμα and ἄθυτόν, respectively). See Milgrom, *Leviticus*, 1:422: "It [פגול] refers to sacred meat that has exceeded its prescribed time limit and thereby become desecrated." Actually, in the LXX of Ezek 4:14, the Greek term ἕωλον, not κοινὸν, translates פגול. Quite interestingly, Delitzsch switches to the Hebrew חל when translating κοινὸν in Acts 10:28. Salkinson and Ginsburg's Hebrew translation of κοινὸν καὶ ἀκάθαρτον in Acts 10:14 as פגול או שקץ טמא. This is pleonastic, if not erroneous. In the LXX, βδέλυγμα normally translates שקץ.

[69] LXX Exod 31:14: the Sabbath is holy, the one who desecrates (ὁ βεβηλῶν) it shall die; Lev 10:10: "to distinguish between the holy and the common, and between the unclean and the clean" (διαστεῖλαι ἀνὰ μέσον τῶν ἁγίων καὶ τῶν βεβήλων καὶ ἀνὰ μέσον τῶν ἀκαθάρτων καὶ τῶν καθαρῶν/להבדיל בין הקדש ובין החל ובין הטמא ובין הטהור); 1 Sam 21:5: "common bread" (ἄρτοι βέβηλοι/לחם חל).

would seem, to forbidden, non-kosher foods. Thus, in 1 Macc 1:47, one learns about the nefarious attempt "to sacrifice swine and other unclean animals (κτήνη κοινά)" in the temple of Jerusalem. The translators of the NRSV have sensed the need here to render κοινά as "unclean" (=ἀκάθαρτος) because the passage would seem to refer to other forbidden or non-kosher animals besides swine.[70] While Goldstein suggests κτήνη κοινά represents kosher animals that were unfit for sacrifices (either because of blemishes or because they were non-sacrificial animals), an even more offensive and deliberate rupture with Mosaic legislation, that is, the offering of other disgusting non-kosher animals in addition to pigs on the altar, might better account for the great distress voiced in 1 Macc over the general apostasy of Jews from the essentials of Judaism (as viewed by its author).[71] Similarly, in 1 Macc 1:62, the author praises the faithfulness of those Jews who "stood firm and were resolved in their hearts not to eat unclean food (κοινά)." These Jews are commended for refusing to defile themselves (μιανθῶσιν=טמא) through the consumption of certain foods (1 Macc 1:63). If these food items were kosher and merely defiled ritually, it is questionable whether their consumption would have prompted such a scandal for the author, since acquiring temporary ritual defilement was not viewed as a major sin. It is probably better, therefore, to view this passage as referring to non-kosher food.[72] Alternatively, it could be that the author of 1 Macc considers the food prepared by any Gentile or Jewish renegade as κοινά and therefore defiling (in an offensive or moral sense), even if, technically, the food item is permitted for a Jew to eat.[73]

---

[70] This is also how Uriel Rappaport, *The First Book of Maccabees: Introduction, Hebrew Translation, and Commentary* [in Hebrew] (Between Bible and Mishnah; Jerusalem: Yad Ben Zvi, 2004), 115, seems to understand the term by translating the Greek as בהמות טמאות.

[71] Cf. 1 Macc 1:48: "They were to make themselves abominable by everything unclean and profane" (βδελύξαι τὰς ψυχὰς αὐτῶν ἐν παντὶ ἀκαθάρτῳ καὶ βεβηλώσει). The verb βδελύξαι corresponds to the Hebrew שקץ. This Maccabean passage recalls the difficult verse in Lev 11:43: "You shall not make yourselves detestable (תשקצו/ βδελύξητε) with any creature that swarms; you shall not defile (תטמאו/ μιανθήσεσθε) yourselves with them, and so become unclean (ἀκάθαρτοι/נטמתם)." It is difficult to know what βεβηλώσει refers to in 1 Macc 1:48. Is it synonymous with κοινά? Rappaport, *The First Book of Maccabees*, 115, renders βεβηλώσει in 1 Macc 1:48 as תועבה.

[72] Cf. Thiessen, *Contesting Conversion*, 128; Rappaport, *The First Book of Maccabees*, 121.

[73] This interpretation of 1 Macc would align itself with Freidenreich's understanding of Dan 1:8. See his *Foreigners and Their Food*, 35–38. The terminology between Dan and 1 Macc is somewhat different, however (Dan 1:8: יתגאל/ ἀλισγηθῇ; 1 Macc 1:63: μιανθῶσιν; 1 Macc 1:48: βδελύξαι). It is possible, therefore, that the author of 1 Macc envisages a transgression of kashrut proper (i.e., the consumption of forbidden meats), since the terminology he employs corresponds more closely to the language of Lev 11.

4 Macc 7:6 praises the priest Eleazar for not defiling (ἐκοινώνησας) his stomach with forbidden foods such as pork. Wahlen believes κοινά and ἐκοινώνησας in 1 Macc and 4 Macc, respectively, refer to kosher food whose ritual purity was held in doubt.[74] Wahlen claims that in 1 Macc 1:62 the word κοινά "cannot be taken to mean the eating of *unclean* animals because this has been clearly referred to already in v. 48."[75] It is true that the language in 1 Macc 1:48 shares affinities with Lev 11:43, which deals with forbidden food items. 1 Macc 1:47, however, possibly uses the term κοινά in reference to other forbidden animals besides pigs, which are viewed as unholy, because they are disgusting and associated with the Gentiles and consequently unfit as sacrificial offerings. At stake in 1 Macc is not halakic hairsplitting over whether Jews can eat permitted food that *might* have been ritually defiled, but far greater departures from the essence of "Judaism" posited over against "Hellenism" as the author sees it: Jews are being led away from the very observance of circumcision, Sabbath keeping, and kashrut, not simply from eating kosher food that has been defiled. Concerning 4 Macc 7:6, Wahlen claims that Eleazar is commended not for his abstinence from defiling (ἐκοινώνησας) his body with pork, but for avoiding eating kosher food that might have become ritually defiled because Gentiles prepared it. Admittedly, in 4 Macc 6:15, Eleazar is offered the opportunity, after explicitly refusing to eat pork, to *pretend* to do so: the king's retinue offers to set before him some "cooked food" (ἡψημένων βρωμάτων) that Eleazar can eat while pretending (ὑποκρινόμενος) it is swine in order to save his life. According to Wahlen, Eleazar is praised for not even eating this kosher food (the king's retinue would have presumably offered him permitted food) because he wonders whether it might have been ritually defiled at some stage of its preparation.

It is questionable, however, whether the concern here involves ritual contamination. Perhaps, the reference to *prepared* (ἡψημένων) food suggests that Eleazar refuses to eat it because it has been *cooked* by non-Jews and is therefore considered as Gentile food.[76] The term βρωμάτων, after all, is a neutral designation that can refer to *any* food, permitted or forbidden. Nevertheless, Eleazar's previous test involved the consumption of a forbidden animal, pork (4 Macc 5:6–8). In addition, one should pay careful attention to the term μιαροφαγία, which appears in 4 Macc 7:6 in conjunction with ἐκοινώνησας. This term can refer to defiling non-kosher meats or

---

[74] Clinton Wahlen, "Peter's Vision and Conflicting Definitions of Purity," *NTS* 51 (2005): 505–18.

[75] Ibid., 512.

[76] This would accord with the comments made by Kraemer, *Jewish Eating and Identity*, 26–29 and Freidenreich, *Foreigners and Their Food*, 35–38, concerning other Second Temple texts.

food offered to idols (4 Macc 5:2–3, 19, 25, 27; 6:19; 8:2, 12, 29; 11:16, 25). Finally, does the author of 4 Macc commend Eleazar for refraining from eating food *cooked* by Gentiles or for abstaining from even *pretending* to eat pork? If Eleazar is praised primarily for refraining from hypocrisy, this would imply that the author of 4 Macc believes Jews *can* eat kosher food prepared by Gentiles. The test, then, for Eleazar would have involved fleeing away from publicly misleading the wider Jewish and non-Jewish communities into thinking that he had complied with the king's coercion to eat pork (which, technically, he would have only "pretended" to eat). Indeed, in 6:17–19, Eleazar seems very disturbed at the prospect of feigning to eat forbidden meat and the precedent this would set for younger people. In the parallel story in 2 Macc 6:21–24, Eleazar is even offered the opportunity to bring food *he himself has prepared*. Nevertheless, he still declines because he wishes not to engage in hypocrisy and mislead the younger generation of Jews.

As noted earlier in this monograph, in Mark 7 and Matt 15, the adjective κοινὸν and the verb κοινόω appear in reference to "impure hands" (Mark 7:2, 5: κοιναῖς χερσίν) and food ritually defiled through such contact (Mark 7:15, 18, 20, 23; Matt 15:11, 18, 20). In Matt and Mark, however, the terms κοινός and κοινόω are used to discuss matters related to the rigorous maintenance of ritual purity through the washing of hands before meals, not kashrut.[77]

The semantic use of κοινός, then, can occasionally overlap with its cousin ἀκάθαρτος, going beyond its literal sense of "common" or "profane" to encompass the domains of impurity and kashrut. Booth suggests that forbidden animals came to be called κοινά in 1 Maccabees because the surrounding nations consumed them, while such foods were deemed impure or forbidden for Jews. Booth argues that this new Jewish extension of κοινός from "profane" to "impure" eventually encompassed discussions dealing with forbidden meats as well as different types of ritual impurity (e.g., impure vessels, liquids, and so on).[78] We could add that the term came to be used to designate *any* food prepared by Gentiles. Such a semantic development seems quite understandable, since the associative dimension of *communion* (κοινωνία), which underlines the term κοινός, easily crosses into the realm of dietary practices. After all, the very *raison d'être*

---

[77] How should Rom 14:14 be understood? "I know and am persuaded in the Lord Jesus that nothing is unclean (κοινὸν) in itself; but it is unclean (κοινὸν) for anyone who thinks it unclean (κοινὸν)"? Does it concern purity, food offered to idols, or food prepared by Gentiles? See Tomson, *Paul and the Jewish Law*, 247–54; Freidenreich, *Foreigners and Their Food*, 89–90.

[78] Booth, *Jesus and the Laws of Purity*, 120–21; cf. Wilfried Paschen, *Rein und Unrein: Untersuchung zur biblischen Wortgeschichte* (SANT 24; Munich: Kösel, 1970), 165–67. See also Meier, *Marginal Jew*, 4:427 n. 4.

for keeping kosher for many Jews in antiquity meant *disassociating* themselves from other ethnic groups, preserving thereby their identity and collective *sanctity* – the very antonym of profaneness. As the Torah "repeats" in Deut the regulations of kashrut, it states: "For you are a *holy* (ἅγιος/קדוש) people to the LORD your God; and the LORD has chosen you to be a people for His own possession *out of all the peoples* who are on the face of the earth" (Deut 14:2; emphasis mine). Prolonged association with other peoples could lead, so some Jews believed, to the abandonment of Jewish identity and transformation into the Gentile "other." "Whoever associates (ὁ κοινωνῶν) with a proud person becomes like him," warns Ben Sira (13:1). This statement, of course, does not deal with dietary laws, but instills in the mind of the reader the need to associate with proper people. In *Joseph and Aseneth* (7:6), Jacob beseeches Joseph and his other sons to keep themselves from foreign women, to not *associate* with them (τοῦ μὴ κοινωνῆσαι αὐτῇ). Not surprisingly, the author of this Diasporan work does not allow Joseph to eat on the same table with his future Egyptian wife so long as she has not converted. In his discussion and defense of the observance of kashrut, the author of the *Letter of Aristeas* provides a rationale for this legislation that is intertwined with the theme of (dis)association (128–130):

> It is my opinion that mankind as a whole shows a certain amount of concern for the parts of their legislation concerning meats and drink and beasts considered to be unclean. For example, we inquired why, since there is one creation only, some things are considered unclean for eating, others for touching – legislation being scrupulous in most matters, but in these especially so. In reply, he began as follows: "You observe, he said "the important matter raised by modes of life and relationships, inasmuch as through bad relationships men become perverted, and are miserable their whole life long; if however they mix with wise and prudent companions, they rise above ignorance and achieve progress in life.

The author of the *Let. Aris.* goes on justifying the practice of Jewish food laws by underscoring how it has kept the Jewish people away from assimilation, idolatry, and polytheism. The Law has "fenced us round with impregnable ramparts and walls of iron, that we might not mingle at all with any of the other nations, but remain pure in body and soul, free from all vain imaginations, worshiping the one Almighty God above the whole creation" (139). Here the themes of association, *kashrut*, and purity intersect to describe the logic and function of Jewish belief and practice.

It is understandable, therefore, that the NRSV and other commentators translate κοινὸν and ἀκάθαρτον as virtual synonyms. Nevertheless, I suggest that Luke makes a fine and important nuance between both terms. Luke conceptually distinguishes between the categories of "purity/impurity" and "holiness/profane" when employing the pair κοινὸν καὶ ἀκάθαρτον. It is critical to understand this distinction already present within the Mosaic

Torah (e.g., Lev 10:10): "Separate from, but related to, the concept of purity is the concept of profaneness. While 'impure' (טמא) is the ontological opposite of 'pure' (טהור), 'profane' (חול) is the ontological opposite of 'sacred' (קדוש)....A 'profanation' (חלול) is a violation of the sacred that is not connected to purity per se."[79] Hayes phrases the distinction in the following way:

> It will be recalled that profanation, or desecration, is simply the transformation of what is holy into what is common. The now common object is not necessarily impure unless the desecration was brought about by contact with a source of impurity. Defilement is the transformation of what is pure into that which is impure, and if the object was formerly holy it will be necessarily common, or profane upon defilement. Profanation of a sanctum, although serious, is not as grave as actual defilement of a sanctum.[80]

Within the Jewish system of thought and practice, a hierarchy, extending from the most profane to the most holy, governs the ways Gentiles, female and male Jews, priests, and high-priests access the realm of the sacred, that is, the temple. According to Josephus, during the Second Temple period, Gentiles could only access the outermost court of the temple where both pure Jewish women and men were also allowed to enter. In the second court, all pure Jews were admitted, whether male or female, while only pure male Jews could enter the third court. To the fourth court entered only the priests, while the sanctuary proper remained accessible only to the high priests (*Ag. Ap.* 2:103). As Hayes points out, pure Jewish women were not excluded from the third court because of a supposed intrinsic ritual impurity ascribed to females, but because they were viewed as more profane than Jewish males. Likewise, a lay Jewish male could not access the fourth court because they were not holy to the same degree as priests. Finally, the high priests enjoyed the greatest degree of sanctity and therefore could access the holiest of holy realms. A spectrum of profaneness-sanctity, ranging from the most profane of persons, Gentiles, to the holiest of individuals, the Jewish high priest, defined and governed relationships between Jews and Gentiles in such spaces and other venues. Vis-à-vis the holy priests, lay Jews were common, but vis-à-vis the Gentiles, as a collective entity, they represented a holy congregation. Accordingly, Gentiles were not excluded from the temple because of their intrinsic ritual impurity, but because of their inherent profaneness. They did not belong to the holy people of Israel; they were profane people.

Within the course of ancient Jewish history, Klawans argues that it was precisely the inherent profaneness ascribed to Gentiles that ultimately

---

[79] Jonathan Klawans, "Notions of Gentile Impurity in Ancient Judaism," *AJSR* 20 (1995): 291–92.

[80] Hayes, *Gentile Impurities*, 230–31 n. 32.

excluded them from the sanctuary of Jerusalem.⁸¹ Ezekiel zealously endorses this position: "O house of Israel, let there be an end to all your abominations in admitting foreigners, uncircumcised in heart and flesh, to be in my sanctuary, profaning (לחלל/ἐβεβήλουν) my temple when you offer to me my food, the fat and the blood" (44:6–7). The author of Ezekiel opposes Gentile participation in the cult because of their inherent profaneness. On the other hand, Isa 56:3–7, whose content and message Luke knows of and embraces, presents an opposing view to Ezekiel's when it recognizes the right for eunuchs and uncircumcised foreigners to participate in the temple cult.

The distinction between profane and impure is useful, I would suggest, for understanding Acts 21:28 and its claim that certain Jews from Asia accused Paul for bringing non-Jews into the temple of Jerusalem, apparently beyond the court of the Gentiles, and consequently *profaned* (κεκοίνωκεν) "the *holy* place" (τὸν ἅγιον τόπον) of Jerusalem. Here the verb κεκοίνωκεν, related to its adjectival cousin κοινός, bears the meaning of making common or profane, not rendering impure,⁸² for a Gentile, in this case a God-fearing follower of Jesus (if the charges against Paul were true), technically could not *defile* the temple of Jerusalem, since Gentiles were not considered to be ritually impure. In this case, Luke would have maintained that Paul's Gentile companion was not even morally impure, since he had presumably abandoned immorality and idolatry.⁸³ This understanding of κεκοίνωκεν becomes clear when the same charge is brought up again against Paul during his hearing before the Roman procurator Felix: "He even tried to *profane* (βεβηλῶσαι) the temple, and so we seized him" (24:6). Here the same charge appears but Luke employs a different, yet in this case synonymous, verb to κεκοίνωκεν. It is precisely βεβηλῶσαι, which is related to the adjective βέβηλος, that the LXX consistently employs to

---

⁸¹ Klawans, "Notions of Gentile Impurity," 292.

⁸² Quite possibly, κοινός in Rev 21:27 and Heb 10:29 also means "profane" rather than "impure." In Rev 21:27, the adjective is used in reference to people who will not enter the *holy* city of Jerusalem. Furthermore, the author of Rev knows and employs the adjective ἀκάθαρτος (16:13; 17:4; 18:2), which means "impure," suggesting that his usage of κοινός with reference to the holy city of the new Jerusalem should be understood in the sense of "profane." Likewise, Heb 10:29 juxtaposes κοινός with the act of *sanctification* (ἡγιάσθη).

⁸³ This is where I differ with Thiessen, *Contesting Conversion*, 130, who understands κεκοίνωκεν in the sense of defilement, that is, rending impure, instead of rendering profane: "According to his accusers in Acts 21, Paul has brought Gentiles into the temple, thus making it impure." But how does a Gentile render the temple impure to begin with (if Klawans and Hayes are right about the point of Gentiles not being intrinsically impure), particularly a God-fearing Gentile follower of Jesus who does not even practice moral impurity?

translate the Hebrew equivalents חלל/חלל ("profane").[84] Interestingly enough, Luke never firmly denies nor affirms that Paul actually brought a non-Jew into the temple.[85] If such a misdemeanor did indeed occur, it would mean that the temple had been profaned, not defiled, unless the Gentile, who after all was a follower of Jesus, had acted in a hostile manner within the temple precincts – a very unlikely scenario in this case.[86]

What Luke is subtly demonstrating in the Cornelius episode is that Gentile followers of Jesus – non-Jews who have abandoned idolatry and other immoral practices – are neither morally impure nor inherently profane. They now enjoy a status similar to Jewish males and females. Consequently, they cannot render the temple in Jerusalem or a sacred realm profane any more than a normal (non-priestly) Jew can.[87] "What God has made

---

[84] Why the Lukan switch of verbs? I suggest because the speech is presented in the narrative to a *non-Jewish* listener, Felix the Roman governor. Luke avoids using the term κεκοίνωκεν because it would have been meaningless for non-Jews in any cultic sense (LSJ only provides Jewish and Christian passages where this verb bears a cultic sense). Hence, the usage of βεβηλῶσαι (cf. Heliodorus, *Aethiopica* 2:25; 10:36; βέβηλος in this sense: Sophocles, Fr. 154; *Anthologia Palatina* 9:298, etc.). See further references in Friedrich Hauck, "βέβηλος," *TDNT* 1:604.

[85] In Acts 21:29, Luke seems to insinuate that the Jews of Asia mistakenly thought that Paul had brought in a certain Trophimus, a non-Jew, with him into the temple. Luke, however, only timidly denies that the Jews of Asia were mistaken over their identification. Could it be that the historical Paul had indeed brought a non-Jew into the temple? Interestingly enough, Luke never has Paul refute this specific charge during his trials. Perhaps, Luke avoids controversy in order to depict Paul in more favorable terms towards a Jewish audience, even while silently acknowledging that Paul had indeed brought a non-Jew into the sacred precincts of the temple. We will never know.

[86] As Hayes, *Gentile Impurities,* 35, points out, in the Hebrew scriptures, Gentile defilement of the temple is only described when *hostile* intentions are involved. So Ps 79:1: "O God, the nations have come into your inheritance; they have defiled your holy temple; they have laid Jerusalem in ruins." On this passage Hayes comments: "The defilement spoken of here need not be a ritual impurity communicated by a ritually impure Gentile but rather the defilement resulting from the rapacious plundering and desecrations of a hostile encroacher of any description" (35). Cf. 1QpHab 12:8–9 (the Jewish Wicked Priest defiling the temple of God, possibly through violent deeds). Otherwise, Gentiles are normally described as *profaning* the temple of Jerusalem (e.g., Ezek 44:5–9).

[87] Mikeal C. Parsons, "'Nothing Defiled AND Unclean': The Conjunction's Function in Acts 10:14," *PRSt* 27.3 (2000): 263–74, makes an original and interesting distinction between κοινὸν and ἀκάθαρτον in Acts 10:14, claiming that "Luke intends his audience to understand κοινός to refer to the Jew who is ritually defiled by association with a Gentile and ἀκάθαρτος to refer to Gentiles who are by nature unclean" (p. 264). Parsons, however, assumes that Gentile can *ritually* defile other Jews. Carlos R. Sosa, "Pureza e impureza en la narrativa de Pedro, Cornelio y el Espíritu Santo en Hechos 10," *Kairós* 41 (2007): 55–78, also works under the assumption that Gentiles could acquire ritual impurity, although he provides a more nuanced description on the matter, positing three differ-

clean (ἐκαθάρισεν), you must not call profane (μὴ κοίνου)," so the heavenly voice insists (10:15). Gentile followers of Jesus are no longer to be viewed as impure and profane but as pure *and* holy with the rest of the congregation of Israel. In contrast to the Temple Scroll (cols. 39–40), which forbade converts from entering the inner courts of the temple,[88] Luke would have maintained that Gentile followers Jesus, purified and sanctified, had the right to do so.[89]

In light of such considerations, we can now fully appreciate the meaning and application of the vision: "God has shown me that I should not call anyone (μηδένα ἄνθρωπον) profane or unclean" (10:28b). The vision is about the purification and sanctification of Gentile believers. Through this declaration, Luke is not completely deconstructing the Jewish categories of pure/impure and holy/profane. Neither is he claiming that the immoral practices of Gentiles in general are not morally defiling. Even after this critical turning point in the narrative of Acts, Luke still has Paul ritually purify himself when he comes to the temple of Jerusalem (21:24, 26). Luke also continues to underscore Paul's moral purity: "I am not responsible (καθαρός, literally "pure") for the blood of any of you" (20:26; cf. 18:6).[90] In addition, the apostles of Jerusalem will issue laws that forbid Gentiles from associating themselves with the morally impure ways of the nations, whether through sexual immorality or idolatry, while simultaneously prohibiting them from eating blood and strangled meat (Acts 15). In the Cornelius episode, Luke is simply stating that Gentile *followers of Jesus* – not all Gentiles – are no longer to be avoided, for they have abandoned their sinful ways and now worship the God of Israel: "I truly understand that God shows no partiality, but in every nation anyone *who fears him* and

---

ent aspects of the Jewish system of purity/impurity (the ethnic, geographical, and ritual dimensions).

[88] Daniel Schwartz, "Jewish Movements of the New Testament Period," in *The Jewish Annotated New Testament*, 528.

[89] Nevertheless, Luke still maintains halakic and ecclesiological distinctions between Jews and non-Jews within Israel (see discussion below). In Luke's day, the theme of the "deprofanization" of Gentiles might have lost some of its radical ring, the temple in Jerusalem no longer operating. However, Luke's model could have been applied to the inner, ecclesiological life of the Jesus movement, granting Gentiles ritual rights and responsibilities normally administered by Jews in synagogues and other settings.

[90] Esler, *Community and Gospel*, 100, under the influence of Alon, interprets καθαρός in a cultic sense as "unpolluted" to mean that Luke's Paul asserts his ritual purity in moving into the house of a Gentile. This seems unlikely. Not only is it debatable to what extent Jews in antiquity would have ascribed an intrinsic ritual impurity to Gentiles, but καθαρός in Acts 18:6 makes sense with the preceding declaration it accompanies, meaning that Paul is morally innocent of the guilt he attaches to the "Jews" ("your blood be on your heads"). Acts 20:26 confirms this interpretation, where, once again, the term καθαρός appears in a very similar statement affirming Paul's moral innocence.

does what is right is *acceptable* (δεκτός) to him" (vv. 34–35; emphasis mine). This declaration underscores Luke's *restrictive* and qualified attribution of moral purification to non-Jews: it only concerns those Gentiles who fear (ὁ φοβούμενος) the God of Israel and practice righteousness (δικαιοσύνην). Only such non-Jews prove "acceptable" (δεκτός) – a Greek term used in the LXX to describe sacrifices that are pleasing (לרצון) before God[91] – while all other Gentiles, those who have not fully abandoned their polytheistic and immoral ways, remain morally impure and profane. The God of Israel, who previously "overlooked the times of human ignorance," now calls all Gentiles to repent from their sinful ways (17:30). Those Gentiles who heed to this call receive a cleansing of the heart (15:8–9), a spiritual transformation that downgrades their profaneness and removes their moral or "inner" impurity.[92]

Thus, Luke only contests with a worldview shared by certain Jews that might deny such a possible reversal in the immoral and profane status of the Gentile. He opposes those who view non-circumcised Gentiles as permanently and intrinsically profane because of their non-Jewish origins.[93] Instead, Luke recalls the common ancestral roots shared by both Jew and Gentile: "From one ancestor he made all nations to inhabit the whole earth" (17:26). For Luke, both Jews and Gentiles belong to the same offspring, implying that the latter can join the former in worshiping the same God: "Since we are God's offspring (γένος), we ought not to think that the deity is like gold, or silver, or stone, an image formed by the art and imagination of mortals" (Acts 17:29). Cornelius, who meets both requirements outlined in this previous verse, he stems from God's "genus" and has fully abandoned idolatry, archetypically embodies the ideal Gen-

---

[91] Lev 1:3; 19:5; Isa 56:7; 60:7. It is quite interesting to see the cultic dimension of this word in use here, as it also appears in Isa 56:7 in reference to the acceptable offerings of Gentiles and eunuchs.

[92] On the Jewish "background" of this passage, see Loren T. Stuckenbruck, "The 'Cleansing' of the Gentiles: Background for the Rationale behind the Apostles' Decree in Acts 15," in *Aposteldekret und antikes Vereinswesen: Gemeinschaft und ihre Ordnung* (ed. Markus Öhler; WUNT 280; Tübingen: Mohr Siebeck, 2011), 65–90.

[93] Hayes, *Gentile Impurities and Jewish Identities*, 89, traces what she coins "genealogical impurity" to the books of Ezra-Nehemiah: "Ezra's innovative holy seed rationale for the prohibition of intermarriage has two effects on the law: First, it renders the prohibition universal. Gentiles by definition and without exception are profane seed – permanently and irreparably – and marriage with them profanes the holy seed of Israel." She locates *Jubilees* and 4QMMT in this trajectory: "Jubilees and 4QMMT can be located at the extreme end of a process that began in postbiblical times, when the geographically (or nationally) based definition of Jewish identity gave way to a religiomoral definition that enabled a higher degree of assimilation of interested foreigners. The extension of a requirement for genealogical purity (in the sense of unmixed lineage) to all Israelites reflects a desire to prevent the assimilation of foreigners, and it occurred in stages" (90).

tile followers of Jesus who can now rightfully and freely associate themselves with the rest of the commonwealth of Israel.[94]

Some of Luke's views on Gentiles, purity, and kashrut side closely with the perspective of the author of the *Letter of Aristeas* as well as Philo. First of all, the author of the *Letter Aristeas* acknowledges that those Gentiles who are favorably disposed toward the essentials of Judaism can enjoy moral purity, since he recognizes that Philocrates possesses a *pure* disposition of the soul (2: ψυχῆς καθαρὰ διάθεσις). The author acknowledges this reality later on in his narrative when he praises the pious attitude and interest of the king of Egypt in the paideia Judaism has to offer – an attestation of the purity of his soul and holy conviction (234: ψυχῆς καθαρότητι καὶ διαλήψεως ὁσίας).[95] In his treatment of Jewish food laws, the author of the *Let. Arist.*, like Luke, affirms in his own way the common origin of all of creation: "we inquired why, since there is one creation only (μιᾶς καταβολῆς οὔσης), some things are considered unclean for eating, others for touching – legislation being scrupulous in most matters, but in these especially so" (129). In this passage, a Gentile embassy inquires about the rationale behind kashrut, wondering why certain foods are deemed impure if all created substance in the end stems from the same (divine) source. The author of this Jewish work from the Diaspora knows and believes that in the beginning God created "the wild animals of the earth of every kind, and the cattle of every kind, and everything that creeps upon the ground of every kind. And God saw that it was *good*" (Gen 1:25). Instead of attributing an innate, ontological impurity to forbidden animals such as swine or camel, this Diasporan Jew finds refuge in the usage of allegory, highlighting the moral etiquettes of kashrut *even while affirming the ongoing necessity of keeping kosher*: "By calling them [i.e., forbidden animals] impure, he has thereby indicated that it is the solemn binding duty of those for whom the legislation has been established to practice righteousness" (147).

---

[94] Cf. Thiessen, *Contesting Conversion*, 138–39. Whereas Thiessen prefers to talk of the genealogical purification of Gentiles, I prefer to see it as a twofold process of moral purification and deprofanization. I think Luke is more set on stressing the common genealogical ancestry both Jews and Gentiles share, even though he preserves a bilateral ecclesiology (Kinzer, *Postmissionary*, 151–79) in which Jews and Gentiles maintain their respective identities. The comparison Thiessen makes with the *Animal Apocalypse* is fascinating and illuminating: both Luke and the *Animal Apocalypse* believe in a restoration of (certain) Gentiles even while Jews continue to retain their particular identity. I would add that their views prove more optimistic, as far as Gentiles are concerned, than the worldview in *Jubilees*, since the latter sees all Gentiles as permanently under the power of impure spirits and hopelessly doomed. See my forthcoming "Forming Jewish Identity by Formulating Legislation for Gentiles." I would like to thank Thiessen for exchanging his thoughts with me on this matter.

[95] On the salvation of Jews and Gentiles in *Aristeas*, see Boccaccini, *Middle Judaism*, 176–79.

Here the author of the *Let. Arist.* sees the usage of (im)purity language in the Mosaic legislation more in a functional than ontological sense. Impurity is imputed, not inherent. His perspective comes close to that of "R. Yohanan b. Zakkai," as represented in a much later midrash, who discards the intrinsic nature of corpse impurity – and by extension all impurity:

> By your life! It is not the dead that defiles nor the water that purifies! The Holy One, blessed be He, merely says: "I have laid down a statute, I have issued a decree. You are not allowed to transgress My decree," as it is written, 'This is the statute of the law (Num 19:2).'"[96]

Whereas the author of the *Let. Arist.* resorts to allegorization in the hope of adequately explaining the *raison d'être* of keeping kosher and purity laws, the rabbinic sages, at least as voiced in the aforementioned tradition, remain agnostic about their logic, denying the innate impurity of any object or person, while nevertheless affirming, in fideistic fashion, the need for Jews to observe such regulations: "God said it, so I do it." Philo's perspective also aligns itself with that of the *Let. Arist.*, since he offers allegorical rationalizations regarding kosher food, partly in response to those who claim swine constitutes the finest of all meats (*Spec.* 4:101).[97]

All of this serves to show that even if Luke understands Peter's vision to mean that all creatures are not to be viewed as intrinsically pure, this need not translate into a license allowing the consumption of all foods, even swine. All foods may be intrinsically pure, but not necessarily *permitted*. Luke, like other Diasporan Jews such as Philo and the author of the *Let. Aris.*, does not roundly state that all meats, such as pork or shrimp, are no longer forbidden. In fact, he does not even seek to abolish the observance of Jewish purity laws. He only reforms purity regulations in order to include Gentiles into the *ekklesia* in more comprehensive terms. He does not align himself with the extreme Jewish allegorizers whom Philo criticizes for completely abandoning the observance of kashrut by focusing on the allegorical kernel of the Torah while dismissing concrete Jewish practice. Neither does he appropriate a Jewish allegorizing hermeneutic *à la Pseudo-Barnabas* in order to conclude that God ordained such laws only for spiritual and ethical edification, while condemning the Jewish people

---

[96] *Pesiq. Rab Kah.* 4:7; *Num. Rab.* 19:8.

[97] Cf. 4 Macc 5:8–9: "When nature has granted it to us, why should you abhor eating the very excellent meat of this animal [i.e., pork]? It is senseless not to enjoy delicious things that are not shameful, and wrong to spurn the gifts of nature." The rabbis were also aware of this polemic directed against the practice of kashrut: "R. Eleazar b. Azariah says: Whence do we learn that one should not say, 'It is not my desire to dress in mixed garments, it is not my desire to eat pork, it is not my desire to commit incest. But it is my desire. What shall I do? And my Father in heaven decreed [the prohibitions] on me thus....'" (*Sifra* Qedoshim Pereq 11:22; translation mine)

for supposedly misunderstanding such legislation by holding onto the literal observance of the Mosaic Torah (*Barn.* 10:2, 9). Luke, like many other Diasporan Jews, tries to makes sense of the Jewish tradition in light of the Greco-Roman environment he inhabits and the unprecedented eschatological influx of the Gentiles into the *ekklesia* even while affirming the literal observance of the Torah.

Entering and Lodging in a Gentile House

As noted earlier, Luke has already prepared his audience through various literary cues for Peter's eventual entry and extensive stay in the house of the Roman centurion. The appearance of a holy angel in Cornelius' house already prefigures Peter's own entrance into the very same territory. Likewise, the stay of the Cornelius' emissaries with Peter in Simon the tanner's house serves as a precedent for what is to come: "So Peter invited them in (εἰσκαλεσάμενος) and gave them lodging (ἐξένισεν)" (v. 23). The usage of the composite verb εἰσκαλεσάμενος probably means that Peter invites these non-Jews to enter the Jewish house where he is staying.[98] Moreover, Peter offers these Gentile visitors lodging – the verb ἐξένισεν stressing the hospitality reserved for guests in ancient society, including table fellowship.

Once again, such a scenario should not arouse drastic surprise among modern readers, as if Peter was the first Jew to host a Gentile in a Jewish house. I have already pointed to the evidence from the *Letter of Aristeas* as well as from the book of Judith, among others, regarding the possibility for Jews to devise ways of eating with non-Jews. In *m. Avod. Zar.* 5:5, the rabbinic sages presuppose that Jews and Gentiles can eat on the same table without assuming that Jews must thereby forsake keeping kosher.[99] Rather, the main concern in such scenarios often (but not only) involved associating with idolatry (cf. *m. Avod. Zar.* 4:6). But since Cornelius' emissaries belong to a "philosemitic" household, and since the encounter between Jew and Gentile occurs here within a controlled, *Jewish* space, Luke sees little reason to defend Peter's action. Hence, his disinterest in deliberating or justifying this initial encounter. It serves rather as a literary device, much like the angel's first visit into Cornelius' house, in order to prepare the reader for Peter's eventual entrance and lodging within a Gentile home.

After a night in Joppa, Luke's Peter, accompanied by some Jewish "brother/sisters" (10:23: ἀδελφῶν) and Cornelius' messengers, makes his

---

[98] The verb εἰσκαλέομαι appears once in Acts, in Josephus, at least five times (*Ant.* 11:252; 17:93; 18:213; 20:46; *J.W.* 1:620), all in reference to the entrance into a court or room.

[99] Cf. *Pesiq. Rab Kah.* 6. Tomson, *Paul and the Jewish Law,* 231.

way to Caesarea.¹⁰⁰ In 11:12, Luke states that these Jewish companions were six in number, forming, along with Peter, a perfect number of seven witnesses. Previously in 9:41, Luke labels these followers with the epithet, ἁγίους ("holy ones"). As *holy* agents they are about to enter into contact with persons normally considered by Jews to be profane.

As noted earlier, Luke gradually describes Peter's approach into Gentile space: he has Peter first enter Caesarea (v. 24), then Cornelius' house (v. 25). This repetition anticipates the apogee of Jewish-Gentile encounter and exchange to occur in 10:48. Upon his arrival into Cornelius' house, Peter openly addresses this controversial issue, declaring: "You yourselves know that it is unlawful (ἀθέμιτόν) for a Jew to associate (κολλᾶσθαι) with or to visit a Gentile (ἀλλοφύλῳ)" (10:28a). Klawans argues that this statement does not imply that ancient Jews viewed contact with Gentiles as forbidden, let alone that Gentiles and their homes were deemed ritually impure.¹⁰¹ Klawans is probably correct, though we have noted that some Jews would have viewed table fellowship with Gentiles as a taboo even if the food served were kosher.¹⁰² Luke seems to address the Jewish concern over *extended, intimate* association and interaction with non-Jews. Thus, in Acts 5:13, Luke speaks of outsiders who did not dare join (κολλᾶσθαι) the Jesus movement in Jerusalem. Such an act would not only require acquiring nominal membership with the burgeoning movement, but also full integration and interaction with its members, including *daily* sharing of bread as well as the common distribution of goods (Acts 4:34–37; 5:1).¹⁰³ The verb denotes more the sense of proximity rather than superficial, formal contact. Elsewhere, the verb is even used to describe the intimate relationship and bodily unification between husband and wife: "For this reason a man shall leave his father and mother and be joined (κολληθήσεται) to his wife, and the two shall become one flesh" (Matt 19:5; cf. Mark 10:7). In these passages, the verb κολλάω corresponds to the Hebrew דבק, "to stick," "cling,"

---

¹⁰⁰ These followers are Jews, since according to 10:45 they belong to "the circumcised believers" (οἱ ἐκ περιτομῆς πιστοί).

¹⁰¹ Klawans, "Notions of Gentile Impurity," 300–1. I disagree, of course, with Klawans' opinion that the author of Acts was a Gentile "who was by no means sympathetic to Jews or Judaism. Thus one can assume that Luke is exaggerating in Acts 10:28" (301).

¹⁰² Ben Witherington III, *The Acts of the Apostles: A Socio-Rhetorical Commentary* (Grand Rapids, Mich.: Eerdmans, 1998), 353, suggests that ἀθέμιτόν "could be translated 'unlawful,' but it probably has its weaker sense of 'taboo' or 'strongly frowned upon.'"

¹⁰³ In a similar vein, Paul, after his recent conversion, tries to join (κολλᾶσθαι) the disciples of Jerusalem (Acts 9:26). Cf. Luke 10:11; 15:15; Acts 8:29; 17:34; Dan 2:43 (LXX); Rev 18:5; *1 Clem.* 15:1; 19:2; 30:3; 31:1; 46:1, 2, 4; 49:5; 56:2; *2 Clem.* 14:5; *Barn.* 10:3, 4, 5, 8, 11; 19:2, 6; 20:2; *Did.* 3:9; 5:2; Herm. *Vis.* 3.6.2; Herm. *Mand.* 10.1.6; *T. Iss.* 6:1.

or "cleave," used to describe the unification between Adam and Eve in Gen 2:24.[104]

Perhaps Luke has in mind very "conservative" Jews, not all Jews, who avoid as much as possible contact with Gentiles. Josephus refers to Essenes who wash themselves even after touching junior members of their own clan, "as if they had intermixed with a foreigner" (καθάπερ ἀλλοφύλῳ συμφυρέντας). Klawans admits that this passage presents evidence that *some* Jews, rather rigorous ones in their observance, considered Gentiles to be ritually impure.[105] In the very anti-Gentile book of *Jubilees*, Jews are strongly exhorted to separate themselves fully from Gentiles by not eating or associating with them (*Jub.* 22:16; cf. CD 11:14–15; 1QS 5:16). But even in this chauvinistic and "primitive" book, as Zeitlin once qualified it,[106] the reason provided for avoiding contact with Gentiles mainly involves disgust over their idolatrous and immoral ways, not their ritual or intrinsic impurity. *One* strand within the rabbinic movement, identified with the Shammaite school of thought, also embraced a distancing attitude toward Gentiles, particularly during and immediately after the First Jewish Revolt.[107]

These passages illustrate how certain Jews avoided, for various reasons, contact with non-Jews as much as possible, even when there was no legal justification for such withdrawal. It is not impossible to imagine that among such Jews were also to be found Jewish followers of Jesus – even in Luke's day. After all, Luke hyperbolically describes the *ekklesia* in Jerusalem as originally comprising several thousand Jewish believers, zealous for the Law (21:20), and we might suppose that a significant body of Jewish followers of Jesus persisted well throughout the end of the first century CE. Of course, Luke's exaggerated "census" should not be taken literally. But once the modern inquirer is ready to abandon the traditional portrait that views insignificant pockets of Ebionites and Nazarenes as the sole surviving representatives of a Torah observant "Jewish Christian" wing in the Jesus movement of the post-70 era, then Luke's concern in addressing this "mighty minority" of Jewish believers, as Jervell puts it,

---

[104] Cf. 1 Cor 6:16–17: "Do you not know that whoever is united (κολλώμενος) to a prostitute becomes one body with her? For it is said, 'The two shall be one flesh. But anyone united (κολλώμενος) to the Lord becomes one spirit with him.'" Cf. Eph 5:31. Interestingly, the Salkinson-Ginsburg Hebrew translation of the New Testament uses the verb דבק to translate κολλᾶσθαι in Acts 10:28.

[105] Klawans, "Notions of Gentile Impurity," 300.

[106] Solomon Zeitlin, "The Book of Jubilees: Its Character and Its Significance," *JQR* 30.1 (1939): 30.

[107] Although in the long run a more lenient attitude, representative of the Hillelite tradition, was embraced by prominent rabbinic sages such as Judah the Patriarch. See Tomson, *Paul and the Jewish Law,* 234–36.

can be fully appreciated. Such zealous Jewish followers of Jesus, Torah observant and secluded from Gentiles, were sufficiently visible even in the post-Bar Kokhba era for Justin Martyr to bother himself in describing and refuting their beliefs.[108] They may not have been too different from the author of *Jubilees* or the Essenes as described in Josephus's writings in so far as their interaction with and attitude toward Gentiles was concerned. In fact, the First Jewish Revolt would have certainly incited further resentment between many Jews and Gentiles in the immediate aftermath of the war and even affected Jewish-Gentile relations among followers of Jesus who were caught in this political tension.[109]

In addition, Luke might also be addressing the concerns of non-"Christian" Jews from the Diaspora who remain suspicious about the extensive Jewish-Gentile interaction within the *ekklesia*, especially if some Jewish followers of Jesus were abandoning Torah observance all together – a rumor, probably not without basis, floating around in Luke's day (e.g., Acts 21:21). Against such rumors, Luke strives not only to portray Paul as a Torah observant Jew, but also to highlight the pious credentials and purification of the Gentiles joining the Jesus movement.

The Baptism of the Sacred Spirit

A *holy* angel (ἀγγέλου ἁγίου) and *holy* Jews have visited the home of a pious Gentile believer (10:22–23).[110] The new anthropological nature Luke attributes to Gentile followers of Jesus, who are no longer to be viewed as morally impure and inherently profane, accounts for such encounters between holy angels, holy Jews, and sanctified Gentiles.[111] Now an even more remarkable visitation occurs near the end of the Cornelius episode: "the sacred spirit" (τὸ πνεῦμα τὸ ἅγιον) falls upon Cornelius and all those

---

[108] In *Dial.* ch. 47, Justin Martyr refers to Jewish followers of Jesus who continue to observe the Torah but refuse to associate with Gentile followers of Jesus unless the latter become circumcised.

[109] So Tomson, *Paul and the Jewish Law,* 236, who addresses the pre-70 situation and aligns James and his followers more closely with Shammaite views, while placing Paul closer to the Hillelite perspective. I suggest such a polarization continued, perhaps even exacerbated, after 70 within the *ekklesia* because of the political-nationalist aspirations and frustrations of that epoch.

[110] Elsewhere in Acts, the followers of Jesus are labeled "the holy ones," including those living in Jaffa where Peter momentarily resides. See Acts 9:13; 9:32, 41. Cf. 1QS 5:13, 18; 8:17, etc. (אנשי\איש הקודש).

[111] Cf. 1QM 7:6: "Any man who is not ritually clean in respect to his genitals on the day of battle shall not go down with them into battle, for holy angels are present with their army." Cf. 1QM 10:9–11; 1QSa (1Q28a) 2:8–9; Sir 42:17; 45:2.

non-Jews present with him (v. 44). I have chosen to translate τὸ πνεῦμα τὸ ἅγιον as "the sacred spirit," rather than "the Holy Spirit." Not only is the latter term entangled in later Trinitarian developments, but also it has become so familiar to the layperson and specialist alike that the epithet, "holy," attached to the noun "spirit," has lost its original *sacred* resonance. Recovering this ascription assists in appreciating the amazement the Jewish disciples express at the event occurring before their eyes: the sacred spirit, which up until this point has fallen only upon select members of the holy people of Israel (some Jews, but also certain Samaritans, perhaps viewed by Luke as "Israelites"), has now fallen upon profane Gentiles. The baptism of the sacred spirit upon Gentile followers of Jesus constitutes definite proof in Luke's eyes that their imputed profaneness no longer exists. *These* (not all) non-Jews can receive the sacred spirit, speak in tongues, and exalt the God of Israel much like the rest of the Jewish *ekklesia* of Jerusalem (2:4).

At such a sight, the Jewish disciples who are with Peter are "out of their wits" (ἐξέστησαν). This Greek verb appears frequently in Acts to describe marvelous expressions of wonder when witnessing a fabulous sign or miracle (cf. 2:7, 12). The Jewish astonishment at the baptism of the sacred spirit upon Gentiles can be fully appreciated when we remember that certain Jews believed non-Jews to be permanently under the control and curse of impure spirits. Such is the extreme view of the author of *Jubilees* who sees no collective hope for the Gentiles: "He made spirits rule over all [i.e., the nations] in order to lead them astray from following him. But over Israel he made no angel or spirit rule because he alone is their ruler" (15:31–32). In contrast to this exceptionally anti-Gentile perspective, Luke depicts certain Gentiles as free from demonic control and capable of enjoying visitations from holy angels and even the sacred spirit.[112] Nothing inhibits these Gentiles, therefore, from also being baptized with water.[113]

Only *after* this miraculous event, does Peter agree to stay at Cornelius' house: "Then they asked him to stay on for a few days" (v. 48). This order of events (baptism followed by lodging in a Gentile house) also occurs in

---

[112] Cf. CD 2:12 where the sacred spirit is granted to a selected group.

[113] Does the baptism with water play any role in the process of the purification and sanctification of the Gentile believer? Or does it merely function as a ritual symbolizing the transformation that God has already *de facto* performed in the heart of the Gentile follower (through the sacred spirit)? Cf. 1QS 3:4, which denies the possibility for immersion through water to purify and sanctify a person whose heart does not express repentance beforehand. Interestingly enough, 1QS 3:7–8 highlights the role the sacred spirit plays in purifying a person who proves upright and humble (see also 1QS 4:20–22; 5:13–14). The parallels with Acts chs. 10–11 are remarkable. Stuckenbruck, "The 'Cleansing of the Gentiles," 78–87, maintains that the material from 1QS 3:13–4:26 is not sectarian in its orientation and describes the condition of *all* humans.

Acts 16:15 where another God-fearing Gentile, Lydia, invites Paul and his companions to lodge in her house after her baptism. By now it should have hopefully become clear that Peter's residence and dining in a Gentile home need not be interpreted as abrogating in any radical sense Jewish praxis, whether in the realm of kashrut or purity matters in general. Peter's acceptance of Cornelius' invitation, which is only implied in the text, signifies that he, or better, Luke, accepts such Gentiles as morally pure. Luke *never* claims that Peter ate non-kosher food during his stay with Cornelius. He operates under the assumption that Jews and Gentiles, purified and sanctified, can enjoy fellowship together without leading the former to forsake their kosher diet.

The Jerusalem Report

As rumor spreads regarding the unprecedented Jewish outreach of the *ekklesia* to the Gentiles, Peter becomes the target of criticism among Jewish believers from Jerusalem. Even here the manner in which their reprimanding is formulated highlights not a concern with the transgression of kosher laws, that is, of eating forbidden food, but with the extensive interaction with Gentiles: "Why did you go to *uncircumcised men* and eat *with them?*" (11:3) The question the Jewish disciples raise concerns itself primarily with *whom* and *where* Peter eats rather than *what* Gentiles serve him on his tray, probably because it would be unthinkable in their minds – and by extension to Luke – that the Jewish apostle would have eaten such reprehensible food items as pork or the like. If there is any apprehension regarding food lurking behind this question, it would probably concern the indirect compromise with idolatry through the consumption of (kosher) food previously offered to idols. Luke addresses this issue when he relates the so-called Apostolic Decree in Acts 15. Alternatively, the zealous Torah observant followers of Jesus from Jerusalem view all Gentile food as forbidden and avoid, therefore, fellowshipping with non-Jews. Nevertheless, the focus throughout the Cornelius episode remains fixed upon *Gentiles* rather than their food.

In any case, Luke never has Peter confirm any allegation over a compromise with kashrut. Neither does he allow Peter's Jewish companions, those who allegedly traveled with him to Caesarea and witnessed the events, to turn against him by testifying that the Jewish apostle did indeed consume forbidden food such as pork. On the contrary, as Luke's Peter recounts the unique events he has recently witnessed (11:4–17), he focuses on the marvelous incident of the sacred spirit falling upon the Gentiles believers. This unique phenomenon is sufficient, at least in Luke's eyes, to justify Peter's temporary residence with non-Jews (vv. 15–17). Thus, upon hearing this report, Luke claims that the Jewish followers in Jerusalem rejoiced, not because of Peter's first taste of bacon, but because "God has given even to the Gentiles the repentance that leads to life" (v. 18). If Luke seeks to show that Peter has consumed forbidden food, he has failed to do so in a clear and unequivocal way. Despite the numerous opportunities he offers himself in the narration of this extended pericope, Luke never claims that Peter or those Jewish followers accompanying him consume the unthinkable. Even when he recounts the Peter-Cornelius encounter, he does so only to reaffirm the purification and sanctification of certain Gentiles.

Conclusion

Far from ever abrogating kashrut or even purity regulations, Luke only argues for the moral purification and deprofanization of Gentile followers of Jesus. Pious Gentiles, who have abandoned their immoral practices and submitted themselves to the God of Israel and the lordship of Jesus, have been purified from their sins and have received an upgrade in their profane status. Luke implies that this metamorphosis of Gentile believers allows them to participate more fully in the ritual-cultic sphere of Judaism without profaning its sanctity. His view on Gentiles aligns itself with a passage from a favorite prophetic book of his: Isa 56:3–7. In the eschatological, redemptive spirit of this passage (cf. Isa 56:1: "soon my salvation will come"), Luke affirms the right for certain Gentiles and eunuchs alike (cf. Acts 8) to come and worship in the "house of prayer for all nations" (Isa 56:7; cf. Luke 19:46; Acts 8:27). Theoretically from Luke's perspective, Gentile followers of Jesus (not all Gentiles!) could enter the courts reserved only for Jewish males and females to offer their sacrifices and offerings without desecrating this sacred space (Acts 21:28; 24:6). Thus, it would seem that Luke would affirm the Mosaic regulation that originally allowed the *ger*, that is, the resident alien living among Israel, to offer his or her burnt offering or sacrifice in the sanctuary (Lev 17:8–9).[114]

Of course, in Luke's day, the temple lay in ruins, but Luke nowhere in his writings expresses loss of hope for the eventual restoration of Jerusalem (Luke 21:24; Acts 1:8). In the meantime, his perspective on the profane and holy could be used for outlining Jewish and Gentile administration of rituals celebrated within the *ekklesia*, not least the celebration of the

---

[114] In the next chapter, I show how the paradigm of Israelite-*ger* relations, as outlined in Lev 17–18, would have served Luke's interests when dealing with the problem of Jewish-Gentile table fellowship within the *ekklesia*.

Eucharist and the fellowship (κοινωνία) to be enjoyed between Jewish and Gentile followers of Jesus alike (cf. Acts 2:42). For Luke, a Gentile follower of Jesus is no longer to be viewed as *koinos* within the *koinonia* shared between Jews and Gentiles in the *ekklesia*. Luke realigns the boundaries between sacred and profane to allow Jewish-Gentile communion and fuller Gentile integration *even while presupposing the maintenance of a kosher diet on the part of the Jewish wing of the Jesus movement.* Such a reformation does not imply that Luke eliminates the lines demarcating the sacred and profane categories as outlined within the Jewish system of purity and holiness. For Luke, Israel collectively continues to be a holy people vis-à-vis the unbelieving nations of the world. It is within the people of Israel proper, that Luke seeks to realign these borders in order to accommodate for the Gentile follower of Jesus, who, like the biblical *ger* from former times, becomes in a real sense part of the Jewish people. But even within Israel, or better, within the *ekklesia* seen as an eschatological miniature model of what the wider house of Israel ought to look like (in Luke's eyes), Luke maintains certain differences between Jews and Gentiles: Gentiles are not required to observe all of the stipulations outlined in the Torah; these are only and continually binding for Jews. The Apostolic Decree presupposes this halakic differentiation, as I underscore in the next chapter.

Chapter 11

The Apostolic Decree

[The law of] the covering up of the blood is binding both in the Land [of Israel] and outside the Land, both during the time of the Temple and after the time of the Temple
(M. Hullin 6:1)

Introduction

The so-called Apostolic Decree appears in the very midst of Acts (ch. 15).[1] The attention Luke devotes in his narrative to this event signals its ongoing importance and relevance for him. Luke repeats the decree and its regulations no less than three times in Acts (15:20; 29; 21:25). The consideration dedicated to this topic in secondary scholarship is even greater.[2] Particularly in this case, the thorny questions concerning the relationship of Acts 15 with Galatians 2, the historicity and accuracy of Luke's portrait, and the relationship between the historical Paul, Peter, and James, on the one hand, and Luke's own depictions of these characters, on the other, will be avoided. The primary aim of this chapter lies in exploring the nature and scope of the stipulations contained in the decree in order to assess Luke's attitude toward Jewish food laws. The question of circumcision is treated in the following chapter, even though controversy over circumcising Gentiles erupts at the beginning of Acts 15 and triggers (according to Luke) an emergency meeting in Jerusalem. In this chapter, I hope to strengthen the thesis posited by a number of scholars who view Lev chs. 17–18 as constituting the backdrop for understanding the contents of the decree. In addition, I suggest that the decree as well as Luke's understanding of this

---

[1] I try to avoid using the term "council" as it projects an anachronistic notion of higher ecclesiological structures and organization upon the burgeoning Jesus movement of the first century. Even the term "Apostolic Decree" is problematic, as it tends to overemphasize universal agreement within the *ekklesia* and overlooks the major differences and tensions existing within the movement from day one. Nevertheless, the term "Apostolic Decree" is used here for the sake of convenience.

[2] The secondary literature is endless. See the rich bibliography at the end of Wehnert, *Die Reinheit,* 285–302, particularly useful for its many references to German works. For an even more recent discussion, see the many articles compiled in Öhler, *Aposteldekret und antikes Vereinswesen.*

legislation presuppose the observance of kashrut in its totality – especially for Jewish and at times even Gentile followers of Jesus, depending on the circumstances. Luke's understanding and application of the decree implies a certain halakic and ecclesiological discrimination: Jewish followers of Jesus keep kashrut, like the rest of the Mosaic Torah, preserving thereby their distinctive Jewish identity; Gentile followers of Jesus observe the stipulations outlined in the Apostolic Decree, but this legislation implies, in Luke's opinion, that they respect Jewish food laws in general *when fellowshipping with other Jews*.

Literary Context

After the Cornelius incident (Acts 10–11:18), Jesus' zealous Jewish disciples continue to disseminate their message, reaching as far as Phoenicia, Cyprus, and Antioch (11:19). In the great metropolis of Antioch, Luke subtly suggests that non-Jews also hear the proclamation regarding the risen Jesus (11:20).[3] Henceforth, Antioch becomes a hub in Acts whence Paul and Barnabas go forth to preach the news to Jew and non-Jew alike throughout the Greco-Roman Diaspora (chs. 13 and 14). It is in the new and blossoming center of Antioch that "certain individuals from Judea," as Luke vaguely puts it, proclaim circumcision as a prerequisite for the salvation of the Gentiles (15:1). This demand creates controversy and is only solved once all of the prominent leaders of the Jesus movement unanimously agree, so Luke claims, that non-Jews need not be circumcised but only observe the four commandments stipulated in the Apostolic Decree.

After their assembling in Jerusalem, the apostles and elders decide to send emissaries in order to instruct those in Antioch about their decision and the contents of the decree (15:22–35). According to Luke, Paul and Barnabas participate in this endeavor, visiting every city where they previously proclaimed the gospel and instructing members of the Jesus movement about the "the decisions that had been reached by the apostles and elders who were in Jerusalem" (16:4).[4] In this way, Luke portrays a complacent Paul who adheres to the decision made in Jerusalem and commits himself to proclaiming and upholding its regulations.

---

[3] The problematic reference to "Hellenists" in 11:20 should be understood as including non-Jews who speak Greek. See Pervo, *Acts,* 291 n. 18 and the many other commentators cited therein.

[4] In Acts 16:1–3, Luke also refers, not accidentally, to the circumcision of Timothy by Paul, a rather striking act, given the historical Paul's opposition to circumcising Gentiles. On this matter, see the following chapter of this book.

In the book of Acts, the meeting in Jerusalem is brought about because of the question raised in Acts 15:1 concerning circumcision as a prerequisite for the salvation of Gentile (male) followers of Jesus. Because in Acts the Apostolic Decree is proclaimed in response to this controversy over soteriology, some commentators argue that its contents have little to do with addressing Jewish-Gentile table fellowship, but only touch upon the eschatological inclusion of Gentiles. According to this view, there would also be little or no connection between the decree and the laws of Leviticus chs. 17–18, at least at the Lukan level.[5] This argument is shortsighted. During the Jerusalem meeting, Luke's Peter refers back to the Cornelius incident (15:7–11). Besides addressing the eschatological inclusion of Gentile believers into God's people, the Cornelius episode, as argued in the previous chapter of this book, also presents the reader with material relevant for solving purity concerns as well as the question of Jewish-Gentile fellowship. It is during his encounter with Cornelius that Luke's Peter notifies the Roman centurion about a Jewish reservation toward entering Gentile homes (10:28). It is also during this episode that Peter abides for several days in the house of the Roman centurion (10:48), leading some Jewish followers of Jesus to accuse him of dining with uncircumcised men (11:3). Furthermore, when Luke has James, the brother of Jesus, repeat the contents of the Apostolic Decree for yet a third time in Acts, this occurs in a context concerned with the perpetuation of Torah observance and Jewish identity (Acts 21:21–25).[6]

The decree, then, proves pertinent not only for addressing the question of Gentile salvation but also concrete issues governing the daily interactions between Jews and Gentiles within the *ekklesia*. Indeed, the two issues cannot be fully divorced from each other. If a proselyte fully follows the regulations of the Torah, he or she will obviously enjoy far greater contact and even complete integration into a Jewish community than a Gentile who remains indifferent or even hostile to Jewish life and practice. Naturally, many Jews will relate more openly and favorably to Gentiles who admire and respect their customs, even if the latter do not observe the Torah in its entirety. Since Luke believes Gentile followers of Jesus enjoy a special status, similar in some ways to that of a full proselyte of Judaism, he hopes that the attitude of other Jewish Torah observant followers of Jesus vis-à-vis such Gentiles will differ from their approach to the average non-Jew, particularly if these Gentile disciples of Jesus observe a body of legislation that removes the fundamental obstacles impeding Jewish-Gentile interac-

---

[5] See, for example, Deines, "Das Aposteldekret," 355–56.

[6] Esler, *Community and Gospel,* 71, has provided a sharp critique of the overemphasis on the theme of the mission to the Gentiles at the cost of appreciating other important issues in Acts such as table fellowship.

tion. If *three out of four* of the regulations in the Apostolic Decree concern themselves in some way with *food*, as we will see, it should come as no surprise that they could assist Luke in addressing the issue of *Tischgemeinschaft* between Jew and Gentile and not merely represent some kind of universal moral code *à la* Noahide Laws used superfluously to justify the eschatological incorporation of Gentile believers into the grander scheme of "salvation history."[7]

The Moral and Ritual Scope of the Decree

Repeatedly throughout the history of research on Luke-Acts, scholars of all stripes and colors have attempted to moralize fully the contents of the Apostolic Decree, often by resorting to textual critical arguments.[8] The textual evidence, however, strongly supports a reading that originally contained an order to abstain from four items: 1) (food) polluted by idols (τῶν ἀλισγημάτων τῶν εἰδώλων) 2) sexual immorality (τῆς πορνείας) 3) what has been strangled (τοῦ πνικτοῦ) and 4) blood (τοῦ αἵματος).[9] It is particularly the third item with its peculiar reference to strangled animals that challenges positing a list originally containing just three ethical com-

---

[7] Cf. Markus N. A. Bockmuehl, *Jewish Law in Gentile Churches: Halakhah and the Beginning of Christian Public Ethics* (Edinburgh: T&T Clark, 2000), 164: "Regardless of one's perspective on the historicity of the account, Luke's report pinpoints the central halakhic problem with great accuracy: should Gentiles who believe in Christ be treated as proselytes or as Noachides? It should be noted carefully that the primary point in this Lucan account is *not* that of table fellowship in mixed congregations (unlike Gal 2.12 and *pace* most commentators), but more generally the halakhic status of Gentiles believers: verse 1 clearly defines the question as being about what Gentiles must *do* to be saved." Bockmuehl, however, acknowledges that the issues of a modus vivendi with Gentiles and soteriology cannot be easily separated (see p. 164 n. 86).

[8] Among others, Thorleif Boman, "Das textkritische Problem des sogenannten Aposteldekrets," *NovT* 7 (1964): 26–36; David Flusser and Shmuel Safrai, "Das Aposteldekret und die Noachitischen Gebote," in *"Wer Tora vermehrt, mehrt Leben." Festgabe für Heinz Kremers zum 60. Geburtstag* (eds. Edna Brocke and Hans-Joachim Barkenings; Neukirchen-Vluyn: Neukirchener, 1986), 173–92; Gotthold Resch, *Das Aposteldecret nach seiner außerkanonischen Textgestalt untersucht* (TUGAL 28.3; Leipzig: J. C. Hinrichs, 1905); Harald Sahlin, "Die drei Kardinalsünden und das Neue Testament" *ST* 24 (1970): 93–112 (especially p. 109); Tomson, *Paul and the Jewish Law*, 179; Wilson, *Luke and the Law*, 79 f.

[9] This is the order and wording of the decree as found in 15:20. In 15:29 and 21:25, the sequence and wording are slightly different and align better with the order of commandments given to the biblical *ger* in Lev chs. 17–18. The positioning in 15:20 of idolatry and sexual immorality at the beginning of the list might represent an orientation toward a Diasporan audience where such issues were viewed by many Jews as the primary iniquities practiced by Gentiles.

mandments, namely, to refrain from idolatry, sexual immorality, and blood(shed). Many have convincingly refuted this moralizing reading of the decree on textual critical grounds, arguing for an original list in Acts that contained all four items, including the peculiar reference to strangled meat.[10]

Besides the textual critical considerations, it is easy to imagine how during the "Gentilizing" course of Christian history a list originally containing regulations stemming from a Jewish framework and mindset concerning purity and dietary considerations could quite easily be converted into a moral charter. Accounting for the reverse process is harder to rationalize.[11] Furthermore, if the decree in Acts originally contained only three cardinal, universal sins (the triad of idolatry, sexual immorality, and bloodshed), one wonders why Luke would bother to have all of the major protagonists of the Jesus movement issue the most obvious of expectations held by most Jews in antiquity. Which Jew would not agree in principle that, ideally, Gentiles should refrain from idolatry, sexual immorality, and violence? There would hardly be a need to summon a "Jerusalem Council" to enforce and inculcate the superfluous.

The ritual dimension of the decree, therefore, cannot be underestimated. Actually, some scholars have rightly sought to transcend the bifurcation of the decree into "moral" and "ritual" components (artificial categories) by claiming that *both* dimensions are present within the apostolic legislation.[12] I try to highlight this dual dimension more fully in the ensuing discussion on each of the four items contained within the decree. Obviously, Gentile followers of Jesus are to avoid idolatry, *porneia,* and blood(shed), because committing such acts is morally impure. Moreover, the decree calls Gentile followers to move beyond these basic demands by abstaining from eating blood and strangled meat. These dietary regulations are viewed as universally binding and quite possibly stem from (moral) purity concerns as well. In this way, the Apostolic Decree removes the obstacles impeding Jewish-

---

[10] Bruce Metzger, *A Textual Commentary on the Greek New Testament* (London: United Bible Societies, 1975), 429–34 (citing many secondary references); Müller, *Tora für die Völker*, 140 f.; Wehnert, *Die Reinheit,* 22–29.

[11] Flusser and Safrai, "Das Apostledekret und die Noachitischen Gebote," 173–92, do not adequately explain how an ethical decree eventually became "ritualized." Positing the existence of two forms of Noahide Laws, one ritual, the other ethical, does not satisfactorily account for explaining this mutation, for the Noahide Laws are entirely moral and theoretical in their orientation, even the command to refrain from eating a limb from a live animal. More on this below.

[12] Bockmuehl, *Jewish Law in Gentile Churches*, 166; Barrett, "The Apostolic Decree of Acts 15.29," *ABR* 35 (1987): 50–59. Also noted by Tomson, *Paul and the Jewish Law,* 179, who, nevertheless, favors the Western text as original, while seeing the Eastern text as an alternative, stricter version issued shortly after in Asia Minor.

Gentile encounters by calling upon Gentile followers of Jesus to preserve their newly acquired moral purity while presupposing that Jews willing to eat with Gentiles will continue to observe their ancestral customs, including Jewish dietary and purity laws.[13]

Lev 17–18 and the Apostolic Decree

A number of scholars have argued that the Apostolic Decree should be understood in light of Leviticus chs. 17–18.[14] Such a correlation can account for the choice and number of regulations outlined in the decree, four in total, which are listed in Acts 15:29 and 21:21 in the same order as the "parallel" commandments given to the Israelite and the *ger* in Lev 17–18. This connection also helps illuminate the function of the decree for its targeted audience: to assist the governance of Jewish-Gentile relations within the Jesus movement. Since Lev chs. 17 and 18 contain commandments that *both* the Israelite and the resident alien must observe, they readily offer material relevant for tackling the many new problems involved in addressing Jewish-Gentile relations within the early *ekklesia*.

Wehnert has made an important contribution to the discussion by drawing upon Targumic passages on Lev 17–18. Surprisingly, scholars have neglected considering the Targumim in their investigation of the Apostolic Decree, even though they constitute a logical source for comparison, given the common language they share with the Aramaic speaking *ekklesia* of Jerusalem.[15] Despite the problems related to dating the traditions embedded within the targumic sources, it is quite justifiable to consult such literature in order to enrich our discussion. The heterogeneous character of

---

[13] It is possible that in Luke's eyes the consumption of blood and carcasses can defile Gentile believers, since according to Lev 17, both the Israelite and the resident alien must wash themselves in the event of eating carrion. Although some ancient Jews thought that Gentiles were exempt from maintaining ritual impurity, as outlined in the Mosaic Torah, the laws in Lev 17–18 were treated differently among certain Jewish followers of Jesus. In the *Pseudo-Clementines*, particularly *Homilies* 7.8.1, there seems to be an expansion of the reach of ritual impurity into the Gentile realm, since this literature calls for Gentile women to keep the laws of menstruation (αὐτὰς μέντοι καὶ ἄφεδρον φυλάσσειν) and for Gentile couples to wash after sexual intercourse (ἀπὸ κοίτης γυναικὸς λούεσθαι). Interestingly enough, these regulations appear in a section of the *Pseudo-Clementine* containing several commandments that overlap with Luke's version of the Apostolic Decree. See discussion below.

[14] Barrett, *The Acts of the Apostles*, 2:734, claims this position to be the majority view. Nevertheless, many have questioned and challenged its premises.

[15] I assume with Wehnert that the so-called Apostolic Decree, because of its peculiar language, does go back to the Aramaic speaking *ekklesia* in Jerusalem and that Luke essentially reaffirms the basic premises of this legislation.

the materials contained in the various Targumim indicates that this corpus of writings contains various traditions, some of which antedate the final composition of the Aramaic translations.[16] Since the discovery of the Dead Sea Scrolls very ancient evidence now attests to the Jewish practice of translating the Hebrew scriptures into Aramaic during the Second Temple period.[17] Gleßmer, among others, has argued for an early provenance of many of the *halakic* materials (in contrast to the haggadic ones) contained within the Targumim, including *Targum Pseudo-Jonathan*.[18] Obviously, this does not mean that all of the halakic traditions recorded within this literary corpus dates from earlier periods. Nevertheless, Wehnert's comparison of the targumic sources on Lev 17–18 with the Apostolic Decree reveals several interesting parallels between *Targum Pseudo-Jonathan* and the Tannaitic works of the Mishnah, the Tosefta, and the halakic Midrash *Sifra*, suggesting that some of the halakic contents in *Targum Pseudo-Jonathan* stem at least from a period prior to the beginning of the third century CE.[19]

Idolatry

Lev 17:8–9 contains a solemn condemnation against the Israelite and the resident alien if they fail to bring their sacrifices and burnt offerings to the tent of meeting. In this way, this section of the Mosaic Torah forbids both the Israelite and the resident alien from sacrificing to other gods.[20] Lev 17:7 presupposes this exclusive devotion to the deity of Israel by prohibiting sacrificing "to goat-demons" (שעירים). Interestingly enough, the LXX translates שעירים with ματαίοις, "idle" or "empty" things. In the LXX, the

---

[16] Wehnert, *Die Reinheit,* 217.

[17] See the Targum of Job (11QtgJob).

[18] See Uwe Gleßmer, *Einleitung in die Targume zum Pentateuch* (TSAJ 48; Tübingen: Mohr Siebeck, 1995). Cf. Peter Schäfer, "Der Grundtext von Targum Pseudo-Jonathan: Eine synoptische Studie zu Gen 1," in *Das Institutum Judaicum der Universität Tübingen in den Jahren 1971–1972* (Tübingen, 1972), 8–29; Robert Hayward, "The Date of Targum Pseudo-Jonathan: Some Comments," *JJS* 40 (1989): 7–30, who also posits early traditions contained within *Targum Pseudo-Jonathan*. For an early dating of *Targum Neofiti*, see Gabriele Boccaccini, "Targum Neofiti as a Proto-Rabbinic Document: A Systemic Analysis," in *The Aramaic Bible: Targums in Their Historical Context* (eds. Derek Robert George Beattie and Martin McNamara; JSOTSup 165; Sheffield: Sheffield Academic Press, 1994), 260–69.

[19] In the English-speaking world, Wehnert's monograph is still neglected. See, however, Markus Bockmuehl, review of Jürgen Wehnert, *Die Reinheit des "christlichen Gottesvolkes" aus Juden und Heiden*, *JTS* 50 (1999): 260–68; Filoramo and Gianotto, *Verus Israel: Nuove prospettive sul giudeo cristianesimo* (preface).

[20] Milgrom, *Leviticus,* 2:1463–9.

Greek μάταιος generally translates Hebrew terms such as הבל, שוא, or כזב. Particularly, the term הבל, sometimes juxtaposed with שוא, is used in reference to pagan deities and the vain devotion (in Jewish eyes) paid to them.[21] In Second Temple Jewish literature, μάταιος appears quite often in passages that reprimand Gentiles for their idolatrous worship of false gods.[22] The usage of ματαίοις in the LXX of Lev 17:7 to translate the narrower Hebrew term "goat demons" can be seen as a Second Temple "update" of the Mosaic legislation discouraging cultic involvement in the idolatrous practices of the surrounding nations.

The targumic materials on Lev 17 testify to a similar trajectory as the LXX but emphasize the link between idolatry and *demon worship*. Thus, *Targum Neofiti* possibly translates שעירים with שדיה ("demons"), but also adds טעוותיה, "idols." The same phenomenon occurs in *Targum Pseudo-Jonathan*: "and they shall not offer their sacrifices *to idols that are like demons*" (לטעוון דמתילין לשידי).[23] As Wehnert observes, the worship of demons in Israelite times is understood here as an *Urbild* for an actual and ongoing problem of (Jewish) involvement with polytheistic cults (cf. *Tg. Ps-J* Lev 19:4 and 20:5).[24] The earliest rabbinic interpretations on the same verse in Leviticus point in the same direction, understanding שעירים more broadly as שדים and comprehensively tying the phrase in Lev 17:7, "to whom they prostitute themselves," to all forms of idol worship.[25]

By the first century CE, many Jews probably read Lev 17:7–10 as a blanket prohibition against idolatry. Already the Jewish thinker Paul, when addressing his Gentile readers, joins in this general and typical type of Jewish derision against idolatry, at times dismissing it as an empty, foolish practice (1 Cor 8:4; 10:19), in line with the "rationalist" perspective on idolatry attested in other Jewish-Diasporan sources written in Greek (LXX; Wis; 3 Macc; *Sib. Or.*; *Let. Aris.*; etc.), or explicitly connecting it with demon worship (Belial: 2 Cor 6:14–16; cf. *1 En.* 99:7; *Jub.* 22:16; Targumim; *Sifra*; etc.).[26] The aforementioned evidence illustrates how the Aramaic

---

[21] Often rendered in LXX with τά μάταια: Jer 2:5; 10:3; 1 Kgs 16:13, 26; 2 Kgs 17:15; Ps 31:6; Amos 2:4; Jon 2:8, etc.

[22] Wis 15:8; 3 Macc 6:11; *Sib. Or.* 3:355; 5:83; 23:31; *Let. Aris.* 134, 136, 139; cf. Acts 14:15; Eph 4:17; 1 Pet 1:18.

[23] Translations of targumic materials are mine.

[24] Wehnert, *Die Reinheit,* 220.

[25] *Sifra* Aharei Mot Pereq 9:8: אין שעירים אלא שדים שנאמר ושעירים ירקדו שם, אשר הם זונים אחריהם לרבות שאר עבודה זרה.

[26] Paul simultaneously displays a supernatural and rational view on idols, while the rabbinic perspective in general follows a rational trajectory (although the demonic dimension is noted at times). See Tomson, *Paul and the Jewish Law,* 156–57; E.E. Urbach, "The Rabbinical Laws of Idolatry in the Second and Third Centuries in Light of Archaeo-

speaking *ekklesia* in Palestine could have applied the prohibitions against the worship of goat demons mentioned in Lev 17 to the current cults of idolatry reigning throughout Greco-Roman and Mesopotamian worlds, prohibiting Gentile followers of Jesus, like Jews, from participating in these polytheistic practices.

The phrase τῶν ἀλισγημάτων τῶν εἰδώλων, which appears in Acts 15:20, may cover not only food items but also the adoration of idols.[27] However, in Acts 15:29 and 21:25, a more restrictive term exclusively tied to food appears: εἰδωλοθύτων, "what has been sacrificed to idols" (NRSV). In the realm of food consumption, the command in Acts to abstain from things polluted by idols would encompass not only *meat* but also others types of food and even drinks offered to idols, particularly wine. Tomson argues that the verb θύω means not only to "slaughter" but also to "offer" or "celebrate," meaning that εἰδωλοθύτων could encompass bloodless food items such as bread or wine.[28]

For a long time, scholars have argued that the diet of the average Jew or non-Jew could not include meat because of its high price.[29] Hence, a command given to Gentiles to refrain merely from eating *meat* offered to idols would not prove a very substantial test of allegiance. Nevertheless, some recent studies are challenging this consensus, positing that at least in Palestine meat may have found its way more often into the average diet than previously thought.[30] If Gentile followers of Jesus were indeed expected to

---

logical and Historical Facts," *IEJ* 9 (1959): 154 n. 19 (for references of primary sources and earlier secondary literature).

[27] Does ἀλισγημάτων qualify only the first item in the Apostolic Decree in Acts 15:20 (i.e., idols) or also the other three remaining ones? Wehnert, *Die Reinheit*, 45, 69, 239–45, highlights the issue of (im)purity as the underlying concern for all four items of the decree. Avemarie, "Die jüdischer Wurzeln des Aposteldekrets: Lösbare und ungelöste Probleme," in *Aposteldekret und antikes Vereinswesen*, 10–12, maintains that ἀλισγημάτων only applies to the first item of the decree, food offered to idols. He also points out that, with respect to sacrifices and the consumption of blood, Lev 17:3–14 does not address purity issues. Even so, we must remember how Jews of the Second Temple period would have viewed such acts, which were described in various ways through the employment of language tied to the concept of impurity. It seems that Luke would have also viewed such acts as defiling, since concepts and language related to (im)purity and sanctity are part and parcel of his worldview, as argued in the analysis of the Cornelius episode in the previous chapter of this book.

[28] Tomson, *Paul and the Jewish Law*, 189. Cf. "θυσία" and "θύω" in *BDAG*; Shulam and Le Cornu, *Jewish Roots of Acts*, 1:836.

[29] See Bockmuehl, *Jewish Law in Gentile Churches*, 170; Safrai, "Home and Family," 747; Tomson, *Paul and the Jewish Law*, 189.

[30] Shimon Dar, "Food and Archaeology in Romano-Byzantine Palestine," in *Food in Antiquity* (eds. John Wilkins, F. D. Harvey, and Michael J. Dobson; Exeter: University of Exeter Press, 1995), 326–35; Justin Lev-Tov, "'Upon What Meat Doth This Our Caesar

abstain from any food or drink offered to idols, this would considerably raise the standards of expectations and test of fidelity to the ideals promoted by the Jesus movement.

Ancient Jewish sources reveal a particular concern with the consumption of Gentile wine. "You cannot drink the cup of the Lord and the cup of demons," declares one radical Jewish thinker of the first century CE in a letter addressing Gentiles (1Cor 10:21; cf. Rom 14:21).[31] Likewise, many passages in the mishnaic tractate, *Avodah Zarah*, focus on the problem of handling Gentile wine, often suspecting such liquid to have been used in a context related to idolatry (e.g., *m. Avod. Zar.* 2:3; 5:9–10).[32] Possibly, Daniel's refusal to "defile (ἀλισγηθῇ/יתגאל) himself with the royal rations of food and wine" of king Nebuchadnezzar could stem in part from a fear that the wine was offered to idols, although the general reference in Dan 1:8 to the royal rations, which presumably would have included permitted foods for Jews to consume (e.g., bread), implies an avoidance of any food prepared by Gentiles (cf. Add Esth C 14:17).[33] The verb used in the book of Daniel to describe defilement with Gentile food and wine, ἀλισγηθῇ, which is related to the noun ἀλισγημάτων appearing in Acts 15:20, may imply that any food processed by Gentiles can defile. Consequently, Daniel and his three friends maintain a diet of vegetables and water, presumably because such products were neither offered to idols nor prepared by Gentiles.[34] In Acts 15:20, however, ἀλισγημάτων, is qualified: Gentile

---

Feed...?' A Dietary Perspective on Hellenistic and Roman Influence in Palestine," in *Zeichen aus Text und Stein*, 420–46; Kraemer, "Food, Eating, and Meals," 406–7.

[31] Other passages on Gentile wine include Jud 12:1, 13, 20; Bel 3, 11.

[32] Avemarie, "Die jüdischer Wurzeln des Aposteldekrets," 15–16, notes that *m. Avodah Zarah* deals little with the question of meat offered to idols, focusing far more on the issue of handling Gentile wine. As Avemarie suggests, this probably stems from the fact that meat offered to idols did not present major problems for Jewish settlements in Palestine as it did in the Diaspora. Determining, on the other hand, the provenance of wine, proved more difficult. For rabbinic attitudes toward Gentile wine, see Rosenblum, *Food and Identity*, 81–83. On the other hand, certain Jews seem to not have been perturbed with purchasing wine produced by Gentiles. See Magness, *Stone and Dung*, 57, for a discussion of archaeological data from Palestine.

[33] Freidenreich, *Foreigners and Their Food*, 36; Kraemer, *Jewish Eating and Identity*, 26–27.

[34] See especially 4 Bar 7:38: Jeremiah offers figs to his people and teaches them to avoid the pollutions of the Gentiles of Babylon (τοῦ ἀπέχεσθαι ἐκ τῶν ἀλισγημάτων τῶν ἐθνῶν τῆς Βαβυλῶνος). Cf. Josephus, *Life* 14: Jewish priests ate only figs and nuts during their stay in Rome. Perhaps, Rom 14:2, with its reference to the "weak" who only ate vegetables, should also be understood in a similar context of Jewish fear over eating food possibly offered to idols and/or prepared by Gentiles. According to Josephus, an Essene, excluded from his community but still bound by oaths, resorted to eating grass until he perished (*J.W.* 2:143). For John the Baptist's diet of *wild* honey (Matt 3:4/Mark 1:6), see

followers of Jesus are not to eat food offered to *idols*. Apparently, the decree allows them to consume food produced by non-believing Gentiles. Another implication of the decree, at least at the Lukan level of understanding, would be that Jewish followers of Jesus should not abstain from eating (kosher) food prepared by Gentile followers of Jesus, since Luke presents several times the occurrence of Jewish-Gentile table fellowship in the book of Acts (e.g., Peter and Cornelius; Paul and various Gentile converts to the Jesus movement).

The demand, then, in the Apostolic Decree to refrain from "things polluted by idols" would require Gentile followers of Jesus to distance themselves from meat, wine, and other food items offered to idols, while also exhorting them to avoid polytheistic rituals and idolatrous practices in general. This was no small demand and could easily disrupt the intricate social, political, and economic ecosystem of delicate Jewish-Gentile coexistence in the Greco-Roman Diaspora, particularly in a post-70 CE environment where tension and suspicion between Jews and Romans would certainly not have ceased after the failure of the First Jewish Revolt. While Romans and other non-Jews could tolerate the right *for Jews* to express their exclusive devotion to their deity and ancestral customs, any conspicuous attempt on the part of Jews to gain Gentile converts to their side by demanding them to distance themselves from the idolatrous and polytheistic practices so intimately tied with various cultic, civic, and family rites could provoke social strife and resentment. Hence, the understandable distancing of the wider Diasporan Jewish communities from messianic Jewish groups of the Jesus movement because of their radical standards of discipleship expected from Gentiles.

Porneia

The command to abstain from πορνεία, which refers loosely to illicit or immoral sexual relations, is the only injunction in the Apostolic Decree that does not concern itself with food. Nonetheless, its inclusion in this legislation is quite understandable in light of the moral dimension of impurity underlining the decree. Leviticus ch. 18 contains a list of forbidden sexual practices that concern both the Israelite and the resident alien (18:26). These include prohibitions against incest (18:6–18), sexual relations with a menstruating woman (v. 19), adultery (v. 20), male sodomy (v. 22), and bestiality (v. 23). From the perspective of Leviticus, all of these sexual acts are viewed as morally defiling: "Do not defile yourselves in

---

chapter 8 of this book dealing with food laws in Matthew. Cf. *Ascen. Isa.* 2:11: Isaiah eats "wild herbs"; 2 Macc 5:27: Judah and company consume "wild herbs."

any of these ways, for by all these practices the nations I am casting out before you have defiled themselves" (18:24). Second Temple Jewish sources continue to stress the defiling force of sexual immorality.[35] Thus, the Enochic tradition emphasizes the pollution arising from the copulation between the Watchers and the "daughters of men" (1 *En.* 10:22; 106:15; cf. *Jub.* 7:20–25). The book of *Jubilees* singles out the moral defilement of the Gentiles because of their sexual immorality.[36] Denunciations of Gentile sexual immorality also appear in Jewish sources from the Greek speaking Diaspora.[37] According to Lev 18, the Canaanite engagement in illicit sexual practices ultimately led to their expulsion from the land of Canaan.[38] While ritual impurity can be removed through rites of purification and atonement, Milgrom notes that "the sexual abominations of Lev 18 (and 20) are not expiable through ritual."[39] In light of this material, the moral cleansing of Gentile believers announced in the Cornelius episode and repeated in Acts 15:9 becomes all the more remarkable. For Luke, the moral purification of Gentile followers of Jesus represents a miraculous working on their behalf.[40] Henceforth, they are to maintain their newly acquired moral purity by avoiding the futility of idol worship as well as the sexual immoralities of the nations.

Wehnert has sought to reinforce the exegetical link between Lev 18 and the command to refrain from πορνεία in the Apostolic Decree.[41] He argues that by the first century CE Lev 18:6–30 could have been viewed as one unit containing a catalogue of commandments prohibiting various illicit sexual relations. Already the Damascus Document (5:9) discusses some of

---

[35] See Klawans, "Notions of Gentile Impurity," 293–97; Hayes, *Gentile Impurities,* 55–58.

[36] See the denunciation of Sodom and Gomorrah for their defilement and sexual immorality (16:5). Cf. *Jub* 9:15; 1QS 4:10, 21.

[37] *Sib. Or.* 3:492, 496–500; 5:168; Wis 14:31; *Let. Arist.* 152; 1 Cor 6:16–20; Rom 1:24, 26, 29.

[38] Although punishment is reserved only for those Gentiles who inhabit the *land* of Canaan, by the Second Temple period, Jews had come to view such sexual practices as universally binding, regardless of geographical location. The attempt, therefore, by Deines, "Das Aposteldekret," 356, to dismiss Lev 17–18 as the basis for understanding the Apostolic Decree because of the *original* confinement of the Levitical legislation to the land of Israel is without basis. Jews from the Second Temple period onward refrained from idolatry, incest, consuming blood and carcasses *regardless of their geographical location.* In rabbinic parlance, the laws in Lev 17–18 are not viewed as "commandments that are dependent on the land of Israel" (מצות התלויות בארץ). In addition, *Jubilees* evinces a universal expansion and application of Lev 17–18 (more on this below).

[39] Milgrom, *Leviticus,* 2:1573.

[40] Cf. Ezek 36:25 f., which describes the purification of Israel by God from all impurities.

[41] Wehnert, *Die Reinheit,* 232–33.

the laws from Lev 18 under the rubric of משפט העריות ("law of incest").[42] Correspondingly, rabbinic tradition at times calls this section of Leviticus עריות ("incest" or "forbidden relations").[43] The Hebrew noun עריות is the plural form of ערוה ("nakedness"), which appears prominently throughout Lev 18. In the Septuagint, ἀσχημοσύνη normally translates ערוה, not πορνεία, which is absent in the LXX version of Lev 18. Rather, the Septuagint often employs πορνεία to translate the Hebrew זנות ("prostitution"), a term missing altogether in the Masoretic Text of Lev 18.

Nevertheless, by the Second Temple period the term πορνεία was used occasionally in the sense of "incest." Thus, in 1 Cor 5:1 Paul states: "It is actually reported that there is sexual immorality (πορνεία) among you, and of a kind that is not found even among pagans; for a man is living with his father's wife." Here Paul's usage of πορνεία corresponds more closely to the rabbinic concept of גילוי עריות (in the restricted meaning of "incest"), since Paul condemns Gentiles from Corinth for engaging in certain kinds of incestuous relationships.[44] It is noteworthy that Lev 18:8 explicitly forbids "uncovering the nakedness" of a father's wife. Elsewhere (e.g., 1 Cor 7:2), Paul uses the term πορνεία in a wider sense to cover a variety of forbidden sexual practices (e.g., adultery). Interestingly, Matt 5:32 (cf. Matt 19:19) renders ערות דבר ("something objectionable") from Deut 24:1, which deals with divorce, as λόγου πορνείας. Probably Matthew understands this term as referring to "those illegitimate sexual acts performed by the wife with a partner other than her husband,"[45] although Meier interprets Matthew's clause as prohibiting incestuous unions among "proselytes."[46]

Given the wide semantic range of the Greek term, capable of covering incest but especially other sexual transgressions such as adultery, it would have proven a most suitable term for encompassing all of the forbidden relationships mentioned in Lev 18, especially for a Jewish *ekklesia* concerned in establishing "sexual halakah" for Gentiles. Even the rabbinic

---

[42] Cf. 4Q251 (4QHalakhah A) which also discusses laws of incest under the rubric "על העריות." Cf. 11QT[a] 66:11–17. For a discussion of these passages, see Aharon Shemesh, "The Laws of Incest in the Dead Sea Scrolls and the History of Halakhah," in *Halakhah in Light of Epigraphy*, 81–99.

[43] *M. Hag.* 2:1; *Sifra* Aharei Mot Pereq 13:1; *Lev Rab.* 24:6. See Tomson, *Paul and the Jewish Law*, 99; Wehnert, *Die Reinheit*, 232.

[44] Tomson, *Paul and the Jewish Law*, 98 n. 5.

[45] Foster, *Community, Law and Mission*, 112.

[46] Meier, *Law and History*, 150. The Vulgate translates the Hebrew ערות דבר of Deut 24:1 as *aliquam foeditatem* ("for any reason of impurity"), which may refer to a prohibition against incestuous relations. See Foster, *Community, Law and Mission*, 111.

עריות in its larger sense can refer more broadly to any prohibited sexual act, not just incest.⁴⁷

Likewise, זנות, normally rendered by πορνεία in the LXX, also enjoys a semantic stretch sufficiently flexible to encompass various illicit practices, including incest, polygamy, and other forbidden relations. In CD 4:20–5:11, the term זנות refers not in a restrictive sense to "harlotry" but polygamy (4:20–5:6), cohabitation with a menstruating women (5:6), and laws of incest (5:7–11) as delineated in Lev 18.⁴⁸ Interestingly, the Damascus Document connects זנות with the concept of impurity (CD 7:1–3), as could be the case in the Apostolic Decree. In MMT, זנות appears four times with meanings not restricted to "harlotry" but applied to various forbidden relations. Section B 75 of this document (as reconstructed by Qimron and Strugnell) deplores the זנות practiced among the holy people of Israel. The term זנות may be translated here as "illegal marriage," rather than "fornication," to condemn intermarriage between priests and lay members, as B 80–82 presents statements condemning priests and sons of Aaron for uniting with partners forbidden for marriage.⁴⁹ Earlier in Section B 9, offerings of Gentiles are even likened to a woman who "has fornicated with him," demonstrating how the term זנות or its counterparts (e.g., זנה) could be used rather loosely to denounce a variety of practices.⁵⁰

---

⁴⁷ Cf. *m. Avod. Zar.* 2:1: "Cattle may not be left in the inns of the gentiles since they are suspected of bestiality; nor may a woman remain alone with them since they are suspected of lewdness (העריות)." Cf. *Sifra* Aharei Mot Pereq 13:1 on Lev 18:6, which understands all of the laws in Lev 18 as applying to both Jew and Gentile (להביא את הגוים שיהיו מוזהרים על העריות כישראל). Nevertheless, rabbinic sages disagree to what extent Gentiles are held accountable to such prohibitions in comparison to Jews. See discussion in Müller, *Torah für die Völker,* 110–16; David Novak, *The Image of the Non-Jew in Judaism: An Historical and Constructive Study of the Noahide Laws* (Toronto Studies in Theology 14; New York: Edwin Mellen, 1983), 199–216. In his discussion of Noahide laws, Maimonides, *Hilkhot Melakhim* 9:5, quoting a baraita in *b. Sanh.* 58a, understands the rubric עריות quite broadly to include incest, adultery, sodomy, and bestiality.

⁴⁸ See Hans Kosmala, "The Three Nets of Belial: A Study in the Terminology of Qumran and the New Testament," *ASTI* 4 (1965): 99. Cf. John C. Endres, *Biblical Interpretation in the Book of Jubilees* (CBQMS; Washington, D.C.: Catholic Biblical Association of America, 1987), 138–39; David W. Suter, "Fallen Angel, Fallen Priest: The Problem of Family Purity in 1 Enoch 6–16," *HUCA* 50 (1979): 115–35.

⁴⁹ Qimron and Strugnell, *Discoveries in the Judaean Desert,* 55. See also the fragmented Section C 5 of MMT, with its vague reference to the destruction of places as a result of violence and זנות.

⁵⁰ Brooke, "Luke-Acts and the Qumran Scrolls," 86–87, in light of the evidence from MMT, suggests that other matters besides incest may be included in the use of πορνεία in Acts 15:20, including a cultic dimension developed by Luke to reconfigure the community of the Jesus movement in continuity with the temple and the Jewish Law. Brooke reaffirms this position in "Acts and the Discourses of the Scrolls from Qumran" (paper presented at the annual meeting of SBL, Chicago, Ill., 18 Nov 2012), 8. I fully concur

Thus, זנות and (גילוי) עריות occasionally overlap and become synonymous when used in a broader sense.[51] Interestingly enough, the term זנות (=πορνεία) appears in Targumim *Neofiti* and *Pseudo-Jonathan* of Lev 18:17 where it replaces the Hebrew זמה ("infamy" or "depravity"), which is used to denounce the practice of uncovering the nakedness of a woman and her daughter or granddaughter. These targumic references demonstrate that certain Jews could find πορνεία (= זנות) to be an appropriate term for describing and denouncing the various illicit sexual practices mentioned in Lev 18. The term would have proven particularly useful to denounce the sexual practices and relationships of the Gentiles on moral grounds, which seems to be the primary aim of the Apostolic Decree.[52] In light of the overlap of πορνεία/זנות with the concept of incest as well as its application to a variety of sexual practices, it is possible that the Apostolic Decree would have demanded Gentiles to abstain from incest (Lev 18:6–18), adultery (18:20), sodomy (18:22), bestiality (18:23), and even sexual intercourse with a woman during her menstruation (18:19).[53] Luke, however, does not specify what is actually covered by the term *porneia*, and so it is possible that he expected Gentile followers of Jesus to abstain primarily

---

with Brooke that there is a fundamental concern in Luke-Act about the proper worship of God and the cultic incorporation of Gentiles (see my discussion of the Ethiopian eunuch in the previous chapter dealing with the Cornelius episode). I would like to thank Brooke for sharing a copy of his paper with me. On the various meanings and usage of זנות in the Dead Sea Scrolls, see John Kampen, "The Matthean Divorce Texts Reexaminzed," in *New Qumran Texts and Studies: Proceedings of the First Meeting of the International Organization for Qumran Studies, Paris 1992* (ed. George J. Brooke with Florentino García-Martínez; STDJ 15; Leiden: Brill, 1994), 149–67, who highlights how the term is employed for discussing various issues related to marriage and sexual relations.

[51] Müller, *Torah für die Völker,* 159 n. 131; Avemarie, "Die jüdischen Wurzel des Aposteldekrets," 24–26, shows that rabbinic usage does not make a sharp distinction between both terms.

[52] Cf. Wehnert, *Die Reinheit,* 233.

[53] The blood of *Gentile* menstruating women is not necessarily viewed by the framers of the Apostolic Decree (and by extension, Luke) as ritually defiling (cf. Lev 15:19–24), because Lev 18 prohibits such kind of intercourse along with other illicit sexual relations. See Klawans, *Impurity and Sin,* v–vi, 7, 107, 173 n. 33; Hayes, *Gentile Impurities,* 22–23, 113, for discussion of this particular issue in Lev 18. Alternatively, the Apostolic Decree could represent a Jewish attestation of a limited extension of ritual impurity to Gentiles (who follow Jesus). *Ps. Clem. Hom.* 7.8.1 appears to view Gentile followers of Jesus as susceptible to ritual impurity, at least in a limited way, when it calls for Gentile women to keep the laws of menstruation (αὐτας μέντοι καὶ ἄφεδρον φυλάσσειν) and for Gentile couples to wash after sexual intercourse (ἀπὸ κοίτης γυναικὸς λούεσθαι). These regulations appear in a section of the *Pseudo-Clementines* containing several commandments that overlap with Luke's version of the Apostolic Decree.

from the immoral sexual acts stereotypically associated with non-Jews (licentiousness, prostitution, adultery, etc.) rather than incest.[54]

Strangled Meat

For generations, the term πνικτός, commonly translated as "strangled," has perplexed scholars and remains shrouded in mystery. Critics who deny seeing any correlation between Lev 17–18 and the Apostolic Decree point to the absence of the term and its Hebrew equivalent (passive form of חנק) not only in Leviticus but also in the entire Pentateuch. Instead, Lev 17:15 only refers to נבלה (*nevelah*), an animal that dies on its own, and טרפה (*terefah*), an animal torn by a wild beast. The Torah forbids consuming both types of dead animals (cf. Exod 22:30; Lev 7:24; 22:8).[55] According to Lev 17:15, in the event that an Israelite or resident alien should eat a *nevelah* or a *terefah*, he or she must undergo purification. "If they do not wash themselves or bathe their body, they shall bear their guilt" (Lev 17:16). The LXX renders both *nevelah* and *terefah* with θνησιμαῖος and θηριάλωτος, respectively, neither of which appear in Acts.

Nevertheless, Lev 17:15 still provides good background for elucidating this particular item of the Apostolic Decree. True, πνικτός is absent from the LXX, but terms from the same word group appear elsewhere in the Septuagint and other ancient Jewish literature written in Greek. Thus, the Masoretic Text of Nah 2:13 states: "The lion has torn (טרף) enough for his whelps and strangled (מחנק) prey for his lionesses; he has filled his caves with prey (טרף) and his dens with torn flesh (טרפה)." The Septuagint renders מחנק ("strangled") with ἀπέπνιξεν (from ἀποπνίγω), a compound verb composed of the preposition ἀπό and the stem πνίγω, which is related to πνικτός.[56] Interestingly, מחנק stands closely in this passage to the verb

---

[54] Avemarie, "Die jüdischen Wurzel des Aposteldekrets," 26–27.

[55] For the various definitions of these terms in the Hebrew Bible and rabbinic sources, see Str-B 2:730–31. In the Hebrew Bible, the *nevelah* refers essentially to an animal that has died on its own through a natural death (cf. Josephus, *Ant.* 3:260: κρέως τοῦ τεθνηκότος αὐτομάτως ζῴου), while in rabbinic literature it may refer to any animal not properly slaughtered according to the laws of *shehitah*. In the Hebrew Bible, *terefah* refers to an animal that has been torn (usually) by a wild beast, whereas in rabbinic literature it describes an animal afflicted by a mortal wound or disease. Upon inspection after slaughter, if one were to find such defects, the animal would be declared *terefah*. See Milgrom, *Leviticus,* 1:653–54 and the ensuing discussion of some of the technicalities involved in these definitions (which are not of major importance for the argument of this chapter).

[56] Cf. LXX to 2 Sam 17:23 translating "he hanged himself" (יחנק) with ἀπήγξατο.

טרף and the noun טרפה – one of the types of carcasses (besides *nevelah*) Israelites and resident aliens are to avoid eating according to Lev 17:15.[57]

Philo provides significant material for the elucidation of strangled meat in *Spec.* 4:119–123. After highlighting the Mosaic prohibition against consuming what "has died on its own" (θνησιμαῖον = נבלה) or "been torn by wild beasts" (θηριάλωτον = טרפה), Philo condemns those who eat meat that has not been ritually slaughtered (ἄθυτα).[58] He condemns them for strangling and throttling (ἄγχοντες καὶ ἀποπνίγοντες) creatures, for burying their blood in their bodies (τυμβεύοντες τῷ σώματι τὸ αἷμα) instead of allowing the "essence of their soul" (τὴν οὐσίαν τῆς ψυχῆς), that is, their blood, to flow freely and unrestrained (ἐλεύθερον καὶ ἄφετον). Of interest here is Philo's reference to animals that have not been properly slaughtered but strangled and throttled prior to consumption (ἀποπνίγοντες being a compound verb related to πνικτός). This comment appears immediately after Philo condemns the consumption of *nevelah* and *terefah*.[59] More importantly, Philo undoubtedly had in mind Lev 17:13–15, which discusses hunting and catching game, when he wrote this section of *De specialibus legibus*. Here Philo refers to the *hunting* practices of Greeks and other non-Jews in conjunction to his discussion on consuming blood, *nevelah*, and *terefah* (*Spec.* 4:120). These items are all brought together in Lev 17:13–15 in the context of hunting:

And anyone of the people of Israel, or of the aliens who reside among them, who hunts down an animal or bird that may be eaten shall pour out its blood and cover it with earth. For the life of every creature – its blood is its life; therefore I have said to the people of Israel: You shall not eat the blood of any creature, for the life of every creature is its blood; whoever eats it shall be cut off. All persons, citizens or aliens, who eat what dies

---

[57] Cf. 4Q169 (4QpNah) 3 + 4 i 4. Nah 2:13, however, does not provide sufficient evidence for subsuming *terefah* (or *nevelah*) under πνικτός, as it renders טרף with ἥρπασεν, while using ἁρπαγῆς for טרפה. Nevertheless, this verse at least shows how a compound verb related to πνικτός with the meaning of "strangled" in reference to meat that has not been properly slaughtered but strangled and torn (by a lion). Furthermore, at least in the Hebraic passage, the synonymous *parallelismus membrorum* between טרפה and מחנק might suggest some kind of conceptual correlation between the two.

[58] This is one way of understanding ἄθυτα to mean that the animal was not slain in a proper manner so as to allow its blood to drain out. In the LXX, θύω can translate both זבח and שחט.

[59] "Now many of the lawgivers both among the Greeks and barbarians, praise those who are skillful in hunting, and who seldom fail in their pursuit or miss their aim, and who pride themselves on their successful hunts, especially when they divide the limbs of the animals which they have caught with the huntsmen and the hounds....But anyone who was a sound interpreter of the sacred constitution and code of laws would very naturally blame them, since the lawgiver of that code has expressly forbidden any enjoyment of carcasses or of bodies torn by beasts for the reasons before mentioned" (*Spec.* 4:120).

of itself or what has been torn by wild animals, shall wash their clothes, and bathe themselves in water, and be unclean until the evening; then they shall be clean.[60]

Philo's reference to the "essence of the soul" of an animal (οὐσίαν τῆς ψυχῆς) in *Spec.* 4:122 also recalls the ψυχὴ πάσης σαρκὸς in the LXX of Lev 17:11, 14, while Philo's call to allow the blood to flow freely and unhindered (ἐλεύθερον καὶ ἄφετον) matches the command in Lev 17:13 to pour out the blood of the captured animal. The connections between *Spec.* 4:119–123 and Lev 17 are manifold.

Wilson has sought to downplay the connection between this Philonic passage and Lev 17 by introducing a very restrained meaning to Philo's usage of the verb ἀποπνίγοντες.[61] Since this verb appears in Philo's text in conjunction with ἄγχοντες, which also means to "strangle," he suggests ἀποπνίγοντες refers to a particular method of preparing or cooking gourmet foods, a practice perhaps peculiar to the area of Alexandria.[62] There is some merit to his proposal, since in the same passage Philo condemns the gluttonous practices of "those like Sardanapalus" (Σαρδανάπαλλοι) – a character who stands for the vices of self-indulgence and greed.[63] However, it is more likely that ἄγχοντες and ἀποπνίγοντες function here simply as a hendiadys in literary symmetry with ἐλεύθερον καὶ ἄφετον, which also appear in the same Philonic paragraph.[64] Philo is thinking primarily about blood trapped in the *corpse* of an animal (τυμβεύοντες τῷ σώματι τὸ αἷμα), which in a certain sense "strangles" or chokes the creature.[65] By using two

---

[60] I fail to understand how A. J. M. Wedderburn, "The 'Apostolic Decree': Tradition and Redaction," *NovT* 35 (1993): 367, can claim that *Spec.* 4:122, with its discussion on hunters, separates itself from Lev 17:14 and 22:18, since Lev 17:13 refers explicitly to the practice of hunting. Philo applies a close reading of Lev 17 even while referring to the Greco-Roman practices of his time.

[61] Cf. Wedderburn, "The Apostolic Decree,'" 362–89.

[62] Wilson, *Luke and the Law,* 90–99. See, however, D. Hans Lietzmann, "Der Sinn des Aposteldekrets und seine Textwandlung," in *Amicitiae Corolla: A Volume of Essays Presented to James Rendel Harris, D. Litt., on the Occasion of His Eightieth Birthday* (ed. H. G. Wood; London: University of London Press, 1933), 203–211, especially 205–206, as well as the further corrective and refutation of Wilson in Klinghardt, *Gesetz und Volk Gottes,* 202–3 n. 43 and 44 and Avemarie, "Die jüdischen Wurzeln des Aposteldekrets," 17: "Denn während die Verbote von Blut und Unzucht sehrt leicht und das Verbot des Götzenopferfleischs überhaupt nur von dem jüdischen Hintergrund des Christentums her zu erklären sind, lässt sich eine Enthaltung von Gedünstetem und Geschmortem weder aus jüdischen noch aus irgendwelchen anderen antiken Tabus herleiten."

[63] See "Sardanapalus," *Dictionary of Greek and Roman Biography and Mythology* (3 vols.; ed. William Smith; Boston: Charles C. Little and James Brown, 1849), 3:711–12.

[64] Wehnert, *Die Reinheit,* 229.

[65] Lietzmann, "Der Sinn des Aposteldekrets," 205–6: "Hier redet Philo von wirklichem 'Erwürgen,' und solches Fleisch ist verboten, weil das Blut darin geblieben ist...." Alternatively, as Klinghardt, *Gesetz und Volk Gottes,* 202 n. 44, suggests,

different verbs to describe the act of strangling, Philo stresses the terrible form (in Greek and Jewish eyes) of putting an animal (or a human) to death through strangulation. Herodotus highlights this awful form of killing animals allegedly practiced among the nomadic Scythians who would tie animals around the neck with a noose, thereby strangling (ἀποπνίγει) their victims (*Hist.* 4:60). Interestingly enough, in other Greek classical passages strangulation represents the worst type of death.[66] Philo appeals to these Greek sensibilities in order to highlight the virtues of Jewish dietary practices.

In addition, literary evidence from Alexandria itself suggests that the term ἀποπνίγοντες was not always understood in the limited sense Wilson seeks to restrict it. In *The Instructor* (*Paedagogus*) 2.17.2, Clement of Alexandria claims that Moses commanded the Jewish people to abstain from animals that "have died (θνηξιμαῖα), or were offered to idols (εἰδωλόθυτα), or have been strangled (ἀποπεπνιγμένα)." Although one could argue that Clement employs the term ἀποπεπνιγμένα in the very restricted sense Wilson suggests, it seems more likely that the ancient Christian writer refers to a more general abstinence from a variety of animals improperly slaughtered or offered to idols, since he juxtaposes ἀποπεπνιγμένα with εἰδωλόθυτα and θνηξιμαῖα (= נבלה) and claims that the prohibition against consuming these three items derives from the Torah of Moses (2.17.1: διὰ Μωυσέως).[67] If this suggestion is correct, ἀποπεπνιγμένα would refer in Clement's writings to any "strangled" meat not properly slaughtered. Its inclusion alongside εἰδωλόθυτα and θνηξιμαῖα would make sense in an environment where many Jews no longer lived in rural areas but in urban towns of the Greco-Roman Diaspora and needed to ascertain whether the meat they purchased had indeed been slaughtered with its blood properly drained.[68] The book of *Joseph and Aseneth*, proba-

---

ἀποπνίγοντες may have a dual sense here denouncing the consumption of blood products as well as the lack of self-restraint.

[66] References can be found in François Hartog, "Self-cooking Beef and the Drinks of Ares," in *The Cuisine of Sacrifice among the Greeks* (eds. Marcel Detienne and Jean-Pierre Vernant; trans. Paula Wissing; Chicago: The University of Chicago Press, 1989), 175. Cf. Sanders, *Judaism: Practice and Belief,* 520 n. 11, who comments on the evidence from Herodotus on the Scythians as well as on Philo, *Spec.* 4:122 and concludes that "we must think that strangling animals with a noose, or garroting them, was practised outside of Scythia, and consequently that Acts 15:20 may refer to it."

[67] Cf. Klinghardt, *Gesetz und Volk Gottes,* 203 and Wehnert, *Die Reinheit,* 228–29.

[68] Wehnert, *Die Reinheit,* 230, suggests that ἀποπνίγοντες, as attested in Philo and Clement, is a traditional term, deriving from the Hebrew חנק, and that the compound form of the word (instead of πνικτός as found in Acts) reflects an alternative way of translating the same Hebrew term. He also suggests that εἰδωλοθύτων came to replace טרפה in the tripartite list as attested in Clement (εἰδωλόθυτα, θνηξιμαῖα, and

bly of Egyptian provenance, may point in this direction as well when it refers to refraining from the "bread of strangulation" (ἄρτον ἀγχόνης) in conjunction to abstaining from idolatry and eating with Gentiles (8:5).

In any case, Wilson's comments do little to elucidate *Luke's* perception of the meaning of πνικτός. It is hardly likely that Luke (and the Aramaic speaking *ekklesia* presumably promulgating this decree) viewed this term as merely prohibiting the consumption of gourmet foods prepared in Alexandria. Different forms of the so-called Apostolic Decree appear in other works that were surely not written in Egypt and show no sign of restricting the term πνικτός to the preparation of delicacies. Certain interesting passages from the so-called *Pseudo-Clementine* literature are of some importance for the consideration of this matter. The version of the *Ps.-Clem.* known as the *Homilies* (7.4.1) contains three items followers of Jesus must avoid: the table of demons (τραπέζης δαιμόνων), dead flesh (νεκρᾶς σαρκός), and blood (αἵματος). In *Hom.* 7.8.2, a longer list of food items appear: the table of demons (τραπέζης δαιμόνων), food offered to idols (εἰδωλοθύτων), dead flesh (νεκρῶν), strangled meat (πνικτῶν), animals torn by a wild beast (θηριαλώτων = טרפה), and blood (αἵματος). Equally interesting is *Hom.* 8.19.1 where a similar list appears with the following overlapping items: dead flesh (σαρκῶν νεκρῶν), an animal torn by a wild beast (θηρίου λειψάνου), an animal that is cut (τμητοῦ)[69] or strangled (πνικτοῦ). Likewise, *Recognitions* 4.36.4 refers to the prohibition of participating in the table of demons (*participare daemonum mensae*), ordering Gentile followers of Jesus to refrain from eating sacrifices (*immolata*), blood (*sanguinem*), or a carcass that is strangled (*morticinum quod est suffocatum*).

These passages from the *Ps.-Clem.*, which as far as we know do not emanate from Alexandria nor concern themselves with gourmet foods, share a certain affinity with the version of the Apostolic Decree recorded in the Acts of the Apostles, although they could represent a later halakic deliberation of its stipulations.[70] They also share a tighter connection with Lev 17, since the terms θηριαλώτων/θηρίου λειψάνου directly correspond to the Hebrew *terefah*, while the references to "dead flesh" (νεκρᾶς σαρ-

---

ἀποπεπνιγμένα) because the issue of eating an "animal torn by a wild beast" became less meaningful in urban areas such as Alexandria.

[69] The term τμητοῦ appears neither in the LXX (but cf. Exod 20:25) nor in the New Testament. For classical references, see *LSJ*. See also Wehnert, *Die Reinheit*, 160: "...bezeichnet ein von einem Tier abgetrenntes oder abgeschnittenes Körperteil, dessen Genuß – im Anschluß an Gen 9, 4 – verboten ist." Should τμητοῦ be tied in any way with the rabbinic, Noahide command not to eat an אבר מן החי (a limb torn from a living animal)?

[70] For a historical discussion and reconstruction, see Wehnert, *Die Reinheit*, 145–86, who tends to views the lists in the *Ps.–Clem.* as reflecting an oral tradition independent from Acts. Cf. Klinghardt, *Gesetz und Volk Gottes*, 203–4.

κός/νεκρῶν/σαρκῶν νεκρῶν) match the Hebrew *nevelah*, "what has died on its own." Remarkably, *Recognitions* connects "dead flesh/carcass" (*morticinum* translates *nevelah* in the Vulgate) with "strangled" meat: *morticinum quod est suffocatum* ("a carcass which is strangled").[71] These different lists clarify what kind of meat is prohibited for Gentiles through the addition of several food items including carcasses, animals torn by wild beasts, and cut or torn limbs, showing that other early followers of Jesus understood the Apostolic Decree as forbidding consuming animals improperly slaughtered, carcasses that "choked" in their own blood.[72]

Wehnert may offer further help by pointing, once again, to the overlooked evidence from *Targum Pseudo-Jonathan*. The Hebrew text of Lev 17:13 commands both Israelite and resident alien to pour out an animal's blood and cover it with earth. *Tg. Ps.-J* adds "and he shall pour its blood in slaughtering (בניכסתא) and if its slaughtering is not ruined (ואין לא מתקלקלא ניכסתיה) he shall cover it with blood." In *Tg. Ps.-J* Lev 17:15, the topic of faulty slaughtering appears again: while the Masoretic Text commands all Israelites and resident aliens to wash themselves in the case

---

[71] In the Vulgate to Acts 15:20, πνικτοῦ is translated with *suffocatis*. Likewise, in the Syriac translation of Acts 15:20, 29 and 21:20, πνικτοῦ is rendered by חניקא suggesting that at least some Aramaic speaking Christians of a later time understood the term literally to mean "strangled," and not in some special restrictive sense limited to fine delicacies. Equally remarkable is an admittedly late passage from *Apostolic Constitutions* 8.47.63: "If any bishop, or presbyter, or deacon, or indeed any one of the sacerdotal catalogue, eats flesh with the blood of its life, or that which is torn by beasts, or which died of itself, let him be deprived; for this the law (ὁ νόμος) itself has forbidden" (translation taken from *Ante-Nicene Fathers*). Wehnert, *Die Reinheit*, 179 n. 119, however, dismisses the relevance of this passage for elucidating the Apostolic Decree, deeming that it reflects the Jewish prohibitions against consuming an אבר מן החי, טרפה or נבלה and are derived directly from the Law of Moses, especially Gen 9:4 and Lev 17:15. Nevertheless, it is questionable whether there is a connection between this passage and the rabbinic Noahidic law, אבר מן החי, since the Christian text forbids Gentiles from eating two additional food items (rabbinic halakah allows for Gentiles, even Noahides, to eat carcasses; cf. Deut 14:21). Perhaps, this Christian text represents an ancient interpretation of the Apostolic Decree that (rightly) understood its connection with Lev 17–18 and by extension Gen 9:4. Cf. *Str.-B* 2:733–34; Barrett, "The Apostolic Decree of Acts 15:29," *ABR* 35 (1987): 50–59.

[72] Cf. Tertullian, *Apology* 9: "Blush for your vile ways before the Christians, who have not even the blood of animals at their meals of simple and natural food; who abstain from things strangled (*propterea suffocatis*) and that die a natural death (*morticinis*), for no other reason than that they may not contract pollution, so much as from blood secreted in the viscera. To clench the matter with a single example, you tempt Christians with sausages of blood, just because you are perfectly aware that the thing by which you thus try to get them to transgress they hold unlawful" (Translation taken from *Ante-Nicene Fathers*). See discussion in Wehnert, *Die Reinheit*, 201–2; Müller, *Tora für die Völker*, 203 n. 21.

of eating *nevelah* or *terefah*, *Tg. Ps.-J* replaces the Hebrew *nevelah* with בישרא דמטלק בקילקול ניבסתא ("flesh that has been thrown out because of a faulty action in slaughtering").[73]

At the very least, these references show that at a later time, at the latest when *Tg. Ps.-J.* acquired its final form, certain Jews had updated the text of Lev 17 (and other pertinent passages in the Mosaic Torah) to forbid the consumption of *any* animal improperly slaughtered. Quite strikingly, Etheridge, in his translation of *Tg. Ps.-J.*, renders the Aramaic term מתקלקלא as *strangled*.[74] Although this translation represents an interpretation of the term, not its literal rendition, it reminds us that certain ancient Jews could have used terminology derived from the roots, קלקל and חנק, to designate meat that was not properly slaughtered.[75] Indeed, the employment of a generalizing rubric such as "strangled" to designate all meats improperly slaughtered could have proven more suitable to the framers of the Apostolic Decree than the adoption of technical and, in certain cases, antiquated terms such as *nevelah* or *terefah* that were no longer meaningful in certain contexts (e.g., in urban areas animals torn by wild beasts would not have been a major issue) or required further clarification.[76] Interesting-

---

[73] Of equal importance are the two references in *Tg. Ps.-J.* Lev 7:24 and Deut 14:21. According to the Hebrew text of Lev 7:24, the flesh of a *nevelah* or *terefah* may be put to any use except for eating. *Tg. Ps.-J.* adds a third item: ותריב חיוא דמיקלקלא בשעת ניכסתא ("and the fat of an animal that is ruined at the moment of slaughtering"). In Deut 14:21, *Tg. Ps.-J.* replaces the Hebrew *nevelah* with דמיקלקלא בניכסא ("what is ruined through [faulty] slaughtering").

[74] John Wesley Etheridge, *The Targums of Onkelos and Jonathan ben Uzziel on the Pentateuch; With the Fragments of the Jerusalem Targum: From the Chaldee* (2 vols.; London: Longman, Green, Longman, and Roberts, 1862–1865), 2:200, 201.

[75] Wehnert, *Die Reinheit*, 231. In a personal communication, Aharon Shemesh suggests considering נחירה, a rabbinic term used to described animals killed by stabbing, as a possible translation of πνικτός.

[76] As Avemarie, "Die jüdischen Wurzeln des Aposteldekrets," 19, points out, by at least the mid-second century CE, if not a generation or two earlier, some rabbinic sages were already redefining the meanings of *nevelah* and *terefah* (e.g., *m. Hul.* 2:4), as the sages mentioned in *m. Hul.* 2:4 all lived at the end of the first and beginning of the second century CE. Interestingly, Schiffman, "Laws Pertaining to Forbidden Foods," 69–72, points to a Qumranic text, 4Q251 (4QHalakha A) 12:4, which might understand *terefah* in the same way as the rabbis do when it states: "[an]imals that have died a natural death or a torn beast that did not live" (נב[לות וטרפה אשר לא חיה]). The verbal phrase, "that did not live," could be translated "and would not live," as suggested by Schiffman. On the other hand, Schiffman suggests that the Temple Scroll (11QT[a] 48:6) views *nevelah* and *terefah* as essentially one (p. 80). It could have been more practical, then, for the framers of the Apostolic Decree to adopt a more generalizing term rather than employing dated terminology from scripture that was currently undergoing halakic and semantic specification. On *terefah* in the Dead Sea Scrolls and rabbinic literature, see further Aharon Shemesh, "Common Halakhic and Exegetical Traditions Shared by DSS

ly, both קלקל and חנק appear in rabbinic literature, though not frequently, including *m. Hul.* 1:1 (מיקלקלא בניכסא = בשחיטתן יקלקלו) as well as *m. Hul.* 1:2, which forbids using a sickle, saw, teeth, or nails to slaughter an animal because these instruments "choke" (חונקין) the creature.[77]

Although many of the passages solicited above derive from later sources, they suggest that the term πνικτός should be understood as encompassing both *nevelah* and *terefah*,[78] or alternatively as a reference to any animal unfit for consumption because of improper slaughtering.[79] Various passages from the earlier literary corpus of the Dead Sea Scrolls show that issues related to the handling and consumption of carcasses, however killed, were important for many Jews of the Second Temple period. We should not imagine that the entire vast corpus of non-scriptural documents discovered in the caves near Qumran merely represents the views of a marginal, extreme sect living in complete isolation from the rest of the world. New research suggests that the religious impact of the non-

---

and Rabbinic Literature," [in Hebrew] in *Zaphenath-Paneah: Linguistic Studies Presented to Elisha Qimron on the Occasion of His Sixty-Fifth Birthday* (eds. Daniel Sivan, David Talshir, and Chaim Cohen; Beer-Sheva: Beer-Sheva University Press, 2009), 383–94.

[77] Wehnert suggests that such terms eventually fell out of use. For the whole *Begriffsgeschichte*, see his extensive analysis in *Die Reinheit*, 221–31. Flusser and Safrai, "Das Aposteldekret und die Noachitischen Gebote," 185–86, point to the overlooked passage, *t. Avod. Zar.* 8:6, which allows a Gentile to strangle (חנקה) and eat a bird smaller than the size of an olive (first the sages wonder whether one may eat a *live* bird smaller than an olive, the minimal size required to acquire impurity from a *nevelah*). However, this passage, which discusses the Noahide commandment against eating a limb from a live animal, does not forbid Gentiles from eating strangled meat. If anything, it allows them to do so. The discussion in the Toseftan passage implies that Gentiles must only refrain from eating blood from a *live* animal. In later rabbinic sources (see section dealing with blood), the sages continue to debate whether Noahides must only refrain from eating a *limb* from a live animal or also abstain from consuming *blood* from a live creature. By contrast, the Apostolic Decree goes further by requiring Gentiles to refrain from eating blood *tout court, even from a carcass* (which rabbinic halakah allows Noahides to eat). Probably the rabbis envisage the act of "strangling" a bird as involving pressing it with one's hands, as suggested by the following statement in *Mek.* Beshallah-Wayehi Parashah 6: "'And on that day the Lord saved Israel from the hand of Egypt' [Exod 14:30]: 'Like a bird that is given in the hand of a person who, were he to squeeze (יכבוש) his hand a little, would immediately strangle it (חונקה)'" (translation mine).

[78] So already Str-B 2:730: "Gemeinsam haben נבלה u. טרפה im AT, daß der Tod des Tieres nicht dadurch eintritt, daß sein im Blut befindliches Leben zugleich mit dem aus dem Körper ausströmenden Blut entflieht – den ein wirkliches Ausströmen des Blutes erfolgt ja weder bei Nebela noch bei Terepha – sondern vielmehr dadurch, daß sein im Blut befindliches Leben im Körper selbst nämlich in dem hier verbleibenden Blut 'erstickt.' Daher kommt es, daß der Ausdruck πνικτόν = 'Ersticktes' im NT beides unter sich befassen kann...."

[79] Wehnert, *Die Reinheit*, 231 n. 61.

biblical works from the Dead Sea Scrolls reached far beyond the "Qumran sectarians." "It is more likely that they [i.e., the scrolls] were brought from several sectarian communities and hidden in the caves in the wilderness at the time of the Jewish Revolt against Rome (66–70 CE), although some presumably belonged to the community at site [i.e., Qumran]."[80] Regev has even argued that several laws attested in Temple Scroll, MMT and *Jubilees* made an impact on Philo and Josephus' halakic perceptions.[81]

With respect to MMT, Brooke notes that several copies of this document were found in Cave 4 and composed principally to convince those lying outside its "sectarian" circle.[82] Interestingly, a rule in MMT B 22–23 bans those who handle carcasses from partaking in sacrificial food, and Brooke suggests that such a ruling might shed light on the Apostolic Decree: its framers as well as Luke were interested in how Gentiles were to relate to and worship God in a proper way.[83] Interestingly, 4Q251 (4QHalakha A) 12:4–5, may not only define *terefah* in the direction taken by the rabbis in the mishnaic tractate *Hullin*, but also rule out the possibility for proselytes from consuming carcasses, although the condition of this fragment does not allow one to ascertain the latter point.[84] 11QT^a 48:5–6, on the other hand, prohibits a proselyte from consuming carcasses by deliberately omitting the ruling in Deut 14:21 that allows an Israelite to give a *nevelah* to a *ger*. Instead, 11QT^a follows Lev 17:15 at this point, which explicitly forbids a *ger* to consume a carcass.[85] The evidence from the Dead Sea Scrolls shows that certain Jews of the Second Temple period showed interest in the laws dealing with carcasses in Lev 17. It also suggests that the Apostolic Decree views Gentile followers of Jesus in ways analogous to proselytes, albeit without requiring circumcision.

---

[80] John J. Collins, *The Dead Sea Scrolls: A Biography* (Princeton, N.J.: Princeton University Press, 2013), vii–viii.

[81] Regev, "From Qumran to Alexandria and Rome: Qumranic Halakhah in Josephus and Philo," in *Halakah in Light of Epigraphy*, 43–63. Some might find it difficult to accept a direct influence of the scrolls on Philo. It is enough though to assume that Philo was aware of similar halakhic stances that were not sectarian.

[82] Brooke, "Acts and Discourses of the Scrolls from Qumran," 8.

[83] Brooke, "Acts and Discourses of the Scrolls from Qumran," 8, suggests that this aspect of the decree has been neglected because of a greater interest among modern commentators of Luke-Acts in the social gospel. Brooke provides an important corrective, although I think the issues of Jewish-Gentile table fellowship and cultic service are not mutually exclusive.

[84] Schiffman, "Laws Pertaining to Forbidden Foods," 71. For 4Q251, see Aharon Shemesh, "4Q251: Midrash Mishpatim," *DSD* 12 (2005): 280–302.

[85] The rabbis deal with the contradiction between Lev 17:15 and Deut 14:21 in a different way by claiming that Lev 17:15 applies to a proselyte, whereas Deut 14:21 addresses a non-Jew who has not converted to Judaism (see discussion below).

It should be noted that there is no indication in Acts suggesting that in Luke's eyes followers of Jesus must procure their meat from a *Jewish* butcher, this despite the fact that a halakah in *m. Hul.* 1:2 declares all animals slaughtered by a Gentile to be *nevelah*. Neither does Luke, in contrast to rabbinic halakah, provide any details about *how* exactly the animal should be slaughtered. This silence underscores a pragmatic orientation toward the conditions experienced by Jewish communities living in the Greco-Roman Diaspora.[86] Probably, many Jews around the Mediterranean basin were content if the blood of the animal was simply poured out upon slaughter and did not care for or were unaware of the halakic intricacies developed (later?) in the mishnaic tractate *Hullin*.[87] Sanders has argued that Jews in the Greco-Roman Diaspora were ready to purchase meat prepared by non-Jews, provided it had been properly slaughtered (blood drained) and had not been offered to idols.[88] Overall, "pagan" methods of slaughtering would have satisfied Jewish demands in the Diaspora: the blood of the animal was removed during the slaughter.[89] This is especially true of Greek techniques of slaughtering, and wherever they were practiced, we may assume that Jews from the Mediterranean Diaspora were

---

[86] Avemarie, "Die jüdischen Wurzeln des Aposteldekrets," 19–20.

[87] Julian the Apostate's admittedly late reference (*Epistulae* 89a line 53; Bidez ed.; cf. Stern, *Greek and Latin Authors,* 2:40) on the abstention from eating flesh whose blood has not been poured out immediately (κρέως του μὴ παραχρῆμα ἀποθλιβέντος) might reflect this Diasporan-Jewish pragmatism toward slaughtering: they did not develop an ornate halakic system concerning *shehitah* as the rabbis did but were content with purchasing meat whose blood had been poured out upon slaughtering.

[88] Sanders, *Judaism: Practice and Belief,* 216, 520 n. 12; *Jewish Law,* 278–82. Cf. Deines, "Das Aposteldekret," 387, although I disagree with his attempt to detach the Apostolic Decree from Lev 17–18. Contrary to what Deines claims, there is no need to imagine *rabbinic* halakic standards lurking behind the term πνικτός in order to posit a link between the Apostolic Decree and Lev 17–18. Here, a distinction should be made between the application of the decree in the vicinity of Palestine and in the greater Diaspora. In the latter territory, where it might be harder to procure meat prepared only by Jews, greater leniency could have been applied to allow the purchase of meat handled by Gentiles, provided it was slaughtered in a way deemed acceptable by the local Jewish populaces.

[89] Sanders, *Jewish Law,* 278; Burkert, *Greek Religion,* 90; Jean-Louis Durand, "Greek Animals: Toward a Topology of Edible Bodies," in *The Cuisine of Sacrifice,* 90–92: "The head, fallen backwards...displaying in full sight the location on the neck of the exact spot where the blade must enter to slit the animal's throat – that is, to cut at least the two carotid arteries if not the trachea...."

willing to purchase such meat.⁹⁰ Like other Greco-Roman Jews living in the Diaspora, Luke probably acted likewise.⁹¹

Blood

The fourth and final item of the Apostolic Decree, blood, overlaps with the previous one, strangled meat. Because of its juxtaposition with strangled meat, the reference to blood cannot be understood only in a moral sense as referring to "bloodshed" (slaughtering humans). Its juxtaposition with strangled meat as well as the reference in the decree to abstain from *food* offered to idols strongly suggests that Gentile followers of Jesus should not *consume* blood *tout court*. Indeed, as Avemarie notes, the verbal command to *abstain* (ἀπέχεσθαι) from blood makes better sense in a discussion dealing primarily with food rather than manslaughter.⁹² Is the Apostolic Decree, then, superfluous, since the reference to strangled meat already addresses the issue of eating blood? Probably not. The reference to "strangled" meat forbids Gentiles to consume animals not properly slaughtered; the mention of blood reminds Gentiles not to consume blood as an item, as Greeks and Romans used it as an ingredient for cooking certain types of food.⁹³

In addition, if the Apostolic Decree does derive from Lev 17–18 and if we also admit a moral dimension embedded in the decree, then this supposed pleonasm becomes all the more understandable: both strangled meats (i.e., *nevelah* and *terefah*) as well as blood are singled out in Lev 17 as food items that Israelites and their Gentile associates must avoid eating. The Apostolic Decree follows the biblical text upon which it builds its legal foundation. Furthermore, the call to refrain from blood emphasizes

---

⁹⁰ See the discussion of Sanders, *Judaism: Practice and Belief,* 216, on Josephus, *Ant.* 14:245.

⁹¹ Perhaps in Palestine, matters could have been observed more strictly, as Jews could presumably have procured meat from Jewish butchers more easily than in the Diaspora, although we know not to what extent the intricate and detailed injunctions for performing kosher slaughtering were in play as reflected in rabbinic halakah. Indeed, according to *m. Hul.* 7:1, some rabbinic sages distrusted Jewish butchers concerning certain matters related to *shehitah*, illustrating how non-rabbinic Jews may have disregarded rabbinic ordinances for quite a while. Cf. Sanders, *Jewish Law,* 278–79. Probably the rabbinic effort to restrict purchasing meat slaughtered by Gentiles (*m. Hul.* 1:1) indicates that there were Jews who remained oblivious to rabbinic legislation.

⁹² Avemarie, "Die jüdischen Wurzeln des Aposteldekrets," 21.

⁹³ Avemarie, "Die jüdischen Wurzeln des Aposteldekrets," 21 n. 68, noting a recipe in Apicius cited by Elisabeth Alföldi-Rosenbaum, *Das Kochbuch der Römer. Rezepte aus der "Kochkunst" des Apicius, eingeleitet, übersetzt und erläutert* (10th ed.; Zurich/Munich: Artemis, 1993), 118–19.

the respect that all humans are to show toward life, which appears prominently throughout the Pentateuch. Already the book of Genesis (9:4–6) commands Noah and his descendants, hence all humans, to refrain from eating blood. Milgrom comments on Gen 9 are worth quoting here at length:

> God's command to Noah and his sons takes the form of a law – the first in the Bible, the first to humanity. And the blood prohibition is the quintessential component of this law. It is the divine remedy for human sinfulness, which hitherto has polluted the earth and necessitated its purgation by blood.... Man's nature will not change; he shall continue sinful (Gen 8:22), but his violence need no longer pollute the earth if he will but heed one law: abstain from blood.... Man must abstain from blood: human blood must not be shed and animal blood must not be ingested. In the Priestly scale of values, the prohibition actually stands higher than the Ten Commandments. The Decalogue was given solely to Israel, but the blood prohibition was enjoined upon all humankind; it alone is the basis for a viable human society.[94]

Werman suggests that in the course of Jewish history a shift took place in certain circles whereby the abominations that defiled the holy land of Israel, as outlined in Leviticus and elsewhere, were eventually applied worldwide: God did not reside simply in the holy land, but throughout the world. This shift is already noticeable in the Deutero-Isaian traditions so dear to Luke:

> For Deutero-Isaiah, the purpose of being chosen is to bring the nations closer to Israel and its religion; that is, it serves a universal purpose. The prophecies even go so far as to envision the alien peoples worshipping in the Temple itself (Isa 61:5–6). The sanctity that the Priestly Code ascribed to the priests alone has now expanded beyond the priesthood to include not only the Israelite nations but the alien peoples as well.[95]

Werman notes that in the book of *Jubilees* the link between the flood story in Genesis and the abominations that defile the holy land is made explicit: the earth was covered by water because of sexual immorality that defiled the *entire world* (*Jub.* 7:20–21). Correspondingly but in a narrower sense, according to Lev 18:25, the Canaanites defiled the holy land through illicit sexual intercourse. But the author of *Jubilees* understands Lev 18:25 in a universal sense. Immoral acts defile "the land in its broadest sense, that is, the soil of the earth."[96] *Jubilees* continues its expansive reading of holiness and purity by claiming that the very consumption of blood can pollute the entire earth. Genesis ch. 9 is read in light of the legislation in Leviticus 17 concerning the handling of blood and impurity. According to *Jubilees,* the consumption *and* the very treatment of blood must be handled carefully by

---

[94] Milgrom, *Leviticus,* 1:705.
[95] Cana Werman, "The Concept of Holiness and the Requirements of Purity in Second Temple and Tannaic Literature," in *Purity and Holiness*, 168.
[96] Werman, "The Concept of Holiness," 168–69.

Noah and his offspring. Noah's descendants must be sure to cover blood that is poured out upon the face of the earth (*Jub.* 7:30 = Lev 17:13).[97] Whereas Lev 17 only forbids the Israelite and the resident alien residing in the holy land of Israel from eating blood, in *Jubilees* this prohibition applies to all of humanity everywhere. If Noah and his descendants fail to respect these injunctions, the land, understood here as the earth, will not be cleansed from its blood (*Jub.* 7:33).

With respect to the Apostolic Decree, Werman declares that the prohibition against eating blood is not "simply a literal repetition of Genesis 9; rather, it is an expansion of Genesis in light of Leviticus 17, which concludes with a warning against eating meat of an animal having been strangled....In Christianity, as in Jubilees, the force of these prohibitions extends beyond the borders of the Land of Israel, concomitant with the belief in the universal divine presence."[98] Werman's findings highlight the concern for purity that underscores the Apostolic Decree, an issue that remained important for Luke in his discussion of the moral purification of the Gentile believers and its ramifications for Jewish-Gentile interaction within the *ekklesia*. Good evidence now exists showing that Jews applied the laws in Lev 17 and 18 to Gentiles. Besides *Jubilees*, I have pointed to 11QT^a 48:5–6. Possibly, 4Q251 12:4–5 might make a similar statement as the Temple Scroll with respect to proselytes and the consumption of carcasses, and Philo *Spec.* 4:123 could also be taken in a similar direction, depending on how the Alexandrian Jew thought his discussion on carcasses and blood should apply to non-Jews.[99]

Luke's perception of Gentiles, however, differs to a certain extent from that of *Jubilees*: whereas the author of *Jubilees* refers to such legislation only to further condemn Gentiles for their failure to observe these universal commandments and to declare their collective and perennial bondage to impure demons (*Jub.* 15:30–32), Luke affirms the eschatological incorporation of Gentile believers who have acquired a moral purification that is preserved through the observance of the Apostolic Decree.

Finally, Luke's formulation of Gentile duties vis-à-vis the Torah also departs from the rabbinic conception of the Noahide Laws on the matter of blood consumption. Because the command to refrain from consuming

---

[97] Ibid., 170–71: "According to Jubilees, the prohibition given to the Israelites and the strangers in Leviticus 17 is given to all mankind anywhere in the world (even more so, since there is no warning against the appearance of blood on the cloak of the slaughtered in Leviticus 17). Moreover, in Jubilees, the punishment for this crime is death by human hands, a punishment not mentioned at all in Leviticus 17."

[98] Ibid., 174.

[99] Wilson, *Luke and the Law,* 86, claims that "there is no evidence that first-century Judaism made Lev. 17–18 part of its demands for proselytes and or godfearers." This is no longer tenable in light of newer studies on certain passages from the Dead Sea Scrolls.

blood appears in Genesis as a regulation given to Noah and his descendants, the rabbis also forbade the Noahides from eating a "limb from a live animal" (*t. Avod. Zar.* 8:6; *b. Sanh.* 59). Nevertheless, this injunction, as the rabbinic concept of the Noahide Laws in general, should not be equated with the Apostolic Decree. The rabbinic prohibition against eating a "limb from a live animal" should be taken *literally* and in an ethical sense to mean that Gentiles should not devour a *live* creature: to tear and eat a limb from a live animal would represent a savage attitude toward animals that eventually could lead to the mistreatment and slaughtering of humans themselves.[100] Apparently, the rabbis understand the Hebrew phrase in Gen 9:4, אך־בשר בנפשו דמו לא תאכלו, in a *functional* sense to mean that Noahides cannot eat the flesh of an animal while its lifeblood is still pulsating in it.[101] But the rabbis permit blood as an *object* of consumption for Noahides. This is especially true with regard to consuming blood from a *dead* animal. While Lev 17:15 clearly forbids a Gentile residing among Israel to eat a *nevelah*, Deut 14:21, by contrast, allows a Gentile resident to eat such food: "You shall not eat anything that dies of itself; you may give it to aliens residing in your towns for them to eat, or you may sell it to a foreigner." The rabbis cleverly "resolve" this contradiction within the Mosaic Torah by claiming that Lev 17:15 refers to a Gentile covert to Judaism (גר צדק), while declaring that Deut 14:21 concerns Gentiles who are not converts (גר תושב) – an indication that according to the rabbinic understanding Noahides can eat meat with its blood (*Sifre Deut* 104; cf. *b. Avod. Zar.* 64b).[102]

---

[100] According to *t. Avod. Zar.* 8:6 (cf. *b. Sanh.* 59a), R. Hananiah also forbids Noahides from eating *blood* (instead of just flesh cut off from an animal) from a *live* animal. However, the sages disagree with his view. Later on, Maimonides (following the majority view) even allows a Noahide to eat blood from a live animal (*Hilkot Melakim* 9:10). See further Müller, *Tora für die Völker,* 128–30.

[101] So Müller, *Tora für die Völker,* 129. Cf. the interpretation of Gen 9:4 by Claus Westermann, *Genesis* (3 vols.; trans. John J. Scullion S. J.; Minneapolis: Augsburg, 1984–1986), 1:465, which coincides with the rabbinic understanding: "The commonly accepted explanation [of Gen 9:4], that the sentence forbids the partaking of blood, is not correct....The sentence is stating rather that the eating of animal flesh is limited to such flesh as no longer has its life in it....B. Jacob has noted correctly: 'It is therefore the pulsating...life-blood of which it is forbidden to partake, immediately after wounding or killing.' ...Blood is understood here not in its objective but in its functional meaning."

[102] Cf. Müller, Tora für die Völker, 164–65; Maimonides, Hilkhot Avodah Zarah 10:6.

Conclusion

It is regrettable that Luke does not expound each item of the Apostolic Decree, which would have allowed for a more precise and nuanced assessment of this most intriguing body of halakic regulations for Gentiles. Nevertheless, positing a link between the decree and Lev 17–18 still proves the most attractive hermeneutical option for clarifying the rationale and function of the decree even at its Lukan level. Lev 17–18 contain laws relevant for both Israelites and residents aliens, and readily presents itself as a model that could be appropriated and adapted for incorporating Gentile followers of Jesus into the early *ekklesia*. All four items in Luke's version of the decree can be paired with laws appearing in Lev 17–18. In fact, the "superfluous" listing of four items rather than a triad of three cardinal sins (i.e., idolatry, *porneia*, and bloodshed) in the decree can be accounted for when the correlation with Lev 17 is fully appreciated: in Lev 17 both the blood and carcasses of animals are forbidden for consumption. In a similar fashion, the Apostolic Decree retains a twofold injunction that prohibits Gentiles from consuming blood and strangled meat: they are to refrain from consuming blood as an ingredient as well as carcasses.

Luke surely thinks that this legislation still carries great importance for governing the life of the *ekklesia* in his own day, given its threefold repetition in Acts (15:21, 29, 21:25). Indeed, the third and last repetition of the contents of the decree in 21:25 suggests that Luke believes its stipulations are relevant for addressing Jewish-Gentile relations and the place of Torah observance among disciples of Jesus. Upon hearing Paul's report about his ministry to the Gentiles, Luke's James delivers the following words to him: "You see, brother, how many thousands of believers there are among the Jews, and they are all zealous for the law. They have been told about you that you teach all the Jews living among the Gentiles to forsake Moses, and that you tell them not to circumcise their children or observe the customs" (21:20–21). Arguably, the concern placed by Luke into James' mouth reflects a contemporary and ongoing suspicion held by a number of Jews after 70 CE who distrust Pauline teaching, claiming it leads Jews away from observing the Torah.[103] Extended interaction and contact be-

---

[103] Particularly at this point it is hard to posit that the Jewish Law has become a "distant" issue for Luke, as if he were only concerned with rehabilitating the image of Paul as a Torah observant Jew without realizing the *contemporary* ramifications of this portrait. The rumors floating around in Luke's day claim that Paul dissuaded Jews from circumcising their *children*. The issue is generational: how are Jews to relate to the Torah in light of the delay of the eschaton? Should they circumcise their children and transmit their ancestral customs to their offspring? The answer, for Luke, is firmly in the positive. Luke emphasizes Paul's fidelity to Torah up to the very end of the narration in Acts, even after the death and resurrection of Jesus and the promulgation of the Apostolic Decree.

tween Gentile and Jewish disciples of Jesus would have only accelerated the propagation of such rumors and further stir the apprehension of those Jews denouncing the apostasy from the Torah generated by a certain interpretation of Paul's teachings.[104] Luke, of course, does everything possible in Acts to dispel such notions, presenting a complacent Paul in complete submission to Jewish custom, while having James, the brother of Jesus, continually reaffirm the binding nature of the Apostolic Decree for the Gentile branch of the *ekklesia*. By collating James' concern for maintaining Jewish identity with the reaffirmation of the Apostolic Decree, Luke reveals his own answer to an ongoing problem concerning the eschatological and ecclesiological integration of the Gentiles into the *ekklesia* and its ramifications for Jewish-Gentile relations.

Some have argued that the proclamation of the Apostolic Decree, as presented in Acts 15, is issued in response to soteriological questions. Consequently, its stipulations carry little weight for addressing social issues of fellowship between Jewish and Gentile followers of Jesus.[105] However, the two issues, salvation and fellowship, cannot be fully separated from each other. They are closely related. A Jew might be more willing to interact with a Gentile who has become a "God-fearer" and showed respect and interest in Jewish customs and beliefs than with a sheer "pagan." Conversion to Judaism could even provide full access into Jewish society. On the other hand, full aversion would naturally translate into a distancing between both sides. By embracing the Apostolic Decree, Luke's solution lies somewhere in the middle of two extremes: Luke affirms that Gentiles can be saved without undergoing circumcision (in the case of males), but expects them to observe a certain number of regulations that preserve their moral purity and allow for a Jewish-Gentile encounters to occur in which Jews faithfully maintain their distinctive identity. Luke calls neither for full assimilation nor complete separation between Jews and Gentiles, only for a reasonable (in his eyes) compromise that guarantees interaction between both entities yet does not eliminate the ethnic and halakic differences that continue exist between both branches of the *ekklesia*.

Here the Conzelmannian tripartite scheme (Israel-Jesus-the church) imposed upon Luke-Acts collapses, for the Law remains largely unaffected in all three periods of Conzelmann's scheme of salvation history.

[104] Whether the historical Paul himself taught that Jews should abandon the Torah is another question, which I happily decide to leave out of this discussion. Probably, it would be helpful to think of several "Pauline schools" in the post-70 era that interpreted Paul's statements regarding the Torah in a variety of ways, some thinking that the Jewish Law should be fully abandoned, others, like Luke, arguing that Paul had never ceased being an observant Jew.

[105] Deines, "Das Aposteldekret," 355–56.

In any case, Luke does connect the question of salvation with the issue of fellowship between Jews and Gentiles, since Peter's speech in Acts 15 clearly alludes to the Cornelius episode (15:8–10). In the previous chapter, I signaled the importance of appreciating the issue of table fellowship for comprehending Luke's narration of the Cornelius incident (cf. Acts 10:28, 48; 11:3). In addition, scenes where Jewish and Gentile followers of Jesus dine and interact together appear prominently throughout Acts, suggesting that the Apostolic Decree could indeed prove important for addressing Jewish-Gentile encounters.[106] More importantly, three out of four of the items in the Apostolic Decree concern *food* (food offered to idols, strangled meat, and blood), not salvation. It is impossible, then, to ignore the import such legislation could carry for addressing Jewish-Gentile relationships. The Apostolic Decree is not simply a moral compilation of universal laws incumbent upon all Gentiles. Unlike the later rabbinic Noahide Laws, which are *entirely* ethical in their orientation, the Apostolic Decree contains dietary components that address the purity concerns of many Jews from the Second Temple period.[107] In Luke's eyes, Gentile followers are more than just "Noahides" (a terminological anachronism); they are more akin to the biblical *gerim* who reside *with* Israel. The Apostolic Decree is designed to address some of the Jewish qualms about interacting with Gentile followers of Jesus who have now invaded Jewish space. After all, Gentiles who embrace the Apostolic Decree commit themselves to forsaking idolatry: they neither worship idols nor consciously acquire and consume food offered to idols. This commitment in itself was no small feat. It was sufficiently conspicuous and unsettling to cause social, political and economic unrest among Jews, Greeks, and Romans, particularly in the

---

[106] For example, Paul stays in Philippi at the house of Lydia (16:15). In Philippi, Paul also eats and lodges at the house of a Gentile jailer (16:34).

[107] As noted above, even the seventh Noahide law, to abstain from eating a "limb from a live animal" reflects a *moral* concern. Likewise, the remaining six Noahide laws are all ethical in their orientation: to maintain justice (דינין), refrain from idolatry (עבודה זרה), blasphemy (קיללת השם), sexual immorality (גילוי עריות), bloodshed (שפיכות דמים), and robbery (גזל). Although the rabbis (ideally) expected Noahides to refrain from idolatry, there is no evidence that this injunction included abstinence from eating food that was offered to idols. Furthermore, unlike the Apostolic Decree, the Noahide legislation seems not to concern itself with Jewish-Gentile *interaction*, but with maintaining clear boundaries between Jews and Gentiles, indeed explicitly forbidding non-Jews from observing any other Jewish custom (e.g., the Sabbath) than the seven Noahide Laws (cf. the rabbinic dictum in *b. Sanh.* 58b, שב ואל תעשה). By contrast, I have suggested in Part I of this book that Luke would not have objected to Gentiles *voluntarily* observing the Sabbath or other Jewish customs. Cf. Müller, *Tora für die Völker,* 165; Novak, "The Origin of Noahide Laws," 26.

tense atmosphere persisting after 70 between Jerusalem and Rome.[108] It is improbable that many non-Christian Jews would have made such uncompromising demands from Gentiles sympathetic to Judaism given these circumstances.[109] Luke's ideal Gentile follower of Jesus, however, refrains not only from idolatry, but also from the other immoral practices of the Gentiles such as *porneia*. In addition, Luke demands that Gentile followers of Jesus abstain from consuming blood and strangled meat. Thus, Luke's ideal Gentile follower of Jesus refrains not only from the triad of cardinal sins normally associated with the nations (idolatry, sexual immorality, and murder), but also from the impurity associated with consuming products containing blood.

Some commentators note that the Apostolic Decree presents only a partial list of dietary laws: no explicit prohibition against eating forbidden foods such as pork appears in Acts.[110] But Luke, like other ancient Jews willing to dine with sympathizing Gentiles, assumes that Gentile followers of Jesus will not serve forbidden items such as pork to fellow Torah observant Jewish believers when they commune together. It is unlikely that Luke envisions the ideal Gentile follower of Jesus (e.g., Cornelius, the friendly Gentile sympathizer toward Jewry *par excellence*) serving a pig that has been ritually slaughtered with its blood properly drained to a Torah observant Jew. Once a pig always a pig! Indeed, at least for Jewish consumption, all non-kosher animals remain *nevelah* even when slaughtered according to the laws of *shehitah*.[111] Wehnert suggests that the Apos-

---

[108] See Acts 16:16–24; 19:19, 24–41, for examples of the social unrest caused by the boycott of idols by followers of Jesus. Saldarini, *Matthew's Christian-Jewish Community*, 158: "Refusal to participate in Greco-Roman worship separated Jews much more decisively from the rest of the Mediterranean world than dietary laws or circumcision."

[109] Paula Fredriksen, "What 'Parting of the Ways'?" in *The Ways That Never Parted*, 55–56: "To have actively pursued a policy of alienating Gentile neighbors from their family gods and native, civic and imperial cults would only have put the minority Jewish community at risk."

[110] Pervo, *Acts,* 376 n. 89: "The decree falls short of *kashrut,* certainly of the sort advocated by the Pharisees. Pork, for example, is not mentioned, nor is there any attention to menstruants as a potential source of impurity or to other purity regulations regarding food." It is debatable whether Jews of this period would have viewed *Gentile* menstruation as source of impurity, though they could have found it disgusting (see references to Klawans, Hayes, Maccoby in the introduction to chapter 8 of this monograph). Of equal interest are the traditions in the *Ps. Clem.* literature mentioned earlier in this chapter that require Gentile women to honor the rules of menstruation and Gentile couples to wash themselves after having sexual intercourse. These traditions merit further consideration and comparison with Second Temple and rabbinic texts dealing with Gentile impurity.

[111] Milgrom, *Leviticus,* 1:654: "…carcasses of impure animals are always termed *nĕbēlâ* no matter how they died – even if they were slaughtered ritually." Cf. Hoffmann, *Das Buch Leviticus*, 1:352, 467. Cf. *m. Hul.* 9:1 and its discussion of slaughtering an impure animal for a Gentile (upon its death it becomes *nevelah*).

tolic Decree was probably accompanied by further instruction elaborating the meaning and application of each item so that Gentile followers of Jesus could learn more fully about Jewish dietary and ritual sensibilities.[112] The terse language of the Apostolic Decree, with its mere listing of four items, certainly calls for further elaboration and clarification. It could also be that Luke only expects Gentiles to refrain from eating forbidden animals *when they commune with Jewish followers of Jesus*. Otherwise, he only requires *Gentiles* to avoid, whenever possible, the four items outlined in the Apostolic Decree. Kashrut, in itself, only carries ongoing relevance for the Jewish wing of the *ekklesia*.[113] Regardless of what one makes of the link between the Apostolic Decree and Lev 17–18, it is quite remarkable that the decree, and by extension, Luke, presupposes an ongoing observance of the Torah in its totality by *Jewish* followers of Jesus. Throughout Acts, Luke always and only discusses the minimal requirements *Gentiles* should observe, while assuming and even affirming that Jewish followers of Jesus will continue observing their customs *in toto*.

---

[112] Wehnert, *Die Reinheit*, 254.

[113] No explicit reference to forbidden (i.e., non-kosher) animals appears in Lev chs. 17–18. But were there Jews of the Second Temple period onward who would have interpreted Lev 17–18 to include kashrut for Gentiles? Probably not. Particularly intriguing is the phrase אשר יאכל in Lev 17:13: "And anyone of the people of Israel, or of the aliens who reside among them, who hunts down an animal or bird that *may be eaten* (אשר יאכל) shall pour out its blood and cover it with earth." The later *Tg. Ps. J.* interprets the phrase as meaning "what is permitted [i.e., kosher] for eating" (דמיכשרין למיכל), assuming that the discussion throughout Leviticus 17 only concerns kosher animals. See also *Sifra* Parashah Aharei Mot Pereq 11:3: אשר יאכל יצא עוף טמא שאינו נאכל; *m. Hul.* 6:2 (discussion between R. Meir and the sages concerning which animals' blood requires covering, basing themselves on Lev 17:13). Milgrom, *Leviticus,* 2:1481, comments on Lev 17:13 in the following way: "Assumed is a knowledge of 11:13–19; 24–28....However, what of the forbidden animals, those whose flesh may not be eaten? Is their blood to be drained and buried? A positive reply must be presumed....The fact, however, that this phrase is used – despite the questions that may arise – indicates that the subject here and throughout the chapter is meat for the table. Indeed, the absence of any reference to predatory (hence, forbidden) animals shows that the notion of hunting as sport is not even envisaged – a far cry from the practices of Israel's neighbors." See also *Rashi* on Lev 17:13.

Part III

Circumcision in Matthew and Luke-Acts

Chapter 12

Circumcision in Matthew and Luke-Acts

"And please circumcise us too, so that we look like Jews...."
(Petronius, Satyricon 102:13–14)

Introduction

Although Jews were not the only people who practiced circumcision in antiquity, classical sources often single out this practice as a distinctive Jewish custom.[1] For Petronius (first century CE), circumcision is a specifically Jewish trait: "and please circumcise us too, so that we look like Jews" (*Satyricon* 102:13–14).[2] Tacitus remarks that the Jewish people "adopted circumcision to distinguish themselves from other peoples by this difference" (*Historiae* V, 5). Besides Sabbath observance and dietary practices, Juvenal also singles out circumcision as a Jewish custom *par excellence* (*Saturae* XIV, 96–106). As Matthew and Luke composed their writings in the shadow of the destruction of the temple, some Jews were trying to evade paying the Roman levy known as the *fiscus Iudaicus*. According to Suetonius, Roman authorities even searched for marks of circumcision in order to identify Jewish evaders.[3]

Many non-Jews, then, viewed circumcision as a quintessential marker of Jewish identity, and any affirmation of this practice on the part of Matthew or Luke could potentially lead them to be qualified as Jewish, at least in the eyes of Greco-Roman outsiders. For Jews, however, simply bearing

---

[1] Stern, *Greek and Latin Authors*, 1:444: "...for Greek and Latin writers the Jews were the circumcised *par excellence*."

[2] Notice the statement made in *Fragmenta* 37, also ascribed to Petronius: "The Jew may worship his pig-god and clamour in the ears of high heaven, but unless he also cuts back his foreskin with the knife, he shall go forth from the people and emigrate to Greek cities, and shall not tremble at the fasts of Sabbath imposed by the law."

[3] See Suetonius, *Domitianus* 12:2: "Besides other taxes, that on the Jews was levied with the utmost vigour, and those were prosecuted who without publicly acknowledging that faith yet lived as Jews, as well as those who concealed their origin and did not pay the tribute levied upon their people. I recall being present in my youth when the person of a man ninety years old was examined before the procurator and a very crossed court, to see whether he was circumcised."

the marks of circumcision was not sufficient a criterion for establishing Jewish identity. After all, other peoples did (and still do) practice circumcision. Recently, Thiessen has made a coherent and compelling argument concerning the importance of the *timing* of circumcision on the eighth day as a means for certain ancient Jews to differentiate themselves from other peoples who also practiced circumcision.[4] He posits that already the narrator of Genesis 17 sought to differentiate Ishmael and those peoples represented by this literary figure vis-à-vis Israel by highlighting their non-eighth-day circumcision.[5] The book of *Jubilees* continues in this trajectory, reaffirming the need for all Jews to circumcise their sons on the eighth day.[6]

It is quite telling that of all canonical gospel authors only Luke devotes attention to the question of circumcision.[7] Quite remarkably, Luke, like the author of *Jubilees*, highlights the timing of circumcision, reporting how both John the Baptist and Jesus entered into the covenant of Israel on the eighth day. Matthew, on the other hand, never explicitly refers to the rite of circumcision, although this certainly has not prevented scholars from speculating about the matter. As Matthew does not refer to circumcision, all comments about his perspective on this matter must remain tentative. Luke, on the other hand, provides a wealth of material that shows how remarkably knowledgeable he is about Jewish halakah. Not only is he well informed about Jewish circumcision and the many rites and practices associated with childbirth: parturient impurity, naming a child on the eighth day, and the redemption of the firstborn. He also affirms the observance of circumcision *for Jews*. Like most Jews of his time, Luke assumes that every Jewish male should undergo circumcision, including Jewish followers of Jesus.

---

[4] Other monographs on circumcision in ancient Judaism and Christianity include: Nina E. Livesey, *Circumcision as a Malleable Symbol* (WUNT 2. 295; Tübingen: Mohr Siebeck, 2010); Simon Claude Mimouni, *La circoncision dans le monde judéen aux époques grecque et romaine: Histoire d'un conflit interne au judaïsme* (Collection de la Revue des études juives 42; Paris: Peeters, 2007); Shaye Cohen, *Why Aren't Jewish Women Circumcised* (Berkeley, Calif.: University of California Press, 2005); Andreas Blaschke, *Beschneidung: Zeugnisse der Bibel und verwandter Texte* (Texte und Arbeiten zum neutestamentlichen Zeitalter 28; Tübingen: Francke, 1998); and Nissan Rubin, *Beginning of Life; Rites of Birth, Circumcision, and Redemption of the First-Born in the Talmud and Midrash* [in Hebrew] (Tel Aviv: Ha-Kibbuts Ha-Meuhad, 1995).

[5] Thiessen, *Contesting Conversion*, 41.

[6] For discussion of the historical contexts of *Jubilees* and its debate about circumcision, see my forthcoming "Forming Jewish Identity by Formulating Legislation for Gentiles."

[7] The gospel of John 7:22–23 mentions circumcision *en passant*, but this occurs only as a secondary motif in a discussion that focuses on healing on the Sabbath and Jesus' authority.

Matthew and the Circumcision Debate in Recent Scholarship

Recently, the question of circumcision in Matthew has acquired a certain profile despite the absence of any explicit reference to this topic in the entire gospel. This state of the evidence does not allow for drawing any definite conclusions on the matter.[8] Unfortunately, Matthew, unlike Luke, did not write his own version of the "Acts of the Apostles" where he could have more clearly outlined his position on the place of circumcision within the *ekklesia*. All that can be posited with reasonable confidence, in light of Matthew's favorable attitude toward the Torah, is an affirmation on his part of circumcision among Jewish followers of Jesus who are to continue observing the Mosaic Law in all of its aspects.

The question concerning Gentile circumcision is far more complicated. A momentary look at the matter through the prism of ancient Judaism might prove illustrative though inconclusive. To the best of my knowledge, it does not seem that many ancient Jews fantasized about a massive and collective (male) circumcision of Gentiles in the days leading toward the eschaton.[9] Instead, many Jews hoped that the nations would eventually abandon their futile devotion to idols and cease practicing sexual immorality, bloodshed, and other disgraceful sins. Others waited for the collective punishment of the nations for their sins and abuse against Israel, although they entertained the possibility that certain non-Jews could be saved, whether through full conversion into Judaism or simply by recognizing and worshiping the one true God of Israel. Müller has done a great service by amassing and analyzing a variety of ancient Jewish texts that condemn the nations for engaging in variety of "cardinal sins," which usually can be subsumed under three categories: idolatry, murder, and sexual immorality.[10] These texts presuppose that Gentiles will continue to live as Gentiles in a righteous way without fully converting to Judaism. This evidence suggests that Matthew could have held a similar view, namely, that Gentile followers of Jesus could acquire a new status enabling them to be included with the eschatologically renewed and reconfigured Israel without having to become Jews.

---

[8] Cf. the cautious reservations made by Hare, "How Jewish is Matthew?" 265–67.

[9] Many of the texts cited in Scot McKnight, *A Light among the Gentiles: Jewish Missionary Activity in the Second Temple Period* (Minneapolis: Fortress, 1991), 47, really only speak about a Gentile confession of the God of Israel that demands abandoning idolatry and other immoral sins rather than full conversion into Judaism. Such texts include Tob 13:11; Sir 36:1–5; *Pss. Sol.* 17:31; *1 En.* 48:4; 50:1–3; 53:1; 90:30–33; 91:14; *T. Sim.* 7:2; *T. Levi* 2:10–11; 4:4–6; 18:2–9; *T. Jud.* 24:6; 25:5; *T. Zeb.* 9:8; *T. Dan* 6:7; *T. Ash.* 7:3; *Sib. Or.* 3:710–730, 767–780; 5:492–500.

[10] Müller, *Tora für die Völker*; Flusser and Safrai, "Das Aposteldekret und die Noachitischen Gebote," 173–92.

Sim, however, has taken Matthew's silence on the question of circumcision as evidence for a Matthean expectation of Gentiles to observe the Torah entirely:

> There is no need to mention circumcision for (male) Gentile converts because Matthew was concerned not with the preliminary step of conversion to the Jewish people, but with the specifically Christian ritual which admitted all Jews, whether by birth or proselytism, to his sectarian Christian Jewish group. It is therefore presumed by author and reader alike that any Gentiles who wished to join their community must proselytise first in order to fulfil the basic requirements for admission.... We can illustrate this point by referring to the admission requirements of a contemporary Jewish sect, the Qumran community. This sectarian group counted proselytes among its members, even though they were ranked at the bottom of the hierarchy (CD 14:4–6). Yet the complex admission procedures of this community, which took years to complete (cf. 1QS 6:13–23), say nothing about circumcision. The reason for this is that the entry requirements of the Qumran community presumed that potential Gentile members would become Jews as a necessary first step.[11]

The analogy drawn by Sim with the "Qumran community" is well made but raises questions that require further attention and clarification. First, it is questionable whether any Gentiles ever joined the Jewish group(s) associated with the Damascus Document or the Community Rule, although these texts may reflect the practices and ideals of several groups of (Essene?) Jews rather than just the views of a small sect living near the Dead Sea.[12] Nonetheless, even if these texts do not reflect social reality, they at least present an *ideal* conception of the commonwealth of Israel as perceived by certain Jews. 1QS 5:6 places Gentile proselytes at the bottom of the social hierarchy of Israel in the following way: "They are to atone for all those in Aaron who volunteer for holiness, and for those in Israel who belong to truth, and for Gentile proselytes who join them in community (והנלוים עליהם ליחד)."[13] This passage from 1QS divides its subjects into three ranks: members of the clan of Aaron, descendants of Israel who are

---

[11] Sim, *The Gospel of Matthew*, 253–54. See his more recent articles on the matter, especially: "Matthew, Paul and the Origin and Nature of the Gentile Mission: The Great Commission in Matthew 28:16–20 as an Anti-Pauline Tradition," *HTS Teologiese Studies/Theological Studies* 64.1 (2008): 377–92. Cf. Levine, *The Social and Ethnic Dimensions*, 178–85, especially 185: "Matthew emphasizes the retention of the Law and continuity between the age of Israel and the age of the church. In this second period of salvation history, the gospel will be preached to the gentiles as well as to the Jews, and the rules for admission into the *Basileia* are extended rather than repealed. Thus it is likely that male gentile members of the church engaged in the rite of circumcision."

[12] On this issue, see Boccaccini, *Beyond the Essene Hypothesis,* 21–49. On the problems with identifying Qumran as an Essene site and relating it with the Dead Sea Scrolls discovered in the caves nearby, see Collins, *The Dead Sea Scrolls,* 20–30; Wise, Abegg, and Cook, *The Dead Sea Scrolls,* 14–35.

[13] Translation taken from Wise-Abegg-Cook, *The Dead Sea Scrolls.*

truthful to the Judaism espoused by 1QS, and other individuals who join the *yahad*. Presumably, נלוים refers to Gentiles who have joined Israel, as the term is used in other Jewish writings with non-Jews in mind.[14] In CD 14:4–6, appear four ranks of people: priests in first place, followed by Levites, Israelites, and *gerim*. In the translation of the Damascus Document provided in the edition by Wise, Abegg, and Cook, the Hebrew term *ger* is rendered as "proselyte." It could be better, however, not to translate the Hebrew *ger* or to render it with words such as "sojourner" or "resident alien," the way *ger* is often translated in the Hebrew Bible. For certain ancient Jews, the impermeability of Jewishness was such that they denied the very possibility of Gentile conversion. Gentiles could not become Jews but were to remain Gentiles, much like the biblical *ger* ("sojourner").[15] 1QS 2:19–23 seems to presuppose that each member of the commonwealth of Israel maintains his or her rank without the possibility of social promotion:

> They shall do as follows annually, all the days of Belial's dominion: the priests shall pass in review first, ranked according to their spiritual excellence, one after another. Then the Levites shall follow, and third all the people by rank, one after another, in their thousands and hundreds and fifties and tens. Thus shall each Israelite know his proper standing in the *Yahad* of God, an eternal society. None shall be demoted from his appointed place, none promoted beyond his foreordained rank.

According to this taxonomy, priests remain priests, ranked among themselves according to their spiritual credentials. Levites appear second in rank, followed by the Israelites. Although the *gerim* are not explicitly mentioned, their presence may be presumed under the category of Israelites who also are called to organize themselves according to their appointed rank. Alternatively, the gerim do not appear in this list because 1QS does not envision their inclusion within the commonwealth of Israel. It is

---

[14] Cf. 4QpNah 3–4 ii:9. Isa 14:1: "But the LORD will have compassion on Jacob and will again choose Israel, and will set them in their own land; and aliens (הגר) will join them (נלוה) and attach themselves to the house of Jacob." Isa 56:3: "Do not let the foreigner joined (הנלוה) to the LORD say, 'The LORD will surely separate me from his people.'" See also Isa 56:6; Esth 9:27 (the Jews established and accepted as a custom for themselves and their descendants and all who joined them [הנלוים]); Zech 2:11 ("Many nations shall join themselves to the LORD on that day, and shall be my people"); Tob 1:8 ("to the converts who had attached themselves to Israel" [προσηλύτοις τοῖς προσκειμένοις τοῖς υἱοῖς Ἰσραηλ]).

[15] Thiessen, *Contesting Conversion*, 17–63, contends that no passage in the Hebrew Bible envisages circumcision as a rite that permits Gentiles to become Israelites. See also Solomon Zeitlin, "Proselytes and Proselytism during the Second Commonwealth and the Early Tannaitic Period," in *Harry Austryn Wolfson Jubilee Volume: On the Occasion of his Seventy-Fifth Birthday* (2 vols.; Jerusalem: American Academy for Jewish Research, 1965), 2:871–82.

equally possible that those Jews responsible for the composition and dissemination of the Damascus Document viewed Gentile circumcision as an exceptional phenomenon that allowed limited integration of certain non-Jews into Jewish society. Elsewhere, the Damascus Document discourages Jews from even associating with Gentiles (CD 11:14–15).[16] To discover a denial in such texts of the possibility for Gentiles to transform into full-blown Jews should come as no surprise. It is in harmony with what we find in other Jewish writings, including the books of *Jubilees* and MMT. These writings deny the very possibility for Gentiles to become Jews, since Jewish membership according to such books is contingent on genealogical purity and, as explicitly stated in *Jubilees,* circumcision on the eighth day. As Hayes states, for "Jubilees, the distinction between and separation of the profane seed of Gentiles and the holy seed of the Israelites is an unalterable fact of the natural order, immune to the remedy of circumcision."[17]

If Matthew expected Gentile (male) followers of Jesus to undergo circumcision, would he have viewed them as "second class" citizens within the *ekklesia*, much like the biblical *ger*, or as full-blown Jews? It is difficult to answer this question with any confidence or precision, since Matthew does not refer to the topic of circumcision.[18] Those exceptional Gentiles who do draw near to Jesus during his earthly ministry, such as the Syrophoenician woman, humble themselves to such a point that one could initially posit a two-tier Matthean system whereby Jews sit at the table with the Gentiles collecting the crumbs underneath them (15:28). On the other hand, Matthew envisages an eschatological banquet composed of Jews and Gentiles who sit at the same table and enjoy fellowship on an equal standing (8:11). This openness toward an eschatological incorporation of Gentiles into the community sets the gospel of Matthew aside from certain writings associated with the community of Qumran and its sister

---

[16] See discussion in Cana Werman, *Attitude towards Gentiles in the Book of Jubilees and Qumran Literature Compared with Early Tanaaic Halakha and Contemporary Pseudepigrapha* [in Hebrew] (Ph.D. diss., The Hebrew University of Jerusalem, 1995), 258–79, 301–2 (on the Damascus Document); 317–19 (on the Temple Scroll and 4QFlorilegium). Werman concludes that both *Jubilees* and the "Qumran sect" were opposed to the idea of conversion.

[17] Hayes, *Gentile Impurities,* 77. Cf. Werman, *Attitude towards Gentiles*, 256. There is good evidence that such views, which negated the possibility of converting to Judaism, continued into the first century CE. See Thiessen, *Contesting Conversion,* 107–10.

[18] What about the genealogy of Jesus in Matthew, which includes four women of non-Israelite background (Tamar, Rahab, Ruth, and Bathsheba) who were integrated into the lineage of Israel? Even a book like *Jubilees* rationalizes in its own way the inclusion of Tamar into the genealogy of Israel that still vouchsafes, at least to the author's satisfaction, the genealogical purity of Israel. On the prominence of matriarchs in *Jubilees,* see Betsy Halpern-Amaru, *The Empowerment of Women in the Book of Jubilees* (JSJSup 60; Leiden: Brill, 1999).

"sects," which treat Gentiles indiscriminately as morally corrupt, doomed to darkness, and under the control of evil spirits.[19]

To be sure, Matthew shares in the common prejudice held by many Jews toward the Gentile world. Gentiles, in Matthew's opinion, utter empty phrases when they pray (6:7). They are overly preoccupied with material concerns and goods (6:31–32). Matthew exhorts his audience to relate to renegades within the *ekklesia* as Gentiles or tax collectors (18:17), as if no Gentiles belonged to his circle. Matthew's Jesus often speaks of the Gentiles in the pejorative plural form, without discrimination (5:47; 20:19, 25). However, the inclusion of the commission at the end of the gospel, the idea of an *active mission* to the Gentile world, sets Matthew's perspective on the Gentile question apart from the worldview(s) expressed in some of the writings composed by the sectarian group(s) who serendipitously bequeathed to us the Dead Sea Scrolls. While some Essenes (or whoever composed the writings traditionally associated with the "Qumran sect") may have been open to the possibility of some exceptional Gentiles joining their communities or at least idealized an Israelite commonwealth in which Gentile *gerim* would follow the Torah according to their ranking, as far as we know, they, like many other ancient Jews, did not engage in an active mission to attract Gentiles to join their circles.[20]

In many ways, Matthew's outlook toward the Gentile world is not too different from the perspective found in *2 Baruch*. Indeed, it is surprising that so little attention has been granted to comparing these two writings, given their mutual interest in the Torah, their contemporaneity (both written after 70), and geographical provenance (both possibly stemming from Palestine).[21] Like Matthew, *2 Bar.* contains its share of prejudice against Gentiles. The nations walk in vanity and are like vapor (*2 Bar.* 14:5; 41:4; 81:4). They act unrighteously and ignore God's Law (48:40; 81:4–5). Their delights should be avoided (83:5).

---

[19] On the other hand, passages in 1 Enoch look forward to the eschatological salvation of Gentiles. See, for example, *1 En.* 90:6–38 and 91:14.

[20] Martin Goodman, *Mission And Conversion: Proselytizing in the Religious History of the Roman Empire* (Oxford: Clarendon, 1994). Matt 23:15 could represent an exception to the rule, showing that some Pharisees did go out of their way to convert Gentiles, although there is no external proof outside of Matthew to confirm this point (see Shaye Cohen, "Did Ancient Jews Missionize?" *BRev* 19.4 [2003]). Matt 23:15 does not contain an aversion to the idea of Gentile circumcision, only an opposition to the conversion of Gentiles into a certain strand of (Pharisaic) Judaism, which renders such non-Jews, in Matthew's eyes, children of hell in a twofold way. In other words, Matthew, like certain other Jews, views Gentiles as already doomed to perdition, and their conversion into Pharisaic Judaism aggravates rather than improves their soteriological standing.

[21] For a preliminary comparison, see Matthias Henze, *Jewish Apocalypticism in Late First Century Israel: Reading 'Second Baruch' in Context* (TSAJ 142; Tübingen: Mohr Siebeck, 2011), 341–47.

On the other hand, the author of *2 Bar.* sees a positive outcome in Israel's temporary exile and subjugation to the nations: in their dispersion, Jews are able to "do good to the nations" or "to bring them news" (1:4).[22] While "Baruch" laments that many of his people have separated themselves from God's statutes and cast away the yoke of the Law, a probable reference to apostasy from Judaism, he rejoices that others have abandoned their vanity and fled under God's wings (41:4). In the aftermath of 70 CE, some Jews probably forsook their Jewish identity, but this passage from *2 Bar.* suggests that Judaism was still attractive enough to draw Gentiles away from their "vanity," as the author puts it, and bring them under the wings of the Most High. It is quite possible that the author of *2 Bar.* envisions here full conversion of Gentiles into Judaism, which, in the case of males, would involve circumcision. In rabbinic literature, to come under the "wings of the *Shekinah*" represents becoming a full proselyte of Judaism.[23] *2 Bar.* understands the imagery of Gentiles coming under God's wings in a similar way, especially since it contrasts the influx of Gentiles into Judaism with an apostasy of Jews from the Torah.

Moreover, circumcision is of extreme importance in *2 Bar.* as is the observance of many other Jewish customs including the Sabbath and festival days (84:8). As the author of *2 Bar.* retells the story of King Josiah in the so-called "apocalypse of the clouds" (chs. 53–76), he underscores the fact that Josiah "left no one un-circumcised" during his reform of Judahite society (66:6). This detail, along with the reference to Josiah establishing "the festivals and the sabbaths" (66:4; cf. 84:8) are not found in the scriptural accounts concerning Josiah's reform.[24] The author of *2 Baruch* may have inferred that Josiah enforced circumcision either from the scriptural reference concerning the king's restoration of the feast of Passover (e.g., 2 Kgs 23:21–23) or the collective renewal of the covenant (2 Kgs 23:3). Nevertheless, there might be more at play here than mere exegetical exercise, since during the aftermath of 70 CE, the time when *2 Bar.* was written, some Jewish males were concealing their signs of circumcision in order to avoid paying the *fiscus Judaicus*, while other Jews were abandon-

---

[22] The Syriac can be construed either way. See Mark F. Whitters, *The Epistle of Second Baruch: A Study in Form and Message* (JSPSup 42; London: Sheffield Academic Press, 2003), 125, for a discussion of the Syriac as well as an excellent treatment of the topic of Gentile inclusion in *2 Bar.* Translations of *2 Bar.* are taken from Charlesworth's edition of the *Old Testament Pseudepigrapha*. Cf. Tob 1:3: "Acknowledge him before the nations, O children of Israel; for he has scattered you among them."

[23] See, for example, the stories about Gentiles who convert to Judaism thanks to the gentleness of Hillel who brought them under the wings of the *Shekinah* (*b. Shabb.* 30b–31a). Cf. Ruth 2:12.

[24] 2 Kgs 22:1–23:30; 2 Chr chs. 34–35; 1 Esd 1:1–33; Sir 49:1–4.

ing Judaism altogether.[25] Out of alarm over this phenomenon, the author of *2 Bar.* brings to the forefront the importance of observing circumcision as well as Jewish festivals and sabbaths.

The evidence from *2 Bar.* demonstrates that some of Matthew's Jewish contemporaries would have welcomed Gentile (circumcised) proselytes into their midst, though even the author of *2 Bar.* claims that the nations that did not know or harm Israel will be spared in the end of time, apparently without having to undergo full conversion into Judaism (72:2–6). Thus, not even an investigation of *2 Bar.* settles the question of Gentile circumcision in Matthew: *2 Bar.* welcomes Gentiles who convert to Judaism, on the one hand, and envisions eschatological salvation without circumcision for the nations that knew not or did not harm Israel, on the other. The question of Gentile circumcision probably continued to be debated in the aftermath of 70 among Jewish followers of Jesus and non-Christian Jews alike.[26] *2 Bar.* suggests that Matthew *may* have welcomed individual Gentile proselytes into his community who underwent circumcision even while hoping for a massive salvation among the nations without such halakic requirements. As noted above, Matthew, like *2. Bar.*, views the Gentile world as a hostile environment. Members of Matthew's community are even to relate to opponents as Gentiles (18:17). Could this verse imply that Gentiles were expected to forsake their identity in order to join the "Matthean community" and participate in the eschatological banquet? It is possible that Matthew believed Gentiles could become entirely "other" (i.e., forsake their "pagan" identity) without undergoing circumcision and transforming into full-blown Jews. The case of the Syrophoenician woman might serve as an example of the renunciation of Gentile identity without the requirement of fully converting to Judaism.

Many questions remain unanswered about Matthew's position on Gentile circumcision, given the state of the evidence. On the other hand, Davies and Allison are probably correct in their treatment of the question of circumcision in the gospel of Matthew, particularly as it relates to Jewish followers of Jesus: "Matthew, despite his insistence on upholding the Jewish law, never mentions circumcision. That he expected Jewish Chris-

---

[25] On Jewish apostasy in response to the Jewish Revolts against Rome, see my forthcoming "Jewish Apocalyptic Expectations during and after the Revolts against Rome," in *The Psychological Dynamics of Revolution: Religious Revolts* (vol. 1 of *Winning Revolutions: The Psychology of Successful Revolts for Freedom, Fairness, and Rights*; ed. J. Harold Ellens; Santa Barbara, Calif.: Praeger, 2014).

[26] As suggested by Josephus' report about the conversion of royal members of the kingdom of Adiabene (*Ant.* 20:35 ff.) and the debate concerning the necessity of circumcision.

tians to circumcise their male children is plausible; but he evidently did not think such necessary for Gentiles."[27]

The Circumcision of John the Baptist and Jesus

Introduction

In the first two chapters of his gospel, which cover the birth of John the Baptist and Jesus, Luke highlights the fidelity of several Jewish protagonists to the Torah.[28] Ironically, Luke's reference in positive terms to the circumcision of Jesus has become a *locus classicus* among a host of New Testament scholars for positing Luke's ignorance of Jewish custom and affirming his Gentile background.[29] These commentators point out that no pre-rabbinic Jewish source refers to the custom of naming a child on the eighth day. Instead of taking the gospel of Luke more seriously as an ancient Jewish source that provides the first attestation of such a practice, they question its reliability. Were the practice of naming a Jewish newborn on the eighth day to be found in a Jewish work like the book of *Jubilees*, one supposes scholars would judge matters quite differently. Nowhere else do the presuppositions concerning Luke's Gentile background govern so strongly the interpretation of his writings. Thus, where Luke describes Jesus' purification and presentation in the temple of Jerusalem, many quickly assert his misunderstanding of basic stipulations from the Mosaic Torah. Since, according to Leviticus 12, apparently only the *mother* of a newborn infant would require purification after giving birth, why does

---

[27] Davies and Allison, *The Gospel according to Saint Matthew,* 3:685. Similarly, Donald Senior, "Between Two Worlds: Gentiles and Jewish Christians in Matthew's Gospel," CBQ 61 (1999): 1–23 (20). Saldarini, *Matthew's Christian Jewish Community,* 156–60, leaves the question open. On the proposal that Matthew conceives of two separate missions, one to the Gentiles (with no requirement of circumcision), another to the Jews (which presupposes Torah observance), see Joel Willits, "The Friendship of Matthew and Paul: A Response to the Recent Trend in the Interpretation of Matthew's Gospel," *HTS Teologiese Studies/Theological Studies* 65.1 (2009): Art. #151, 8 pages. Cf. Axel von Dobbeler, "Die Restitution Israels und die Bekehrung der Heiden: Das Verhältnis von Mt 10,5b.6 und Mt 28,18–20 unter dem Aspekt der Komplementarität: Erwägungen zum Standort des Matthäusevangeliums," *ZNW* 91.1–2 (2000): 18–44. I would like to thank Brian Tucker for sharing these references with me.

[28] For a more detailed analysis of the Law in Luke's Infancy Narrative, see Salo, *Luke's Treatment of the Law,* 45–63.

[29] As Salo, *Luke's Treatment of the Law,* 46 n. 11, notes, the theme of the Jewish Law in the Infancy Narrative of Luke has been largely ignored because of a greater interest in matters more central to Christian theology such as the virgin birth and the divinity of Jesus.

Luke refer to Jesus' purification as well? Furthermore, shouldn't Luke know better that there would be no need for Jesus' parents to present their child in person in the temple of Jerusalem in order to have him redeemed as a firstborn Israelite? Brown's magisterial commentary on the Infancy Narratives of Matthew and Luke represents just one prominent voice that embraces such a critique of Luke. Brown believes that Luke probably was a Gentile proselyte before becoming a "Christian," because he reveals only a "bookish" knowledge of Judaism, acquired through his reading of the Septuagint, when he reports the circumcision, purification, and redemption of Jesus.[30] One wonders, however, how a Gentile of the first century CE could become a proselyte to Judaism only through an individual and private reading of the LXX. Presumably, conversion into Judaism would involve a certain form of *integration* into and interaction with a Jewish *community* made of human flesh and blood. Even if Luke were a Gentile convert to Judaism, which cannot be proven, he could not have acquired his knowledge about Jewish life merely through a private reading of the Septuagint. Conversion into Judaism was (and still is) as much, if not more, a social and communal phenomenon as it is a religious and individualized experience.

The contemporary projection of Gentileness upon Luke goes one step further: Luke's narration about John the Baptist and Jesus' circumcision would be colored by "pagan" practices.[31] Since no Second Temple Jewish source mentions the custom of naming a Jewish boy at the time of circumcision, though this is the case today among practicing Jews, Luke must have imposed his non-Jewish baggage upon a scenery that in all other respects remains completely focused on conveying to its readers a sense and atmosphere of Jewish piety and practice.[32] All such assertions, however, reveal a lack of halakic imagination and acquaintance with extra-biblical Jewish works relevant for deciphering Luke's sources and redactional project. In the following section, I will try to dismantle this final stronghold, which has firmly guarded Luke's Gentile identity for so long, by arguing that Luke actually possesses an intimate knowledge about halakah that he accurately incorporates into his narrative in order to present the families of John the Baptist and Jesus as pious Jews.

---

[30] Brown, *The Birth of the Messiah*, 449 n. 14.

[31] I do not deny that Greco-Roman culture has shaped Luke's worldview. Nevertheless, it is unlikely to discover an intentional intrusion of non-Jewish practices at a point of Luke's narration where he is set on portraying Jesus and the John the Baptist as Jews *par excellence*.

[32] On Greek and Roman customs of naming the child a few days after birth, see Wiefel, *Das Evangelium nach Lukas*, 61.

Passage

1:59: "On the eighth day they came to circumcise the child [i.e., John the Baptist], and they were going to name him Zechariah after his father."

2:21–24: "After eight days had passed, it was time to circumcise the child; and he was called Jesus, the name given by the angel before he was conceived in the womb. When the time came for their purification according to the law of Moses, they brought him up to Jerusalem to present him to the Lord (as it is written in the law of the Lord, 'Every firstborn male shall be designated as holy to the Lord'), and they offered a sacrifice according to what is stated in the law of the Lord, 'a pair of turtledoves or two young pigeons.'"

Redactional Analysis

Luke probably had access to sources when composing his narrative about the births of John and Jesus.[33] A major challenge involves discerning how of much this section of Luke's gospel is imbued with redactional creativity. It could be that Luke 1:59, which reports the circumcision and naming of John the Baptist on the eighth day, stems from a source. On the other hand, the literary parallelism, easily discernible between the births of John the Baptist and Jesus, suggest redactional activity at several points. Undoubtedly, Luke has at least enhanced the literary symmetry between both reports about the circumcision and naming of John the Baptist and Jesus. Parallels between the birth stories of these two major protagonists abound in Luke's narrative. For example, both Zechariah and Mary receive angelic visitations announcing the future birth and special calling of both John and Jesus. Both births are brought about through divine will and intervention. John's birth, according to Luke, is miraculous: his parents, like Abraham and Sarah, could not have children because of their elderly age. For Luke, like Matthew, Jesus' conception is also out of the ordinary (1:35). Luke even claims that John the Baptist and Jesus are relatives, strengthening thereby the link between both birth episodes. Many of these connections undoubtedly stem from Luke's pen. Luke 2:21–24 contains many Lukan words and phrases, including:

ἐπλήσθησαν (2:21 and 22): "were fulfilled" or elsewhere in Luke "were filled." This verb appears in the plural passive aorist form seven times in Luke (1:23; 2:6; 4:28; 5:26; 6:11) and five times in Acts (2:4; 3:10; 4:31; 5:17; 13:45); only twice in the LXX, there with the meaning of to be "filled" (2 Kgs 4:6 and Ps 37:8); once in Herm. *Vis.* 2.2.2; 1x *Jos. Asen.* 8:8. In conjunction with ἡμέραι, ἐπλήσθησαν appears only in Luke (1:23; 2:6, 21, 22).

ὀκτώ: The reference to eighth days in relation to circumcision is of importance for Luke (1:59; 2:21; Acts 7:8: ὀγδόῃ). Cf. Gen 17:12; 21:4; Lev 12:3; *Jub.* 15:12, 14, 25, 26; 16:14; Philo, *QG* 3:38, 49; 52; Phil 3:5; Josephus, *Ant.* 1:192, 214.

---

[33] For a discussion on Luke's usage of sources in the Infancy Narratives, see especially Brown, *The Birth of the Messiah*, 244–45.

περιτεμεῖν: "To circumcise." Not particularly Lukan, but the topic is of extreme interest for Luke (1:59; 2:21; Acts 15:5; 21:21; cf. Acts 7:8; 11:2; 16:3).

συλλημφθῆναι: "to become pregnant." Luke uses this verb elsewhere to describe the pregnancy of Elizabeth (Luke 1:24, 31, 36). The verb is missing in Matthew's Infancy Narrative. In 2:21, Luke also employs the term κοιλία (so too in 1:15, 41, 42, 44; 2:21; cf. 11:27; 23:29; 3:2; 14:8), which Matthew does not use in his narrative of Jesus' birth (but see Matt 12:40; 15:17; 19:12).

καθαρισμοῦ: "purification." This noun appears a few times in the LXX (Lev 15:13; Num 14:18; cf. 1 Chr 23:28; Neh 12:45; Job 7:21; Prov 14:9; Sir 51:20; Dan 12:6). It appears frequently in 2 Macc (1:18; 1:36; 2:16; 2:19; 10:5; cf. 4 Macc 7:6), often in reference to the purification of the temple. Otherwise, the term is rather rare in early Jewish and Christian literature (Mark: 1x; John: 2x; Heb: 1x; 2 Pet: 1x; *1 Clem.*: 1x; *T. Lev.* 14:6). In Luke, the term appears only twice: once in 2:22; the other in 5:14, which derives from Mark 1:44.

κατὰ τὸν νόμον Μωϋσέως: "according to the Law of Moses." In all of Luke-Acts, this cluster appears only here. However, Luke enjoys employing synonymous constructions using the preposition κατά followed by various nouns that refer in one way or another to Jewish laws and customs: κατὰ τὸν νόμον κυρίου (Luke 2:39); κατὰ τὸ ἔθος τῆς ἱερατείας (Luke 1:9); κατὰ τὸ εἰθισμένον τοῦ νόμου (Luke 2:27); κατὰ τὸ ἔθος τῆς ἑορτῆς (Luke 2:42); κατὰ τὸ εἰωθός (Luke 4:16; Acts 17:2); κατὰ τὴν ἐντολήν (Luke 23:56); κατὰ ἀκρίβειαν τοῦ πατρῴου νόμου (Acts 22:3); κατὰ τὸν νόμον (Acts 22:12; 23:3); κατὰ τὴν ἀκριβεστάτην αἵρεσιν τῆς ἡμετέρας θρησκείας (Acts 26:5). Cf. 2 Kgs 23:25; 2 Chr 35:19; Sus 1:3, 62 (κατὰ τὸν νόμον Μωυσῆ); Tob 6:13; Heb 9:19.

ἀνήγαγον: literally, "they brought/led up." Like other Jews, Luke knows well that, regardless of one's geographical location, one always "goes up" to Jerusalem. The verb is too common though to qualify as redactional. Nevertheless, it appears in this form (third personal plural aorist indicative active voice) three times in Luke-Acts (2:22; Acts 7:41 and 9:39), and is rarely attested in early Jewish and Christian literature (a few times in the LXX; cf. *T. Gad* 8:5; *T. Benj.* 12:3; Josephus, *J.W.* 4:115).

Ἱεροσόλυμα: Surprisingly, Luke uses here the Hellenistic form for naming Jerusalem rather than the Hebraicizing Ἰερουσαλήμ, which he usually prefers (27x in Luke; 37x in Acts versus Ἱεροσόλυμα: only 3x in Luke; 11x in Acts). In 2:25, Luke reverts to the Hebraicizing Ἰερουσαλήμ. Luke is not entirely consistent in his usage of both forms.[34]

ἐν τῷ νόμῳ κυρίου: literally, "in the law of the Lord." As the term appears only in Luke 2:23 and 24, it is hard to determine whether it is traditional or redactional.

Luke 2:21–24 contains many unique literary features, though it is not always possible to distinguish with full confidence between Lukan (i.e., deriving from a special Lukan source or tradition) and redactional layers. With Salo, I tend to view much of Luke 2:21–24 as redactional.[35] Some of the unique literary elements highlighted above, the literary and thematic parallelism between 2:21 and 1:59 (Jesus and John's circumcision and naming), and Luke's deep interest in the temple point toward some type of redactional activity. Indeed the interest in the temple of Jerusalem leads

---

[34] For a rationale accounting for Luke's usage of both forms to describe the same city, see my redactional analysis of Acts 1:12 in chapter 7 of this book.

[35] Salo, *Luke's Treatment of the Law*, 49.

Luke to place the reference to Jesus' circumcision next to the pericope announcing his purification and redemption (2:22–24). Noteworthy is the resemblance between the openings of 2:21 and 2:22:

Καὶ ὅτε ἐπλήσθησαν ἡμέραι ὀκτὼ τοῦ περιτεμεῖν αὐτὸν (2:21a)
Καὶ ὅτε ἐπλήσθησαν αἱ ἡμέραι τοῦ καθαρισμοῦ αὐτῶν (2:22a)

By attaching 2:21 to 2:22–24, Luke enriches the halakic dimension of a pericope, which, as shall be shown, is full of *accurate* references to Mosaic practices such as the purification of the parturient and her infant as well as the redemption of the firstborn.

Naming and Circumcising Jewish Boys

As noted earlier, no passage in any Jewish work prior to Luke refers to the custom of naming a Jewish infant on the eighth day. The first rabbinic attestation to this practice appears only in the late work known as *Pirqe de Rabbi Eliezer* 48.[36] This silence in the ancient Jewish sources, coupled by the mainstream presupposition that Luke is not a Jew but a Gentile, has led many to conjecture that Luke has colored his narrative with Greco-Roman pastels. But were one to assume that Luke was a Jew informed about his Jewish heritage and ancestral customs, his writings would probably be viewed with different lenses as potentially constituting the first Jewish attestation to the custom of naming a Jewish child on the eighth day.[37]

First, it must be acknowledged that foreign custom, Greco-Roman or other, may have led ancient Jews to name their children on the eighth day. If this is the case, Luke would constitute the first written attestation of the Jewish appropriation of this foreign custom. As Jews (un)consciously adopted and adapted this custom from surrounding cultures, they may have searched for biblical "precedents" they thought legitimated its practice. As Cohen and others note, biblical passages such as Gen 17 could have even encouraged associating the naming of the child with the rite of circumcision, since both Abram and Sarai receive their new names, Abraham and Sarah, in the same pericope where God orders Abraham's household and descendants to undergo circumcision.[38] Likewise, the circumcision and

---

[36] "Rabbi Nathaniel said: The parents of Moses saw the child, (for) his form was like that of an angel of God. They circumcised him on the eighth day and they called him Jekuthiel" (translation taken from Gerald Friedlander, *Pirkê de Rabbi Eliezer* [London: Kegan Paul, Trench, Trubner & Co. Ltd., 1916], 378).

[37] Interestingly, Jewish scholars tend to accept Luke's reference to the naming of a child on the eighth day as the earliest attestation to this Jewish practice. So Cohen, *Why Aren't Jewish Women Circumcised,* 34 and Rubin, *The Beginning of Life,* 129–30.

[38] Cohen, *Why Aren't Jewish Women Circumcised,* 34; Léopold Sabourin, S. J., *L'Évangile de Luc: Introduction et commentaire* (Rome: Editrice Pontificia Università Gregoriana, 1985), 78 "Aux temps de Jésus, c'est au moment de la circoncision que

naming of Isaac are placed next to each other in the same chapter of Genesis (21:2–4), providing suggestive material for ancient Jews to correlate the naming of the male infant with his circumcision on the eighth day.[39] Although some ancient cultures named their infants on the day of birth, others did so near the time of birth, while some adults even altered their names later on to commemorate significant events in their lives.[40] Circumcision, which represents an important moment of transition for the male Jewish infant officially entering into the covenant, would have proven a most appropriate time for publicly announcing the name of child. Such factors might have led ancient Jews to combine the official announcement of the child's name with eighth-day circumcision.

Some have tried to downplay Luke's twofold repetition of John the Baptist and Jesus' circumcision by subordinating it to the allegedly more important act of their *naming*. In other words, Luke is set on signaling the fact that both John and Jesus received their appointed names at the time of their births as foretold by the angel Gabriel (1:13, 31). Circumcision only provides a decorative element to a scene focused on announcing this prophetic fulfillment.[41] Who though would claim that Isaac's circumcision, which also appears right next to his naming (Gen 21:3,4), is an incidental detail subordinate to Abraham and Sarah's naming their son in accordance with divine forecast (Gen 17:19; cf. Gen 18:12–15)? Undoubtedly, Luke wishes to show that Gabriel's oracles materialized once John the Baptist and Jesus officially received their respective names. But Luke also goes out of his way to frame this event with the equally important Jewish rite of eighth-day circumcision. The gospel writer could have simply stated: "And

---

l'enfant mâle recevait son nom. On pouvait appuyer cette coutume sur le fait que Dieu avait changé les noms d'Abram et de Sarai en relation avec la déclaration sur la loi de la circoncision (Gn 17,5.15).''

[39] Of course, this is not the "plain" sense of Gen 21:2–4, which reads more naturally as consisting of two consecutive steps: the naming of Isaac at the time of birth (21:3), followed by his circumcision on the eighth day. Nevertheless, ancient Jews could have understood these texts in a way that does not correspond to modern "scientific" readings.

[40] Rubin, *The Beginning of Life,* 110.

[41] So already Frédéric Louis Godet, *Commentaire sur l'évangile de saint Luc* (2 vols.; Neuchâtel: Librairie générale de Jules Sandoz; 1871), 1:184: "Le poids du récit porte-t-il non sur la circoncision qui, à proprement parler, n'est pas même mentionnée, mais sur le nom donné à l'enfant à cette occasion. . . ."; L. Legrand, "On l'appela du nom de Jésus," *RB* 89 (1982): 483; Gerhard Schneider, *Das Evangelium nach Lukas* (2 vols; ÖKT; Gütersloh: Mohn, 1984), 1:60: "Der Zug der Erzählung hebt aber plastisch die Besonderheit der gottverfügten Namengebung hervor"; Wiefel, *Das Evangelium nach Lukas*, 77; Wilson, *Luke and the Law,* 21: "They are incidental details, predictable within the thoroughly Jewish context of the narratives...." More recently, Andrews S. Jacobs, *Christ Circumcised: A Study in Early Christian History and Difference* (Divinations: Rereading Late Ancient Religion; Philadelphia: University of Pennsylvania, 2012), 29.

it came to pass that when the child was born, they named him John /Jesus." To mention circumcision twice in a narrative that emphasizes in so many other respects the Jewish piety of some of the foundational figures of the Jesus movement certainly bears some significance, especially since Luke returns to the topic of circumcision several times in the book of Acts.[42]

The Importance of Eighth-Day Circumcision

The eighth-day circumcision of John the Baptist and Jesus enables them to pass the highest and strictest standards of assessing Jewishness in antiquity. Even the most stringent of ancient Jews would recognize their Jewishness since they were circumcised on the eighth day and were genealogically pure. As noted in the introduction to this chapter, certain Jews denied the possibility for Gentiles to become Jews because they were not of a pure Jewish stock. But Luke's John and Jesus enjoy a remarkable Jewish pedigree. John the Baptist stems from a distinguished priestly lineage, while both of Jesus' human parents are Jewish.[43] Mary, in Luke's eyes, can possibly even boast of Levitic ancestry, given her alleged kinship with Elizabeth (1:5, 36). Joseph, for his part, belongs to the royal and Davidic clan of the tribe of Judah (1:26, 32; 2:4).

For Luke, the circumcision of John the Baptist and Jesus might even serve as a model for all Jewish followers of Jesus of his time to emulate and embrace.[44] The polemical charges embedded in Acts 21:21, which were circulating in Luke's day, should not be overlooked for appreciating the significance of Luke's twofold reference to John and Jesus' circumcision. Far from teaching "all the Jews living among the Gentiles to forsake Moses, and…not to circumcise their children or observe the customs" (Acts 21:21), Luke contends throughout his writings that the Jewish con-

---

[42] Others wonder why during John the Baptist's birth Luke refers to the custom of naming the child after the father's name. There are, however, several references to such a practice, including *t. Nid.* 5:15; *y. Naz.* 4:6 53c (R. Haninah b. Haninah), Matt 16:17; 1 Esd 5:38; Neh 7:63; *Jub.* 11:14 (Greek fragment); Josephus, *Life* 4; *Ant.* 14:10; *J.W.* 5:534. *Ant.* 20:197 and *J.W.* 4:160 refer to a priestly family naming the son after the father (Ananus). Cf. Papyri Yadin 5, 12–17, and 27 (Yeshua b. Yeshua and Yosef b. Yosef) from the Babatha archive; P. Yadin 45 (Elazar b. Elazar b. Hitta) from the Bar Kokhba period, all cited and surveyed in Hanan Eshel, "A Survey of the Refuge Caves and Their Legal Documents," in *Halakhah in Light of Epigraphy*, 121–29. Rubin, *The Beginning of Life,* 111–13, concludes that it was customary in pre-exilic times to give a child a new name, but beginning in the Second Temple period Jews would often name a child after an ancestor, either after the parent or grandparent.

[43] Luke traces Jesus' genealogy through his human father, Joseph, back to God (Luke 3:23–38).

[44] See especially Jacob Jervell, *The Unknown Paul: Essays on Luke-Acts and Early Christian History* (Minneapolis: Augsburg, 1984), 138–45.

stituency of the *ekklesia* should continue to uphold the rite of circumcision. Read against this backdrop, the two pairs of parents, Zechariah-Elizabeth and Joseph-Mary, who faithfully circumcise their sons, could even serve as exemplary role models for Jewish followers of Jesus to imitate. Circumcising not only circumscribes John the Baptist and Jesus within the sphere of Torah practice and covenantal duties, but also serves as a model for the Jewish branch of the Jesus movement in Luke's day to follow: Jewish believers are not to leave their children uncircumcised, contrary to the ongoing rumors about Paul encouraging Jews to abandon Judaism, but must uphold this ancient tradition in the same way that the parents of John the Baptist and Jesus did.[45]

The Purification of the Parturient and Her Child

After mentioning the naming and circumcision of Jesus, Luke states that "when the time came for *their* purification according to the law of Moses," Joseph and Mary brought Jesus to Jerusalem "to present him to the Lord" (2:22). Leviticus 12 states that a mother remains impure for forty days after giving birth to a boy (eighty days if she has a girl). During the first seven days after giving birth to a boy (or fourteen days for a girl), the mother's impurity is reckoned "as the days of the menstruation of her

---

[45] Remarkably, in a context divorced from the process of *Auseinandersetzung* that dominated Jewish-Christian relations in the Greco-Roman world, the Ethiopian Orthodox Christian church till this very day practices eighth day circumcision, apparently in imitation of Christ's circumcision. This obviously does not prove my point about Luke's historical situation. Neither do I claim that circumcision among Ethiopian Orthodox Christians originated from an independent and exclusive reading of Luke. Indeed, Herodotus already refers to the practice of circumcision among Ethiopians (*Histories* 2:104), and the Ethiopian Christians probably drew from other biblical passages to justify their custom, including the story in Genesis 17 on the circumcision of Abraham and his household. Ethiopian Christian circumcision only serves as a hermeneutic device to illustrate how some Christians from a later time and different region understood Luke's writings along similar (but not identical) lines to the ones I suggest for appreciating Luke's appreciation of circumcision. However, unlike the Ethiopian Christian interpretation that applies Christ's circumcision to *all* Christians, Luke only intended that followers of Jesus of *Jewish* ethnicity undergo this rite, not *Gentile* followers of Jesus – a bilateral ecclesiological and ethnic differentiation I suppose (though am not certain) would not prove meaningful in the Ethiopian Orthodox tradition. On circumcision and other "Judaic" practices in the Ethiopian Christian tradition, see Edward Ullendorff, "Hebraic-Jewish Elements in Abyssinian (Monophysite) Christianity," *JSS* 1 (1956): 216–56; Maxine Rodinson, "Sur la question des 'influences juives' en Éthiopie," *JSS* 9 (1964): 11–19; Kirsten Stoffregen Pedersen, "Is the Church of Ethiopia a Judaic Church?" *Warszawskie Studia Teologiczne* 12 (1999): 203–16. On the reception and interpretation of Luke's circumcised Christ among Late Antique Christians, see Jacobs, *Christ Circumcised*.

sickness" (כימי נדת דותה).⁴⁶ The book of Leviticus likens these first seven days of impurity after childbirth with the period of impurity acquired during menstruation. Pursuing this analogy, one could infer that once the first seven days after childbirth had been completed, the parturient would have to immerse herself in water in order to remove this form of impurity. She would remain, however, in a state of reduced impurity for the remaining thirty-three days (or sixty-six days in the case of an infant girl) vis-à-vis the sacred realm and all things holy. In other words, the parturient would not be able to access the sanctuary or touch a holy object, but could perhaps interact more freely with the common realm and participate in other routines of daily life (Lev 12:4).⁴⁷ After the forty (or eighty) days were over, the parturient would then bring to the sanctuary a lamb as a burnt offering and a pigeon or turtledove as a sin offering (Lev 12:6). If she could not afford such offerings, she could bring two pigeons or turtledoves (Lev 12:8).

As many have pointed out, the main problem in Luke's description of the visit of Jesus' family to the temple concerns his reference to the process of *their* purification (2:22: καθαρισμοῦ αὐτῶν). The LXX to Leviticus 12:4 (cf. 12:2b) only explicitly speaks of the days of the *mother's* purification (καθάρσεως αὐτῆς), while never referring to the potential impurity the infant could acquire during or after the infant's birth.⁴⁸ Does the usage of the pronoun in the plural possessive form confirm the position that Luke is ignorant about Judaism? Recently, Thiessen has made a compelling argument that challenges such notions.⁴⁹ His mains points are worth briefly summarizing in order to strengthen the thesis advocated throughout this chapter.

Thiessen first shows how the silence of the text of Lev 12 does not preclude viewing the infant as also susceptible to acquiring the parturient's impurity. Scholars such as Milgrom have pointed out that the text of Leviticus is by no means exhaustive and does not outline its legislation in the fullest detail. Often the laws in Leviticus appear in terse and elliptical form, requiring further elucidation through analogy, inference, and ac-

---

⁴⁶ See Milgrom, *Leviticus*, 1:749, for the elucidation of this phrase.

⁴⁷ Although Leviticus 12 does not explicitly refer to immersion after the first seven days, Milgrom, *Leviticus,* 1:746, argues that this ritual is certainly implied.

⁴⁸ Without the vocalization, the Masoretic Text of Lev 12:4 proves more ambiguous: both דמי טהרה and ימי טהרה could be read without the *mappiq* on the final *he* to mean "blood of purification" and "days of purification," respectively, rather than the blood and days of *her* purification. The Masoretes add a *mappiq* to the second nominal construction to clarify that the text is speaking of "days of her purification."

⁴⁹ Matthew Thiessen, "Luke 2:22, Leviticus 12, and Parturient Impurity," *NovT* 54 (2012): 16–29. I thank Thiessen for sharing this article with me before its publication.

quaintance with the Levitical system as a whole.[50] As noted earlier, Lev 12 does not even refer to the ablution of the parturient after the first seven (or fourteen) days, although this ritual is certainly implied based on what is known about the rest of the purity system in Leviticus. It is certainly possible, then, that the laws concerning the impurity of the parturient also applied to the infant even if this point is not mentioned in Leviticus.

Thiessen also appeals to cross-cultural studies in order to strengthen his case. In other ancient cultures, including Egyptian, Hittite, and Greek, both the mother and the newborn were considered impure. Hittite law even distinguishes between the length of impurity depending on whether the child is male (three months) or female (four months).[51] Might not Israelite practice have resembled in this instance the customs of the surrounding nations, especially since Lev 12 also bases itself on the gender of the new born in order to determine the length of the parturient's impurity, suggesting that this form of impurity is in some way linked to the child?[52]

One should note that at least one (Dosithean) Samaritan voice applies Lev 12 to both the parturient and the child in the same way. It is impossible to determine with any precision the antiquity of Samaritan practice, though it is certainly possible that many of its rituals stem from the Second Temple period. At the very least, the Dosithean opinion illustrates how Lev 12 can invite a reading that incorporates the infant and the mother under the same degree of impurity. There is no need to blame certain Samaritans, as has been the case with Luke, for misunderstanding Mosaic legislation.[53] Indeed, more than silence in the sources could lead a Jewish

---

[50] Thiessen, "Luke 2:22," 16–29, citing Mary Douglas, *Leviticus as Literature* (Oxford: Oxford University Press, 1999), 39; Milgrom, *Leviticus,* 1:976–1000; Erhard S. Gerstenberger, *Leviticus: A Commentary* (OTL; Louisville, Ky.: WJK, 1993), 147.

[51] See further, Aylward M. Black, "Purification: Egypt," *ERE* 10:476–482; Milgrom, *Leviticus,* 1:763–65; David P. Wright, *The Disposal of Impurity: Elimination Rites in the Bible and Hittite and Mesopotamian Literature* (SBLDS 101; Atlanta: Scholars, 1987).

[52] Cf. Milgrom, *Leviticus,* 1:746, who wonders: "In other cultures, the new born child is also impure, for instance, among the Hittites. What of the Israelite child? Is he (or she) rendered impure by contact with the mother? The text is silent. Nor is there even a hint from the laws of *niddâ*, or must we assume that the child's impurity is taken for granted, that the child is isolated with the mother during the seven (or fourteen) days, and that at the termination of this period it undergoes immersion with her? There is no clear answer." However, Milgrom departs from his uncertainty and later confidently states that "Leviticus leaves no room for doubt that only one person needs be purified: the new mother" (1:762; cf. 1:746, 1750).

[53] See Iain Ruairidh Mac Mhanainn Bóid, *Principles of Samaritan Halachah* (SJLA 38; Leiden: Brill, 1989), 258, 327. Ethiopian Jews have their infants immersed on the fortieth or eightieth day, depending on the gender, but this may be due to other reasons besides purity concerns. See Aaron Zeev Aescoly, *Sefer ha-Falashim: Yehude Habash, Tarbutam u-Mesorotehem* (Jerusalem: Reuben Mass, 1943), 41–44.

or Samaritan reader of the Second Temple period to interpret Lev 12 as referring to the impurity of the mother as well as the infant. If the impurity of a parturient is comparable to the impurity of a menstruant, then it is reasonable to infer that both types of impurity are imparted in similar ways. Since a husband who lies with her wife during her menstruation is defiled for seven days (Lev 15:24), a Second Temple Jew could reasonably conclude through analogy and inference that an infant could acquire impurity from her mother through contact with the blood emitted during childbirth.[54] In fact, Thiessen and others before him have argued that *Jubilees* as well as 4Q265 and 4Q266 extend the impurity of the parturient to the infant.[55] *Jubilees* 3:8–13 refers to a curious story concerning the entry of Adam and Eve into the Garden of Eden. Adam has to wait until forty days are over before entering the Garden of Eden. Likewise, Eve waits until eighty days before making her entry. Elsewhere in *Jubilees*, the Garden of Eden is likened to the temple (*Jub.* 8:19). The connections with the legislation of Lev 12 are obvious, and, as Thiessen suggests, the author of *Jubilees* probably viewed newborn children as impure, having to wait forty or eighty days before entering the sacred realm, as Adam and Eve, "newborn" creatures, as it were, wait until the time of their impurity is fulfilled before entering the sanctuary of Eden.[56]

In his reconstruction and reading of 4Q265, Baumgarten concludes that this fragment, like *Jubilees,* links the legislation of the parturient in Lev 12 with the entry of Adam and Eve into Eden, viewing the primordial garden as a holy place that functions as a paradigm for the "acceptance of newly born infants of both sexes into the sacred sphere."[57] Most interesting is 4Q266 6 ii 10–11, which prohibits a mother from nursing her newborn child and requires instead the service of a wet nurse. Thiessen maintains that unlike *Jubilees* and 4Q265, this text denies that a newborn acquires impurity at the moment of childbirth but assumes that an infant can subse-

---

[54] Indeed, this is how Samaritan halakah understands the matter. See, for example, *Kitâb Al-Kâfi* ch. XIII (Bóid, *Principles of Samaritan Halachah*, 153–54) and its discussion to what extent a male infant who has not been cleansed before circumcision renders a Samaritan "*mohel*" impure.

[55] Joseph M. Baumgarten, "Purification after Childbirth and the Sacred Garden in 4Q265 and Jubilees," in *New Qumran Texts and Studies*, 3–10; Hannah K. Harrington, *The Purity Texts* (Companion to the Qumran Scrolls 5; London: T&T Clark, 2004), 62, 100; William R. G. Loader, *The Dead Sea Scrolls on Sexuality* (Grand Rapids, Mich.: Eerdmans, 2009), 229 n. 126.

[56] Thiessen, "Luke 2:22," 16–29.

[57] Baumgarten, "Purification after Childbirth," 5. Admittedly, this is a possible, though not necessary, extension of *Jubilees* as well as 4Q265. The authors of these ancient Jewish texts may simply be tying Lev 12 to primeval times in order to highlight the importance for Jewish *mothers* to respect the laws of impurity related to childbirth.

quently become impure through contact with the mother during her days of impurity.⁵⁸ Basing herself on this Qumranic evidence, Himmelfarb concludes that "P must have shared the view that the parturient conveyed impurity to those who touched her during the first stages of impurity. Surely it would not have escaped P's notice that the newborn baby could not avoid such contact."⁵⁹ She explains the silence of the issue in Leviticus 12 in the following way: "The consequences of impurity as specified in Leviticus 12 are hardly relevant to a newborn, who is most unlikely to have the opportunity to enter the sanctuary or touch holy things and who is certainly incapable of eating sacrificial meat and other kinds of consecrated food."⁶⁰

Since Luke is set on presenting Jesus in the temple, he cannot do so before the days of impurity of *both* the mother and the infant are over. Otherwise, Luke would run the risk of implying that Jesus and his family defiled the temple of Jerusalem by entering therein before the days of purification had been completed.⁶¹ Thankfully, Luke was sufficiently familiar with all of these halakic intricacies to save himself from such embarrassment.

The Presentation and Redemption of the Firstborn

Having dismissed claims concerning Luke's ignorance of the laws of impurity of the parturient, there remains the issue of the redemption of Jesus

---

⁵⁸ Thiessen, "Luke 2:22," 11–12. This is one possible reading of this fragmentary text. Alternatively, 4Q266 views the infant as impure upon birth, but requires that the (male) infant be removed immediately so as to be washed on the same day and be purified in time for circumcision on the eighth day. Samaritan halakah posit that a parturient's blood during the first seven days (i.e., during and immediately after the birth of a male infant) can impart impurity for seven days to the infant or other persons (e.g., midwife) that come into its contact. Thus 4Q266 might be advocating the immediate removal of the infant boy so he can be cleansed in time for circumcision on the eighth day, the first day after the end of the seven day cycle of first degree impurity. See Bóid, *Principles of Samaritan Halachah*, 153–54; 242.

⁵⁹ Martha Himmelfarb, "Impurity and Sin in 4QD, 1QS, and 4Q512," *DSD* 8 (2001): 26.

⁶⁰ Himmelfarb, "Impurity and Sin," 26.

⁶¹ The reference to "their purification" in Luke 2:22 could refer to the impurity of the mother and the father (rather than the infant), since "their purification" is followed by ἀνήγαγον αὐτὸν ("they [i.e., Mary and Joseph] brought him up"), which might suggest that both parents were impure. However, as Salo, *Luke's Treatment of the Law*, 52–53 and Sabourin, *L'Évangile de Luc*, 99 note, "their purification" lies closer to the previous verse describing *Jesus'* birth and circumcision, allowing, therefore, for a reading that interprets καθαρισμοῦ αὐτῶν as referring to Mary and Jesus. Is Joseph's impurity (to a lesser degree) implied as well since he could have entered into contact with Mary and Jesus during their journey to the temple?

as firstborn son (פדיון הבן). Once again, many have disproportionately blamed Luke for his supposed ignorance about the legislation concerning the redemption of the firstborn, claiming that it was unnecessary in the Second Temple period for Jews to bring their firstborn sons to the temple for redemption. These same commentators also criticize Luke for failing to mention the payment of the five shekels necessary for finalizing this rite. In fact, some go as far as claiming that Luke has confused the regulations concerning the purification of the parturient with the rite of redeeming the firstborn:

> The Lucan combination of the two customs has often been thought to reflect popular practice in the Judaism of NT times, i.e., for the sake of convenience, the observance of two different religious duties at the same time. But that explanation does not cover the inaccuracies in the Lucan description of the combined customs. Luke seems to think that both parents needed to be purified, since in 22 he modifies Lev 12:6 to read "when the time came for *their* purification." He seems to think that the reason for going to the Temple was the consecration or presentation of Jesus (vs. 27), when only the law concerning the purification of the mother mentions the custom of going to the sanctuary. (And it is dubious that a journey to the Temple was still practiced to any great extent in the Judaism of NT times.) He mentions nothing of the price (five shekels) required for redeeming the firstborn child from the service of the Lord; rather he connects with that event the sacrifice of the two doves or pigeons which was really related to the purification of the mother.[62]

We already noted that Luke understands perfectly well the regulations related to the purification of the parturient and her infant. Furthermore, it is not so dubious, as Brown asserts, that many Jews would travel to the temple, even in the first century CE, to perform such rituals as the redemption of the firstborn. Alon has amassed a number of primary texts from the Second Temple period demonstrating that certain Jews continued to bring their first fruits, tithes, and other offerings – money for the redemption of the firstborn included – directly to the temple rather than presenting them to a local priest.[63] Surveying some of this evidence can assist in understanding Luke's reason for mentioning and locating the execution of this rite in the temple of Jerusalem.

According to the Mosaic Torah, every firstborn Israelite male was to be dedicated to the God of Israel (Exod 13:12). The rationale provided in the Torah for this practice draws directly from the Exodus story:

> When in the future your child asks you, "What does this mean?" you shall answer, "By strength of hand the LORD brought us out of Egypt, from the house of slavery. When

---

[62] Brown, *Birth of the Messiah*, 447.

[63] Gedalyahu Alon, *Jews, Judaism and the Classical World: Studies in Jewish History in the Times of the Second Temple and Talmud* (trans. Israel Abrahams; Jerusalem: Magnes, 1977), 91–93. See also Rubin, *The Beginning of Life,* 125–30, who concurs with Alon.

Pharaoh stubbornly refused to let us go, the LORD killed all the firstborn in the land of Egypt, from human firstborn to the firstborn of animals. Therefore I sacrifice to the LORD every male that first opens the womb, but every firstborn of my sons I redeem" (Exod 13:14–15).

In earlier history all firstborn Israelite sons were dedicated to serve the God of Israel, but eventually the Levites assumed this priestly task (Num 3:11–13). Henceforth, non-Levite firstborn sons would be exempted or redeemed from their priestly duties through the payment of five shekels (Num 18:15–16). Exodus 34:20 could imply that one of the parents had to redeem the firstborn son *in person at the sanctuary where the God of Israel resided*: "All the firstborn of your sons you shall redeem. No one shall appear before me (פני) empty-handed" (Exod 34:20).[64] This verse presupposes that one of the parents (with the child?) had to be present at the sanctuary, the Hebrew noun פני indicating that the rite was to take place in the sanctum where the God of Israel resided.

Such a procedure was possible as long as the Israelites and, later on, the Judeans resided near the sanctuary and could bring their first fruits, tithes, and other offerings in person or at least have them sent to Jerusalem (cf. Neh 12:44 and 2 Chr 31:5–6). Nehemiah 10:36 implies that Judeans living in the vicinity of Jerusalem would bring their firstborn sons to the temple for the purpose of redemption: "…also to bring to the house of our God, to the priests who minister in the house of our God, the firstborn of our sons and of our livestock, as it is written in the law, and the firstlings of our herds and of our flocks." There is evidence that the practice of bringing tithes, first fruits, and other gifts to Jerusalem persisted among certain Jews throughout the Second Temple period. Thus, in 1 Macc 3:46–50, the Judeans who regather at Mizpah wonder whither they shall bring their first fruits and tithes after losing control over the temple of Jerusalem (cf. Jdt 5:13). Interestingly, LXX 1 Sam 1:21 states that, in addition to offering his yearly sacrifice and paying his vow, Elkanah, the father of Samuel, also brought the tithes of his land to the sanctuary rather than giving them to a local Levite or priest (cf. Josephus, *Ant.* 5:346).

Philo provides the most important reference to the ongoing practice of bringing money for the firstborn directly to the temple, since he not only lived during the first century CE, but also resided in Egypt – far away from the temple. After discussing the laws about the first fruits and the firstborn (*Spec.* 1:131–151), Philo claims that the Torah commands lay people to bring their first fruits (τὰς ἀπαρχὰς) *to the temple* (εἰς τὸ ἱερὸν) so that the priests can take these gifts privately at their own discretion, thereby avoiding public reproach and embarrassment:

---

[64] See Rubin, *The Beginning of Life*, 125, 128, for a discussion about the responsibility of the father, rather than the mother, for redeeming the firstborn.

For it was suitable to the nature of God, that those who had received kindness in all the circumstances of life, should bring (ἀνάγειν) the first fruits as a thank-offering, and then that he, as a being who was in want of nothing, should with all dignity and honor bestow them on the servants and ministers who attend on the service of the temple; for to appear to receive these things not from men, but from the great Benefactor of all men, appears to be receiving a gift which has in it no alloy of sadness (*Spec.* 1:152).[65]

As Alon and Rubin note, Philo assumes in this passage that Jews could bring their own tithes and offerings – including the money for redeeming the firstborn – directly to the temple.[66] One early rabbinic passage seems to confirm this impression when it refers to Jews from the Diaspora who tried to bring offerings to the temple only to have them rejected:

> Nittai of Tekoa brought Dough-offerings from Be-ittur and they would not accept them. The men of Alexandria brought their Dough-offerings from Alexandria and they would not accept them....Ben Antigonus brought up Firstlings from Babylon and they would not accept them....Ariston brought his First-fruits from Apamia and they accepted them from him, for they said: He that owns [land] in Syria is as one that owns [land] in the outskirts of Jerusalem (*m. Hal.* 4:10–11).

Commenting on this passage from the Mishnah, Alon states: "Although they did not accept the dough-offerings from them in these instances, yet there can be no doubt that it was the ancient custom to bring the dough-offering from outside Eretz-Israel to Jerusalem, only the later Halakha enacted not to accept the dough-offering nor the heave-offerings and tithes that came from outside Eretz-Israel."[67]

Because of the long distances involved in traveling all the way to the temple of Jerusalem, it became customary to offer money for the redemption of the firstborn son to a local priest. Nevertheless, it would have still been considered an *ideal* practice to bring an offering or other gift directly to the temple. Any effort to perform a pilgrimage to Jerusalem in order to make a personal offering or fulfill a vow would have certainly been viewed as a commendable and pious act by many Jews. The evidence surveyed by Alon, who also takes Luke's reference seriously into account, leads him to conclude on this matter with the following words:

> ...during the greater part of the Second Temple era, the people were accustomed to bring the heave-offering and tithes to the Temple store-house, where they were distributed to the priests (and Levites) *pro rata*. And even at the end of the Temple period, when the Halakha permitted the gifts to be given to a priest or Levite anywhere and without the

---

[65] Cf. *m. Sheqal.* 5:6 with its reference to a "chamber of secrets" in the temple filled with gifts for the needy who could help themselves privately without having to confront the donors.

[66] Alon, *Jews, Judaism and the Classical World,* 102; Rubin, *The Beginning of Life,* 129–30.

[67] Alon, *Jews, Judaism and the Classical World,* 93–94.

supervision of the central authority at Jerusalem, it was still apparently deemed the ideal way of fulfilling the commandment to bring the gifts up (if possible) to the Temple.[68]

The Lukan pericope, then, seeks to present Jesus' family as ideal Jews who not only carefully follow the Levitical purity laws but also go up to Jerusalem in person in order to present their child in the temple. In this way, Luke shows that Jesus' parents surpass the halakic expectations of their time.[69]

Rubin suggests that Jews who went up to Jerusalem during the Second Temple period might have taken advantage of this unique opportunity to perform several commandments at the same time in the temple.[70] This proposal would account for Luke's combination of the fulfillment of two commandments, namely, the purification after childbirth and the redemption of the firstborn. It is clear that Luke's main goal in this pericope is to have the infant Jesus brought to the temple, a site of extreme importance throughout Luke-Acts. Nevertheless, Jesus' presentation could not occur before the forty days of purification of the parturient and her newborn were completed. Luke takes advantage of this halakic opportunity to highlight the Torah observance of Jesus' family by indicating that they waited until the days of purification were over before redeeming their firstborn son at the temple. Numbers 18:16 declares that a firstborn male could be redeemed "*from* one month of age" (מבן־חדש). Rabbinic exegesis interpreted this phrase to mean that a firstborn could not be redeemed before the age of thirty days.[71] Thirty-one days, of course, is too early a date to bring the infant Jesus into the temple since he would still be impure. The first opportunity to present Jesus in the temple would occur after the completion of the forty days of impurity. Some rabbinic passages claim that a firstborn can be redeemed after the thirty-first day.[72] Indeed, the wording of Num 18:16 allows one to infer that the redemption can take place anytime from the age of thirty days onward. Based on the limited evidence at

---

[68] Alon, *Jews, Judaism and the Classical World*, 91. So also, Rubin, *The Beginning of Life*, 129–30.

[69] Luke's precise knowledge of Jewish practice does not prove the historicity of the events he relates. This is another matter altogether and is not the concern of this inquiry.

[70] Rubin, *The Beginning of Life*, 125.

[71] *Sifre Num* 118; cf. *b. Bek.* 10b; 12b: an infant cannot be redeemed before the age of thirty days. According to *t. Shabb.* 15:7, an infant younger than thirty days was not considered a person (because of the high mortality rates of that time).

[72] *M. Bek.* 8:6; *b. Bek.* 51b: a father must redeem a son who died after thirty days if he had not yet done so. See also *t. Bek.* 6:10, which allows for the postponement of the redemption in certain circumstances (cf. *b. Qidd.* 29b). According to *b. Bek.* 12b, if the father did not redeem his firstborn at the right time, he may do so "forever" (עד עולם). See Rubin, *The Beginning of Life*, 128–29.

our disposal, Luke's description and timing of the performance of the redemption of the firstborn make good sense halakically.

The only minor problem awaiting resolution involves the absence of any reference in Luke 2:22–24 to the *payment* of the five shekels for the redemption of Jesus. However, the payment for the redemption may be implied in Luke 2:27: "the parents brought in the child Jesus, *to do for him* what was customary under the law." More importantly, Luke does not mention this financial transaction because he wants to emphasize the *presentation and dedication* of Jesus in the temple to his special calling (2:22: παραστῆσαι τῷ κυρίῳ). Luke wishes to portray Jesus as a unique and gifted child (2:47) dedicated and set apart for an important mission, not as any firstborn Jew exempted from fulfilling his priestly service to the God of Israel. In a certain sense, Luke implies that Jesus never really was redeemed from his obligation of carrying out his mission on behalf of Israel (and the nations). This becomes clear later on when Luke presents Jesus once again in the temple, this time at the age of twelve, "sitting among the teachers, listening to them and asking them questions" (2:46). Jesus' bewildered parents, who search endlessly for their lost child, fail to comprehend his retort when they finally find him in the temple: "Why were you searching for me? Did you not know that I must be in my Father's house (ἐν τοῖς τοῦ πατρός μου)?" (2:49) The Greek phrase ἐν τοῖς τοῦ πατρός μου is ambiguous and could alternatively be rendered as "about my Father's work." Regardless, the sentence proclaimed by Luke's adolescent Jesus still implies a dedication to a particular mission that will bring him into the realm of the temple in Jerusalem throughout the Lukan narrative.

The parallels between Luke's presentation of Jesus and the story of Samuel's birth and childhood are also noteworthy, even if they do not always perfectly align with each other.[73] Hannah, the future mother of Samuel, vows to dedicate her child to serve in the sanctuary, should her barrenness be removed. Her miraculous impregnation recalls the Lukan episode relating the birth of John the Baptist whose parents were also unable to have children. Her personal journey also mirrors Mary's story: both find favor from above; both offer hymns of praise thanking God for intervening on their behalf; both give birth to child prodigies. However, unlike Joseph and Mary, Hannah does not immediately bring her newborn to the sanctuary, but waits until he is weaned (1 Sam 1:22). Only when Samuel becomes a lad (נער) does she bring him to the sanctuary to serve God. But like Samuel, Luke's Jesus also finds himself at young age in the temple fulfilling his mission. And like Samuel's distinguished career, Luke's Jesus' ministry also bears a prophetic stamp though not a priestly

---

[73] For a list of the many parallels, see Brown, *Birth of the Messiah*, 450–51.

one.⁷⁴ Quite interestingly, Josephus claims that Samuel started his prophetic career at the age of twelve, the same age when the adolescent Jesus in Luke finds himself in the temple announcing the debut of his service to his heavenly Father (*Ant.* 5:348).

Did Luke Believe in Genealogical Impurity? Circumcision in Acts 7:8

Thiessen's thesis regarding Luke's perception of Gentiles as genealogically impure has already been noted in this work.⁷⁵ His argument is intertwined with the practice of eighth-day circumcision: Luke believes Gentile adult males cannot become Jews because they were not circumcised as infants on the eighth day and because of their non-Jewish origins. Thiessen leans on the references to the eighth-day circumcision of John the Baptist and Jesus in Luke chs. 1–2 to make his argument. He also underscores another reference to eighth-day circumcision that appears in Stephen's speech in Acts 7. In a terse retelling of Israel's history, Luke's Stephen speaks of the "covenant of the circumcision" (διαθήκην περιτομῆς), how "Abraham became the father of Isaac and circumcised *him on the eighth day*" (Acts 7:8: τῇ ἡμέρᾳ τῇ ὀγδόῃ). It is remarkable to see Luke mention this chronological detail in a speech that recounts in only a few verses several hundred years of Israelite history. All the more so, since, as is widely acknowledged, the speeches within Acts stem largely from the literary creativity of Luke, conveying his impression about the significance of the narrated events.⁷⁶

For Thiessen, the reference to eighth-day circumcision in Stephen's speech appears in Acts because of Luke's belief in the proper timing of the rite and its connection with genealogical purity.⁷⁷ Luke focuses on *Isaac*, the patriarch who received the covenant of circumcision on the *eighth* day (καὶ ἔδωκεν αὐτῷ διαθήκην περιτομῆς), rather than Abraham, who was circumcised at an elderly age. Luke prefers to mention Isaac's circumcision because he believes Jews should be circumcised on the eighth day, whereas highlighting Abraham's circumcision could potentially lead to the

---

⁷⁴ Luke claims that Mary was a cousin of Elizabeth who belongs to a priestly clan. However, Luke does not exploit this motif. Instead, he underscores Joseph's Judahite and Davidic origins.

⁷⁵ See chapter 10 dealing with the Cornelius episode.

⁷⁶ Stephen's speech, however, may be one of the exceptions, with some scholars positing a source behind its formulation. Nevertheless, Pervo, *Acts,* 178, remarks: "If he has not completely assimilated his source, Luke has shaped it to meet his goals."

⁷⁷ Thiessen, *Contesting Circumcision,* 117.

misunderstanding that (male) Gentile followers of Jesus should undergo full conversion into Judaism through circumcision.[78] The fact that the prepositional phrase in Acts 7:8, "on the eighth day" (τῇ ἡμέρᾳ τῇ ὀγδόῃ), quite possibly derives from the LXX of Gen 17:14 and Lev 12:3, rather than Gen 21:4, would strengthen Thiessen's argument that Luke is not simply retelling Isaac's story but highlighting the importance of performing the most central of rituals for Jewish male infants at its proper time.[79]

Thiessen has certainly come up with an original and intriguing thesis on the question of circumcision in Luke-Acts. Nevertheless, his proposal raises several important issues that require further consideration. First, some might feel uncomfortable with the implication that Luke would hold a similar conception of Gentile impurity as the extremely anti-Gentile author of *Jubilees*.[80] Further exploration is also of order for understanding the question of genealogical (im)purity in the Greek speaking Diaspora in which Luke most likely resided and composed his works. Even the LXX of Gen 17:14, unlike the Masoretic Text, emphasizes that circumcision should be performed on the eighth day. But does this mean that Greek speaking Jews of the Diaspora, who used the Septuagint as their primary text, de-

---

[78] Ibid. Cf. *Song of Songs Rab.* 1.2.5: "Abraham received the command of circumcision. Isaac inaugurated its performance on the eighth day" (cf. *Pesiq. Rab Kah.* 12:1; *Midr. Proverbs* 31). See also Philo, *QG* 3:38.

[79] In addition, Thiessen proposes supplying the verb περιτέμνω to the rest of Acts 7:8, rather than γεννάω as most English translations do: "Then he gave him the covenant of circumcision. And so Abraham begot (ἐγέννησεν) Isaac and circumcised (περιέτεμεν) him on the eighth day; and Isaac [circumcised] Jacob [on the eighth day], and Jacob [circumcised] the twelve patriarchs [on the eighth day]." The Greek text does not contain any verbs attached to the subjects Isaac and Jacob, reading simply καὶ Ἰσαὰκ τὸν Ἰακώβ, καὶ Ἰακὼβ τοὺς δώδεκα πατριάρχας. Most English translations have understood the last part of this verse as referring to the "begetting" (γεννάω) of Jacob and the twelve patriarchs. Thiessen thinks it is more likely that περιτέμνω should be supplied instead, or better, that both verbs are implied. In this way, Luke intertwines genealogy with circumcision. Thiessen, *Contesting Circumcision*, 117–18. Cf. Jürgen Roloff, *Die Apostelgeschichte übersetzt und erklärt* (17th ed.; Göttingen: Vandenhoeck & Ruprecht, 1981), 120; Pervo, *Acts,* 181 n. 71.

[80] In a personal communication, Thiessen informs me that Luke's perspective on the genealogical impurity of the Gentiles need not be understood in negative terms. After all, the Mosaic Torah outlines a genealogical distinction between Israelite priests and laity. This discrimination is not negative. It only means that the stipulations in the Torah apply to both groups in different ways. In Luke's case, the unbridgeable genealogical gap between Jew and Gentile could be viewed in a similar vein as part of God's created order. After all, impure animals, which, Thiessen argues, are analogous to Gentiles (Acts 10–11:18), were created by the God of Israel and therefore are good in their place. I thank Thiessen for sharing his thoughts with me on this matter, although I think Luke conceives of Gentile impurity more along ethical or moral lines, like other Greek speaking Jews of the Diaspora.

nied, like the author of *Jubilees,* the possibility that Gentiles could convert to Judaism? This question also applies to the writings of Philo who highlights eighth-day circumcision when he states that Isaac was "the first man who existed of our nation according to the law of circumcision, being circumcised on the eighth day" (*QG* 3:38). Despite his emphasis on eighth-day circumcision, Philo can speak elsewhere in positive terms of proselytes who have come (προσεληλυθέναι) "to a new and God-fearing constitution, learning to disregard the fabulous inventions of other nations, and clinging to unalloyed truth" (*Spec.* 1:51). Philo also claims that such people should have "an equal share in all their [i.e., of Israel] laws, and privileges, and immunities, on their forsaking the pride of their fathers and forefathers" (*Spec.* 1:53; cf. *Spec.* 1:308; *Praem.* 152). The last statement could be taken as an indication that Philo believes in the possibility for proselytes to assimilate fully into Jewish society.[81]

Regardless of what one makes of Philo's statements, other texts from the Diaspora such as the *Letter of Aristeas,* whose traditions may indeed have shaped Luke's worldview,[82] do not refer to the genealogical impurity of Gentiles but point to the possibility for non-Jews to become morally pure (e.g., *Let. Aris.* 2). Indeed, the book of *Joseph and Aseneth* could prove quite relevant for the clarification of this issue and merits an entire monograph comparing its views with Luke-Acts. After undergoing a "mystical" transformation (chs. 14–18), equivalent in some way to a moral purification, Aseneth is able to marry Joseph (chs. 19–21). Her condition as a Gentile, therefore, is not irreversible. She becomes a Jewess in the fullest sense of the term after her spiritual metamorphosis. This work from the Diaspora may suggest that Luke also believed in the possibility for non-Jews to transform fully into Jews even though he was convinced that such a path was *unnecessary* for the masses of Gentiles entering the *ekklesia*. It is clear that Luke does not hold that Gentiles need to convert to Judaism in order to be saved. But does he think Gentiles *cannot* become Jews because of an irreversible and impermeable genealogical-ethnic gap separating both groups? Hopefully, the case of Timothy's circumcision can shed some light on this discussion.

---

[81] The matter cannot be fully addressed in this chapter. On Philo and conversion, see Ellen Birnbaum, *The Place of Judaism in Philo's Thought: Israel, Jews, and Proselytes* (Brown Judaic Studies 290; Atlanta: Scholars, 1996).

[82] See chapter 9 on food laws in Luke and the commission of the seventy-two, which draws from the legendary story about the translation of the Septuagint.

Paul's Circumcision of Timothy: Acts 16:1–3

Luke's reference to Paul's circumcision of Timothy has intrigued scholars for generations. How different Luke's compliant Paul appears to be from the adamant figure we discover in Paul's own letter to the Galatians! "Listen! I, Paul, am telling you that if you let yourselves be circumcised, Christ will be of no benefit to you" (Gal 5:2). Against his opponents demanding Gentile circumcision, Paul delivered the following scathing words: "I wish those who unsettle you would castrate themselves!" (Gal 5:12; cf. 6:12, 13) The gap between the historical Paul and Luke's Paul seems so great at this juncture that it has led some to dismiss the historicity of the report about Timothy's circumcision in Acts altogether.[83] But perhaps the abyss is not as deep in this instance as some have imagined, since in his letter to the Galatians Paul attacks those who were compelling *Gentiles* to be circumcised, whereas Luke refers here to a borderline case, someone whose multicultural, Jewish-Gentile background defies classification. Unlike Titus, who is only qualified as a Greek in Gal 2:3, Timothy, according to Luke, shares a dual background: his mother is Jewish; his father Greek. His ancestry is deemed problematic enough for Luke to claim that Paul circumcised him in order to accommodate to local Jewish sensibilities. How might this puzzling text complement our understanding of Luke's attitude toward circumcision?

Any discussion of this passage must deal with the question of Jewish descent and identity in antiquity. It can no longer be assumed that, before the rise of the rabbis, Jewishness was determined across the spectrum according to the matrilineal principle. Cohen has argued extensively

---

[83] This was the position of the so-called Tübingen School. See W. Ward Gasque, *A History of the Criticism of the Acts of the Apostles* (BGBE 17; Tübingen: Mohr Siebeck, 1975), 66. However, some like Gerd Lüdemann, *The Acts of the Apostles: What Really Happened in the Earliest Days of the Church* (Amherst, N.Y.: Prometheus Books, 2005), 208–209; Blaschke, *Beschneidung*, 460–64, accept the historicity of the tradition. Others think that a rumor about Paul teaching circumcision (based on Gal 5:11) influenced Luke's composition or that he used an unreliable tradition. See Haenchen, *The Acts of the Apostles*, 482. A redactional analysis hardly settles the issue. Weiser, *Die Apostelgeschichte,* 400, reaches the conclusion that Luke drew from a tradition, which is reflected in vv. 1b and 3a, but redacted vv. 1a, 2, 3bc, 4 and 5. I find it unlikely that Luke made up such a peculiar episode. The option remains open, therefore, that Luke drew from a tradition that related Timothy's circumcision. The historical reliability of the tradition though is another question. On the relationship between Paul and Luke-Acts, see David P. Moessner, et al., eds., *Paul and the Heritage of Israel: Paul's Claim upon Israel's Legacy in Luke and Acts in the Light of the Pauline Letters* (Library of New Testament Studies 452; London: T&T Clark, 2012).

against this notion, claiming that, prior to the composition of the Mishnah, many Jews did not view the matrilineal principle as a meaningful criterion for establishing Jewish identity.[84] It is unclear, therefore, whether Luke views Timothy as Jewish because of his mother's Jewish background. Levinskaya, however, argues that Acts should be taken as evidence that Jews from Asia Minor did in fact use the matrilineal criterion for establishing one's Jewishness.[85] Her proposal is not entirely without merit, since Luke does bother to mention the Jewish origins of Timothy's mother.[86] Levinskaya also points to 2 Tim 3:15, which states that Timothy had been instructed in the holy scriptures since his childhood.[87] If this statement is historically reliable, it would mean that Timothy had been brought up in a Jewish way despite his mother's marriage to a Greek husband. It could mean that some local Jews from Asia Minor might have considered Timothy Jewish because of his upbringing even though they knew he was not circumcised, possibly because of his father's objection to such an undertaking. Paul, therefore, according to Acts, would not have been compelling a "pure" Gentile to be circumcised, but converting a "semi-Gentile," someone who, arguably, qualified as Jewish in the eyes of some. It is only because of Timothy's dual heritage that Luke permits himself to depict Paul as a "mohel" without compromising his fundamental belief that Gentiles need not become circumcised.[88] Timothy's is a borderline case, lying

---

[84] Cohen, *Beginnings of Jewishness,* 273; See also Cohen's article, "Was Timothy Jewish? (Acts 16:1–3): Patristic Exegesis, Rabbinical Law, and Matrilineal Descent," *JBL* 105 (1986): 251–68.

[85] Irina Levinskaya, *The Book of Acts in Its Diaspora Setting* (vol. 5 of *The Book of Acts in Its First Century Setting;* ed. Bruce W. Winter; Grand Rapids, Mich.: Eerdmans, 1996), 12–17. Similarly, Cristopher Bryan, "A Further Look at Acts 16:1–3," *JBL* 107 (1988): 292–94; Mimouni, *La circoncision dans le monde judéen,* 208–10.

[86] Moreover, the earliest rabbinic evidence for a matrilineal principle is nearly contemporaneous with Acts, since Cohen concludes that it appears "in the first quarter of the second century C.E. at the latest" ("Was Timothy Jewish?" 266). *M. Bik.* 1:4, however, implies that in certain circumstances even a child of a Jewish mother had to convert: "These may bring the First-fruits but they may not make the Avowal: the proselyte may bring them but he may not make the Avowal since he cannot say, *Which the Lord swore unto our Fathers to give us.* But if his mother was an Israelite he may bring them and make the Avowal." Like the case of Timothy in Acts, this mishnaic passage implies that there were individuals of Jewish descent through the mother who, in certain circumstances, needed to convert to Judaism.

[87] Levinskaya, *The Book of Acts,* 15–16.

[88] The Greek text could suggest that Paul performed the circumcision: καὶ λαβὼν περιέτεμεν αὐτόν. To my knowledge, the Hebrew Bible and all other Second Temple sources do not refer to specialists who would perform this operation. Rubin, *The Beginning of Life,* 88–91, provides a useful discussion of the matter in biblical and rabbinic sources. He concludes that the Hebrew Bible holds the father responsible for guaranteeing that the circumcision is carried out, although he suggests there were already special-

somewhere in between the Jewish-Gentile gulf. This exceptional occurrence proves Luke's general rule: Gentiles do not have to be circumcised; Jews do.

Luke focuses not so much on the Jewish ancestry of Timothy's mother but on his father's Greek background.[89] Twice Luke refers to the Greek heritage of Timothy's father (16:1, 3). The second reference to Timothy's Greek father explains, somewhat elliptically, why Paul, according to Acts, has the circumcision performed: he wants to take Timothy along with him as a fellow worker and has him circumcised because of the Jews in those places who all "knew that his father was a Greek" (16:3).[90] Paul needs a colleague to accompany him as he goes about Asia Minor. The Jews from that region, however, allegedly know about Timothy's origins and would have blamed Paul for not having him circumcised. Luke, unfortunately, does not provide further details that could clarify the logic lying behind this localized Jewish objection.[91]

---

ists at that time who performed the rite because of the dangers involved (87). 1 Macc 1:61 might point in this direction ("and their families and those who circumcised them"). In rabbinic literature, the father is responsible for assuring that the infant is circumcised: "All the obligations of a father towards his son enjoined in the Law are incumbent on men but not on women" (*m. Qidd.* 1:7). *T. Qidd.* 1:11 explicitly includes circumcision as one of the father's obligations toward the son (cf. *y. Qidd.* 1:7 61a; *b. Qidd.* 29a). An uncircumcised Jewish male is responsible for his own circumcision once he becomes an adult. Amoraic sages debate whether women can be responsible for having their sons circumcised (e.g., *b. Avod. Zar.* 27a). Some rabbinic passages suggest that women did indeed assume this responsibility, including a passage about a woman from Cappadocia discussed below. One should also note 1 Macc 1:60 ("they put to death the women who had their children circumcised"). Rabbinic passages refer to specialists who perform circumcision. *Gen. Rab.* 46:9 and *y. Yevam.* 8:1 8d even specifies that the Jewish "mohel" should himself be circumcised. Rabbinic sages occasionally refer to instances where a Gentile or Samaritan performed the circumcision, probably because no Jewish specialist was available (*t. Avod. Zar.* 3:12–13; *b. Avod. Zar.* 26b; *b. Menah.* 42a).

[89] Commenting on the phrase in Acts 16:3 ("for they all knew that his father was Greek"), Conzelmann, *Acts of the Apostles,* 125, claims "…a reference to the mother – instead of the father – would have been better! Apparently, Luke does not have a precise understanding of Jewish law." This statement no longer carries any basis and represents the classical distrust of Luke as a reliable source of information on ancient Judaism. It is now clear that the matrilineal principle was not established throughout Jewry before at least the third century CE.

[90] As noted above, the twofold reference to Timothy's Greek father might also explain why Timothy was not circumcised in the first place: his Greek father opposed this act. Once the father passed away (as suggested by the Greek verb ὑπῆρχεν in 16:3), and in order to avoid controversy, Luke's Paul has Timothy circumcised.

[91] Would they have objected to the idea of a Gentile proclaiming a message in their synagogue or participating therein in tasks normally reserved for Jews? Of course, there were Gentiles (so-called God-fearers, proselytes, etc.) who attended synagogues. But to what extent were they allowed to participate in tasks that other Jews performed in this

The missiological dimension embedded in this pericope might be of some service, although its import should not be overemphasized at the cost of overlooking Luke's appreciation of the observance of the Law. Acts 16:1–3 appears in a wider section that reports Paul's visit to communities he had previously established in Syria and Cilicia (15:36–40). More significantly, after having Timothy circumcised, Paul and his new circumcised disciple "went (διεπορεύοντο) from town to town" and "delivered (παρεδίδοσαν) to them for observance the decisions that had been reached by the apostles and elders who were in Jerusalem" (Acts 16:4). The verbs in the Greek appear in the plural and imply that Timothy participated in the proclamation of the *Apostolic Decree*. The major decision that had been reached in Jerusalem, according to Luke, was that Gentiles did not need to be circumcised but only observe the commandments of the Apostolic Decree. Of course, in Luke's eyes, this decision presupposes that Jewish followers of Jesus continue to observe the Torah *in toto*, including circumcision. An uncircumcised follower of Jesus, whose mother was Jewish and father Greek, might not have proved the most adequate candidate for proclaiming the Apostolic Decree. On the contrary, Timothy's ambiguous background could raise further halakic questions and headaches: As an uncircumcised Jew (to those who would have considered him as such), did he necessitate circumcision or not? Could his non-circumcised status imply that Jewish followers of Jesus need not circumcise their children, precisely the rumor spreading around in Luke's day about Paul's teachings (Acts 21:21)? The circumcision of Timothy resolves this ambiguity and allows Luke at the same time to refute the allegations directed against Paul concerning his alleged abrogation of Torah observance for Jews. If Luke's Paul is even willing to circumcise a "semi-Gentile," how much more would he affirm the circumcision of Jews.[92] Timothy's circumcision provides a buffer protecting Paul against accusations stating to the contrary that he opposed Jews who upheld the Torah.

Thiessen suggests that Luke is not in favor of Timothy's circumcision because he does not consider him to be Jewish in the first place. Only males of a pure Jewish genealogical stock who have been circumcised on the eighth day qualify as Jewish in Luke's eyes. Gentiles, therefore, should not and *cannot* become Jewish. "In Luke's eyes, non-eighth-day circumcision is as good as uncircumcision."[93] This interpretation, while attractive

---

space? Since in Acts Paul addresses the gospel not only to Gentiles but also to Jews, it might have been viewed as inappropriate to have a non-Jewish ambassador instructing Jews. Cf. Jervell, *Die Apostelgeschichte,* 412–13: "[I]n der Apg gibt es nur jüdische Missionare...."

[92] Cf. Jervell, *Die Apostelgeschichte,* 412; Wehnert, *Die Reinheit,* 88–89, 98.

[93] Thiessen, *Contesting Circumcision,* 122–23.

and ingenious, raises several questions, some of which have been already discussed above. Other Jews of the Greek speaking Diaspora certainly were open to the possibility that Gentiles or "semi-Jews" could become Jewish, as the text of Acts 16:1–3 implies. It is of course possible that Luke held a different view about this matter than his Jewish counterparts from the Greco-Roman Diaspora. *T. Shabb.* 15:8 could support this point, as it reports an interesting debate about the practice of eighth-day circumcision allegedly occurring in Asia Minor:

R. Nathan said: "When I was in Mazaca of Cappadocia one woman was there who would give birth to males and they would be circumcised and die. She circumcised the first one and he died; the second and he died; the third she brought him to me. I saw that he was green. I examined him and did not find in him the blood of the covenant. They said to me: 'Are we to circumcise him?' I said to them: 'Wait for him until blood enters him.' They waited for him and circumcised him and he lived. And they called him Nathan the Babylonian after my name."[94]

This passage from the Tosefta, however artificial it may be, claims some Jews in Cappadocia would not wait beyond the eighth day to circumcise their sons. Only after a rabbinic sage intervened did they decide to postpone the time of circumcision. Nevertheless, the passage only reveals a concern to circumcise *Jewish* male *infants* on the eighth day in accordance with the mandate in the Mosaic Torah. Accordingly, it explores the possibility of postponing briefly this surgical procedure should the Jewish infant prove too fragile.[95] The passage does not preclude the possibility that Jews in Cappadocia or elsewhere believed Gentile male adults could undergo circumcision and become Jewish.

Luke suggests that Paul thought it unnecessary that Timothy undergo this procedure in the first place and only performed it to accommodate to local Jewish sensibilities. This Lukan portrait seems to match Paul's own perspective on the matter: "…let each of you lead the life that the Lord has assigned, to which God called you. This is my rule in all the churches. Was anyone at the time of his call already circumcised? Let him not seek to remove the marks of circumcision. Was anyone at the time of his call uncircumcised? Let him not seek circumcision" (1Cor 7:17–18). Luke might have imagined that Paul was reluctant to circumcise Timothy because he knew about Paul's own position on such matters: Jews were not

---

[94] Translation mine. Cf. *b. Shabb.* 134a; *b. Hul.* 47b; *b. Yevam.* 64b. See Lieberman, *Tosefta Ki-Fshuta,* 3:250, for further parallel passages. See the brief discussion of this passage in Cohen, *Why Aren't Jewish Women Circumcised,* 23.

[95] Rashi, in his commentary on the story, as it appears in *b. Shabb.* 134a, adds that besides the health risks the very validity of the circumcision was under threat since the child was "green" and consequently the issuance of the "covenantal blood" (דם ברית; citing Zech 9:11) required during the circumcision would by no means be guaranteed under such conditions.

to undergo epispasm in order to remove their marks in an attempt to free themselves from their Jewish identity, just as Gentiles (and maybe even non-circumcised Jews?) were not to undergo circumcision in order to become Jewish and be bound to the Law.[96] This statement could imply that Paul as well as Luke would have recognized the Jewishness of a Gentile male once he had undergone circumcision. Otherwise, how could Paul assert in his letter to the Galatians that every man allowing himself to be circumcised was obliged to obey the entire Law (Gal 5:3)? And why did the historical Paul complain about being persecuted if he was "still preaching circumcision?" (Gal 5:11). Perhaps by this latter statement Paul meant that he still upheld circumcision for Jewish males, and Luke's report about Timothy's circumcision illustrates how this incident as well as Paul's position on the matter served to no avail in eliminating the rumors continuously circulating about Paul's supposed abrogation of Jewish circumcision (Acts 21:21).[97]

Conclusion

Matthew's position on the circumcision of Gentiles, as I suggested above, may not have lied very far from Luke's: Matthew did not require Gentiles to undergo circumcision in order to join the Jesus movement, although he certainly expected Jews to continue honoring this covenantal rite. Regarding Luke, I tried to show that, far from proving to be a Gentile ignorant about Jewish praxis, in his narrative about John and Jesus' births, he reveals a remarkable and accurate knowledge on laws and practices related to purity, circumcision, child naming, and the redemption of the firstborn. Luke relies on his expertise on the Jewish Law in order to depict the central protagonists of the Infancy Narrative as faithful members of the house of Israel who pass the highest and strictest standards of Jewish observance. In a pericope dense with halakic features and references to Mosaic legislation, Luke presents Jesus and his parents as the ideal type of Jews. Like John the Baptist, Jesus is circumcised on the *eighth* day and stems from a distinguished Jewish lineage (tribe of Judah, clan of David). In addition, Luke's Jesus is presented (and redeemed) *in person* at the temple *after* the forty days of his impurity (and that of his mother's) are over. This is the

---

[96] Cf. David J. Rudolph, *A Jew to the Jews: Jewish Contours of Pauline Flexibility in 1 Corinthians 9:19–23* (WUNT 2.304; Tübingen: Mohr Siebeck, 2011), 23–27.

[97] James Dunn, *The Epistle to the Galatians* (Peabody, Mass.: Hendrickson, 1993), 278–79: "Paul was accused by...other missionaries of being inconsistent: that although he preached a circumcision-free gospel to the Galatians, he continued to 'preach circumcision' among Jews."

appropriate and earliest moment in the narrative where Luke can present Jesus in the temple. Placing the parturient and her infant inside the temple anytime before the completion of their impurity would imply that they defiled the temple.

It is possible that Luke bothers to describe the births of John the Baptist and Jesus, their circumcision, and Jesus' presentation in the temple by his parents in such a Jewish way in order to present such foundational characters as paradigms for Jewish followers of Jesus to emulate.[98] Polemics over the question of circumcision continued to abound in the Jesus movement even after 70 CE. We must abandon the notion that the importance of the Jewish Law for the *ekklesia* vanished after the first generation of Jewish followers of Jesus (Paul, Peter, James, etc.) passed away. On the contrary, Luke's writings show that the issue and place of circumcision as well as the observance of the rest of the Torah within the Jesus movement had hardly been settled by the end of first century CE, as witnessed by several writings from around Luke's time that deal in various ways with these questions (e.g., *Barnabas, Didache, Dialogue with Trypho*, etc.).[99] There were probably several takes on this complicated issue. On one extreme stood some Jewish followers of Jesus who demanded that Gentiles become circumcised. At the other end of the spectrum could be found Jews who were abandoning the rite altogether as well as Gentile followers of Jesus who were opposed to the idea that Jews could continue to maintain their Jewish identity once they became followers of Jesus.[100] By presenting John the Baptist and Jesus as circumcised Jews, Luke places himself somewhere in between these two poles: he dismisses the notion that Gentiles must be circumcised, as the Apostolic Decree makes clear (Acts 15), but also refutes the idea that the *ekklesia* should teach "*Jews* living among the Gentiles to forsake Moses" and not "circumcise *their children* or observe the customs" (Acts 21:21).[101]

---

[98] Cf. Jervell, *The Unknown Paul*, 141; Thiessen, *Contesting Conversion*, 115–16.

[99] Murray, *Playing a Jewish Game*, has gathered and discussed the relevant texts from the first *and* second centuries CE that speak on behalf of an ongoing attraction toward Jewish practices among Gentile Judaizers.

[100] If Luke-Acts was written in the beginning of the second century CE, could some of these opponents of Jewish praxis stem from Marcionite circles? Tyson, *Marcion and Luke-Acts*, 75, reads Acts 21:21 in light of the Marcionite controversy with the author of Acts opposing Marcion's view that Paul did not observe the Torah. On the other hand, Tyson (pp. 125–28) is careful not to posit Marcion as entirely anti-Judaic, though it is hard to imagine that he would have tolerated any follower of Jesus persisting in showing attachment to customs that originated, after all, from the Hebrew scriptures.

[101] Might this proposal prove even more compelling if Luke wrote his Infancy Narrative after he had composed Luke-Acts? Brown, *Birth of the Messiah*, 239–40, suggests that Luke did indeed write this section of his narrative after he composed the rest of Luke and Acts. If this is true, it is noteworthy that Luke consciously chooses to portray the

Because of his apocalyptic vision and belief in the imminent return of Jesus, the historical Paul did not deal with many of the long term questions pressing the administration of the *ekklesia* during the delay of the Parousia, including the transmission of Torah observance to future generations of Jewish followers of Jesus living during Luke's day. "Was anyone at the time of his call already circumcised? Let him not seek to remove the marks of circumcision. Was anyone at the time of his call uncircumcised? Let him not seek circumcision" (1 Cor 7:18). Paul treated the question of circumcision, convinced that the "impending crisis" (1 Cor 7:26) or "the appointed time" (v. 29) had drawn near and that the present world was "passing away" (v. 31). Caught in this eschatological excitement, Paul did not deal extensively with the question of raising families and transmitting Jewish values to *subsequent generations.* A Jewish follower of Jesus should remain Jewish; a Gentile follower of Jesus Gentile. Paul left unanswered how Jewish followers of Jesus should raise their children, given his fervent belief in the immediate arrival of the "day of wrath" and the Parousia. If anything, Paul believed that, ideally, followers of Jesus should remain single or "as if" they were unmarried (vv. 8, 29). There is little room within such an ideology to deal with the "anxieties" of marriage and children (vv. 28, 32). Paul's apocalyptic worldview should never be left out of sight, however important he has become for the subsequent development of Christian systematic theology.

It was up to Luke, therefore, who only represents *one* possible interpretation of Paul's ambiguous and complex, if not contradictory, thought, to tackle some of the ongoing questions left unanswered during the delay of the Parousia. In such circumstances, Luke's Jesus – circumcised, purified, and redeemed, the Jew *par excellence* – could serve as a role model for Jewish followers of Jesus to follow as they transmitted their Jewish identity to their children.

Making sense of Acts 16:1–3 is a challenging task because its terse language presents the modern reader with a character of liminal stature. Does Luke believe that Timothy's circumcision was unnecessary because his father was not Jewish (the patrilineal principle) or because he was genealogically impure (both parents needed to be Jewish) and not circumcised on the eighth day? Alternatively, like his predecessor Paul, does Luke believe that an individual, whether circumcised or uncircumcised, should remain in that status unchanged? More than Paul, Luke is consistent and clear throughout his writings about the ongoing obligations of Jewish followers of Jesus vis-à-vis the Torah, including the transmission of such values to their children. If Paul believed that Jew and Gentile should not

---

families of John the Baptist and Jesus as Torah observant Jews after considerably exerting himself in presenting Paul in similar light.

seek to alter their status, subsuming the relevance of this question to the primary importance of being prepared for the imminent arrival of the Parousia and withdrawal from this world, Luke, living a generation or two after Paul, could no longer postpone the resolution of this problem: Jews were not only to keep their acquired marks of circumcision intact, but were to perpetuate this practice by circumcising their children. Eschatological delay led Luke to affirm the halakic prolongation and maintenance of the ancestral customs observed by Jewish people for subsequent generations. Gentile followers of Jesus, for their part, were to continue in their non-circumcised yet morally purified and sanctified status during the interim period between post-paschal resurrection and parousian crystallization.

Chapter 13

Conclusion

"I came to the research for this commentary fresh from a period of ten years in which the Gospel of Luke had dominated my horizons. The transition from the one to the other was initially quite a shock. After the urbane humanity of Luke, Matthew seemed very narrow and Jewish. And it was hard at first to find in Matthew the generosity of spirit that I had come to value so much in Luke.... Matthew may not have been the urbane world citizen that Luke was, but he shows the same generosity of spirit and he recognises the comprehensive significance of Jesus for the world every bit as much as Luke.... The shock of transition from Luke to Matthew was real enough. A major cultural adaptation is involved in moving from the one to the other."
(John Nolland, *The Gospel of Matthew*, xvii)

My experience reading Matthew and Luke-Acts has been different from Nolland's, whose works I have found very useful and instructive. In any case, Nolland also detects commonalities between both gospel writers. I have been struck by the remarkable overlap between Matthew and Luke and confounded by the dichotomies that continue to separate these Jewish works into discrete categories of "Jewish/particularistic" vs. "Gentile/universalistic," problematic terms to say the least. Matthew, for one thing, appears to me to be just as "universalistic," if we may momentarily use such nomenclature, as Luke.[1] Already in his birth narrative, which in all respects proves to be quite Jewish, Matthew introduces elements that hint toward the universal: he includes the names of four women who were all possibly of non-Israelite origins into a genealogy (Matt 1:1–17) that

---

[1] The usage of the terms "particularistic" and "universalistic" are problematic and misleading for several reasons. In a certain way, Christianity became a "particularistic" movement by denying salvation to anyone outside of its system, while Judaism became "universalistic" by recognizing the possibility for all humans to gain a legitimate standing before God without embracing Judaism but simply following the Noahide Laws. Boccaccini, *Middle Judaism*, 265: "...if universalism means the capacity of attaching value to being different, then its opposite is not particularism or nationalism, but dogmatism and intolerance, namely, the pretense of possessing the whole truth or of having the only key to salvation." See also Robert Goldenberg, "The Place of Other Religions in Ancient Jewish Thought, with Particular Reference to Early Rabbinic Judaism," in *Pushing the Faith: Proselytism and Civility in a Pluralistic World* (ed. Martin E. Marty and Frederick E. Greenspahn; New York: Crossroad, 1988), 40; Hirshman, "Rabbinic Universalism in the Second and Third Centuries," 101–15; *Torah for the Entire World*, 40.

traces Jesus' ancestry back to Abraham, the progenitor of Israel, but also, let us not forget, the "father of a multitude of nations" through whom "all the families of the earth shall be blessed" (Gen 12:3; 17:5).[2] Only Matthew refers to the visit of the Gentile magi who travel from distant foreign lands to pay their devotion to Jesus (2:1–12). Matthew occasionally describes the attitudes of certain Gentiles in favorable terms (e.g., the Canaanite woman in 15:22–28; the Roman centurion in 8:5–13).[3] He looks forward to the day when Jew and Gentile alike will share in the same eschatological banquet (8:11–12). Finally, after his resurrection, Matthew's Jesus exhorts his disciples to go forth among the nations teaching and baptizing Gentiles (28:18–20).[4]

Luke, for his part, constructs the most Jewish of infancy narratives. No Gentile characters figure prominently throughout Luke's description of John the Baptist and Jesus' births. Instead, Luke immerses his readers into the most Jewish atmosphere possible where priests, prophets, and Jewish shepherds celebrate the birth of these two prominent figures who are circumcised and, hence, fully circumscribed within the Jewish parameters of halakic and covenantal duties. Throughout this portion of his narrative, Luke announces the salvation of *Israel* (1:68; 2:38). Admittedly, Luke also

---

[2] Tracing Jesus' origins back to Abraham could be seen as an exclusive act, since Abraham is the ancestor of the Israelite people. Nevertheless, I agree with those commentators who view Abraham's inclusion into Jesus' genealogy, along with the foreign women, as an inclusive move on the part of Matthew. See Kent Sparks, "Gospel as Conquest: Mosaic Typology in Matthew 28:16–20," *CBQ* 68 (2006): 651–63. For a more detailed discussion of the roles of the women in Matthew's genealogy, see Edwin D. Freed, "The Women in Matthew's Genealogy," *JSNT* 29 (1987): 3–19; A. T. Hanson, "Rahab the Harlot in Early Christian Tradition," *JSNT* 1 (1978): 53–60; Wim J. C. Weren, "The Five Women in Matthew's Genealogy," *CBQ* 59 (1997): 288–305; Jason Hood, *The Messiah, His Brothers, and the Nations (Matthew 1:1–17)* (Library of New Testament Studies 441; London: T&T Clark, 2011).

[3] As Sparks, "Gospel as Conquest," 653, correctly notes, Matthew's portrayal of the Roman centurion is more inclusive than Luke's, since the latter goes through great pains to justify the centurion's encounter with Jesus.

[4] For a further discussion of the universal themes in Matthew, See Luis Sánchez Navarro, "La Escritura para las naciones. Acerca del universalismo en Mateo" in *Palabra de Dios, Sagrada Escritura, Iglesia* (eds. Vicente Balaguer and Juan Luis Caballero; Pamplona: Ediciones Universidad de Navarra, 2008), 187–203 and his *Testimonios del Reino: Evangelios Sinópticos y Hechos los Apóstoles* (Madrid: Ediciano Palabra, 2010). I agree with Navarro's affirmation of the universal dimension in Matthew but do not accept his reduction of the Jewishness of Matthew to an "estilo semítico de composición" that denies Matthew's "judaizing" tendencies (as Navarro puts it) and attachment to the Law of Moses ("La Escritura para las naciones," 202). Navarro forgets that even the Hebrew prophets, who proclaim light to the nations, do not assume that Israel forsakes its identity by opening itself to the Gentiles. I would like to thank prof. Juan Carlos Ossandón for informing me about Navarro's work.

declares in his infancy narrative that Jesus will bring salvation to the nations (e.g., 2:32), but this process occurs via the circumcised messiah and his Jewish emissaries who invite Gentiles to ally themselves with Israel. "*Extra Israel nulla salus est*."[5]

Many point to the universal texture of Jesus' genealogy in Luke, which goes all the way back to Adam, the son of God (3:23–38).[6] We cannot, however, overlook the *Enochic* provenance and Jewish structure of this genealogy: Jesus is the *seventy-seventh* descendant of Adam, the one destined to bring redemption and a new age during the seventh part of the eleventh week, that is, the seventy-seventh generation (cf. *1 En.* 10:12; *1 En.* 91:15–17).[7] Long ago according to Enochic tradition, the mythical Enoch, the seventh descendant of Adam living right before the time of Noah's flood, had predicted that the final judgment would occur seventy generations after his departure (1 *En.* 93:3; Luke 3:37). Interestingly, for Luke, the days of Noah prefigure the events to come at the end of times before the return of the Son of Man (Luke 17:26–27).[8] Even Luke's genealogy must be deemed just as Jewish as Matthew's.[9]

Throughout his gospel, Luke, more than Matthew, carefully avoids having Jesus enter into contact with Gentiles. No encounter occurs between Luke's Jesus and the Canaanite woman. When Jesus meets the Roman centurion, Luke is most cautious in his approach, stressing more than Matthew the social-halakic gulf existing at that time between Jew and

---

[5] Jacob Jervell, "The Future of the Past: Luke's Vision of Salvation History and Its Bearing on His Writings of History," in *History, Literature, and Society in the Book of Acts* (ed. Ben Witherington III; Cambridge: Cambridge University Press, 1996), 123.

[6] Bock, *Luke,* 1:360, overlooks the significant parallels with Jewish tradition, opining: "Jesus is not some isolated minister to Israel; he does not merely minister to a tiny nation of subjected people seeking political deliverance from a dominating Rome....In him, as well, the fate of all divinely created humans is bound together." Bovon, *Luke 1,* 134–5, states that "Matthew's perspective is dominated by the privileged status of Abraham's descendants; Luke shows a universalistic tendency," but then goes on to recognize the apocalyptic dimension of Luke's genealogy; Green, *The Gospel of Luke*, 189: "The reference to Adam as son of God presents the divine origin of the human race and indicates Jesus' solidarity with all humanity."

[7] According to the *Apocalypse of Weeks*, the final judgment occurs at the end of the *tenth* week, that is, during the seventieth generation (*1 En.* 93:3–10; 91:11–17). Nevertheless, *1 En.* 10:12 refers to seventy generations of history to occur *after* Enoch, the seventh descendant of Adam. The genealogy in Luke, therefore, reckons the end as occurring at the end of *eleven* weeks, namely, during the seventy-seventh generation. Cf. *4 Ezra* 14:11.

[8] See especially Richard Bauckham, *Jude and the Relatives of Jesus in the Early Church* (Edinburgh: T&T Clark, 1990), 320–26, for a discussion about the Enochic features in the Lukan genealogy as originating from Palestinian tradition.

[9] The Davidic messiahship, singled out by Matthew in his genealogy, is also of special importance for Luke (1:27, 32; 3:31; 20:41–44; Acts 2:30; 13:23; 15:16).

Gentile. It is almost as if Luke chooses to follow Matthew's Jesus' command to "go nowhere among the Gentiles, and enter no town of the Samaritans" but "rather to the lost sheep of the house of Israel" (Matt 10:5–6). Almost. For Luke's Jesus does eventually send out emissaries to Samaria, but this outreach probably happens because these people qualify as Israelites in Luke's eyes. Even then, Luke's attitude toward the Samaritans is marked by ambivalence (9:52; Acts 1:8; ch.8).[10] Only after his resurrection does the Lukan Jesus turn his attention to the Gentiles (Acts 1:8), much like the Matthean Jesus in his final commission after the resurrection. The schemes of *Heilsgeschichte* in both Matthew and Luke prove quite similar as far as the proclamation of the gospel to the Gentiles is concerned, with the Jewish Law remaining in force throughout.

On three important accounts, I have found Luke to be as Jewish and affirmative as Matthew concerning the observance of the Law: Sabbath keeping, kashrut, and circumcision – three central markers of Jewish identity. Along the way, I noted and discussed other aspects of Jewish praxis, including matters related to purity (hand washing, impurity of the parturient, corpse impurity, etc.), burial, naming and redeeming Jewish children, in which I found nothing to substantiate the claims that either Matthew or Luke announces the abrogation of the Jewish Law. Some might get frustrated with this work for not finding in it a more "sophisticated" and nuanced differentiation between Matthew and Luke's perspectives on the Law. However, this project strives not to nuance but to question problematic categories and dichotomies that continue to subsist and govern the ways in which we read and comprehend these texts. Only in the aftermath of this deconstruction, can we then refine our approaches and perspectives on these documents and understand their fuller significance within the Jewish matrices that were constantly shifting and realigning themselves partly in response to the traumatic destruction of the temple in 70 CE.

In the meantime, I only offer some considerations for further investigation that move beyond the *intra/extra muros* debate and explore what types of strands of Judaism Matthew and Luke represent. First, I suggest the differences between Matthew and Luke, as far as the question of the observance of the Law is concerned, might lie more in their respective social and regional settings than in their theological stances. This point is not made to embrace some kind of harmonizing agenda that rejects the undeniable theological diversity pervading the Jesus movement since day one, only to recognize and recover the strong Jewish element persisting within its veins even after 70 CE. If Matthew includes the categorical and systematic statement, "do not think that I have come to abolish the law or the prophets; I have come not to abolish but to fulfill. For truly I tell you, until

---

[10] See my treatment of the literary context of Luke 10:1–11 in chapter 9 of this book.

heaven and earth pass away, not one letter, not one stroke of a letter, will pass from the law until all is accomplished" (5:17–18), Luke has Jesus declare, "it is easier for heaven and earth to pass away, than for one stroke of a letter in the law to be dropped" (16:17). If Matthew's Jesus can reprimand his Pharisaic opponents for not practicing justice, mercy, and faith, yet exhort them not to abandon the observance of "lighter" commandments such as the tithing of herbs, the Lukan Jesus can equally affirm this principle: "you tithe mint and rue and herbs of all kinds, and neglect justice and the love of God; it is these you ought to have practiced, *without neglecting the others*" (11:42).

Matthew and Luke's overall perspectives on the Jewish Law may have differed on theological and cultural grounds. Nevertheless, in practical terms, I suggest they could have shared the same table, as both recognized the importance of providing a space for Jewish followers of Jesus to continue observing their ancestral traditions. Accordingly, I suggest we further explore the *Sitz im Leben* of both authors. Why does Matthew show such animosity toward the Pharisees when his Jesus clashes with them over halakic matters? Why, on the other hand, does Luke's portrait of the Pharisees prove more subdued in these instances and elsewhere? In addition, what leads Luke to portray Paul as a Pharisee? Does this discrepancy between the two gospel authors stem in part from Matthew's ongoing clash with Pharisees in a locale, Syria or Palestine, where the Pharisaic reach of power could be felt more effectively? In such circumstances, Jesus readily becomes for Matthew and his readers the halakic model, the embodiment of Torah and normative point of reference dictating how Jewish life is to be observed. If this is the case, the retelling of Jesus' Sabbath healings could well represent a contemporary Matthean position on Sabbath keeping: Matthew's followers, like Jesus, are entitled to treat minor diseases on the Sabbath. Likewise, Jesus' argument about hand washing before meals could reflect Matthew's own opposition, or at least indifference, toward such a practice: Jesus' disciples need not observe this rite. In Matthew's eyes, it represents a Pharisaic innovation. In other words, as many suggest, Matthew's gospel reflects an ongoing debate between Pharisees and Matthean Jews (and some Gentiles), maybe even an intra-Pharisaic clash between Pharisees and former "Christian Pharisees" who now belong to Matthew's circle.[11]

---

[11] Anders Runesson, "Behind the Gospel of Matthew: Radical Pharisees in Post-War Galilee?" *CurTM* 37.6 (2010): 460–71; "Rethinking early Jewish Christian Relations," 95–132. I agree with Runesson in moving beyond the *intra/extra muros* debate about Matthew and instead pinpoint his specific brand of Judaism, which is undeniably close yet firmly opposed to Pharisaic Judaism. Luke's brand of Judaism, I would argue resem-

Luke, on the other hand, possibly gazes at the Pharisaic party from a certain *geographical* distance. He writes somewhere in the Greco-Roman Diaspora beyond the immediate grasp of Pharisaic power. He, like other Diasporan Jews, is aware, however, of the reputation of the Pharisees for being "accurate" in their approach to the Law and for their influence among the Judeans living in the area of Palestine. He also knows that Paul himself once belonged to the Pharisaic camp. He taps on this information, depicting Paul as an *ongoing* Pharisee (Acts 23:6) in order to argue that the apostle to the Gentiles always remained faithful to the Law and that this legislation continues to enjoy a special place within the Jesus movement, particularly for Jewish followers of Jesus. Luke can remain more nuanced, occasionally even favorable toward the Pharisees than Matthew, for he is not caught in the same polemical dynamics as his synoptic cousin vis-à-vis this particular Jewish group. Consequently, he seems more willing to accommodate to Pharisaic halakic sensibilities: unlike Matthew, he does not seek to dissuade Jewish believers from washing before eating (11:38–41). He does not even disapprove of this pharisaic innovation. He only disagrees with "Christian Pharisees" (Acts 15:5) who refuse to interact with non-circumcised Gentile followers of Jesus because they focus so much on the preservation of their own purity while failing to acknowledge the marvelous moral purification experienced by Gentile followers of Jesus.

Likewise, the Sabbath healing episodes in Luke provide not so much a justification for the administration of minor cures on the Sabbath, though they might have, but present Jesus as an exalted messianic figure full of authority. It is quite telling that Luke never portrays any of Jesus' disciples in Acts as performing healings on the Sabbath despite the fact the he includes more Sabbath healing episodes performed by Jesus than any other gospel. How far Luke is willing to accommodate to halakic sensibilities, provided they do not exclude Jewish-Gentile fellowship. If Matthew is "anti-Pharisaic," Luke is "pro-Pharisaic" (these are hyperboles). Ultimately, Luke's social and theological concerns are shaped by relations with the "Jews" of Asia Minor and other regions of the Mediterranean basin. He struggles with the disheartening reality that many Diasporan Jews do not recognize the messianic credentials of Jesus. "Lukan Judaism" is more "Hellenistic" and Diasporan in its outlook; "Matthean Judaism" more Galilean, Palestinian, and (anti-)Pharisaic.

All of these observations, however, might be granting too much weight to external matters at the cost of overlooking the internal evidence provided by the primary sources under examination. I am, of course, aware of the

---

bles more a "Hellenistic-Diasporan" type of Jewish expression, though highly informed by Palestinian traditions.

methodological problems involved in identifying texts with groups. Even Luke betrays a remarkable dependence on Jewish traditions that ultimately stem from Palestine. Consequently, the "Hellenistic" (if we ascribe a geographical dimension to this term) background should not be overstated. Besides his genealogy on Jesus, which draws from the Enochic tradition, he emphasizes, like the author of *Jubilees,* the importance of eighth-day circumcision, extends the impurity of the parturient to the infant just as *Jubilees,* 4Q265, and 4Q266. He also upholds the Apostolic Decree, which also originates from Palestine, and, like *Jubilees,* views the prohibition against consuming blood as universally binding: failure to handle blood properly can defile not only the Land of Israel but also the whole earth. He might have even been to Palestine, especially if he composed the so-called "we sections" in Acts. He enjoys a cosmopolitan experience similar to that of Paul of Tarsus, whom he does not follow blindly on every point, or of Flavius Josephus, familiar with Jewish life in Palestine and the Diaspora. He exemplifies a unique blend, a hybridization of Jewish and Greek culture – a consequence of his own experience and acquaintance with synagogue life in the Mediterranean context.

The *communis opinio* on Luke as a "Gentile Christian," a God-fearer, or even a proselyte to Judaism operates under certain presuppositions about the author that select specific verses from Acts, particularly 15:10, read occasionally in conjunction with 13:38–39,[12] as the hermeneutical key governing the interpretation of Luke's perspective on the Law as a whole. For many, Acts 15:10 represents a Gentile perspective on the Law, written by someone "distant" from Judaism, a "pagan," a "Gentile Christian" or a God-fearer insufficiently acquainted with Jewish teachings.[13]

---

[12] Schneider, *Die Apostelgeschichte,* 2:140: "Anders als Paulus selbst stellt Lukas das Ungenügen des Gesetzes so dar, daß seine Befolgung zu schwer war."

[13] Haenchen, *The Acts of the Apostles,* 446: "It would be more correct to say that the Gentile Christian Luke, who is speaking here, has lost sight of the continuing validity of the law for Jewish Christians...because all that matters to him is to demonstrate Gentile Christian freedom from the law." On 446 n. 3, Haenchen adds: "Here however we have the law seen through Hellenistic Gentile Christian eyes, as a mass of commandments and prohibitions which no man can fulfil. Luke here is obviously speaking for himself and transmitting the view of his age and milieu." Pervo, *Acts,* 374, follows in the steps of Conzelmann, *Acts,* 117: "It expresses the view of a Christian at a time when the separation from Judaism already lies in the past." Conzelmann continues on the same page: "On this basis we can also understand why Luke does not draw the conclusion which logic demands, that this yoke should also be removed from Jewish Christians. For Luke Jewish Christianity no longer has any present significance, but it is of fundamental significance in terms of salvation history." Schneider, *Die Apostelgeschichte,* 2:181, following Haenchen and Conzelmann: "Lukas denkt dabei wohl an die Vielzahl der gesetzlichen Verpflichtungen." Similarly, Weiser, *Die Apostelgeschichte,* 2:381.

Acts 15:10, however, really betrays a Jewish perspective and bitter recognition of Israel's corporate and historical failure to observe the Torah: "Now therefore why are you putting God to the test by placing on the neck of the disciples a yoke that neither our ancestors nor we have been able to bear?" Luke's Peter's reference to the Law as a yoke is not negative. He blames *Israel* for failing to fulfill the Law, not the supposedly overwhelming stipulations contained in the Mosaic Torah.[14] Interestingly, Luke's reference to the Law as a yoke is matched by a *contemporaneous* Jewish work, surprisingly overlooked, written after 70 CE in response to the tragic event of the destruction of the temple: "For behold, I see many of your people who separated themselves from your statutes and who have cast away from them the yoke of your Law. Further, I have seen others who left behind their vanity and who have fled under your wings" (*2 Baruch* 41:3–4).[15] The author of *2 Baruch* is aware of the apostasy of some Jews from the Torah and cognizant of the historical failure of Israel as whole in living up to the high covenantal standards expected from a chosen and holy people. Nevertheless, the author of *2 Baruch* remains optimistic that, by God's grace, a sufficient number of people among the Jewish people will eventually gather themselves and successfully carry the yoke of the Law: "In you we have put our trust, because, behold, your Law is with us, and we know that we do not fall as long as we keep your statutes…And that Law that is among us will help us" (48:22–24).[16] By contrast, certain traditions contained in the book of *4 Ezra* remain far less hopeful about this positive outcome, suspecting that only a select few will be saved and pass the final judgment: "The Most High made this world for the sake of many, but the world to come for the sake of few…Many have been created, but few will be saved" (8:1–3).[17]

---

[14] For a refreshing view on Acts 15:10, see John Nolland, "A Fresh Look at Acts 15.10," *NTS* 27 (1980): 105–15.

[15] As noted in the previous chapter on circumcision, the references to forsaking vanity and fleeing under God's wings point to proselytes converting to Judaism. Cf. *2 Bar.* 1:4; 14:5; 42:5. Ruth 2:12; *b. Shabb.* 31a.

[16] Cf. 44:2–8; 46:5–6; 51:3–4, 7; 54:5; 66:5–6; 77:15–17; 78:7; 79:2; 84:1–11; 85:3, etc.

[17] In the end of *4 Ezra* (e.g., 14:22), the author seems to align himself more or less with the position of *2 Baruch*. However, the perspective on the Law in *4 Ezra* is complex, presenting differing views as voiced by Uriel and Ezra (before and after his "conversion"). This matter has received its ample share of attention in the history of research as well as at the Enoch Seminar in Milan (2011). For a summary of the discussion and the history of research on *4 Ezra*, see Karina Hogan, *Theologies in Conflict in 4 Ezra: Wisdom, Debate, and Apocalyptic Solution* (Supplements to the Journal for the Study of Judaism 130; Leiden: Brill, 2008), 1–40. Here I draw statements from *4 Ezra* to illustrate how certain Jews doubted the adequacy of their covenantal and theological systems for addressing the question of theodicy and the awful reality of Jewish suffering confronting

Luke joins the authors of *2 Baruch* and *4 Ezra* and other Jewish thinkers of his time in recognizing that history confirms Israel's collective failure to follow God's Law.[18] "O look not upon the sins of your people, but at those who have served you in truth" is the cry of a Jewish prayer confessing Israel's sins in the midst of the existential turmoil and posttraumatic distress generated by the failure of the First Jewish Revolt (*4 Ezra* 9:26). Luke, on the other hand, prays the Jewish people look to the risen Jesus, their heavenly and Davidic messiah reigning high above, who announces release from sin to Israel and the pious Gentiles and will soon return to pronounce his final judgment upon this world as the vindicated and victorious Son of Man. What Israel needs, in Luke's eyes, is a *supplement* (not a supplanter!) to the Torah to assist in fulfilling its vocation and destiny.

This inquiry began analyzing the *texts* of Matthew and Luke with the aim of demonstrating that Luke and Acts are just as Jewish as Matthew, as far as their perspectives on the observance of the Law are concerned. As I conclude this chapter, I would like to go a step further by embracing the motto, "Jewish till proven Gentile," to affirm the Jewishness of the very *authors* of these documents. However problematic it may prove to make "positivistic" pronouncements about an author's identity based solely on a reading of their writings (what other evidence can we work with?), there is a certain urgency, in my opinion, to question the longstanding consensus about Luke's Gentile background and to invite a reading of Luke-Acts as well as Matthew that operates under the assumption that their authors were born and raised in a Jewish environment. The classical approach has led many to view the canonical gospel authors, particularly Luke, as ignorant about Judaism. This assumption, which runs deep in the history of research, in turn, governs how the entire literary corpus of Luke-Acts is understood and placed within the mosaics of the burgeoning Jesus movement and early Judaism. Not surprisingly, these readers then find confir-

---

them in the post-70 era. Luke joins in this conversation to say that a solution to these problems for Israel, as a collective entity, must lie in part elsewhere, since, historically, the Jewish people has failed to live up to its special calling.

[18] Cf. 1QS 1:24–26: "[Al]l the initiates into the Covenant are to respond by confessing, 'We have been wicked,[tr]ansgressed and [sin]ned. We have been wicked – we [and] our [f]athers before us – walking [...] of truth and righteousness, [wherefore Go]d has judged us, both we and [our] fathers.'" The confession here is very close to Acts 15:10. Like Luke's Peter, the initiates confess their shortcomings as well as those of their ancestors. Like Luke, the Qumranic charter stipulates a (re)new(ed) covenant that does not renounce Israel's call to observe the Torah (cf. Luke 22:20). Later on 1QS 11:1–2 underscores personal shortcomings and recognizes that justification and perfection are only possible through God's righteousness and loving kindness. The perspective on the Law in Acts 15:10 and 13:38–39 is very Jewish indeed.

mation of the Gentile identity they posit for the author as they go about reading these documents. By exploring the perspectives of the gospel of Matthew and Luke-Acts on various Jewish practices without sharing this set of assumptions, I have become increasingly impressed at the remarkable knowledge and affirmation of the Torah contained in these writings to the point of convincing me that Luke should not be viewed simply as a God-fearer (i.e., a Gentile who sympathized with certain precepts of Jewish teaching) or even a full convert (proselyte) to Judaism. I suggest, therefore, that both Matthew and Luke were born and raised Jewish.[19] They both observed the Torah and were of Jewish parentage. This understanding of Matthew and Luke's Jewishness corresponds to Mimouni's (older) definition of "Jewish Christians":

> Ancient Jewish Christianity is a recent formulation designating Christians of Jewish origin who have recognized the messiahship of Jesus, who have recognized or not recognized the divinity of Christ, but who all continue to observe the Torah.[20]

By reclaiming Luke's Jewishness, I am by no means denying the obvious impact of Greco-Roman thought and culture upon the shaping and molding of his worldview, which can be easily detected throughout his writings, just as I do not deny the same process of acculturation perceptible among

---

[19] Wolter, *Das Lukasevangelium*, 9–10, has come to the same conclusion about Luke's Jewish origins, although he underestimates Luke's affirmation of the Torah and his knowledge of halakah, which would only further undergird his thesis: "Seine ausgezeichnete Kenntnis der Septuaginta, die sogar so weit ging, dass er Septuaginta-Stil imitieren konnte, und die ihn in die Lage versetzte, seine Jesusgeschichte als Fortsetzung der Geschichte Israels zu erzählen, seine Kenntnis der Lehrdifferenzen zwischen Pharisäern und Sadduzäern (Apg 23,6–8), seine präzise Schilderung jüdischer Milieus in Lk 1–2 und vor allem das herausragende Interesse an der Israelfrage, das Lukas allererst veranlasst haben dürfte, die Geschichte der Trennung von Christentum und Judentum als Bestandteil der Geschichte Israels zu schreiben, sprechen dafür, dass der Verfasser der LkEv in einer jüdischen Familie aufgewachsen ist und wie Paulus nicht nur seine primäre, sonder auch seine sekundäre Sozialisation in einem jüdischen Milieu erfahren hat."

[20] My translation of Mimouni, *Le judéo-christianisme ancien*, 15: "Le judéo-christianisme ancien est une formulation récente désignant des chrétiens d'origine juive qui ont reconnu la messianité de Jésus, qui ont reconnu ou qui n'ont pas reconnu la divinité du Christ, mais qui tous continuent à observer la Torah." In a more recent paper delivered at SBL in San Francisco, Mimouni slightly alters his definition of *judaïsme chrétien* to include Gentiles who observe parts or all of the Torah: "Aujourd'hui, au regard des changements de la recherche historique, j'ai tendance à reformuler ma définition de la manière suivante: 'le judaïsme chrétien est une formulation désignant des chrétiens d'origine judéenne et d'origine non judéenne qui ont reconnu la messianité de Jésus, qui ont reconnu ou qui n'ont pas reconnu la divinité du Christ, mais qui tous continuent à observer en totalité ou en partie la Torah'" ("Christian Judaism: A Question Still Open for Discussion" [paper presented at the annual meeting of the SBL, San Francisco, Calif., 20 November 2011], 6).

other Jewish authors who wrote in Greek such as Aristobulus, the author of the *Letter to Aristeas,* Philo, Paul, Matthew, and Josephus. All Jews of the Greco-Roman world were to various degrees "Hellenized." Even the most anti-Gentile Jew such as the author of the book of *Jubilees* could not avoid the inroads of Hellenization.[21] I am mainly concerned with the neglect of seriously studying ancient Jewish sources, with a misunderstanding of ancient Judaism that enables the Gentile Christian profile of Luke to distort the comprehension of central themes within Luke-Acts. Often when interpreters claim a Gentile Christian background for Luke, they then go on to search for elements in his writings that allegedly prove his "Mosaiophobia" and ignorance of halakah. In reality, as the following inquiry hopefully demonstrated, Luke reveals a very precise understanding of Jewish Law, as much as his cousin Matthew, making it unlikely that he stems from a Gentile background. So my aim is not to perpetuate false dichotomies such as "Jewish vs. Greek" or "Palestinian vs. Hellenistic," nor to downplay the significance of appreciating the classical Greco-Roman sources for the understanding of the formation of early "Christianity." Indeed, I find it hermeneutically helpful to imagine Luke as a Jew, much like Philo or Josephus, living in the Greco-Roman Diaspora and contemplating the place and significance of Israel's ancestral customs and traditions for Jew and non-Jew alike. Luke was Hellenized and rather comfortable in writing in Greek but equally knowledgeable about and indebted to Jewish traditions of Palestinian and Diasporan provenance.[22]

By highlighting a different pair of verses, rather than Acts 13:37–38 and 15:10, as a hermeneutical guide through the halakic and theological forests of Luke-Acts, my conclusions about Luke's perspective on the Law prove to be rather different. If we begin with the reasonable assumption that in Luke's eyes Paul did nothing against the ancient customs of the Jewish people as he claims at the very end of Acts in front of a Jewish delegation from Rome (Acts 28:17), are able to detect a concern for the Torah

---

[21] Several scholars have extensively studied the usage of Ionian geography in *Jubilees*' description of world geography. For a summary of the various contributions on the topic by scholars such as Hölscher, Uhden, Schmidt, and VanderKam, see Isaac. W. Oliver and Veronika Bachmann, "The Book of Jubilees: An Annotated Bibliography from the First German Translation of 1850 to the Enoch Seminar of 2007," *Henoch* 31 (2009): 123–64.

[22] A proselyte of that time could probably acquire the knowledge of Judaism Luke showcases in his own writings, but I hold onto my motto of "Jewish till proven Gentile" in my exploration of Christian literature stemming from earlier periods when the parting of the ways between Judaism and Christianity had not fully germinated, especially since the image of Luke as a God-fearer or a proselyte has led many to postulate his ignorance about Jewish halakah. My affirmation of Luke's Jewish background is pronounced more for rhetorical effect to unlock news ways of understanding his writings.

throughout Luke-Acts, and even discover along the way a Torah observant Jew in the very figure of the Lukan Jesus, then we have succeeded, so I argue, to comprehend one of Luke's main contentions, namely, that circumcision and the Mosaic package appended to this covenantal sign enjoy ongoing relevance for the Jewish children of Israel, even those who have become followers of Jesus (Acts 21:21).

Of course, for Luke, the observance of the Law as such does not in itself possess soteriological powers. We would do well, however, to avoid diminishing the incentive for observing the Torah to soteriological compensation – this represents a particular kind of reading (and reduction) of the function and purpose of keeping the Law of Moses. The Torah provides Jews with moral instruction, wisdom and insight, a rich set of symbols, festivals, and rituals to perform, a particular vocation, and much more. Correspondingly, it furnishes the Jesus movement with an ecclesiological identity to be lived out in distinctive ways within its respective Jewish and Gentile branches:

> Luke refers repeatedly to Jews charging Christians with apostasy, with having abandoned the law...Luke rejects the accusations as baseless and false....This is something far more to Luke than a description of something which happened in the church long before his own time, a purely historical matter. The question of the law is a burning problem to him, and he returns to it again and again, for it has to do also with the identity of the church.[23]

In his argumentation on behalf of Luke's observance of Yom Kippur, Stökl points to the relevance of festivals and other rituals as cultural symbols that serve to forge collective identities. He cites Bell who states: "In [fasting and feasting rites] people are particularly concerned to express publicly – to themselves, each other, and sometimes outsiders – their commitment and adherence to basic religious values."[24] For Luke, the rituals and commandments outlined in the Mosaic Torah continue to grant the *ekklesia* a unique identity and heritage that mark her off from the rest of the nations who stand in need of recognizing the lordship of Jesus and sovereignty of the God of Israel. Luke's affirmation of the Law may not be grounded on soteriological foundations but they are built on solid ecclesiological and cultural considerations – no small endorsement for a follower of Jesus living after 70 CE.

Luke the Gentile is dead. Today we can instead discover a remarkable Jewish writer who joined Matthew in affirming the ongoing relevance of the Torah for followers of Jesus living after 70 CE. Both Matthew and Luke-Acts preserve and reflect the rich diversity of early Judaism that

---

[23] Jervell, *The Theology of Acts,* 54.

[24] Catherine Bell, *Ritual: Perspectives and Dimensions* (New York: Oxford University Press, 1997), 120, cited in Daniel Stökl Ben Ezra, "Whose Fast is It? The Ember Day of September and Yom Kippur," in *The Ways That Never Parted,* 261.

persisted after 70: "Matthean Judaism" more akin yet in conflict with Pharisaic Judaism; "Lukan Judaism" closer to the Hellenistic strands of Jewish expression from the Greek speaking Diaspora yet deeply indebted to Jewish traditions emanating from Palestine and the *ekklesia* in Jerusalem. If my thesis is correct, we will have to reconsider the nature and composition of the Jesus movement and early Judaism after 70. When scholars discuss "Jewish Christianity/Christian Judaism," they will no longer be able to focus on the pockets or remnants of sectarian groups such as the so-called Ebionites and Elkasaites, on excavating and recovering the lost "Jewish Christian" gospels such as the "The Gospel according to the Hebrews" or "The Gospel of the Nazareans." They will have to look beyond the primitive stages of the *ekklesia* of Jerusalem, spearheaded by James, the brother of Jesus. They will have to search for the "Jewish Christian" writings standing within the New Testament: the gospel of Matthew, but also the gospel of Luke and the Acts of the Apostles.

Bibliography

Primary Sources and Books of Reference

Aland, Barbara, Kurt Aland, Johannes Karavidopoulos, Carlo M. Martini, and Bruce M. Metzger, eds. *The Greek New Testament*. 4th ed. Stuttgart: Deutsche Bibelgesellschaft, 1993.

Aland, Barbara, Kurt Aland, Johannes Karavidopoulos, Carlo M. Martini, and Bruce M. Metzger, eds. *Novum Testamentum Graece*. 27th ed. Stuttgart: Deutsche Bibelgesellschaft, 2001.

Bauer, Walter, Frederick W. Danker, William F. Arndt, and F. Wilbur Gingrich. *Greek-English Lexicon of the New Testament and Other Early Christian Literature*. 3d ed. Chicago, University of Chicago Press, 2000.

Baumgarten, Joseph M. *Qumran Cave 4. XIII: The Damascus Document (4Q266–273)*. Discoveries in the Judean Desert XVIII. Oxford: Clarendon, 1996.

Berenbaum, Michael, and Fred Skolnick, eds. *Encyclopaedia Judaica*. 2d ed. 22 vols. Detroit: Macmillan Reference USA, 2007.

Bible de Jérusalem. N.p.: Cerf, 1973.

Biblia Hebraica Stuttgartensia. 5th ed. Stuttgart: Deutsche Bibelgesellschaft, 1997.

Bidez, J. *L'empereur Julien. Œuvres complètes*. 2d ed. Vol. 1.2. Paris: Les Belles Lettres, 1960.

Blackman, Philip. *Mishnayot*. 7 vols. London: Mishna, 1951–1956.

Blass, F., and A. DeBrunner. *A Greek Grammar of the New Testament and Other Early Christian Literature*. Translated by Robert W. Funk. Chicago: University of Chicago Press, 1961.

Boccaccini, Gabriele. Online: http://www.4enoch.org.

Borgen, Peder, Kåre Fuglseth, and Roald Skarsten, eds. *The Philo Index: A Complete Greek Word Index to the Writings of Philo of Alexandria*. Grand Rapids, Mich.: Eerdmans, 2000.

Botterweck, G. Johannes, and Helmer Ringgren, eds. *Theological Dictionary of the Old Testament*. Translated by John T. Willis. 15 vols. Grand Rapids, Mich.: Eerdmans, 1974–2006.

Bromiley, W. G., ed. *The International Standard Bible Encyclopedia*. Rev. ed. 4 vols. Grand Rapids, Mich.: Eerdmans, 1979–1988.

Brown, Francis, S. R. Driver, and Charles A. Briggs. *The Brown-Driver-Briggs Hebrew and English Lexicon: With an Appendix Containing Biblical Aramaic*. Oxford: Clarendon, 1907.

Buber, Solomon. *Midrash on Psalms*. Vilna: Romm, 1892.

Buck, Carl Darling. *A Dictionary of Selected Synonyms in the Principal Indo-European Languages*. Chicago: University of Chicago Press, 1949.

Bushell, Michael S., Michael D. Tan, and Glenn L. Weaver. *BibleWorks*. 8th ed. Norfolk: BibleWorks, LLC., 2008. BibleWorks v.8.

Cancik, Hubert, and Helmuth Schneider, eds. *Der neue Pauly: Enzyklopädie der Antike*. Stuttgart: Metzler, 1996–.

Chantraine, Pierre. *Dictionnaire étymologique de la langue grecque*. Klincksieck, 2009.
Charles, Robert H., ed. *The Apocrypha and Pseudepigrapha of the Old Testament, Volume Two: Pseudepigrapha*. Oxford: Clarendon, 1913.
Charlesworth, James H., ed. *The Old Testament Pseudepigrapha*. 2 vols. New York: Doubleday, 1983.
Danby, Herbert. *The Mishnah*. London: Humphrey Milford, 1938.
Delitzsch, Franz. *Sifre Haberit Hahadashah*. Forest Falls, Calif.: The Society for Distributing Hebrew Scriptures, 1966.
Die Bibel: Die Heilige Schrift des Alten und Neuen Bundes. Freiburg im Breisgau: Herder, 2005.
Einheitsübersetzung der Heiligen Schrift. Stuttgart : Katholische Bibelanstalt, 1980.
Elberfelder Bibel revidierte. Wuppertal: R. Brockhaus, 1994.
English Standard Version. Wheaton, Ill.: Crossway Bibles, 2007.
Epstein, Isidore. *Hebrew-English Edition of the Babylonian Talmud*. London: Soncino, 1960.
Etheridge, John Wesley. *The Targums of Onkelos and Jonathan ben Uzziel on the Pentateuch; With the Fragments of the Jerusalem Targum: From the Chaldee*. 2 vols. London: Longman, Green, Longman, and Roberts, 1862–1865.
Evans, Craig A. *The Greek Pseudepigrapha*. N.p.: OakTree Software, 2008. BibleWorks v.8.
Evans, Craig A., Danny Zacharias, Matt Walsh, and Scott Kohler, trans. *The Pseudepigrapha (English)*. N.p.: OakTree Software, 2008. BibleWorks v.8.
Finkelstein, Louis. *Siphre ad Deuteronomium*. Berlin: Jüdischer Kulturbund in Deutschland, 1939.
Freedman, David Noel, ed. *Anchor Bible Dictionary*. 6 vols. New York: Doubleday, 1992.
Freedman, Harry, and Maurice Simon. *Midrash Rabbah*. 10 vols. 3d ed. London: Soncino, 1983.
Friedlander, Gerald. *Pirkê de Rabbi Eliezer*. London: Kegan Paul, Trench, Trubner & Co. Ltd., 1916.
Hastings, James, ed. *Encyclopedia of Religion and Ethics*. 13 vols. New York: Scribner, 1908–1927.
Higger, Michael, and Chaim M. Horowitz. *Pirke Rabbi Eliezer*. New York: Horev, 1944–1948.
Hoffmann, David. *Midrash Tannaim*. 2 vols. Tel Aviv, 1962.
Holman Christian Standard Bible. Nashville, Tenn.: Holman Bible Publishers, 2004.
Horovitz, Haim S. *Siphre de-be Rab: Fasciculus primus – Siphre ad Numeros adjecto Siphre Zutta*. Leipzig: Gustav Fock, 1917.
Horovitz, Haim S., and Israel A. Rabin. *Mechilta deRabbi Ismael: Cum variis lectionibus et adnotationibus*. 2d ed. Jerusalem: Wahrmann, 1970.
Jastrow, Marcus. *A Dictionary of the Targumim, the Talmud Babli and Yerushalmi, and the Midrashic Literature*. 2d ed. Peabody, Mass.: Hendrickson, 2005.
João Ferreira de Almeida, Revista e Atualizada. 2d ed. N.p.: Sociedade Bíblica do Brasil. 1993.
Josephus, Flavius. *The Works of Josephus: Complete and Unabridged*. Translated by William Whiston. Peabody, Mass.: Hendrickson Publishers, 1987.
Kittel, Gerhard, and Gerhard Friedrich, eds. *Theological Dictionary of the New Testament*. Translated by Geoffrey W. Bromiley. 10 vols. Grand Rapids, Mich.: Eerdmans, 1964–1976.

Kluser, Theodor, et al., eds. *Reallexikon für Antike und Christentum*. Stuttgart: Anton Hiersemann, 1950–.

Koehler, Ludwig, Walter Baumgartner, and Johann Jakob Stamm. *The Hebrew and Aramaic Lexicon of the Old Testament*. Translated by M. E. J. Richardson. 5 vols. Leiden: Brill, 1994–2000.

La Biblia de nuestro pueblo: Biblia del peregrino. Bilbao: Ediciones Mensajero, 2007.

La Bible en Français courant, édition révisée. N.p.: Société biblique française, 1997.

La Nuova Diodati. Brindisi: La Buona Novella, 1991.

La Sacra Bibbia Nuova Riveduta. 3d ed. N.p.: Società biblica di Ginevra, 1996.

La Santa Biblia Reina-Valera Actualizada. N.p.: Casa Bautista de Publicaciones, 1989.

La Sainte Bible: Traduite des textes originaux hébreu et grec par Louis Segond. Nouvelle édition de Geneva. N.p.: Société Biblique de Geneva, 1979.

Levy, Jacob. *Wörterbuch über die Talmudim und Midraschim*. 4 vols. Berlin und Wien: Benjamin Harz, 1924.

Liddell, Henry George, Robert Scott, Henry Stuart Jones, and Roderick McKenzie. *A Greek-English Lexicon: With a Revised Supplement*. 9th ed. Oxford: Clarendon, 1996.

Lieberman, Saul. *The Tosefta*. 5 vols. New York: Jewish Theological Seminary, 1955–1988.

Lightfoot, J. B. *The Apostolic Fathers*. Edited by J. R. Harmer. 2d ed. London: Macmillan, 1898.

Louw, Johannes E., and Eugene A. Nida. *Greek-English Lexicon of the New Testament: Based on Semantic Domains*. 2 vols. 2d ed. New York: United Bible Societies, 1989.

Lust, Johan, Erik Eynikel, and Katrin Hauspie. *Greek-English Lexicon of the Septuagint*. Rev. ed. Stuttgart: Deutsche Bibelgesellschaft, 2003.

Luther, Martin. *Die gantze Heilige Schrifft Deudsch. Wittenberg 1545*. 2 vols. Darmstadt: Wissenschaftliche Buchgesellschaft, 1972.

Mandelbaum, Bernard. *Pesikta De-Rav Kahana*. New York: Jewish Theological Seminary of America, 1962.

Martínez, Florentino García, and Eibert J. C. Tigchelaar. *The Dead Sea Scrolls Study Edition*. 2 vols. Brill: Leiden, 1997–1998.

Metzger, Bruce. *A Textual Commentary on the Greek New Testament*. London: United Bible Societies, 1975.

Miller, Robert J., ed. *The Complete Gospels*. Rev. and enl. ed. San Francisco, Calif.: HarperSanFrancisco, 1994.

Muenchener Neues Testament Version. Düsseldorf: Patmos, 1998.

Neusner, Jacob. *The Tosefta Translated from the Hebrew*. 6 vols. New York: Ktav, 1977–1986.

–. *The Talmud of the Land of Israel: A Preliminary Translation and Explanation*. 35 vols. Chicago Studies in the History of Judaism. Chicago: University of Chicago Press, 1982–1994.

–. *Sifre to Deuteronomy: An Analytical Translation*. 2 vols. Brown Judaic Studies 98, 101. Atlanta: Scholars, 1987.

–. *Sifra: An Analytical Translation*. Brown Judaic Studies 138–40. Atlanta: Scholars, 1988.

New International Reader's Version. Colorado Springs, Colo.: International Bible Society, 1998.

New Revised Standard Version Bible. New York: Division of Christian Education of the National Council of the Churches of Christ in the United States of America, 1989.

Nuovissima Versione della Bibbia, San Paolo Edizione (IEP). Roma: San Paolo Edizione, 1996.

Parry, Donald W., and Emanuel Tov, eds. *The Dead Sea Scrolls Reader*. 6 vols. Leiden: Brill, 2004–2005.
Philo. *The Works of Philo: New Updated Edition*. Translated by C. D. Yonge. N.p.: Hendrickson, 1993.
Qimron, Elisha, and John Strugnell, eds. *Discoveries in the Judaean Desert X, Qumran Cave 4, V, Miqsat Ma'ase Ha-Torah*. Oxford: Clarendon Press, 1994.
Rahlfs, Alfred. *Septuaginta: Id est Vetus Testamentum iuxta LXX interpretes edidit Alfred Rahlfs*. Stuttgart: Deutsche Bibelgesellschaft, 1935.
Rehm, Bernard. *Die Pseudoklementinen II: Rekognitionen*. Die Griechischen christlichen Schriftsteller der ersten Jahrhunderte. Berlin: Akademie, 1965.
–. *Die Pseudoklementinen I: Homilien*. 3d ed. Die Griechischen christlichen Schriftsteller der ersten Jahrhunderte. Berlin: Akademie, 1992.
Roberts, Alexander, and James Donaldson, eds. *Apostolic Fathers English Translation from the Ante-Nicene Fathers*. Buffalo, N.Y.: The Christian Literature Publishing Co., 1896.
Roberts, Alexander, James Donaldson, Philip Schaff, and Henry Wace, eds. *The Ante-Nicene, Nicene, and Post-Nicene Fathers*. 39 vols. New York: The Christian Literature Publishing Co., 1885.
Robertson, A. T. *A Grammar of the Greek New Testament in Light of Historical Research*. Leicester: Hodder & Stoughton, 1919.
Salkinson-Ginsburg Hebrew New Testament (1886), 1999 Revision. Hitchin, England: The Society for Distributing Hebrew Scriptures, 1999.
Schechter, Salomon. *Aboth de Rabbi Nathan: Edited from Manuscripts with an Introduction, Notes and Appendices*. Vienna: Knöpflmacher, 1887. Repr., Hildesheim, 1979.
Schlachter, Franz Eugen. *Die Bibel*. Geneva: Genfer Bibelgesellschaft, 2002.
Schürer, Emil, Geza Vermes, Fergus Millar, and Matthew Black. *The History of the Jewish People in the Age of Jesus Christ*. 3 vols. Rev. English ed. Edinburgh: T&T Clark, 1973–1987.
Smith, William, ed. *Dictionary of Greek and Roman Biography and Mythology*. 3 vols. Boston: Charles C. Little and James Brown, 1849.
Spicq, Ceslas. *Theological Lexicon of the New Testament*. Translated and edited by J. D. Ernest. 3 vols. Peabody, Mass.: Hendrickson, 1994.
Stern, Menahem. *Greek and Latin Authors on Jews and Judaism*. 3 vols. Jerusalem: The Israel Academy of Sciences and Humanities, 1984.
Tanakh, A New Translation of the Holy Scriptures According to the Traditional Hebrew Text. Philadelphia: Jewish Publication Society, 1985.
Targumim (Aramaic Old Testament) (Comprehensive Aramaic Lexicon). N.p.: Hebrew Union College. BibleWorks v.8.
Targum Neofiti (Aramaic Old Testament) (Comprehensive Aramaic Lexicon). N.p.: Hebrew Union College. BibleWorks v.8.
Targum PseudoJonathan (Aramaic Old Testament) (Comprehensive Aramaic Lexicon). N.p.: Hebrew Union College. BibleWorks v.8.
Thayer, Joseph. *A Greek-English Lexicon of the New Testament (Abridged and Revised Thayer Lexicon)*. Ontario, Canada: Online Bible Foundation, 1997.
The English Bible in Basic English 1949/1964. Cambridge: Cambridge University Press, 1965.
The Holy Bible: New International Version. Colorado Springs, Colo.: International Bible Society, 1984.
The Interpreter's Dictionary of the Bible. 5 vols. New York: Abingdon, 1962.

The Jewish Encyclopedia: A Descriptive Record of the History, Religion, Literature, and Customs of the Jewish People from the Earliest Times. 12 vols. New York: Ktav, 1964.

The New American Bible with Revised New Testament and Revised Psalms, and with Roman Catholic Deutero-Canon. Washington, D.C.: Confraternity of Christian Doctrine, 1991.

The New American Standard Bible. La Habra, Calif.: The Lockman Foundation, 1988.

The New English Translation Bible. N.p.: Biblical Studies Press, LLC., 1996.

The New International Reader's Version. Grand Rapids, Mich.: Zondervan, 1996.

The New Interpreter's Dictionary of the Bible. 5 vols. Nashville, Tenn.: Abingdon, 2006–2009.

The New King James Version. Nashville, Tenn.: T. Nelson, 1982.

The New Living Translation. Wheaton, Ill.: Tyndale, 2004.

The Peshitta. N.p.: British and Foreign Bible Society, 1905.

Today's New International Version. Grand Rapids, Mich.: Zondervan, 2005.

Traduction Œcuménique de la Bible. 11th ed. Paris: Cerf, 2010.

Vacant, A., E. Mangenot, and Emile Amann, eds. *Dictionnaire de théologie catholique.* 15 vols. Paris: Letouzey et Ané, 1899–1950.

VanderKam, James C. *The Book of Jubilees.* 2 vols. Corpus scriptorum christianorum orientalium 510–511. Scriptores Aethiopici 87–88. Leuven: Peeters, 1989.

Vermes, Geza. *The Dead Sea Scrolls in English.* 5th ed. London: Penguin, 1997.

Vigouroux, F., ed. *Dictionnaire de la Bible.* 5 vols. Paris: Letouzey et Ané, 1895–1912.

Wansbrough, Henry, ed. *New Jerusalem Bible.* New York: Doubleday, 1985.

Weiss, Isaac H. *Sifra de-ve Rav hu sefer torat kohanim.* Vienna: Shlosberg, 1862.

Windfuhr, Walter. *Die Tosefta: Band 6, Seder Toharot. 8. Heft, Ahilot/Negaim.* Edited by Gerhard Kittel and Karl H. Rengstorf. Stuttgart: W. Kohlhammer, 1956.

Wise, Michael O., Martin G. Abegg Jr., and Edward M. Cook. *The Dead Sea Scrolls: A New Translation.* San Francisco: HarperSanFrancisco, 2005.

Yalqut Shimoni. Warsaw, 1878.

Zlotnick, Dov. *The Tractate "Mourning."* New Haven, Conn.: Yale University Press, 1966.

Zuckermandel, Moses Samuel. *Tosefta.* 2d ed. Jerusalem: Wahrmann, 1970.

Secondary Sources

Aescoly, Aaron Zeev. *Sefer ha-Falashim: Yehude Habash, Tarbutam u-Mesorotehem.* Jerusalem: Reuben Mass, 1943.

Aichinger, Hermann. "Quellenkritische Untersuchung der Perikope vom Ährenraufen am Sabbat. Mk 2,23–28 par Mt 12, 1–8 par Lk 6, 1–5." Pages 111–53 in *Jesus in der Verkündigung der Kirche.* Edited by Albert Fuchs. Studien zur Umwelt des Neuen Testaments A1. Linz: A. Fuchs, 1976.

Albeck, Chanoch. *Shisha Sidre Mishnah.* 6 vols. Jerusalem: Bialik Institute, 1952–1959.

Alföldi-Rosenbaum, Elisabeth. *Das Kochbuch der Römer. Rezepte aus der "Kochkunst" des Apicius, eingeleitet, übersetzt und erläutert.* 10th ed. Zurich/Munich: Artemis, 1993.

Alkier, Stefan, and Jürgen Zangenberg, eds. *Zeichen aus Text und Stein: Studien auf dem Weg zu einer Archäologie des Neuen Testaments.* Texte und Arbeiten zum neutestamentlichen Zeitalter 42. Tübingen: Francke, 2003.

Allen, Willoughby C. *The Gospel according to S. Matthew*. 3d ed. International Critical Commentary. Edinburgh: T&T Clark, 1977.

Alon, Gedalyahu. *Jews, Judaism and the Classical World: Studies in Jewish History in the Times of the Second Temple and Talmud*. Translated by Israel Abrahams. Jerusalem: Magnes, 1977.

Anderson, Hugh. "Broadening Horizons: The Rejection at Nazareth Pericope of Luke 4.16–30 in Light of Recent Critical Trends." *Interpretation* 18 (1964): 259–75.

Avemarie, Friedrich. "Jesus and Purity." Pages 255–79 in *The New Testament and Rabbinic Literature*. Edited by Reimund Bieringer, Florentino García Martínez, Didier Pollefeyt, and Peter J. Tomson. Supplements to the Journal for the Study of Judaism 136. Leiden: Brill, 2010.

–. "Die jüdischer Wurzeln des Aposteldekrets: Lösbare und ungelöste Probleme." Pages 5–32 in *Aposteldekret und antikes Vereinswesen: Gemeinschaft und ihre Ordnung*. Edited by Markus Öhler. Wissenschaftliche Untersuchungen zum Neuen Testament 280. Tübingen: Mohr Siebeck, 2011.

Aviram, J., G. Foerster, Ehud Netzer, and Guy Stiebel, eds. *Masada VIII: The Yigael Yadin Excavations 1963–1965*. Jerusalem: Israel Exploration Society, 2007.

Bacchiocchi, Samuele. *From Sabbath to Sunday: A Historical Investigation of the Rise of Sunday Observance in Early Christianity*. Rome: Pontifical Gregorian University, 1977.

–. *Divine Rest for Human Restlessness*. Rome: Pontifical Gregorian University Press, 1980.

Back, Sven-Olav. *Jesus of Nazareth and the Sabbath Commandment*. Åbo: Åbo Akademi University Press, 1995.

Bammel, Ernst. "The Cambridge Pericope: The Addition to Luke 6:4 in Codex Bezae." *New Testament Studies* 32 (1986): 404–26.

Banks, Robert. *Jesus and the Law in the Synoptic Tradition*. Society for New Testament Studies Monograph Series 28. Cambridge: Cambridge University Press, 1975.

Barnes, Timothy David. "The Date of Ignatius." *Expository Times* 120 (2008): 119–30.

Barrett, C. K. "The Apostolic Decree of Acts 15.29." *Australian Biblical Review* 35 (1987): 50–59.

–. *The Acts of the Apostles*. International Critical Commentary. 2 vols. Edinburgh: T&T Clark, 1994.

Barth, Gerhard. "Matthew's Understanding of the Law." Pages 58–164 in *Tradition and Interpretation in Matthew*. Edited by Günther Bornkamm, Gerhard Barth, and Heinz Joachim Held. Translated by Percy Scott. Philadelphia: Westminster Press, 1963.

Basser, Herbert W. *The Mind behind the Gospels: A Commentary to Matthew 1–14*. Boston: Academic Studies Press, 2009.

Bauckham. Richard. "The Lord's Day." Pages 221–50 in *From Sabbath to Lord's Day: A Biblical, Historical, and Theological Investigation*. Edited by Daniel A. Carson. Grand Rapids, Mich.: Zondervan, 1982.

–. *Jude and the Relatives of Jesus in the Early Church*. Edinburgh: T&T Clark, 1990.

–. ed. Vol. 4 of *The Book of Acts in Its First Century Setting*. Edited by Bruce W. Winter. Grand Rapids, Mich.: Eerdmans, 1995.

Bauernfeind, Otto. *Die Apostelgeschichte*. Theologischer Handkommentar zum Neuen Testament 5. Leipzig: A. Deichert, 1939.

Baumgarten, Albert I. "*Korban* and the Pharisaic *Paradosis*." *The Journal of the Ancient Near Eastern Society* 16–17 (1984–1985): 5–17.

–. "The Pharisaic Paradosis." *Harvard Theological Review* 80 (1987): 63–77.

–. "Graeco-Roman Associations and Jewish Sects." Pages 93–111 in *Jews in a Graeco-Roman World*. Edited by Martin Goodman. Oxford: Clarendon, 1998.

Baumgarten, Albert I., Hanan Eshel ז"ל, Ranon Katzoff, and Shani Tzoref, eds. *Halakhah in Light of Epigraphy*. Journal of Ancient Judaism Supplements 3. Göttingen: Vandenhoeck & Ruprecht, 2011.

Baumgarten, Joseph M. "Purification after Childbirth and the Sacred Garden in 4Q265 and Jubilees." Pages 3–10 in *New Qumran Texts and Studies: Proceedings of the First Meeting of the International Organization for Qumran Studies, Paris 1992*. Edited by George J. Brooke with Florentino García-Martínez. Studies on the Texts of the Desert of Judah 15. Leiden: Brill, 1994.

–. "The Religious Law of the Qumran Community." *Qadmoniot* 30 (1997): 97–100. [Hebrew]

Baur, Ferdinand Christian. *The Church History of the First Three Centuries*. Translated by Allan Menzies. 2 vols. London: Williams and Norgate, 1878.

Beare, Francis Wright. "The Sabbath Was Made for Man?" *Journal of Biblical Literature* 79 (1960): 130–36.

–. *The Gospel according to Matthew*. Oxford: Basil Blackwell, 1981.

Beattie, Derek Robert George, and Martin McNamara, eds. The *Aramaic Bible: Targums in Their Historical Context*. Journal for the Study of the Old Testament: Supplement Series 165. Sheffield: Sheffield Academic Press, 1994.

Becker, Adam H., and Annette Yoshiko Reed, eds. *The Ways That Never Parted*. Minneapolis: Fortress, 2007.

Becker, Michael. *Wunder und Wundertäter im frührabbinischen Judentum: Studien zum Phänomen und seiner Überlieferung im Horizont von Magie und Dämonismus*. Wissenschaftliche Untersuchungen zum Neuen Testament 2.144. Tübingen: Mohr Siebeck, 2002.

Bell, Catherine. *Ritual: Perspectives and Dimensions*. New York: Oxford University Press, 1997.

Ben David, Arye. *Talmudische Ökonomie: Die Wirtschaft des jüdischen Palästina zur Zeit der Mischna und des Talmud Vol. 1*. Hildesheim: Olms, 1974.

Benoît, Pierre. *Exégèse et théologie III*. Cogitatio fidei 30. Paris: Cerf, 1968.

Berger, Klaus. "Jesus als Pharisäer und frühe Christen als Pharisäer." *Novum Testamentum* 30 (1988): 231–62.

Bergmann, J. "Zur Geschichte religiöser Bräuche." *Monatsschrift für Geschichte und Wissenschaft des Judentums* 5/6 (1927): 161–71.

Betz, H. D. *The Sermon on the Mount: A Commentary on the Sermon on the Mount, Including the Sermon on the Plain (Matthew 5:3–7:27 and Luke 6:20–49)*. Hermeneia. Minneapolis: Fortress, 1995.

Bieringer, Reimund, Florentino García Martínez, Didier Pollefeyt, and Peter J. Tomson, eds. *The New Testament and Rabbinic Literature*. Supplements to the Journal for the Study of Judaism 136. Leiden: Brill, 2010.

Birnbaum, Ellen. *The Place of Judaism in Philo's Thought: Israel, Jews, and Proselytes*. Brown Judaic Studies 290. Atlanta: Scholars, 1996.

Black, Matthew. *An Aramaic Approach to the Gospels and Acts*. 3d ed. Oxford: Clarendon, 1967.

Blaschke, Andreas. *Beschneidung: Zeugnisse der Bibel und verwandter Texte*. Texte und Arbeiten zum neutestamentlichen Zeitalter 28. Tübingen: Francke, 1998.

Blomberg, Craig L. *Matthew*. New American Commentary. Nashville, Tenn.: Broadman, 1992.

Boccaccini, Gabriele. *Middle Judaism: Jewish Thought, 300 B.C.E. to 200 C.E.* Minneapolis: Fortress, 1991.

–. "Targum Neofiti as a Proto-Rabbinic Document: A Systemic Analysis." Pages 260–69 in *The Aramaic Bible: Targums in Their Historical Context*. Edited by Derek Robert, George Beattie, and Martin McNamara. Journal for the Study of the Old Testament: Supplement Series 165. Sheffield: Sheffield Academic Press, 1994.

–. *Beyond the Essene Hypothesis: The Parting of the Ways between Qumran and Enochic Judaism.* Grand Rapids, Mich.: Eerdmans, 1998.

–. *The Roots of Rabbinic Judaism.* Grand Rapids, Mich.: Eerdmans, 2002.

–. ed. *Enoch the Messiah Son of Man: Revisiting the Book of Parables.* Grand Rapids, Mich.: Eerdmans, 2007.

Bock, Darrell L. *Luke.* 2 vols. Baker Exegetical Commentary on the New Testament 3. Grand Rapids, Mich.: Baker Books, 1994.

Bockmuehl, Markus N. A. Review of Jürgen Wehnert, *Die Reinheit des "christlichen Gottesvolkes" aus Juden und Heiden. Journal of Theological Studies* 50 (1999): 260–68.

–. *Jewish Law in Gentile Churches: Halakhah and the Beginning of Christian Public Ethics.* Edinburgh: T&T Clark, 2000.

Bohak, Gideon. "Jewish Exorcism before and after the Destruction of the Second Temple." Pages 277–300 in *Was 70 CE a Watershed in Jewish History? On Jews and Judaism before and after the Destruction of the Second Temple.* Edited by Daniel R. Schwartz and Zeev Weiss. Ancient Judaism and Early Christianity 78. Leiden: Brill, 2012.

Bóid, Iain Ruairidh Mac Mhanainn. *Principles of Samaritan Halachah.* Studies in Judaism in Late Antiquity 38. Leiden: Brill, 1989.

Boman, Thorleif. "Das textkritische Problem des sogenannten Aposteldekrets." *Novum Testamentum* 7 (1964): 26–36.

Bonnard, Pierre. *L'évangile selon saint Matthieu.* Commentaire du Nouveau Testament 1. Neuchâtel: Delachaux & Niestlé, 1963.

Booth, Roger P. *Jesus and the Laws of Purity: Tradition History and Legal History.* Journal for the Study of the New Testament: Supplement Series 13. Sheffield: University of Sheffield, 1986.

Bornkamm, Günther. "End-Expectation and Church in Matthew." Pages 15–51 in *Tradition and Interpretation in Matthew*. Edited by Günther Bornkamm, Gerhard Barth, and Heinz Joachim Held. Translated by Percy Scott. Philadelphia: Westminster Press, 1963.

–. "The Authority to 'Bind' and 'Loose' in the Church in Matthew's Gospel: The Problem of Sources in Matthew's Gospel." Pages 37–50 in vol. 1 of *Jesus and Man's Hope*. Edited by Donald G. Miller. 2 vols. Pittsburgh, Pa.: Pittsburgh Theological Seminary, 1970–1971.

Bornkamm, Günther, Gerhard Barth, and Heinz Joachim Held, eds. *Tradition and Interpretation in Matthew.* Translated by Percy Scott. Philadelphia, Pa.: Westminster Press, 1963.

Bottini, G. Claudio, Leah Di Segni, and L. Daniel Chrupcala, eds. *One Land – Many Cultures: Archaeological Studies in Honour of Stanislao Loffreda.* Jerusalem: Franciscan, 2003.

Bourgel, Jonathan. "'On Both Sides of the Borderline': The Portrayal of the Samaritans in the Third Gospel." Paper Presented at the Eighth Congress of the Société d'Études Samaritaines. Erfurt, Germany, July 15–20, 2012.

Bovon, François. *L'Évangile selon saint Luc*. 4 vols. Commentaire du Nouveau Testament. Deuxième série. Geneva: Labor et Fides, 1991–2009.

–. "*Fragment Oxyrhynchus* 840, Fragment of a Lost Gospel, Witness of an Early Christian Controversy over Purity." *Journal of Biblical Literature* 119 (2000): 705–28.

–. *Luke 1*. Hermeneia; Minneapolis: Fortress, 2002.

–. *Luke the Theologian: Fifty-five Years of Research (1950-2005)*. 2d ed. Waco, Tex.: Baylor University Press, 2006.

Boyarin, Daniel. *A Radical Jew: Paul and the Politics of Identity*. Berkeley, Calif.: University of California Press, 1994.

–. "'After the Sabbath' (Matt 28:1) – Once More into the Crux." *Journal of Theological Studies* 52 (2001): 678–88.

–. *Borderlines: The Partition of Judaeo-Christianity*. Philadelphia: University of Pennsylvania Press, 2004.

–. "Rethinking *Jewish Christianity*: An Argument for Dismantling a Dubious Category (To Which is Appended a Correction of My Borderlines)." *Jewish Quarterly Review* 99 (2009): 7–36.

–. *The Jewish Gospels: The Story of the Jewish Christ*. New York: New Press, 2012.

Brawley, Robert L. *Luke-Acts and the Jews: Conflict, Apology, and Conciliation*. Society of Biblical Literature Monograph Series 33. Atlanta: Scholars, 1987.

Brocke, Edna, and Hans-Joachim Barkenings, eds. *"Wer Tora vermehrt, mehrt Leben." Festgabe für Heinz Kremers zum 60. Geburtstag*. Neukirchen-Vluyn: Neukirchener, 1986.

Brooke, George J. "Luke-Acts and the Qumran Scrolls: The Case of MMT." Pages 72–90 in *Luke's Literary Achievement: Collected Essays*. Edited by Christopher M. Tuckett. Journal for the Study of the New Testament Supplement Series 116. Sheffield: Sheffield Academic Press, 1995.

–. "Acts and the Discourses of the Scrolls from Qumran." Paper presented at the annual meeting of SBL. Chicago, Ill., 18 Nov, 2012.

Brooke, George J., with Florentino García-Martínez, eds. *New Qumran Texts and Studies: Proceedings of the First Meeting of the International Organization for Qumran Studies, Paris 1992*. Studies on the Texts of the Desert of Judah 15. Leiden: Brill, 1994.

Brown, Raymond. *The Gospel according to John*. 2 vols. Anchor Bible 29–29A. Garden City: Doubleday, 1966–1970.

–. "Not Jewish Christianity and Gentile Christianity but Types of Jewish/Gentile Christianity." *Catholic Biblical Quarterly* 45 (1983): 74–79.

–. *The Birth of the Messiah: A Commentary on the Infancy Narratives in the Gospels of Matthew and Luke*. Anchor Bible Reference Library. New York: Doubleday, 1993.

Bruce, Frederick F. *Commentary on the Book of Acts*. New International Commentary on the New Testament. Grand Rapids, Mich.: Eerdmans, 1968.

Bryan, Cristopher. "A Further Look at Acts 16:1–3." *Journal of Biblical Literature* 107 (1988): 292–94.

Bultmann, Rudolf. *The History of the Synoptic Tradition*. Translated by John Marsh. Oxford: Basil Blackwell, 1963.

Burkert, Walter. *Greek Religion*. Translated by John Raffan. Cambridge, Mass.: Harvard University Press, 1985.

Busse, Ulrich. *Die Wunder des Propheten Jesus: Die Rezeption, Komposition und Interpretation der Wundertradition im Evangelium des Lukas*. Forschung zur Bibel 24. Stuttgart: Katholisches Bibelwerk, 1977.

–. *Das Nazareth-Manifest: Eine Einführung in das lukanische Jesusbild nach Lk 4, 16–30*. Stuttgarter Bibelstudien 91. Stuttgart: Katholisches Bibelwerk, 1978.

Cadbury, Henry J. "Some Lukan Expressions of Time (Lexical Notes on Luke-Acts VII)." *Journal of Biblical Literature* 82 (1963): 272–78.

Caird, G. B. *The Gospel of St. Luke*. Pelican New Testament Commentaries. Baltimore: Penguin Books, 1963.

Carmona, Antonio Rodríguez. *Evangelio de Mateo*. Bilbao: Desclée De Brouwer, 2006.

Carson, Daniel A., ed. *From Sabbath to Lord's Day: A Biblical, Historical and Theological Investigation*. Grand Rapids, Mich.: Zondervan, 1982.

–. "Jesus and the Sabbath in the Four Gospels." Pages 57–97 in *From Sabbath to Lord's Day: A Biblical, Historical and Theological Investigation*. Edited by Daniel A. Carson. Grand Rapids, Mich.: Zondervan, 1982.

Carter, Warren. "Matthew's Gospel: Jewish Christianity, Christian Judaism, or Neither?" Pages 155–80 in *Jewish Christianity Reconsidered: Rethinking Ancient Groups and Texts*. Edited by Matt Jackson-McCabe. Minneapolis: Fortress, 2007.

Casey, M. "Culture and Historicity: The Plucking of the Grain (Mark 2:23–28)." *New Testament Studies* 34 (1988):1–23.

Charlesworth, James H. *The Historical Jesus*. Nashville, Tenn.: Abingdon, 2008.

Chilton, Bruce. "Announcement in Nazareth: An Analysis of Luke 4.16–21." Pages 147–72 in *Gospel Perspectives: Studies of History and Tradition in the Four Gospels. Vol. 2*. Edited by R. T. France and David Wenham. Sheffield: JSOT, 1981.

Clark, Kenneth Willis. "The Gentile Bias in Matthew." *Journal of Biblical Literature* 66 (1947): 165–72.

Cohen, Shaye J. D. "Was Timothy Jewish? (Acts 16:1–3): Patristic Exegesis, Rabbinical Law, and Matrilineal Descent." *Journal of Biblical Literature* 105 (1986): 251–68.

–. *The Beginnings of Jewishness: Boundaries, Varieties, Uncertainties*. Berkeley, Calif.: University of California Press, 1999.

–. "Did Ancient Jews Missionize?" *Bible Review* 19.4 (2003).

–. *Why Aren't Jewish Women Circumcised?* Berkeley, Calif.: University of California Press, 2005.

Cohen, Yehezkel. "Attitude to the Gentile in the Halacha and in Reality in the Tannaitic Period." Ph.D. diss., Hebrew University, Jerusalem, 1975. [Hebrew]

Cohn-Sherbok, Dan. "An Analysis of Jesus' Arguments concerning the Plucking of Grain on the Sabbath." *Journal for the Study of the New Testament* 2 (1979): 31–41.

Collins, Adela Yarbro. *Mark*. Hermeneia. Minneapolis: Fortress, 2007.

Collins, John J. *The Dead Sea Scrolls: A Biography*. Princeton, N.J.: Princeton University Press, 2013.

Colpe, Carsten. *Das Siegel der Propheten: historische Beziehungen zwischen Judentum, Judenchristentum, Heidentum und frühem Islam*. Arbeiten zur neutestamentliche Theologie und Zeitgeschichte 3. Berlin: Institut Kirche und Judentum, 1990.

Conzelmann, Hans. *The Theology of St. Luke*. Translated by Geoffrey Buswell. New York: Harper & Row, 1961.

–. *Acts of the Apostles*. Hermeneia. Translated by James Limburg, A. Thomas Kraabel, and Donald H. Juel. Philadelphia: Fortress, 1987.

Crossan, John Dominic. *Who Killed Jesus? Exposing the Roots of Anti-Semitism in the Gospel Story of the Death of Jesus*. San Francisco: HarperSanFrancisco, 1995.

Cuvillier, Élian. "Torah Observance and Radicalization in the First Gospel. Matthew and First-Century Judaism: A Contribution to the Debate." *New Testament Studies* 55 (2009): 144–59.

Daniélou, Jean. *Judéo-Christianisme: Recherches historiques et théologiques offertes en hommage au Cardinal Jean Daniélou.* Recherches de science religieuse. Paris: Éditions Beauchesne, 1972.
–. *Théologie du judéo-christianisme.* 2d ed. Tournai: Desclée, 1991.
Dar, Shimon. "Food and Archaeology in Romano-Byzantine Palestine." Pages 326–35 in *Food in Antiquity.* Edited by John Wilkins, F. D. Harvey, and Michael J. Dobson. Exeter: University of Exeter Press, 1995.
Davies, W. D., and Dale C. Allison. *The Gospel according to Saint Matthew.* 3 vols. International Critical Commentary. London: T&T Clark, 1988–1997.
Deines, Roland. *Jüdische Steingefäße und pharisäische Frömmigkeit: Ein archäologisch-historischer Beitrag zum Verständnis von Joh 2,6 und der jüdischen Reinheitshalacha zur Zeit Jesu.* Wissenschaftliche Untersuchungen zum Neuen Testament 2.52. Tübingen: Mohr Siebeck, 1993.
–. "Das Aposteldekret – Halacha für Heidenchristen oder christliche Rücksichtnahme auf jüdische Tabus?" Pages 323–98 in *Jewish Identity in the Greco-Roman World.* Ancient Judaism and Early Christianity 71. Edited by Jörg Frey, Daniel R. Schwartz, and Stepanie Gripentrog. Leiden: Brill, 2007.
–. "Not the Law but the Messiah." Pages 53–84 in *Built upon the Rock: Studies in the Gospel of Matthew.* Edited by Daniel M. Gurtner and John Nolland. Grand Rapids, Mich.: Eerdmans, 2008.
Delebecque, Édouard. "Les épis 'égrenés' dans les synoptiques." *Revue des études grecques* 88 (1975): 133–42.
Delobel, Joël. "Luke 6,5 in Codex Bezae: The Man Who Worked on Sabbath.'" Pages 453–77 in *À cause de l'évangile. Études sur les synoptiques et les Actes offertes au P. Jacques Dupont, O.S.B., à l'occasion de son 70e anniversaire.* Lection divina 23. Paris: Cerf, 1985.
Denaux, Adelbert. "L'hypocrisie des Pharisiens et le dessein de Dieu. Analyse de Lc. XIII, 31–33." Pages 155–95 and 316–21 in *L'évangile de Luc/The Gospel of Luke.* Edited by F. Neirynck. 2d ed. Bibliotheca ephemeridum theologicarum lovaniensium 32. Leuven: Leuven University Press, 1989.
Denaux, Adelbert, Reimund Bieringer, Gilbert van Belle, and Jozef Verheyden, eds. *Luke and His Readers: Festschrift A. Denaux.* Bibliotheca ephemeridum theologicarum lovaniensium 182. Leuven: Leuven University Press, 2005.
Derrett, J. Duncan M. "Luke 6:5D Reexamined." *Novum Testamentum* 37 (1995): 232–48.
–. *Studies in the New Testament Vol I: Glimpses of the Legal and Social Presuppositions of the Author.* Leiden: Brill, 1977.
Detienne, Marcel and Jean-Pierre Vernant, eds. *The Cuisine of Sacrifice among the Greeks.* Translated by Paula Wissing. Chicago: The University of Chicago Press, 1989.
Deutsch, Celia. *Hidden Wisdom and the Easy Yoke: Wisdom, Torah, and Discipleship in Matthew 11.25–30.* Journal for the Study of the New Testament: Supplement Series 18. Sheffield: JSOT, 1987.
Dibelius, Martin. *Studies in the Acts of the Apostles.* Translated by Mary Ling. London: SCM Press, 1956.
Dimant, Devorah, and Uriel Rappaport, eds. *The Dead Sea Scrolls: Forty Years of Research.* Studies on the Texts of the Desert of Judah 10. Leiden: Brill, 1992.
Disraeli, Isaac. *The Genius of Judaism.* London: Edward Moxon, 1833.
Dobbeler, Axel von. "Die Restitution Israels und die Bekehrung der Heiden: Das Verhältnis von Mt 10,5b.6 und Mt 28,18–20 unter dem Aspekt der Komplementarität:

Erwägungen zum Standort des Matthäusevangeliums." *Zeitschrift für die neutestamentliche Wissenschaft und die Kunde der älteren Kirche* 91.1–2 (2000): 18–44.

Doering, Lutz. *Schabbat: Sabbathhalacha und –praxis im antiken Judentum und Urchristentum*. Texte und Studien zum antiken Judentum 78. Tübingen: Mohr Siebeck, 1999.

–."Much Ado about Nothing? Jesus' Sabbath Healings and their Halakhic Implications Revisited." Pages 217–41 in *Judaistik und neutestamentliche Wissenschaft*. Edited by Lutz Doering, Hans-Günther Waubke, and Florian Wilk. Forschungen zur Religion und Literatur des Alten und Neuen Testaments 226. Göttingen: Vandenhoeck & Ruprecht, 2008.

–. "Sabbath Laws in the New Testament." Pages 207–54 in *The New Testament and Rabbinic Literature*. Edited by Reimund Bieringer, Florentino García Martínez, Didier Pollefeyt, and Peter J. Tomson. Supplements to the Journal for the Study of Judaism 136. Leiden: Brill, 2010.

Doering, Lutz, and Annette Steudel, eds. *Fundamenta Judaica: Studien zum antiken Judentum und zum Neuen Testament*. Studien zur Umwelt des Neuen Testaments 25. Göttingen: Vandenhoeck & Ruprecht. 2001.

Doering, Lutz, Hans-Günther Waubke, and Florian Wilk., eds. *Judaistik und neutestamentliche Wissenschaft*. Forschungen zur Religion und Literatur des Alten und Neuen Testaments 226. Göttingen: Vandenhoeck & Ruprecht, 2008.

Douglas, Mary. *Leviticus as Literature*. Oxford: Oxford University Press, 1999.

–. "Impurity of Land Animals." Pages 33–45 in *Purity and Holiness: The Heritage of Leviticus*. Edited by Marcel J. H. M. Poorthuis and Joshua Schwartz. Jewish and Christian Perspectives Series 2. Brill: Leiden, 2000.

Draper, Jonathan A. "The Holy Vine of David Made Known to the Gentiles through God's Servant Jesus: 'Christian Judaism' in the *Didache*." Pages 257–84 in *Jewish Christianity Reconsidered: Rethinking Ancient Groups and Texts*. Edited by Matt Jackson-McCabe. Minneapolis: Fortress, 2007.

Dunn, James D. G. *Jesus, Paul and the Law*. Louisville, Ky.: Westminster John Knox, 1990.

–. *The Epistle to the Galatians*. Peabody, Mass.: Hendrickson, 1993.

–. *The Acts of the Apostles*. Narrative Commentaries. Valley Forge, Penn.: Trinity Press International, 1996.

–. *The Partings of the Ways between Christianity and Judaism and Their Significance for the Character of Christianity*. 2d ed. London: SCM, 2006.

Dupont, Jacques. *Jésus aux origines de la christologie*. Bibliotheca Ephemeridum Theologicarum Lovaniensium 40. Leuven/Louvain: Leuven University Press, 1975.

Durand, Jean-Louis. "Greek Animals: Toward a Topology of Edible Bodies." Pages 87–118 in *The Cuisine of Sacrifice among the Greeks*. Edited by Marcel Detienne and Jean-Pierre Vernant. Translated by Paula Wissing. Chicago: The University of Chicago Press, 1989.

Easton, Burton Scott. *The Gospel according to St. Luke*. Edinburgh: T&T Clark, 1926.

Ehrman, Bart D. *The New Testament: A Historical Introduction to the Early Christian Writings*. Oxford: Oxford University Press, 2008.

Eliav, Yaron Z. Review of Seth Schwartz, *Imperialism and Jewish Society*. *Prooftexts* 24 (2004): 116–28.

Eisenbaum, Pamela Michelle. *Paul Was Not a Christian: The Real Message of a Misunderstood Apostle*. New York: HarperOne, 2009.

Elgvin, Torleif. "Jewish Christian Editing of the Old Testament Pseudepigrapha." Pages 278–304 in *Jewish Believers in Jesus: The Early Centuries*. Edited by Oskar Skarsaune and Reidar Hvalvik. Peabody, Mass.; Hendrickson, 2007.

Elitzur, Yoel. "Ritual Pools for Immersion of Hands." *Cathedra* 91 (1991): 169–72. [Hebrew]

Endres, John C. *Biblical Interpretation in the Book of Jubilees*. Catholic Biblical Quarterly Monograph Series. Washington, D.C.: Catholic Biblical Association of America, 1987.

Ennulat, Andreas. *Die "Minor Agreements": Untersuchungen zu einer offenen Frage des synoptischen Problems*. Wissenschaftliche Untersuchungen zum Neuen Testament 62. Tübingen: Mohr Siebeck, 1994.

Epstein, Jacob Nahum. *Introduction to Tannaitic Literature: Mishna, Tosephta and Halakhic Midrashim*. Jerusalem: Magnes, 1957. [Hebrew]

Ernst, Josef. *Das Evangelium nach Lukas*. 6th ed. Regensburger Neues Testament. Regensburg: Friedrich Pustet, 1993.

Eshel, Hanan. "A Survey of the Refuge Caves and Their Legal Documents." Pages 103–53 in *Halakhah in Light of Epigraphy*. Edited by Albert I. Baumgarten, Hanan Eshel ז"ל, Ranon Katzoff, and Shani Tzoref. Journal of Ancient Judaism Supplements 3. Göttingen: Vandenhoeck & Ruprecht, 2011.

Evans, Craig A. *Jesus and the Ossuaries*. Waco, Tex.: Baylor University Press, 2003.

Falk, Daniel K. "Jewish Prayer Literature and the Jerusalem Church in Acts." Pages 267–301 in *The Book of Acts in Its Palestinian Setting*. Edited by Richard Bauckham. Vol. 4 of *The Book of Acts in Its First Century Setting*. Edited by Bruce W. Winter. Grand Rapids, Mich.: Eerdmans, 1995.

Festugière, A. J. Review of Paul Lemerle, *Philippes et la Macédoine orientale à l'époque chrétienne et byzantine*. *Revue Biblique* 54 (1947): 132–40.

Fiedler, Peter. *Das Matthäusevangelium*. Theologischer Kommentar zum Neuen Testament 1. Stuttgart: W. Kohlhammer, 2006.

Filoramo, Giovanni, and Claudio Gianotto. "Introduzione." Pages 9–18 in *Verus Israel: Nuove prospettive sul giudeocristianesimo. Atti del Colloquio di Torino (4-5 novembre 1999)*. Edited by Giovanni Filoramo and Claudio Gianotto. Brescia: Paideia Editrice, 2001.

–. eds. *Verus Israel: Nuove prospettive sul giudeocristianesimo. Atti del Colloquio di Torino (4-5 novembre 1999)*. Brescia: Paideia Editrice, 2001.

Fine, Steven, ed. *Jews, Christians, and Polytheists in the Ancient Synagogue*. Baltimore Studies in the History of Judaism. London: Routledge, 1999.

Fitzmyer, Joseph A. "The Aramaic Qorban Inscription from Jebel Hallet et-Tur and Mark 7:11/Mt 15:5." *Journal of Biblical Literature* 78 (1959): 60–65.

–. *The Gospel according to Luke*. 2 vols. Anchor Bible 28–28A. Garden City, N.Y.: Doubleday, 1981–1985.

–. *The Acts of the Apostles*. Anchor Bible 31. New York: Doubleday, 1998.

Flusser, David. "Do You Prefer New Wine?" *Immanuel* 9 (1979): 26–31.

–. *Die rabbinischen Gleichnisse und der Gleichniserzähler Jesus*. Judaica et Christiana 4. Bern: Peter Lang, 1981.

–. *The Sage from Galilee: Rediscovering Jesus' Genius*. 4th ed. Grand Rapids, Mich.: Eerdmans, 2007.

–. "Anti-Jewish Sentiment in the Gospel of Matthew." Pages 351–53 in *Judaism of the Second Temple Period. Vol. 2: The Jewish Sages and Their Literature*. Translated by Azzan Yadin. Grand Rapids, Mich.: Eerdmans, 2009.

–. *Judaism of the Second Temple Period. Vol. 2: The Jewish Sages and Their Literature*. Translated by Azzan Yadin. Grand Rapids, Mich.: Eerdmans, 2009.

Flusser, David, and Shmuel Safrai. "Das Aposteldekret und die Noachitischen Gebote." Pages 173–92 in *"Wer Tora vermehrt, mehrt Leben." Festgabe für Heinz Kremers zum 60. Geburtstag*. Edited by Edna Brocke and Hans-Joachim Barkenings. Neukirchen-Vluyn: Neukirchener, 1986.

Foster, Paul. *Community, Law, and Mission in Matthew's Gospel*. Wissenschaftliche Untersuchungen zum Neuen Testament 2.177. Tübingen: Mohr Siebeck, 2004.

–. Review of Patricia Walters, *The Assumed Authorial Unity of Luke and Acts*. *Expository Times* 121 (2010): 264–65.

France, R. T. *The Gospel of Matthew*. New International Commentary on the New Testament. Grand Rapids, Mich.: Eerdmans, 2007.

France, R. T., and David Wenham. *Gospel Perspectives: Studies of History and Tradition in the Four Gospels. Vol. 2*. Sheffield: JSOT, 1981.

Frankemölle, Hubert. *Matthäus: Kommentar*. 2 vols. Düsseldorf: Patmos, 1997.

Franklin, Eric. *Luke: Interperter of Paul, Critic of Matthew*. Journal for the Study of the New Testament: Supplement Series 92. Sheffield: JSOT Press, 1994.

Freed, Edwin D. "The Women in Matthew's Genealogy." *Journal for the Study of the New Testament* 29 (1987): 3–19.

Freidenreich, David M. *Foreigners and Their Food: Constructing Otherness in Jewish, Christian, and Islamic Law*. Berkeley, Calif.: University of California Press, 2011.

Frey, Jörg, Daniel R. Schwartz, and Stephanie Gripentrog, eds. *Jewish Identity in the Greco-Roman World*. Ancient Judaism and Early Christianity 71. Leiden: Brill, 2007.

Fuchs, Albert, ed. *Jesus in der Verkündigung der Kirche*. Studien zur Umwelt des Neuen Testaments A1. Linz: A. Fuchs, 1976.

Furstenberg, Yair. "Defilement Penetrating the Body: A New Understanding of Contamination in Mark 7.15." *New Testament Studies* 54 (2008): 176–200.

Gager, John G. *Reinventing Paul*. New York: Oxford University Press, 2000.

–. "Did Jewish Christians See the Rise of Islam?" Pages 361–72 in *The Ways That Never Parted*. Edited by Adam H. Becker and Annette Yoshiko Reed. Minneapolis: Fortress, 2007.

Gander, Georges. *L'Évangile pour les étrangers du monde: Commentaire de l'Évangile selon Luc*. Lausanne, 1986.

Garland, David E. *The Intention of Matthew 23*. Supplements to Novum Testamentum 52. Leiden: Brill, 1979.

Gasque, W. Ward. *A History of the Criticism of the Acts of the Apostles*. Beiträge zur Geschichte der biblischen Exegese 17. Tübingen: Mohr Siebeck, 1975.

Gaston, Lloyd. *No Stone on Another: Studies in the Significance of the Fall of Jerusalem in the Synoptic Gospels*. Supplements to Novum Testament 23. Leiden: Brill, 1970.

–. *Paul and the Torah*. Vancouver: University of British Columbia Press, 1987.

Geddert, Timothy J. *Watchwords: Mark 13 in Markan Eschatology*. Journal for the Study of the New Testament: Supplement Series 26. Sheffield: Sheffield Academic Press, 1989.

Gerstenberger, Erhard S. *Leviticus: A Commentary*. Old Testament Library. Louisville, Ky.: WJK, 1993.

Gibson, Shimon. "Stone Vessels of the Early Roman Period from Jerusalem and Palestine: A Reassessment." Pages 287–308 in *One Land – Many Cultures: Archaeological Studies in Honour of Stanislao Loffreda*. Edited by G. Claudio Bottini, Leah Di Segni, and L. Daniel Chrupcala. Jerusalem: Franciscan, 2003.

Gils, Félix. "Le sabbat a été fait pour l'homme." *Revue Biblique* 69 (1962): 516–21.

Ginzberg, Louis. *An Unknown Jewish Sect*. Moreshet Series 1. New York: Jewish Theological Seminary of America, 1970.

Gleßmer, Uwe. *Einleitung in die Targume zum Pentateuch*. Texte und Studien zum antiken Judentum 48. Tübingen: Mohr Siebeck, 1995.

Gnilka, Joachim. *Das Evangelium nach Markus*. 2 vols. Evangelisch-katholischer Kommentar zum Neuen Testament 2. Zurich: Neukirchener, 1978.

–. *Das Matthäusevangelium*. 2 vols. Herders theologischer Kommentar zum Neuen Testament. Freiburg: Herder, 1986.

Godet, Frédéric Louis. *Commentaire sur l'évangile de saint Luc*. 2 vols. Neuchâtel: Librairie générale de Jules Sandoz, 1871.

Goldenberg, Robert. "The Place of Other Religions in Ancient Jewish Thought, with Particular Reference to Early Rabbinic Judaism." Pages 27–40 in *Pushing the Faith: Proselytism and Civility in a Pluralistic World*. Edited by Martin E. Marty and Frederick E. Greenspahn. New York: Crossroad, 1988.

Good, R. S. "Jesus Protagonist of the Old, in Lk 5:33–39." *Novum Testamentum* 25 (1983): 19–36.

Goodfriend, Elaine Adler. "Could *Keleb* in Deuteronomy 23:19 Actually Refer to a Canine?" Pages 381–97 in *Pomegranates and Golden Bells: Studies in Biblical, Jewish, and Near Eastern Ritual, Law, and Literature in Honor of Jacob Milgrom*. Edited by David P. Wright, David Noel Freedman, and Avi Hurvitz. Winona Lake, Ind.: Eisenbrauns, 1995.

Goodman, Martin. *Mission and Conversion: Proselytizing in the Religious History of the Roman Empire*. Oxford: Clarendon, 1994.

–. *Rome and Jerusalem: The Clash of Ancient Civilizations*. London: Allen Lane, 2007.

–. ed. *Jews in a Graeco-Roman World*. Oxford: Clarendon, 1998.

Goulder, M. D. *Midrash and Lection in Matthew*. London: SPCK, 1974.

Grappe, Christian. "Jésus et l'impureté." *Revue d'Histoire et de Philosophie Religieuses* 84 (2004): 393–417.

Green, Joel B. *The Gospel of Luke*. New International Commentary on the New Testament. Grand Rapids, Mich.: Eerdmans, 1997.

–. Review of Patricia Walters, *The Assumed Authorial Unity of Luke and Acts*. *Review of Biblical Literature* [http://www.bookreviews.org] (2009).

Grossberg, Asher. "The *Miqva'ot* (Ritual Baths) at Masada." Pages 95–126 in *Masada VIII: The Yigael Yadin Excavations 1963–1965*. Edited by J. Aviram, G. Foerster, Ehud Netzer, and Guy Stiebel. Jerusalem: Israel Exploration Society, 2007.

Grundmann, Walter. *Das Evangelium nach Matthäus*. Theologischer Handkommentar zum Neuen Testament. Berlin: Evangelische Verlagsanstalt, 1968.

Gundry, Robert Horton. *Mark: A Commentary on His Apology for the Cross*. Grand Rapids, Mich.: Eerdmans, 1993.

–. *Matthew: A Commentary on His Handbook for a Mixed Church under Persecution*. 2d ed. Grand Rapids, Mich.: Eerdmans, 1994.

Gurtner, Daniel M., and John Nolland, eds. *Built upon the Rock: Studies in the Gospel of Matthew*. Grand Rapids, Mich.: Eerdmans, 2008.

Guthrie, W. K. C. *The Greek Philosophers from Thales to Aristotle*. New York: Harper & Row, 1975.

Guy, Fritz. "The Lord's Day in the Letter of Ignatius to the Magnesians." *Andrews University Seminary Studies* 2 (1964): 1–17.

Haam, Ahad. *Kol Kitve Ahad Haam*. Tel Aviv: Dvir, 1965.

Haber, Susan. *"They Shall Purify Themselves": Essays on Purity in Early Judaism*. Edited by Adele Reinhartz. Society of Biblical Literature Early Judaism and Its Literature 24. Atlanta: Society of Biblical Literature, 2008.

Hachlili, Rachel. *Jewish Funerary Customs, Practices and Rites in the Second Temple Period*. Supplements to the Journal for the Study of Judaism 94. Leiden: Brill, 2005.

Haenchen, Ernst. *The Acts of the Apostles: A Commentary*. Translated by Bernard Noble, Gerald Shinn, Hugh Anderson, and R. McL. Wilson. Oxford: Blackwell, 1971.

Hagner, Donald A. *Matthew*. Word Biblical Commentary 33A–B. Dallas: Word Books, 1993–1994.

–. "Matthew: Apostate, Reformer, Revolutionary." *New Testament Studies* 49 (2003): 193–209.

–. "Matthew: Christian Judaism or Jewish Christianity?" Pages 263–82 in *The Face of New Testament Studies: A Survey of Recent Research*. Edited by Scot McKnight and Grant R. Osborne. Grand Rapids, Mich.: Baker Academic, 2004.

–."Paul as a Jewish Believer – According to His Letters." Pages 96–120 in *Jewish Believers in Jesus: The Early Centuries*. Edited by Oskar Skarsaune and Reidar Hvalvik. Peabody, Mass.; Hendrickson, 2007.

Hamilton, John J. "The Chronology of the Crucifixion and the Passover." *Churchman* 106 (1992): 323–38.

Hanson, A. T. "Rahab the Harlot in Early Christian Tradition." *Journal for the Study of the New Testament* 1 (1978): 53–60.

Hanson, R. P. C. *The Acts in the Revised Standard Version*. The New Clarendon Bible. Oxford: Clarendon, 1967.

Hare, Douglas R. A. "How Jewish is the Gospel of Matthew?" *Catholic Biblical Quarterly* 62 (2000): 264–77.

Harland, Philip A. "Acculturation and Identity in the Diaspora: A Jewish Family and 'Pagan' Guilds at Hierapolis." *Journal of Jewish Studies* 57 (2006): 222–44.

Harnack, Adolf von. *The Acts of the Apostles*. Translated by J. R. Wilkinson. Crown Theological Library 27. London: Williams & Norgate, 1909.

Harrington, Daniel J. *The Gospel of Matthew*. Sacra pagina 1. Collegeville, Minn.: Liturgical, 1991.

Harrington, Hannah K. *The Purity Texts*. Companion to the Qumran Scrolls 5. London: T&T Clark, 2004.

Hartog, François. "Self-cooking Beef and the Drinks of Ares." Pages 172–82 in *The Cuisine of Sacrifice among the Greeks*. Edited by Marcel Detienne and Jean-Pierre Vernant. Translated by Paula Wissing. Chicago: The University of Chicago Press, 1989.

Hayes, Christine E. *Gentile Impurities and Jewish Identities: Intermarriage and Conversion from the Bible to the Talmud*. Oxford: Oxford University Press, 2002.

–. *The Emergence of Judaism: Classical Traditions in Contemporary Perspective*. Minneapolis: Fortress, 2011.

Hayward, Robert. "The Date of Targum Pseudo-Jonathan: Some Comments." *Journal of Jewish Studies* 40 (1989): 7–30.

Heemstra, Marius. *The Fiscus Judaicus and the Parting of the Ways*. Wissenschaftliche Untersuchungen zum Neuen Testament 2.277. Tübingen: Mohr Siebeck, 2010.

Hengel, Martin. *Crucifixion in the Ancient World and the Folly of the Message of the Cross*. Translated by John Bowden. Philadelphia, Minn.: Fortress, 1977.

–. *Acts and the History of Earliest Christianity*. Translated by John Bowden. London: SCM Press, 1979.

Henze, Matthias. *Jewish Apocalypticism in Late First Century Israel: Reading 'Second Baruch' in Context*. Texte und Studien zum Antiken Judentum 142. Tübingen: Mohr Siebeck, 2011.

Heschel, Abraham Joshua. *The Sabbath: Its Meaning for Modern Man*. New York: Noonday, 1997.

Hezser, Catherine, ed. The *Oxford Handbook of Jewish Daily Life in Roman Palestine*. Oxford: Oxford University Press, 2010.

Higgins, A. J. B. *New Testament Essays: Studies in Memory of Thomas Walter Manson*. Manchester: Manchester University Press, 1959.

Hill, David. "The Rejection of Jesus at Nazareth (Luke iv 16–30)." *Novum Testamentum* 13 (1971): 161–80.

–. False Prophets and Charismatics: Structure and Interpretation in Matthew 7:15–23. *Biblica* 57 (1973): 327–48.

–. "On the Use of and Meaning of Hosea VI. 6 in Matthew's Gospel." *New Testament Studies* 24 (1978): 107–19.

Himmelfarb, Martha. "Impurity and Sin in 4QD, 1QS, and 4Q512." *Dead Sea Discoveries* 8 (2001): 9–37.

Hirsch, Emanuel. *Die Frühgeschichte des Evangeliums*. 2 vols. Tübingen: J. C. B. Mohr, 1941.

Hirshman, Marc G. *Torah for the Entire World*. Tel Aviv: Ha-Kibbutz ha-Me'uhad, 1999. [Hebrew]

–. "Rabbinic Universalism in the Second and Third Centuries," *Harvard Theological Review* 93 (2000): 101–15.

Hoffmann, David Z. *Das Buch Leviticus*. 2 vols. Berlin: Poppelauer, 1905.

Hoffmann, Paul. *Studien zur Theologie der Logienquelle*. 2d ed. Neutestamentliche Abhandlungen 8. Münster: Aschendorff, 1972.

Hogan, Karina. *Theologies in Conflict in 4 Ezra: Wisdom, Debate, and Apocalyptic Solution*. Supplements to the Journal for the Study of Judaism 130. Leiden: Brill, 2008.

Hood, Jason. *The Messiah, His Brothers, and the Nations (Matthew 1:1–17)*. Library of New Testament Studies 441. London: T&T Clark, 2011.

Hooker, Morna D. *A Commentary on the Gospel according to St Mark*. Black's New Testament Commentaries. London: A&C Black, 1991.

Horst, Pieter W. van der. "Was the Synagogue a Place of Sabbath Worship before 70 C.E.?" Pages 18–43 in *Jews, Christians, and Polytheists in the Ancient Synagogue*. Edited by Steven Fine. Baltimore Studies in the History of Judaism. London: Routledge, 1999.

Hübner, Hans. *Das Gesetz in der synoptischen Tradition: Studien zur These einer progressiven Qumranisierung und Judaisierung innerhalb der synoptischen Tradition*. 2d ed. Göttingen: Vandenhoeck & Ruprecht, 1986.

Hübner, Reinhard. "Thesen zur Echtheit und Datierung der sieben Briefe des Ignatius von Antiochen." *Zeitschrift für Antikes Christentum* (1997): 44–72.

Hummel, Reinhart. *Die Auseinandersetzung zwischen Kirche und Judentum im Matthäusevangelium*. Beiträge zur evangelischen Theologie 33. Munich: Chr. Kaiser, 1966.

–."Thesen zur Echtheit und Datierung der sieben Briefe des Ignatius von Antiochen." *Journal of Ancient Christianity* (1997): 44–72.

Hvalvik, Reidar. "Paul as a Jewish Believer – According to the Book of Acts." Pages 121–53 in *Jewish Believers in Jesus: The Early Centuries*. Edited by Oskar Skarsaune and Reidar Hvalvik. Peabody, Mass.: Hendrickson Publishers, 2007.

Instone-Brewer, David. *Feasts and Sabbaths: Passover and Atonement*. Traditions of the Rabbis from the Era of the New Testament Volume 2A. Grand Rapids, Mich.: Eerdmans, 2011.

Jackson-McCabe, Matt. "What's in a Name? The Problem of 'Jewish Christianity.'" Pages 7–38 in *Jewish Christianity Reconsidered: Rethinking Ancient Groups and Texts*. Edited by Matt Jackson-McCabe. Minneapolis: Fortress, 2007.

–. ed. *Jewish Christianity Reconsidered: Rethinking Ancient Groups and Texts*. Minneapolis: Fortress, 2007.

Jacobs, Andrews S. *Christ Circumcised: A Study in Early Christian History and Difference*. Divinations: Rereading Late Ancient Religion. Philadelphia: University of Pennsylvania, 2012.

Jacquier, Eugène. *Les Actes des apôtres*. Études Bibliques 18. Paris: J. Gabalda, 1926.

Jaffee, Martin S. *Early Judaism*. Upper Saddle River, N.J.: Prentice Hall, 1997.

Jaubert, Annie. *La date de la Cène. Calendrier biblique et liturgie chrétienne*. Paris: Gabalda, 1957.

Jellicoe, Sidney. "St. Luke and the Seventy-Two." *New Testament Studies* 6 (1960): 319–21.

–. "St. Luke and the Letter of Aristeas." *Journal of Biblical Literature* 80 (1961): 149–55.

Jeremias, Joachim. Review of Matthew Black, *An Aramaic Approach to the Gospels and Acts*. Göttingische gelehrte Anzeigen 210 (1956): 1–12.

–. *The Eucharistic Words of Jesus*. Translated by Norman Perrin. New York: Scribner, 1966.

Jervell, Jacob. *Luke and the People of God: A New Look at Luke-Acts*. Minneapolis: Augsburg, 1972.

–. "The Mighty Minority." *Studia theologica* 34 (1980): 13–38.

–. *The Unknown Paul: Essays on Luke-Acts and Early Christian History*. Minneapolis: Augsburg, 1984.

–. "The Church of the Jews and Godfearers." Pages 11–20 in *Luke-Acts and the Jewish People: Eight Critical Perspectives*. Edited by Joseph B. Tyson. Minneapolis: Augsburg, 1988.

–. "Retrospect and Prospect in Luke-Acts Interpretation." Pages 383–404 in *Society of Biblical Literature 1991 Seminar Papers*. Edited by Eugene H. Lovering. Society of Biblical Literature Seminar Papers 30. Atlanta: Scholars, 1991.

–. "The Future of the Past: Luke's Vision of Salvation History and Its Bearing on His Writings of History." Pages 104–26 in *History, Literature, and Society in the Book of Acts*. Edited by Ben Witherington III. Cambridge: Cambridge University Press, 1996.

–. *The Theology of the Acts of the Apostles*. Cambridge: Cambridge University Press, 1996.

–. *Die Apostelgeschichte*. Kritisch-exegetischer Kommentar über das Neue Testament (Meyer-Kommentar). Göttingen: Vandenhoeck & Ruprecht, 1998.

Jewett, Paul K. *Lord's Day: A Theological Guide to the Christian Day of Worship*. Grand Rapids, Mich.: Eerdmans, 1971.

Johnson, Luke Timothy. *The Gospel of Luke*. Sacra pagina Series 3. Collegeville, Minn.: Liturgical, 1991.

–. *The Acts of the Apostles*. Sacra pagina 5. Collegeville, Minn.: Liturgical, 1992.

Jones, Stanley F., ed. *The Rediscovery of Jewish Christianity: From Toland to Baur*. History of Biblical Studies 5. Atlanta: Society of Biblical Literature, 2012.

Joosten, Jan, and Menahem Kister. "The New Testament and Rabbinic Hebrew." Pages 335–50 in *The New Testament and Rabbinic Literature*. Edited by Reimund Bieringer,

Florentino García Martínez, Didier Pollefeyt, and Peter J. Tomson. Supplements to the Journal for the Study of Judaism 136. Leiden: Brill, 2010.

Juel, Donald. *Luke-Acts: The Promise of History.* Atlanta: John Knox, 1983.

Kampen, John. "The Matthean Divorce Texts Reexaminzed." Pages 149–67 in *New Qumran Texts and Studies: Proceedings of the First Meeting of the International Organization for Qumran Studies, Paris 1992.* Edited by George J. Brooke with Florentino García-Martínez. Studies on the Texts of the Desert of Judah 15. Leiden: Brill, 1994.

Kaufmann, Asher S. "Determining the Length of the Medium Cubit." *Palestine Exploration Quarterly* 116 (1984): 120–32.

Kazen, Thomas. *Issues of Impurity in Early Judaism.* Coniectanea biblica: New Testament Series 45. Winona Lake, Ind.: Eisenbrauns, 2010.

–. *Jesus and Purity Halakhah: Was Jesus Indifferent to Impurity?* Coniectanea biblica: New Testament Series 38. Winona Lake, Ind.: Eisenbrauns, 2010.

Kehati, Pinhas. *The Mishnah.* 23 vols. Jerusalem: Department for Torah Education and Culture in the Diaspora of the World Zionist Organization, 1987–1996.

Kelhoffer, James A. "Did John the Baptist Eat like a Former Essene? Locust-Eating in the Ancient Near East and at Qumran." *Dead Sea Discoveries* 11 (2004): 293–314.

King, Karen L. *What is Gnosticism?* Cambridge, Mass.: Harvard University Press, 2003.

Kinzer, Mark. *Postmissionary Messianic Judaism: Redefining Christian Engagement with the Jewish People.* Grand Rapids, Mich.: Brazos, 2005.

Klawans, Jonathan. "Notions of Gentile Impurity in Ancient Judaism." *Association for Jewish Studies Review* 20 (1995): 285–312.

–. *Impurity and Sin in Ancient Judaism.* New York: Oxford University Press, 2000.

Klein, Hans. *Das Lukasevangelium.* Kritisch-exegetischer Kommentar über das Neue Testament (Meyer–Kommentar) 1.3. Göttingen: Vandenhoeck & Ruprecht, 2005.

Klein, Samuel. *Tod und Begräbnis in Palästina zur Zeit der Tannaiten.* Berlin: Itzkowski, 1908.

Klinghardt, Matthias. *Gesetz und Volk Gottes.* Wissenschaftliche Untersuchungen zum Neuen Testament 2.32. Tübingen: Mohr Siebeck, 1988.

–."The Marcionite Gospel and the Synoptic Problem: A New Suggestion." *Novum Testamentum* 50 (2008): 1–27.

Koet, Bart J. *Five Studies on Interpretation of Scripture in Luke-Acts.* Studiorum Novi Testamenti Auxilia 14. Leuven: University Press, 1989.

–. "Purity and Impurity of the Body in Luke-Acts." Pages 93–106 in *Purity and Holiness: The Heritage of Leviticus.* Edited by Marcel J. H. M. Poorthuis and Joshua Schwartz. Jewish and Christian Perspectives Series 2. Brill: Leiden, 2000.

Kosmala, Hans. "The Three Nets of Belial: A Study in the Terminology of Qumran and the New Testament." *Annual of the Swedish Theological Institute* 4 (1965): 91–113.

Kraemer, David. *The Meanings of Death in Rabbinic Judaism.* London: Routledge, 2000.

–. *Jewish Eating and Identity through the Ages.* New York: Routledge, 2007.

–. "Food, Eating, and Meals." Pages 403–19 in *The Oxford Handbook of Jewish Daily Life in Roman Palestine.* Edited by Catherine Hezser. Oxford: Oxford University Press, 2010.

Kraft, Robert A. "In Search of 'Jewish Christianity' and its 'Theology': Problems of Definition and Methodology." *Recherches de science religieuse* 60 (1972): 81–92.

Krauss, Samuel. "Die Zahl der biblischen Völkerschaften." *Zeitschrift für die alttestamentliche Wissenschaft* 19 (1899): 1–14.

–. *Talmudische Archäologie.* Hildesheim: Olms, 1966.

Laansma, Jon. *I Will Give You Rest: The Rest Motif in the New Testament with Special Reference to Mt 11 and Heb 3–4*. Wissenschaftliche Untersuchungen zum Neuen Testament 2.98. Tübingen: Mohr Siebeck, 1997.

Lagrange, P. M.–J. *Évangile selon saint Matthieu*. 4th ed. Paris: Librairie Lecoffre, 1927.

Lechner, Thomas. *Ignatius Adversus Valentinianos? Chronologische und theologiegeschichtliche Studien zu den Briefen des Ignatius von Antiochen*. Supplements to Vigiliae Christianae 47. Leiden: Brill, 1999.

Le Cornu, Hilary, with Joseph Shulam. *A Commentary on the Jewish Roots of Acts*. 2 vols. Jerusalem: Academon, 2003.

Legrand, L. "On l'appela du nom de Jésus." *Revue Biblique* 89 (1982): 481–91.

Lemerle, Paul. *Philippes et la Macédoine orientale à l'époque chrétienne et byzantine*. Bibliothèque des Écoles françaises d'Athènes et de Rome 158. Paris: É. de Boccard, 1945.

Leon, Harry Joshua. *The Jews of Ancient Rome*. Philadelphia: Jewish Publication Society of America, 1960.

Lev-Tov, Justin. "'Upon What Meat Doth This Our Caesar Feed...?' A Dietary Perspective on Hellenistic and Roman Influence in Palestine." Pages 420–46 in *Zeichen aus Text und Stein: Studien auf dem Weg zu einer Archäologie des Neuen Testaments*. Edited by Stefan Alkier and Jürgen Zangenberg. Texte und Arbeiten zum neutestamentlichen Zeitalter 42. Tübingen: Francke, 2003.

Levine, Amy-Jill. *The Social and Ethnic Dimensions of Matthean Salvation History: "Go nowhere among the Gentiles..." (Matt. 10:5b)*. Studies in Bible and Early Christianity 14. Lewiston, N.Y.: The Edwin Mellen Press, 1988.

Levine, Amy-Jill, and Marc Zvi Brettler, eds. *The Jewish Annotated New Testament*. Oxford: Oxford University Press, 2011.

Levine, Etan. "The Sabbath Controversy according to Matthew." *New Testament Studies* 22 (1975/76): 480–83.

Levine, Lee I. *The Ancient Synagogue: The First Thousand Years*. 2d ed. New Haven, Conn.: Yale University Press, 2005.

–. ed. *The Galilee in Late Antiquity*. New York: Jewish Theological Seminary of America, 1992.

Levinskaya, Irina. *The Book of Acts in Its Diaspora Setting*. Vol 5 of *The Book of Acts in Its First Century Setting*. Edited by Bruce W. Winter. Grand Rapids, Mich.: Eerdmans, 1996.

Lewis, Richard B. "Ignatius and the Lord's Day." *Andrews University Seminary Studies* 6 (1968): 46–59.

Lichtenberger, Hermann. "The Dead Sea Scrolls and John the Baptist: Reflections on Josephus' Account of John the Baptist." Pages 340–46 in *The Dead Sea Scrolls: Forty Years of Research*. Edited by Devorah Dimant and Uriel Rappaport. Studies on the Texts of the Desert of Judah 10. Leiden: Brill, 1992.

Lieberman, Saul. *Tosefta Ki-Fshutah: A Comprehensive Commentary on the Tosefta*. 10 vols. 2d ed. Jerusalem: The Jewish Theological Seminary of America/The Maxwell Abbell Publication Fund, 1992. [Hebrew]

–. *Tosefeth Rishonim: A Commentary*. 4 vols. New York: The Jewish Theological Seminary of America, 1999. [Hebrew]

Lietzmann, D. Hans. "Der Sinn des Aposteldekrets und seine Textwandlung." Pages 203–211 in *Amicitiae Corolla: A Volume of Essays Presented to James Rendel Harris, D. Litt., on the Occasion of His Eightieth Birthday*. Edited by H. G. Wood. London: University of London Press, 1933.

Lieu, Judith. *Neither Jew nor Greek? Constructing Early Christianity*. Studies of the New Testament and Its World. London: T&T Clark, 2002.

Lindsey, Robert L. *A Hebrew Translation of the Gospel of Mark*. Jerusalem: Dugith Publishers, 1973.

Livesey, Nina E. *Circumcision as a Malleable Symbol*. Wissenschaftliche Untersuchungen zum Neuen Testament 2.295. Tübingen: Mohr Siebeck, 2010.

Loader, William R. G. *Jesus' Attitude towards the Law*. Wissenschaftliche Untersuchungen zum Neuen Testament 2.97. Tübingen: Mohr Siebeck, 1997.

–. *The Dead Sea Scrolls on Sexuality*. Grand Rapids, Mich.: Eerdmans, 2009.

Lohfink, Gerhard. *Die Sammlung Israels: Eine Untersuchung zur lukanischen Ekklesiologie*. Munich: Kösel, 1975.

Lowe, Malcolm, and David Flusser. "Evidence Corroborating a Modified Proto-Matthean Synoptic Theory." *New Testament Studies* 29 (1983): 25–47.

Lüdemann, Gerd. *The Acts of the Apostles: What Really Happened in the Earliest Days of the Church*. Amherst, N.Y.: Prometheus Books, 2005.

Lührmann, Dieter. *Das Markusevangelium*. Handbuch zum Neuen Testament 3. Tübingen: Mohr Siebeck, 1987.

Luz, Ulrich. *Matthew*. 3 vols. Hermeneia. Minneapolis: Fortress, 2001–2007.

Maccoby, Hyam. "The Washing of Cups." *Journal for the Study of the New Testament* 14 (1982): 3–15.

–. *Early Rabbinic Writings*. Cambridge Commentaries on Writings of the Jewish and Christian World, 200 B.C. to A.D. 200. Vol. 3. Cambridge: Cambridge University Press, 1988.

–. *Ritual and Morality: The Ritual Purity System and Its Place in Judaism*. Cambridge: Cambridge University Press, 1999.

MacLennan, Robert S., and A. Thomas Kraabel. "The God-Fearers – A Literary and Theological Invention." *Biblical Archaeology Review* 12 (1986): 47–53.

Magness, Jodi. *Stone and Dung, Oil and Spit: Jewish Daily Life in the Time of Jesus*. Grand Rapids, Mich.: Eerdmans, 2011.

Malina, Bruce. "Jewish Christianity or Christian Judaism: Toward a Hypothetical Definition." *Journal for the Study of Judaism in the Persian, Hellenistic, and Roman Periods* 7 (1976): 46–57.

Mann, Jacob. "Jesus and the Sadducean Priests: Luke 10. 25–37." *Jewish Quarterly Review* 6 (1915–1916): 415–22.

Marcus, Joel. *Mark*. Anchor Bible 27–27A. New York: Doubleday, 2000–2009.

Marguerat, Daniel. *Les Actes des apôtres (1–12)*. Commentaire du Nouveau Testament Va. Deuxième série. Geneva: Labor et Fides, 2007.

Marshall, I. Howard. *The Gospel of Luke: A Commentary on the Greek Text*. New International Greek Testament Commentary. Exeter: Pater Noster, 1978.

–. *The Acts of the Apostles: An Introduction and Commentary*. Grand Rapids, Mich.: Eerdmans, 1980.

Marshall, John W. "John's Jewish (Christian?) Apocalypse?" Pages 233–56 in *Jewish Christianity Reconsidered: Rethinking Ancient Groups and Texts*. Edited by Matt Jackson-McCabe. Minneapolis: Fortress, 2007.

Marty, Martin E., and Frederick E. Greenspahn, eds. *Pushing the Faith: Proselytism and Civility in a Pluralistic World*. New York: Crossroad, 1988.

Marxsen, Willi. *Mark the Evangelist: Studies on the Redaction History of the Gospel*. Nashville, Tenn.: Abingdon, 1969.

Mason, Steve. "Jews, Judaeans, Judaizing, Judaism: Problems of Categorization in Ancient History." *Journal for the Study of Judaism* 38 (2007): 457–512.

Mateos, Juan, and Fernando Camacho, *El Evangelio de Mateo lectura comentada*. Lectura del Nuevo Testamento. Madrid: Cristiandad, 1981.

Matthews, Shelly. *First Converts: Rich Pagan Women and the Rhetoric of Mission in Early Judaism and Christianity*. Stanford, Calif.: Stanford University Press, 2001.

Mayer-Haas, Andrea J. *"Geschenk aus Gottes Schatzkammer (bSchab 10b)": Jesus und der Sabbat im Spiegel der neutestamentlichen Schriften*. Neutestamentliche Abhandlungen 43. Münster: Aschendorff, 2003.

McArthur, Harvey K., and Robert Morris Johnston. *They Also Taught in Parables: Rabbinic Parables from the First Centuries of the Christian Era*. Grand Rapids, Mich.: Academie Books, 1990.

McCane, Byron. *Roll Back the Stone: Death and Burial in the World of Jesus*. Harrisburg, Pa.: Trinity Press International, 2003.

McKay, Heather A. *Sabbath and Synagogue: The Question of Sabbath Worship in Ancient Judaism*. Leiden: Brill, 2001.

McKnight, Scot. *A Light among the Gentiles: Jewish Missionary Activity in the Second Temple Period*. Minneapolis: Fortress, 1991.

McKnight, Scot, and Grant R. Osborne. *The Face of the New Testament Studies: A Survey of Recent Research*. Grand Rapids, Mich.: Baker Academic, 2004.

Meier, John P. *The Vision of Matthew: Christ, Church, and Morality in the First Gospel*. New York: Paulist, 1979.

–. *Matthew*. Collegeville, Minn.: Liturgical Press, 1990.

–. "The Historical Jesus and the Plucking of Grain on the Sabbath." *Catholic Biblical Quarterly* 66 (2004): 561–81.

–. *A Marginal Jew: Rethinking the Historical Jesus. Volume Four: Law and Love*. New Haven, Conn.: Yale University Press, 2009.

Mello, Alberto. *Evangelo secondo Matteo*. Magnano: Edizioni Qiqajon, 1995.

Merkel, Helmut. "Israel im lukanischen Werk." *New Testament Studies* 40 (1994): 371–98.

Metzger, Bruce. "Seventy or Seventy-Two Disciples?" *New Testament Studies* 5 (1959): 299–306.

Milavec, Aaron. *The Didache: Faith, Hope, and Life of the Earliest Christian Communities, 50–70 C.E.* Mahwah, N.J.: Newman, 2003.

Milikowsky, Chaim. "Reflections on Hand-Washing, Hand-Purity and Holy Scripture in Rabbinic Literature." Pages 149–62 in *Purity and Holiness: The Heritage of Leviticus*. Edited by Marcel J. H. M. Poorthuis and Joshua Schwartz. Jewish and Christian Perspectives Series 2. Brill: Leiden, 2000.

Milgrom, Jacob. *Leviticus*. 3 vols. Anchor Bible 3–3B. New York: Doubleday, 1991–2001.

Miller, Chris A. "Did Peter's Vision in Acts 10 Pertain to Men or the Menu?" *Bibliotheca Sacra* 159 (2002): 302–317.

Miller, Donald G. *Jesus and Man's Hope*. 2 vols. Pittsburgh, Pa.: Pittsburgh Theological Seminary, 1970.

Miller, Geoffrey D. "Attitudes towards Dogs in Ancient Israel." *Journal for the Study of the Old Testament* 32 (2008): 487–500.

Mimouni, Simon Claude. *Le judéo-christianisme ancien: essais historiques*. Paris: Cerf, 1998.

–. *Le judéo-christianisme dans tous ses états: Actes du Colloque de Jérusalem 6-10 1998*. Paris: Cerf, 2001.

–. *La circoncision dans le monde judéen aux époques grecque et romaine: Histoire d'un conflit interne au judaïsme*. Collection de la Revue des études juives 42. Paris: Peeters, 2007.

–. "Christian Judaism: A Question Still Open for Discussion." Paper presented at the annual meeting of the SBL. San Francisco, Calif., November 20, 2011.

Moessner, David P., Daniel Marguerat, Mikeal C. Parsons, and Michael Wolter, eds. *Paul and the Heritage of Israel: Paul's Claim upon Israel's Legacy in Luke and Acts in the Light of the Pauline Letters*. Library of New Testament Studies 452. London: T&T Clark, 2012.

Moore, George Foot. "Conjectanea Talmudica." *Journal of the American Oriental Society* 26 (1905): 315–33.

–. "Christian Writers on Judaism." *Harvard Theological Review* 14 (1921): 197–254.

Mor, Menahem. *The Bar-Kochba Revolt: Its Extent and Effect*. Israel Exploration Society. Jerusalem: Yad Izhak Ben-Zvi, 1991. [Hebrew]

–. "The Geographical Scope of the Bar Kokhba Revolt." Pages 107–32 in *The Bar Kokhba War Reconsidered: New Perspectives on the Second Jewish Revolt against Rome*. Edited by Peter Schäfer. Texte und Studien zum antiken Judentum 100. Tübingen: Mohr Siebeck, 2002.

Morris, Leon. *The Gospel according to Matthew*. Grand Rapids, Mich.: Eerdmans, 1992.

Moskala, Jirí. *The Laws of Clean and Unclean Animals of Leviticus 11: Their Nature, Theology, and Rationale (an Intertextual Study)*. Adventist Theological Dissertation Series 4. Berrien Springs, Mich.: Adventist Theological Society Publications, 2000.

Müller, Klaus. *Tora für die Völker: Die noachidischen Gebote und Ansätze zu ihrer Rezeption im Christentum*. Studien zu Kirche und Israel 15. Berlin: Institut Kirche und Judentum, 1994.

Müller, Mogens. "Luke–the Fourth Gospel?" Pages 231–42 in *Voces Clamantium in Deserto: Essays in Honor of Kari Syreeni*. Edited by Sven-Olav Back and Matti Kankaanniemi. Studier exegetik och judaistik utgivna av Teologiska fakulteten vid Åbo Akademi 11. Åbo: Teologiska fakulteten vid Åbo Akademi, 2012.

Murmelstein, Benjamin. "Jesu Gang durch die Saatfelder." *Angelos* 3 (1930): 111–20.

Murray, Michele. *Playing a Jewish Game: Gentile Christian Judaizing in the First and Second Centuries CE*. Studies in Christianity and Judaism/Études sur le christianisme et le judaïsme 13. Waterloo, Ontario: Wilfrid Laurier University Press, 2004.

Murray, Robert. "Defining Judaeo-Christianity." *Heythrop Journal* 15 (1974): 303–10.

Mussner, Franz. *Apostelgeschichte*. Die neue Echter Bibel. Kommentar zum Neuen Testament mit der Einheitsübersetzung 5. Würzburg: Echter, 1984.

Nanos, Mark. *The Mystery of Romans: The Jewish Context of Paul's Letter*. Minneapolis: Fortress, 1996.

–. *The Irony of Galatians: Paul's Letter in First-Century Context*. Minneapolis: Fortress, 2002.

Navarro, Luis Sánchez. "La Escritura para las naciones. Acerca del universalismo en Mateo." Pages 187–203 in *Palabra de Dios, Sagrada Escritura, Iglesia*. Edited by Vicente Balaguer and Juan Luis Caballero. Pamplona: Ediciones Universidad de Navarra, 2008.

–. *Testimonios del Reino: Evangelios Sinópticos y Hechos los Apóstoles*. Madrid: Ediciano Palabra, 2010.

Neil, William. *Acts*. New Century Bible Commentary. Grand Rapids, Mich.: Eerdmans, 1981.

Neirynck, F. "Jesus and the Sabbath. Some Observations on Mk II, 27." Pages 227–70 in *Jésus aux origines de la christologie*. Edited by Jacques Dupont. Bibliotheca ephemeridum theologicarum lovaniensium 40. Leuven/Louvain: Leuven University Press, 1975.

–. ed. *L'évangile de Luc/The Gospel of Luke*. 2d ed. Bibliotheca ephemeridum theologicarum lovaniensium 32. Leuven: Leuven University Press, 1989.

Nepper-Christensen, Poul. *Das Matthäusevangelium, ein judenchristliches Evangelium?* Acta theologica danica 1. Aarhus: Universitetsforlaget, 1958.

Nestle, Eb. "Zu Acta 1:12." *Zeitschrift für die neutestamentliche Wissenschaft und die Kunde der älteren Kirche* 3 (1902): 247–49.

Neusner, Jacob. *The Development of a Legend: Studies on the Tradition concerning Yohanan ben Zakkai*. Studia post-biblica 16. Leiden: Brill, 1970.

–. *From Politics to Piety: The Emergence of Pharisaic Judaism*. Engledwoods Cliff, N.J.: Prentice Hall, 1973.

–. *Rabbinic Traditions about the Pharisees before 70*. 3 vols. Leiden: Brill, 1973.

–. *The Idea of Purity in Ancient Judaism*. Studies in Judaism in Late Antiquity 1. Brill: Leiden, 1973.

–. *A History of the Mishnaic Law of Purities*. 22 vols. Studies in Judaism in Late Antiquity 6. Leiden: Brill, 1974–1976.

–. "First Cleanse the Inside: The 'Halakhic' Background of a Controversy-Saying." *New Testament Studies* 22 (1976): 486–95.

–. "The Formation of Rabbinic Judaism: Yavneh from A.D. 70–100." *Aufstieg und Niedergang der römischen Welt: Geschichte und Kultur Roms im Spiegel der neueren Forschung* 19.2:3–42. Part 2, *Principat,* 19.2. Edited by Hildegard Temporini and Wolfgang Haase. New York: de Gruyter, 1979.

Noam, Vered. "'The Gentileness of the Gentiles': Two Approaches to the Impurity of non-Jews." Pages 27–42 in *Halakhah in Light of Epigraphy*. Edited by Albert I. Baumgarten, Hanan Eshel ל"ז, Ranon Katzoff, and Shani Tzoref. Journal of Ancient Judaism Supplements 3. Göttingen: Vandenhoeck & Ruprecht, 2011.

Nolland, John. "A Fresh Look at Acts 15.10." *New Testament Studies* 27 (1980): 105–15.

–. *Luke*. 2 vols. Word Biblical Commentary 35A–C. Dallas: Word Books, 1989–1993.

–. *The Gospel of Matthew: A Commentary on the Greek Text*. New International Greek Testament Commentary. Grand Rapids, Mich.: Eerdmans, 2005.

Novak, David. *The Image of the Non-Jew in Judaism: An Historical and Constructive Study of the Noahide Laws*. Toronto Studies in Theology 14. New York: Edwin Mellen, 1983.

Öhler, Markus, ed. *Aposteldekret und antikes Vereinswesen: Gemeinschaft und ihre Ordnung*. Wissenschaftliche Untersuchungen zum Neuen Testament 280. Tübingen: Mohr Siebeck, 2011.

Oliver, Isaac W. "Breaking Passover to Keep the Sabbath: The Burial of Jesus and the Halakic Dilemma as Embedded within the Synoptic Narratives." Paper presented at the annual meeting of the Midwest Region of the SBL. Bourbonnais, Ill., February 12, 2011.

–. "Simon Peter Meets Simon the Tanner: The Ritual Insignificance of Tanning in Ancient Judaism." *New Testament Studies* 59 (2013): 50–60.

–. "Forming Jewish Identity by Formulating Legislation for Gentiles." *Journal of Ancient Judaism* 4 (2013): 105–32.

–. "Jewish Apocalyptic Expectations during and after the Revolts against Rome." Forthcoming in *The Psychological Dynamics of Revolution: Religious Revolts*. Vol. 1 of *Winning Revolutions: The Psychology of Successful Revolts for Freedom, Fairness, and Rights*. Edited by J. Harold Ellens. Santa Barbara, Calif.: Praeger, 2014.

–. "Jewish Followers of Jesus and the Bar Kokhba Revolt: Re-examining the Christian Sources." Forthcoming in *The Psychological Dynamics of Revolution: Religious Revolts*. Vol. 1 of *Winning Revolutions: The Psychology of Successful Revolts for Freedom, Fairness, and Rights*. Edited by J. Harold Ellens. Santa Barbara, Calif.: Praeger, 2014.

Oliver, Isaac. W., and Veronika Bachmann. "The Book of Jubilees: An Annotated Bibliography from the First German Translation of 1850 to the Enoch Seminar of 2007." *Henoch* 31 (2009): 123–64.

Olsson, Birger, Dieter Mitternacht, and Olof Brandt, eds. *The Synagogue of Ancient Ostia and the Jews of Rome*. ActaRom–4o.57. Stockholm: Paul Åströms, 2001.

O'Neill, J. C. *The Theology of Acts in its Historical Setting*. 2d ed. London: S. P. C. K., 1970.

Oppenheimer, Aharon. *The ʿAm Ha-Aretz: A Study in the Social History of the Jewish People in the Hellenistic-Roman Period*. Arbeiten zur Literatur und Geschichte des hellenistischen Judentums 8. Leiden: Brill, 1977.

Orlov, Andrei, and Gabriele Boccaccini, eds. *New Perspectives on 2 Enoch: No Longer Slavonic Only*. Studia Judaeoslavica 4. Leiden: Brill, 2012.

O'Toole, Robert F. "Some Exegetical Reflections on Luke 13, 10–17." *Biblica* 73 (1992): 84–107.

Ottenheijm, Eric. "Impurity between Intention and Deed: Purity Disputes in First Century Judaism and in the New Testament." Pages 129–47 in *Purity and Holiness: The Heritage of Leviticus*. Edited by Marcel J. H. M. Poorthuis and Joshua Schwartz. Jewish and Christian Perspectives Series 2. Brill: Leiden, 2000.

–. "Genezen als goed doen. Halachische logica in Mt 12, 9–14." *Bijdragen: Tijdschrift voor filosofie en theologie* 63 (2002): 356–65.

Overman, J. Andrew. *Matthew's Gospel and Formative Judaism: The Social World of the Matthean Community*. Minneapolis: Fortress, 1990.

Paget, James Carleton. "The Definition of the Terms Jewish Christian and Jewish Christianity in the History of Research." Pages 22–48 in *Jewish Believers in Jesus: The Early Centuries*. Edited by Oskar Skarsaune and Reidar Hvalvik. Peabody, Mass.: Hendrickson, 2007.

Parker, Robert. *Miasma: Pollution and Purification in Early Greek Religion*. Oxford: Clarendon, 1983.

Parsons, Mikeal C. "'Nothing Defiled AND Unclean': The Conjunction's Function in Acts 10:14." *Perspectives in Religious Studies* 27 (2000): 263–74.

Paschen, Wilfried. *Rein und Unrein: Untersuchung zur biblischen Wortgeschichte*. Studien zum Alten und Neuen Testaments 24. Munich: Kösel, 1970.

Pedersen, Kirsten Stoffregen. "Is the Church of Ethiopia a Judaic Church?" *Warszawskie Studia Teologiczne* 12 (1999): 203–16.

Pervo, Richard I. *Dating Acts: Between the Evangelists and the Apologists*. Santa Rosa, Calif.: Polebridge, 2006.

–. *Acts: A Commentary*. Hermeneia. Minneapolis: Fortress, 2009.

–. Review of Patricia Walters, *The Assumed Authorial Unity of Luke and Acts: A Reassessment of the Evidence*, *Review of Biblical Literature* [http://www.bookreviews.org] (2009).

Pesch, Rudolf. *Das Markusevangelium*. 2 vols. Wege der Forschung 411. Darmstadt: Wissenschaftliche Buchgesellschaft, 1979.

–. *Die Apostelgeschichte*. 2 vols. Evangelisch-katholischer Kommentar zum Neuen Testament 5. Zurich: Benziger, 1986.

Pettem, Michael. "Luke's Great Omission and His View of the Law." *New Testament Studies* 42 (1996): 35–54.

Philipps, John. *Exploring Acts: Volume One Acts 1–12*. Chicago: Moody Press, 1986.

Pirot, Louis, and Albert Clamer. *La Sainte Bible: Texte latin et traduction française d'après les textes originaux avec un commentaire exégétique et théologique*. 12 vols. Paris: Letouzey, 1946.

Plümacher, Eckhard. *Lukas als hellenistischer Schriftsteller. Studien zur Apostelgeschichte*. Studien zur Umwelt des Neuen Testaments 9. Göttingen: Vandenhoeck & Ruprecht, 1972.

Plummer, Alfred. *The Gospel according to Luke*. 5th ed. ICC. Edinburgh: T&T Clark, 1989.

Poirier, John C. "Why Did the Pharisees Wash their Hands?" *Journal of Jewish Studies* 47 (1996): 217–33.

–. "Purity beyond the Temple in the Second Temple Era." *Journal of Biblical Literature* 122 (2003): 247–65.

Poorthuis, Marcel J. H. M., and Joshua Schwartz, eds. *Purity and Holiness: The Heritage of Leviticus*. Jewish and Christian Perspectives Series 2. Brill: Leiden, 2000.

Powell, Mark Allan. "Do and Keep What Moses Says (Matthew 23:2–7)." *Journal of Biblical Literature* 114 (1995): 419–35.

Qimron, Elisha. "Chickens in the Temple Scroll (11QTc)." *Tarbiz* 54 (1995): 473–76. [Hebrew]

Rappaport, Uriel. *The First Book of Maccabees: Introduction, Hebrew Translation, and Commentary*. Between Bible and Mishnah. Jerusalem: Yad Ben Zvi, 2004. [Hebrew]

Rawlinson, Alfred E. J. *The Gospel according to St Mark*. 6th ed. Westminster Commentaries. London: Methuen, 1925.

Reed, Jonathan L. "Stone Vessels and Gospel Texts: Purity and Socio-Economics in John 2." Pages 381–401 in *Zeichen aus Text und Stein: Studien auf dem Weg zu einer Archäologie des Neuen Testaments*. Edited by Stefan Alkier and Jürgen Zangenberg. Texte und Arbeiten zum neutestamentlichen Zeitalter 42. Tübingen: Francke, 2003.

Reed, R. *Ancient Skins, Parchments and Leathers*. London: Seminar Press, 1972.

Regev, Eyal. "Non-Priestly Purity and Its Religious Aspects according to Historical Sources and Archaeological Findings." Pages 129–47 in *Purity and Holiness: The Heritage of Leviticus*. Edited by Marcel J. H. M. Poorthuis and Joshua Schwartz. Jewish and Christian Perspectives Series 2. Brill: Leiden, 2000.

Repschinski, Boris. *The Controversy Stories in the Gospel of Matthew. Their Redaction, Form and Relevance for the Relationship between the Matthean Community and Formative Judaism*. Forschungen zur Religion und Literatur des Alten und Neuen Testaments 189. Göttingen: Vandenhoeck & Ruprecht, 2000.

Resch, Gotthold. *Das Aposteldecret nach seiner außerkanonischen Textgestalt untersucht*. Texte und Untersuchungen zur Geschichte der altchristlichen Literatur 28.3. Leipzig: J. C. Hinrichs, 1905.

Rice, George E. "Luke 4:31–44: Release for the Captives." *Andrews University Seminary Studies* 20 (1982): 23–28.

Riesenfeld, H. "Sabbat et jour du Seigneur." Pages 210–218 in *New Testament Essays: Studies in Memory of Thomas Walter Manson*. Edited by A. J. B. Higgins. Manchester: Manchester University Press, 1959.

Rodinson, Maxine. "Sur la question des 'influences juives' en Éthiopie." *Journal of Semitic Studies* 9 (1964): 11–19.

Roloff, Jürgen. *Die Apostelgeschichte übersetzt und erklärt*. 17th ed. Göttingen: Vandenhoeck & Ruprecht, 1981.

Rordorf, Willy. *Sunday: The History of the Day of Rest and Worship in the Earliest Centuries of the Christian Church*. Translated by A. A. K. Graham. London: SCM Press, 1968.

Rosenblum, Jordan D. "Kosher Olive Oil in Antiquity Reconsidered." *Journal for the Study of Judaism* 40 (2009): 356–65.

–. *Food and Identity in Early Rabbinic Judaism*. Cambridge: Cambridge University Press, 2010.

–. "'Why Do You Refuse to Eat Pork?' Jews, Food, and Identity in Roman Palestine." *Jewish Quarterly Review* 100 (2010): 95–110.

Rubin, Nissan. *Beginning of Life; Rites of Birth, Circumcision, and Redemption of the First-Born in the Talmud and Midrash*. Tel Aviv: Ha-Kibbuts Ha-Meuhad, 1995. [Hebrew]

Rudolph, David J. *A Jew to the Jews: Jewish Contours of Pauline Flexibility in 1 Corinthians 9:19–23*. Wissenschaftliche Untersuchungen zum Neuen Testament 2.304. Tübingen: Mohr Siebeck, 2011.

Runesson, Anders. *The Origins of the Synagogue: A Social-Historical Study*. Coniectanea biblica: New Testament Series 37. Stockholm: Almqvist & Wiksell, 2001.

–. "Water and Worship: Ostia and the Ritual Bath in the Diaspora Synagogue." Pages 115–29 in *The Synagogue of Ancient Ostia and the Jews of Rome*. Edited by Birger Olsson, Dieter Mitternacht, and Olof Brandt. ActaRom–4o.57. Stockholm: Paul Åströms, 2001.

–. "Rethinking Early Jewish-Christian Relations: Matthean Community History as Pharisaic Intragroup Conflict." *Journal of Biblical Literature* 127 (2008): 95–132.

–. "Behind the Gospel of Matthew: Radical Pharisees in Post-War Galilee?" *Currents in Theology and Mission* 37 (2010): 460–71.

Rutgers, Leonard Victor. "Archaeological Evidence for the Interaction of Jews and non-Jews in Antiquity." *American Journal of Archaeology* 96 (1992): 101–18.

–. *Making Myths: Jews in Early Christian Identity Formation*. Leuven: Peeters, 2009.

Ruzer, Serge. "Jesus' Crucifixion in Luke and Acts: The Search for a Meaning vis-à-vis the Biblical Pattern of Persecuted Prophet." Pages 173–91 in *Judaistik und neutestamentliche Wissenschaft*. Edited by Lutz Doering, Hans-Günther Waubke, and Florian Wilk. Forschungen zur Religion und Literatur des Alten und Neuen Testaments 226. Göttingen: Vandenhoeck & Ruprecht, 2008.

Sabourin, Léopold S. J. *L'Évangile de Luc: Introduction et commentaire*. Rome: Editrice Pontificia Università Gregoriana, 1985.

Safrai, Shmuel. "Home and Family." Pages 728–92 in *The Jewish People in the First Century*. Edited by Shmuel Safrai and Menahem Stern. 2 vols. Compendia rerum iudaicarum ad Novum Testamentum. Amsterdam: Van Gorcum, 1976.

Safrai, Shmuel, and Menahem Stern, eds. *The Jewish People in the First Century*. 2 vols. Compendia rerum iudaicarum ad Novum Testamentum. Amsterdam: Van Gorcum, 1976.

Safrai, Ze'ev, and Chana Safrai ל"ז. "Papyrus Oxyrhynchus 840." Pages 255–82 in *Halakhah in Light of Epigraphy*. Edited by Albert I. Baumgarten, Hanan Eshel ל"ז, Ranon Katzoff, and Shani Tzoref. Journal of Ancient Judaism Supplements 3. Göttingen: Vandenhoeck & Ruprecht, 2011.

Sahlin, Harald. "Die drei Kardinalsünden und das Neue Testament." *Studia theologica* 24 (1970): 93–112.

Saldarini, Anthony. "Interpretation of Luke-Acts and Implications for Jewish-Christian Dialogue." *Word & World* 12 (1992): 37–42.

–. "The Gospel of Matthew and Jewish-Christian Conflict in Galilee." Pages 23–38 in *The Galilee in Late Antiquity*. Edited by Lee I. Levine. New York: Jewish Theological Seminary of America, 1992.

–. *Matthew's Christian-Jewish Community*. Chicago Studies in the History of Judaism. Chicago: University of Chicago Press, 1994.

Salmon, Marilyn. "Insider or Outsider? Luke's Relationship with Judaism." Pages 76–82 in *Luke-Acts and the Jewish People: Eight Critical Perspectives*. Edited by Joseph B. Tyson. Minneapolis: Augsburg, 1988.

Salo, Kalervo. *Luke's Treatment of the Law: A Redaction-Critical Investigation.* Annales Academiae scientiarum fennicae. Dissertationes humanarum litterarum 57. Helsinki: Suomalainen Tiedeakatemia, 1991.

Sanders, E. P. *Paul and Palestinian Judaism: A Comparison of Patterns of Religion*. Philadelphia: Fortress, 1977.

–. "Jesus and the Constraint of the Law." *Journal for the Study of the New Testament* 17 (1983): 19–24.

–. *Jesus and Judaism*. London: SCM Press, 1985.

–. "Jewish Association with Gentiles and Galatians 2:11–14." Pages 170–88 in *The Conversation Continues: Essays on Paul and John Presented to J. Louis Martyn*. Edited by Robert Fortna and Beverly Gaventa. Nashville, Tenn.: Abingdon, 1990.

–. *Jewish Law from Jesus to the Mishnah*. Philadelphia: Trinity Press International, 1990.

–. *Judaism: Practice and Belief 63 BCE–66 CE*. Philadelphia: Trinity Press International, 1992.

Sanders, E. P., and Margaret Davies. *Studying the Synoptic Gospels*. London: SCM, 1989.

Sanders, Jack T. *The Jews in Luke-Acts*. Philadelphia: Fortress, 1987.

Sandmel, Samuel. *Anti-Semitism in the New Testament?* Philadelphia: Fortress, 1978.

Sandt, Huub van de. "'Do Not Give What Is Holy to the Dogs' (Did 9:5D and Matt 7:6A): The Eucharistic Food of the Didache in Its Jewish Purity Setting." *Vigiliae christianae* 56 (2002): 223–46.

Sandt, Huub van de, and Jürgen K. Zangenberg, eds. *Matthew, James, and Didache: Three Related Documents in their Jewish and Christian Settings*. Society of Biblical Literature Symposium Series 45. Atlanta: Society of Biblical Literature, 2008.

Sariola, Heikki. *Markus und das Gesetz: Eine redaktionskritische Untersuchung*. Annales Academiae scientiarum fennicae. Dissertationes humanarum litterarum 56. Helsinki: Suomalainen Tiedeakatemia, 1990.

Schäfer, Peter. "Der Grundtext von Targum Pseudo-Jonathan: Eine synoptische Studie zu Gen 1." Pages 8–29 in *Das Institutum Judaicum der Universität Tübingen in den Jahren 1971–1972*. Tübingen, 1972.

–. *Der Bar Kokhba-Aufstand: Studien zum zweiten jüdischen Krieg gegen Rom*. Texte und Studien zum antiken Judentum 1. Tübingen: Mohr Siebeck, 1981.

–. ed. *The Bar Kokhba War Reconsidered: New Perspectives on the Second Jewish Revolt against Rome*. Texte und Studien zum antiken Judentum 100. Tübingen: Mohr Siebeck, 2002.

Schaller, Berndt. "Jesus und der Sabbat. Franz-Delitzsch-Vorlesung 1992." Pages 125–47 in *Fundamenta Judaica: Studien zum antiken Judentum und zum Neuen Testament*. Edited by Lutz Doering and Annette Steudel. Studien zur Umwelt des Neuen Testaments 25. Göttingen: Vandenhoeck & Ruprecht. 2001.

Schiffman, Lawrence H. "Laws Pertaining to Forbidden Foods in the Dead Sea Scrolls." Pages 65–80 in *Halakhah in Light of Epigraphy*. Edited by Albert I. Baumgarten,

Hanan Eshel ז"ל, Ranon Katzoff, and Shani Tzoref. Journal of Ancient Judaism Supplements 3. Göttingen: Vandenhoeck & Ruprecht, 2011.
–. *The Halakhah at Qumran*. Studies in Judaism in Late Antiquity 16. Leiden: Brill, 1975.
Schlatter, Adolf. *Der Evangelist Matthäus*. 2d ed. Stuttgart: Calwer Verlag, 1933.
Schmithals, Walter. *Das Evangelium nach Lukas*. Zürcher Bibelkommentare: Neues Testament 3.1. Zurich: Theologischer, 1980.
Schnackenburg, Rudolf. *Matthäusevangelium*. 2 vols. Die Neue Echter Bibel. Würzburg: Echter, 1985–1987.
Schneider, Gerhard. *Die Apostelgeschichte*. 2 vols. Herders theologischer Kommentar zum Neuen Testament 5. Freiburg im Breisgau: Herder, 1980–1982.
–. *Das Evangelium nach Lukas*. 2 vols. Ökumenischer Taschenbuch-Kommentar zum Neuen Testament. Gütersloh: Mohn, 1984.
Schonfield, Hugh J. *Proclaiming the Messiah: The Life and Letters of Paul, Envoy to the Nations*. London: Open Gate, 1997.
Schröter, Jens. *Erinnerung an Worte Jesu: Studien zur Rezeption der Logienüberlieferung in Markus, Q und Thomas*. Wissenschaftliche Monographien zum Alten und Neuen Testament 76. Neukirchen-Vluyn: Neukirchener, 1997.
Schwartz, Daniel R. "The end of the ΓΗ (Acts 1:8): Beginning or End of the Christian Vision?" *Journal of Biblical Literature* 105 (1986): 669–76.
–. "The Futility of Preaching Moses (Acts 15, 21)." *Biblica* 67 (1986): 276–81.
–. "Jewish Movements of the New Testament Period." Pages 526–30 in *The Jewish Annotated New Testament*. Edited by Amy-Jill Levine and Marc Zvi Brettler. Oxford: Oxford University Press, 2011.
Schwartz, Daniel R., and Zeev Weiss, eds. *Was 70 CE a Watershed in Jewish History? On Jews and Judaism before and after the Destruction of the Second Temple*. Ancient Judaism and Early Christianity 78. Leiden: Brill, 2012.
Schwartz, Joshua. "Dogs in Jewish Society in the Second Temple Period and in the Time of the Mishnah and Talmud." *Journal of Jewish Studies* 55 (2004): 246–77.
Schwartz, Seth. *Imperialism and Jewish Society, 200 B.C.E. to 640 C.E.* Princeton, N.J.: Princeton University Press, 2001.
Schweizer, Eduard. *Das Evangelium nach Matthäus*. Das Neue Testament Deutsch 2. Göttingen: Vandenhoeck & Ruprecht, 1981.
Segundo, Juan L. *El Caso Mateo: Los comienzos de una ética judeo-cristiana*. Colección Presencia Teológica 74. Santander: Editorial Sal Terrae, 1994.
Selwyn, Edward Carus. *St. Luke the Prophet*. London: Macmillan, 1901.
Senior, Donald. *What Are They Saying about Matthew?* Rev. and enl. ed. New York: Paulist, 1996.
–. "Between Two Worlds: Gentiles and Jewish Christians in Matthew's Gospel." *Catholic Biblical Quarterly* 61 (1999): 1–23.
Shemesh, Aharon. "4Q251: Midrash Mishpatim." *Dead Sea Discoveries* 12 (2005): 280–302.
–. "Common Halakhic and Exegetical Traditions Shared by DSS and Rabbinic Literature." Pages 383–94 in *Zaphenath-Paneah: Linguistic Studies Presented to Elisha Qimron on the Occasion of His Sixty-Fifth Birthday*. Edited by Daniel Sivan, David Talshir, and Chaim Cohen. Beer-Sheva: Beer-Sheva University Press, 2009. [Hebrew]
–. "The Laws of Incest in the Dead Sea Scrolls and the History of Halakhah." Pages 81–99 in *Halakhah in Light of Epigraphy*. Edited by Albert I. Baumgarten, Hanan Eshel ז"ל, Ranon Katzoff, and Shani Tzoref. Journal of Ancient Judaism Supplements 3. Göttingen: Vandenhoeck & Ruprecht, 2011.

Sigal, Phillip. *The Halakhah of Jesus of Nazareth according to the Gospel of Matthew.* Society of Biblical Literature 18. Leiden: Brill, 2007.

Sim, David C. *Apocalyptic Eschatology in the Gospel of Matthew.* Society for New Testament Studies Monograph Series 88. Cambridge: Cambridge University Press, 1996.

–. *The Gospel of Matthew and Christian Judaism: The History and Social Setting of the Matthean Community.* Studies in the New Testament and Its World. Edinburgh: T&T Clark, 1998.

–. "Matthew, Paul and the Origin and Nature of the Gentile Mission: The Great Commission in Matthew 28:16–20 as an Anti-Pauline Tradition." *Hervormde Teologiese Studies/Theological Studies* 64 (2008): 377–92.

–. "Reconstructing the Social and Religious Milieu of Matthew: Methods, Sources, and Possible Results." Pages 13–41 in *Matthew, James, and Didache: Three Related Documents in their Jewish and Christian Settings.* Edited by Huub van de Sandt and Jürgen K. Zangenberg. Society of Biblical Literature Symposium Series 45. Atlanta: Society of Biblical Literature, 2008.

–. "Matthew's Use of Mark: Did Matthew Intend to Supplement or to Replace His Primary Source?" *New Testament Studies* 57 (2011): 176–92.

Simon, Marcel. *Verus Israël. Études sur les relations entre chrétiens et juifs dans l'empire romain (135-425).* 2d ed. Paris: É. de Boccard, 1964.

–. "Problèmes du judéo-christianisme." Pages 1–16 in *Aspects du judéo-christianisme: Colloque de Strasbourg 23–25 avril 1964.* Bibliothèque des centres d'études supérieures spécialisés: Travaux du centre d'études supérieures d'histoire des religions de Strasbourg. Paris: Presses Universitaires de France, 1965.

Skarsaune, Oskar. "Jewish Believers in Jesus in Antiquity – Problems of Definition, Method, and Sources." Pages 3–21 in *Jewish Believers in Jesus: The Early Centuries.* Edited by Oskar Skarsaune and Reidar Hvalvik. Peabody, Mass.: Hendrickson, 2007.

Skarsaune, Oskar, and Reidar Hvalvik, eds. *Jewish Believers in Jesus: The Early Centuries.* Peabody, Mass.: Hendrickson, 2007.

Soler, Jean. *Sacrifices et interdits alimentaires dans la Bible. Aux origines du Dieu unique.* Paris: Hachette, 2004.

Sosa, Carlos R. "Pureza e impureza en la narrativa de Pedro, Cornelio y el Espíritu Santo en Hechos 10." *Kairós* 41 (2007): 55–78.

Sparks, Kent. "Gospel as Conquest: Mosaic Typology in Matthew 28:16–20." *Catholic Biblical Quarterly* 68 (2006): 651–63.

Staats, Reinhart. "Die Sonntagnachmittaggottesdienste der christlichen Frühzeit." *Zeitschrift für die neutestamentliche Wissenschaft und die Kunde der älteren Kirche* 66 (1975): 224–63.

Stählin, Gustav. *Die Apostelgeschichte.* Das Neue Testament Deutsch 5. Göttingen: Vandenhoeck & Ruprecht, 1980.

Stanton, Graham N. "The Origin and Purpose of Matthew's Gospel: Matthean Scholarship from 1945–1980." *Aufstieg und Niedergang der römischen Welt: Geschichte und Kultur Roms im Spiegel der neueren Forschung* 25.3:1889–1951. Part 2, *Principat*, 25.3. Edited by Hildegard Temporini and Wolfgang Haase. New York: de Gruyter, 1985.

–. *A Gospel for a New People.* Edinburgh: T&T Clark, 1992.

–. *The Gospels and Jesus.* 2d ed. Oxford: Oxford University Press, 2002.

Stegemann, Wolfgang. *Zwischen Synagoge und Obrigkeit: Zur historischen Situation der lukanischen Christen.* Forschungen zur Religion und Literatur des Alten und Neuen Testaments 152. Göttingen: Vandenhoeck & Ruprecht, 1991.

Stendahl, Krister. *The School of St. Matthew*. Acta seminarii neotestamentici upsaliensis 20. Uppsala: C. W. K. Gleerup, Lund, 1954.

Stiebel, Guy D. "'Meager Bread and Scant Water' – Food for Thought at Masada." Pages 283–303 in *Halakhah in Light of Epigraphy*. Edited by Albert I. Baumgarten, Hanan Eshel ז"ל, Ranon Katzoff, and Shani Tzoref. Journal of Ancient Judaism Supplements 3. Göttingen: Vandenhoeck & Ruprecht, 2011.

Stökl Ben Ezra, Daniel. "'Christians' Observing 'Jewish' Festivals of Autumn." Pages 53–73 in *The Image of the Judaeo-Christians in Ancient Jewish and Christian Literature*. Edited by Peter J. Tomson and Doris Lambers-Petry. Wissenschaftliche Untersuchungen zum Neuen Testament 158. Tübingen: Mohr Siebeck, 2003.

–. *The Impact of Yom Kippur on Early Christianity: The Day of Atonement from Second Temple Judaism to the Fifth Century*. Wissenschaftliche Untersuchungen zum Neuen Testament 163. Tübingen: Mohr Siebeck, 2003.

–. "Whose Fast is It? The Ember Day of September and Yom Kippur." Pages 259–82 in *The Ways That Never Parted*. Edited by Adam H. Becker and Annette Yoshiko Reed. Minneapolis: Fortress, 2007.

–. "Markus-Evangelium." *Reallexicon für Antike und Christentum* 24 (2010): 173–207.

Strack, Hermann L., and Paul Billerbeck. *Kommentar zum Neuen Testament aus Talmud und Midrasch*. 6 vols. Munich: C. H. Beck, 1922–1961.

Strand, Kenneth. "Another Look at the 'Lord's Day' in the Early Church and in Rev. 1:10." *New Testament Studies* 13 (1965): 174–81.

Strecker, Georg. *Der Weg Gerechtigkeit: Untersuchung zur Theologie des Matthäus*. Forschungen zur Religion und Literatur des Alten und Neuen Testaments 82. Göttingen: Vandenhoeck & Ruprecht, 1962.

Streeter, Burnett Hillman. *The Four Gospels*. London: Macmillan, 1924.

Strelan, Rick. *Luke the Priest: The Authority of the Author of the Third Gospel*. Burlington, Vt.: Ashgate, 2008.

Stuckenbruck, Loren T. "The 'Cleansing' of the Gentiles: Background for the Rationale behind the Apostles' Decree in Acts 15." Pages 65–90 in *Apostledekret und antikes Vereinswesen: Gemeinschaft und ihre Ordnung*. Edited by Markus Öhler. Wissenschaftliche Untersuchungen zum Neuen Testament 280. Tübingen: Mohr Siebeck, 2011.

Suter, David W. "Fallen Angel, Fallen Priest: The Problem of Family Purity in 1 Enoch 6–16." *Hebrew Union College Annual* 50 (1979): 115–35.

Talbert, Charles H. *Reading Luke: A Literary and Theological Commentary on the Third Gospel*. Reading the New Testament Series. New York: Crossroad, 1986.

–. *Reading Acts: A Literary and Theological Commentary on the Acts of the Apostles*. Reading the New Testament Series. New York: The Crossroad Publishing Company, 1997.

–. *Matthew*. Paideia Commentaries on the New Testament. Grand Rapids, Mich.: Baker Academic, 2010.

Tannehill, Robert C. "Varieties of Synoptic Pronouncement Stories." *Semeia* 20 (1981): 101–19.

–. *The Narrative Unity of Luke-Acts: A Literary Interpretation*. Vol. 1.: *The Gospel according to Luke*. Foundations and Facets. Philadelphia, Pa.: Fortress, 1986.

Taylor, Vincent. *The Gospel according to St Mark*. London: Macmillan, 1935.

Theissen, Gerhard. *The Miracle Stories of the Early Christian Tradition*. Translated by Francis McDonagh. Edinburgh: T&T Clark, 1983.

Thiessen, Matthew. *Contesting Conversion: Genealogy, Circumcision, and Identity in Ancient Judaism and Christianity*. Oxford: Oxford University Press, 2011.

–. "Luke 2:22, Leviticus 12, and Parturient Impurity." *Novum Testamentum* 54 (2012): 16–29.

Thompson, William. "An Historical Perspective on the Gospel of Matthew." *Journal of Biblical Literature* 93 (1974): 243–62.

Tobias, Nicklas. "Das Agraphon vom 'Sabbatarbeiter' und sein Kontext: Lk 6:1–11 in der Textform des Codex Bezae Cantabrigiensis (D)." *Novum Testamentum* 44 (2002): 160–75.

Tomson, Peter J. *Paul and the Jewish Law: Halakha in the Letters of the Apostle to the Gentiles.* Compendia rerum iudaicum ad Novum Testamentum 3. Jewish Traditions in Early Christian Literature 1; Assen, Netherlands: Van Gorcum, 1990.

–. *'If this be from Heaven...' Jesus and the New Testament Authors in Their Relationship to Judaism.* Sheffield: Sheffield Academic Press, 2001.

Tomson, Peter J., and Doris Lambers-Petry, eds. *The Image of the Judaeo-Christians in Ancient Jewish and Christian Literature*. Wissenschaftliche Untersuchungen zum Neuen Testament 158. Tübingen: Mohr Siebeck, 2003.

Trautmann, Maria. *Zeichenhafte Handlungen Jesu. Ein Beitrag zur Frage nach dem geschichtlichen Jesus*. Forschung zur Bibel 37. Würzburg: Echter, 1980.

Trilling, Wolfgang. *Das wahre Israel: Studien zur Theologie des Matthäus-Evangeliums.* Studien zum Alten und Neuen Testaments 10. Munich: Kösel, 1964.

Trocmé, Etienne. *Le livre des Actes et l'histoire.* Paris: Presses Universitaires de France, 1957.

Tuckett, Christopher M., ed. *Luke's Literary Achievement: Collected Essays*. Journal for the Study of the New Testament Supplement Series 116. Sheffield: Sheffield Academic Press, 1995.

Turner, Max M. B. "The Sabbath, Sunday, and the Law in Luke/Acts." Pages 99–157 in *From Sabbath to Lord's Day: A Biblical, Historical, and Theological Investigation.* Edited by Daniel A. Carson. Grand Rapids, Mich.: Zondervan, 1982.

Tyson, Joseph B. "Acts 6:1–7 and Dietary Regulations in Early Christianity." *Perspectives in Religious Studies* 10 (1983): 145–61.

–. *Luke, Judaism, and the Scholars: Critical Approaches to Luke-Acts*. Columbia, S.C.: University of South Carolina, 1999.

–. *Marcion and Luke-Acts: A Defining Struggle.* Columbia, S.C.: University of South Carolina Press, 2006.

–. ed. *Luke-Acts and the Jewish People: Eight Critical Perspectives*. Minneapolis: Augsburg, 1988.

Ullendorff, Edward. "Hebraic-Jewish Elements in Abyssinian (Monophysite) Christianity." *Journal of Semitic Studies* 1 (1956): 216–56.

Ulmer, Rivka. *The Evil Eye in the Bible and in Rabbinic Literature*. Hoboken, N.J.: Ktav, 1994.

Uro, Risto. *Sheep among the Wolves: A Study of the Mission Instructions of Q*. Annales Academiae scientiarum fennicae. Dissertationes humanarum litterarum 47. Helsinki: Suomalainen Tiedeakatemia, 1987.

Urbach, E. E. "The Rabbinical Laws of Idolatry in the Second and Third Centuries in Light of Archaeological and Historical Facts." *Israeli Exploration Journal* 9 (1959): 149–65, 229–45.

Vahrenhorst, Martin. *"Ihr sollt überhaupt nicht schwören." Matthäus im halachischen Diskurs*. Wissenschaftliche Monographien zum Alten und Neuen Testament 95. Neukirchen-Vluyn: Neukirchener, 2002.

Verheyden, Jozef. "How Many Were Sent according to Lk 10,1?" in *Luke and His Readers: Festschrift A. Denaux*. Edited by Adelbert Denaux, Reimund Bieringer, Gilbert van Belle, and Jozef Verheyden. Bibliotheca ephemeridum theologicarum lovaniensium 182. Leuven: Leuven University Press, 2005.

Vermes, Geza. *Jesus the Jew: A Historian's Reading of the Gospels*. Philadelphia: Fortress, 1981.

Vouga, F. *Jésus et la Loi selon la tradition synoptique*. Le Monde de la Bible. Geneva: Labor et Fides, 1988.

Wahlen, Clinton. "Peter's Vision and Conflicting Definitions of Purity." *New Testament Studies* 51 (2005): 505–18.

Walker, Rolf. *Heilsgeschichte im ersten Evangelium*. Forschungen zur Religion und Literatur des Alten und Neuen Testaments 91. Göttingen: Vandenhoeck & Ruprecht, 1967.

Walters, Patricia. *The Assumed Authorial Unity of Luke and Acts: A Reassessment of the Evidence*. Society for New Testament Studies Monograph Series 145. Cambridge: Cambridge University Press, 2009.

Wedderburn, A. J. M. "The 'Apostolic Decree': Tradition and Redaction." *Novum Testamentum* 35 (1993): 362–89.

Wehnert, Jürgen. *Die Reinheit des "christlichen Gottesvolkes" aus Juden und Heiden*. Forschungen zur Religion und Literatur des Alten und Neuen Testaments 173. Göttingen: Vandenhoeck & Ruprecht, 1997.

Weiser, Alfons. *Die Apostelgeschichte*. 2 vols. Ökumenischer Taschenbuch-Kommentar zum Neuen Testament 5.1–2. Gütersloh: Gütersloher Verlaghaus Gerd Mohn, 1982–1985.

Weiss, Herold. *A Day of Gladness: The Sabbath among Jews and Christians in Antiquity*. Columbia, S.C.: University of South Carolina Press, 2003.

Weren, Wim J. C. "The Five Women in Matthew's Genealogy." *Catholic Biblical Quarterly* 59 (1997): 288–305.

Werman, Cana. *Attitude towards Gentiles in the Book of Jubilees and Qumran Literature Compared with Early Tanaaic Halakha and Contemporary Pseudepigrapha*. Ph.D. diss., The Hebrew University of Jerusalem, 1995. [Hebrew]

–. "The Concept of Holiness and the Requirements of Purity in Second Temple and Tannaic Literature." Pages 163–79 in *Purity and Holiness: The Heritage of Leviticus*. Edited by Marcel J. H. M. Poorthuis and Joshua Schwartz. Jewish and Christian Perspectives Series 2. Brill: Leiden, 2000.

Westermann, Claus. *Genesis*. 3 vols. Translated by John J. Scullion S. J. Minneapolis: Augsburg, 1984–1986.

White, L. Michael. "The Gospel of Matthew: Jesus as the New Moses." No Pages. Cited 13 February, 2012. Online: http://www.pbs.org./wgbh/pages/frongline/shows/religion/story/matthew.html.

White, Robert J. *The Interpretation of Dreams: The Oneirocritica of Artemidorus*. Park Ridge, N.J.: Noyes, 1975.

Whitters, Mark F. *The Epistle of Second Baruch: A Study in Form and Message*. Journal for the Study of the Pseudepigrapha: Supplement Series 42. London: Sheffield Academic Press, 2003.

Wiefel, Wolfgang. *Das Evangelium nach Matthäus*. Theologischer Handkommentar zum Neuen Testament. Leipzig: Evangelische Verlagsanstalt, 1998.

Wilkins, John, F. D. Harvey, and Michael J. Dobson, eds. *Food in Antiquity*. Exeter: University of Exeter Press, 1995.

Williams, Margaret H. "Palestinian Jewish Personal Names in Acts." Pages 79–113 in *The Book of Acts in Its Palestinian Setting*. Edited by Richard Bauckham. Vol. 4 of the

The Book of Acts in Its First Century Setting. Edited by Bruce W. Winter. Grand Rapids, Mich.: Eerdmans, 1995.

Willits, Joel. "The Friendship of Matthew and Paul: A Response to the Recent Trend in the Interpretation of Matthew's Gospel." *Hervormde Teologiese Studies/Theological Studies* 65.1 (2009): Art. #151. 8 pages.

Wilson, Stephen G. *Luke and the Law.* Society for New Testament Studies Monograph Series 50. Cambridge: Cambridge University Press, 1983.

Winger, J. Michael. "When Did the Women Visit the Tomb?" *New Testament Studies* 40 (1994): 284–88.

Witherington III, Ben, *The Acts of the Apostles: A Socio-Rhetorical Commentary.* Grand Rapids, Mich.: Eerdmans, 1998.

–. ed. *History, Literature, and Society in the Book of Acts.* Cambridge: Cambridge University Press, 1996.

Wolter, Michael. *Das Lukasevangelium.* Handbuch zum Neuen Testament 5. Tübingen: Mohr Siebeck, 2008.

Wong, E. K. C. "The Matthean Understanding of the Sabbath: A Response to G. N. Stanton." *Journal for the Study of the New Testament* 44 (1991): 3–18.

Wright, David P. *The Disposal of Impurity: Elimination Rites in the Bible and Hittite and Mesopotamian Literature.* Society of Biblical Literature Dissertation Series 101. Atlanta: Scholars, 1987.

Wright, David P., David Noel Freedman, and Avi Hurvitz, eds. *Pomegranates and Golden Bells: Studies in Biblical, Jewish, and Near Eastern Ritual, Law, and Literature in Honor of Jacob Milgrom.* Winona Lake, Ind.: Eisenbrauns, 1995.

Yang, Yong-Eui. *Jesus and the Sabbath in Matthew's Gospel.* Journal for the Study of the New Testament: Supplement Series 139. Sheffield: Sheffield Academic Press, 1997.

Young, Brad H. *Jesus and His Jewish Parables: Rediscovering the Roots of Jesus' Teaching.* Theological Inquiries. New York: Paulist Press, 1989.

–. *The Parables: Jewish Tradition and Christian Interpretation.* Peabody, Mass.: Hendrickson, 1998.

Zeitlin, Solomon. "The Book of Jubilees: Its Character and Its Significance." *Jewish Quarterly Review* 30 (1939): 1–32.

–. "The Beginning of the Jewish Day during the Second Commonwealth." *Jewish Quarterly Review* 36 (1946): 403–14.

–. "Proselytes and Proselytism during the Second Commonwealth and the Early Tannaitic Period." Vol. 2:871–82 in *Harry Austryn Wolfson Jubilee Volume: On the Occasion of his Seventy-Fifth Birthday.* 2 vols. Jerusalem: American Academy for Jewish Research, 1965.

Ziesler, John A. "Luke and the Pharisees." *New Testament Studies* 25 (1978/79): 146–57.

Zmijewski, Josef. *Die Apostelgeschichte.* Regensburger Neues Testament. Regensburg: Friedrich Pustet, 1994.

Index of Ancient Sources

Hebrew Bible/Old Testament

Genesis		46:27	31
1	107		
1:5	223, 229	Exodus	
1:20–25	326	1:5	313
1:24	341	3:3	340
1:25	355	11:4	226
2:1–3	187	12:6	149
2:4	106	12:16	153
2:24	359	12:18	223
3:8	342	13:12	422
6:20	326	13:14–15	423
8:22	244, 391	14:24	225
9	275, 391–92	14:30	387
9:4	244, 385, 393	16:23	187
10	309–10	16:25	80
10:11	310	16:29	56, 199, 233
10:14	310	20	274
10:22	310	20:2	136
12:3	440	20:8	56
15:1	340	20:9	135
17	402, 414, 417	20:11	187, 215
17:5	440	20:12	267, 270
17:12	412	20:25	384
17:14	428	21:1	248
17:19	415	21:17	267, 270
18:1	340	22:30	380
18:12–15	415	23:5	123
18:25	342	23:12	187
19	304	23:19	245
19:7	342	28:29	340
21:2–4	415	29:39	227
21:4	412, 428	30:18–21	258
22:2	343	31:12	193
28:20–22	268	31:13–14	107
32:33	245	31:14	56, 345
37:28	122	31:15	187
46:2	340	31:16	56

31:17	45, 187	15:11	258
34:20	106, 423	15:13	413
34:26	245	15:19–24	379
35:2	187	15:24	252, 420
40:31	258	17	244–45, 275
		17:3–14	373
Leviticus		17:7	371–72
1:3	354	17:7–10	372
2:2, 9, 16	340	17:8–9	363, 371
3:17	245	17:10	245
5:2	330	17:10–16	272
6:8	340	17:11	382
7:15	229	17:13	245, 385, 392, 398
7:18	345	17:13–15	381
7:21	330	17:14	382
7:23–25	245	17:15	380, 381, 388, 393
7:24	330, 380, 386	17:16	380
10:10	345, 350	17–18	213, 363, 370–71, 376, 380, 385, 389, 390, 392, 394, 398
11	242–44, 252, 272, 275, 282, 285, 300, 326, 341	18	252, 375–80
11:3	243, 341	18:6	378
11:4	251, 284	18:6–18	379
11:4–7	341	18:6–30	376
11:8	331	18:8	377
11:8, 39–40	330	18:19	252, 379
11:10	251	18:20	379
11:20	284, 341	18:22	379
11:21–22	284	18:23	379
11:22	341	18:25	379
11:29	243	19:5	354
11:29–30	243, 285	19:7	345
11:29–35	288–89	20:18	252
11:29–38	243	20:25	252
11:32	300	21:1–3, 11	25
11:33–36	285	22:8	380
11:39	330	22:18	382
11:39–40	243, 329	22:28	229
11:41	285	23:3	187
11:41–44	285	23:24, 29	153
11:43	346–47	23:32	223
11:44	286	24:8	93
12	418–21	25:10	75, 187
12:2	418	25:35	51
12:3	412, 428	27:2, 8	268
12:4	418	27:30	283
12:6	418, 422	27:34	343
12:8	418		
12–15	249, 252	Numbers	
13:45–46	252	3:11–13	423

5	252	Judges	
6:7	25	5:13	122
9:2	134	7:19	225
11:25–26	313	11:30	268
12:6	340	16:3 (LXX A)	226
14:18	413	16:3 (LXX B)	226
18:15–16	423	17:8	88
18:16	425		
19	252	Ruth	
19:2	276, 356	2:12	408, 446
19:5	271		
19:11–22	291	1 Samuel	
19:14–15	289	1:21	423
28:2	134	1:22	426
28:3–4, 8	227	11:11	225
28:18	153	12:23	342
30	268	17:43	280
31:19–23	289	20:2, 9	342
35:4–5	233	21	92–93
		21:2–10	92
Deuteronomy		21:3	92
2:23	310	21:5	93
5	274	21:6	93
5:12	56	22:15	342
5:13	135	24:7	342
5:15	136, 187	24:14	280
5:16	267, 270	26:11	342
6:7	229		
8:3	274	2 Samuel	
10:22	313	3:8	280
12	275	9:8	280
12:16, 23	245	12:3	123
13:2–4	343	16:9	280
14	242, 275, 345	17:23	380
14:2	244, 349		
14:3–20	326	1 Kings	
14:7	284	13:4	117
14:21	245, 330, 385, 386, 388, 393	14:11	280
		16:4	280
14:22	283	16:13, 26	372
14:23	283	21:19, 23	280
18:16	342	23:38	280
20:20	53, 231		
21:22–23	159	2 Kings	
22:4	123	4:6	412
23:1	321	8:13	280
23:21–23	268	17:15	372
23:35	89	22:1–23:30	408
24:1	377	23:3	408
30:12	343–44	23:21–23	408

23:25	413	Isaiah		
		11:12	341	
1 Chronicles		14:1	405	
23:28	413	29:13	269	
		48:7	106	
2 Chronicles		49:6	197	
10:4	85	55:3	206	
10: 9, 10, 11, 14	85	56:1	363	
31:5–6	423	56:3	405	
34–35	408	56:3–7	321, 354, 363	
35:19	413	56:6	405	
		56:7	321, 354, 363	
Nehemiah		58:6	55, 71, 74–75, 78–	
7:63	416		79, 188	
10:36	423	59:10	226	
12:44	423	60:7	354	
		61	75–76	
Esther		61:1	75, 188	
8:5	241	61:1–2	56, 71, 74–75, 78	
9:27	405	61:5–6	391	
		66:6	342	
Job		66:23	86	
7:21	413			
34:36	297	Jeremiah		
37:3	341	2:5	372	
		2:20	84	
Psalms		5:5	84	
22:17	280	10:3	372	
29	342	17:21	56	
31:6	372	17:21–27	199	
37:8	412	38:10, 13	122	
40:3	122			
59:7, 15	280	Lamentations		
79:1	352	2:19	225	
		3:27	84	
Proverbs				
1:22	297	Ezekiel		
10:21	297	4:12, 15	342	
14:9	413	4:14	34, 345	
14:18	297	4:15	342	
17:12	297	4:9–12	342	
21:20	297	14:7	296	
21:21	338	36:25	376	
22:3	297	44:5–9	352	
27:12	297	44:6–7	321, 351	
		46:13–15	227	
Qohelet				
10:10	241	Daniel		
11:6	241	1:8	249, 250, 346, 374	
		1:17	340	

2:1, 7, 26, 28, 36	343	9:7	310
2:19	340	9:11–12	211
2:43	358		
6:18	121	Jonah	
7:1	340	1:14	342
7:7	340		
7:13	340	Micah	
7:15	340	6:9	341
8:2	340	7:6	176
8:13	340		
8:15	340	Nahum	
8:17	340	2:13	380
8:26	340		
8:27	340	Habakkuk	
9:21	227	1:15	121–21
12:6	413		
		Zephaniah	
Hosea		3:9	84
6:6	96–98, 110, 113		
		Zechariah	
9:14	117	2:11	405
		9:11	434
Amos		11:17	117
2:4	372		

New Testament

Matthew		8:16–17	61, 65–69
1:1–17	439	8:22	25
3:4	250, 292, 374	8:29b	55
4:4	274	9:12	84
4:13	55	9:13	85, 97
4:23	57	9:14	265
4:24a	55	9:14–17	99, 191
5:1	55	9:15	191
5:8	275	9:35	57
5:17–20	10	10:1–14	306
5:19	270, 289	10:5–6	442
5:21–48	24	10:10	313
5:32	377	10:17	57
6:1–4	298	10:31	124
6:26	124	11:5	84
7:6	276–88	11:25–30	81–87, 98, 182, 186–87
7:15–23	172, 181		
7:28–29	54–61	12:1	56
7:29	57	12:1–8	80–99
8:1–13	61	12:2	88, 109, 116, 190
8:14–15	61–65	12:7	117, 183

492   *Index of Ancient Authors*

12:9–14	114–24	24:6–7a	173
12:11	116, 121, 123, 143–45	24:9–14	180
		24:11–12	181
12:14	123, 125	24:15	172–73
12:15–21	81	24:15–28	173, 175
12:34	275	24:20	40, 124, 170–82, 183
12:40	413		
13:11	82	27:57	161
13:53–58	69	27:58–60	158
13:54	57, 69	27:62	165
14:13–21	253, 254, 255	27:57–28:1	147–69
14:25	229	28:1	162–65, 229
15:1	265	28:20	102
15:1–20	255–75, 292		
15:2	83	Mark	
15:8	270	1:6	250, 292, 374
15:11	274	1:14 f.	69
15:12	273, 275	1:21	55, 56, 57, 115
15:17	413	1:21a	55
15:18	274	1:21–28	54
15:18–19	270	1:21–39	54
15:20	275	1:22	55, 57
15:26	280	1:23	58, 115
15:26–27	256	1:23–28	60
15:29–39	253	1:24	55
16:14	212	1:28	55
16:17	416	1:31	67
17:9	340	1:32	67
18:16	275	1:32–34	65–69
19:5	358	1:44	413
19:12	413	2:3	67
19:17	270	2:18–20	191
19:19	377	2:18–22	99
21:5	85	2:20	191
21:16	275	2:23	234
22:36	270	2:23–26	95
22:38	270	2:24	126, 141
22:40	270	2:25	104, 109
23:2–3	269, 275, 277	2:27	105–12, 184
23:4	83	2:28	110
23:15	407	3:1	115
23:16–26	273	3:1–6	50
23:23	85, 97, 180, 183, 278, 282, 283, 287	3:2	116
		3:4	116, 119, 125, 126, 141
23:24	276–88, 292		
23:25–26	288–92, 300	3:5	125
23:26	298	3:6	116, 125
23:27	271	6:1–2	70
23:27–28	291	6:1–6	69
24:3	173	6:6b–13	306

6:7	307	1:77	75
6:11	307, 318	2:6	412
6:15	212	2:21	421
6:30–44	253	2:21–22	204
6:45–8:26	295	2:21–24	412–14
7:1–23	255, 292, 295	2:22	73, 204, 413, 417– 21
7:2	348		
7:2–4	266	2:22–24	414, 426
7:4	299, 300	2:25	148, 196, 413
7:5	266, 348	2:27	413, 426
7:6	276	2:32	441
7:6–7	276	2:38	196, 440
7:11	267, 268	2:39	413
7:15–23	181	2:41–42	204
7:17	273	2:42	70, 73, 413
7:19b	32, 256, 275	2:44	198
7:21–22	274	2:45	198
7:27	280	2:46	426
7:27–28	256	3:3	75
8:1–10	253, 255	3:7	131
8:27	212	3:23–38	416, 441
8:35	126	3:31	441
9:18	117	4:4	274
10:7	358	4:15	212
13	35	4:16	56, 73, 132, 186, 204, 210, 221, 413
13:4	170		
13:14	172	4:16–21	71, 135, 142, 221
13:18	170	4:16–30	54, 55, 60, 61, 69–79, 136, 184, 186, 187, 205, 210, 220, 234
13:19	174		
14:1–2	151		
14:3–8	160		
14:12	149	4:18	210
15:42–16:2	147–69	4:18–19	55, 71, 74–75
15:43	148	4:18–21	74–77, 185, 206
15:43–46	158	4:23–27	210
16:1–2	163	4:28	412
16:2	222	4:31	55–57, 104, 131, 234
Luke		4:31–37	54–69, 76, 184, 187
1:3	195	4:31–39	136, 211
1:9	413	4:31–41	184, 186
1:16	196	4:32	57
1:23	412	4:33	58
1:24	306, 413	4:35	59, 62, 132, 185
1:27	441	4:36	57, 62
1:35	412	4:38–39	61–65, 184, 187
1:49	301	4:39	55, 59, 62, 132
1:54–55	196	4:40	65, 68
1:59	204, 412	4:40–41	65–69, 184
1:68	196, 440	4:41	59

5:1–11	55, 65	10:8	307–8, 315
5:5	55	10:9a	308
5:26	412	10:11	318, 358
5:27	306	10:17–20	305
5:33–39	99–102, 191	10:21–22	81, 83
5:35	105, 191	10:25	140
6:1	56, 88, 90, 103, 109, 128, 234	10:26	212
		10:60	25
6:1–5	99–105	11:5	226
6:2	88, 104, 109, 190	11:15–20	139
6:3–4	104, 184	11:37–41	255, 294–303, 338
6:5	109, 127, 133	11:38	297, 300
6:5D	185	11:39–52	284
6:6	56	11:39b–44	295
6:6–11	124–27	11:40	297
6:7	128, 140	11:41	283, 298, 302, 319, 339
6:9	64, 68, 125, 126, 127, 139, 140, 141, 184		
		11:42	248, 297, 303, 314
		11:43	212
6:11	125, 127–30, 142, 296, 297, 412	11:45	140
		11:46	84
6:18	132	12:1	269
6:20	74, 275	12:4	306
6:42	269	12:6–7	135
6:45	275	12:27	135
6:49	57	12:36–40	226
7:2	307	12:38	228
7:21	132	12:56	269
7:22	74	13:8	342
7:30	140	13:10–17	76, 130–38, 140
8:1, 4	212	13:13	51, 67
8:26–29	60	13:14	68, 209
8:38	142	13:15	143, 184, 269
8:39	301	13:15–16	135, 137, 142, 188
8:49	133, 209	13:16	68, 76, 144, 185
9:2, 6	59	13:18–19	138
9:5	305, 318	13:22	212
9:8	212	13:22–30	138
9:19	212	13:31	128
9:28	306	13:31–33	138, 148
9:31	307	14:1	56
9:35	342	14:1–6	136–45
9:37–43a	60	14:3	141
9:51–56	304–6	14:4	51, 185, 188
9:51–18:34	304	14:5	70, 119, 121, 122, 138, 143, 144, 184
9:52	304, 305, 307, 442		
		14:13, 21	74
9:57–62	304	14:18–21	76
10:1–11	304–18	15:15	358
10:7	305, 308, 313, 314, 319	16:20, 22	74

16:29, 31	212	20:19–23	233
17:8	306		
17:26–27	441	Acts	
18:4	306	1:1	195
18:12	191, 222	1:3	201
18:20	215	1:6	139, 195
18:22	74	1:7	197
19:8	74	1:8	27–28, 197, 208, 306, 321, 363, 442
19:29	198		
19:44	304	1:9–11	197
19:46	321, 363	1:12	194–204, 218, 229, 233, 413
20:20	140		
20:41–44	441	1:12–14	197
20:46	212	1:14–16	339
21:20	173	1:24	307
21:24	28, 139, 172, 196, 363	2:1–42	321
		2:7, 12	361
21:37	131, 198	2:22	301
22:20	447	2:30	441
22:35–36	312–13	2:38	75
23:44–46	228	2:42	364
23:50–51	148	3:1	227
23:50–24:1	147–69	3:17	129
23:52–53	158	4:3	224
23:53	158	4:24	216, 301
23:54	150, 161, 227	4:31	339
23:54–57	227	4:34–37	358
23:56	73, 145, 161, 162, 166, 186, 204, 413	5:1	358
		5:13	358
24:1	201, 221	5:31	75
24:13	198	5:33–39	148
24:21	196	5:34	130
24:27	70, 75, 210	6:2	254
24:30	233	6:3	260
24:50–53	195	6:5	318
		7:8	412, 413, 427–29
John		7:14	313
1:3	106	7:31	350
1:10	106	7:32	297
5:3	117	7:41	413
5:10	126	7:50	301
6:1–15	253	8	306
7:22–23	402	8:5–25	321
9:6	51	8:15	339
11:44	150	8:27	321, 363
19:14	150	8:30	210, 212
19:31	155	9:4	342
19:39–40	160	9:24	140
20:1	222	9:36	338
		9:39	413

10–11:18	320–64	15	15, 29, 365–98
10:2	227, 298, 302, 317	15:1	367
10:2–4	227	15:4	301
10:7	337, 340	15:5	299, 319, 413, 444
10:9	228	15:7	212
10:14	341, 342, 343, 345, 352	15:7–9	323, 325
		15:7–11	367
10:15	298, 353	15:8–10	396
10:22	28, 207, 219, 326, 340	15:10	445–47
		15:12	301
10:28	326, 345, 353, 358, 359, 367, 396	15:13–21	211
		15:16	306, 441
10:35	207, 219, 337	15:17	212
10:38	132	15:19–20	212
10:43	75	15:20	212, 213, 365, 368, 373, 374, 378, 383, 385
10:48	326, 358, 367		
11	27, 28		
11:2	326, 339, 413	15:21	70, 210, 211–16, 234, 235, 394
11:3	396		
11:8	350, 352	15:29	370, 373, 385
11:9	342	15:36	212, 306, 307
11:10	121	15:36–40	433
11:15	296	16:1–3	7, 366, 430–35, 437
11:17	28	16:3	28, 413, 432
11:23	207	16:4	366, 433
11:26	16	16:11–40	216
12:4	168, 228	16:12–15	222–26
13:2, 3	101, 105	16:13	56, 70, 218, 219, 234
13:4	70		
13:13–52	210	16:15	317, 362, 396
13:14	56, 204–11	16:16	132
13:14–15	28, 71	16:16–24	397
13:15	70, 133, 306	16:18	236
13:23	441	16:25	226, 339
13:27	204–11, 212, 213, 221	16:34	317, 396
		17:1	226
13:29	158	17:1–2	72
13:37–38	449	17:2	70, 73, 220–22, 413
13:38	75, 77, 188	17:4	207, 208, 219, 317
13:38–39	211, 445, 447	17:5	317
13:42	204–11	17:12	219
13:43	207, 219	17:17	220
13:44	56, 204–11	17:24	216, 301
13:50	219	17:26	301, 354
13:51	318	17:29	354
14:1	204, 207, 219	17:30	354
14:15	215, 301, 372	18:1	220, 306
14:22	207	18:4	207, 219, 220–22, 234
14:23	101, 105		
14:27	301	18:6	353

18:7	207, 219, 317	2:20	297
18:8	133, 209, 318	14:1–2	249
18:24–28	220	14:2	374
19:1–20	220	14:14	348
19:19	397	14:21	374
19:24–41	397	16:21	317
19:40	140		
20:6	203, 230, 231, 232	1 Corinthians	
20:7–12	222–37	5:1	377
20:16	28, 203, 222, 230	6:16–17	359
20:23	212	6:16–20	376
20:26	353	7:2	377
20:31–32	224	7:18	437
21:4	231	7:26	437
21:7–12	236	7:29	437
21:9	230	7:31	437
21:19	301	8:4	372
21:20–21	394	9:14–18	313
21:21	131, 186, 214, 322, 339, 360, 370, 413, 416, 433, 435, 436, 450	10:19	372
		10:27	307, 308, 315
		10:28	315
		11:8–9	106
21:24	28, 353	15:36	297
21:25	365, 368, 373, 394		
21:28	321, 351, 363	2 Corinthians	
21:29	352	6:14–16	372
22:3	413	11:7–11	313
22:6–21	333	11:16, 19	297
22:12	73, 413	11:23–25	2
23:6	299, 444	12:6, 11	297
23:6–10	148		
23:9	128	Galatians	
23:23	228, 234	2	273, 365
24:5	17	2:3	430
24:6	321, 351, 363	2:12	368
24:12	212	5:2	430
26:5	73, 148, 413	5:3	435
26:9–20	325	5:11	212, 430, 435
26:18	75	5:12	430
26:28	16, 207	6:5	84
27:8–9	202	6:12, 13	430
27:9	28, 202, 203		
27:10	84	Ephesians	
27:27	226	4:17	372
28:14	231	5:17	297
28:17	28, 186, 214, 299, 322, 339, 449	5:31	359
		Philippians	
Romans		3:2	280
1:24, 26, 29	376	3:5	412

Colossians		1 Peter	
1:16	106	1:18	372
		2:15	297
1 Timothy			
5:18	313	2 Peter	
		2:22	282
2 Timothy			
3:15	431	Revelation	
		1:10	189
Hebrews		7:1	341
1:2	106	17:6	297
4	86	18:5	358
9:19	413	21:27	351
10:29	351	22:15	280
11:3	106		
13:11	294		

Apocrypha

Bel		1:61	432
3	374	1:62	245, 346, 347
11	374	1:63	346
		2:39–41	49
1 Esdras		3:46–50	423
1:1–33	408		
5:38	416	2 Maccabees	
		1:18	413
Additions to Esther		1:36	413
C 14:17	250, 374	2:16	413
		2:19	413
Epistle of Jeremiah		5:19	106
27	152	5:27	249, 292, 375
32	152	6:18–7:42	281
		6:21–24	348
Judith		7:25	342
12:1–2	250	10:5	413
12:19	316	15:2	342
5:13	423	15:36	342
8:14	342		
9:1	339	3 Maccabees	
		3:4	246
1 Maccabees		6:11	372
1:1–10	8	6:30	247
1:44–50	281	6:34	247
1:47	346, 347	6:40	247
1:47–48	245	7:20	217
1:48	346, 347		
1:60	432		

4 Maccabees

5	281
5:2	246
5:2–3	348
5:6	246
5:6–8	347
5:8–9	356
5:19	348
5:25	348
5:27	348
6:15	247
6:19	348
7:6	347, 413
8:2	348
8:12	348
8:29	348
11:16	348
11:25	348

Sirach

3:30	303, 339
6:30	84
22:11–12	152
29:12	303
31:16	315
36:1–5	403
38:16–23	153
38:32	334
40:24	303
42:17	360
45:2	360
49:1–4	408
51:20	413
51:26	84

Tobit

1:3	408
1:8	405
1:10–13	250
2:9	258
4:10	303
5:16	280
6:13	413
10:8	342
11:4	280
12:9	303
12:12	338
13:11	403

Wisdom of Solomon

3:12	297
5:4	297
14:31	376
15:8	372

Old Testament Pseudepigrapha

Ascension of Isaiah

2:11	250, 375

2 Baruch

1:4	446
14:5	407
14:18	106
32:2–7	176
41:3–4	446
41:4	407
42:5	446
48:22–24	446
66:4	408
66:6	408
72:2–6	409
81:4	407
84:8	408

1 Enoch

7:5	245
10:12	310, 441
10:22	376
48:4	403
50:1–3	403
53:1	403
89:59	309, 311
90:6–38	407
90:22	309, 311
90:25	309, 311
90:30–33	403
91:11–17	441
91:14	403, 407
91:15–17	450
93:3	441
93:3–10	441
98:4	25

98:11	245	Life of Adam and Eve	
99:7	372	51:2	86
106:15	376		

Letter of Aristeas

2 Enoch
33:1–2   86

		2	355, 429
4 Ezra		50	310
8:1–3	446	128–130	349
9:26	447	134	372
14:11	441	136	372
14:22	446	139	349, 372
14:46	310	145–147	341
		181–188	247, 321
Joseph and Aseneth		234	355
7:6	349	305	217, 258
8:5	245, 384	306	258
8:8	412	307	310
14–18	429		
19–21	429	Psalms of Solomon	
		7:9	84
Jubilees		8:15	197
2:19–21	45, 193	17:30	84
2:28	106	17:31	403
2:30	106		
3:8–13	420	Sibylline Oracles	
7:20–21	391	3:355	372
7:20–25	376	3:492	376
7:28–33	245	3:496–500	376
7:30	392	3:591–593	222
7:33	392	3:710–730	403
8:19	420	3:767–780	403
9:15	376	4:165	217
11:14	416	5:83	372
11:20	310	5:168	376
15:12	412	5:492–500	403
15:14	412	23:31	372
15:25	412		
15:26	412	Testament of the Twelve Patriarchs	
15:30–32	361, 392	T. Ash. 7:3	403
16:14	412	T. Benj. 12:3	413
22:16	250–51, 359, 372	T. Dan 6:7	403
44:34	309, 311	T. Gad 8:5	413
50:9–11	96	T. Iss. 6:1	358
50:12	49, 52, 53	T. Jud. 24:6	403
50:13	105	T. Jud. 25:5	403
		T. Levi 2:10–11	403
Liber antiquitatum biblicarum		T. Levi 4:4–6	403
63:2	92	T. Levi 18:2–9	403
		T. Sim. 2:12	117
		T. Sim. 7:2	403
		T. Zeb. 9:8	403

Dead Sea Scrolls and Related Texts

Damascus Document (CD)
2:12	361
3:6	245
4:20–5:11	378
6:15	302
7:1–3	378
8:5	302
10:14–16	162
10:19	51
10:21	89, 199
10:22	90
11:5	89, 134, 199
11:11	67
11:13–14	120, 121
11:14	122, 144
11:14–15	359, 406
11:15–17	145
11:16–17	50, 53
12:11–13	285, 286
12:14–15	292
12:15–18	262
12:19–20	286
14:4–6	404, 405
16:14–20	268

Genesis Apocryphon (1Qap Gen^{ar})
20:28–29	67

Pesher Habakkuk (1QpHab)
8:10–13	302
10:6–11:2	269
12:7–10	302
12:8–9	352

Rule of the Community (1QS)
1:24–26	447
2:19–23	405
3:4	361
3:7–8	361
3:13–4:26	361
4:10	376
4:19	302
4:20–22	361
4:21	376
5:6	404
5:7–9	24
5:13	360
5:13–14	361
5:16	259, 359
5:18	360
6:13–23	404
8:17	360
11:1–2	447

Rule of the Congregation/
Eschatological Rules (1QSa/1Q28a)
2:8–9	360

War Scroll (1QM)
7:6	360
10:9–11	360

Pesher Nahum (4QpNah/4Q169)
3–4 i:4	381
3–4 ii:9	419
3–4 iii:5	84

4QHalakha A (4Q251)
12:5	245
12:4	386
12:4–5	388, 392

4QHalakha B (4Q264a)
1:1	89
1:5–8	51

4QMisc Rules (4Q265)
6:5–6	122
6:5–6	120, 121, 144
6:6–7	50, 53
6:6–8	145
7:4	89, 134

4QD^a (4Q266)
6 ii:10–11	420

Miqtsat Ma'aseh HaTorah (MMT)
B 22–23	388
B 60–62	321
B 75	378
B 80–82	378
C 5	378

4QMMT^a (4Q394 3–10)
2 (3–7 ii): 2–4   331

4QMMT^d (4Q397)
2:2–3   279
3:11–13   331

4QMMT^e (4Q398)
2–3:1–3   331

4QWays of Righteousness^b (4Q421)
13:1   89

4QMessianic Apocalypse (4Q521)
2 ii + 4:1–13   75

11QMelchizedek (11Q13)
2:12–25   75

11QTemple^a (11Q19)
46:15   332
47:15–17   331
48:5–6   388, 392
48:6   386
48:11–14   152
49:5–21   152
49:13–16   262
66:11–17   377
50:5–9   152
50:16–17   262
51:4–5   331

11QTemple^c (11Q21)
3:2–5   279

Philo

Hypothetica
7:358   268

In Flaccum
41   217
45   217
95–96   281
96   246
111   228
122   217

Legatio ad Gaium
152   217
156–157   71, 209
180   231
311–313   71, 209
360   246

De vita Mosis
2:21   51
2:22   91
2:41–42   247
2:214   219

De opificio mundi
89   45, 106, 135, 193

De praemis et poenis
152   429

Quod omnis probus liber sit
81   194
81–83   71, 209

Quaestiones et solutiones in Genesin
3:38   412, 428, 429
3:49   412
3:52   412

De somniis
2:127   71, 209

De specialibus legibus
1:51   429
1:53   429
1:131–151   423
1:151   329
1:152   424
1:308   429
4:95–131   246
4:101   356
4:119–123   381, 382
4:120   381
4:122   382, 383
4:123   245, 392

De Virtutibus
143–144   245

Josephus

Against Apion
1:167   268
2:10   217
2:103   350
2:148   246
2:175   71, 209
2:205   152
2:258   246
2:282–284   193

Jewish Antiquities
1:192   412
1:214   412
2:259   121
3:237   227
3:251   141
3:260   380
4:73   268
5:223   229
5:346   423
5:348   427
6:242   92
8:213   85
11:252   357
12:11–118   312
12:57   312
12:86   312
12:89–90   334
12:107   312
12:146   331
12:253   281
12:276   49
13:243   281
13:252   126, 141, 200, 218, 231
14:10   416
14:65   227
14:226   200, 218, 231
14:245   390
14:258   217
15:196–200   152
15:259   141
16:43   71, 209
16:163   150, 168
17:93   357
18:213   357
18:356   229
20:35   409
20:46   357
20:113–117   71
20:169   198, 200
20:197   416
20:200–203   148
20:268   141

Jewish Wars
1:620   357
1:673   152
2:129   299
2:135   24
2:143   250, 374
2:147   332
2:228–231   71
2:262   198
3:437   152
4:115   413
4:160   416
4:317   159
4:582   229
5:70   198, 200
5:99   149
5:510   229
5:534   416
6:423   141

Life
4   416
11   292
13–16   231
14   249, 374
276–279   51
280   217

Rabbinic Literature

Mishnah
Avodah Zarah
2:1   378
2:3   374
2:7   316
3:5   86
4:6   357
5:5   316, 357
5:9–10   374

Avot
1:1   267
4:1   39

Bava Batra
2:9   333, 336

Bava Qamma
7:7   279, 281

Bekhorot
8:6   425

Berakhot
1:1   229
1:2   229
2:2   86
4:1   227

Bikkurim
1:4   431
2:1   259

Eruvin
4:1   59
4:1–2   230
4:3   199
4:7   199
5:7   199

Hagigah
2:1   377
2:5   262, 300
2:7   300

Hallah
4:10–11   424

Hullin
1:1   387, 390
1:2   387, 389
1:6   283
2:4   266, 386
3:6   341
5:5   229
6:1   365
6:2   398
7:1   390
8:1   245, 269
9:1   339, 397
9:2   331
9:3   336
9:4   330

Kelim
8:18   289
9:3   289
10:1   262
10:9   289
25:1   289, 290
25:6   290
25:7   289, 290
26:5   334
26:8   335

Ketubbot
7:10   329

Kila'yim
9:4   150

Ma'aserot
1:1   283
4:5   283
5:12   150

Megillah
1:5   155
3:2   329, 333

Menahot
10:1   96

Mikwa'ot			5:6	424
1:1	290			
5:4	336		Sotah	
5:6	290		7:7, 8	209
6:2	290			
			Ta'anit	
Nazir			4:1	223
7:1	25			
			Teharot	
Nedarim			2.2	261
1:4	268		9:5	259
2:5	268		10:4	259
4:6	268			
5:6	268		Temurah	
			6:5	279
Ohalot				
18:6	336		Yadayim	
			1–2	262
Pesahim				
1:1–3	149		Yom Tov	
3:8	90		3:2	155, 320
4:8	91		5:2	155
Qiddushin			Yoma	
1:7	432		6:4	89
			8.6	50, 63
Rosh HaShanah				
2:5	89		Zevahim	
			6:1	229
Sanhedrin				
2:4	88		Tosefta	
4:1	169		Avodah Zarah	
6:5	167		3:12–13	432
11:4	167, 169		8:6	387, 393
Shabbat			Bava Qamma	
1:2	331, 334, 336		8:17	281
1:8	335			
4:1	332		Bekhorot	
4:2	334		6:10	425
5:4	331			
14:3	50		Berakhot	
14:4	50		1:1	229
16:8	53		5:13	260
20:2	284		5:26	260
22:6	50		6:6	285
23:5	160			
			Eruvin	
Sheqalim			3:7	53
5:1	312			

Index of Ancient Authors

Nedarim
2:7   150

Niddah
5:15   416

Ohalot
18:2   336

Pesahim
3:19, 21   90

Qiddushin
1:11   432

Shabbat
7:23   64
13:13   231
14:3   50, 120, 144
14:11   103
15:7   425
15:8   434
15:11   50
16:22   52, 114
18:1   134

Terumot
7:11   285
9:6   292

Yom Tov
3:2   320

Yerushalmi
Berakhot
1:9 2d   229

Mo'ed Qatan
3:5 82a   157, 166

Nazir
4:6 53c   416

Qiddushin
1:7 61a   432

Shabbat
1:8 4a   231

Shevi'it
6:1 36c   300

Yevamot
8:1 8d   432

Yoma
8:6 45b   112

Bavli
Avodah Zarah
26b   432
27a   432
46a   280
64b   393

Bava Batra
9a   303
10a   303, 338
19b   303
21b   333

Bava Metzi'a
59b   344

Bava Qamma
82a   223

Bekhorot
10b   425
12b   425
51b   425

Berakhot
3a   229
3a–b   230
22b   334
25a   332
25b   334
51b   343
57b   87

Eruvin
6b–7a   343
13b   355
20b–21a   134
30a–b   90
51a   199

Hagigah
13a   280
18b   266

Index of Ancient Authors

Hullin
- 47b — 434
- 67a — 241, 284
- 117b — 330

Ketubbot
- 68a — 303
- 111a — 280

Megillah
- 7b — 280
- 14a — 343

Menahot
- 42a — 432
- 95b — 93

Mo'ed Qatan
- 19b — 154
- 20a — 154

Pesahim
- 65a — 334
- 66a — 134
- 114a — 343

Qiddushin
- 29a — 432
- 29b — 425
- 82a — 329, 333

Rosh HaShanah
- 14b — 343

Sanhedrin
- 35a–36a — 156
- 58a — 378
- 58b — 193, 396
- 59a — 393
- 101a — 63

Shabbat
- 12a — 284
- 19a — 231
- 30b–31a — 408
- 31a — 446
- 49a–b — 335
- 52b — 264
- 54a — 134
- 79a — 335
- 104a — 343
- 113b — 51
- 119b — 45
- 128a — 91
- 128b — 120, 123, 144
- 134a — 434
- 139a–b — 156
- 150a — 51

Sukkah
- 49b — 303
- 55b — 312

Temurah
- 30b — 279

Yevamot
- 14a — 343
- 64b — 434

Yom Tov
- 6a — 156
- 22a — 156

Yoma
- 67b — 276
- 81a–b — 162
- 85b — 193

Mekilta de-Rabbi Yishmael
Beshallah Wayassa
- Parashah 1 — 223
- Parashah 4 — 80

Beshallah-Wayehi
- Parashah 6 — 387

Ki Tissa-Shabbeta
- Parashah 1 — 107, 193

Mishpatim-Neziqin
- Parashah 1 — 248

Yitro-BaHodesh
- Parashah 7 — 223

Sifra
Aharei Mot
- Pereq 9:8 — 372
- Pereq 11:3 — 398

Pereq 13:1	377, 378	34:8	303
		34:16	51
Qedoshim			
Pereq 11:22	356	Num. Rab.	
		19:8	257, 276, 356
Shemini			
Parashah 10:3–6	330	Deut. Rab.	
Pereq 4:8–9	331	1:21	193
Sifre Numbers		Eccl. Rab.	
Pisqa 118	425	1:9	281
Sifre Deuteronomy		Song of Songs Rab.	
Pisqa 104	393	1.2.5	428
Pisqa 203	53, 231		
Pisqa 258	334	Midrash Proverbs	
Pisqa 344	86	31	428
Midrash Tannaim		Midrash Psalms	
Deut 20:20	53, 231	92	107
Deut 32	312		
		Pesiqta of Rab Kahana	
Avot of Rabbi Nathan		4:7	256
A 4	97	6	357
A 34	281	12:1	428
B 8–9	97	28:9	312
Kallah Rabbati		Pirqe Rabbi Eliezer	
7:1	332	11	97
		16	97
Midrash Rabbah		48	414
Gen. Rab.			
11:8	193	Semahot	
46:9	432	4:6	155
55:7	343	4:7	155
		7:4	154
Exod. Rab.		7:5	153
25:11	193		
		Yalqut	
Lev. Rab.		130 1 Sam 21:5	93
2:4	312	310 Jer 30	97
13:5	281	522 Hos 6	97
24:6	377		

Targumim

Neofiti		Lev 18:17	379
Lev 17:7	372		

Pseudo-Jonathan		Lev 18:17	379
Exod 16:29	199	Lev 19:4	372
Lev 7:24	386	Lev 20:5	372
Lev 17:7	372	Deut 14:21	386
Lev 17:13	385, 398	Deut 32:8	312
Lev 17:15	385		

Apostolic Fathers

Barnabas		6:2–3	193, 282
2:5–6	188	7:4	105
10	282	8:1	105, 191, 223
10:2	357	9:5	279, 281
10:3	358	11–13	314
10:4	358	13:2	313
10:5	358	14:1	223
10:8	358		
10:9	357	Shepherd of Hermes	
10:11	358	Mandate	
15:9	188	10.1.6	358
19:2	358		
19:6	358	Similitude	
20:2	358	9.2.4	84
1 Clement		Vision	
15:1	358	3.6.2	358
19:2	358	2.2.2	412
30:3	358		
31:1	358	Ignatius	
46:1	358	Magnesians	
46:2	358	8:1	189
46:4	358	9:1	189
49:5	358	10:3	189
56:2	358		
		Philadelphians	
2 Clement		6:1	189
14:5	358		
16:4	105	Romans	
		9:3	212
Didache			
1:3	105	Martyrdom of Polycarp	
3:9	358	5:1	212
5:2	358	7:2	105
6:2	85		

New Testament Apocrypha and Pseudepigrapha

Apostolic Constitutions and Canons
8.47.63 385

Gospel of Peter
2:5 151, 162
6:24 160

Gospel of Thomas
6 298
14 298, 307
47 100
89 297

90 81
93 278, 282

Pseudo-Clementines
Homilies
7.4.1 384
7.8.1 370, 379
7.8.2 384
8.19.1 384

Recognitions
4.36.4 384

Greek and Latin Patristic Works

Augustine
De civitate Dei
VI, 11 46
XVI, 3 311

Clement of Alexandria
Paedagogus
2.17.1–2 383

Cyril of Alexandria
Contra Julianum
9:318–319 320

Eusebius
Historia ecclesiastica
3.39.16 20

Irenaeus
Adversus haereses
3.22.3 311

Justin Martyr
Dialogus cum Tryphone
47 360

Origen
Commentarium in evangelium Matthaei
11:3 253

Tertullian
Apologeticus
9 385

De jejunio Adversus psychicos
16 218

Ad nationes
1:13 218

Greek and Latin Classical Works

Aeschylus
Agamemnon
607 279
896 279

Anthologia palatina
9:298 352

Index of Ancient Authors

Aristophanes
Equites
1023 — 279

Aristotle
Historia animalium
IX, 1 — 279

Diogenes Laertius
4:27 — 140

Heliodorus
Aethiopica
2:25 — 352
10:36 — 352

Herodotus
Historiae
2:104 — 417
4:60 — 383

Homer
Odyssea
17:291 — 279

Julian ("Apostata")
Epistulae
89a — 389

Juvenal
Satirae
XIV, 96–99 — 46
XIV, 96–106 — 401
XIV, 104–105 — 46

Ovid
Remedia Amoris
219 — 219, 231

Petronius
Satyricon
102:13–14 — 401

Plato
Theaetetus
152A — 108

Timaeus
86B — 129

Pliny the Elder
Naturalis historia
8:143 — 279
8:147 — 279

Pliny the Younger
Epistulae
10:96 — 224

Seneca
De Superstitione (Augustine, Civ.)
VI, 10 — 46

Sextus Empiricus
Adversus mathematicos
7:60 — 261

Sophocles
Fr. 154 — 352

Suetonius
Domitianus
12:2 — 402

Tacitus
Historiae
V, 4–5 — 246
V, 5 — 401

Tibullus
Carmina
I, 3:15–18 — 219, 231

Varro
De re rustica
2.4.3 — 281

Xenophon
Oeconomicus
13:8 — 279

Papyri

P. Egerton
2 l 51   129

P. Oxyrhynchus
840   282

P. Plond
1.130.39   163

P. Yadin
5   416
12–17   416
27   416
45   41

Index of Modern Authors

Aescoly, A. Z. 419
Aichinger, H. 103, 109
Albeck, C. 333
Alföldi-Rosenbaum, E. 390
Alkier, S. 262
Allen, W. C. 265, 266, 271
Allison, D. C. 81, 82, 83, 86, 95, 99, 108, 116, 149, 160, 165, 166, 179, 253, 255, 256, 257, 272, 275, 277, 278, 281, 409, 410
Alon, G. 422, 424
Anderson, H. 71
Avemarie, F. 260, 262, 373, 374, 379, 380, 382
Aviram, J. 300

Bacchiocchi, S. 72, 76, 77, 86, 189, 214, 223, 224, 225
Bachmann, V. 449
Back, S. O. 34, 81
Bammel, E. 185
Banks, R. 61, 96, 177, 178
Barkenings, H. J. 181, 368
Barnes, T. D. 189
Barrett, C. K. 195, 197, 199, 201, 208, 221, 222, 227, 228, 232, 322, 325, 337, 343, 345, 369, 370, 385
Barth, G. 19, 178
Basser, H. W. 20
Bauckham, R. 189, 337, 339, 441
Bauernfeind, O. 202
Baumgarten, A. I. 241, 267, 268, 295, 300
Baumgarten, J. 162, 420
Baur, F. C. 11–12.
Beare, F. W. 108, 274
Beattie, D. R. G. 371
Becker, A. H. 2
Becker, M. 64
Bell, C. 450

Ben David, A. 199
Benoît, P. 88
Berger, K. 252
Bergmann, J. 59
Betz, H. D. 277
Bieringer, R. 67
Billerbeck, P. 38, 159, 328, 331
Birnbaum, E. 429
Black, M. 144
Blaschke, A. 402, 430
Blomberg, C. L. 178, 302
Boccaccini, G. 1, 3, 8, 9, 86, 98, 355, 371, 404, 439
Bock, D. L. 26, 441
Bockmuehl, M. N. A. 368, 371, 373
Bohak, G. 59
Bóid, I. R. M. 419, 420, 421
Boman, T. 368
Bonnard, P. 91, 94, 95, 99, 123, 124, 277
Booth, R. P. 259, 260–61, 266, 300, 348
Bornkamm, G. 19, 58
Bottini, G. C. 264
Bourgel, J. 306
Bovon, F. 18, 30, 57, 62, 69, 100, 126, 129, 132, 136, 139, 140, 142, 161, 227, 233, 254, 282, 306, 307, 441
Boyarin, D. 1, 2, 5, 9, 10, 15, 24, 32, 95, 110, 112, 162, 164, 243, 256, 266, 292
Brawley, R. L. 29
Brocke, E. 181, 368
Brooke, G. J. 322, 378–79, 388
Brown, R. 14, 26, 74, 233, 411, 412, 422, 426, 436
Bruce, F. F. 195, 232, 320, 328
Bryan, C. 431
Bultmann, R. 11, 80, 81, 115, 131, 190, 265, 279

Burkert, W. 259, 389
Busse, U. 55, 69

Cadbury, H. J. 228
Caird, G. B. 25, 66
Camacho, F. 99, 117, 123, 165, 178
Carmona, A. R. 96
Carson, D. A. 66, 77, 82, 178
Carter, W. 24
Casey, M. 91
Charlesworth, J. H. 176, 262, 408
Chilton, B. 71
Chrupcala, D. 264
Clamer, A. 224
Clark, K. W. 20
Cohen, C. 387
Cohen, S. J. D. 6, 9, 10, 37, 402, 407, 414, 430–31, 434
Cohen, Y. 247
Cohn-Sherbok, D. 93, 95, 97, 134
Collins, A. Y. 63, 66, 110, 115, 148, 159, 160, 173
Collins, J. J. 388, 404
Colpe, C. 10
Conzelmann, H. 21, 22, 196, 197, 200, 203, 213, 395, 432, 445
Crossan, J. D. 168
Cuvillier, E. 19

Daniélou, J. 12–14, 16
Dar, S. 373
Davies, W. D. 81, 82, 83, 86, 95, 99, 108, 116, 149, 160, 165, 166, 179, 253, 255, 256, 257, 272, 275, 277, 278, 281, 409, 410
Deines, R. 31, 252, 254, 261–64, 289, 309, 324, 367, 376, 389, 395
Delebecque, E. 88, 89, 90
Delobel, J. 185
Delabaux, A. 138, 309
Derrett, J. D. M. 87, 88, 89, 160, 185
Detienne, M. 383
Deutsch, C. 85
Dibelius, M. 211, 325, 326
Dimant, D. 292
Di Segni, L. 264
Disraeli, I. 45
Dobbeler, A. 410
Dobson, M. J. 373

Doering, L. 36, 46, 47, 49, 50, 51, 52, 53, 64, 65, 67, 88, 89, 90, 91–92, 93, 94, 95, 96, 99, 103,104, 106, 107, 108, 117, 118, 120, 121, 122, 123, 124, 125, 126, 130, 133, 134, 135, 141, 144, 149, 150, 164–65, 177, 178, 182, 185, 199, 200, 219, 230, 231
Douglas, M. 241, 243, 419
Draper, J. 85, 282
Dunn, J. D. G. 3, 203, 256, 435
Dupont, J. 106
Durand, J. L. 389

Easton, B. S. 138
Eliav, Y. 9
Eisenbaum, P. M. 26
Elgvin, T. 8
Elitzur, Y. 300
Endres, J. C. 378
Ennulat, A. 109
Epstein, J. N. 63, 64, 65, 263
Ernst, J. 296, 309, 314
Eshel, H. 416
Evans, C. A. 22, 25, 305

Falk, D. K. 339
Festugière, A. J. 218
Fiedler, P. 266, 269, 272, 275
Filoramo, G. 15, 16, 371
Fine, S. 235
Fitzmyer, J. A. 65, 67, 71, 72, 129, 131, 138, 142, 144, 145, 151, 161, 195, 201, 218, 223, 225, 226, 233, 254, 268, 306, 307, 345
Flusser, D. 1, 20, 63, 101, 102–3, 118, 130, 181, 196, 368, 369, 387, 403
Foster, P. 18, 24–25, 33, 35, 36, 172, 181, 377
France, R. T. 15, 71, 110, 116, 118, 149, 151, 213, 268, 272, 313
Frankmölle, H. 96, 115
Franklin, E. 32–33
Freed, E. D. 440
Freidenreich, D. M. 36, 247, 249, 250, 347, 348, 374
Frey, J. 31
Fuchs, A. 104
Furstenberg, Y. 243–44, 259, 260, 261, 262, 271

Gager, J. G. 26–27
Gander, G. 309, 314
Garland, D. E. 283
Gasque, W. W. 430
Gaston, L. 26, 173
Geddert, T. J. 173
Gerstenberger, E. S. 419
Gianotto, C. 15, 16, 371
Gibson, S. 264
Gils, F. 108
Ginzberg, L. 90
Gleßmer, U. 371
Gnilka, J. 63, 81, 83, 84, 85, 88, 98, 122, 160, 173, 177, 275, 279
Godet, F. L. 415
Goldenberg, R. 439
Good, R. S. 101
Goodfriend, E. A. 280
Goodman, M. 6, 26, 300, 407
Goulder, M. D. 277
Grappe, C. 252
Green, J. B. 35, 309, 441
Grossberg, A. 300
Grundmann, W. 178, 272
Gundry, R. H. 63, 66, 149, 178, 255, 272, 274, 278
Gurtner, D. M. 254
Guthrie, W. K. C. 108
Guy, F. 189

Haam, A. 45–46
Haber, S. 258, 259, 262
Hachlili, R. 150, 160
Haenchen, E. 31, 213, 221, 228, 323, 345, 430, 445
Hagner, D. A. 2, 23, 85, 172, 256, 265, 276, 283
Hamilton, J. J. 168
Hanson, A. T. 440
Hanson, R. P. C. 203
Hare, D. R. A. 287, 403
Harland, P. A. 158
Harnack, A. 328, 467
Harrington, D. 83, 84, 87, 275
Harrington, H. K. 420
Hartog, F. 383
Hayes, C. E. 6, 36, 247, 248, 249, 251, 302, 329, 332, 350, 351, 352, 354, 376, 379, 397, 406
Hayward, R. 371

Heemstra, M. 4
Hengel, M. 168, 328
Henze, M. 407
Heschel, A. J. 180
Hezser, C. 9
Higgins, A. J. B. 223
Hill, D. 71, 97, 172
Himmelfarb, M. 421
Hirsch, E. 178, 342
Hirshman, M. 193, 280, 439
Hoffmann, D. Z. 244, 397
Hoffmann, P. 307
Hogan, K. 446
Hood, J. 440
Hooker, M. D. 66, 150, 152
Horst, P. W. 235
Hübner, H. 109
Hübner, R. 189
Hummel, R. 98, 116, 269
Hvalvik, R. 2, 7, 16, 203

Instone-Brewer, D. 155

Jackson-Mcabe, M. 10
Jacobs, A. 415, 417
Jacquier, E. 203
Jaffee, M. S. 7, 8.
Jaubert, A. 151
Jellicoe, S. 312
Jeremias, J. 144, 159, 160, 168
Jervell, J. 21, 29–31, 195, 196, 203, 206, 214, 219, 222, 359, 416, 433, 436, 441, 450
Jewett, P. K. 76, 215
Johnson, L. T. 313, 345
Johnston, R. M. 101
Jones, S. F. 12
Joosten, J. 122
Juel, D. 29

Kampen, J. 379
Kankaanniemi, M. 34
Kaufmann, A. S. 200
Kazen, T. 25, 36, 248, 249, 252, 259, 260, 261, 262, 263, 264, 271, 288, 291, 295, 296, 298, 308
Kehati, P. 333
Kelhoffer, J. A. 292
King, K. L. 11
Kinzer, M. 181, 256, 282, 355

Klawans, J. 36, 244, 247, 302, 329, 350, 351, 358, 359, 376, 379, 397
Klein, H. 306, 307, 310
Klein, S. 160
Klinghardt, M. 18, 30, 34, 46, 72, 95, 102, 112, 124, 131, 133, 140, 162, 184, 206, 207, 224, 225, 227, 233, 234, 235, 237, 326, 327, 338, 382, 383, 384
Koet, B. 25, 252
Kosmala, H. 378
Kraabel, A. T. 207
Kraemer, D. 9, 36, 40, 152, 161, 242, 245, 249, 250, 251, 347, 374
Kraft, R. A. 13
Krauss, S. 160, 310, 311, 331, 334, 335, 336

Laansma, J. 83–85
Lagrange, P. M.-J. 266
Lechner, T. 189
Le Cornu, H. 27, 196, 197, 203, 218, 232, 339, 340, 373
Legrand, L. 415
Lemerle, P. 218
Leon, H. J. 46
Lev-Tov, J. 373
Levine, A. J. 20, 22, 30, 404
Levine, E. 96
Levine, L. I. 23, 209, 217
Levinskaya, I. 431
Lewis, R. B. 189
Lichtenberger, H. 292
Lieberman, S. 103, 153, 156, 157, 336, 434
Lietzmann, D. H. 382
Lieu, J. 2
Lindsey, R. L. 102
Livesey, N. E. 402
Loader, W. R. G. 18, 28, 30, 60, 62, 72, 85, 95, 100, 101, 104, 110, 116, 124, 128, 131, 166, 196, 283, 313, 314, 337, 420
Lohfink, G. 31
Lowe, M. 103
Lüdemann, G. 430
Lührmann, D. 58
Luz, U. 55, 57, 83, 91, 94, 96, 97, 115, 118, 123, 149, 160, 164, 178, 179, 254, 256, 269, 271, 277, 278, 283, 284

Maccoby, H. 1, 36, 118, 243, 244, 247, 271, 284, 286, 287, 288, 289, 290, 302, 329, 332, 397
MacLennan, R. S. 207
Magness, J. 105, 160, 168, 217, 241, 262, 264, 279, 285, 286, 287, 292, 316, 331, 332, 374
Malina, B. 10
Mann, J. 25
Marcus, J. 149, 150, 173, 256, 263, 266, 268, 275
Marguerat, D. 227, 228, 320, 329
Marshall, I. H. 72, , 195, 196
Marshall, J. W. 16
Marty, M. E.439
Marxsen, W. 173
Mason, S. 5
Mateos, J. 99, 117, 123, 165, 178
Matthews, S. 208
Mayer-Haas, A. J. 31, 36, 47, 53–54, 57, 58, 60, 62, 66–67, 69, 71, 72, 73, 77, 83, 91, 93–94, 97, 101, 102, 103, 104, 107, 108, 109, 112, 117, 124, 126, 130, 135, 137, 139, 142, 143, 144, 149, 160, 161, 162, 164, 166, 177, 180, 181, 199, 201, 208, 215, 218, 223
McArthur, H. K. 101
McCane, B. 152–53, 160, 168
McKay, H. A. 46, 71, 235
McKnight, S. 23, 403
McNamara, M. 371
Meier, J. P. 20, 47–54, 63, 65, 92, 178, 190, 263, 268, 270, 272, 348, 377
Mello, A. 93, 94, 110, 118, 142, 149, 180
Merkel, H. 57
Metzger, B. 309, 369
Milavec, A. 191
Milikowsky, C. 259, 264
Milgrom, J. 36, 241, 242, 243, 244, 262, 280, 289, 330, 332, 341, 345, 371, 376, 380, 391, 397, 398, 418, 419
Miller, C. A. 329, 344
Miller, D. G. 19
Miller, G. D. 280

Mimouni, S. C. 10, 11, 14, 16, 282, 402, 431, 448
Moessner, D. P. 430
Moore, G. F. 1, 164
Mor, M. 3
Morris, L. 101, 178
Moskala, J. 242, 244
Müller, K. 245, 369, 378, 379, 385, 393, 396, 403
Müller, M. 34
Murmelstein, B. 88, 93
Murray, M. 13, 436
Murray, R. 13
Mussner, F. 195

Nanos, M. 1, 26
Navarro, L. S. 440
Neil, W. 328
Neirynck, F. 106, 112, 131, 138, 144
Nepper-Christensen, P. 20
Nestle, E. 200
Neusner, J. 30, 38, 261, 262, 263, 290
Noam, V. 247
Nolland, J. 65, 110, 118, 119, 124, 126, 132, 148, 160, 161, 227, 233, 254, 296, 298, 302, 308, 315, 439, 446
Novak, D. 378, 396

Öhler, M. 354, 365
Oliver, I. W. 3, 107, 449
Olsson, B. 217
O'Neill, J. C. 37
Oppenheimer, A. 53, 83
Orlov, A. 86
Osborne, G. R. 23
O'Toole, R. F. 131
Ottenheijm, E. 117, 118, 121, 252
Overman, J. A. 22, 23

Paget, J. C. 10
Parsons, M. C. 352
Paschen, W. 348
Pedersen, K. S. 417
Pervo, R. I. 3, 17, 22, 35, 37, 195, 201, 202, 205, 213, 222, 227, 302, 309, 320, 366, 371, 397, 427, 428, 445
Pesch, R. 173, 200, 208
Pettem, M. 295
Philipps, J. 328
Pirot, L. 224

Plümacher, E. 211
Plummer, A. 100, 132, 138, 227
Poirier, J. C. 261, 262, 263
Poorthuis, M. J. H. M. 241, 252
Powell, M. A. 277

Qimron, E. 229, 279, 378

Rappaport, U. 292, 346
Rawlinson, A. E. J. 66
Reed, A. Y. 2
Reed, J. L. 66
Reed, R. 334–35
Regev, E. 258, 262, 388
Repschinski, B. 33, 93, 95, 102, 190–91, 192, 237, 265
Resch, G. 368
Rice, G. E. 55
Riesenfeld, H. 223
Rodinson, M. 417
Roloff, J. 428
Rordorf, W. 72, 215, 224
Rosenblum, J. D. 36, 244, 251, 281, 316, 374
Rubin, N. 37, 402, 414, 415, 416, 422, 423, 424, 425, 431
Rudolph, D. J. 435
Runesson, A. 25, 57, 71, 115, 217, 443
Rutgers, L. V. 4, 246–47
Ruzer, S. 196

Sabourin, L. 414, 421
Safrai, C. 282, 300
Safrai, S. 160–61, 181, 368, 369, 373, 387, 403
Safrai, Z. 282
Sahlin, H. 368
Saldarini, A. J. 4, 22, 23, 24, 96, 97, 99, 111, 119, 121, 180, 275, 397, 410
Salmon, M. 29
Salo, K. 18, 72, 73, 100, 410, 413, 421
Sanders, E. P. 1, 29, 36, 38, 49, 50, 51, 63, 118, 133, 242, 245, 247, 248, 251, 259–63, 265, 266, 283, 285–86, 299, 316, 383, 389, 390
Sanders, J. T. 296
Sandmel, S. 1, 33, 320
Sandt, H. 37, 279
Sariola, H. 58

Schäfer, P. 3, 8–9, 371
Schaller, B. 64
Schiffman, L. H. 90, 122, 245, 285, 386, 388
Schlatter, A. 123
Schmithals, W. 25
Schnackenburg, R. 274
Schneider, G. 200, 327, 337, 415, 445
Schonfield, H. J. 17
Schröter, J. 307–8
Schwartz, D. R. 31, 197, 212, 213, 353
Schwartz, J. 241, 252, 280, 281
Schwartz, S. 2, 9
Schweizer, E. 265, 272, 273, 274
Segundo, J. L. 93, 98, 119
Selwyn, E. C. 202
Senior, D. 18, 410
Shemesh, A. 377, 386, 387
Shulam, J. 27, 196, 197, 203, 218, 232, 339, 340, 373
Sigal, P. 88, 91, 96
Sim, D. 23, 33, 37, 57, 171, 172, 173, 175, 181, 273, 275, 280, 404
Simon, M. 14–15
Skarsaune, O. 2, 7, 16, 17, 203
Soler, J. 242
Sosa, C. R. 352
Sparks, K. 440
Staats, R. 223, 227
Stählin, G. 328
Stanton, G. N. 18, 19, 51, 57, 177, 178
Stegemann, W. 207, 218
Stendahl, K. 19, 270
Stern, M. 122
Stiebel, G. D. 241
Stökl Ben Ezra, D. 16, 28, 32, 202, 203, 450
Strack, H. L. 38, 159, 328, 331
Strand, K. 189
Strecker, G. 20, 179, 190
Streeter, B. H. 173
Strelan, R. 18, 27, 31
Stuckenbruck, L. T. 354, 361
Suter, D. W. 378

Talbert, C. H. 82, 304, 309, 312, 329
Tannehill, R. C. 29, 80, 115, 190
Taylor, V. 66
Theissen, G. 115

Thiessen, M. 6, 7, 30, 37, 346, 351, 355, 402, 405, 406, 418, 419, 420, 421, 427–28, 433, 436
Thompson, W. 34, 171, 172
Tobias, N. 185
Tomson, P. J. 16, 52, 121, 130, 139, 247, 348, 357, 359, 360, 368, 369, 372–73, 377
Trautmann, M. 190
Trilling, W. 20
Trocmé, E. 213
Tuckett, C. M. 322
Turner, M. M. B. 72, 78, 202, 302
Tyson, J. B. 18, 29, 35, 320, 436

Ullendorff, E. 417
Ulmer, R. 64
Uro, R. 308, 311
Urbach, E. E. 372

Vahrenhort, M. 123
Vernant, J. P. 383
Verheyden, J. 309
Vermes, G. 1, 51, 63, 118, 122, 264, 283
Vouga, F. 111

Wahlen, C. 347
Walker, R. 179
Walters, P. 35
Wedderburn, A. J. M. 382
Wehnert, J. 16, 30, 31, 198, 212, 213, 326–27, 365, 369, 370–87, 397–98, 433
Weiser, A. 326, 327, 328, 430, 445
Weiss, H. 45, 47, 77, 106, 111, 149, 163, 169
Weren, W. J. C. 440
Werman, C. 391–92, 406
Westermann, C. 393
White, L. M. 22
White, R. 333
Whitters, M. F. 408
Wiefel, W. 275, 279, 411, 415
Wilkins, J. F. D. H. 373
Williams, M. H. 337
Willits, J. 410
Wilson, S. G. 132, 137, 368, 382–83, 392, 415
Winger, J. M. 163

Witherington III, B. 358, 441
Wolter, M. 62, 112, 125, 127, 129, 130, 131, 132, 135, 138, 141, 142, 144, 203, 227, 228, 233, 296, 297, 304, 309–14, 448
Wong, E. K. C. 178, 180–81
Wright, D. P. 280, 419

Yang, Y. E. 47, 58, 60, 66, 69, 72, 74, 78, 81, 82, 83, 84–85, 91, 92, 93, 95, 96, 116, 122, 131, 178, 179
Young, B. H. 101

Zangenberg, J. 37, 262
Zeitlin, S. 230, 359, 405
Ziesler, J. A. 102, 139, 148, 296
Zmijewski, J. 199, 202, 217, 222

Index of Subjects

Almsgiving/Charity 97, 114, 298, 302–3, 317, 319, 338–39
Angels 339–40, 357, 360–61, 414, 415
Anti-Judaism 3, 20, 26, 27, 178, 217, 220, 269
Apostolic Decree 15–16, 29, 41, 193, 212–15, 235, 236, 245, 250, 252, 255, 299, 315, 317, 318, 323, 362–63, 365–98, 433, 436, 445

Baptism 218–219, 299, 317, 322, 325–26, 361–62
Bar Kokhba Revolt 2–3, 9, 13, 35, 360
Burial
– anointing bodies 160–61
– criminals 167–68
– Gentiles 156–58
– obligation to bury 25
– secondary burial 25, 305
– spices 162–63
– timing 150, 159
– washing bodies 160
– wrapping bodies 150

Christology 23, 29, 95, 96, 108, 110–11, 112, 127, 133, 184
Circumcision
– eighth day 6–7, 402, 414–17, 427–29, 433–34
– Gentiles 403–10
– Jesus 410–17, 435–38
– Jewish identity 6–7, 401–2, 433–34
– John the Baptist 410–17, 435–38
– *Mohel* 431–32
– Sabbath 107
Commandments
– ethical/moral vs. ritual 37, 248, 270, 276, 282–83, 328, 368–70
Commission 111, 197, 255, 294, 305–6, 311–13, 318, 321, 404, 407, 442
Common/Profane 245–46, 322, 334, 345–57, 358, 360–61, 363–64, 406

Cornelius 28, 208, 219, 227, 255, 298, 302, 316–17, 323–25, 326, 337–40, 354, 360, 362, 367, 375, 397

David 92–95, 98, 104, 112–13, 205–6, 435, 441
Dogs 176, 178, 279–82, 332

Ebionites
– Gospel of Ebionites 12
– "sect" 8, 12, 13, 16, 359, 451
Ecclesiology 29, 171, 181–82, 192, 235, 355, 364, 395
Elkasaites 451
Enochic Movement and Traditions 9, 376, 441, 445
Eschatology 10, 86–87, 170–77, 184, 195–97, 362, 406–7, 409
Essenes 9
– calendar 150–51
– oaths 24–25, 250
– Gentiles 360
– purity 249, 299–300, 303, 332, 359
– Qumran 24, 404, 407
– Torah observance 52, 250
Ethiopian Eunuch 320–21, 325
Ethiopian Jews 419
Ethiopian Orthodox Church 417
Eucharist 222–23, 231–33, 235, 254, 281–82, 364
Exorcism
– exorcism as healing 58–59, 62, 132
– laying hands 67
– Sabbath 58–60

Fasting 99–102, 105, 191, 223, 338, 450
First Jewish Revolt 2, 51, 200, 208, 359–60, 375, 447
Fiscus Judaicus 4, 408
Food Laws/Kashrut
– blood 244–45, 275, 370, 390–93

- camels 284–87
- carcasses 243–44, 329–31, 342, 370, 380–90, 397
- "detestable" creatures 242–43, 284–87
- fish sauce 316
- gnats 284–87
- eight vermin 243, 284–87, 289
- Gentiles 244, 316, 391
- idols 315
- (im)purity 251
- Jewish Identity 245, 264
- locusts 292
- pork 246, 250, 256, 275, 281, 346, 356, 362, 397
- table fellowship between Jews and Gentiles 246–47, 249–50, 253, 307–8, 316–18, 324, 349, 357–58, 362, 365, 367–68, 396
- wine 249–50, 285, 316, 373–75

Form Criticism 18, 47–48, 80–81, 115

Galilean Customs 53, 71, 103, 123, 217, 264
Gemilut Hasadim 97–98, 117
Gentiles 108, 111, 156–58, 181, 197, 214, 219, 244, 281, 304, 316, 350–51, 360–62, 403–10
Gentile Christians 5, 20, 181, 192, 214
Gentile Sympathizers/"God-Fearers" 28, 31, 214, 219, 318, 337, 395, 397, 445, 448–49
Ger 362–64, 368, 370, 388, 393, 396, 405–7
Gezerah Shavah 93, 134, 138
Gnosticism 11
Gospel of the Hebrews 12, 118

Hannah 426
Healing (See "Sabbath")
Heilsgeschichte/Salvation History 21, 179, 185, 256, 442
Hillel (House of) 117, 245, 259, 290, 359, 408
Historical Jesus 1, 4, 18, 30, 40, 47, 48, 49, 51, 63, 106, 118, 140, 144, 167, 178, 179, 189, 265, 268, 272
Holy/Sacred 345–57, 358
Holy Days (Yom Tov) 121, 153–56, 167

Holy Spirit 301, 303, 321, 325, 339, 344, 360–62

Idolatry 215, 250, 302, 315, 357, 371–75, 397, 403

James, Brother of Jesus 11, 13, 16, 148, 211–14, 237, 360, 365, 367, 394, 395, 436, 451
Jerusalem 27–28, 139, 195–97, 198, 304, 320–21, 331, 350–51, 362
Jerusalem Council 21, 148, 211, 212, 215, 325, 327, 367, 369
Jewish Christian(ity)/Christian Jew 7, 10–18, 23, 26–27, 29, 445, 448, 451
Jewish Identity/Jewishness
- circumcision 6–7, 401–2, 433–34
- ethnicity 6–8
- genealogy 6–7, 437
- matrilineal/patrilineal ancestry 6–7, 430–31, 437
- Torah observance 7–10
John the Baptist 77, 99–101, 191, 204, 206, 250, 292, 299, 402, 410–17, 426, 427, 435–36, 440
Joseph of Arimathea 147–48, 158, 161–63

Liberation 187–188, 196, 206–9, 210–11
Luke-Acts
- audience 68, 130–31, 200, 202–4, 210, 211, 214, 233–35
- author(ship) 4, 25, 29, 31, 111, 202, 210, 233, 306, 410–12, 444–49
- date 35, 37
- "Jews" 206, 220
- Gentile Christian 25, 68, 111, 121–22, 281, 410–12, 445
- Great Omission 295
- Jewish Christian 29, 281, 448
- history of research 20–22, 25–32
- provenance 27–28
- unity 35
Lydia 216, 219, 317, 362, 396

Mark
- audience 266
- date 171
- Food Laws 256

Index of Subjects

- Sabbath keeping 58
- Torah observance 32–33
- Two-Source Hypothesis 32, 34

Matthew
- authorship 4, 111, 447
- audience 177, 180, 190–91, 192, 443
- date 37, 171
- Gentile Christian 20, 179
- history of research 19–20, 22–25
- provenance 177, 443–44, 451

Narrative Criticism 35–36
Nazarenes/Nazareans
- Gospel of the Nazareans 12, 451
- "sect" 17, 359

Noahide Laws 244, 253, 369, 385, 392–93, 396

Parting of the Ways 2–4, 19, 23–27, 57–58, 189–90, 417, 442
Passover/Festival of Unleavened Bread
- burial 150–60
- meal 149
- purchasing 150, 159–60
- traveling 203, 222, 230

Paul
- historical Paul vs. Lukan Paul 26, 28, 365, 430, 433–35, 437–38
- Pharisee 299
- synagogue attendance 74, 124, 204, 210, 220, 234
- Torah observance 9, 26, 230–34, 317–18, 360, 366, 394–95, 417, 431

Pentecost 28, 153, 158, 203, 222, 230, 234, 321
People of the Land/Am Haarets 53
Peter 27–28, 29, 55, 65, 73, 237, 273, 298, 316–17, 323–25, 328, 340–45, 367

Pharisees
- Christian Pharisees 301, 319, 338–39, 443–44
- relationship to Rabbinic Judaism 30, 259–60
- tradition of the elders 83, 266–69
- Luke-Acts 57, 105, 125, 127–28, 130, 138–40, 142, 145, 148, 295–99
- Matthew 115–16, 148, 165–66, 169, 191, 265, 277, 443

- Vows 267–69

Porneia 375–80, 397, 403
Prayer 227, 258–59, 323–24, 339
Proselytism 208–9, 220–21, 234, 407
Purity/Impurity
- carcasses 243–44, 329–31, 342, 370, 380–90, 397
- corpse 25, 258, 271, 276, 289, 291
- feces 332, 342
- genealogical (im)purity 6–7, 355, 427–29
- Gentiles 247–49, 250, 301, 347–48
- hand washing 257–64, 266, 299–300
- immersion 259, 299–300
- inner vs. outer 271, 288–92, 300–301, 354
- intrinsic 302, 350–53, 355–56
- land 391–92
- liquids 260, 284–87, 292
- menstruation 249, 252, 370, 379, 397, 417–18, 420
- moral (im)purity 244, 252, 302, 339, 353–54
- parturient 410–11, 417–21
- permanent 242
- ritual (im)purity 250, 252, 302, 339, 346–48
- seaside 258, 336
- sexual relations 258, 370
- vessels 262, 288–92, 300, 316
- tanning 327–37
- urine 332
- *Zav* 252, 289

Qal Vahomer 97, 116–17, 120, 135, 143–44
Qumran 24, 83, 121, 134, 145, 152, 171, 199, 285–86, 387–88, 404, 406–7

Rabbinic Judaism and Literature
- methodological and historical problems 37–39, 152–53, 261, 262–63
- relationship to Pharisaic Judaism 30, 52

Redaction Criticism/Composition Criticism 18, 21, 27, 33–34, 236–37
Redemption of the Firstborn 421–27

Replacement Theology/Supersessionism 11–12, 24, 25, 86
Roman Empire/Rome 21, 26–28, 196, 197, 208–9, 231, 246, 281, 375, 397, 409, 441

Sabbath
- animals 120–23, 133–35, 138, 143
- burial 149
- carrying 50, 66–67
- circumcision 107
- creation 52, 106–7
- eschatology 75–78, 86–87, 98, 135–37, 182–83
- exorcism 58–60, 62, 132
- Gentiles 108, 111, 193, 214–16, 219
- healing 47–50, 118–120, 140, 211, 236
- Jewish identity 45–46
- liberation 187–88
- mercy 85, 96–98, 110, 113, 117, 123–24, 183
- piquah nefesh 49, 63–64, 94, 107, 118, 124, 126–27, 140, 143, 145, 178, 183
- plucking 80, 89–91, 96, 103
- priestly service in the temple 95–96
- purchasing 149
- rest 187–88
- rubbing 103
- Sabbath limits 66–67, 164–65, 199–200, 218, 224–25
- sunset 161–65, 224, 227
- synagogue 70, 72–73, 216
- talk 51–52
- travel by boat 52, 230–32
- travel by foot 87–89, 164–65, 178, 183, 199–204
- tying/untying 133–35
- universality, 45–46, 106, 111, 193
- warfare 45, 136
- worship 58
Sadducees 17, 116, 118, 148
Samaritans 304, 306, 311, 321, 325, 339, 361, 419–20, 442
Samuel 426–27
Sanhedrin 27, 138, 148, 167, 168, 299
Septuagint 211–12, 233, 306, 309–12, 345, 371–72

Shammai (House of) 122, 259, 290, 359, 360
Social Criticism 22
Son of Man 98, 104–5, 108, 110, 133, 304–5
Sunday/Lord's Day 188–89, 222–23, 235
Synagogue
- Diaspora 71–72, 209, 216
- head of the synagogue 133, 209, 210
- Pharisaic 71–72, 115–16
- prayer 216–19, 258
- readings 71–72, 204, 209
- sanctity 333
- teaching 124, 132, 204, 209
- worship 58, 235
Synoptic Problem 34, 102–3, 108–10

Tanners 327–37
Temple 9, 21, 23, 28, 35, 95–98, 112–13, 117, 131, 167, 170–76, 183, 198, 218, 227–28, 233, 259, 262, 268, 272, 320–21, 331, 332, 346, 350–53, 362, 378, 391, 411, 413–14, 420–27, 435–36, 442, 446
Ten Commandments 215, 244, 248, 267, 274, 391
Time
- Jewish 223–230
- Roman 223–230
Timothy 21, 28, 225, 366, 430–35, 437
Tithes 268, 282–84, 287, 288, 300, 422–25, 443

Universalism vs. Particularism 439–42

We Sections (Acts) 203, 216, 218, 222, 445
Women 219, 333, 350, 406

Yom Kippur 16, 28, 153, 202–3, 230, 450
Yoke 29, 82–86, 193, 275, 408, 445–46

www.ingramcontent.com/pod-product-compliance
Lightning Source LLC
Chambersburg PA
CBHW080530300426
44111CB00017B/2663